The Golden Oriole

The Golden Oriole

Childhood, Family and Friends
in India

RALEIGH TREVELYAN

OXFORD UNIVERSITY PRESS
1988

Oxford University Press, Walton Street, Oxford OX2 6DP

Oxford New York Toronto
Delhi Bombay Calcutta Madras Karachi
Petaling Jaya Singapore Hong Kong Tokyo
Nairobi Dar es Salaam Cape Town
Melbourne Auckland

and associated companies in
Berlin Ibadan

Oxford is a trade mark of Oxford University Press

First published 1987 by Secker and Warburg
First issued as an Oxford University Press paperback 1988

British Library Cataloguing in Publication Data
Trevelyan, Raleigh, 1923–
The golden oriole: childhood, family and
friends in India.—(Oxford paperbacks).
1. Great Britain. Trevelyan, Raleigh, 1923–
I. Title
941.082'092'4
ISBN 0–19–282573–9

Printed in Great Britain
at the University Printing House, Oxford
by David Stanford
Printer to the University

Once, on this earth, once, on this familiar spot of ground, walked other men and women, as actual as we are today, thinking their own thoughts, swayed by their own passions, but now all gone, one generation vanishing after another, gone as utterly as we ourselves shall shortly be gone like ghosts at cockcrow.

G. M. Trevelyan,
An Autobiography and Other Essays, 1949

The existing connection, between two such distant countries as England and India, cannot, in the nature of things be permanent; no effort of policy can prevent the natives from ultimately regaining their independence. But there are two ways of arriving at this point. One of these is through the medium of revolution; the other, through that of reform. In one, the forward movement is sudden and violent; in the other it is gradual and peaceable.

C. E. Trevelyan,
On the Education of the People of India, 1838

Contents

List of Illustrations

1 to 19, 21 to 23, 25 to 34, 37, 38, 64 to 66, copyright of the author; inset to 37, Virginia Trower; 20, National Geographic Society; 24, Mrs Leila Phillips; 35, 36, Alan Walker; 41, National Portrait Gallery; 43, Kate Forbes; 44, 45, 46, 55, 60, India Office Library and Records; 51, 52, 53, Library of the University of Newcastle upon Tyne; 54, Richard John Barter Snow; 56, 57, 59, Lady Trevelyan; 61, Mrs Theo Robertson; 62, 63, Julian Wathen; 39, 42, 50, 58 are engravings from the *Oriental Journal* 1834–5.

FOR THOSE WHO STILL REMEMBER SHANGRI-LA

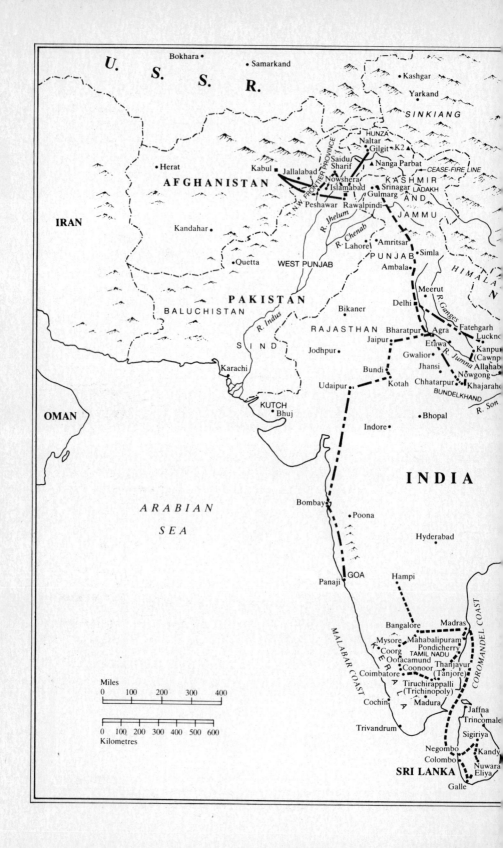

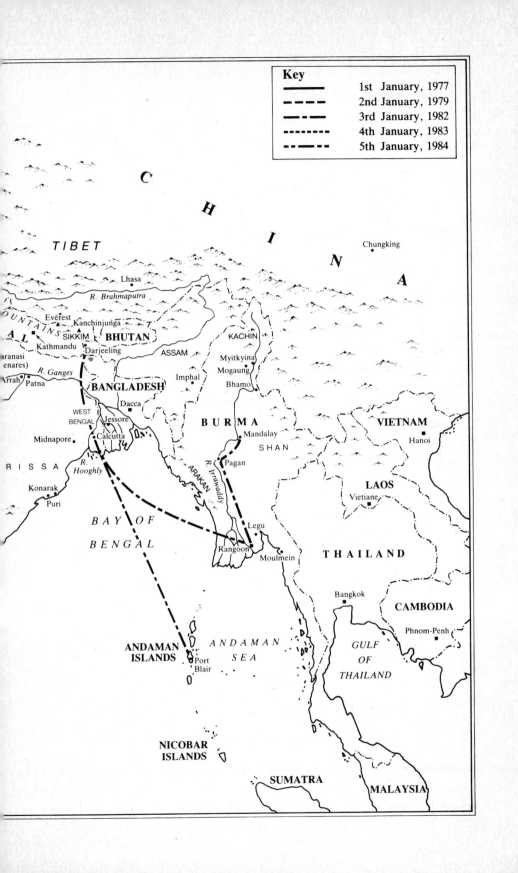

C H I N A

TIBET

Chungking

Lhasa

R. Brahmaputra

OUNTAINS

Everest Kanchinjunga

SIKKIM BHUTAN

AL Kathmandu Darjeeling ASSAM

KACHIN

Myitkyina

Mogaung

ranasi
enares)

R. Ganges

Arrah Patna

BANGLADESH

Dacca

Imphal

Bhamo

WEST
BENGAL Jessore

Midnapore Calcutta

BURMA

Mandalay

VIETNAM

Hanoi

SHAN

R. Hooghly

R. Irrawaddy

ARAKAN

Pagan

RISSA

Konarak

Puri

LAOS

Vietiane

BAY OF

BENGAL

Legu

Rangoon Moulmein

THAILAND

Bangkok

CAMBODIA

Phnom-Penh

ANDAMAN
ISLANDS

ANDAMAN

Port
Blair

SEA

GULF

OF

THAILAND

NICOBAR
ISLANDS

SUMATRA

MALAYSIA

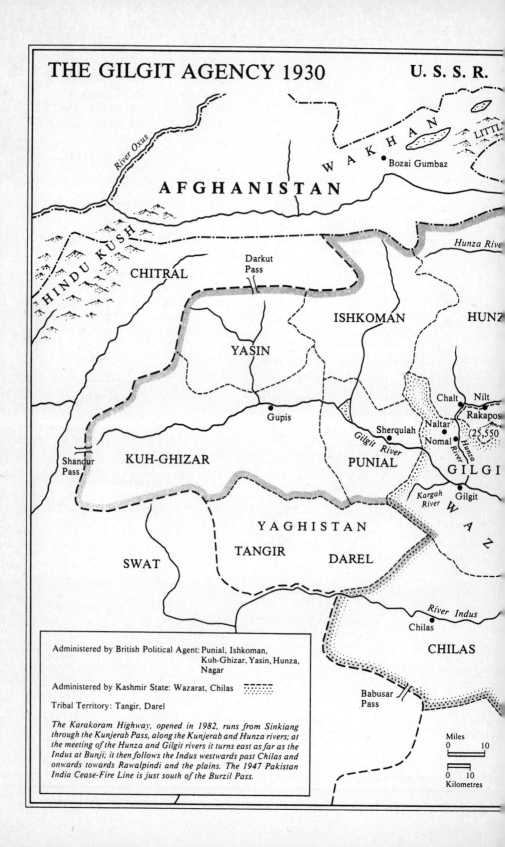

THE GILGIT AGENCY 1930

U. S. S. R.

River Oxus

WAKHAN

LITTL

• Bozai Gumbaz

AFGHANISTAN

HINDU KUSH

CHITRAL

Darkut
Pass

Hunza Rive

ISHKOMAN

HUNZ

YASIN

Chalt Nilt

• Gupis

Sherqulah

Naltar

Rakapos

(25,550

Nomal

Shandur
Pass

KUH-GHIZAR

Gilgit River

PUNIAL

Hunza River

GILGI

Kargah
River

Gilgit

YAGHISTAN

W
A
Z

SWAT

TANGIR

DAREL

River Indus

Chilas

CHILAS

Administered by British Political Agent: Punial, Ishkoman,
Kuh-Ghizar, Yasin, Hunza,
Nagar

Administered by Kashmir State: Wazarat, Chilas

Tribal Territory: Tangir, Darel

*The Karakoram Highway, opened in 1982, runs from Sinkiang
through the Kunjerab Pass, along the Kunjerab and Hunza rivers; at
the meeting of the Hunza and Gilgit rivers it turns east as far as the
Indus at Bunji; it then follows the Indus westwards past Chilas and
onwards towards Rawalpindi and the plains. The 1947 Pakistan
India Cease-Fire Line is just south of the Burzil Pass.*

Babusar
Pass

Miles
0   10

0   10
Kilometres

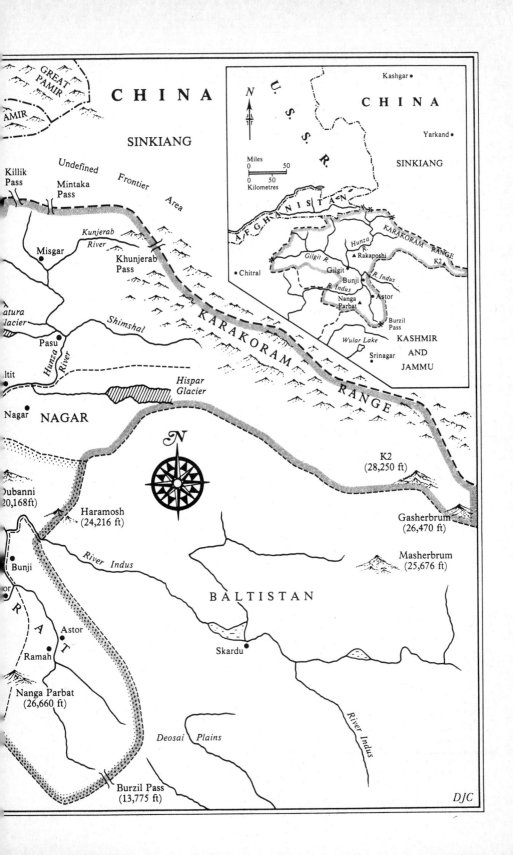

GREAT PAMIR

AMIR

CHINA

SINKIANG

Killik
Pass

Mintaka
Pass

Undefined

Frontier

Area

Kunjerab
River

Misgar

Khunjerab
Pass

atura
lacier

Shimshal

Pasu

Hunza River

ltit

Nagar   NAGAR

Hispar
Glacier

KARAKORAM

RANGE

N

Dubanni
20,168ft)

Haramosh
(24,216 ft)

K2
(28,250 ft)

Gasherbrum
(26,470 ft)

River Indus

Masherbrum
(25,676 ft)

Bunji

or

R
A
T

Astor

Ramah

BALTISTAN

Skardu

Nanga Parbat
(26,660 ft)

River Indus

Deosai Plains

Burzil Pass
(13,775 ft)

DJC

Inset map

Kashgar

CHINA

U.S.S.R.

N

Yarkand

SINKIANG

Miles
0   50
0   50
Kilometres

AFGHANISTAN

KARAKORAM RANGE

Hunza R.

Rakaposhi

K2

Gilgit R.

Chitral

Gilgit

Bunji

R Indus

R Indus

Nanga
Parbat

Astor

Burzil
Pass

Wular Lake

KASHMIR
AND
JAMMU

Srinagar

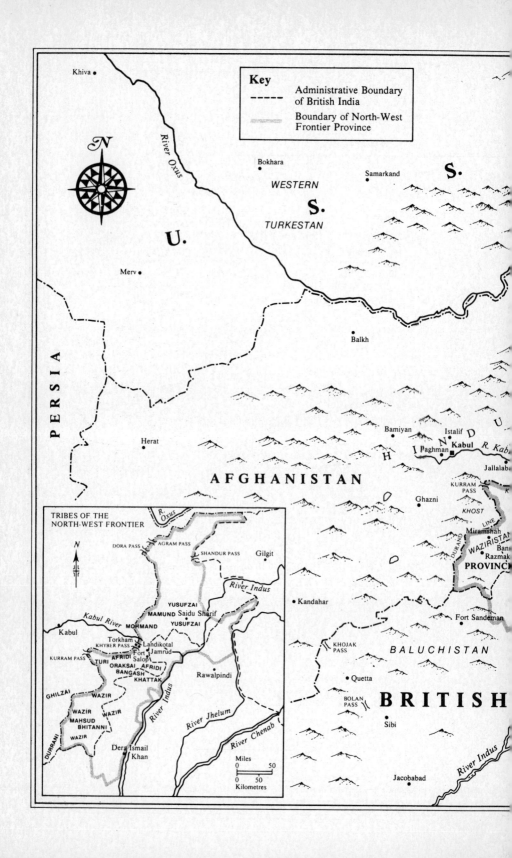

Key
- - - - - Administrative Boundary of British India
〰〰〰 Boundary of North-West Frontier Province

Khiva

N

River Oxus

Bokhara

Samarkand

S.

WESTERN

S.

TURKESTAN

U.

Merv

Balkh

PERSIA

Herat

Bamiyan   Istalif

H   Paghman Kabul R. Kab

I   N   Jallalaba

D   KURRAM PASS   K

AFGHANISTAN   KHOST

Ghazni   LINE   Miramshah

DURAND   WAZIRISTAN   Bann

U   Razmak

PROVINC

TRIBES OF THE
NORTH-WEST FRONTIER

R. Oxus

N

DORA PASS   AGRAM PASS

SHANDUR PASS   Gilgit

River Indus

YUSUFZAI

MAMUND Saidu Sharif

Kabul River MOHMAND   YUSUFZAI

Kabul

Torkham   Landikotal

KHYBER PASS   Fort   Jamrud

KURRAM PASS   AFRIDI Salop

TURI   ORAKSAI AFRIDI

BANGASH

KHATTAK   Rawalpindi

GHILZAI

WAZIR

WAZIR   WAZIR

MAHSUD

BHITANNI

DURRANI   WAZIR

Dera Ismail
Khan

River Indus

River Jhelum

River Chenab

Miles
0   50

0   50
Kilometres

Kandahar

Fort Sandeman

KHOJAK
PASS   BALUCHISTAN

Quetta

BRITISH

BOLAN
PASS

Sibi

Jacobabad

River Indus

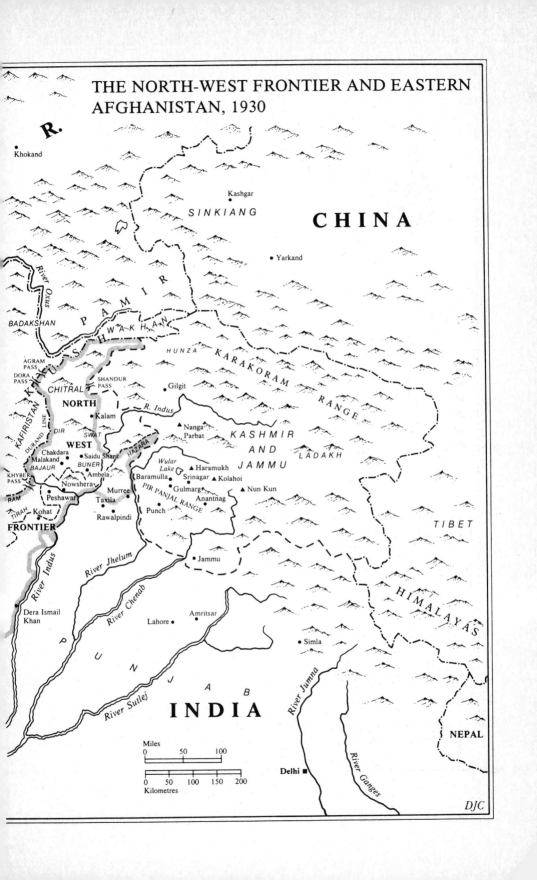

THE NORTH-WEST FRONTIER AND EASTERN AFGHANISTAN, 1930

R.

Khokand

SINKIANG

CHINA

Kashgar

Yarkand

River Oxus

PAMIR

BADAKSHAN

WAKHAN

HINDU KUSH

HUNZA

KARAKORAM RANGE

AGRAM PASS
DORA PASS
CHITRAL
SHANDUR PASS
Gilgit

NORTH
Kalam
R. Indus

▲ Nanga Parbat

KASHMIR AND JAMMU

LADAKH

DURAND LINE
DIR
SWAT
WEST
Chakdara
Malakand
Saidu Sharif
BAJAUR
BUNER
Ambela
HAZARA

KAFIRISTAN

Wular Lake
▲ Haramukh
Baramulla
Srinagar ▲ Kolahoi
Gulmarg
▲ Nun Kun

KHYBER PASS
Nowshera
Ambela

Murree
Taxila
Punch
PIR PANJAL RANGE
Anantnag

RAM
Peshawar
TIRAH
Kohat
FRONTIER

Rawalpindi

Jammu

TIBET

River Indus

River Jhelum

River Chenab

Dera Ismail Khan

P
U
N
J
A
B

Lahore •
Amritsar •

HIMALAYAS

• Simla

River Sutlej

INDIA

River Jumna

NEPAL

Miles
0   50   100

Delhi ■

River Ganges

0   50 100 150 200
Kilometres

DJC

SOME FAMILY RELATIONSHIPS I

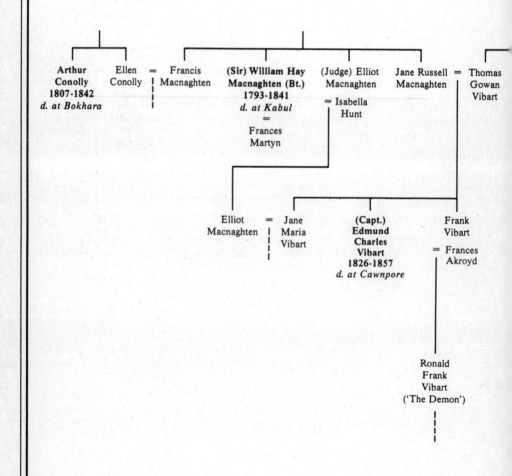

Arthur Conolly 1807-1842 *d. at Bokhara* — Ellen Conolly = Francis Macnaghten — **(Sir) William Hay Macnaghten (Bt.)** 1793-1841 *d. at Kabul* = Frances Martyn — (Judge) Elliot Macnaghten = Isabella Hunt — Jane Russell Macnaghten = Thomas Gowan Vibart

Elliot Macnaghten = Jane Maria Vibart — **(Capt.) Edmund Charles Vibart** 1826-1857 *d. at Cawnpore* — Frank Vibart = Frances Akroyd

Ronald Frank Vibart ('The Demon')

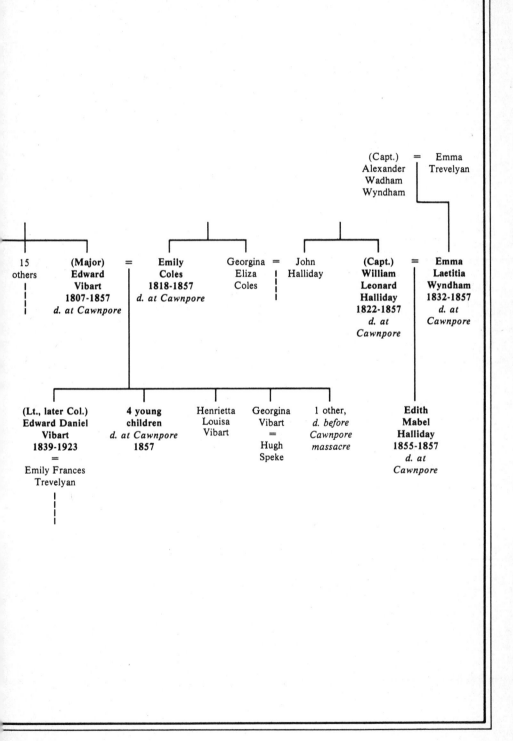

(Capt.) = Emma
Alexander Trevelyan
Wadham
Wyndham

15 (Major) = Emily Georgina = John (Capt.) = Emma
others Edward Coles Eliza Halliday William Laetitia
Vibart 1818-1857 Coles Leonard Wyndham
1807-1857 *d. at Cawnpore* Halliday 1832-1857
d. at Cawnpore 1822-1857 *d. at*
d. at *Cawnpore*
Cawnpore

(Lt., later Col.) 4 young Henrietta Georgina 1 other, Edith
Edward Daniel children Louisa Vibart *d. before* Mabel
Vibart *d. at Cawnpore* Vibart = *Cawnpore* Halliday
1839-1923 1857 Hugh *massacre* 1855-1857
= Speke *d. at*
Emily Frances *Cawnpore*
Trevelyan

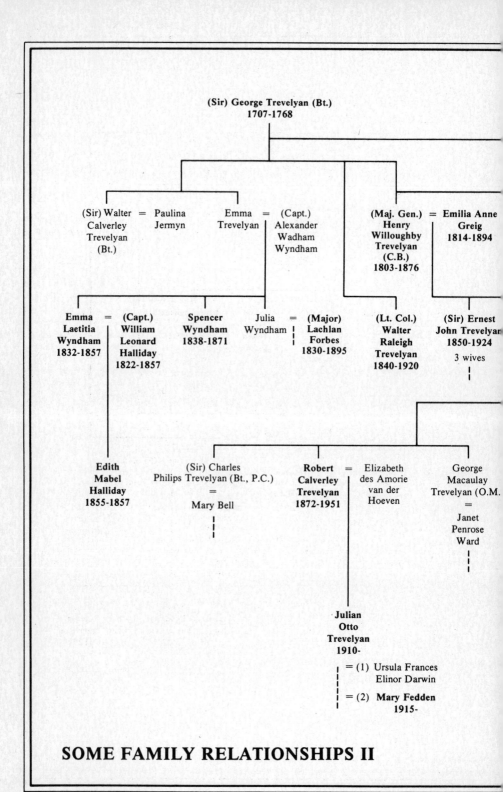

(Sir) George Trevelyan (Bt.)
1707-1768

(Sir) Walter = Paulina
Calverley Jermyn
Trevelyan
(Bt.)

Emma = (Capt.)
Trevelyan Alexander
Wadham
Wyndham

(Maj. Gen.) = **Emilia Anne**
Henry **Greig**
Willoughby **1814-1894**
Trevelyan
(C.B.)
1803-1876

Emma = (Capt.)
Laetitia **William**
Wyndham **Leonard**
1832-1857 **Halliday**
1822-1857

Spencer
Wyndham
1838-1871

Julia = **(Major)**
Wyndham **Lachlan**
Forbes
1830-1895

(Lt. Col.)
Walter
Raleigh
Trevelyan
1840-1920

(Sir) Ernest
John Trevelyan
1850-1924

3 wives

Edith
Mabel
Halliday
1855-1857

(Sir) Charles
Philips Trevelyan (Bt., P.C.)
=
Mary Bell

Robert = Elizabeth
Calverley des Amorie
Trevelyan van der
1872-1951 Hoeven

George
Macaulay
Trevelyan (O.M.)
=
Janet
Penrose
Ward

Julian
Otto
Trevelyan
1910-

= (1) Ursula Frances
Elinor Darwin

= (2) **Mary Fedden**
1915-

SOME FAMILY RELATIONSHIPS II

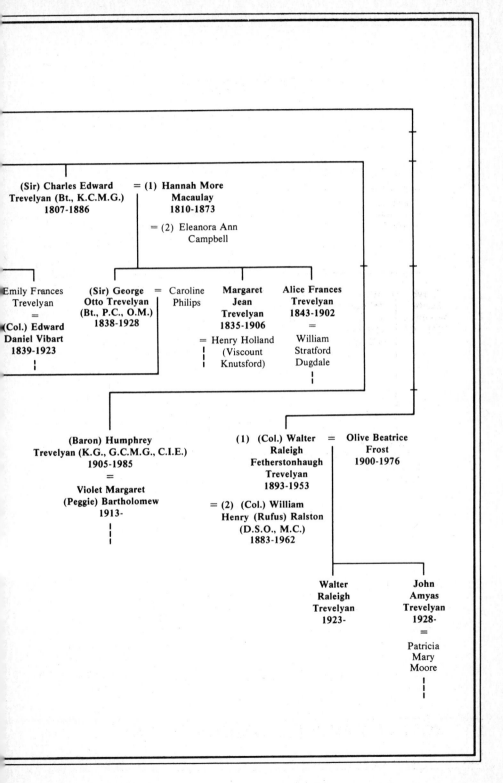

(Sir) Charles Edward = (1) Hannah More
Trevelyan (Bt., K.C.M.G.)   Macaulay
1807-1886   1810-1873

= (2) Eleanora Ann
Campbell

Emily Frances   (Sir) George = Caroline   Margaret   Alice Frances
Trevelyan   Otto Trevelyan   Philips   Jean   Trevelyan
=   (Bt., P.C., O.M.)   Trevelyan   1843-1902
(Col.) Edward   1838-1928   1835-1906   =
Daniel Vibart   William
1839-1923   = Henry Holland   Stratford
¦   (Viscount   Dugdale
                                        Knutsford)   ¦

(Baron) Humphrey   (1) (Col.) Walter = Olive Beatrice
Trevelyan (K.G., G.C.M.G., C.I.E.)   Raleigh   Frost
1905-1985   Fetherstonhaugh   1900-1976
=   Trevelyan
Violet Margaret   1893-1953
(Peggie) Bartholomew
1913-   = (2) (Col.) William
¦   Henry (Rufus) Ralston
¦   (D.S.O., M.C.)
                               1883-1962

                                    Walter   John
                                   Raleigh   Amyas
                                  Trevelyan   Trevelyan
                                    1923-   1928-
                                                       =
                                                   Patricia
                                                     Mary
                                                     Moore
                                                       ¦

In Limbo

'HE WAS BORN in the East, I suppose?'

This question by the grand, pearl-necklaced mother of a friend of mine bothered me a little when it was reported back, not just because I knew she was being condescending but because I was sure she was a witch. What was the peculiarity that she had divined in me? Something odd in my manner, my face, my complexion? Was I like that child in *The Secret Garden*, with 'a little thin face and a little thin body, thin light hair and a sour expression ... the most disagreeable-looking child ever seen?' Did I smell of curry?

Ever since then, when I meet others of pre-Second World War vintage who like me were born in the territories of the British Raj, I find myself scanning them for that tell-tale aura or mark. Nearly all of us were sent home to boarding-schools around the age of seven or eight (I was eight), and therefore separated from our families for several years, being farmed out to Misselthwaite Manors for holidays. So most of our childhoods were solitary ones. Maybe it is true that it taught us to be independent. To me the whole experience of my life between the ages of eight and fourteen seems now to be summed up by a sentence that I was supposed not to have overheard: 'It's your turn to have Raleigh for Christmas.' Which is perhaps why I have loved my quiet Christmases on my Cornish creek, without illuminated trees, tinsel or fuss.

I often feel that I belong to a tribe that is becoming extinct. Air travel of course means that families no longer have to endure those drastically long separations if a child is sent 'home' when the father is stationed abroad. By no means all my coevals however, as I have discovered, share, or shared, my longing to go back to India. Some would hate to do so. I have a friend who ran away twice from a convent school at Darjeeling. Not for her another glimpse of the superb Kanchinjunga. Another friend gives a guilty smile when he admits to having been born in Calcutta, thinking perhaps the listener immedi-

I

ately has a vision of deformed beggars and the hospitals of Mother Teresa. At least I can claim an exotic spot for my birthplace: Port Blair in the Andaman Islands, an appendage of the then Indian Empire not far from the coast of Burma. What is more, I can boast that Port Blair was a penal settlement. When I was born, in July 1923, my mother was carried on a litter or 'dandy' to the hospital by two murderers. My first ayah was a Burmese murderess called Mimi. Our servants were murderers.

My father, then a captain, was in charge of the garrison at Port Blair. He was in the 93rd Burma Infantry, later to be known as the 5th Battalion of the 8th Punjab Regiment. Many of the prisoners had committed crimes of passion which did not entail the death penalty; they were hanged only if they murdered one another, a guard or an European. There were also some political prisoners, whom we now acknowledge as freedom fighters, though there were many more in the next decade, after our time. It was an enclosed life socially for the Europeans at Port Blair, as there were so few of them, but my parents enjoyed themselves. My mother collected some gorgeous butterflies, and my father took some rather good photographs. Because of the danger from sharks they and others of the officer class swam inside a large net which was below the Club House. Other ranks and their wives had to take their chance without nets. Nearly all the islands were covered in jungle, where there were orchids, parrots and hornbills, and the original inhabitants were said to be or have been cannibals. My father took pictures of some Andamanese: anxious-looking, semi-pygmy negritos, rather like Papuans. The men and women were naked except for little sacks in front. Some parts of the islands were too dangerous to visit, as they were inhabited by the Jarawas, also negritos but normal size, better-looking and very fierce. South of the Andamans were the Nicobar Islands. My father's photographs show the natives there were of the semi-mongoloid type, like Malaysians, usually totally naked though evidently fond of wearing hats.

All these photographs made me anxious to visit the place of my birth. I liked the idea of being born near a tropical beach among coconut palms. As for memories of the Andamans, I had absolutely none, for we left when I was only a few months old. I was christened in Rangoon Cathedral where my parents had been married. Before going to the Andamans they had been in Bhamo, in the north of Burma near the Chinese province of Yunnan. Here again my father had taken intriguing pictures, including some of the giraffe-necked women of the Padaungs. In December 1923 he was sent to the North-West Frontier of India to take part in the Waziristan campaign, which was then coming to a close but nevertheless earned him a medal. Meanwhile my mother took me to England to show me to her parents near Chester, and in due course my father joined us.

At this stage it is easier to refer to my mother and father by their Christian names, which were Olive and Walter. Both disliked these names. 'Olive' derived from olive branch, because she had been born when the Boer War was at its most depressing. As a little girl she had called herself 'Woggie' or 'Wog', and this was how she was usually known for the rest of her life by her family and old friends: a nick-name which caused raised eyebrows in what could be called *Jewel in the Crown* circles. 'Walter', like 'Raleigh' for me, was due to a connec-tion with the great Elizabethan, always a bit embarrassing to have to admit.

Walter's mother had just died. He was a self-contained individual, rather silent and not good at keeping up with people, even his mother. The excuse was that his childhood had been an unhappy one, as his parents had been divorced when divorce was a matter of scan-dal, and he had been 'allocated' to the Trevelyans while his sister remained with the mother. It is true that my grandmother was rather wild Anglo-Irish, always falling in love, especially with good horse-men, but those particular Trevelyans – Walter's father, grandmother, uncles and aunts – were (with one special exception) a selfish and quarrelsome lot, inhabiting two gloomy houses near one another in Onslow Gardens in South Kensington. Walter never wrote to his grandmother when he was in the Army, which annoyed her, so she cut him out of her will. Another relation in Ireland who was intend-ing to leave him her property became fed up for the same reason. In fact the very possibility of inheriting anything from these two would have stopped him from writing as a matter of principle. In our years of pinching and scraping after the last war, when he was living on his Army pension, he may have regretted this attitude; certainly the rest of us did. His mother also virtually disinherited him. She had mar-ried a 'bounder' as her second husband but had been separated from him. There was a lawsuit between Walter and this man when she died, and Walter lost, because – so I used to be told – the case was heard in Dublin at the time of the Troubles (which sounded rather like a non-sequitur). Whenever Walter spoke of his mother to us, his eyes would go red with tears, and I am sure that it was nothing to do with money.

I acquired a nanny from Liverpool, Norah Spicer, who also became a kind of governess. She had dark hair and dark soft eyes. She loved me and I loved her. I suppose she must have been in her late thirties, even over forty, but whenever her birthday came along she

3

always laughingly would say that she was twenty-one. I think by the time I left India I probably loved her nearly as much as Olive, and certainly more than Walter.

Walter had ginger hair, or the remains of it, for he was bald on top, the consequence he would say of having had to wear a tin hat during the Great War in Mesopotamia. His complexion was florid, unsuitable really for the Indian climate. He was considered to have rather a fine face, with a 'typical' Trevelyan nose, which seems to derive from a Huguenot connection way back in the eighteenth century. My nose is more like Olive's, her worst feature. Although she photographed badly and sometimes looked awful in hats, she was by general consent attractive, vivacious, energetic, always well and usually expensively dressed, even in her riding clothes. 'I think she had more charm than anyone I knew,' one of her oldest friends wrote to me after she died. Once, in middle age, someone stopped her in Edinburgh and asked her if she was Marlene Dietrich, something that forever afterwards was good for a laugh. I used to be teased by the others in the family because I was the only one whose hair was not fair, but now that I have seen Walter's early photographs of Olive I realize that she had darkish hair like mine, and that she suddenly became an ash blonde on her return from that trip to England in 1924.

Olive was born in 1900, Walter in 1893. Her father's family, the Frosts, were well-to-do millers in Chester. We were always conscious of the intellectual and political reputations of other branches of the Trevelyan family, and by association Macaulay, so we teased her a little about the Frosts, as if they were philistines, which they certainly were not, one for instance being a collector of Pre-Raphaelite pictures. Among near antecedents Olive's mother's side was the most interesting for me, 'Phiz' having been my great-great uncle, and Constable and David Roberts thus connected by marriage; there was also a rumour of illegitimate descent from Mrs Jordan in her pre-Clarence days, which I hope was true.

Olive had been spoilt as a child, as she always admitted, and she inherited her extravagance from her father. Indeed she had been brought up in a largish country house in the Edwardian period, which is now of course a byword for luxury – for those who were rich that is. The Frosts and the Onslow Gardens Trevelyans were friends, and so it was that Olive met Walter in 1920 when he came on leave looking for a wife. She followed him out to Burma for the wedding, travelling alone with her three dogs. At the end of her life she admitted to me that when she saw Walter waiting for her on the quay she wondered if she had made a mistake. In many ways it had been an attraction of opposites, revealed perhaps in their very different hand-

4

writings: Walter confident and neat, Olive sprawling and untidy, yet sophisticated.

Walter's battalion moved to Lahore, where we remained a couple of years before he was transferred to Nowshera, after another period of leave in England. I find it hard to dissociate any scattered memories of that cantonment life from the photographs in Walter's and Nanny Spicer's albums. In the Lahore time I certainly do remember a children's picnic in the Shalimar Gardens, when we wore garlands and hunted for sugared almonds instead of Easter eggs. All the nannies wore white cloche hats, white dresses, white stockings and white shoes – or do I *imagine* I remember this part, after seeing a photograph? By and large what I do recall from my early childhood are shocks, not things like picnics, though later on picnics became a high spot of my life in India. But perhaps the beauty of the Shalimar Gardens was a kind of shock, just as I also have a vivid memory of being taken to the Taj Mahal (though I thought the approach far too long and tiring). Once I was 'stolen' and there was an uproar. That I certainly do remember. An Indian woman – they said she was mad, but I found her boring – wheeled me away, and under a mud wall in a long dirty road she filled my pram with French marigolds, the smell of which I still detest.

Olive loved parties and bridge, but living in a cantonment and being a regimental wife was the side of India she hated (some people of course thought that it was a simply wonderful life). She had quite a flair for interior decoration, which usually meant no clutter or Victoriana, and made the most of any place we inhabited. Walter on the other hand cared little about possessions. He was a soldier through and through, and being keen on polo and hunting enjoyed Lahore and Nowshera. Both my parents were more at ease in really wild country (Olive so long as she could have her bridge). Our cantonment bungalows never seemed like home to me, and if places like them are the sole memories for others who spent their childhoods in India I can understand their reluctance to return. In the back of my mind I can see dull anonymous nursery rooms with lizards on cream walls, very high ceilings, arched verandahs all round the house, brown grass, mynah birds with yellow beaks, green parakeets, kites, rows of flowerpots instead of flowerbeds, cannas; also lots of servants each with special jobs: the bearer or general servant, the khansama or cook, the bhisti or water-carrier, the dhobi or laundry-man, and the lowly mehtar or sweeper for emptying the thunder boxes – we seemed never to be *alone*.

The biggest upheaval in Nowshera as far as I was concerned was the disappearance of the Pemberton children, a boy and a girl, next door. They were left playing in their garden by their nanny, but when she went to fetch them for tiffin they were gone. I was cross-questioned, indeed grilled, because I had been with them for a while, and not believed when I said I did not know where they had gone. There was a hue and cry all day, Mrs Pemberton sobbing etc. Then that evening there they were, as if nothing had happened, back in the garden and – even more strangely – still thinking it was morning. 'Just like *Mary Rose*,' Olive kept on saying, referring to the J. M. Barrie play she had seen in London.

My brother John was born in 1928 in Srinagar during the hot weather, which we used to spend in the hill-station of Gulmarg above the Vale of Kashmir, Srinagar having had the nearest hospital of consequence. Some months later Lady Hailey, a small brown Italian, the wife of the Governor, was invited to our house in Nowshera and dutifully leant over John's cot to admire him. He snatched at her pearls and swallowed quite a few. So he was given castor oil, and sure enough that night they reappeared. Lady Hailey especially intrigued me; I was told she liked sliding down banisters.

I never liked 'early starts', still a feature of travel in India. One morning I was aroused when it was dark, and rushed to Peshawar in order to see the aeroplanes that had brought the King of Afghanistan and his wives to safety after a revolution in Kabul. I was taken inside one of the planes, stuffy and smelling like old laundry baskets; all over the floor were bits of cotton wool which had been in the wives' ears. Not being mechanically minded, I am ashamed to admit that I was hardly thrilled by my first sight of an aeroplane, which I now know to have been a Hinaidi, and a lumbering old thing it was. On another occasion in Nowshera I was woken up suddenly when it was hardly light because some men from Turkestan had arrived on camels – oonts we called them, from the Hindustani word. I was given a ride on a camel, and enjoyed the experience far more, even though I caught a flea, and camels are really rather silly munching animals with bad breath, not as comfortable as elephants.

Our excitement at Nowshera was crossing the bridge of boats over the Kabul River. I used to like to watch clouds gathering before monsoons. Once, sitting in a chair in our garden, I was sure I could see a small white figure bobbing up and down like an uvula. I rushed in to tell Nanny Spicer but she only smiled, and that hurt me a bit. Of course when I returned it had gone, but for a long while I was convinced I had seen one of my father's brother officers, a Major Haycraft, who had recently been murdered by a Sikh and was trapped up there in the clouds.

In 1929 Walter was appointed military adviser in Gilgit to the

Maharajah of Kashmir; or, more precisely, he was Special Service Officer, Kashmir State Infantry. The most practical way of reaching Gilgit, which was on the edge of the Karakoram and near 'where three empires meet', was from the south over the always dreaded Burzil Pass, nearly 14,000 feet. We set off from Srinagar early in September on a two and a half weeks' trek over the mountains, with ninety ponies and several coolies carrying supplies for eight months, including water for the journey. As Olive would say, in an offhand way: 'It was quite easy really. You thought of how much salt you wanted for a month, and multiplied it by eight.' To which would be added a supply of potassium permanganate ('pinky pani'), in which vegetables would have to be boiled. I suppose her wardrobe would have added considerably to the ponies' loads. Since both she and Walter were keen gardeners, they brought with them shrubs and daffodil bulbs, specially sent out from England. She also took a supply of Balkan Sobranie cigarettes and bottles of gin and Cointreau, as she had a passion for White Lady cocktails, plus masses of silver spoons and forks ('I can't bear not eating off silver') and a bone china tea-set for twenty, even though the European inhabitants of Gilgit, including nannies and children, numbered less than that. John, aged fifteen months, was carried in a doolie, a wickerwork bed with a canvas roof. I had my own pony, Tommy. Then began a time that afterwards for the rest of all our lives seemed like a fragmented dream.

Walter's turn of duty ended in 1933, but I had to go to school in England in 1931. For most of the year in Gilgit we were completely cut off from civilization by snow, although dak runners would get through somehow with the mail (often soaked) and there was a telegraph connection with the British Residency in Srinagar. When the snows melted early in June we returned over the Burzil to spend our summer at Gulmarg, and there would be for me a much too hectic round of fancy dress parties, tea parties, Wolf Cub outings and golf lessons. We had a bungalow entirely lined with bark. It was known as Hut 46a, quite a humble place, even ramshackle, like most bungalows at Gulmarg. But it was spectacularly placed on the edge of a khud or mountainside, covered with pines, with a vast view over the Vale to the glorious sight, when the clouds lifted, of a whole range of Himalayan peaks: Haremukh, Gudhai, Kalaho and, far away, Machai, 19,620 feet. We could even see, further round to the left, Nanga Parbat, the ninth highest mountain in the world, looming up on its own, away from the Great Himalaya chain and the Pir Panjal. To me nostalgia for Gulmarg means not a crush of children dressed as columbines and pierrots (and how I suffered once under a mask at a fancy dress party when I went as Felix the Cat) but going for rides in

the pine forests and across the flower meadows on Tommy, or picnics and trout fishing expeditions in the Ferozepur nullah where the
thrilling noise and swirl of the water made talking difficult, and
where the white spray dazzled; or looking for tussocks of a minute
white and pink androsace.

But Gilgit was our real home. Our house was not an imposing
place by any means: just a dun-coloured bungalow with swinging net
doors on the verandah and a bay window. Olive and Walter had
mostly laid out the sloping garden and planted the trees. In front of us
were the barren grey-ribbed mountains with violet shadows, and up
the valley were the irrigation channels, lined with tamarisks. There
was not much rain in Gilgit, and the winters were mild, so those
channels called khuls were a great feature of the valley. There were
apricot trees, poplars, mulberries and pomegranates. In the distance
were the great peaks of Dubanni and Haramosh, always covered with
snow. I loved the call of the chukor, a kind of red-legged partridge, in
the fields behind, and the great silences as evening fell, when we
knew that the markhor, a wild goat, would be coming down the
mountainsides to drink. Sometimes in the afternoon we would hear
the excited rhythm of drums and pipes; this would mean that a polo
match was in progress on the other side of the bazaar.

The Political Agent, Heb Todd, to whom Walter was also Military
Assistant, lived next door, and he had two daughters, called Heather
and Lavender, who were the only two children of about my age for
me to play with, apart from the sons of mirs and rajahs whom I only
saw at intervals when their fathers came on official visits to Gilgit.
My best friend was Amin Khan, the youngest son of the Mir of
Hunza; we used to have jumping competitions on our ponies. When
the Mir came to dinner with us he brought his dancing girls, who
were really boys in long greasy wigs made from hair from Kashgar
and with bells round their ankles. He was always inviting me to
Hunza so that I could ride a yak, but as the journey involved crossing
the river by a rope bridge my parents would not allow it, and this
made me lose face in front of Amin. Everyone liked the old Mir. He
was a 'card', and was amused and perplexed by the way that every
year Olive's skirts were a different length: one year short, one year
long, one year short in front and long behind.

Needless to say, I was in ignorance of the manoeuvres in the Gilgit
area at the end of the nineteenth century to block the Russians from
British India. There was no danger from Russians in our time,
though one of Walter's jobs was to visit the northern passes occasionally. His military obligation could hardly have been all that exacting.
Indeed I know that for him it was an ideal life. He played polo and

tennis, fished, went on shoots and stalked snow leopard, measured glaciers, paid courtesy visits to mirs and rajahs and was entertained by them. He also collected skins for the Natural History Museum in South Kensington, and had a lynx named after him, Lynx trevelya-nii. In the drawing-room we had the skins of two black bears he had shot, and dotted round the bungalow were heads of markhor and ibex – not liked at all however by Olive ('so barbaric'). I never saw him much. Sometimes he would be away for weeks. Olive told me after he had died that she used to say to him: 'Do try to see more of Raleigh.' After so many separations in subsequent years he and I seemed to have less and less in common. He would have liked me to have been a regular soldier, and to me that was an anathema. I was a bad shot, hated blood sports in fact, and was bad at golf and tennis (because of a broken elbow, badly mended). Long-distance running and rowing were my forte at school. I respected him for his extra-ordinary, almost obtuse integrity, and began only to understand what he meant to me as a father when he was on his death-bed.

With Olive it was different; she was demonstrative, and 'believed' in me. She sacrificed a lot to give me a good education. She also had ambitions for me, but they were usually not my ambitions, so when I began to grow up I found myself being over-organized, particularly in the matter of meeting the right girls. When she and Walter went to Quetta, a friend of theirs told me that Olive took her to her room to look at a photograph of me at school. 'This is my first love,' she had said.

It would be unkind to the various relations and friends with whom I boarded during the holidays, in the years of blankness after leaving India, to say that I was unhappy with them. I had an aunt who lived in a splendid house overlooking the Killarney lakes, which after all are one of the world's beauty spots. I did loathe having to stay in the gri-miness of mid-Victorian South Kensington, and Onslow Gardens still seem to me the Slough of Despond. My feelings for Henley-on-Thames, though, are quite different, and I think of it in terms of endless summer days; I used to spend many holidays near there as a paying guest at the house of one of Olive's old school-friends, who had a daughter of my own age in whom I could confide and whom I could trust absolutely. It is only looking back that I have realized what I missed by not having had a home for six years.

Olive made the journey with my brother John from India to see me most summers. I knew that our partings were agony for her, and would make it worse on purpose by crying out when on the last even-ing she would come to see me in bed: 'Don't leave me, don't leave me.' In the Killarney days she was worried because I had some bad accidents, but she did not realize that my Irish cousins used to force me to do dangerous things like diving off haystacks into straw, or jumping into a lake to see if I could swim. There was a nice rich old American called Mr Harrington who had bought and beautified the house and gardens at Dunloe Castle. One night some men came and cut down all the young trees along the drive, and he had a heart attack and died. All this turned me against Killarney.

Much as Olive had loved Gilgit and Kashmir, she was tired of the life of the wife of an Indian Army officer and dreaded another cantonment. John was coming up to school age and she could not bear the thought of being separated from both him and me, and of being split in two, between husband and children. So she insisted that Walter should retire early, which he did in 1937. We settled in Essex, but he was still on the reserve list and when the war came had to return to India. In 1942 I joined the Army, went to North Africa and Italy, and was demobilized at the end of 1946. By that time Walter and I were almost strangers.

Walter could not stand what he considered to be the semi-urban life of Essex, and our house there was too large to run on his pension. Besides he was not well. Overwork during the Bengal Famine of 1943 had caused him to be invalided home halfway through the war. By an extraordinary stroke of luck he was able to acquire what the historian G. M. Trevelyan described as our Cornish *Stammhaus*, a converted farmhouse called Trevelyan from which the family had originally taken its name. It stood on a windy hill, with a great view down a creek leading off the River Fowey and towards the pyramids of the St Austell china clay mines. He was perhaps more at peace there than at any time in his life, but after two years he died, aged fifty-nine.

Olive went to live abroad, to be followed by John after his marriage. So the house Trevelyan became mine. I could not possibly live there, being dependent on a job in London, and I let it. Nevertheless owning that little house, with all its sentimental family associations, gave me – at last – a sense of having roots. Walter had had so few possessions – a few books, cuff-links, a blotter made from a crocodile he had shot, and of course the photograph albums. I looked through those albums, trying to establish that I really did have a bond with him when I was a child. I failed, but when I saw again those wonderful pictures of the country around Gilgit I knew that some day I must return there. Could any place have been so beautiful? Could I ever have been so happy? I had a yearning to make that trek again, even to cross the Burzil Pass. I wanted to make the night journey by houseboat from Srinagar across the Wular Lake, waking in the early morning among the reeds and lotus flowers, and seeing the clouds and mountains reflected in the blue-milk water. I wanted to ride again up through those pine forests, stay in those musty rest-houses made of logs, and after dark hear the panthers purring like sawmills outside. If I were to go in summer, there would be the flowers, if in autumn the blaze of sumac contrasting with the bark of silver birch, each day bringing one closer to some of the grandest scenery of the world. If I were lucky, as we reached the tundra, I would hear marmots calling, and see them popping up like big brown ferrets on their hind legs . . .

The wars between India and Pakistan, cutting what had been regarded as Kashmir into two, soon made that journey even more of a pipe-dream. But I went on hoping. Then a strange thing happened: I had a letter from an unknown man telling me that he was emigrating to Canada and wanted to give me some ciné films which he believed had something to do with my family. It turned out that during the war, when our house in Essex had been in the direct line for bombing raids on London, Olive had been told that photographic material was especially inflammable. We had had several incendiary bombs dropped close to us, so she had thrown away some films she had taken in Gilgit and Gulmarg. These had been rescued by the dustman, and given to a home movies enthusiast, who twenty-five years later was now approaching me.

Suddenly to be confronted by a replay of part of one's life such a long while ago is almost as though one were already dead, a kind of ghost, or anxious uvula-figure bobbing in the clouds. There before me was the trek across the Burzil, polo matches, jumping fences on Tommy, the Mir's dancing girls, sword-dances, a tug-of-war between Hunza and its rival Nagar at the annual Jhalsa or durbar in Gilgit. Nostalgic fool that I was, and am, I nearly wept.

A Quest

I CANNOT RECALL having seen many shelves of books in the houses we inhabited in India, Essex or Cornwall, or for that matter pictures, apart from prints and watercolours of game-birds and foxhunting scenes. I suppose that in India we would have left most of our books behind for the libraries. The first adult work I read was called *I Like a Good Murder*, and that was at the age of nearly eight on my last trek across the mountains. When I began to collect material for this book I had no idea how many murders would come my way.

Olive used to say that she did not like novels, and she therefore read biographies. It was Walter who introduced me to the Mowgli stories and various other books about animals which I always loved. He was a passionate admirer both of Kipling and of R. L. Stevenson, whose works in twenty volumes he owned. The more august branches of the Trevelyan family had a reputation as radical-Liberals, and in the early part of this century were certainly not known as churchgoers, but Walter was right-wing and after the last war became not only a campaigner for the Tories but religiously inclined. Thus he collected Winston Churchill's works and possessed Money-penny and Buckle's life of Disraeli. *Pilgrim's Progress* became one of his favourite books (also *The Compleat Angler*). He was always thinking of ways to make more money – out of growing apples, vegetables or flowers for Covent Garden, or pigs and poultry – and would buy heaps of instructional books, which he would study minutely. He wrote occasional articles and letters to the press, and attempted a novel which he read out to us and was I am afraid very dull. He was an intensely patriotic person, as distinct from chauvinist. The fact that we were related to George Macaulay Trevelyan and his father George Otto Trevelyan was always a source of pride to Walter and a stimulus to his own writing. We therefore possessed various Tre-velyana (or trevelyanii), in particular George Otto's first two books – *Cawnpore: The Story of a Massacre* and *The Competition Wallah*. In this way I became aware of the fact that Trevelyans had a long association with India, and not necessarily a military one.

G. M. Trevelyan and his two brothers were always kind to me, and when I was in hospital in Italy G.M. wrote me little notes from Cambridge recommending poems or books, which were impossible to get hold of in those circumstances. To be accepted by this trio compensated for the prejudice I felt against my immediate Onslow Gardens Trevelyan forebears. In Italy it was thanks to them that I met people like Bernard Berenson and the family of Benedetto Croce. Oddly, so it seemed to me then, but not so much now, Walter disapproved of those friendships, and I had a letter from him about the dangers of becoming a 'sponger'.

After the war I used to be summoned at yearly intervals by G.M. to have lunch at the Master's Lodge at Trinity. I must admit that I did feel that once he had heard a potted account of my year's activities he would seem suddenly anxious to get on to other more important matters of his own. At the end of his life, he appeared pleased by my first book, which was autobiographical and about my experiences in the army in Italy, and asked me what else I had in mind to write. I said that one day perhaps I would write about Gilgit and places I had remembered in India. To which he replied: 'You could add something about other Trevelyans in India. Find out about my grandfather, the Governor of Madras. He was a great man.' Whether he meant it seriously or not, I was encouraged. 'If only Walter could have heard that,' Olive said when I told her (Walter having been dead some years). Her words were like a dagger, and I think that was the first real occasion on which I understood how much Walter had been disappointed in me.

The book that I vaguely had in my mind to write was a nostalgic one about going back and what it was like to have lived in such remote places. Gradually this also developed into a kind of quest, not for identity, but proof of existence. Of course I now had Cornwall, where I was beginning to dig myself in and discover some comforting family associations. I also had many Anglo-Irish and Irish forebears on both my grandmothers' sides, but much as I loved the beauty of Ireland I felt that the country had failed me – it would always have sad memories. I certainly did not feel a Londoner or an Essex man.

As I began to read books inspired by the Raj, including typescript memoirs of old military buffers and civil servants in my job as a publisher's editor, I was struck by their intensity of feeling, something that is hardly to be found from other outposts of Empire (one great exception being Arthur Grimble's *A Pattern of Islands*). Then, on rereading *Kim*, I became fascinated by the Great Game, which was the term given to the rivalry between Russia and Britain in Central Asia throughout most of the nineteenth century. I came to realize how important Gilgit, 'where three empires meet', had been in all this, and inevitably I found myself drawn to accounts of the first two Afghan wars and the clashes with the tribes of the North-West Frontier. It was hard not to conclude that the territorial aspirations of Tsarist Russia were similar to those of the Soviets.

Which led me on to thinking generally about imperialism: now a dirty word. Whilst I could easily understand the reaction of a new generation to the imperial mystique and the 'white man's burden' (actually Kipling wrote the poem with those fatal words in 1899 to warn Americans of their responsibilities in the Philippines), from my own limited experience I knew that it had not all been hypocrisy, exploitation, lust and plunder, but that there had also been a degree of selflessness among a great many who had served in India and given their lives to it. I wanted, not to contrast British and Russian imperialist behaviour, but to write a little about the work of the generation previous to mine, not only my immediate relatives.

G. M. Trevelyan's grandfather was Sir Charles Edward Trevelyan, who was born in 1807 and died in 1886. I became interested in him whilst doing some research among family papers at Newcastle, where there were fifty-four volumes of his correspondence and much else. In recent years Sir Charles has come under fire (not altogether fairly) for his role at the Treasury during the Irish Potato Famine. Because of the Northcote–Trevelyan report of 1854 he is still known as the father of the modern Civil Service. Anyone wanting to describe Charles will inevitably turn to Macaulay, whose sister Charles married in Calcutta in 1834: 'Zeal boils over in all his talk. His topics even in courtship are steam navigation, the education of the natives, the equalisation of the sugar duties, the substitution of the Roman for the Arabic alphabet.'

'Not a type but an individual,' G.M. said of him. 'My grandfather was one of those utterly fearless and disinterested men, who have their own standards and always act to them.' He also added: 'Inconsiderate rashness in pursuit of a scheme of public welfare sometimes brought him into conflict with the authorities.'

He was meaning that Charles had been recalled from Madras under a cloud. On the other hand, when in due course I met an historian from Madras, I found a firm and convinced admirer of Charles's record there: Charles, he said, had done more for Madras than any

British Governor; he had had a true feeling for the benefit of the Indian population, and his name in Madras was still remembered and respected. Wilfrid Scawen Blunt went to Madras in 1883, and discovered, twenty-three years after the recall, that Charles had been the only Governor 'who had left a really good impression on the natives'.

But I also discovered a connection between Charles and the early stages of the Great Game. So my idea for a book gradually came to be more ambitious. I became interested in the impact of India on the British, and their reactions to events at various points in history. Most British people have had relatives who served in India, whether in the Army or the Civil Service, stretching back at least to the eighteenth century. I began to see myself as inescapably belonging to a wider context, and not just for reasons of having been born in India.

Charles went out to India three times. During his last period he was Finance Member of the Supreme Council at Calcutta, and he took with him his son George Otto; *Cawnpore* and *The Competition Wallah* resulted. George Otto (as he is always referred to now, instead of George alone as his contemporaries called him) did not love India in the way his father had, and never wanted to return. Ten of our relations – or more properly kinsmen – died in massacres at Cawnpore in 1857. G. M. Trevelyan's brother Bob, R. C. Trevelyan the poet, travelled with E. M. Forster and Lowes Dickinson on Forster's first trip to India in 1912–13; they stayed at Chhatarpur with the eccentric maharajah who appears in J. R. Ackerley's wicked little classic *Hindoo Holiday*. And there were others in the family with Indian connections: Humphrey Trevelyan, for instance, who worked with Nehru and became an ambassador in Moscow.

Instead therefore of simply planning to revisit haunts of my childhood – Kashmir, the Andamans and the equivalent of what is now northern Pakistan – I decided I must travel to other parts of the subcontinent. Indeed I was to make five journeys, which included parts of Afghanistan, Burma and Sri Lanka. I was not able to go to nearly all the places I would have liked, sometimes because I was debarred for political reasons, sometimes for lack of cash or time, sometimes because I allowed myself to be lured to spots such as Hampi or Goa which had nothing to do – or hardly anything to do – with my theme or themes. In so doing I have learnt a little about the sub-continent that was unknown to me as a child. But I have so much more to learn, or even to understand. An Indian from Cawnpore, or Kanpur as it now is, said to me in 1984: 'I am an Indian, and have never left India, but I still do not understand India.' And Clement Attlee once said: 'India is not a tabula rasa, but a paper much scribbled over.' Travelling around India and Pakistan aroused or revived in me a number of questions, most of them unanswerable, but it has not been my aim to give grand overviews about for instance whether we should have been in India at all.

The result is a kind of kaleidoscope, going backwards and forwards in time, depending on my whereabouts on my travels. It amuses me now to think of what Nanny Spicer would have said if she had seen me walking barefoot in the bazaar at Tiruchirappalli. Little English boys were not allowed to go into bazaars in Raj days. When I was in the slit trenches of Anzio I had a letter from her which said: 'I don't know, dear, how you can stand up to all this. You were so carefully brought up.' How grateful I am to her for leaving me her Gilgit diary and albums in her will.

The First Journey

I

I BEGAN TO make serious plans for returning to Gilgit in 1973. By then the dispute between India and Pakistan over the ownership of Kashmir appeared to be in abeyance. There was still the cease-fire line between Pakistan-occupied north and Indian-occupied south, created in 1948 after the coups d'état in Gilgit and Skardu that had brought both those areas under Pakistani control. Pakistan also occupied a strip known as Azad or Free Kashmir, only a few miles west of Gulmarg. In my innocence I thought of adapting my original dream of following our old trek, by making two separate trips, one down from Gilgit to the Burzil and the other up from Srinagar. Soon I discovered that there was a large military zone on each side of the cease-fire line, and that tourists were not welcome in either.

It was hard to get much information about conditions in Gilgit, whether for instance there was even a reasonable hotel. I assumed that our bungalow would have been destroyed in the fighting after Independence. Naturally I also wanted to get to Hunza, as it had been forbidden to me as a child, but even that now seemed problematical after reading in *The Times* about Chinese plans for building a road there from Sinkiang, and then extending it along a branch of what had been the original Silk Road from China to Gilgit.

I decided that I must pull strings at the Pakistan High Commission, where at least I had a friend of a friend. The thought had also occurred to me that it might even be safer if I travelled with official backing. To my surprise, my approach was welcomed with enthusiasm, if rather slight, by the High Commissioner himself. Pakistan, it seemed, had at last realized that there was income in tourism. Perhaps I would write articles? An itinerary, in some ways elaborate, in some ways suspiciously impressive, began to be drawn up, and I was soon uneasy in case this trip would be less à la recherche than a tour of Pakistan's modern marvels. I had, for instance, no particular reason for wanting to go to Karachi, but my sponsors were anxious for me to

17

see some factories there. Still a free passage was mooted... At the Carlton Tower Hotel in London I was invited to meet the quaintly named Minister of Minorities and Tourism, described to me over the telephone as 'gent of Pakistan' and who turned out to be a handsome Rajah with Nepalese features – hailing, so I was told, from East Pakistan (now of course Bangladesh). The Rajah had only just arrived from a conference on tourism in Rio and was crushed by jet-lag. Yes, he said, wearily and anxious to get rid of me, I was to be the guest of Pakistan. Not entirely convinced that he meant what he had said, I nevertheless had my cholera, typhoid, smallpox and other jabs, and on the assumption that staying in Gilgit might be rough bought such things as water-purifying tablets, a sheet sleeping-bag, a torch, and the all-important anti-diarrhoea pills.

Then began the frustrations, with evasive excuses relayed to me about not being sure precisely when I could get out. For three weeks I was waiting for the tickets to arrive, and when they did, I would have to be at five days' notice to leave. March became April and April became May, and I could endure the suspense no longer. After all, I had my office work to consider, and the weather out there would soon be getting too hot. So I decided to scrap the whole plan of going to Pakistan in 1973, and it was just as well, because soon after that decision I read that Pakistani commandos, some of them from Gilgit, had been captured by Indians in southern Kashmir. Next came the news that Pakistan had been given or was about to be given a hundred and fifty tanks by China. Not only that, but Pakistan seemed bent on having its own nuclear bomb. Mr Bhutto was talking about 'sharpening knives' against India. Then it was announced that Gilgit was a restricted zone, and that intending tourists would have to make special application to the Ministry of Defence in Karachi. I was beginning to lose hope of ever getting back to what had been British-Indian Kashmir, north or south.

I consoled myself with books about the Great Game in Central Asia. I also attempted to get at the mind of Charles Trevelyan.

A fair amount has been written about the achievements, political, literary, or in the public service, of his branch of the Trevelyans, and especially of course about his brother-in-law Macaulay. Nevertheless I came to realize that there was still a great deal to be unearthed about Charles's stormy and so often controversial career, and that such details were more suitable for an academic work. In any case my interest remained always in what it was *like* to have lived in India at different times. I admit too that I was intrigued by Charles's character partly because I could see aspects reflected in his descendants and even in my nearer relatives.

After reading Macaulay's description of Charles's obsessions with domestic matters in India, it was almost a surprise to discover that, at the time of their first meeting at Calcutta, he was in the Secret and Political, that is Foreign, Department, and thus concerned with agents operating in and around Afghanistan and Turkestan. In Walter's desk I had discovered a letter from the by then aged George Otto with a sentence which until I started reading about the Great Game meant nothing to me: 'My father never wanted to speak about Conolly's death.' George Otto was referring to Arthur Conolly, who had such a gruesome end at Bokhara in April 1842. Eleven years before Conolly had been working with the young Charles Trevelyan on official reports, so full of alarming prophecies about the encroaching Russian menace and the likelihood of invasion that they are still regarded as an important – indeed key – step in British thinking about the defence of India during the nineteenth century. It was Conolly who was credited with inventing the phrase the Great Game.

Walter, I could see, was particularly interested in Conolly and other agents, or spies, who had worked in central Asia because part of his job at Gilgit was keeping a watch on the northern passes through the Karakoram and the Pamirs. The accounts of these intrepid men were of use to him even a hundred years later. Occasionally, too, White Russian refugees would struggle up to our house at Gilgit, one group having come from Bokhara.

Chinese in Hunza. A Russian envoy at Simla in the time of the Mrs Gandhi–Zulfikar Ali Bhutto agreement. Russian 'technicians' at Kabul. American aid for Pakistan. Territories still held by the Chinese after the Sino-Indian war. Russian aid for India. And across the Indian Ocean, Russians in Aden and Ethiopia. If there was still a Game with Russia, it seemed to be in a new and sinister form. I thought of Walter, not in those carefree Gilgit days, but when he was doing his stints with the battalion in Waziristan and along the North-West Frontier, and of his grim pictures of dusty encampments and snipers at the ready . . .

Hayward at Yasin

There was another British agent, operating much later than Conolly, whose name we all knew at Gilgit. This was George Hayward, who was also murdered, at Yasin in 1870.

Yasin is one of the northernmost states of what in our time had been the Gilgit Agency, now under the political control of Pakistan.

In Walter's albums there were photographs with captions such as
'Ravine in which Hayward was murdered', 'An old man who witnessed the murder', and 'Site of Hayward's grave – apricot tree in
background has never borne fruit since the murder'. I did vaguely
remember seeing Hayward's grave in the Gilgit cemetery, though
this was a verboten subject for children, like the murder in Nowshera
of Major Haycraft, whose name was so confusingly and to me
disturbingly alike.

By 1870 not only Bokhara but Samarkand had been captured by
the Russians. Their advance across Siberia had been spectacular. Hayward's activities were the more significant because of rumours of
Russian spies in Srinagar.

In Walter's albums there were other pictures of Yasin: Olive and a
group of local men on horses splashing through the river, followed
by our golden retriever Amber; an enormous tent, with folding
chairs and a table, among poplars, willows and pencil pines on the
bank of the river; the Rajah's son in a tightly buttoned Western-style
jacket and smart riding boots. Olive afterwards had brought back
some wild gentian roots for our garden at Gilgit. It had all been such
fun.

That Rajah's son, though, was he related to Mir Wali, the man
most suspected of having arranged Hayward's murder? There has
always been a mystery about the actual circumstances in which Hayward died, but it seems to be certain that he asked to watch the sun
rise before being beheaded. If only Walter had written down what
that old man had told him!

It is hard, however, not to think of Hayward, courageous though
he was, as other than obstinate, foolhardy and a bit of a masochist and
poseur. After his first visit to Yasin, in 1869, he had himself photographed in Yasini clothes with a markhor's head at his feet. He was a
Gold Medallist of the Royal Geographical Society and probably the
first Englishman to have passed through Gilgit. Walter had a guidebook to Kashmir by a Lieutenant-Colonel Joshua Duke, published in
1910. Here it was said that Hayward had sat up writing all during his
last night, with his rifle by his side. When dawn came, he felt sleepy
and his head dropped on the table. Immediately the men who had
been watching rushed forward and pulled away the tent poles. The
tent enveloped Hayward like a net. He was dragged out, bound, and
told he was going to be killed. As a favour he begged to be allowed to
see the sun rise, and gave his word that if he was allowed to go up on a
mound nearby he would return of his own accord. This request was
granted and his hands were unbound. So he went up to the mound
and knelt down and prayed, facing the rising sun. After a short while

he returned to his murderers, quite calmly. They then drew their swords and began a war dance round him. Suddenly a sword swept, then another, and another.

Reading this account, I remembered with a kind of chill, one of Olive's ciné films, which had a long sequence of a sword dance, the men like dervishes, whirling, twisting, writhing in a circle, increasing in tempo, their choga sleeves flapping, swords swiping at a furious speed, on a hill-top against a panorama of a superb mountain range. And those men were waving scimitar-shaped swords and carrying studded shields, dressed exactly as in the photograph of Hayward. Could it have been possible that they were reenacting the scene for my parents?

Hayward's body was later taken to Gilgit to be buried. The public in England was outraged, and a dramatic poem about the murder was written by Henry Newbolt. But no avenging mission was sent to Yasin. It was all too embarrassing for the Government. Besides, the Maharajah of Kashmir was believed to have been behind the plot to kill Hayward, whose visits were no doubt rightly suspected as having been a preliminary to a British invasion. To allay such rumours the Maharajah paid for the erection of the tombstone, on which his own name was also inscribed.

Undaunted by any dire reflections on Hayward *et al.*, I had concluded by 1977 that if I wanted to go to Gilgit I had better make my own arrangements. And if I could move about under some official panoply, well and good, but I would certainly pay for the trip myself. Two friends would join me: Raúl Balín, Spanish but living in England, and John Guest, publisher and writer. Raúl was hoping to be the first Spaniard to set foot in Gilgit.

It was an American friend, the author Allen Drury, who had given me the final encouragement. He and a group of hardy San Franciscans had been on a tour of Pakistan and Afghanistan in 1976, and they had stayed in Gilgit. Allen had written to me afterwards:

Gilgit today is composed of one long unpaved main street, presently being resurfaced, at a casual pace, with chunks of stone put in place by moderately energetic natives. Bit by bit the work progresses, while donkeys, camels, tourists, dogs and natives learn to sidestep skilfully when the rock trucks come by.

We stayed at a hotel called the Varshi-Goom, which is a small 20-room motel-type with a cold pail of water and a dipper for a shower, reasonably good meals, and a general air of being amiable and trying awfully hard. Very likeable people we thought – life is

hard and threadbare, but everybody seems cheerful and hospitable . . . We were awakened each morning at 4.30 by the muezzin,
now assisted by the marvels of modern amplification, so that the
voice booms across the valley from loudspeakers strategically
located. That, and the dogs constantly barking, are my chief impressions of Gilgit night-life. The Chinese are building a road on
the other side of the river, for reasons other than philanthropic I
think.

I therefore once more made approaches to the Pakistan High Commission in London, and courteous – though, as expected, vague –
promises about help were received. It also seemed impossible to find
out about what our costs would be . . . We made our bookings to
Islamabad, whence we would fly to Gilgit on May 14. Then trouble
broke out again in Pakistan. It was announced by the opposition
parties that Mr Bhutto's success in the elections had been rigged; presumably the example of Mrs Gandhi's defeat in India had spurred
these parties on. There were riots in Karachi, then in Lahore. People
were shot. Curfew, press censorship, and martial law in Karachi and
Lahore, as well as in Hyderabad, were imposed. So we became
alarmed. The news that all alcohol was banned was not encouraging
either. We thought of switching to Afghanistan only, or to India,
aiming for Srinagar and Gulmarg, but it was too late and we were
told that if we cancelled our flights to Pakistan we would forfeit a
large part of our fares.

Not long before we were due to set out I met another American
friend, Martha Gellhorn, at a party. She was looking splendid, like a
portrait by Wyndham Lewis, all in black with a long rope of pearls.
When I told her where we were going, her eyes gleamed. Danger!
What luck! I felt ashamed of our qualms. Would we be there at the
time when two million people were proposing to march on Bhutto's
house in Islamabad? She hoped so. She just could not understand, she
said, how any police would be persuaded to fire on their own compatriots.

On May 3 I jotted in a notebook: 'Everything seems under control
in Pakistan; most of the main leaders of the opposition are in prison.
We are told that, when people arrived for the march, plain clothes
police persuaded them to get into vans and buses, and then drove
them far out into the country where they were dumped.'

A day or two later there was a small paragraph in *The Times*: tribesmen had attacked Chinese workers on the road near Gilgit.

So we arrived having travelled in a plane that was half empty
because of the political scares. And we found ourselves in a half-

empty, half-built motel near Islamabad, in a setting that reminded me of the Central African bush. The other guests were a collection of grim-looking Chinese, all identically dressed, middle-aged and determined not to notice us. Islamabad itself had a half-empty, half-built look; it did not seem like a capital city, but we knew that it was unfair to criticize so soon after its conception. An ageing white hippy, with silly staring eyes, offered us a flower. There were lorry-loads of soldiers, getting ready for the riots, we supposed, when people came out of the mosques – a favourite time for violence. Dizzy with jet-lag we tried to sort out this business of costs in Gilgit, how much hiring a jeep would be for instance. 'No problem, no problem,' was as far as we got. We tried to telephone our contacts at the Ministry of Tourism, but soon realized that we might as well forget any official interest in us. People just then were more concerned with holding on to their jobs.

We took a taxi to the new concrete British High Commission, with its distant views of the Russian and US Embassies, and even more distant views of the hazy indigo-coloured Murree hills. Some weeks ago, we were told, a young Englishman from Henley, trekking alone in the mountains east of Gilgit, had disappeared without trace. We were beginning to feel like innocents abroad. There was not much to see in Islamabad, so we walked round the rose and jasmine garden, all the plants labelled in English, and tried to avoid squashing little frogs. The sky looked stormy, and we wondered if we would ever get away the next morning, as the plane would only take off in perfectly clear weather. 'The second most dangerous journey in the world,' Mr No Problem had encouragingly told us. What was the first? The journey to Skardu. A Japanese team was getting ready to climb K2, he said, and we would probably see them at the airport; their base camp was at Skardu.

At the hotel Raúl tried to speak to the Chinese. He wanted to know what they felt about the Gang of Four, by then in prison. 'No! No!,' they cried, and scurried out of the lobby.

'Woke 5.15 a.m.,' I wrote the next day. 'No early call as requested. John complained of jackals howling. Our hotel bill was all wrong, so we had to rouse the manager. Then anxieties about the car, which arrived late. Thank God, a perfectly clear day. To airport, plane luckily very late too. Crowd into room full of lean Chinese roadworkers doing exercises and Pakistani men in crumpled pyjamas. Women in special purdah box. Bales of luggage everywhere. Skardu plane turned back. Japs very despondent.'

But we made it, and were given the best seats in the plane. Soon we were up in the morning light, with the deep blue sky and approaching those incredible peaks in their solemn cathedral procession. We could see the Indus, and were heading for the Babusar Pass. There were patches of cultivation, which seemed to have no conceivable access. One by one we were allowed into the cockpit, where the two young pilots thought it all a tremendous lark. Did we know, they asked, such and such a restaurant in the Earls Court Road? And then, at last, we were approaching Nanga Parbat, the Naked Mountain, 26,600 feet, in many ways the symbol of my Kashmir childhood, of a height and a remoteness impossible to grasp, a mountain which I used to be told had claimed more lives than any other. The shadows on the snow were blue-black, the pines on the lower crests entirely black. The despair of the unreachable, Rabindranath Tagore said about mountains.

I had been rereading a book by a less erudite author than Tagore, *Lost Horizon*, and as the clouds began suddenly to threaten I thought of a passage at the beginning of it: 'The icy rampart of the Karakoram was now more striking than ever against the northern sky, which had now become mouse-coloured and sinister, the peaks had a chill gloom, utterly majestic and remote, their very namelessness had dignity ... "I wouldn't be surprised if that mountain is Nanga Parbat, the one Mummery lost his life on." ... There are heaps of places on this frontier where you might crash and not be heard of afterwards.'

Mummery had died on Nanga Parbat in 1895, after reaching 20,000 feet. In 1932 two Germans had got to nearly 23,000 feet but had been beaten back. In 1934 three Germans had died, and in 1937 an expedition of sixteen had been crushed to death in an avalanche. Hermann Buhl had at last scaled the unreachable in 1953, without oxygen, and had returned delirious.

Our pilots whirled us round the big teeth of the mountain, dodging the clouds. Some of the sides were too steep to carry snow. As I drank my coffee out of a plastic cup I saw a whole corner of an ice ridge break off and crumble into an avalanche. It was magnificent.

The Gilgit Agency

Now that I count up the number of Europeans who were in Gilgit at the end of 1929, I find that we were nineteen, including five children and eight women. As I have said, the Political Agent was Heb, later Sir Herbert, Todd, and I cannot do better than quote his own description of his responsibilities:

Gilgit village itself came under the administration of the Kashmir

State and they had a Kashmiri magistrate – a Wazir he was called –
who ran the civil, criminal and revenue administration of the
Agency at Astor and Bunji [to the south] and the lands of the village of Gilgit itself [known as the Wazarat]. Beyond the narrow
confines of the village the administration came under the Political
Agent up to the frontiers of China, Russia, Afghanistan and Chitral. In this Agency area I had six tribal chiefs: Punial, Ishkoman,
Kuh-Ghizar, Yasin, lying in the mountain valleys running down
into the Gilgit River, and, up the Hunza River, the Mirs of Hunza
and Nagar, whose lands ran up to China [Sinkiang] to the north
and Ladakh to the north-east.

These chiefs administered their tribes pretty well autono-
mously, but with a fatherly supervision by the Political Agent. I
ran them on a loose rein only interfering if there arose discontent in
a tribe at some misjudgement by the Chief. The chiefs ran their
tribes with the support of a council of 'greybeards', a benevolent
paternalism to which the tribesmen were very amenable.

To the west of Agency territory was the large tribal area of
Tangir and Darel which was quite unadministered either by the
Political Agent or the Kashmir Government. It was called 'Yaghi-
stan', which being interpreted means 'land of outlaws'.

Heb had an assistant political agent at Chilas, which was within
Wazarat territory and used as a watching post for any threatened
tribal incursions, usually because of blood-feuds and vendettas, from
Tangir and Darel. Some maintain that Kipling was really thinking of
Tangir and Darel when he wrote *The Man Who Would Be King*,
though the Kafiristan he refers to seems just as likely and certainly as
dangerous a place.

Apart from Hunza and Nagar, nominally the chieftaincies outside
the Wazarat acknowledged the suzerainty of Kashmir, paying tributes in gold dust, grain or horses. Chilas was five marches downstream from Gilgit and about one march along the Indus gorge from
Bunji, where a British military adviser and an 'artillery chap' were
stationed. This criss-crossing of responsibilities and spheres of
influence between the Wazir and Heb Todd could at times be an
embarrassing arrangement.

Walter, then a captain, was military adviser in the Agency proper,
and in command of the Kashmir State garrison, so in a sense also
answerable to the Maharajah of Kashmir – another anomaly. The
other troops stationed in Gilgit were the Gilgit Scouts, local levies, a
typically British creation, which had a separate British commander,
again a captain. Then there were an officer in charge of supplies and

transport, an Agency surgeon, and – temporarily – a sapper officer, George Clark, who like Walter kept an eye on the northern passes. The civil surgeon for the Agency was an Indian major.

The whole Agency was reckoned at 15,000 square miles with a scattered population of 165,000. The first Agent, or officer on Special Duty, had been Colonel John Biddulph in 1877, but he had been withdrawn in 1881. Heb Todd and his family inhabited the bungalow that Biddulph had built, and we were next door. In 1889, because of Russian activity in the Pamirs and Sinkiang, not to mention in Hunza, the Agency had been reestablished under Colonel Algernon Durand, who became famous shortly afterwards in the war against Hunza and Nagar. Durand had extended Biddulph's bungalow.

Kashmir – or Kashmir and Jammu as it was known – formed a self-governing state under the Maharajah, Hari Singh, who had his summer headquarters at Srinagar and went for the winter to Jammu, which was on the borders of the Punjab. The British kept a Resident, Heb's immediate boss, at Srinagar. Hari Singh had only recently become Maharajah and was in an anti-British mood because of a much publicized sex scandal, the 'Mr A. Case'. In 1929 he was trying forlornly to recover control of the entire Agency from the British; in fact in 1935, because of fresh British fears of Russian influence in Sinkiang, he was to be forced to hand over the Gilgit Wazarat on a sixty-year lease. He was a Hindu, but most of his subjects were Muslims. In Gilgit they were chiefly Sunni Muslims with a few Shiahs, though the majority of the shopkeepers were Hindus and Sikhs. The people of Hunza, the Hunzakuts, belonged mainly to the Ismaili sect and were followers of the Aga Khan.

In Gilgit the local language was Shina, but in Hunza they spoke Burushaski, which had no known roots or comparisons with other languages. The Gilgitis had quite fair skins and sometimes reddish hair and hazel eyes. They had a complicated and tiresome class structure, and were generally regarded as rather idle. Their usual dress was the choga, a rough loose garment, like a dressing-gown, off-white, and a rolled woollen cap or koi. All the tribes in the Agency had markedly different characteristics, the Ishkomani being regarded as the dregs, but the Hunzakuts were a race apart from all of them, more intelligent and tougher, expert mountaineers, with quite Mediterranean features. The tradition always was that the Hunzakuts were descended from Alexander's soldiers, and both the Mirs of Hunza and Nagar claimed to be descended from Alexander the Great himself, who had mated with a mountain fairy.

Gilgit, at the confluence of two rivers known as the Gilgit and the Hunza, was 5,000 feet above sea-level and had very little rainfall. Its extraordinarily green, almost emerald, 'oasis', between the bare but to me always friendly mountain ranges, was fed by streams of melted ice- and snow-water, and by swiftly running irrigation channels, one of which was eleven miles long. There was scarcely any snow in Gilgit during the winter, but in July and August the heat was so unpleasant (as were the sand-flies and mosquitoes) that those British women and children who had not already decamped to the social razzmatazz of Gulmarg were removed to higher valleys. No doubt Gilgit was much more bleak in the days of Biddulph and Durand. Or indeed still later, in 1907, when it was described as 'very expensive and unattractive'. My memories are of lots of trees: poplars, willows, mulberries, pomegranates, apricots, and along the khuls tamarisks. One could grow nearly all kinds of English fruit and vegetables there, as well as citrus fruit and vines. Apricots were the most important diet of the Gilgitis, and they would be dried on the roofs of houses. In the spring the whole valley was filled with the bluish white haze of apricot blossom. Occasionally we felt small earth tremors.

The journey up in 1929

Although I made four journeys to and from Gilgit, the first – in September and October 1929 – sticks most in my mind. I was aged six, and have to admit that my memories have been jogged not only by Walter's pictures but by Nanny Spicer's diary. All the same, just a single image has often been enough to set off a whole new train, somehow stored away in the dusty shelves of my mind.

Then there has been Leila Blackwell's diary. Leila was in her early twenties, a major-general's daughter. She came to Gilgit in 1929 to look after a small child called June Lloyd, whom I always considered a bore – unfairly, as she wasn't even two years old – the daughter of the supplies and transport officer. I confess that my recollection of Leila then is somewhat dim. All I can visualize now are bobbed hair, a man's tie and jodhpurs. She was far too energetic I thought, roping me at once into the Wolf Cubs when we reached Gilgit. I was the only white child in the pack; I didn't mind that, but I did resent the silly games she forced us to play, like the Jungle Dance of Kaa the Serpent, the Howl, and Knocking the Blob.

Leila and the Lloyds were in the group that immediately followed us on the 240-mile trek from Srinagar to Gilgit. There had been floods in Srinagar, which had made transport arrangements more difficult. We left by houseboat overnight so as to arrive on the north shore of the Wular Lake before the inevitable afternoon storm. We woke to the cries of wild geese. Our mules and ponies, tough little things from Yarkand in central Asia, were waiting for us, and the coolies began scrambling for the lightest loads. Sixty pounds' weight was a coolie's limit, a hundred and twenty for a mule or pony. The leather-covered boxes we had were called yakdans.

My brother John was put in his doolie. My parents were riding their rather prized horses (as distinct from ponies). 'Poor Raleigh,' Nanny wrote, 'his pony galloped away with him, being a bit fresh. What a fright I got. However a man managed to stop him.' I was given a new, less 'barbary' pony temporarily, and she then wrote: 'Topping canter with Raleigh.' But she was scolded by Olive for leaving John on his own with the coolies.

Then came the long steady climb for our cavalcade, through the solemn forests, their scent mixed with the smell of horses' sweat and saddles, and seas of wild delphiniums, as blue as sapphires Nanny wrote; to the first pass, the beautiful Tragbal, 9,340 feet, like a grassy plain with deep shadows from deodars. I had never heard of Kim then, but now I think of him and his lama climbing the terraces of Doon... There were so many butterflies on the way up. Leila in a later diary noted that the flowers were even 'more glorious' on the trek back from Gilgit in June, and listed meconopsis, columbines, eremurus, forget-me-nots, geraniums, monkshood, white clematis, hollyhocks, and the more prosaic rhubarb, and 'lots of things I didn't know'.

The view of the Vale of the Kashmir was just like a relief map, until it disappeared into the heat haze, and the birches and sumac that late September were turning gold and crimson. The first rest-house was not much fun though, with its smoking fire, and the fleas made a meal of us. There was no glass in the windows, so we had to close the shutters 'to keep the panthers out'. That afternoon I watched Olive and Nanny Spicer disinfecting the wounds of a pony which had been clawed by a panther dropping on it from a tree.

We now reached dwarf junipers and copses of jasmine. We saw gentians and blue anemones. The clouds began to boil and tumble, and we knew that could mean snow. Nanny Spicer was thrown from her pony when her saddle slipped, but not badly harmed. I remember well the silences of that trek, only disturbed by the tread of the coolies and their curses at the mules as they tried to bite one another, and by the creaking of the doolie. We passed some wild-looking villagers, but they hardly seemed to notice us. Emerging from the Gurais valley, at 12,000 feet, along a ridge, my pony Tommy and I suddenly felt a tremendous exhilaration in that diamond-bright air, and we broke into a canter. Nanny was terrified.

Karagbal was about our fourth or fifth rest-house, and quite a pleasant one, at any rate flealess. Our meal as usual was cooked on a Primus stove. When Leila and the Lloyds reached it a few days after us, a lone Englishman, looking distressed and bedraggled, with a few coolies in attendance, turned up in search of a room. The bedrooms were full up, so Mrs Lloyd suggested that he put his camp bed in the dining-room. He had ridden thirty miles, he said, and had come from Ladakh. That evening by the light of hurricane buttees – oil lamps – chestnuts were roasted over the fire, using his pencil. Not until he had gone the next morning did they discover from a note he had left that he was the Earl of Aylesford. (As a footnote to this story, I can add that in 1932 he came to stay at our bungalow in Gilgit. When he returned to England he brought back several skins of bears and snow leopards, as well as some live wolves, which I went to see near Coventry. He was killed near Dunkirk in May 1940, just a month after his marriage.)

Among my favourite flowers was – and still is – Primula denticulata, in spite of an incident which occurred on a later journey. There were still a few of these primulas as we approached the Burzil Pass in 1929, but on that other occasion there were masses of them among patches of snow, and I longed to pick some. My mother forbade me to walk in the snow, so I hopped from one melted patch to another. Of course my shoes got wet just the same, and when I presented a bunch of the flowers to Olive she beat me.

Then there were the marmots. The sad unearthly shrieks of their sentinels were so appropriate to the landscape. I wanted to stop and watch them that day in 1929, but it was too chilly. Gold was to be found thereabouts, we were told, and I am sure that the traveller G. T. Vigne was right in 1835 when he thought that these marmots must have been the originals of Herodotus's gold-digging ants, 'as big as foxes'.

Some snowflakes fell, and the higher peaks were ominously white. Far below we could see the bright green of a river, among the autumn-tinted trees. My nanny wrote on October 1st:

We set off at 8.30 a.m. to go over the Burzil Pass. During the night there had been a snowstorm, so you can imagine how cold it was. It snowed on us the whole 17 miles. Oh dear, how wretched we felt, and we got so stiff sitting on our ponies, but everybody tried to be cheerful. When we got to the top of the Pass (13,775 feet) we found a little stone hut, so we went in and had some coffee from the Thermos. Poor Raleigh, I felt so sorry for him, the little chap had set off so bravely but after the climb up he got so cold and his hands began to pain, and he started to cry. Leaving the hut we all had a sharp walk downhill to get warm. We had sent the servants ahead to light fires and get a warm lunch ready.

The incident of my hands hurting in that horrible dank hut now fills me with shame. I was in agony as they thawed, and very frightened. One of our bearers seized them in his and began blowing on them. I snatched my hands away, revolted by his dirtiness.

There was another hut nearby, a crow's nest on stilts thirty-five feet high, such was the depth of the snow in winter when the mail runners came through. I hated the Burzil and I am not surprised to read that in 1891 a hundred Gurkha soldiers were frostbitten there, and that some died. It was so cold that several of our ponies lost the hair on their hocks. The mail used to reach us every six weeks at Gilgit, generally sopping wet.

Away to the east were the Deosai Plains, regarded as a place of utter abomination. Beyond was Baltistan, otherwise known as Little Tibet. As we descended from the Burzil the sun came out, and Nanny Spicer's face and lips suddenly burst into blisters: not unusual for Europeans, Burzilitis it used to be called. There was also some alarm lest coolies would go snowblind. We whites all wore 'glares', as Olive called sun-glasses, and some of the coolies had yaks' tails over their faces for a protection.

We met a big caravan of Kashgari pilgrims on their way to Mecca. The men had slit eyes and wore round furry hats; real Tartars. Their women were on ponies and completely bundled up in grey sacks with two peep-holes; we hoped they were wearing furs underneath, and even more that they had brought some cooler clothes for the Arabian desert.

We were over the watershed, and there was a dramatic change in the scenery. Everything was much more austere, barren, but with a new sort of beauty. There were immense dark brown boulders, and occasionally in the distance we had glimpses of the Nanga Parbat range. We were in the realms of black bear and ibex. Walter used to go out after chukor partridge as soon as we reached a rest-house. I remember in particular the perils of a suspension bridge so shaky that all ninety ponies had to be led over singly.

The unfortunate Nanny Spicer had her face tied up with cotton wool and bandages, making her look like 'an Egyptian mummy in specs'. She said it was agony to put her face on the pillow. Before reaching Astor, we were met by a welcoming party, including the local rajah – yet another who claimed direct descent from Alexander the Great – bringing gifts. There was a band of pipes and drums, and our coolies immediately dropped their loads and began that peculiar skipping dance that we got to know in its various forms throughout 'Dardistan'. Astor was awesome, at the junction of two gigantic gorges, with an endless roar of torrents. Every now and then you heard the groans of landslides.

Dashkin was a village of box-like mud and log huts and tiny terraced fields, with one poplar on guard. I liked it, but Nanny thought it a 'mess-heap'. The zigzag track, cut into the face of the mountain, became ever more spectacular, and eventually we reached the notorious Hattu Pir cliff, which on occasions was two thousand feet above the Indus. One part of the Hattu Pir was known as the Seven Chukkas, and danger spots were shored up by poles. The track being only a few feet wide, I was ordered to dismount in case my pony stumbled. Not surprisingly more literary personages than my nanny have invoked the Twelfth Canto of the *Inferno* as they braved the Hattu Pir. 'Stupendous scenery,' wrote Leila. 'Every conceivable shade of grey, sandy yellow, soft reddish brown, chocolate, the whole washed in pale violet. Dazzling ranges above.' Caper plants like sprawling octopi were almost the only vegetation; some skeletons of pack ponies down the precipices were noted.

The next stage was wearisome though, miles of stony desert and scuds of dust, and it was a relief when we reached the green of Bunji. A pile of letters was waiting for Walter and Olive. It had already been to Gilgit, but had been sent back to greet us.

Bunji was a real oasis for travellers, with green millet fields and poplars, set in the centre of a group of huge mountains. The two British liaison officers stationed there, Captains Cooper and Eldred, had a pub sign outside their bungalow, 'Ye Olde Pigge and Whistle', and there were other jokes such as 'Park your car here' and a signpost showing how many miles to London and Peking. Below the bungalow was the Indus, looking deceptively placid.

Actually the 'Pigge and Whistle' sign was there when Lord Curzon passed through Bunji in 1894, and he records that he spent a night of horror in a flea-haunted bedroom. The young officers then had pin-ups of Society ladies such as Lady Warwick round the walls, and visitors were expected to write their names against the portrait they thought most beautiful.

We stayed two nights at Bunji, cleaning up and having laundry done by the dhobi. Our hosts had a gramophone, and the first night a table was laid for dinner with flowers, asparagus fern and silver. They even provided us with hair-brushes. At night there was a chorus of pi-dogs, and some would even come into the tents, darting round our beds and snarling at one another. Leila recorded that when she was there she spent the night getting up and throwing stones at the animals.

I quote again from Nanny Spicer's diary:

Oct 8th. Captain Eldred has brought a small boat all the way from the plains. The natives do not like it, and have asked Mr Todd the Political Agent at Gilgit to have it removed, as the fairies of the mountains will be annoyed and it will bring harm to them. Capt E. saw us off over the ferry, which he called 'Gin and Angostura'. The pack ponies had to cross by the suspension bridge higher up. The current was very swift and we were swept downstream 100 yards. Afterwards we ran into a sandstorm, very horrid.

That ungainly ferry was on inflated buffalo skins and oared by eight men. We could see the mighty Indus gathering speed as it swept into the long defile towards Chilas. Its colour was slate-grey, but the Gilgit River that flowed into it was clear and blue. Caverns measureless to man. From source to mouth the Lion River was 1,430 miles long. In 1929 there was a big drama when it became blocked up in Ladakh by a glacier sliding down a mountainside and causing a lake and floods.

The glory of Bunji that last day was its view of Nanga Parbat; untouched, towering, glistening, brilliantly clear, calm, with a personality of its own. 'To feast my eyes on Nanga Parbat,' said Sir Francis Younghusband in the 1890s, 'was a perpetual delight.' He wrote of its 'purity, dignity and repose'; and at sunset it was a 'pearly island rising from an ocean of ruddy light' – but to see it by moonlight was an experience that 'rivalled the Taj Mahal'. And he was right.

There were only two more marches before Gilgit, the final one being eighteen miles. Excitement was growing as the landscape softened and there were willows by the road. We passed through villages, the suburbs of Gilgit. At last Walter and Olive could bear the suspense no more, and cantered on ahead. It was annoying for me to be left behind. We followed on with the baggage train and doolie, slowly, too slowly.

At this stage it is appropriate to add an extract from Nanny Spicer's diary of some weeks later:

December 1 1929. This was the day on which Captain Eldred was drowned. He was on his way to Gor with his partner Captain Cooper to a shoot there. They were both crossing the river in Capt. E's motor boat when it struck a rock and they were thrown into the water. They got on to the rock and then decided to swim to the shore. Capt. E was drowned but Capt. C managed to get ashore. The body was found washed up on a bank far down the river six weeks afterwards. It was carried to Gilgit by coolies on a bed and buried in the English cemetery.

When the weather improved Captain Eldred's mother made the journey over the mountains to see her son's grave. Her husband stayed behind, as he had a bad heart. She had brought her own tent, and I still have a photograph of her: a tragic face, a strong face, intelligent. In the picture she wears long spats and a cravat, and holds a topee with a veil round it for keeping off the insects. Apparently she had never before ridden astride.

Back to 1977. As our plane flew down from Nanga Parbat towards the Gilgit valley, I began to recognize the contours of the mountains. There were the twin teeth of Haramosh, with its skein of cloud, 24,000 feet, and there the white pyramid of Dubanni, on the route to Hunza and where Walter used to go on ibex shoots. The Gilgit River was not blue as at Bunji but a more familiar – to me – olive green, and I could see the old suspension bridge, claimed now to be the longest in Pakistan, with its concrete Arcs de Triomphe at each end. How often had I ridden across it! When, at the airport barrier, I saw the rolled Gilgit caps and the chogas, and caught the whiff of damp oily wool, I thought to myself, this is home.

We were met by Naunihal Shah, who wished to be known as Shah. He turned out to be the great-grandson of the Mir of Hunza of my childhood days, the Mir having died in 1938 aged ninety-five, a ripe enough age even if Hunzakuts are by repute expected to pass their century. The son therefore of my friend Amin, I asked? To my surprise he had never heard of Amin; he would 'ask' about him. Shah may have been our courier, but he was an aristocrat, in looks and manner. He had never been further than Rawalpindi and Islamabad, but he could easily have passed as belonging to some grand Florentine or Bavarian family.

But was this really home? So many jeeps, so many lorries, covered in naïve paintings like old-fashioned English barges. Military everywhere, though not one Chinaman. We found that we were indeed staying at Allen Drury's hotel, the Varshi-Goom, on the outskirts of the bazaar. It was pretty well as Al had described it: little rooms round a courtyard full of hens under the control of a randy cock, ancient loos that sent up waterspouts whenever anyone else pulled the plug along the line, cold showers with a bucket, cockroaches. The waiter was a dwarf who looked as if he had just finished stoking furnaces. Still, we were thankful not to be in the Jubilee Hotel, with its broken panes of glass replaced with cardboard, and reached by a plank bridge over an open drain.

The pomegranates were in flower. I saw bee-eaters and tamarisks, and the orange and cerise saris of women working in the fields. All that was home. The main street of the bazaar was rough but seemed as though any work on it was now over. A squashed pi-dog appeared to have been there for some days. We saw an idiot dressed as a woman. Some Marks and Spencer pullovers were for sale in the stalls, also Ulster tea-towels, and a lot of brightly coloured buckets from Czechoslovakia; rather more local products included stiff-looking fox skins, displays of sweets in alarming colours that were attractive to flies, and framed photographs of fat film stars. Restaurants were blackened holes. People were very friendly, wanting to practise their English and inviting us to tea. 'You are my brothers,' said one student with enthusiasm. Perhaps he meant Raúl, who was the youngest of us three. When he looked at me, in my fifties, and John Guest, in his sixties, and saw our grey hairs, he corrected himself: 'I mean my fathers.'

It was still early in the day, and I was determined to find our bungalow. Obviously the bazaar had grown vastly in recent years, and was considered to be the metropolis for the whole of what was now called the Northern Provinces. I found myself continually glancing up at the tremendous bare, pure mountains that I had loved . . .

The British colony, 1929

I have mentioned that we were nineteen within Gilgit itself, and our household consisted of five people. Next door were the Todds in what was necessarily the grandest bungalow, since Heb was the P.A., Political Agent. They accounted for another five. The Todd girls, Heather and Lavender, were near my age, and thus were my chief friends apart from my brother John, Amin when he was not in Hunza, and the orderly Multana who went with me on rides. Multana was a naik or corporal. Unfortunately Heather and Lavender had a Yorkshire nanny, Miss Hardie, who disapproved of me, and the reason was not my fault (well not absolutely); the girls asked me to pee in front of them, and had then reported me to Miss Hardie.

I can still visualize Heb Todd, with his trim moustache, in the spruce white uniform and helmet that he wore at the Jhalsa, the gathering of the chiefs every March. It was thanks to him that we were such a happy community – under his predecessor things had not been quite the same. His wife Nancy I remember as smiling, plumpish and in flowing pale clothes, a natural hostess: a Queen Mother figure.

The channel of command for my father was through the P.A. to the Resident at Srinagar (Sir George Ogilvie) and then to the Maharajah.

On the other side of the Todds' bungalow lived Maurice and Mollie Berkeley. Maurice was a captain in command of the Gilgit Scouts, consisting of eight highly trained and mobile companies of eighty men, each proud of his silver ibex cap badge; two companies were from Hunza, two from Nagar, and one each from Gilgit, Yasin, Kuh-Ghizar and Punial. He was therefore known as the 'Commanding Sahib'. Mollie, the 'Commanding Memsahib', was Olive's closest friend, being also a bridge fiend, and I was fond of her too. Olive used to go to the Berkeleys' house to let off steam. 'Your mother was always so lively and full of life. We called her the Hot Gospeller,' Mollie told me many years later. 'She would stand on the mat and hold forth. The first time I met her she was making a fuss about losing a mackintosh from Fortnums. We had lost *all* our clothes on the trek up from Srinagar, and had to borrow warm ones.' The Todds left Gilgit in 1931, and were succeeded by people of a different type, without much sense of humour. It was noted that these newcomers, called Gillan, had brought with them several crates of champagne, but none was ever offered to a visitor at the Political Agent's bungalow. Be that as it may, Mollie and Olive were both sent 'chits' saying that they were treating the Gillans like social lepers. Perhaps the Gillans didn't like bridge? (At any rate George Gillan was eventually knighted and rose to the heights of Resident both at Gwalior and for Rajputana.)

Maurice wore a monocle, which appealed to me. He and Walter often used to go down to their respective officers' messes after dinner. Olive would get bored with being left alone. One night, before going to bed, she rearranged the furniture in the drawing-room, so that when Walter came home half-drunk and groping his way in the dark, he was completely lost.

I might add that, contrary to the legend that the British in remote places abroad even when alone dressed for dinner, Olive and Walter would dine in dressing-gowns, and I think this was usual in most outposts of the Indian Empire.

There were three pianos in Gilgit, one being a baby grand. All had been brought in pieces over the passes on the backs of mules, and all were in need of tuning. Generally speaking, however, furniture was made locally and was left as legacies, like the pianos, to succeeding residents.

I have absolutely no memory of the Agency Surgeon, Pyper, and his wife, except that on the annual Gor shoot she got a pellet in her eye – 'a ghastly affair,' Heb has said. Then there was the Lloyd household, including that tremendously active Leila Blackwell.

Finally there was George Clark, a bachelor and younger than Olive. Everyone thought they were having a flirtation. Now when I try to probe the memories of Gilgit survivors, they just smile at me and say: 'Yes, of course we knew all about it.' There was one occasion when I did feel jealous because George and Olive seemed to get on so well. This was when Olive, my brother and I had been asked to tea at his bungalow, and John got his fingers covered with honey. George gave him some chukor feathers to hold which he couldn't get rid of. I felt it was wrong that someone not in the family should make fun of John. I also remember Olive coming back from a ride with George, looking flustered. She said that her horse had bolted, and George had saved her life by seizing the bridle. I was shocked when Walter said that he couldn't care less.

George certainly was handsome and amusing. Olive used to say that he was just her 'tame cat'. For years afterwards he would send her a birthday present of her favourite Chanel No. 5. He was so young and gauche then, he has since said, that he thought a bottle of port and two bottles of whisky would last him a year at Gilgit. (Olive went to the other extreme. She ordered a gross of Bromo lavatory paper, and it had to be carried over the Burzil by a train of mules.)

George had originally come to Gilgit as Divisional Engineer, in linear descent so to speak from a colourful character named Conky Bill Turner. But the Maharajah, being very anti-British at the time, said that the appointment had been made without his permission, and anyway could be performed just as well by a Kashmiri. 'It was a perfectly reasonable argument,' George has said, 'though there were aspects of the job which could not however properly have been carried out by a civilian. So I was eventually kept up in Gilgit on "Special Duties".' These duties included trying to construct forts and keeping an eye on the passes into Sinkiang and Afghanistan with Walter. The expeditions to the passes sometimes lasted a couple of weeks; whatever the gossip, he and Walter got on well together. Needless to say, a main pleasure of their jaunts was the chance of going after game, which included both types of bear, red and black, snow leopard and – I regret to say – the even rarer Ovis poli, the Marco Polo sheep, which could have a horn span of over five feet.

I never felt lonely in Gilgit. Perhaps I spent half the day on my pony, usually with Multana. I had a great number of pets, always fluctuating and including a fox cub, a wolf cub, a young markhor, a cat and some geese. We also had two dogs. Every now and then I would be told that one of my pets had died, I hoped honourably. The poor cat, however, got its head stuck in an empty condensed milk tin and went careering into the water garden where it drowned.

Almost in a state of trance, and followed obediently by Raúl and John, I walked up the slope in the direction where I knew our bungalow lay.

Behind a plastered wall and among trees there was a moderately well kept building, obviously a relic of British times. I was sure that it had been George Clark's.

Then, just beyond, we came upon a primitive water-mill. We stooped inside the dim room, and as soon as I smelt and saw the flour funnelling into a goatskin, and heard the millstones bumping away, I recognized it as the very place where Multana used to take me on our rides together for some illicit tea – illicit because not under Nanny Spicer's supervision.

We passed a cluster of new Army huts, and above them I saw clearly the Todds' house; it seemed to me absolutely unchanged. The garden was a little more bare than I remembered, but I could see the same flaking eucalyptuses, the same flagpole, the same children's swing. Yes, I was told by a guard, this was still the Political Agent's residence; the house further up the lane – ours – was the General's, but he was away.

I had ridden along that lane a thousand times, a thousand years ago. The low crumbling wall, the fields with the sprouting maize, the goats and the chickens, even the dust, were familiar to me. Then at last we came to our entrance, and the drive up to the bungalow.

I had loved that house, and I knew that I loved it still. I could see the verandah with its mosquito netting, and the bay window with the mock Tudor window panes, just as I had longed to see them. Some white-painted stones lined the drive. My mother would not have allowed that, even if she had tolerated the Tudor windows.

Two little soldiers, probably from Baluchistan, were sentries. They were bewildered when I strode inside, Raúl and John in train. The garden was as my parents had laid it out, even to the irises on the bank. Over there was the spiraea we had brought from Srinagar; there was the rockery. Were there King Alfred daffodil bulbs still beneath that grass? On my last day in Gilgit, before returning to England and school, Olive had called me out into the garden: 'Quick, look, there's a golden oriole in the chinar tree.' I had looked and peered, and had at last seen the oriole. All during the trek south, across the Burzil and over the Wular Lake, my brother, by then almost four, had whistled the oriole's song: four notes – two long, two short.

An oriole was singing in that same tree.

The trees had seemed huge to me in those days. They had grown of course, but were still huge.

The two soldiers did not dare stop me. I ordered them to open the net doors. Facing me on the walls were some horns of ibex. I recognized them: they had been shot by Walter and still hung as we had left them. Below were two wickerwork armchairs. I knew them too, they had been ours.

I went from room to room, followed by the now alarmed soldiers, and by Raúl and John in silence. Again I was recognizing features – the shape of a fireplace, an alcove – and each brought back a memory of no conceivable interest to anybody but me. Here we had had a Christmas tree, here there had been the skin of a black bear with a snarling face. Here on a sofa a mysterious Indian woman had told my fortune. In the corner of the tiny dining-room Olive used to perform the occasional ritual of making a French omelette on a Primus stove, according to the recipe of her cookery guru Boulestin, with whom she had taken lessons when last in London. For me the air seemed suddenly full of voices: Walter's, as he came back muddy and sweaty from polo, in his white stock, topee and jodhpurs, complaining that a pony's mouth was like iron; Nanny Spicer's, telling me to hurry or we'd be late for the picnic tiffin in the Kargah nullah.

I burst into the General's bedroom. I was sure that his double bed must have been my parents'. Then we went into his bathroom, perhaps a little grander than in our days – no thunder box for instance – and inspected his range of toothpaste and ointments. I found the small room in which I had slept. Every morning the khansama used to carry chota hasri, early morning tea, for Olive and Walter past my window.

So we left the house, to the relief of the soldiers. I could see our orchard; the blossom was over. Then I noticed the ugly concrete fountain which one of our predecessors had created. One day I had bathed in it naked, and Nanny Spicer had rushed for her Brownie camera to 'snap' me. 'Cross your legs!' I had obeyed, and had wondered why that had been necessary.

As we walked back towards the bazaar I suddenly realized that a derelict field covered in cow-pats was the British cemetery. I looked for Eldred's grave, and there it was: 'In loving memory of our only son Harold S. Eldred SSO, Captain Sikh Pioneers Kashmir Infantry. Accidentally drowned in the Indus near Bunji, Dec. 1 1929 aged 33. Until the day breaks and the shadows flee away.'

Then there were the graves of Captain Shaw Johnson, 'killed out shooting by falling down a cliff', and Captain Claye Ross Ross of the 14th Sikhs who died on March 10 1895 with 'forty-five brave Sikhs killed at the same time'. One stone simply said: 'Remember Ian and Mary Galbraith.'

Ian Galbraith, so I was told later, had been Political Agent in the late Thirties. On leaving Gilgit he had insisted on going down the river with his wife in a rubber dinghy. She had not wanted to do this, and the children had been sent ahead. Within fifteen minutes the dinghy had been overturned and both had been drowned in the icy turbulent water.

. . . But where was the famous grave of George Hayward, who had 'fallen among thieves' in 1870? Nobody I asked could help: 'Must have been taken by the Dogras.'

The Dogras. I was to learn that they were the Gilgitis' chief enemies. Dogras were lurking 'out there', over the mountains, beyond the Burzil, beyond the cease-fire line, ready to strike at any moment.

'Dogra' had barely impinged on me as a child. It happened that a tea-stained Oxford Dictionary lay in the Varshi-Goom dining-room, so I looked up the word: 'Member of a warlike Hindu race of N-West India (many of whom enlisted in the Indian Army)'. Later, in a British Army manual, I found the Dogras described as of high caste, manly, noted for their loyalty, very shy and apt at first to be distrustful of strangers; also never forgiving or forgetting an abuse.

Down in the Shina gardens, by the Gilgit River, we found a memorial to those who had died in the 'War of Liberation' against the Dogras in 1947–8. Few people I met, however, seemed inclined to talk politics in this frontier state atmosphere, apart from a young man who ran the bookstore and sat barefoot and cross-legged on its counter. Perhaps he felt detached because his family had been refugees from Burma after Independence. 'You come back tomorrow,' he said, 'and I shall tell you all about Mr Bhutto's speeches.' We decided that we would probably not accept this invitation.

The Dogra Maharajahs

'The Lion of the Punjab is crouching to seize his prey.' Charles Trevelyan wrote this in his memorandum for the Governor-General,

Lord Auckland, in 1836. The Lion was Ranjit Singh, one of the ablest and shrewdest of all Indian princes in the nineteenth century, a Sikh, lord of huge domains including the Vale of Kashmir that he had wrested from the Afghans. His prey in this case was Sind, at the mouth of the Indus, which Charles considered so essential to the defence of India against Russian ambitions.

'Exactly like an old mouse,' Auckland's brilliant sister Emily Eden was to describe Ranjit Singh, 'with grey whiskers and one eye.' It was a piercing bloodshot eye, the other having been lost from smallpox. The golden throne on which she saw him sit cross-legged at his capital Lahore is now in the Victoria and Albert Museum; and his Koh-i-noor diamond, again from the Afghans, is part of the British Crown jewels. He knew what might happen to the Punjab after his death. When he looked at a map of India, showing British territories in red, he is said to have remarked: 'All will one day be red,' meaning the whole sub-continent. 'No native prince,' Charles had added, 'has ever understood the real nature and extent of our power so well.'

Ranjit Singh died in 1839, at the beginning of the Afghan War. There was an immediate struggle for supremacy in the Punjab among the Sikh chieftains, and a succession of murders. One assassination would automatically involve the deaths of many other human beings; when Emily Eden's 'dandy of the Punjab', Suchet Singh, was slain, three hundred and ten women had to be burnt alive in his honour.

Long before this period of confusion the states of Kashmir and Jammu had been put under the control of a Hindu Dogra, Gulab Singh, as a reward for his help in getting rid of the Afghans – Jammu being regarded as the home of the Dogras, a Rajput race. In the late 1830s Gulab Singh extended his rule to Ladakh and Baltistan. Then in 1842 an army was sent to Gilgit to drive out Yasini invaders.

In that same memorandum Charles also pessimistically wrote: 'We are, I fear, notwithstanding all our efforts for the good of the people, an unpopular domination. We cannot afford to lose a battle. The first defeat would be the signal for a general rising.' He was not of course by any means alone in realizing this, and the British annexation of Sind in the wake of the Afghan disaster was an essential show of strength. Next the British turned their attention to the Punjab, which – with great slaughter – they subdued.

The Sikhs however were soon to rise again, but were once more crushed. During the short intervening period of peace Gulab Singh played his trump card. At first he had declared himself neutral, then he had offered to mediate. Finally, so it would seem, he had actually participated in fighting against his original protectors. In return for independent sovereignty over Kashmir and Jammu – including Ladakh, Baltistan and Gilgit – he offered to pay the British the equivalent of about a million pounds. This was confirmed by the treaty of Amritsar in March 1846. Gulab Singh was now Maharajah.

The Dogra dynasty was not able to keep anything like adequate control over Gilgit and its neighbouring states, in spite of persecution and cruelty of a type which horrified George Hayward. Like the Kashmiris of the south, the people were mainly Muslims, for which they were made to suffer. Indeed in 1852 the Dogras suffered a disaster almost parallel to that of the British troops at Kabul: nearly two thousand men were exterminated, and only one person, a soldier's wife, escaped. It was eight years before they could recross the Indus to Gilgit.

Gulab Singh was succeeded by Ranbir Singh as Maharajah in 1857, the year of the Mutiny. The British became alarmed by rumours of Ranbir Singh's flirtations with the Russians, and this resulted in the planting of the first Political Agent, Biddulph, at Gilgit in 1877.

Ranbir Singh's successor on his death in 1885 was his son Pratab Singh. More tribal unrest in addition to suspicious manoeuvres by the Russians, particularly in Hunza, induced the British not only to reestablish the Agency, but to send a combined force of British, Kashmiri-Dogra, Sikh and Gurkha troops against both Hunza and Nagar in 1891–2. Meanwhile a British Resident had been established at Srinagar, and Pratab Singh was temporarily deposed.

By 1901, the British had fully reorganized the civil and military administration of the Gilgit Agency, and the situation vis-à-vis the Wazarat and the other districts was much as it was when we arrived in 1929. The Gilgit Scouts were formed in 1913.

In 1925 Pratab Singh was succeeded by his nephew Hari Singh, to whom Walter was military adviser. Soon after Hari Singh's succession there were ominous signs of unrest among the Muslims in the Vale of Kashmir.

Revolution in Gilgit

Only much later, after leaving Pakistan, did I hear a version of the happenings of 1947–8 in Gilgit. This was from a relative of the brigadier who had been deputed by Maharajah Hari Singh as Governor. Having realized that this account could be biased, I sought a Pakistani alternative and tried to fit the two together.

Well before Independence (midnight on August 15 1947) the

Maharajah began enlarging his army with Dogras and Sikhs, to the alarm of the Muslim League which had always considered the whole of the Kashmir territories as essentially part of its concept of Pakistan, over three-quarters of the population being Muslim. Then came the fearful post-Independence riots and massacres – of Muslims, Hindus and Sikhs – particularly in the Punjab, in Lahore and Amritsar. There was a pogrom in Jammu, during which the Muslim element, some say about half a million, was eliminated, most having fled, after some murders. Further north, near Poonch, villages were indiscriminately burnt down after a rising.

Enraged Pathan tribesmen, from Waziristan and other areas along the Afghan frontier, now marched into western Kashmir to avenge their Muslim brethren. On October 26 they sacked the town of Baramulla, not distinguishing between Hindus, Muslims or Christians, and threatened Srinagar. The Maharajah fled; he had not made up his mind at Independence whether to opt for Pakistan or India, but the invasion of tribesmen made him decide in favour of India. So on October 27 Indian troops were airlifted to Srinagar.

Such, briefly, were the events that led up to the Gilgit revolution. The Gilgit Scouts were still at that stage being commanded by a British officer, Major Willie Brown, a tall dark Scot, aged twenty-four, and there was another British officer, Captain Mathieson, stationed at Chilas. My Indian informant claimed that these two 'organized the coup d'état', having already decided in favour of Gilgit for Pakistan, and that the Maharajah's Governor, a Rajput Dogra called Brigadier Gansar Singh, had realized this even before he reached Gilgit. Naturally Gansar Singh had installed himself in the Todds' bungalow. When news of the Maharajah's decision in favour of India reached Gilgit, the mullahs began preaching a holy war, and there were rumours of imminent invasions from the provinces of Swat and Chitral, already part of Pakistan. The 6th Kashmir Infantry was stationed at Bunji, but one of the companies was Muslim. The Hindu and Sikh shopkeepers in Gilgit, who had always hitherto been respected, and perhaps numbering about one hundred and fifty, asked Gansar Singh to summon the 6th Kashmir to protect them, but he realized that the troops' arrival would constitute as great a danger to them and himself as did the Scouts and the local people. He told them to be ready to shoot their womenfolk when the emergency came.

The two young British officers were quite alone, isolated from the rest of the world and with no reliable superior to consult. Brown gave orders for the Indus crossings to be manned, so that the 6th Infantry could not advance from Bunji. There was some fighting, with casualties. At midnight on the 31st about a hundred Scouts surrounded Gansar Singh in his bungalow. Some tried to break down a bathroom door. The brave Brigadier and three others fired back, killing two. As there was a moon he was able to keep the besiegers at bay across the open lawns until daybreak, when Willie Brown was able to persuade him to leave under guard for the Scouts' lines, where he was kept prisoner. Meanwhile, according to my Indian account, some of the shopkeepers were murdered (one does not know what happened to the women), and Muslims of the 6th Infantry turned on their commanders, who either were killed or fled south, to be slaughtered by villagers or die from exposure around the Burzil. According to the Pakistani version, the revolution in Gilgit was bloodless, and a demand by a mullah that Brown should be killed was suppressed. The Scouts took over the telegraph and wireless station, and Brown informed Peshawar by wireless that Gilgit had acceded to Pakistan.

Brown's troubles were by no means over. The tribesmen were for Pakistan, but a new and independent 'Provisional Government of the Republic of Gilgit-Astor' was proclaimed, complete with its own president, commander-in-chief and chief commissioner.

Brown continued to command the Scouts, and was in a sense the official administrator of the area. He is quoted as having said that it was several weeks until a Pakistani political agent flew in to take over, but the Pakistanis say that their flag was hoisted at Gilgit on November 14, and soon afterwards at Skardu also. The 'Provincial Government' was not heard of again.

Mountain warfare between Pakistani and Indian forces continued until the cease-fire in December 1948. Gansar Singh remained a captive in Gilgit for sixteen months, and at least everyone seems agreed that he was well treated, being even allowed to watch polo matches.

So it is clear to me that the Gilgitis not the Dogras must have been to blame for the disappearance of Hayward's gravestone, in view of its inscription mentioning 'His Highness the Maharajah of Kashmir'. (In 1981 I was to learn that a new gravestone was erected on behalf of the Royal Geographical Society, almost a replica but tactfully leaving off any reference to the Maharajah.)

At the Varshi-Goom Hotel I had two shocks. Naunihal Shah had found out about his relation, my friend Amin Khan, the son of the old Mir of Hunza. At the age of ten, the year after I had left Gilgit therefore, he had accidentally killed himself with a .22 rifle.

Then Shah had had confirmation, quite definitely, that we would not be allowed into Hunza: the Chinese would not permit it. The new road, known as the Karakoram Highway, colloquially KKH, had just reached Gilgit, but there had been some trouble with tribesmen, as we had indeed already seen in *The Times*: the road had been blocked in six places. This was one reason why foreigners had to be kept away. It was a miserable disappointment for me.

I heard the howling of Allen Drury's dogs all night. I could not sleep, partly I admit for fear of cockroaches dropping on my face – the beasts were about ten times the size of those in New York. I went out into the moonlight, and saw a shooting star in the great blue-black cavern of the sky. Bats chittered. I was still awake for the muezzin. 'I love to hear the priest calling people to pray, away up in the mountain,' Nanny Spicer had written.

Shah had arranged for us to go by jeep to Punial, north of Gilgit. The Rajah there had invited us to tea, though we had to bring our own cakes.

Punial had been created as a buffer state between Gilgit and Yasin in the time of the second Dogra Maharajah, Ranbir Singh. The British had always considered its people especially loyal, and Punial troops had fought against Hunza and Nagar in 1892. To me Punial meant the Sherqulah 'rope' bridge, known as a jhula, a fearsome affair actually made of intertwined birch branches, about seventy yards long, anchored at each end by tree trunks and boulders. It had been so narrow that you had to walk with one foot in front of the other, though luckily there had been balustrades of a sort (rope again) to hang on to, as you swayed over the rapids. The Rajah used to stand at the end of the bridge to greet his guests. It was his joke that on arrival they were always forced to stoop in front of him. He also had the reputation of being the best polo player in the Agency.

Raúl and John were alarmed by the twisting narrow track above the ravine of the Gilgit River, and more so by a home-made suspension bridge with a few slats missing – even a donkey refused to step over the gap. If they had but known, there were to be far more dangerous roads ahead on our future excursions; I being Gilgit bred was of course unruffled, the old hand. It was my first sight of a landscape that I had known so well in trekking days: patches of brilliantly green fields among the alluvial stones; mulberries, vines, walnut trees, poplars, shimmering willows; cattle standing on flat roofs made of thatch; irrigation channels – khuls; gigantic boulders round which the river foamed and sprayed; sheer mountain walls, without any vegetation whatsoever, generally a reddish brown garnet colour with lighter strata showing their volcanic beginnings; scree from landslides; and, always, in the distance the majestic peaks, below the snowlines a diluted turquoise blue gradually deepening into shadow. It was rather cold, like November Shah said.

The Sherqulah rope bridge was, however, no more. Instead there was a suspension bridge, all its slats mercifully intact. The Rajah was the son of the great polo player. If not so athletic-looking, he was otherwise the image of his parent who featured so often in Walter's photographs, with his great fleshy nose and moustachios dyed black. He smiled a lot; there was a sad, serene atmosphere about the place. We admired his roses and his cherry trees, the fort and the broken-down fretwork of the wooden mosque. We heard about the deposition of the rajahs in 1974; the shock was supposed to have killed the Mir of Hunza. The Rajah told us that in recompense for his loss of power he now received a subsidy of three thousand rupees a month. He had nine brothers, nine sisters, and two wives and two daughters. Shah was related to him. His family had lived in that same spot for at least a thousand years. We went into his dining-room, piled with rug upon rug (perhaps the one at the bottom was the best?), and there among the plastic flowers and photographs of himself, taken by tourists, our cakes were laid out. We were shown a visitors' book, and in it we found the names of Allen Drury and his Californian ladies. No Spaniards. Italians yes, Japanese yes, one Finn. The Rajah enjoyed our cakes. He gave us his card: 'Rajah Jan-Alam, Sherqulah Punial, Where Heaven and Earth Meet'. Only as we said goodbye did we find out that we must have been Wolf Cubs together.

That evening we had visitors at the Varshi-Goom. One was the very distinguished-looking Wazir Hamayoun Beg, who came from Hunza and had dyed hair, again black. He had been Heb Todd's secretary and remembered Walter as a good polo player. Polo, he said, had not originated at Gilgit, as some people said, but at Bokhara, where Tamerlane had played with the skulls of his enemies. Walter and Heb had tried to change the rules, but without success. Once Hamayoun Beg had been the local librarian, but the library had been looted – by the Dogras of course. Polo was played far less now in Gilgit, but always on November 1, the anniversary of the defeat of the Dogras, and again in June to please the tourist office.

Then Ashraf Aman came, also a Hunzakut. We took to him at once. He was a mountaineer, born in 1953, small, virile, shortly to join the Japanese expedition to K2, one of four Pakistanis in a team of about fifty. He had vowed not to think of marriage until he had 'achieved something' in mountaineering. And he certainly managed to achieve something. Later that year he sent us some newspaper cuttings about the expedition. Ashraf, the 'Himalayan tiger', was the first Pakistani to reach the top of K2. In the process three toes were frost-bitten and had to be amputated. In 1980 he was on the Royal

Geographical Society expedition to the Karakoram, with Lord Hunt, Keith Miller, and other distinguished RGS characters. As a result in 1982 he was invited to London.

Ashraf said that his father had died in his late nineties, and that his grandfather had lived until a hundred and thirty. I asked what was the secret of this famous Hunza longevity. He said that you must have been suckled on your mother's milk, and that afterwards you should only drink Hunza mountain water (so silty that the Chinese workers would not touch it) or yak's milk, never tea or coffee. Honey and apricot kernel oil were also essential parts of the diet.

I remembered hearing from Olive that it had once been the custom in Hunza to put old women into sacks and throw them into the river. Apparently old men, if too decrepit, also shared the same fate. Shah told us that before 1892 when a mir died his strongest son would be selected as successor. The other sons would be taken for a quiet walk and then shoved over a precipice; this was why there were so few in the Hunza royal family now, although the dynasty had been in existence for nine hundred years.

We also discussed the position of women. In Hunza they could go unveiled, but not in Gilgit. Even the Varshi-Goom manager's wife, who was from Karachi, could not go unveiled in the Gilgit bazaar.

We talked about Kashgar, supposed to be the furthest city from the sea in the world. Shah had been there in a caravanserai once; obviously it was no land of Cockaigne, for he had not been allowed to wander about. He told us about a Kashgari man who had come to Gilgit and opened a shop. After some years he had gone back to Kashgar but had been refused permission to see his wife and son. Unknown to him, however, his son had recognized him from a distance and knew that he was still alive. The man had returned to Gilgit and married again, never expecting to see his original family. Suddenly the first wife, his son and daughter-in-law had permits to join him in Gilgit. The daughter-in-law wore trousers in the Chinese fashion, and was not veiled; there was an uproar in the bazaar. She became so unhappy that she went back to Kashgar.

The Chinese had closed all the mosques in Kashgar, we were told, because praying was a waste of time. They had also had to withdraw road-girls from working on KKH because they so upset the natives.

At one time there had been 10,000 Chinese working on the road. Because of landslips, avalanches, earthquakes and other 'problems', usually from blasting, five hundred Pakistani and Chinese workers had so far died in its construction. It was wide enough for two tanks to pass one another, but of course the pass into Sinkiang was only usable during the summer: this was the Khunjerab, 15,400 feet, 1,700 higher than the Burzil.

John announced that he had caught a chill on the jeep journey to Punial. He kept all us inhabitants of the Varshi-Goom awake with his constant hawking and spitting.

I was determined to take photographs of our old bungalow and garden, and obviously this time would have to have a permit. John had had enough of nostalgia, and said he would walk up the valley, to photograph the view whilst the sun was right. So Raúl and I set off in search of that permit, and not unexpectedly soon found ourselves plunged into red tapery. Having at last reached a hut belonging to the 'Northern Area Works Department' I hit on the idea of invoking my father's regiment, the 8th Punjab, which I knew still to be in existence and based at Lahore. This at once made all the difference, and amid smiles tea was produced.

As we were sitting there, doing our best to be charming, an American youth was hustled in under arrest. He had been caught trying to photograph the bridge over the Gilgit River, the greatest conceivable crime apparently, even if the bridge had been in existence in 1906 and featured on all the tourist brochures. The boy didn't look like a spy, and as Raúl and I had already generated an atmosphere of bonhomie, he was forgiven and offered tea. 'Let's hope John won't be next,' Raúl whispered.

A Lieutenant-Colonel would meet us at the bungalow in the late afternoon, we were told. Much relieved, Raúl and I returned to the Varshi-Goom. 'Other sahib no well,' the dwarf said, looking very worried. And sure enough there John was in bed, looking pale and harassed. 'I've been arrested,' he told us weakly. We rushed for the duty-free vodka and mango juice (a mixture to be recommended), and soon heard the whole dreadful story. He had been walking in the direction of the airfield, and had asked a policeman if it was allowed to go along a certain road. The policeman had nodded, probably not understanding English, and on rounding the corner John had immediately been pounced upon by two soldiers, who had bundled him into a passing lorry. In due course he found himself in the bazaar jail.

John must qualify as among London's great raconteurs, and has often since dined out on this story of his arrest. There were beggars and prostitutes clinging to the bars all round, he says. He had not brought his passport, neither could he remember the names Varshi-Goom or Naunihal Shah. Presumably with his silver hairs he did not look like a spy either. The magistrate released him, having said that he was lucky not to have been sentenced to ten years in jail or to have had a hand chopped off; so John says.

I tried to cheer John up by telling him about a Dareli tribesman in the Thirties who had killed his wife and her paramour, and had ridden through Gilgit swinging their heads by the hair. Even he had been set free, because he had done his duty according to local law. So Gilgit magistrates did have a lenient side to them. But John was not comforted; he felt nervous throughout the rest of our time in Pakistan, convinced that sooner or later higher authorities would catch up with him.

He was in no mood for further walks, so after lunch Raúl and I went up on to the slopes above what had been the British bungalows. We walked along the main khul, about ten feet wide, then sat for a while under a mulberry tree and watched the shadows on the mountains opposite. The river now looked silver as it wound through the ravine towards Punial and Yasin. *Out of the mist and hum of that low land*. Directly below us had been my parents' stables. Somewhere along here Nanny Spicer and I had had what she described as a nasty experience, though I think she overdramatized it. I see in her diary that we had been 'attacked by a native, a hill man'. I do vaguely remember the incident, and suppose that he must have made some kind of pass at her. I remember just thinking that he seemed friendly, rather nice if ragged. I have stronger memories of especially beautiful sunshine on that walk and some very large caterpillars.

On the slopes above the khul there was a hermit who lived in a cave. He was always somebody who haunted my imagination, though I was never allowed to go and look for him. He was supposed to have been born with a hoof instead of a left foot, and I was told that he only came out at night, when he would go skipping about the rocks like a wild animal. Now I wonder whether it was this man, hoofed or not, whom Nanny Spicer and I met.

At 5.30 Raúl and I went down to meet the Colonel at the bungalow. He was courteous and correct, a bit formidable, in civilian clothes and wearing dark glasses. Raúl and he sat in deckchairs while I rushed round taking photographs. Then I rejoined them, as the light faded and that old, old silence descended on the mountains across the river. If a markhor were to stumble on the other side, a mile away, we surely would have heard it. The snow on the Dubanni peak was turning pink. The shadows were like curtain folds. An oriole began to sing in the chinar tree: four notes; again and then again. The Colonel was polite, and we talked in low voices; I explained about the old days and how my parents had laid out this garden. He kept nodding

and was anxious for us to go. I understood. The past was past. I was
the ghost now.

Polo in Gilgit

In British times there used to be polo every Thursday and Sunday. At
dawn on those days, whistles would be blown, competing with the
muezzin; then the drumming would begin, building up into a frenzied tension. Polo was the national sport and a thrilling, invigorating
sight, though also often alarming since few holds were excluded and
there were frequent accidents. Every village in the Agency had its
polo ground, usually about 125 feet long. The smallest children
would play a so-called polo on foot, a kind of hockey without rules,
and the highest polo ground in the world, used by shepherds, was in
the Killik Pass, on the Hunza–Sinkiang border.

Walter wrote an article on Gilgit polo for *Blackwood's Magazine*,
that great outlet for pukka sahibs' reminiscences. He maintained that
it had been played in Persia in Alexander's time and had spread into
India. 'But it is a strange fact that it completely disappeared for some
centuries except around Gilgit and Chitral and in Manipur – two
parts of the world where the mutual difficulties of terrain would
appear to be greater.'

The ponies were usually Badakshis from northern Afghanistan,
sturdy little things of about thirteen hands, of 'unbelievable stamina'
and extraordinarily sure-footed, on mountain tracks too. Only stallions were used; sometimes they fought each other during a chukka,
which all added to the excitement. These ponies could be bought for
the equivalent of fifteen pounds. The Gilgits would remove cartilage
from their nostrils to help with the breathing.

The polo sticks were quite short with heads made of wild almond
or mulberry. Sometimes these heads broke loose and would go
whizzing towards the spectators, who would be squatting on the
stone walls or sitting in trees. The ball would be carved from the root
of a mulberry tree, or it might even be a stone. There were six players
on each side and the chukka would continue perhaps for two hours
until nine goals had been scored. All the while the crowd would be
shouting advice or abuse, and bands would be screeching out local
tunes, meant to encourage the ponies, and adding to the general
frenzy and sense of recklessness.

'The game,' said Walter, 'is like our own polo, but eliminating all
the rules making for safe play and adding several features of its
own . . . Perhaps the most bizarre is the manoeuvre called
"Tambak". When a goal is scored, a player, generally he who hit the

goal, takes the ball in his hand and gallops with it to the centre of the field, where he throws it forward and, whilst it is still in the air, hits it with all his might towards the opposing team's goal.' The Rajah of Punial would frequently score a goal from his 'Tambak'. 'To see it well done is a very pretty sight, the ball soaring high up in the air and falling over or between the goal-posts.'

A player could even throw the ball through the goal, but as he galloped along his bridle was liable to be grabbed by an opponent or by several opponents, who would then wrestle with him and try to drag him off his pony. 'My goodness, sir,' a visiting Indian said, 'these men must be made of rubber.' At the Jhalsa of 1931 tremendous tension was generated because Hunza was to play Nagar. As Walter wrote: 'Local feeling is too strong for even the tradition of the national sport. They [Hunza and Nagar] have been rivals, not too friendly, for centuries, and what Hunza gained on the battlefield Nagar can generally avenge on the polo-ground.' It happened that in each of the teams there had been men who had been enemies for years: 'Sarwar, a swaggering Nagari with the dash and conceit of a rough-riding sergeant, and Imamyar Beg of Hunza, less dashing in appearance but no less tough in a scrap.' On that occasion Sarwar, in what might or might not have been an unfortunate lapse, followed through with an immense backhander full into Imamyar's face. 'The latter, spluttering teeth and threats, was hauled before the Political Agent with his antagonist, and the game was stopped. Sarwar was held to blame and left the field, possibly fortunately as Imamyar stated he would have killed him had he remained.'

On another occasion Walter had to intervene when a full-scale riot broke out after a Yasin man, dismounted because of a broken rein, had put out his stick as one of the opposing team dashed past with the ball, hitting him in the face and knocking out his front teeth.

After a long game it was the custom for ponies to be tied to a tree whilst still sweating, with their heads held so high that they were literally 'on their toes'. They would be kept there until they had 'staled' twice, and then would be watered and fed.

The Jhalsa, 1930

The Jhalsa was the great event of the Gilgit year: a ceremonial durbar, with entertainments, livestock shows and sports, notably polo. My first Jhalsa was in 1930 and it started on March 24.

Every Mir and Rajah came in turns to pay calls on the sahibs, usually with a retinue of about twelve followers. They arrived in order of seniority, the most important (and the most popular) being the Mir of Hunza. Then would come the Mir of Nagar, followed by the Rajahs of Punial, Yasin etc. 'Rajah' was really a Hindu title, but nobody seemed to mind.

The Mir of Hunza, Sir Mohammed Nazim Khan KBE, was well fleshed and jolly, very fond of jokes and a contrast in character to his hereditary rival, the more serious and thinner Mir of Nagar, Sir Shah Sikhander (i.e. Alexander) Khan KBE. The difference between the temperaments of the people of Hunza and Nagar was put down to the fact that Hunza was on the sunny side and Nagar on the shady side of a valley. Also at Hunza they made and drank wine, which at Nagar they didn't.

Throughout the Jhalsa week the sahibs would invite the chiefs to dinner, as repayment for past hospitality when out on trek and for other favours: for instance, at Christmas the Mir of Hunza, as he knew we were sick of mutton, would send us meat that tasted very like the forbidden beef (perhaps it was yak), and we would always tactfully thank him for mutton. When he came to dinner he would bring Amin and another son, much older, Ghazan Khan, his heir, whose funny stories nobody believed and who fascinated me because of his red moustache and black hair. There was never any question of being at a loss at what to say when the Mir of Hunza came to dinner.

In 1930 we combined Nagar with Punial at dinner. Nagar obviously felt the strain of late nights by the end of that week. He was not much at home with a knife and fork, and loved tinned fruit and boiled sweets. The sahibs used to make their guests play parlour games. 'I think they thought we were a bit dotty,' one ex-sahib has since said to me. Hunza brought his own orchestra: two men with instruments like lutes and another with a pair of cymbals – and a rug for sitting on. They sang in Persian and their music was supposed to be from Kashgar. Then under a master of ceremonies (actually the Mir's cook) four nautch boys came in, dressed as girls, with pillbox hats and tresses that reached below their knees. They wore long white pantaloons and Kashgari silk coats, pink and white, and hopped, skipped, waved their arms about, and clapped their hands, moving round the room in a series of jerks, sometimes kneeling and bumping along the ground. Every now and then the musicians uttered sounds like Ha, ha, ha. Nanny Spicer never realized that the dancers were male. Indeed the Mir of Hunza was known to 'like boys'.

The son of the Mir of Nagar, Shanhat Ali, was also my age, but simpered rather and was a bit wet I thought. But he did give me a falcon as a present. Nearly every morning before breakfast that week I would go jumping with Amin. Although we liked each other we couldn't communicate much as he only spoke Burushaski, and my Urdu was limited. He gave me presents: an embroidered cap and a dagger. I hope I was not responsible for giving him the .22 that killed him.

In the afternoons we all would go down to watch sports on the parade ground. We had wire netting put up in front of our tent, as if we were in an aviary, because the games tended to be so violent. We had a display of archery at the gallop: a survival from an ancient Persian sport evidently. Then there was the popinjay – riders dashing madly past firing at a dead bird on a pole. The big excitement on the first day, however, was a fight between Gilgit Scouts and Walter's Kashmiri soldiers about some question of seating arrangements. One man was concussed, and another broke his leg; as they were carried away on stretchers, spectators cheered and laughed. Polo would always be the last item of entertainment of the day, and afterwards the losing team would be made to dance.

On the second morning we crossed the river to the desert-like 'right bank' and watched khud races: men scrambling up and down the scree of the mountain, the winners being welcomed with kisses and hugs by their friends. Then there would be a competition between sahibs and chiefs, firing at moving 'markhor' targets. In 1930 it was a tie between Walter and the eldest son of the Mir of Nagar, the elegant Mahbub; people teased Leila Blackwell as she was supposed to have a soft spot for him.

That same afternoon in 1930 we had to put on our best clothes, memsahibs in fashionable coalscuttle hats. I remember Nancy Todd's dress in particular, because it went down in points and floated about like a fairy's in a book her daughters had. 'We ladies and children,' Nanny Spicer wrote, 'had to meet Major Pyper at 4.20 p.m. by the hospital.'

We felt like school children waiting for a bus. We were then escorted down to the Durbar. We ladies had to sit at the side of the main dais under an awning and in order of seniority. The chiefs were in a large semi-circle, and costly rugs were laid on the ground. The chiefs were all very dignified. The Mir of Hunza was in blue with medals under a gorgeous green cloak with gold brocade. The Mir of Nagar wore purple velvet with gold sunbursts. He sat very straight. At 5 p.m. Mr Todd came all in white, with a sword and medals and on a black horse. He inspected the guard and then walked up to the dais followed by the officers. Captain Trevelyan then declared the Durbar open in Hindustani. Mr Todd read a long speech in Hindustani. He is quite the little god here.

After all this the State and Scout officers marched up to present their swords, which Heb Todd touched. Next came the wazirs with their gifts – nuggets of gold wrapped in silk – followed by the Mirs and Rajahs, also with gifts. The tributes were again touched by Heb. Those from Hunza and Nagar were to be kept, because they were for the British; the others were for the Maharajah of Kashmir. Next, there were presents from King George V for each of the chiefs and for various members of their families, as well as for head men of villages and policemen; these gifts included saddles, firearms, binoculars and scented soaps. Afterwards Walter declared the durbar over.

At night the Scouts, dressed in their best Black Watch tartan, instead of the usual grey shirt and khaki shorts, danced by the light of two huge bonfires, which fantastically illuminated the bright colours of the chogas of the spectators squatting around. Most of the dances were mime, a favourite being the shooting of a markhor.

In the following afternoons there were some polo matches, fiercely contested, 'almost fights to the death', Nanny said. In the match between Ghizar and Astor a pony collapsed from exhaustion. We also watched tent pegging displays, tug-of-wars, climbing greasy poles and pony races. In the evenings there were more dances round bonfires and braziers. We had the Yasin sword dance and the Chilas vulture dance, and some boys gave an Indian club display. 'Those flashing eyes!' Nanny Spicer wrote. Alas, on one dread afternoon the Wolf Cubs had to do a jungle dance, followed by leap-frogging, tug-of-war and an obstacle race, in which I am delighted to learn 'Raleigh did very well'.

On April 1st the chiefs departed in swirls of dust to the accompaniment of divers bands. The Jhalsa was over. 'Now we can have a holiday,' the Mir of Nagar said without a smile.

White Russians

From time to time, particularly in the period after I had gone to school in England, pathetic characters would turn up in Gilgit claiming to be White Russian refugees. It was Walter's job to screen them in case they were spies. I personally encountered only one of them. He suddenly appeared in our garden, in 1931, dressed in filthy sheepskins and with such glaring eyes that he frightened me and my brother. When I asked Nanny why he was shaking so much, she told me that he didn't want to be sent back to Russia.

Now that I have looked up records in the India Office Library, I see that the man's name was Kizhniak, that he came from Kiev, had been working on railways since the Revolution, and was thought by Walter to have been of upper middle-class origin. The great difficulty for Walter was always the question of language. Kizhniak was at first suspected of being a Soviet agent, but the official reports say that: 'Trevelyan considers him intelligent and willing to give information.' And later on he certainly did provide the British authorities with a quantity of information, including much about OGPU, the secret police, and Soviet agents in Afghanistan.

My brother remembers White Russian refugees in tents on our lawn. This would have been in 1933, when there was a civil war in Sinkiang. Mollie Berkeley says that some died in the snow of the passes before reaching Hunza and Gilgit, and that others were sent back: 'Oh the heartache having to refuse to allow some to go on. It wasn't believed possible for the ones who had to go back to survive. I also remember that an interpreter had to be found to trek up from Delhi.'

There had been several White Russian colonies in Sinkiang following the Russian Revolution, particularly in Kashgar. It had been obvious for years that the Soviets were poised to take over the whole province, and during the anti-Chinese riots in Sinkiang there was panic among the Whites. The ridiculous anomaly was that White Russian mercenaries had been fighting for the so-called Provincial Government in the north, which was being subsidized by the Soviets. By 1933 Kashgar had been taken over by a group of rebels opposed to both Chinese and Soviets, and a new Muslim republic had been proclaimed. So the White Russians in the city found themselves caught between two perils: a possible Soviet invasion and attack on Kashgar, and reprisals because other White Russians had been helping the enemy in the north.

Meanwhile lone refugees continued to struggle over the 'high Pamere' and Hindu Kush ranges from Soviet Turkestan. I have a haunting photograph still of one called Seraphim Vorokiev, born in Moscow in 1907. The face is refined though rather sly, with fair hair smoothed back, a little beard and a drooping eyelid. My parents had liked him. I see from the records that he was in due course arrested in Karachi as a vagrant. Evidently a number of White Russian refugees were shipped to Brazil, unless they managed to be claimed by relatives already in France. Nothing specific is divulged in these records about the eventual fate of these wretches.

In January 1934 there was a flutter in Gilgit when a party of five arrived, including a man of about thirty who was referred to as 'Romanov' and who claimed to be the Tsarevich, Alexei Nicolaievich. A companion of his said he was Prince Sviatopolk-Mirski from Petrograd. The Russian royal family, according to this Romanov, had not been murdered at Ekaterinburg but had all escaped, thanks to 'loyal retainers'. The Tsar had poisoned himself in 1920, but the Tsarina and Grand Duchess Tatiana were still in hiding in the Rayeski desert. Olga was in a lunatic asylum, and Maria had 'gone away' when her father died. As for Anastasia, Romanov had found her in Samara married to a man called Buistrow. She had died in childbirth. The story was full of contradictions, although details of Romanov's wanderings, escapes and arrests were moderately convincing. He wrote letters from Gilgit to King George V, Monsieur Poincaré and Grand Duke Cyril, very ungrammatically. 'Dear King,' he began, 'I am writing you a second letter to London. I wrote you one from the town of Kashgar in the name of Alexei Nicolaievich Romanov, the Tsarevich of Russia, but have no reply. Dear George, I have arrived in your country, India, where I have to live until the month of March, but my life is very difficult. I am living in very bad circumstances.' He had no chair or stove, he said, and was starving.

The British Consul-General in Kashgar was consulted about his case. He knew about Romanov and thought he was a Soviet agent. Some 'credulous women' in Kashgar had believed in the Tsarevich story, and he had even spoken about the man to the Soviet Consul, who had just shrugged and said: 'He is mad.' As usual in the official records there is no clue as to what happened to Romanov and his friends, whether they were sent back across the passes to Kashgar or the USSR, or were shipped to Brazil, or merely popped into Karachi jail.

In 1938, it seems China still regarded Hunza as a tributary state. This was because the Mir, according to custom, used to send the Chinese presents. In that year there was an 'incident' when a flock of Hunza sheep strayed into Sinkiang; not only were six of these sheep killed by Chinese soldiers but the shepherds were detained.

Peter Fleming wrote about White Russians in Kashgar and the civil war in Sinkiang in *News from Tartary*. If, as he put it, Sinkiang was the 'last home of romance in international politics', it was a pretty gory Ruritania. Nevertheless the Soviet Consul was thought by him to be charming, though obviously disconcerted by Peter; he allowed him and his travelling companion, the French dynamo Ella – alias Kini – Maillart, to use his swimming-pool and tennis court. The British consulate was a delightful place too, even if the year before the

Consul's wife Mrs Thomson-Glover – a 'peculiarly indomitable sort of person' – whilst standing on the terrace had been shot through the shoulder by a soldier.

Kini, shock-haired and in long boots, a champion skier and champion hockey player, made a sensation when she arrived in Gilgit, and a banquet was arranged at the Political Agent's bungalow. In her own book she was scornful about an Englishwoman she met there, who had been seen wearing beach pyjamas in the bazaar, and who arrived in full evening dress, complaining about having had to drink rancid butter tea in Ladakh.

Kini's fame lingered on in Gilgit. In 1939 Eric Shipton's Karakoram expedition arrived, and there was some consternation when it was announced that she was 'around'. So another banquet was arranged at the Political Agent's house. The Shipton party was kept waiting for a long time. Finally there was a noise of someone dismounting outside. Everyone stood up in anticipation. The message came that Mlle Maillart was 'powdering her nose'. Another long wait. At last the legendary tomboy made her entrance, vividly made up, wearing a kind of turban and a Gilgit choga hitched round her waist. The effect was spoiled by her stumbling and falling 'flat on her fanny'. She recovered quickly and began flirting with Eric Shipton in a peculiarly abandoned way. Then he looked up and saw people writhing with laughter – for this Kini Maillart was none other than his colleague Peter Mott in drag. Shipton was not amused, indeed was furious, because the departure from Gilgit had been purposely delayed by a day.

Shipton afterwards went to Kashgar as Consul-General. Sinkiang was still an uncertain place for Europeans to live in. In 1940 or 1941 an American missionary and his wife were found floundering in the snows of the Mintaka Pass (15,400 feet) on the Hunza border. They had been running their mission for twenty years and had now been expelled, deliberately during the worst period of the winter.

In due course the British consulate in Kashgar was closed by the Sinkiang authorities. One effect of the war in Europe was that Russia had less time for intriguing in eastern Tartary.

At the Varshi-Goom hotel we were told by Naunihal Shah that he had arranged for us to spend three nights in a rest-house at Naltar, the last valley before the forbidden Hunza. It was 10,000 feet up, and we would have to bring our own food. The name Naltar was familiar to me, because some of the Anglo-Gilgiti women and children used to be sent up there for July and August.

Meanwhile we had another visitor at the Varshi-Goom. This was

Daulat Shah, who said he had worked for Walter. He wore curled up embroidered slippers and a grey astrakhan 'Jinnah' cap, and had a long slightly hennaed beard. I was to find many references to him in Leila Blackwell's diary, E. O. Lorimer's *Language Hunting in Karakoram* and elsewhere. He also was a Hunzakut. He was so dignified and courteous that we could not believe that he had ever done any menial jobs.

That night we gave a vodka and mango juice party, and learnt some more Hunza folklore. Before 1892 the Mir could ask for any woman he liked, and the woman would consider it an honour to be chosen. It used then to be the custom to offer your wife to your guest. Since many illegitimate children were the result, infanticide had not been considered a crime. Butter, buried for a hundred years, we also heard, was still considered a great delicacy in Hunza.

In the morning a box of food, mostly packets of Italian spaghetti it seemed, was roped on to our jeep, and off we went across the river. We would be travelling along a branch of the original silk road of the merchant caravans from China, on the opposite side of the ravine to KKH. Allen Drury had said in his letter that he and his group of Californians had started off on that same route but had been forced back because of a landslide. Nicholas Monsarrat, of *The Cruel Sea* fame, had had the same experience.

We emerged from an exceedingly dreary area composed of barracks and parade grounds into a large alluvial fan at the point where the Hunza River emerged. Alluvial fans are a feature of the Karakoram, some being cultivable, though this one was not. It had been the scene of one of the great sensations of my time in Gilgit: the arrival of the first planes, three Wapitis, in April 1931, during Jhalsa week. George Clark had been in charge of clearing the site of stones, with the help of coolie labour, for a landing strip. Instead of windsocks there had been a couple of bonfires so that the pilots could get an idea of the direction of the wind from the smoke. The planes had flown from Risalpur near Peshawar over the Babusar Pass; Heb Todd had had a 'flash wire' saying that they had taken off, and George had had to gallop frantically to the strip to get the fires lit. It had been thrilling for us all to see the arrival of those black specks, like determined bumblebees, across the snow ranges, and even more thrilling to watch them swooping down on such dangerous ground: a very different experience for me from visiting those stuffy hen-coops which had brought the King of Afghanistan's family from Kabul.

As we saw later, the pilots had taken superb photographs of Nanga Parbat and the whole Gilgit valley. At first it had been quite cloudy for them and they had been afraid that they might have to turn back.

So like *Lost Horizon*:

All afternoon the plane had soared through the thin mists of the upper atmosphere, far too high to give clear sight of what lay beneath. Sometimes, at longish intervals, the veil was torn for a moment, to display the jagged outline of a peak, or the glint of some unknown stream.

Then:

Far away, at the very limit of distance, lay range upon range of snow-peaks, festooned with glaciers, and floating, in appearance, upon vast levels of cloud.

Schemes for getting planes to Gilgit had started in 1926, not just to improve communication but to impress the tribes, for a Soviet plane had recently been reported in the region of Murghab in the Pamirs. There was always trouble with the unadministered republics of Darel and Tangir, but in 1926 it had been worse, after a raid by the Tangiris into the neighbouring state of Kuh-Ghizar. A jehad, holy war, had been declared against the British, who in retaliation had started a blockade. The non-payment of gold dust as tribute had also been a sore point. In Srinagar there had been worries lest the Tangiris might buy rifles with all the money that they were making out of cutting down their forests. 'We do not want a second Waziristan,' I read now in the Residency records. Added to all of this there had been complications reminiscent of the days of George Hayward in Yasin, involving the odd murder and deposed chieftains in exile threatening invasion. Perhaps it would have been reassuring for Political Agents in Gilgit to read a further remark in a Residency document: 'Judged by Pathan standards the Tangiri is a very poor fighter.'

The only European, apparently, who had hitherto dared enter Tangir and Darel – if one does not count the Man who would be King – had been (in disguise) Sir Armine Dew, Agent in Gilgit between 1908 and 1912, and usually described as looking like a rugby international. Even today there probably would be risks for a lone traveller, however powerfully built.

Quite why it took five years for these Wapitis finally to arrive in Gilgit is not clear at all. In November 1927 Heb Todd was writing to Srinagar that the failure of the planes to reach Gilgit had caused 'surprise and comment' among the chiefs. 'Some action may have to be taken to convince the Tangiris that we really mean business.' The eventual, intermediate, action seems to have been in the nature of preventing the Tangiris from taking their flocks to graze in Punial during the summer months.

A flu epidemic broke out in Gilgit soon after the arrival of the Wapitis, and it was immediately assumed that it was the fault of the planes. There was a deputation to stop any more of them arriving.

But to return to our jeep journey to Naltar. We reached a stony desert under the peak of Dubanni, over which some threatening cumulus clouds were running away towards the east. 'Perhaps there will be an earthquake,' Shah encouraged us. But as a scene of desolation it was superb. We came to the famous gorge, like a vast gash in the mountains, and our jeep began to climb. 'Marco Polo went this way,' Shah said, but we did not feel convinced, and indeed he was wrong. Nor did I believe that Chinese silk and spice caravans could often have used such an arduous route, seeing that for centuries the Hunza people had been notorious as robbers and slave-traders, and ambushes would have been easy. The huge diagonal shadows ahead, the bleakness and inscrutability of the landscape, the swollen milky waters of the river, the sight of little Chinese trucks buzzing along KKH a quarter of a mile away, had an overwhelming and silencing effect on us. KKH kept to a lower level, nearer to the river. When we reached a kind of oasis on a mountain ledge, we found ourselves looking down on a Chinese encampment, composed of perhaps about fifty khaki bell tents. There was no sign of human movement. I insisted on stopping and taking a spy's photograph. John was horrified. 'You're mad! They'll be watching us through fieldglasses!'

As we climbed higher, the road seemed almost to turn into a mule-track. The precipices were frightful, so were the bends, and there was no pretence of a parapet; in some cases trunks of trees or brushwood shored up piles of boulders where there had been a landslip. The driver went at a crazy speed, and from the back I could almost see John's and Raúl's hair rising. When we reached a bridge, apparently made of telegraph cables, over a drop of some two hundred feet, and saw the usual slats missing, they leapt out. And so did I.

Rock falls, the small ones, sounded like horses galloping. It was not much fun to see boulders the size of lorries thundering into the deep grey valley, especially as we reached the Chaicar Pari, the most precipitous slope of all and the one most usually swept by avalanches; it was three times the height of the Grand Canyon, so Shah said. Turner's *Pass of St Gotthard* could not even compare for savagery. We reached a mini-glacier, dirty chunks spilling across the road. 'I think it best you walk,' the driver advised this time. At last, with some relief, we came to a verdant terraced valley. We saw purple irises, berberis and clumps of wild pink roses, and walnuts, apricots and poplars. Lots of magpies. Nomal was our first halt, straggling along the river. We were eighteen miles from Gilgit.

Ahead we could just see the summit of the superb Rakaposhi, loveliest of all the Karakoram peaks, perhaps in the entire Himalayan chain. Then, fourteen miles on, we reached the village of Chalt on the Hunza frontier, and guards stopped us: Chalt, where in November 1891 Colonel Algy Durand's troops had gathered before the attack on Hunza and Nagar – a campaign in which three Victoria Crosses had been won.

Journeys to Hunza and Nagar, 1891 and 1930

After the 1930 Jhalsa in Gilgit the round of pleasure continued for the British colony. First there was the opening of the trout fishing season with elaborate picnics, when newly caught fish would be grilled on open fires. Then everybody had invitations to visit Hunza and Nagar. Not all of us could go of course, especially not children and nannies. The weather had been unusually bad, resulting in avalanches and bridges being washed away, but all this made no difference to the acceptances. Maurice Berkeley, as commandant of the Gilgit Scouts, had also to stay behind, to be in charge of the garrison. Arthur Lloyd and Leila Blackwell were to be in the first party, accompanied by Daulat Shah as factotum. Then would come Olive, Walter and the Todds and finally George Clark.

Leila kept her diary going in her same zestful and vivid style, and Walter's record as usual was a photographic one. The Mirs never questioned the propriety of Leila travelling alone with Arthur, and merely assumed – so Mrs Lloyd was amused to learn later – that Leila was his senior memsahib. The trip had a particular excitement for Leila when she reached Chalt. For it was here that her gallant cousin Fenton Aylmer, one of the heroes of the 1891 campaign against Hunza and Nagar, had 'thrown' a bridge across the river. Aylmer, whom Durand had described as a man not with nerves of an ordinary mortal, was still alive in 1930, retired as a major-general and living in England. A sapper, he had also constructed temporary bridges at Gilgit and across the Indus at Bunji.

The Mir of Hunza in 1891 had been Safdar Ali. By 1888 Russian plotting could not be ignored by the British Government, and in that same year a Captain Grombchevtski and twelve Cossacks had spent a week in Hunza. Safdar Ali had recently murdered his father, and just to be on the safe side had also disposed of two brothers, in addition – so some said – to his mother. Patricide was well in the family tradition, for his father had not only murdered some of his own brothers, an uncle and a few other relatives, but had had his own father killed, using the novel expedient of giving him a present of a robe infested with smallpox. Safdar Ali had also reinstated the age-old Hunza tradition of raids on caravans.

Across the valley Nagar was under the control of its Mir's heir-apparent, Uzr Khan, no less distrustful of the British. Durand had visited both in 1889 after the Gilgit Agency had been reestablished, and had found Safdar Ali in particular truculent and arrogant, and had left convinced that he ought to be punished. Preparations for war were well advanced when in May 1891 Durand heard that Uzr Khan had murdered his two younger brothers and was intending to attack the garrison at Chalt. At once Durand took the opportunity of moving up four hundred men and a mountain battery. Aylmer's new bridge was thus a preliminary to invasion.

Soon afterwards there was an incident which *The Times* correspondent described as 'equivalent to a declaration of war'. In August Francis Younghusband was expelled in an undignified manner from a remote spot called Bozai Gumbaz, the 'Gibraltar of the Pamirs', by a party of Russians which also announced that the Pamirs had been annexed by Russia. Younghusband had been surveying the passes in the Pamirs and the Karakoram for the past few years, and had been attempting to persuade the Chinese and Afghans to agree on a frontier, in order to thwart the Russians' seemingly relentless advance. This incident was regarded as a major setback to British policy, and Durand was now instructed to inform Safdar Ali that his government claimed free access into Hunza. A defiant reply to this ultimatum was received (as expected), even if phrased in quaint language. Chalt, Safdar Ali said, was more precious to him than the strings of his wives' pyjamas. The British were like 'camels without nose-rings', and he was ready to chop off Durand's head and send it to Simla. Such supreme confidence in himself was due to the tradition that Mirs of Hunza had magic powers and were therefore invincible.

So on December 1 the British force crossed Aylmer's bridge. Hunza and Nagar might have been hereditary enemies, each with claims on Chalt, but they were now united against the British, and had a combined force of perhaps 5,000 tribesmen. Apart from Aylmer, who was 'jolly' enough, Durand's officers were a high-spirited lot, longing for a 'good scrap' and lured on no doubt by stories of the loose morals of the Hunzakuts. They included Curly Stewart and Charlie Townshend, who played the banjo and carried with him copies of the magazine *La Vie Parisienne*, and who later became elevated to the rank of national hero at the sieges of Chitral and Kut. There was also the splendid *Times* special correspondent, E. F. Knight; he had brought his golf clubs, and was to find himself leading a platoon of Pathan warriors. 'Surely,' Knight wrote, 'no military expedition ever before penetrated into so sublime a mountain region as that which now lay before us.'

The east bank of the river at Chalt is Nagar territory. A stiff climb follows; the reason for the crumbling of the rocks here, apparently, is the prevalence of iron pyrites which rain turns into sulphuric acid – a geologically-minded friend assures me this is true. The next stop after Chalt is Nilt, and it was at this place that Leila noted in her diary that Fenton Aylmer won the VC. 'Heavens! It must have been a ghastly place to take, with enemy breastworks all over the place.'

The tribesmen in 1891 had regarded Nilt, on the edge of a chasm, as an impregnable fortress. Leila saw the remains of the gate that Aylmer had blown up, but the bricks of the fort had been used for houses. You could still see an old apple tree from which a sniper had taken 'pot-shots'. Aylmer had crept up under the walls to place gun-cotton by the gate; the fuse had failed to go off, and in spite of being badly wounded in the leg he had returned to reignite it. 'While doing this,' E. F. Knight wrote, 'he received another wound, his hand being terribly crushed by a stone that was thrown from the battlements.' Another VC was won by Lieutenant Boisragon, in the hand-to-hand fighting that followed, and a third, after a hold-up of several days, by Lieutenant Manners-Smith who, in his white Wolseley helmet, had scaled what Leila called 'that awful cliff' to the neighbouring fortress of Maiun. Other medals were won in the campaign. It was not surprising therefore, to quote a *Blackwood's Magazine* article, that Chalt, Nilt and Gilgit came to be regarded by all adventure-seeking officers of the Indian army as 'favoured spots where honour was to be clutched by the stout-hearted and dragged from every rock, and where the heavens dropped awards alike upon the colonel and upon the subaltern'.

Durand was also wounded at Nilt, by a bullet made from a garnet, garnets being plentiful around Hunza. As for Aylmer, he struggled on 'as jolly as ever', and went on designing bridges 'as soon as he could crawl'.

Leila wrote that Arthur Lloyd had no head for heights, so the journey was 'rather agonising', especially when the ponies got difficult and began biting one another. The whole valley of Nagar was billowing with apricot and almond blossom, 'an unbelievable sight', with the dazzling snow ranges and 'blue blue' sky above. Old men in chogas were lined up to salaam Arthur and Leila, and there were camels frisking about, 'making an awful row'. The people were light-skinned, looking as if they were slightly sunburnt – but maybe that was due to the Nagaris' aversion to washing. That night Arthur and Leila had dinner with the Mir, 'a very pious Muslim', under an 'ornate' ceiling. One wall of the room had a display of heads of the bharal, known also as the blue sheep, though in point of fact it is neither sheep nor goat, and another had coloured pictures of George V and Queen Mary. There was also a collection of ancient guns, eight or nine feet long. A pink and white chandelier overhead was 'pretty ghastly'. In the corner was an English bedstead, complete with mosquito nets. The menu consisted of soup, rissoles, chicken pilaff, curry, baked custard, stewed pears, coffee, sweets and walnuts. Arthur and Leila knew that it was tactful to tell the Mir how like his profile was to the heads of Alexander the Great on Greek coins.

The muezzin, next morning, was wonderful to hear, echoing backwards and forwards across the valley. Leila, accompanied by Daulat Shah, climbed 2,000 feet over a wild tangle of rocks to look at the Hispar glacier, 'composed of enormous ice ridges, quite thin and sharp, twenty to thirty feet high'. There was a constant sound of booms and crashes as bits of the glacier melted. The colour of the ice was steely blue. It was quite eerie. 'Couldn't spot any ibex though.'

Leila gave the Rani presents: necklaces ('Woolworth!'), a ring, some scent and soap. In return she received an embroidered cap and bag to match. Daulat Shah told Leila how his grandfather had been shot dead by the Nagaris when he swam across the river to rescue a cow. That was in the time of Safdar Ali. So the grandfather's brother had swum over and captured two Nagari youths, who were later sold as slaves in the Pamirs. (In Durand's book *The Making of a Frontier* there is a perhaps significant reference to a Daulat Shah who was 'the scoundrel son of the old chief's headman'.)

The way to Hunza from Nagar was over a wobbly 'acrobatic' rope bridge, really two bridges, that sagged in the middle and swung 'madly' over the frothy water. 'Poor Arthur!' On the Hunza side 'large shaggy yaks were waiting to take us up the hill – the horns removed otherwise they would have savaged us'. It was a hard climb up to the Mir's new guest house, a chalet designed by himself, and the broad-backed yaks ('so slow it wasn't true') sounded like chugging trains. Nagar had seemed greener than Hunza, because of the pines, but Hunza was by far the most spectacular, with the view of the Mir's palace of Baltit romantically built on a kind of pinnacle surrounded by a 'hive' of flat-roofed houses, and a huge dark valley yawning mysteriously behind under barren peaks. All around were 'tiny terraced fields, poplars, neat stone walls, belts or orchards full of blossom'. 'Enchanting.' And, presiding over all, the timeless Rakaposhi, more than a mountain, with a personality of its own, 'just one sharp peak, not like Nanga Parbat'. Shangri-La at last! 'The hillside was dotted with people watching our triumphant entry. We were greeted by a band playing its loudest and brightest, and women were singing a strange wailing song. We were met by the Mir's son, Ghazan Khan, who piloted us up some steps, at the top of which, under a stone arch, surmounted by two white clay tigers with pink tongues hanging out, stood the Mir, Sir Mohammed Nazim Khan.'

There had been no welcoming Mir of course when the British entered Hunza early in December 1891, for the invincible 'Saffy' – like Uzar Khan – had fled with all his wives. E. F. Knight had found the people of Nagar very friendly, and the Hunzakuts were 'fair, sturdy-looking men, with a fresh fearless mien'; they had rather cruel mouths and were sometimes quarrelsome, though jovial and 'fond of boisterous merry-making over the flowing bowl'. Townshend had been designated Military Governor, so the palace was commandeered. It was a 'curious rambling old place', some five storeys high, well built out of sun-dried mud, stones and timber; at the top were galleries of 'tastefully carved wood', and in each room there was a ladder by means of which you climbed to the floor above. Apart from some illuminated Korans, the loot had been disappointing. The new Governor soon livened the place up with strumming his banjo.

Mohammed Nazim Khan was the half-brother of Safdar Ali. How he had escaped the fratricidal slaughter was not clear. Leila noted that his beard had been dyed blue-black for the visit and was now curled outwards on each side at the bottom. He produced a copy of Curzon's *Leaves from a Viceroy's Notebook* from which she saw that in 1898 he had worn ringlets, hanging from his rolled cap.

Leila and Arthur were invited to dinner at the palace, and also had to climb ladders. The view at the top was 'the most marvellous one could find anywhere'. 'Below us each house had a large square hole in the middle to let the light in and smoke out, and most of the inhabitants were squatting on the roof-tops.' The walls of the dining-room were hung with Khotan rugs. There were pictures of Queen Victoria and the Aga Khan, a Nativity, and an advertisement for Mellin's food, 'for Infants and Invalids, untouched by human hands', 1899. Overhead was a pink chandelier 'with bangles'. 'The Mir is such a wag.' He said that his brother Safdar Ali was still alive and living on a plot of land in Yarkand (actually he died that year, 1930). Uzar Beg, however, had gone into more comfortable exile in Srinagar, fratricide being no 'problem' in the 1890s. He also told them how he had been invited to Calcutta for the Durbar in 1911. He had gone out on a ship – quite amazing, nothing but sky and water everywhere, and he hadn't known in which direction he was going; suddenly he had found himself back where he had started from.

The dancing girls gave their performance, and my friend Amin was there to watch. The new Rani was just a child, not nearly as pretty as the last one, her sister, the Mir said. She wore baggy trousers, a knee-length pink brocaded shirt and an embroidered cap. As Leila was wearing a Fair Isle waistcoat, knitted by herself, she was asked to show the Rani how to make a similar pattern on her husband's socks. Leila spent some time with the girl on the purdah terrace. When she went for walks she was always followed by a mob of children. 'The Pied Piper wasn't in it! I must be a queer-looking fish! Daulat Shah held an umbrella over me while I sketched. One little girl was so intrigued by the nails on my boots that she kept stroking them. Most of the children are fair-skinned and pretty. The women are nearly all shy and hide their faces when you approach.'

Even more dramatic than Baltit was the fort at Altit, 'a real medieval robber's nest'. From here Leila and Arthur watched an avalanche. 'It was like a coloured breaker, dashing against a cliff, going downwards instead of up. It spread out all over the place like a giant fan, and made me realize how utterly awful and helpless one would feel if one saw an avalanche approaching. The noise lasted ten minutes, then nothing was visible in a cloud of powdered snow ... A perfectly wonderful sight. We heard avalanches all through the day, like guns.'

Then it was back across the rope bridge, and the Mir of Nagar was waiting for them. On the way to Nilt they met the Trevelyans and the Todds, and had about an hour's 'chin-wag'. Later they ran into George Clark, who had been after ibex. 'He'd got a good one. He said he was going to join Heb and Walter, in order to get up to the Shimshal Pass beyond Hunza, if that could be managed. Brave fellows! At Nilt I wrote to Fenton Aylmer, sending him both Mirs' salaams.' Down in the gorge she noticed khuraputs, gold-washers, busily at work.

In the event, George, Heb and Walter did not go to the Shimshal Pass, because of the unsettled weather, and it was probably just as well with its reputation for being one of the most dismal places of the world, leading to a spot that was designated 'blank on the map' and is still virtually unexplored. Instead George and Walter headed for the Mintaka and Killik, further to the north-west and eighty miles from Hunza – Mintaka was the pass taken by the defeated Mir in 1891. The ragged Doré-like teeth opposite the entrance to the Shimshal valley have been compared to the Aiguilles near Chamonix. From there onwards the scenery is pretty desolate; not that Walter would have minded, for he was after Ovis poli and snow leopard. He took a few photographs, but rather more when he returned with Maurice Berkeley and Jamal Khan, the old Mir's grandson, in 1932. Jamal Khan was to be the last Mir to rule in Hunza, and it was he who died of a reputedly broken heart in 1976.

Olive and the Todds stayed behind in Hunza with the dogs, which had had to be carried across the rope bridge in sacks, and later travelled back to Gilgit together. They watched polo, yak fights and sword-dances by firelight. Olive collected some garnets, which I still have. There is a photograph of her in her best hat, which didn't suit her, sitting in the spring sun on the Mir's terrace at Baltit, looking down on the panorama of the valley with Heb, who is wearing a topee and smoking a pipe. For me this simple picture of happiness – although I never went to Hunza – sums up everything that I remember and still feel about the Karakoram.

Olive after an experience in the early 1920s had sworn never to go again on a 'major' shooting expedition with Walter. They had crossed the Deosai Plains to Baltistan, where she had kept a diary but to my dismay destroyed it just before she died 'because it was too silly'. I often heard her story, which went something like this: 'We had a tent in *the* most ghastly valley, with sun literally one hour a day. Walter used to go out at dawn and come back dog-tired, not wanting to talk. I had nothing to do except keep this deadly diary about the weather, or write letters to anybody I could think of in England, and collect dried yak's dung for fires. We had to have fires going all night, the temperatures dropped so fast. I was also frightened of bears.'

Three glaciers feed into the Shimshal valley and spread right across it in severe winters. The danger is that snow will block the free flow of water, causing lakes to be formed. Traditionally a flood takes place every seven years (one hopes that the Chinese when constructing KKH took due account). It did not happen when we were there, though in previous years there had been some disastrous floods, but Alec Redpath, who was assistant P.A. in Gilgit from 1939, has described how a twenty-foot wall of foaming brown water, full of boulders, roared down the Hunza River, sweeping the banks and carrying everything before. 'As it reached the Gilgit river it seemed to pause before swirling away to the east and down to the Indus. He saw part of the bank crumbling, and then in slow motion thousands of tons from the mountainside broke loose and subsided into the river, which providentially was not blocked...' A bonanza for the gold-washers.

Walter and George stopped at Pasu, which E. F. Knight, with the force pursuing Safdar Ali, described as a densely populated rabbit-warren. Pasu really marks the end of the Karakoram range. The people there speak a Persian-based language called Wakhi instead of the curious Burushaski of Hunza, and in Knight's day cheerfully admitted to having been the hereditary robbers of the region and the terror of merchants on the old silk road. Legends of man-eating giants up in the Shimshal valley cannot have made the route any more attractive to travellers. Just beyond Pasu is the Batura glacier, thirty-six miles long, up to one and a half miles wide, supposed to be the fifth largest glacier in the world, and probably one of the most unprepossessing – of very little interest, by all accounts, to anybody except geomorphologists and maybe spies. It has been suggested that it could be six hundred feet thick. At Gulmit there is a cliff which is still pointed out as the one over which the fleeing Safdar Ali threw and killed yet another of his brothers. Then comes the Khunjerab River, 'the river of blood', too swollen to ford in the summer and even in the spring full of pot-holes, so forcing horses to swim. When Curzon passed over it in 1894 his sturdy Hunzakuts stripped themselves and swam unconcerned in the freezing water.

Beyond the village of Misgar, which is the point where KKH now turns up to the Khunjerab Pass, is the land of the Khirgiz shepherds: real Tartars, 'tough as anything', nomad shepherds, with flat faces but high cheekbones, slit eyes, thin beards and moustaches, and in winter dressed in long sheepskin or quilted coats and round black sheepskin hats like helmets with earflaps. The Khirgiz lived in felt tents with rugs hung inside, and with a circular hole at the top to let the smoke out from fires of dried dung and lavender.

The last stretch up to the snows had in 1930 to be made on yaks. Was it then that Walter became slightly snowblind? Certainly from his 1932 photographs I realized that Walter loved it all. For him it was the real life. He had two special triumphs in 1932. One was a photograph of the Killik, 15,870 feet, icy and to me hideous, much bleaker than described by Curzon, and looking straight across to the Afghan, Soviet and Sinkiang frontiers, although now the pass is inside Sinkiang. The Roof of the World. Ultima Thule. Where Three Empires Meet. You could just see Nanga Parbat from there apparently. But how could Gromchevtski have reported back to Moscow that the pass was 'exceedingly easy, so that a cart with a full team of horses could follow it'? In this very place Curzon, intent on finding the source of the Oxus (which he identified in the Wakh-jir glacier), had sat down and written a letter to *The Times*. Walter's second triumph was the shooting of a Marco Polo sheep, which was decapitated, the head being carried back to Hunza.

Now that Ovis poli have become so rare, in part thanks to the slaughter by workers on KKH, I wonder whether Walter would have been quite so exultant about his bag. I think probably not. He did get his snow leopard: two snow leopards in fact. The skin of one was sent to the Natural History Museum, South Kensington, joining that of Lynx trevelyanii and others of a polecat, a marten, a wolf, a wild cat and a fox that he had also shot. The soft grey skin of the other snow leopard used to lie for a long while on the floor of our drawing-room in Essex, until Olive decided to have it turned into a fur coat. Walter told me I remember, that bear steak was very good, 'better than mutton'.

I forget now whether an almost fatal accident to Olive occurred in the Karakoram or further south in Kashmir near Gulmarg. She was crossing a glacier, evidently quite a smooth-surfaced one, with Walter, and slipped. 'I would have gone sliding away for miles and miles,' she used to say, 'but luckily I hit a rock.' The result was that she broke her 'tail-bone' and had to have it removed.

Because, presumably, Naunihal Shah was of royal Hunza blood and therefore to be trusted, the guards at Chalt allowed us to cross the border into Hunza territory as far as a view of Rakaposhi – though a police escort was insisted upon.

We drove in our jeep for about a mile, half expecting to run into angry Chinese. And there she was, the fabled peak, haunt of fairies and giants, and maybe of the Yeti, unconquered by mountaineers until the year 1958, 25,500 feet rising to a triangular point of frozen snow without the hint of a cloud. At least 15,000 feet of her rose sheer before us. In the warmth and brightness of that upland air we sat among the boulders and bushes of wild roses and stared at her for a full hour, hardly speaking.

Then we returned to Chalt for tea. Apart from the flies in the café we felt we were in a garden of Eden looked down upon by glittering snowtopped ranges. The people were smiling, as if trying to forget the frontier feeling of Chalt.

We retraced the horrible road to Nomal, and then drove up to Naltar, where we found ourselves in a valley of meadows and pines, like dark green plumes, rather Swiss apart from the flat-roofed huts made of logs. There was even a ski-lift, because we were told Pakistani airborne troops came to train there in the winter. Our hut had a corrugated roof, sloping, with two bedrooms, a dining-room and a wire fence outside to keep away the many grazing buffaloes, whose dark brown meringues dotted the hillside. It was homelier than the rest-houses I used to know, but our first thought was to have all the bedding, including mattresses, put out to air on the fence. We had a houseboy and a cook allocated to us, the one tall and giggly, rather camp, and the other small and anxious.

Shah was keen to be off to Hunza, as his wife was expecting a baby. Before he left he arranged for a chicken to be beheaded in our honour that evening. We took his advice to trek next day up to an apparently beautiful lake called Kuto. It would be useful to take a guide, he said, 'because of the tribesmen'. Remembering the recent experiences of Chinese roadworkers on KKH, we agreed to this too.

A short while after Shah had gone we spotted some jeeps and motor cycles approaching across the valley. 'Very important General,' the cook warned us. We watched the fuss as the General and some other officers, accompanied by women in expensive saris, were decanted from the jeeps, and as the houseboy rushed out arranging chairs in the sun, taking some from our bedrooms. The General settled in front of our drying mattresses and asked for tea, which rather to our indignation was taken from our rations. We were paying good money for the hire of this hut and its amenities, and were beginning to feel annoyed. John decided to put on a British Raj act, and advanced grandly down the steps to shake hands with every member of the party in turn, including the outriders. 'Please don't get up,' he said to the General. 'Do make yourselves at home. It's all right, we're just going for a walk.' He then said to the ADC: 'When the sun goes down, would you mind asking your men to carry in our blankets and mattresses?'

This incident has also become another of John's dining out stories. He is convinced that the extremely courteous General was General Zia, which was indeed a possibility, as I do remember a thin black moustache and staring eyes.

I had hoped that at last we would find some alpine flowers on our walk, but the season was still too early, and in any case the buffaloes would have munched them up. We did however meet some men with Primula denticulata stuck in their caps, a Gilgit fashion. We also were shown some female markhors in a compound: 'Very good milk. No TB.' Through fieldglasses I saw a pair of lammergeiers, hardly moving their wings as they glided at an extraordinary speed over the ridges. There also were a few choughs with yellow beaks, and we found some wild gooseberries. The people mostly had long faces, like the Nagaris, with hooked noses.

It became cold as soon as the sun went out of sight, and as we had seen the General's party leave we returned to our hut. The bedding had been taken in. Each bedroom had a stove in the middle with funnels made of welded tins going up through the ceiling. Fires had been lit, but realizing that fuel would soon run out we found some sacks and went out in the dusk to collect fir cones. The houseboy, Balihan, scolded us. 'Red bears. Too many,' he said.

The darker it became, the more the peaks gleamed, like ghosts of ghosts. The only sound outside was a waterfall. We were about a hundred miles from the Killik Pass and the Pamirs. I knew that in the 1930s local women used to weave charms against the British when their families came here for the summer. There used to be guards of course, but the fact that women and children could be left alone for days or weeks on end was typical of the confidence one felt even in such remote places.

Our headless hen duly appeared, with a pile of spaghetti and some chapattis, both brownish because the water was brown. The servants squatted on the floor watching us eat. Next morning, on unbarring the doors, we found we had a levee of about eight strangers, who seemed ready to follow us into the bathroom. Raúl complained that he could not perform in front of spectators, so I had an idea: 'Photograph! Everybody out!' This worked splendidly.

A boy of about fifteen wearing a ragged army coat was introduced as Pakihan, or Paki. He was to be our guide to Lake Kuto and protector against any troublesome tribesmen. How far was this lake, we asked? Nine miles. And how much higher did we have to climb? About two thousand feet. Enough, certainly, at this altitude. Any glaciers to cross? Only one.

For our picnic we took biscuits and tins of bully beef and cheese, with a can of drinking water laced with Puritabs. The climb was not that arduous and the glacier more of a moraine. In a pinewood by the river we saw what appeared to be a Very Serious Conference, a circle of men around their chief, a jirga explained Paki (consulting about the threat of Chinese roadworkers?) – they were too intent to look round when we passed. We ran into two of Paki's friends who had a brown and white sheep on a rope; they joined us, and the sheep had to trot beside us all the way to Lake Kuto. As we approached the snowline we came into a realm of birches and junipers. A cataract tumbled among boulders. There were giant forget-me-nots of a pure cobalt blue, and giant marsh marigolds. Here, in the dappled shade of pine forests, we found a village which seemed to be made entirely of brushwood. The women began shouting at us, whether to entice us in, or out of anger, we could not decide, but rather thought the latter, and as there were several barking dogs we kept our distance. Six of the filthiest and poorest children I had ever seen now joined the party; their nails were like broken claws, as if they were accustomed to scrabble for roots. So now we were eleven, plus the sheep. My field-glasses were in perpetual demand, sternly supervised by Paki.

Lake Kuto was at the head of the pass and indeed startlingly beautiful, a pool of turquoise and bright apple green, the colours set off against the bark of the birch trees and the snow patches. I was amazed to see fish in the lake, and thought I heard frogs. Someone had made a rough bridge over to an island, like the willow pattern design on plates. We settled down to our picnic on the island, when yet more urchins arrived, obviously hungry. So we cut up some bully and dropped pieces into a dozen dirty paws. Before, however, any of our guests could begin to eat, Paki snapped at them and everybody at once dropped the food as if it were poisoned. We tried to tell Paki it was only yak meat but he would not relent. We offered cheese and biscuits, without more success. We therefore left some cheese on a rock in the hope that the boys would sneak over to it after we had gone.

Streams bubbled over fine green moss. We were conscious always of that intense silence one only gets at great heights. It was a slog back, but our friend the sheep, which should surely have been acclimatized to the altitude, felt the journey more than we did. John however did seem exhausted at the end. Raúl and I began to worry about him, and braved the red bears once more to bring in twenty loads of fir-cones, so that he could keep his stove fed all night. In due course there were several squalls of rain, turning into a downpour. We had not realized that there were gaps in the roof around the funnels of the stove; water came down, hissing and spitting on to the stoves and splashing on to our beds, especially John's. But he was none the worse next morning, and in bouncing form for the usual levee.

A quiet day wandering in the hills was called for. My most vivid memory of those beautiful walks will be not so much of the evening smoke of the villages, or of clouds sailing along the valleys, as the sight of a farmer letting loose two horses, a mare and a stallion, and watching them careering in mad abandon down a steep slope. The stallion was randy, trying to mount at the gallop and squirting when he failed.

Raúl volunteered to cook the spaghetti that evening in the hope – fond, as it turned out – of boiling it in less mud-coloured water. The cook was understandably reluctant to admit us into his witches' cavern of a kitchen, and on entering it we were quite surprised that the spaghetti had not been black instead of brown. We noted that the chicken's head was still lying in the washing-up place.

Our day of departure was overshadowed by a panic over the cook's wife getting ill. It sounded like pneumonia. I presented him with my only spare clothing, a pair of pyjamas, and two aspirins – being afraid that if I gave him more she would swallow the lot. We wondered what else we could dispose of, we had brought so little and they were so poor. The houseboy had been thrilled when I had left an old razor-blade and a squeezed out toothpaste tube in the bathroom. He seemed content with the present of a plastic bag inscribed Victoria Wine Company.

The Haardt–Citroën Expedition, 1931

I was on the brink of leaving for England when the French expedition to central Asia arrived in Srinagar, on its way to Hunza and Gilgit via the Burzil. It was late June and we were up in Gulmarg packing when suddenly the summons came from the Maharajah of Kashmir for my parents to meet Georges-Marie Haardt, the leader of this very grand, lavishly equipped, stylish and much publicized group. It was the third of M. Haardt's great expeditions by Citroën tracked vehicles, the other two having been across Africa. The plan now was to meet other Citroën cars which had set out in February from Peking in the direction of the Gobi Desert. The vague idea was to follow the old silk road 'in the steps of Marco Polo' and perhaps open it to modern means of transport, preferably Citroën tracked vehicles. Various French scientific institutions, as well as Pathé-Nathan and the National Geographical Society of Washington, were helping to sponsor the trip. The Maharajah had made available a number of bell tents in Srinagar as well as two houseboats and fifty servants. Walter and Olive went to a luncheon at his country palace, and a reception and tea given by the British Resident in the Shalimar Gardens.

There is a picture of Olive, looking slightly flirtatious I must admit, with the elegant M. Haardt, in front of the Golden Scarab and Silver Crescent, the names of the two vehicles which were to make the journey to Gilgit and beyond. Haardt had started his journey in Beirut and had travelled across Persia and Afghanistan. One imagines that Walter could hardly have been encouraging about his prospects in darkest Dardistan, even less when he learnt that there was a plan to cross the Killik into Sinkiang.

An advance party had already been sent out by Haardt to scout the route. As it happened it had been met by George Clark, who had been on his way to see the Resident in Srinagar. Since he was a sapper, by rights his advice ought to have been taken seriously, but...

'Somewhere near Astor,' George has said:

I met a Vicomte de Something or Other and told him that they hadn't got a hope of being able to drive even their tracked machines even down the final bit of road to the Bunji plain. He was most indignant and, I gather, later expressed his disbelief by demanding who 'ce petit garçon' was who had dared to criticize the vehicles' ability. Anyway I continued my journey south and, a day or two after reaching Kashmir, went out to see the main body of the expedition by then in their camp near the Wular Lake. They were just about to start off. I spent a pleasant couple of weeks in Gulmarg and then went on the return journey myself, and was amused to catch up with them at the Rest House just before one drops down into the Indus valley and Bunji. They were by then in a state of disarray, having been forced to realize that my pessimism was justified, and were in the process of dismantling their vehicles and trying to make the bits and pieces into coolie loads! This time the opinion of the 'petit garçon' carried more weight and they did, in fact, dine me and wine me most hospitably that evening. Next morning I waved them goodbye and set off on my pony, and had been in Gilgit some weeks before they all trailed in. I was the only English person present in Gilgit when they arrived, as Heb etc were in the coolth of Naltar.

The Burzil had been negotiated all right, in spite of ponies sinking up to their girths in snow, and in spite of recent storms, but the drama for the expedition had occurred on a narrow ledge overlooking the Astor River. The driver of the Golden Scarab had suddenly felt himself sinking.

    'Don't move!'

    'For God's sake, what am I sitting on?'

    'Thin air, mon vieux.'

The retaining wall of the path had slid down the precipice. While the two-ton car was suspended hundreds of feet over the torrent, with the terrified driver still inside, some 'improvised engineering' took place underneath it. After five hours it was hauled back to its companion on solid ground. The expedition struggled on, shoring up dangerous spots on the path, breaking up rocks with mallets, levering others out of the way, and observing the occasional skeletons of ponies. Only four miles a day could be managed. At Astor, in a 'chaos of boulders' and 'deafened by the thundrous roar'· of the river, they felt like 'struggling beetles in a bottomless pit'. After reaching a full-scale landslide at the Hattu Pir, a 'glissade of loose rubble', it was decided to dismantle the vehicles altogether.

Meanwhile there had been bad news from the Peking party. A

Muslim rebellion had broken out in Sinkiang – the tail end of which, a few years later, Peter Fleming and Ella Maillart were to endure – and the Frenchmen had been arrested at Urumchi, a hundred miles or so from Outer Mongolia.

Even after Haardt had reassembled his vehicles, there were ordeals in that 'hellish country': dysentery, no shade, rocks as hot as clinkers, clouds of sandflies. The arrival of the first motor cars in Gilgit was a huge excitement for the locals, who had never even seen a bicycle, and as sensational as the appearance of the planes the year before. Heb abandoned his coolth and came hurrying down to lay on 'traditional British hospitality'. But Haardt could not linger; he was anxious about the fate of his friends at Urumchi. Not only the petit garçon but Heb and everyone else had now convinced him that his vehicles would have to be left behind in Gilgit. So ponies were hired, and in due course there was more traditional hospitality at Hunza, in the form of Scotch whisky originally presented to the Mir by Heb and performances by the dancing girls. Haardt in return offered handsome presents, which were graciously accepted. The Mir then suggested that any money which the expedition might be intending to offer to his retainers should instead be given to him. 'As for those,' he added, introducing with a vague gesture a group of dignitaries, who bowed low, 'they are the most important functionaries in my State, and I authorize them to receive presents directly from your generous hands.'

Haardt and his companions reached the Roof of the World, and on a rock found a half-effaced inscription marking the frontiers. It seemed to him, on that high plateau, almost as if the mountain had shrunk, to reveal nothing except the 'pale blue of the heaven'. 'Silence and solitude, broken only by the shrill cries of marmots, brooded over the vast sloping sheets of virgin snow.' Finally on October 8 at a place called Aksu beyond Kashgar the grand reunion took place with the China group, which had been released by the rebels though it was under surveillance still, unscathed and fit apart from one man who was suffering from what all travellers to remote places must dread: appendicitis.

The four 'Chinese' vehicles were in such good condition that they looked as though they had come straight from the factory, a splendid advertisement for Citroën. Back in Gilgit the Golden Scarab was being dismantled again, and it eventually found its way to the Citroën museum in Paris. The Silver Crescent was presented to the Government of India and remained therefore in Gilgit, to the joy of the village children whose toy it became. My brother John well remembers seeing it in 1934.

In 1977 I asked what had happened to the Silver Crescent. 'The Dogras took it.'

Haardt died at Hong Kong on his way home to France, on March 16 1932.

Ramah, the Gor shoot and Chilas

An alternative hot weather resort to Naltar was Ramah, which was near Astor, below Nanga Parbat. Leila went there with the Lloyds for July and August 1930. She thought it just like a miniature Gulmarg: a flat grassy maidan or open space, surrounded by pines and snowclad hills. Much of this maidan was polo-ground, and some of it was bog. The camp was quite luxurious, and Heb Todd as 'boss' had his own hut, Union Jack flying over it, with a dining-room and a spacious living-room. There were tents (double-roofed) for his office, kitchen and servants. 'It was fascinating – and could there have been a more lovely place to camp?' The running up of the Union Jack every morning was quite a ceremony.

The Lloyds brought two cows with them, but eggs were the difficulty; in the end there was only one hen which could 'oblige' – the others had to go 'into the pot'. Every morning before breakfast there would be a chukka of polo with the servants and locals, and Leila had lessons in the game. The Lloyds made their own nine-hole golf course, and there were two deck-tennis courts. 'No lack of exercise!' There were also 'lots of fascinating walks', with a glacier to explore. Because of wolves, which attacked the sheep, two bonfires were kept going all night, and 'we would sit round them before dinner sipping drinks and eating potato crisps'. The sheep and goats kept wandering into tents; 'needless to say, they didn't wipe their feet.' Sometimes there was dancing in the mess tent after dinner, and Arthur Lloyd and Pinky Greenwood, who was now stationed at Bunji after Eldred's death, would do funny turns. 'Oh, we had all sorts of fun!' Pinky was a card; the story was that as a boy he had run away to join the Canadian Mounties. Because of his nickname it soon followed that the unfortunate Walter, with his high complexion, was sometimes referred to as Purple.

'One day,' Leila went on, 'we were unexpectedly entertained by travelling dancers from Srinagar, who were in the district before going on to Skardu. The troupe consisted of two small boys and a larger one (a cut-throat looking villain), all of whom had long hair and were dressed like girls, in red skirts, coloured waistcoats and saris. The party was completed by three venerable old men who provided the (?!) music. Then poor Mrs Eldred arrived and stayed with us for a few days. She had been to Bunji to see where her son had been drowned in the Indus, and was on her way in that awful heat down below to see the grave.'

At the turn of the century, and indeed long before, the country round Astor was recognized as a sportsman's paradise. The Astor markhor was a special breed with larger and more widely flowing corkscrew-like horns. Its rutting season was in October, when it went through a short period of madness, and this was regarded as a good time to 'nab' a male – which seems a bit unfair. There were also urial, a kind of sheep, and at a much greater height ibex and bear. Walter shot two black bears near Astor, and it was their skins that lay on our Gilgit drawing-room floor, to the terror of my small brother.

Around Christmas Heb organized another camp at Gor, which was on the other side of the Indus valley, facing Nanga Parbat, on the way to Chilas. This was one of the year's chief social occasions, and the little band of British officers from Gilgit, Bunji and Chilas assembled there, 'plus wives where applicable' – children and nannies having been left behind.

Chukor, hill partridge, was the quarry at Gor. Woodcock, snipe and duck, particularly teal, were plentiful in season near Gilgit, which seemed to be on the main migration route between central Asia and the swamps of India and possibly of East Africa. There were chukor of course at Gilgit, but nothing like the quantities at Gor. Tents were pitched on flat terraces. 'We bought straw from the villagers,' Heb has said, 'on which to spread our bedding rolls for the night. It was very cold at that height, being winter, so our servants kept a roaring fire going in the middle of the camp. During the day we organized beats along the hillside and had some excellent shooting. If you went up to ten or eleven thousand feet, you might get a "Monal" pheasant, which had bright metallic blue markings and feathers which we used for fishing flies.'

Apart from the incident when Joanna Pyper got a pellet in her eye, it was a supremely enjoyable time, as Walter's photographs of picnics round those roaring fires make plain. When the headman of Gor came to pay his respects to Heb, he did a special dance. Men from Chilas would also do a vulture dance, imitating birds of prey circling round and swooping on their prey.

Heb's assistant P.A. at Chilas, which was two days' ride from Bunji and not far from Gor, was Lovell Wooldridge, known as Wooly. He lived there quite alone in a house which he called Journey's End with three dogs – a springer, an Afghan hound and a Yorkshire terrier – and some pets including an acrobatically-inclined lynx, to which the Yorkshire terrier was an anathema. He used to bring the Afghan hound to Gilgit; this 'pyjama dog', as I called it, was a great favourite of mine. Actually I always used to think Wooly looked rather like an Afghan hound. Walter and George visited him in Chilas quite a bit and played polo – 'the gold-sifters were the backbone of the Chilas polo team'. Once Walter accidentally hit Wooly in the eye with his polo stick, and Wooly thought he'd lost it. 'We used to have ibex hunts,' he has told me. 'We would hide in an ice-cave until light faded and it was an absolute rush to get up the damn slopes in time. The ibex always had a sentinel, but they had a bad eye in the semi-dark. One was so fit! The Gor shoot was a pretty idle way of shooting, too easy. The beaters were on the hillside above, and you just sat on your bum, and chukor came roaring overhead. Almost took your hat off.'

It was an odd experience for me, after hearing reminiscences about the Gor shoot and polo with the natives of Chilas, to read the last chapter of Durand's *The Making of a Frontier*. The subjugation of Hunza and Nagar in 1891 had been followed by some more vicious fighting against the tribesmen of Chilas, who had been supported by their ever belligerent neighbours in Darel and Tangir: this time not quite so glorious an affair for the British, and no Victoria Crosses were awarded. By the 1930s Gor was considered to be part of the territory of Chilas, but previously it had been a separate republic, and one ostensible reason for troops being sent up the Indus valley in 1892 was that the headman of Gor (no angel) had asked for protection against the Chilasis, who – said Durand – were 'confirmed disturbers of the peace', fanatical Sunni Muslims 'under the influence of the mullahs of Swat' and therefore not happy with being tributary to the Hindu Maharajah of Kashmir. Indeed, in earlier years the Kashmiris had hit on an easy way of disposing of their convicts, who would be dumped on the Chilas side of the Indus, either to be slaughtered immediately by the tribesmen or taken into slavery.

By 1892 the whole tribal area to the north-west and west of Gilgit looked as if it were about to explode, the chiefs being thoroughly suspicious of the British. Anglo-Afghan relations were going through another tense stage. The Russian foreign minister may have said, after the British capture of Hunza, 'Ils nous ont fermé la porte au nez,' but Russians had reappeared at Bozai Gumbaz and had destroyed a Chinese fort near the Killik. The Chinese were as usual claiming that Hunza was within their sphere, and were suspected of being in collusion with the Russians. A series of murders and counter-murders were rapidly producing anarchy in Chitral. So an uprising along the

Indus valley, during the 'second Pamir crisis', could hardly have been more inconvenient for Durand, the Warden of the Marches as he now styled himself.

The Gilgit garrison's strength had been increased to twenty-three British officers, and Captain Aylmer VC's bridges were now complete. Quite clearly, Bunji was the vital strategic spot, commanding the road to the Burzil and Kashmir, and the beginning of the defile to Gor, Chilas ('our sheet-anchor') and down to the Punjab. If, Durand reasoned, a road could be made along that torrid valley it would be a valuable alternative to the Burzil route. But the Chilasis said that they would never permit such a road. For good measure, they also expelled the Kashmir agent, after trying to murder him.

Durand's friend, Surgeon-Major George Scott-Robertson, later to become Political Agent in Gilgit and a man of 'fiery courage and stern determination who would brook no failures', set out for Gor, where he was well received by those 'inoffensive' people. However, for fear of assault, he took it upon himself to advance further up the valley. And there, with only about eighty men, he was indeed attacked by 'thousands' of tribesmen. He won through, and the enemy was routed. In the excitement of the chase the Kashmiri soldiers took off their trousers in order to run better. The village of Chilas was reached and burnt down with all its grain supply. A garrison, including Gurkhas, was established in a new fort on a mountain crag above, seven hundred feet above the Indus. All this, so a British participant claimed, was 'simply a raid', not a war: 'a thoroughly important and sporting move which included fighting'. Sporting, because a certain amount of chukor had been bagged en route. Robertson departed for Chitral, where the situation had become far worse, and a holy war against the British had been announced.

Algy Durand now set about having his road made from Bunji to Chilas. The tribesmen reacted at once, and reoccupied the ruined village of Chilas. In the ensuing fighting there were many casualties on each side, including one British and three Indian officers. But without their grain the Chilasis were for the time being defeated, although for the British the place remained a 'military nightmare' and a possible death-trap. 'The Chilas business would I knew raise a storm,' said Durand, and he was right. All references to it were omitted from the Parliamentary Blue Book.

A photograph taken by a Wapiti airman in 1931 certainly does show the valley of the Indus to be a thoroughly desolate spot, like a huge trough in the empty quarter of Arabia. A Major Bruce, who was on Robertson's expedition, described it as the abomination of desolation: 'enormous, hideous, and terrific, and when red-hot, as it is during the summer months, to be avoided like the plague.' It is also an area noted for severe and frequent earthquakes.

By 1931 there were threats of troubles again from the always smouldering Darel and Tangir – it seemed that, far from being impressed by aeroplanes flying over their territories to Gilgit, and by the possibility of another landing strip at Chilas, the tribesmen had become alarmed and angry. Needless to say, in Walter's albums all seems to have been idyllic at Journey's End in 1931, with Wooly, Walter, Olive and George photographed in deckchairs and impeccably dressed – Olive in cardigan, plaid skirt and her favourite 'cantilever' shoes, and the men wearing ties; the Afghan hound and our retriever Amber are with them. It seems to me now that Wooly's situation, isolated and quite alone in a spot where once no European would have dared enter without the protection of an army, was typical of one aspect of the administration of British India. He had his gramophone records sent from Regent Street – 'not one arrived broken' – and his Christmas fare, such as ham and Wensleydale cheese, from Quetta. He was respected by the local people and perfectly content on his own, living the 'larger and nobler life that man should live', as E. F. Knight so grandiloquently put it.

The Chilasis may have been staunch Muslims but they also believed in fairies. 'Every Friday they would wash themselves, put on blue clothes and go and speak to them.' When Leila had been at Hunza she jokingly asked the Mir if his people still murdered one another. 'Not now,' he had said. 'They only do it in Chilas – over women.' 'Such damned ugly women too,' Pinky Greenwood had said when he heard this.

And now I add a footnote: the completed KKH follows Durand's dream of an Indus valley route, passing Bunji and through Chilas to Rawalpindi, and so beyond. In theory one can now drive from Peking to Karachi.

On our return from Naltar to Gilgit we looked down from on high on the Chinese encampment by the side of KKH. This time it seemed alive with little drab termites, scurrying hither and thither in what would have seemed a nonsensical way had not some of them been pushing wheelbarrows. In that landscape of the moon the scene seemed more sinister and science fiction than ever.

At the Varshi-Goom we were confronted by the sight of another energetic but very different group: five or six wizened septuagenarian American women, game old things. They were on their way to Gupis, which by all accounts had accommodation somewhat rougher than at Naltar. Gupis is in Kuh-Ghizar on the way to Chitral. As a name it had amused me as a child. I also knew of it because Charles Townshend 'of Chitral and Kut' had been stationed there before the famous expedition in 1895 to Chitral, where he had been besieged with 543 men.

Gupis and Townshend

In his letters home Townshend did not make Gupis sound attractive ('this most awful place'), which was one reason why we declined the invitation of the Americans to join them there. 'Of course,' he had written, 'I try to live as little as possible like John the Baptist, although I *am* in the desert.' He had also had to endure a tremendous earthquake: 'like skating on a ship's deck in a heavy wind'. Curzon called on him in 1893, finding a 'somewhat unusual host', well versed in Clausewitz and the strategy of Hannibal, but decorating the walls of his mud dwelling with 'daring coloured illustrations from Parisian journals of the lighter type'. The future Viceroy was also 'regaled' with French songs to the accompaniment of the banjo.

Curly Stewart, Townshend's chum, was in Yasin in a house he called the Adelphi. Townshend's house was the Garrick, from which he wrote to his sister. It is dated November 9 1893:

> ... There is actually a lady now in Gilgit. I think it awful rot and nonsense. A fellow in the Transport Corps (the fellows in that corps are *all* married) has brought his wife up. I call it turning the place into a regular Punch and Judy show! Gilgit will be getting quite suburban, and lines of dubious-looking lingerie, I suppose, hung out to dry, like you see in the outskirts of London, as you approach in the train.

As usual in 1893 there had been the yearly Pamirs crisis, but hard bargaining over frontiers in other people's domains was in progress between London and St Petersburg. At last there was a settlement, and a narrow corridor of territory, the Wakhan, stretching from the Hindu Kush to the Little Pamirs, was assigned to Afghanistan as a demilitarized buffer between the Russian and British Indian empires. However, the British still had tribes to pacify: in Chitral, there was a never-ending 'hotbed of disaffection'. Only three days after the signing of the Russo–British Pamirs settlement, on March 14 1895, orders had to be given for a force of 15,000 men to be sent to relieve the British garrison under Townshend.

In our time in Gilgit there was a particular reason for Walter being interested in Gupis, since as a young lieutenant in Mesopotamia in

1916 he had been in the relief force when Townshend had been besieged in Kut. Actually, I have a feeling that Walter did not altogether
approve of Townshend's performance at Kut compared to that of
Chitral – though I have to admit that as a child I took very little interest in the details of my father's experiences in the Great War, even
if he was awarded a mention in despatches for his bravery in the campaign. For me Walter in Mesopotamia had meant four things: the
reason for his baldness, a horrid story he used to tell about the stench
of Turkish prisoners, a lizard tattooed on his left forearm which
Olive was ashamed of, and one of his favourite books which was too
'grown-up' for me, *The Witch of En-Dor*.

Walter and George crossed the ten-mile Shandur Pass into Chitral,
following Townshend's route. The Mehtar or ruler of Chitral had
been murdered on January 1 1895 by his half-brother, whose claim to
the throne was being threatened by Umra Khan, a Pathan who was
married to one of the previous Mehtar's seventy children. This had
been pretext enough for Townshend's expedition, in which he was
accompanied by George Scott-Robertson, by then Political Agent in
Gilgit. There was a force of Afghan troops at that time in the Chitral
River valley, nominally holding tribesmen in check during discussions over boundary demarcations, and it is probable that when
the siege began some of them assisted the Chitralis. While the main
British relief force advanced from the south, another set off from
Gilgit, under Colonel Kelly, consisting of about six hundred men,
mostly the 32nd Punjab Pioneers and composed of the lowest castes
and Untouchables, and a mountain battery of two guns. Colonel
Kelly's epic march, without any tents, also took him over the Shandur Pass, then in deep snow, but he was the first to reach Chitral and
easily defeated the Chitralis opposing him. He had achieved what
seemed to be the impossible, and the relief came only just in time. At
least, for a change, there is no evidence of Russian entanglement in
the affair.

The ordeals, so heroically endured, inside the ramshackle fortress
of Chitral, were not to compare with those in Kut, which lasted over
three times as long and in scorching heat, with the British force being
reduced from 15,000 to under 7,000. The youthful Townshend in
Chitral summed up his predicament in a typical way: 'Mud, stinks,
dirt . . . Our tobacco is all finished and cheroots only exist in the imagination. No whisky. No liqueurs. Nothing!' Townshend, twenty
years older in Kut, wrote in a quite different style: 'Our duty stands
out plain and simple. It is our duty to our Empire, and to our beloved
King and Country, to stand here and hold up the Turkish Army
advance as we are doing now, and with the help of all, heart and soul

and me together, we will make the defence one to be remembered in history as a glorious one.'

With the defeat of Umra Khan in Chitral the whole state could safely be painted red on the map and become part of the North-West Frontier Province of British India, more closely under the control of the Indian Government even than Gilgit. A British garrison was kept in the south of Chitral, but in typical British fashion outlying posts were soon handed over to local levies. The new tame Mehtar, Shuja-al-Mulk, like the Mirs of Hunza and Nagar, was invited to the Delhi Durbar in 1903.

The boundary from Baluchistan to Chitral between British India and Afghanistan was known as the Durand Line, after Sir Mortimer Durand, the Viceroy's Foreign Secretary and brother of Colonel Algy. The Afghans were never however to lose their interest in Chitral, and were always ready to fan political unrest. The Dora Pass in the Hindu Kush runs across the Durand Line and remained a favourite passage for gun-runners and smugglers; in *Kim* it is mentioned as the easiest route for secret agents into central Asia. Since the Russian occupation of Afghanistan in 1979, the position has, at long last, been reversed; even the Afghan corridor of Wakhan is now under firm Russian control, within easy range of KKH.

The Kargah nullah

There was one remembered spot that I had to see before we left Gilgit, and this was the Kargah nullah, if only because of the picnics we used to have there, particularly at the opening of the trout fishing season. I also used to ride out there with Multana.

After the Jhalsa practically the entire Anglo-Gilgiti colony would ride out to the nullah, followed by orderlies and bearers bringing tents, cooking equipment, folding tables and chairs for a stay of two nights. According to Heb brown trout were originally introduced by a predecessor of his in 1904. Well-established trout streams and hatcheries were by then already in existence in Srinagar, and spawn was carried up to Gilgit by relays of coolies, carrying kerosene tins with holes in them that had to be dipped into streams whenever possible. 'But that experiment failed, so my predecessor built a small hatchery in Gilgit and managed to bring up small fry from Srinagar. When large enough he drafted them to the Kargah nullah where they soon began to propagate. The streams that fed the Gilgit river all came down from the high Pamirs to the north, and those grasslands seemed to bring ample feed for the trout. So we all became enthusiastic fishermen, and in the trout season we always breakfasted on one-pound to one and a half pound fresh trout.' It was so easy to get the fish that he had to lay down a maximum catch of seven per rod, all to be twelve inches or over.

At the entrance of the nullah there was something that had made a big impression on me: a Buddha sitting high on the mountainside. There was a legend about this Buddha which people joked about, but the mystery to me always was how it could have been carved in the rock when it was so far from the ground. The legend concerned a giant female demon who the Gilgitis believed used to prey on men. One day she pounced on a holy man, who turned her into stone – hence the Buddha. He had told the grateful villagers that when he died he must be buried beneath her, otherwise she would come alive again and get up to her tricks once more. The Gilgitis were naturally alarmed about this. What if the holy man died far away and they did not even know? They solved the problem there and then by chopping off the holy man's head, and burying him beneath the Buddha.

There had been both Buddhists and Hindus originally ruling in Gilgit, and it was always assumed that the former had been wiped out by raiders from Turkestan. Sahi princes had erected various Buddhist stupas in the area. A number of Muslim saints had been active at conversion in Gilgit in the twelfth century, but some Hindu customs were still prevalent in many places, such as a ban on eating beef. There were also plenty of relics of more primitive religions – the belief in mountain fairies for instance. Durand had found a pagan altar, still in use, hidden in a cave. The sprinkling of fresh goat's blood was common, as a way of keeping off evil spirits or for purification.

Walter brought back some Buddhist relics which had been found in Yasin. Very shortly afterwards, in 1931, there was a sensational new discovery, close to the Kargah nullah.

Some shepherd boys had seen an old post sticking out of a heap of stones, and their father had come to dig it out for firewood. In point of fact it was the site of a Buddhist stupa, and the man found a small underground chamber in which were hundreds of white plaster votive offerings like Thermos flasks. He had then come across a wooden box containing a great number of pothis, sacred Buddhist writings on brick bark, in very good condition.

There was immense excitement. One of the votive offerings was given to me, and whether by design or not the top came off. Inside was a coin wrapped in a crumbling brown leaf. Very shortly afterwards that great orientalist and archaeological explorer Sir Aurel Stein arrived from one of his expeditions to Sinkiang. He pronounced the writing to be in Gupta script. Since then his comments have been published:

> The manner of the deposit, the writing etc., correspond to those of Buddhist Turkestan. No single 'find' of such magnitude has ever been made there, and in India. I do not know of any find of this kind ... If the discovery had been made when I passed through Gilgit in 1900, I might well have undertaken the complete clearing of the Stupa and of three smaller ones still intact which closely adjoin it. But under the changed conditions the matter must be left to the Kashmir authorities. Entre nous, I was able to acquire specimens which had passed into villagers' hands and then to save them from dispersal.

George Clark has this to say about the fate of the pothis:

> Sir Aurel Stein asked that he might be allowed to take charge of them so that he could take them down to Srinagar and hand them to the Museum authorities there. But the Maharajah was still in a b-minded mood and wouldn't allow them to be moved from the Wazarat. A few months later, when I happened to be in the Wazir's office, I saw the box, with its lid wide open and bits of ms scattered all over the place. Some bits looked as if they had been used to light cigarettes or a fire. It was a disgraceful sight, but nothing could be done about it, of course, as the mss had been found in Kashmiri territory and were the property of the State.

In 1982 I went to see an Indian Manuscripts exhibition at the British Museum, and there to my delight saw some of the Gilgit pothis on display. These specimens, I read, were dated sixth–seventh century AD, and it was stated that some of the others had even been fourth-century. The find had been 'one of the greatest literary discoveries of this century', since it had included not only the rules of monastic discipline in Sanskrit of the Mulasarvastivadins, compiled in about the fourth century, but a large number of illustrative stories, thus forming 'one of the most important sources for the study of early Indian narrative literature'. Hitherto this work had only been known from its Tibetan and Chinese translations.

'The remainder of the ms,' I also read, 'is in the National Archives, New Delhi, and a private collection in Lahore.'

'Typical markhor country' had been Walter's caption under his picture of the Kargah nullah, and he did shoot a giant markhor with 46-inch horns.

Yes, the Buddha was still there, with the holy man's tomb beneath. Needless to say, the scale of everything was much smaller than I had thought. The Buddha was only nine feet high and thirty feet above the ground. The top half was far better excavated than the lower, and there was indeed something superficially female about the breasts and long ear-rings on the weathered and thus apparently naked body. No doubt it has escaped mutilation because it was in such an inaccessible place. Scaffolding of some sort must have been used when it was carved.

I also could see the remains of a stupa.

We drove in our jeep up the narrow, spectacular nullah. The clear water of the river rushed and swirled over the dancing rocks, forming pools, and the sun was as blindingly bright as it always used to be. There was a narrow footbridge, made of pieces of tin, falling to bits. At the top a new hydro-electric plant was being built, and we were held up for a long time by a train of men carrying concrete blocks, far heavier than the coolie loads that used to be thought permissible. What I wondered would be the fate of the trout? And the markhor? Did anybody care?

That evening we gave another clandestine vodka and mango juice party for some new Hunzakut friends. Penalties were becoming stricter, we heard, for drinking alcohol. John was alarmed again, but was told that if you were caught it would only mean the lash. We were assured that the production of Hunzakut wine would carry on regardless.

It was our last day. I steered Raúl and John back to my old bungalow. The guards were not pleased to see us again, so we wandered on. I could not hear the oriole. Oleanders were in bloom. A man in a jeep stopped and asked if we wanted a lift. We said no, but a hundred yards further on we found him waiting for us on the path and wanting us to come into his house, a large new bungalow with a view up the valley and to the peaks in the west. The garden was full of young trees and annual plants, and extremely well watered. Suddenly we were surrounded by about a dozen small children, including a beautiful little girl of about ten in a flaming red pyjama suit. The man had blue eyes and said that his grandfather's brother had been Mir of Nagar. He wrote down his name as Nasr uddin. Whilst we drank tea, we were aware of being watched and of women's whispers behind the curtains. How many people were living in this bungalow? Forty. We heard again about the genealogical descent from Alexander the Great. The blue eyes of course!

We walked back past my bungalow again, the guards scowling. But the oriole was singing.

The Golden Oriole

I like to think that the oriole is still singing in the garden, even though I am not there, and shall probably never return.

GURKHAS

II

34 ELGIN ROAD: that had been my parents' address at Lahore. I had no special wish to search for our house, but after so much mountain scenery I felt I could have done with some good architecture at Lahore: the Shish Mahal especially, and with it old Ranjit Singh's tomb. I would also have liked to have seen, or – to be exact – revisited, the Shalimar Gardens. Lahore, however, in May 1977 was still under martial law. News was vague, and one felt one would learn more about the political situation from British newspapers, if one could even find such things. Actually, in my mind's eye the strongest picture I had of Lahore was unappealing: not from the Raj days but from reading Paul Theroux, who had evoked a city of pimps, jostling crowds and 'venereal' suburbs.

So it was decided to keep to the north of Pakistan and to head for Peshawar, via Swat. As far as I knew, Swat had no particular association with Charles Trevelyan, my parents or any other member of the Trevelyan family. Who, why, which or what was a good enough reason for wanting to go there. Another was because of Alexander the Great; I was re-reading Mary Renault's *The Persian Boy*. And Swat was said to be extremely beautiful.

We were in the time of year when British wives and children used habitually to flee to the hill-stations. The heat was indeed stunning. A car, from the curious half-built city of Islamabad, had been hired to drive John, Raúl and me to Swat, and we left at 4.30 am, along the Grand Trunk Road – shades of *Kim*. Personally, and a little shame-facedly, I have to admit that I find the archaic dialogue in *Kim* a barrier to my full enjoyment of it, though I do recognize it as Kipling's chef d'oeuvre. His descriptions of the Grand Trunk Road will always have for me the tang of the old India: the India of the plains of course, not of the mountains – 'the green-arched, shade-flecked length of it, the white breadth speckled with slow-pacing folk', 'people and new sights at every stride . . . bustling and shouting, the beating of bul-

87

locks and creaking of wheels, lighting of fires and cooking of food'. To which one might add the shiny bodies of naked fishlike children and of wallowing buffaloes, bathing together in dark brown canals; and now of course the transport lorries with their fantastic crude paintings of springing tigers, Swiss scenes in winter and the Taj Mahal.

Taxila was on our way to Swat, and this was a place where I had to stop a while. In 1936, when Olive left India for good, she brought back a clay head of a Buddha. It had the usual topknot, and you could see that the lips had been coloured. I was always intrigued by it, and when I asked Olive how she had got hold of it she was a little offhand. 'I was out on a picnic, and the Brigadier took me for a walk up to some fort. There were a lot of these heads lying around, and the Brigadier said to me: "If you like them so much why don't you take one?" So I did.' After Walter died, she gave the head to me, and I took it to be identified. I was told that it was Gandharan. According to Buddhist tradition, Taxila had been the capital of Gandhara during the Buddha's lifetime, around 500 BC. Gandharan sculpture, however, has obvious Greek affinities, and Alexander the Great reached Taxila in 326 BC. Apollonius of Tyana compared Taxila to Nineveh.

By and large ancient Gandhara included the valley of the Kabul River from Peshawar to the Indus, and what eventually became the North-West Frontier Province. Taxila was on the eastern border, its importance due to its being at the meeting of three trade routes. By about AD 603 Gandhara was part of Afghanistan, but Taxila was subject to Kashmir. The Hindu Shahis ruled Gandhara and the Punjab from about AD 879 until the dynasty was destroyed by the Muslims a hundred and fifty years later.

A serious archaeologist would no doubt wish to spend at least two days among the Taxila ruins, originally the sites of three separate cities covering twenty-five square miles. Frankly, in that terrific heat, one hour trying to visualize Nineveh among some carefully marked foundations and bases of shrines was ample, especially with the thought of a long journey still ahead. Here Alexander had held his durbar, and had met the wise men, the Gymnosophists, who sensibly went about stark naked. I tried to conjure up Mary Renault's picture of King Omphis's welcome: 'his whole army drawn up on the plain, flashing and bright, with its scarlet standards, its painted bedizened elephants, its clashing cymbals and booming gongs'. But the place seemed to me to be soaked in the blood of massacres, not of pageantry. I could only think of the slaughter of the gentle Buddhist Gandharans by Bactrians, Scythians and Kushans. I was not surprised to learn either that in this very month of May Alexander had opted to leave baking Taxila, never to return, but leaving behind him a garrison and a settlement for invalid soldiers.

The very good – amazingly good – Taxila museum, with its cooling fans indoors and pretty shady garden outside, was a relief. The foundation stone, I noted, had been laid by Lord Chelmsford, whom I have always thought one of the dullest of the Viceroys. I came to realize that my Gandharan head was of a Bodhisattva and, admittedly, only a minor example of a great art, which undoubtedly had Indian elements in it, as well, and possibly Iranian. I also realized that Olive's 'fort', which I had understood to have been in the region of the Khyber Pass, had undoubtedly been a monastery.

We bypassed Nowshera. That was a place I had absolutely no desire to revisit. From a distance it seemed neat, green, military, and doleful. There was no point in wasting time looking at the cantonment area, which I knew was going to be just like scores of others that I would be coming across in my journeying around the Indian subcontinent. We drove through Malakand and past Chakdara Fort on the Swat river. At Malakand in 1897 the 45th Sikhs had been attacked by the 'Mad Fakir' of Swat on yet another jehad. Winston Churchill had been six weeks with the Malakand Field Force and had written despatches for the *Daily Telegraph*. Our driver told us that Gunga Din had been killed on a ridge near Chakdara. All right, we believed him, but I had been brought up to understand that the original Gunga Din had been an Untouchable bhisti (water-carrier) called Juma attached to the Corps of Guides at the siege of Delhi in 1857. We imagined that we could see Gunga Din prototypes everywhere at Chakdara.

> The uniform 'e wore
> Was nothin' much before
> An' rather less than 'arf o' that be'ind . . .

The Malakand Pass, although not as dramatic, and less bleak, moved me more than the offshoot of the old silk road between Gilgit and Hunza. We could see the route that Alexander and his Macedonians would have taken two thousand years ago: so easy to be ambushed. The tribesmen's forts, Mary Renault said, had clung to the crags like martens' nests. A pretty obvious image maybe; all the same, although she had never been in this part of the world, I was always being surprised by the way she caught the landscape.

The capital of Swat is Saidu Sharif, and in effect Swat is mostly a broad fertile valley, indeed beautiful. In ancient times Swat was known as Uddiyana, which meant (appropriately) garden. A wide river runs through the centre from the melted snows, and at the lower end there are rice, clover and saffron fields, with high mountains on each side. There are quantities of Buddhist remains, easily seen from the road. We had arrived when the prickly pears were covered with sulphur-yellow flowers, and along the main road there were great bushes of pink roses, double. The light was clear, as at Chalt on the road to Hunza, and the air invigorating after the stultifying heat of the plains.

Our hotel had been a royal building: white with long verandahs. It reminded me strongly of the set for Tony Harrison's play *Phaedra Britannica*, which I had enjoyed. The rooms were pure Raj; only the punkahs were missing. The garden was full of jacarandas, frangipani, bougainvillaea and lantana, and distantly we could see the snow tops of the Hindu Kush. Because of the political crisis only two other guests were staying in the hotel, at a time when it would normally have been full. We thought it was one of the most delightful hotels we had ever been in.

Was there, we asked hopefully, still an Akond of Swat? People looked blank at this question. The ex-'king' had been known as the Wali. Later we found that our pronunciation had been at fault. In the middle part of the nineteenth century there had been an Akhund of Swat, with a hard A, a very holy, famous and ascetic man who had preached a jehad in 1863. Although he had been the son of a herdsman, he had been the spiritual leader for thirty years. We should have known really. The Akhund's tomb was pointed out as an unascetic, domed marble pavilion with openwork screens; it was a place of pilgrimage.

> Is he tall or short, or dark or fair?
> Does he sit on a stool or a sofa or chair,
>   or SQUAT,
>   The Akond of Swat?
>
> Does he wear a white tie when he dines with his friends
> And tie it neat in a bow with ends,
>   or a KNOT,
>   The Akond of Swat?

We were depressed about our finances. Our Gilgit trip had cost us fifty per cent more than we had bargained for, and John claimed that our stay at Naltar had been as expensive as Claridge's. Suddenly there was an explosion of Spanish fire on the part of Raúl, who had been ominously quiet for some while. It seemed that John and I were truly in the doghouse for not handling money matters properly. We denied it of course. Resolved henceforward Raúl would be in command of communal finances. We had all learnt bitter lessons which were to hold good for any of our other trips round the sub-continent: always be clear in advance about costs, with no loopholes, even for a short rickshaw ride; be unashamedly ready to bargain, even over the price of rooms in the smartest hotels.

We wanted to drive the next day up the valley, especially to the Wali's summer villa at Miandara. Our financial comptroller discovered that if we hired a local car, instead of the one that had driven from Islamabad, we would only pay two hundred and twenty rupees as against four hundred. Our original driver was perfectly happy to have the day off. We suspected that he had a girl friend in Saidu, even if as a Punjabi he was rude about Pathans, the Swatis being Pathans. He told us some horrific tales about Pathan behaviour. We must not stray out of the hotel grounds after dark, or we would be knifed. It was unsafe to drive after dark between Nowshera and Peshawar because of dacoits. It would even be unsafe for us to wander round the bazaars of Peshawar. Etc., etc. 'Afridi tribesmen in Peshawar,' he said. 'Very wicked people.'

Then something occured as if to prove his point about the impulsiveness of Pathan behaviour. We happened to be drawn up by the Saidu hospital. We heard a tremendous sound of wailing, and a woman dashed out beating her head. An armed policeman stopped one of the many garishly bedecked motorbike taxis, rudely hustled out the passengers, two veiled women, and shoved in this screaming female and some others. The taxi then tore off in a cloud of exhaust. It turned out that the woman's husband had died after a fall. Some moments later a stretcher covered with red cloth was carried out of the hospital, and its bearers ran down the hill with it, following the taxi, for instant burial.

We had observed a great number of graves and cemeteries in this land of Pathans. They were often covered with clumps of wild cannabis, as common in Swat as nettles in England.

Our local driver, the next day, was a swarthy Pathan who quite openly was smoking hashish. He explained to us how hash was made, but all I remember now is that you had to dry and bury the weed for a while to let it mature

or ROT?

We declined some puffs from his cigarette.

The strong smell of clover from the fields compensated a little for the whiffs of hash. Miandara was some two and a half thousand feet above the valley, the hillsides green and terraced, with ochre-coloured earth, thin firs and larches: very like traditional Chinese paintings. The villa was a small bungalow with a Georgian style portico and a verandah, with a separate house for the harem across a shady lawn. The Wali's venerable gardener was still in charge. We admired his special roses, and the larkspur and love-in-a-mist. I asked him about Pir-Sar, 'the peak of the holy man', which Sir Aurel Stein had identified as the 'bold spur' of Aornus, and up which Alexander had had himself hauled by a rope. The old man waved vaguely eastwards: monkeys, bears and panthers lived there, he said. Then I recalled that Stein had approached Pir-Sar from the Indus, which would have meant returning south through the Malakand Pass. It had been probably the most daring action in Alexander's entire military history. Aornus had been thought impregnable; even the god Heracles had been unable to capture it.

Three youths, who looked like Pathans but said they were Baluchis, emerged from the villa. They produced revolvers and invited us to join in some shooting practice. We complied, firing against the wall of the villa, the shots sending the plaster flying and echoing into the quiet Chinesey landscape. As we left the gardener came up with six roses. The young men put theirs behind their ears and continued with their shooting.

We realized that our taxi-driver was definitely high on his hash, as we bucked and zigzagged down to the valley, and we began to wonder whether after all it had been worth saving a hundred and eighty rupees. Two things sobered our moustachioed pirate however. The first was when our car was stoned by a madman, and he leapt out and stoned the madman in retaliation. The other was when he saw we were excited by some hoopoes in a field; he took out his catapult and seemed totally mystified when we showed horror at the very idea of killing any of these favourite birds of mine.

We stopped to watch some boys throwing hand-nets into the Swat river for fish. Like the poplars along the bank, they were black silhouettes against the dazzle of the water.

We drove to Kalam, in an amphitheatre of mountains about 7,000 feet up, up a road more suitable for jeeps. It was like a shabby Swiss resort, with various derelict-looking modern houses waiting to be smartened up for the summer season. We walked to a precipice, and far below saw the whirling river and a cluster of wooden houses built in tiers. Perhaps in Alexander's time the hill tribesmen, knowing that prisoners could expect no quarter, would have fled here before going on to Aornus.

If only for the sake of its Raj associations we had to stay at Dean's Hotel in Peshawar.

The First Journey

I had a photograph, dated February 1936, with the caption 'O. and the Studebaker outside Dean's'. And what a Studebaker! Spare tyre strapped to the side, canvas folding roof, headlamps like goggles, and a horn to honk. Olive very fashionable as usual, calf-length skirt this time, bicoloured shoes, scarf and tightly waved blonde hair: Scott Fitzgerald à la Raj, almost. It was the last picture before she left India for good, and the last time she and Walter were able to live in such affluence together.

After Gilgit my parents had gone to Quetta, and it was then that Olive had decided that she had had enough of India and had persuaded Walter to retire from the Army. It was a big decision, since Walter would only have a major's pension. He was forty-two. However he would still be on what was known as the SUL, Supplementary Unemployed List, which meant that he would have to be called up in the event of war.

Olive was above all *bored* by India, by Indian Army life and, I am afraid, by Indians. She was fed up with the climate and the dirt, unless she could be somewhere exceptional like Gilgit. She adored the scenery, the flowers, the birds, the riding. Perhaps there was an element of snobbery in her dislike of cantonment life; she used to say that anyone who used words like tiffin or pukka was common. But if she was a snob, her snobbery was not of the kind that goes chasing after titles. On the other hand commonness to her was not necessarily to do with class. It was an attitude to life, a question of having some indefinable spark. Here I am speaking only of Europeans. As for the Indians, she hated the palm-greasing and the graft and the smells. She hated curry. She fussed about seeing starving cows wandering in streets, about tonga ponies with sores, and pi-dogs. I cannot recall her ever being a *real* friend of an Indian who was not of the family of a Mir or a Rajah, unlike Walter who got on well with his Indian fellow officers of a lower rank. But then Army wives (places like Gilgit excepted) lived a much more circumscribed life than wives of political officers or government servants in cities such as Delhi or Calcutta, and matters like taboo foods made entertaining difficult – for some Hindus of high caste a shadow over their food would make it uneatable. At Gilgit there were no Indian friends to be had besides Mirs, Rajahs and Wazirs. Nowadays, perhaps, it is hard to understand a statement like that.

Dean's Hotel, founded in 1899 by ex-Regimental Sergeant-Major Dean, turned out to be a group of semi-detached bungalows, or had developed into such. Naturally on arrival we were directed to the luxury suites, but Raúl soon discovered that 'economy' rooms were to be had, with overhead fans instead of air-conditioning, and we opted for those, particularly as they seemed unchanged in décor since prewar days. We also decided that they had probably been for non-commissioned officers and their wives. Perhaps the rooms were rather dark, but each had a small garden with jasmine and stephanotis bushes. Our room 'boy' looked like an aged military orderly from the Guides or the Tochi Scouts. In the evening scores of crows flew noisily to roost in a peepul tree nearby, as we sipped our chota pegs in John's garden. Kites wheeled in the sunset, with pitiful cries, like kittens missing their mothers.

Peshawar is on the edge of Afridi country. The Afridis control most of the ranges to the south of the Khyber Pass and had the reputation in Raj days of being the least trustworthy of the Pathan tribes. The Mohmands are to the north of the Pass, and could be counted as the most fanatical. The Chitralis, who inhabit what is strategically the most important part of the North-West Frontier Province, are not Pathans, whose common language is called Pushtu. The Pathans stretch from Dir, Swat and Buner, and the Yusufrais and Mohmands in the north, to Waziristan in the south, where there are two tribes, the Wazirs and Mahsuds, the latter by tradition being the most ferocious and the cruellest. And there are other tribes and subdivisions of tribes. When the Durand Line was agreed in 1893, marking the political boundary between India and Afghanistan, it cut right through tribal territories and remained a sore point forever afterwards.

Ruthlessness, war as the supreme sport, allegiance to no one, cruelty, arrogance, blood feuds: these are the attributes usually associated with Pathans. To which are added courage, good humour and loyalty. The Pathans were once so desperately poor, up in those barren mountains, that raids for plunder were considered a legitimate way of life. Since several wives were allowed per man, these raids could also include the abduction of women. Writers also refer, in an embarrassed sort of way, to their propensity towards homosexuality. Women for duty, a boy for pleasure, a goat for choice. The unwritten Pathan code of honour is Pakhtunwali, the two most important rules being the necessity of revenge for insults received – murder being permissible – and the obligation to give hospitality to anyone who needs or asks for it. Walter used to say that if ever he had to choose a lifelong bodyguard he would take a Pathan. I think though, of all the races in British India, he preferred the Sikhs.

When I got to Peshawar in 1977, I heard a great deal about 'Pakhtunistan', which meant in effect independence for all the Pathans of the North-West Frontier and Afghanistan, though in practice the Pakistanis knew quite well that it was a ruse for the whole territory to become part of Afghanistan. The Russians were said to be behind the Afghans, just as they were also promoting the idea of an 'independent' Baluchistan, since there were also Baluchis both in Afghanistan and Iran.

Peshawar under the Sikhs

At the beginning of the nineteenth century Peshawar had been the second city of Afghanistan after Kabul. Ranjit Singh, the wily 'lion of the Punjab', had taken advantage of the overthrow of the Durrani dynasty in Afghanistan by its rivals the Baraksais, and in 1818 had threatened the city. He had bided his time however, and in the following year had secured Kashmir, which had been under the Afghans for sixty-seven years. In 1823 his troops were back at Peshawar, and this time he laid it waste, destroying its main buildings, many of them ancient, though contenting himself with leaving a Baraksai in charge as his nominal vassal.

Ranjit Singh had not reckoned with the temper of the Pathan tribesmen. There also appeared a religious firebrand, Sayyid Zaman Shah, back from a pilgrimage to Mecca. When Charles Trevelyan at the time of the First Afghan War wrote his confidential report after the disasters in 1842, he said:

> The Yusufrais and other tribes fled to Sayyid in thousands, and he made several campaigns against Ranjit Singh, and fought several pitched battles against him, retiring to the mountains when he was hard pressed, and reappearing when he had gathered sufficient strength to take to the field again.

An all too familiar story, as British infidels were to discover over the course of a century.

The rule of the Punjab Sikhs over the northern Muslim regions is still remembered for its repression and cruelty, and was probably even responsible for some of the atrocities at Independence in 1947. Charles's purpose in mentioning Sayyid had been to warn against the danger of the Afghans rushing to seize Peshawar, and also of Muslims generally rising up to support their co-religionists. In the time of Sayyid, he added:

> The holy war was preached in all the great towns in our provinces; hundreds of crusaders hoisted the green flag and proceeded to join

him from Benares, Patna and even from Calcutta and Madras, and those whose circumstances prevented them from assisting in person, sent supplies of money.

The loss of Peshawar remained a severe blow to the pride of the Afghans, and the city is still regarded as the prize of Pakhtunistan. It was the Sikhs who built the famous fort of Jamrud, covering the entrance to the Khyber Pass and proving always to be impregnable.

'Ranjit Singh could never be persuaded to advance beyond Peshawar,' Charles Trevelyan had written. He was warning of the dangers of sending the 'Army of Retribution' through the Khyber. As it happened, General Pollock did – amazingly – manage to force the Pass, by the then novel means of sending out patrols to cover the overhanging heights, and Kabul was reentered by the British, who exacted their own brand of revenge.

In 1849, after the two Sikh Wars, the British annexed the entire state of Punjab, as enlarged by Ranjit Singh, and including Peshawar, which immediately became the most important military command in India.

The Cassandra-like peroration of Charles's memorandum, if read after the great Mutiny of 1857, would indeed have seemed apt:

The political feeling against us in India as foreigners and as destroyers of the independence of so many races and states is very strong ... The religious feeling against us, and particularly the religious feeling of the Mohammedans, is a still more dangerous element. We have succeeded, in some degree, in quieting the apprehensions of the Hindus, but the religious animosity of the Mohammedans burns as fiercely as ever against us. It breaks out from time to time, even in times of profound peace, in the dependent native states, in our own provinces, in our own regiments; and any event which held out a prospect of success, or appeared to the natives to do so, might make it burst out in flames all over India.

The question for us now was: after Peshawar, where we meant to stay a few days, should we go to Chitral, Quetta or Kabul? I felt that Chitral would be a kind of extension of Gilgit, and rather favoured it. Besides I would have liked to have seen the 'black' Kafirs (non-Muslims and as unique as the Hunzakuts), and above all the fort where Townshend had been besieged. Quetta, off the tourist beat, might have been more adventurous, but would be like an oven in May. Raúl and John, having heard that the mountain roads in Chitral were even more perilous by jeep than the ones we had already experienced, opted strongly for Kabul; so I gave in.

Three murders, and a namesake

Such 'family' links as I had with Kabul were all to do with murders of the most fearful sort. There was Sir William Macnaghten, who had been Charles's superior at Calcutta and although an opponent of Macaulay's educational policies much praised by him; he had been the Resident, and in January 1842 his head had been chopped off and put in a bhoosa bag at the entrance of the main bazaar. In the previous month Sir Alexander Burnes, Charles's 'truly noble friend', had been slashed down by a mob, and bits of his body hung from trees in his garden; some people in England were to place part of the blame for the war on Burnes for giving the wrong advice but Charles who had once worked on his secret reports came angrily to his defence. Charles's views at that time that the most likely attack by the Russians would be through the Kashmir passes, and that Kashmir should therefore be turned into an 'English fortress', were also influenced by Burnes.

In September 1879 during the Second Afghan War the Resident at Kabul, Sir Louis Cavagnari, was murdered. His head was also cut off and paraded through the bazaar. Like Alexander Burnes, Cavagnari was 'mercurial', boastful but brilliant. Just as Burnes and Charles Trevelyan seem opposites in character, so I have always found it peculiar that Cavagnari should have been the friend of my namesake, Walter Raleigh Trevelyan of the Bombay Staff Corps, a stuffy old bachelor with muttonchop whiskers who retired as a colonel to Penzance, where he was known as the Chocolate Soldier.

This Walter Raleigh, as is clear from his diary, loathed India. His role in the Second Afghan War had merely been concerned with supplies at what he called the 'wretched doghole' of Quetta. I quote from his first impressions of Quetta:

5000 ft. Pop. 4500, mainly Pathan, sullen rascals. Fort of mud on small hill has been improved a little by our troops. A few guns and howitzers mounted. Water plentiful, drainage evil. Hospital full of cholera cases. Pitched our tents in an orchard north of fort, out of wind. Roads heavy with dust. A few small houses for officers and messes. Two good shops only in bazaar. Mud walls round town. Mud houses. Carcasses of camels. Extraordinary effect of sunset on mountain peaks. Some mulberries but few trees. Hateful place.

97

Two griffs dead. Cholera. A horrid torture – vomiting, cramp,
lips blue.

Griffs or griffins were names given to young officers fresh from Britain.

If at Penzance in later years you had been trapped in his boarding-
house rooms, packed with mementoes such as hog-spears, hookahs
and tusks, you would never have guessed that his experience of India
had been anything but Taj Mahals, babus, elephants, tiger hunts,
sunsets over the Himalayas, paddle-steamers on the Ganges, naughty
memsahibs and Parsees. But Walter Raleigh never boasted about the
military side of his career.

Most of the banks at Peshawar had had their windows broken some
twenty days before our arrival, and a bus had been burnt. Otherwise
the city was said to be quiet. Ignoring the warnings of our Punjabi
driver at Swat, we took a tonga to the old bazaar, and on the way
passed a small, orderly anti-Bhutto demonstration. Thanks to Ranjit
Singh in 1823 there are no great monuments within the walls of the
city, but it is a fascinating mishmash: lopsided wooden houses perhaps four storeys high, terrible fire risks; telegraph poles everywhere,
wires, placards, awnings; bicycles, carts, tongas; purdah women, but
only a few tribesmen carrying rifles; acrid smoke mixed with
incense, exhaust fumes, sizzling kebabs (rather enticing), hubble-
bubbles, tea shops; knife shops, embroidered slipper shops, scarf
shops, rows of shops selling exactly the same things; mounds of fly-
infested sweets, mounds of water melons three or four feet high;
mosques, alleys; boys peeing in gutters, horse shit, rummaging pi-
dogs. The Mahabat Khan mosque with its tall white minarets and
sugar front stood out as the most decorative building, but the ancient
carved doors and arches were almost the most interesting architectural features, perhaps pre-Ranjit Singh. We noted the nicely named
Hotel Decent in the midst of all this, but were mightily glad that we
had not opted to stay there.

We did get bored with being asked if we were carrying copies of
Playboy magazine. We found ourselves lured into a copperware shop
by a persuasive man with the name of Ali, and were shown photographs of many famous individuals including presidents and kings
who (he said) had bought his copper jugs and trays. We joined in
some pat jokes about Ali Baba, Ali Khan, Mohammed Ali and other
Alis, and eventually extracted ourselves without buying anything. I
think it was in the Street of the Storytellers that Raúl bought some
lapis stones and mangoes. John, in the Street of the Partridges (was

it?), was tempted by a gold-threaded skull cap, but instead bought a Jinnah cap, which we wondered if he would ever wear.

Raúl, typically, insisted on our plunging into a dim smoke-filled courtyard. It was full of Fellini-type grotesques who beckoned to us in a drunken way. We realized that we had wandered into a hashish den.

In a mosque I was admiring some painted walls, which looked like fake pietra dura work, when I tripped over an old man who had been asleep. At once he seemed to become my dearest friend. 'We Pakistanis and you English have a lot in common,' he told me. I agreed. At that moment there was a fight in the street. When a man brought out a hatchet, we decided it was time to get back to Dean's Hotel and to whatever was left of the panoply of the Raj.

We went early to the bank, to avoid the great heat. John had suddenly been struck by gout, so was not really in a walking mood. One had the impression that half 'new' Peshawar was unfinished – streets and buildings – but in a different sense to Islamabad: work had simply been abandoned. Soldiers with rifles guarded the entrance to the bank.

Outside the hotel we had seen a pseudo fakir encamped, a derelict with hideously matted hair and about five hundred cigarette stubs littered around him. A little further along there had been a bundle of rags piled against a wall. 'Those rags moved,' John, hobbling along, said appalled. 'Someone's underneath.' On our way back we found who it was: a European girl. Her hair too was matted and she was now sitting up, examining her naked crotch.

At the hotel we found a young Englishman whom we had seen on our plane from London. He was pink-faced with a strip of a moustache, the perfect box wallah as in the old days traders disparagingly used to be called. Although he had been in Pakistan for such a short while, he had become an expert on its politics. He was also starved for talk.

We produced our duty-free booze, and heard that he was advising on some sugar project. He was contemptuous about the average Pakistani's desire to work. In the factory where he was, eighteen hundred men were doing the work of three hundred. He also told us that the tourist season had been a disaster.

We moved on to the subject of Afghanistan. All this talk of Afghans invading Pakistan was rubbish, our friend said. 'Mind you,' he told us grandly, 'I wouldn't be surprised if its president took advantage of this anti-Bhutto unrest in some way or other'; even if the Afghan President, Daoud, was too busy 'sucking up' to the Shah of Persia; 'and that's not going to please the Russians'. Bhutto had been to see Daoud in 1976, and had hoped then that the Durand Line would be reconfirmed in return for the release of some insurgent leaders now in gaol. The idea had been for Bhutto to revisit Kabul after the March 1977 elections, but of course because of the present crisis this had been impossible.

'Bhutto began to think he was God. He used to be very popular with the ordinary people, even if he did sack a few independently minded journalists. Most ordinary Pakistanis are illiterate anyway, so what did that matter? He came from an important family [in Sind, that I knew – his daughter had spoken of a descent from Tamerlane and Genghis Khan], but broke down the cliques of wealthy land-owners and went electioneering himself in the bazaars. Then his head was turned, and what with the country's economic problems his old supporters are fed up.'

I mentioned the charge of vote-rigging, which had not yet been proved. Our friend was convinced that it *was* true. 'Bhutto's the sort of guy who just can't be content with an overall majority. He wants to see on paper that ninety-nine per cent of the people are with him.' But wasn't one of the big reasons for the present crisis due to his getting across the Islamic hard-liners, and in particular the military?

It was past midnight and my mention of Islamic hard-liners reminded us of the restrictions on alcohol and the need to conserve our last bottle of gin.

Policies on the Frontier

The 'Forward' Policy, begun in Lord Lytton's Viceroyalty, had been continued on the Frontier after the Second Afghan War, into the 1880s and 1890s. Roads had been pushed into tribal areas, a railway had been built through the Bolan Pass to Quetta. Fear of Russian intentions increased as more of Turkestan was engorged, eventually reaching the northern Afghan border. For some while there seemed a real danger of war with Russia, or even a partition of Afghanistan. Tribesmen's raids and ambushes, and the occasional murder of a political agent or police officer, became part of the way of life on the Frontier.

In 1897 the territories of the Pathans from Swat to Waziristan blazed into savage revolt. In the heart of the Khyber the fortress of Landikotal was for a while lost to the Afridis, and indeed this period could be counted as the grimmest in the history of the Khyber Pass in modern times. The British had to send 40,000 troops to suppress the Afridis.

Under Curzon the whole policy towards the tribes was reversed. He believed that they could be effectively controlled by political agents of strong personality, behaving firmly and consistently. So troops were withdrawn from forward areas, and tribal militias, similar to the Gilgit Scouts, were introduced, though the corps of Khyber Rifles was already in existence. New units such as the Tochi Scouts, the North Waziristan Militia and the Kurram Militia were thus ready as striking forces in case of trouble.

Curzon was also responsible for the formation of the North-West Frontier Province, separate from the Punjab and with its own Chief Commissioner in Peshawar. In the tribal territories, beyond the 'administrative boundary', no taxes were levied, and by and large the tribes were left to themselves, the mode of control being between deputy commissioners and jirgas or assemblies of elders. In essence Curzon was following the precedent of great figures on the Frontier, such as Warburton and Sandeman, whose personalities and integrity had won the confidence of the tribes. (Not, it must be added, that the raids, kidnappings and murders of the odd European ceased.) Everything depended on the assumption that Britain was ultimately invincible.

The signing of the St Petersburg Convention in 1907 is generally regarded as the curtain call of the Great Game. Britain had found itself bereft of allies in Europe as a result of reaction against the Boer War, and Russia had been weakened by its defeat in the Japanese war and by revolution at home. It was therefore in the interest of both finally to settle their differences. Spheres of influence were agreed upon; Britain would not occupy any part of Afghanistan, and any dealings by Russia with the Amir would be solely through the British.

In effect the 'Backward Policy', or 'Peaceful Penetration', in the NWFP remained in force until 1923, though it had begun to fail long before then, notably in South Waziristan after the Third Afghan War. The system of quick punitive raids on tribes that had misbehaved was colloquially known either as 'Butcher and Bolt' or 'Burn and Scuttle'.

At least the Third Afghan War was not launched by the British. It was a piece of opportunism by the new Amir, or King as he preferred to be called, Amanullah. After the Great War the British were weak as seldom before. Riots in the Punjab – that led to General Rex Dyer's notorious Amritsar Massacre – and general unrest elsewhere in India, especially in Peshawar, were other incentives for the Afghans to invade. In Kabul a group of revolutionaries had set up what they called 'The Provincial Government of India'. And besides all this, there was a general alarm among Muslims over the defeat of the Turkish empire and the consequent occupation by Christians of some holy places of Islam.

In the event the Afghans were soon defeated, though the British had used troops which would otherwise have been demobilized after service in Mesopotamia and France (though Walter was spared). Jallalabad and Kabul, including the tomb of Amanullah's father and grandfather, were bombed. Ironically it was General Dyer, ill and already under a cloud as a result of the Amritsar affair, who commanded the final victorious attack. At the peace treaty they did however obtain the right to conduct their own affairs as a fully independent state; in return the Durand Line was reaffirmed.

In 1920 Amanullah signed a friendship treaty with Russia. It was the end of Afghanistan's isolation, and Amanullah soon showed that he was determined to 'modernize' the country.

The war had set off serious unrest among the Wazirs and Mahsuds, initially as a result of a rumour that the British were intending to hand over Waziristan to Afghanistan. The British explained that they had no intention of doing this, but the tribes in any case did not want peace. Large-scale raids began, and the clashes continued for some years, earning Walter his campaign medal as a result of his brief appearance in Waziristan at the end of 1923.

Military bases were created by the British at Razmak and Wana, and there was a RAF camp and aerodrome at Miramshah, immortalized by the arrival there in 1928 of Aircraftman Shaw, alias T. E. Lawrence. The Forward Policy was back again.

Perils of cantonment life, 1923

One of the sights since Independence for tourists who come to Peshawar has always been the village of Darra Adam Khel, where practically every house has a rifle factory. Needless to say, it is in Afridi country. On our visit to Peshawar in 1977 both John and I decided that we had seen enough of rifles in Italy in 1944, so did not feel inclined to go there, even if – as our pontificating sugar friend at Dean's Hotel had said – hash, opium and cigarette lighters had become alternative industries to weapons. Sten guns could cost £100, he had warned us, as if we were seriously thinking of buying one, but we might pick up a good sharp dagger, with a barb, for £15.

I almost wish, in view of the eventual Russian invasion of Afghanistan in 1979, that I had had a look at these rifle factories, just to get an idea of the frenetic activity that must have gone on there. Darra is twenty-five miles south of Peshawar, on the way to Kohat, where there used to be a fairly large British cantonment. Sir Olaf Caroe, the last British Commissioner in Peshawar, and the author of a definitive book on the Pathans, described Kohat as sheer delight, green and well-watered, neat and clean. Apples, mangoes, vines and raspberries grew there, and violets were so profuse that they 'haunted the memory'. Kohat was where Cavagnari had his domed house before he went to Kabul.

The cantonment stood around a kind of green. The gardens were full of acacia trees, roses and of course violets. It was here that in 1923 one of the great sensations of the Frontier province took place, though nothing to do with Afghans or Russians: the kidnapping of Molly Ellis.

The name Molly Ellis impinged on me as a child because whenever something like a kidnapping was mentioned I would hear Olive say darkly: 'I do hope it is not going to be another Molly Ellis.' In a previous generation the Ellises, who lived in south Devon, had been family friends or at least acquaintances.

It had all begun after a gang of Afridis, suspected of having been the murderers of a Major and Mrs Foulkes, had daringly stolen some forty rifles from Kohat fort. The murders could not be proved, so there had been no charge. Molly herself has said this to me:

The theft was a few months before my kidnap. Eventually the Frontier Constabulary was able to trace the culprits to their village, which one night was raided and searched. At first nothing was found, then in the circle of the womenfolk who were all standing outside the police noticed that two of them had very large feet, and sure enough these were two men in disguise. They had some of the rifles hidden under their clothes, and the rest were found under the mud floor of a house. The women then taunted their men, who were furious and swore that they would carry out a revenge for the insult and get one up on the British Raj.

It had been in fact decided to kidnap one of two miss-sahibs at Kohat, Barbara Markham or Molly Ellis, aged nineteen and seventeen, both daughters of majors and great friends. As Major Ellis was up the line, the tribesmen picked on Molly, a small, pale, dark girl – 'appealing', so they described her in Devon. 'There was nothing personal in this decision,' Molly said. 'It was done for notoriety and a ransom.'

The Ellises' bungalow was next to that of General Jacob, the local Commander-in-Chief. Mrs Ellis was a 'dear', everyone thought, but inclined to be nervous. So the General said: 'You needn't be afraid.

I'll give you a whistle. Keep it under your pillow, and if you're frightened blow the whistle and the guards will come.' In the middle of the night Molly was woken by the sound of a violent struggle. She could just see her mother fighting and kicking in the next bed, under the same mosquito net.

'Give me the whistle,' she cried out. 'You've got it!' Mrs Ellis screamed back. Molly felt under her pillow, but it wasn't there. Then she heard a kind of gasp, and there was silence. At once the mosquito net was ripped away and she was roughly dragged out of bed and into the garden.

As her friend Barbara has succinctly put it: 'So they cut the mother's throat, and pinched poor old Molly. When I came round in the morning for our usual ride, I found their house surrounded by troops. "What on earth's going on?" I said. They told me, and there was nothing I could do but to turn my horse round and go home.'

Molly's version of the reason for her mother's murder is this: 'They were in a hurry to get away safely and could not manage to take more than one of us, so killed my mother to facilitate their departure.' Presumably they had not bargained for mother and daughter being in the same room.

Molly at the time was not sure of her mother's fate. Eventually she was given a cotton jacket and a piece of pugree cloth to wind round her feet. The journey from village to village over crags and mountains lasted four days, but they moved only at night-time. She had guessed that her captors wanted ransom money and was terrified that she was to be taken to Kabul, after hearing the place mentioned.

A hue and cry immediately flared up throughout India and in the press in Britain. It was Sir John Maffey, the Chief Commissioner for Peshawar, who hit on a way of getting Molly released. He now knew that she was in the Tirah, where no European had ever dared go, and it was obvious that any white male emissary would be murdered at once. So he decided to send a woman, and approached a Mrs Lillian Starr, a remarkable and brave missionary working in a hospital. Mrs Starr's husband, a doctor, had been stabbed to death before her eyes by Afridis in 1918 but she had continued to work in the hospital, nursing local people, and was thus particularly respected by Pathans. She at once agreed to go.

On the eighth day after the kidnap Mrs Starr found Molly, and after some delicate bargaining managed to get possession of the girl. Molly, she was relieved to find, had not been molested or harmed in any way. In addition to some ransom money being agreed upon, it was decided that two of the men's friends – petty thieves – would be released from prison.

As soon as she could, Mrs Starr said: 'Molly, I'm very sorry. I'm afraid your mother's dead.' Molly had felt all along that she had known this, but it was the first time that she was able to cry.

Sir John Maffey held a jirga, and got the elders to agree to outlaw the kidnappers and place a fine on the tribes which had sheltered Molly during the journey through the mountains. One of the villages would be burnt down.

As Molly has said: 'In the end my kidnappers did not get any ransom money for me. They were never caught either. In fact they returned to their village and were treated as local heroes.' Now among Pathans her name has gone into folklore, and songs have been made up about her – how she fell in love with a handsome chieftain and so on.

'For Pete's sake, or should I say for the love of Allah, don't take photographs in the wrong places in the Khyber, or you'll be sniped,' was the cheerful advice from our friend at Dean's. 'And keep away from the women.'

He then added: 'I suppose you've read "The Young British Soldier" in *Barrack Room Ballads*, last verse?' Yes, I had read it, or at least I had heard Walter recite it. For good measure here are the last two verses:

> If your officer's dead and the sergeants look white,
> Remember it's ruin to run from a fight.
> So take open order, lie down, and sit tight,
>   And wait for supports like a soldier.
>   Wait, wait, wait like a soldier . . .
>
> When you're wounded and left on Afghanistan's plains,
> And the women come out to cut up what remains,
> Jest roll to your rifle and blow out your brains
>   An' go to your Gawd like a soldier.
>   Go, go, go like a soldier,
>   Go, go, go like a soldier,
>   Go, go, go like a soldier,
>   So-oldier *of* the Queen!

Our driver said he would take us to the Afghan frontier, a distance of some seventy kilometres, for a ridiculously low fee – there simply weren't enough tourists in Peshawar by way of competition. He was a gloomy fellow called Abdul, long due for a shave and wearing chapplis, or sandals, and the usual white baggy trousers which in the

wind revealed all the shapes of his anatomy. We passed Jamrud, de-
fiantly crouching in a desert of stones like a castle of Outremer: as
unpleasant-looking and menacing as when Walter had photographed
it in 1936, though now it had evidently turned into some kind of
market village or emporium. It had three encircling walls. A great
castellated archway had just been built over the road nearby. 'Bab-el-
Khyber', Abdul said it was. The arch seemed a bad omen to me, as if
it were the first stage in commercialization of the Khyber. But then
could one blame the Pakistanis for wanting to make the most of what
most tourists longed to see?

Far away we could make out new tribal villages laid out in geometric patterns, complete with mud walls and watchtowers. It reminded me a little of south of the Atlas in Morocco. Ahead were the
forbidden highlands of the Afridis and the Mohmands: the mountains were the colour of hard baked crust, with scrub like spots of
mould, all under a deep blue sky. Somewhere up there was another
Shangri-La that only tribesmen could visit – Maidan, which Abdul
said was as beautiful as Kashmir. He picked a yellow flower, the
Prophet's flower he said, and showed us five fingerprints on it, marks
of the Prophet.

I asked about Fort Salop. This was where Walter had been
stationed, and I knew it was supposed to be a few miles from Jamrud.
Abdul had never heard of it, not surprisingly perhaps, as Walter's
photographs had shown merely a cluster of corrugated huts, a low
stone wall, barbed wire and a watchtower with a machine-gun
mounted among sandbags.

Almost I wished I had not come to see the Khyber. There was a
slight feeling of going back to bad memories in the last war. We
would miss seeing the Khyber train, Abdul said, as it only ran on Fri-
days. I was sorry about that, as the sight of it huffing and puffing, in
and out of the thirty-two tunnels, would have jollied us up (or me
up). The single-track line, built by the British, went only as far as
Landikotal, not to the Afghan frontier, and the train had to have
engines at both ends. Was it true that the tunnels were full of bats, I
asked, remembering Paul Theroux's description of tribesmen passengers swatting at them with sticks? Abdul looked at me as if I were
mad.

As we entered the famous jaws, we could see newish pillboxes and
gun emplacements here and there. Because of the threatened 'war'
over Pakhtunistan, I again asked? This time Abdul did not bother to
answer. Somehow all seemed to be on a smaller scale than I had
visualized. I had also expected miles of sheer cliffs on either side.
Instead the road zigzagged upwards through a wide bleak valley of

Walter and Olive Trevelyan: the wedding picture, Rangoon, April 6 1921

Walter in Kashmir

Olive at Bhamo

Raleigh Trevelyan in his doolie, Lahore

Nanny Spicer at the Burzil Pass

Captains Bill Cooper and Bill 'Pinky' Greenwood
at Ye Olde Pigge and Whistle, Bunji

Crossing the Burzil Pass, 13,775 feet. The crow's nest was a shelter for
telegraph linesmen and mail coolies in winter

The Trevelyans' bungalow at Gilgit

Gilgit from the air, 1931. The Political Agent's bungalow is in the centre, the
Trevelyans' to the right. On the left is the Agency Office

One of the first aeroplanes to Gilgit passes Nanga Parbat, April 1931

Residents and visitors at Gilgit, April 1931. Left to right: back row, Miss Hardie (Todds' nanny), Nanny Spicer, Arthur Lloyd (Supply and Transport), Bill Greenwood (from Bunji), Maurice Berkeley (Commandant Gilgit Scouts), Ram Pal (Kashmiri Divisional Engineer), George Clark (Sapper); 2nd row, 4 R.A.F. officers, 'Morny' (friend of the Lloyds), Lovell Wooldridge (from Chilas); 3rd row, Lt. Freer (Asst. Scouts Commandant), Lucy Lloyd, Olive, Heb Todd, Nancy Todd, John Pyper (Surgeon), Walter; 4th row, Lavender Todd, John, Raleigh, Heather Todd, June Lloyd

Heb Todd, Walter by his side, takes the salute at the march of the Gilgit
Scouts, led by Maurice Berkeley

Sir Mohammed Nazim Khan KCIE, Mir of
Hunza, 1932

The Mir of Hunza's dancing 'girls'

Near the Killik Pass: Walter returns in triumph on a yak, after bagging his Marco Polo sheep

Olive crossing a rope bridge near Gilgit

Fording the Kunjerab River

The 1st Gilgit Wolf Cubs pack: Raleigh second from right

The vulture dance of Chilas: preparing to swoop on the prey

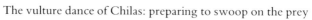

toothy crags and boulders – perfect cover for snipers no doubt. Everywhere one saw little forts and watchtowers, mostly crumbling, and occasionally a ruined stupa. We also saw those much remarked on regimental badges carved on rocks: Royal Sussex, 1st Bn the Cheshires, the Dorsetshire Regiment. Memorials of death, sweat and horror, but placed there, of course, in pride. Echoes. Menace. Mules, Maxim guns, Gatling guns, Wolseley pith helmets, the tramp of feet, Highlanders in filthy torn kilts and gaiters, Gurkhas and bugles, drums, kukri knives; long-barrelled jezails ... 'Heavy losses were inflicted on the enemy'; 'A gallant rearguard action was fought'; 'The tribesmen hit back with great fanaticism'; 'The ridge was held on a bitter night without food or blankets'; 'We regret to announce the sad loss of a most outstanding and popular officer.' I could almost smell the cordite. Go to your Gawd like a soldier.

I tried to switch my mind to the possibility that Alexander the Great's Hephaestion might have passed this way. The great Moghul Babur had certainly come along here; but not in pomp and circumstance. Instead I kept thinking of the arguments over the role of General Tuker of the 4th Indian Division at Monte Cassino in Italy in 1944. How, as a result of his experience in mountain warfare here on the NWFP, and following the precedent of General Pollock in the First Afghan War, he had advocated bypassing the Monastery and had *not* wanted the frontal attack ... I looked up at the stratified rocks, yellowish brown, split by dry watercourses, and wondered if some day tea houses and restaurants for the hoped for flocks of tourists would be built there, with trees and gardens laid out; just as in Italy the Calypso nightclub and the 'Voo-Doo Snack Bar' now stand near Anzio exactly where ... Suddenly a series of crazily painted lorries trundled past, gasping with exhaust and jammed with workmen who waved and shouted, enjoying themselves.

We reached the narrower defile or throat, the sides almost vertical, which I had always thought the Pass ought to look like. The large pink-walled Shagai Fort, which the British had built for the Khyber Rifles in the 1920s, was apparently still in tip-top condition. We came to a place where photography was permitted. Far below at the foot of the again wide valley we could see a line of men doggedly driving mules. 'Smugglers,' Abdul told us. When we laughed, he smiled wearily. The men were in tribal territory, he said, so the Pakistan government could not interfere with them. But what kind of smuggling we asked, half imagining that it would be Bokhara rugs, sandalwood from Samarkand, myrrh, apes, peacocks and sweet white wine. Oh, refrigerators, cigarettes, that sort of thing. Guns of course. Yes, perhaps drugs.

At Landikotal we stopped for tea at a café, but not the notorious one, alas, where the counter is made from the gravestone of Drummer James Pinfold. We could see from the eagle noses and nut-brown eyes that the people around us were real Afridis. Nearly everyone carried rifles and bandoleers. 'They wear them like jewellery,' John said. Landikotal is supposed to be full of millionaires linked with the Mafia in Sicily and New York. If that was true, the hideous concrete blocks didn't look like millionaires' houses. Actually those nut-brown eyes all seemed perfectly friendly, even gentle, though watchful. We felt uneasy and pressed on, reaching another cleft in the Pass, even more sinister.

The Afghan end of the Khyber had a vaguely softer landscape. The farms on the way were real fortresses, as if expecting a long siege. The actual frontier post at Torkham was by no means awesome, indeed rather comic. We enjoyed watching Khyber Riflemen arguing with the better dressed travellers while grizzled tribesmen in straggly turbans and carrying huge burdens were allowed through without a glance. A leathery old crone appeared with some goats and strode through as if she were the frontier queen. All the while, about half a mile to the north, lines of 'smugglers' moved in both directions, mostly with heavily heaped mules though with the occasional camel. The Durand Line was marked out in white.

We had our picnic in a glade overlooking Afghanistan: like a huge amphitheatre, one would almost think unmapped. Near to hand it was all quite pastoral. Goat bells tinkled. Then soldiers appeared bringing a table and folding chairs for a Pakistani officer who had evidently chosen the same spot to impress a girl friend, dressed as for a ball, or a soap opera, in a crimson and gold sari. A transistor was switched on. We did not want to spoil the romance, and he was grateful when we left.

On our way back we spotted a small British cemetery and asked to visit it. The chowkidar was an Afridi of the Afridis, enormous, so fierce-looking and so loaded with weapons as to be almost a caricature. He was very proud of his cemetery. Barbed wire had to be untwisted. There were only about a dozen graves (no more?), mostly of soldiers who had died of cholera in 1919. I wanted to ask the chowkidar's permission to photograph him, but John thought that the very suggestion might cause trouble. He said something to our driver and I asked what it was. 'He asks if you want to see the haunted picquet. No Englishman who went up there ever came back.' Even the Spaniard decided against.

Later when we were 'eating the evening air', as they used to say at Simla, in the garden of Dean's, a coach arrived full of elderly Americans. Tourists at last. They leapt out with cries of 'Oh, oh, oh,' and began taking ciné films of this relic of the Raj, with us three fossilized in the foreground.

Memories of a Political Agent in Baluchistan

Before his posting to Gilgit, Heb Todd had been assistant Political Agent first at Sibi and then at Kalat, eventually succeeding to the post of Political Agent itself at Kalat. I often think of him now as just the sort of stalwart whom Curzon had envisaged for the North-West Frontier, even though in point of fact both Sibi and Kalat were in Baluchistan. Walter had a great admiration for Heb, and my parents' paths were to coincide with the Todds' in many unexpected ways in the years after Gilgit.

Sibi was near the Bolan Pass and had the reputation of being one of the hottest places in India in the pre-monsoon months. One of Heb's predecessors used to hold his weekly municipal meetings in a bath of cold water.

When I spoke to Heb about those days, he had reached his ninetieth year. At Sibi he had become deeply interested in tribal affairs, he said, 'which were based on the necessity in a tribal society to settle both civil and criminal cases by appeasing the aggrieved defendant rather than rewarding the plaintiff'. This made sense, for in the tribal lands where there were no government magistrates or government police it was essential to prevent the spread of a blood feud by settling the claim of the aggrieved, or he or his family would pursue the feud. 'The practice of running the country through jirgas or councils of elders of the tribe was the linchpin of Sir Robert Sandeman's policy in Baluchistan. Sandeman had been the Deputy Commissioner of the British Indian district of Jacobabad and had been the first official to make contact with the neighbouring unadministered Baluchistan in 1867. Raiders from Baluchistan were frequently invading the British India districts of Sind, Dera Ghazi Khan and Dera Ismail Khan, so Sandeman decided to make personal contact with these marauding tribes and try to come to some modus vivendi with them.'

Heb would receive petitions in Urdu or Persian in his office, and then call on the jirga to hear the evidence and give opinions. The really important cases, which local jirgas were unable to settle, were heard at 'Shahi' jirgas in Quetta. In the Marri country, when evidence was not conclusive, Heb saw cases settled by a challenge to take the oath with a hand placed on the sirdar or chief man's head. Other oaths which were much revered were those of 'fire and water'. One party would accept the other's claim if he would take a sheet of paper on which some verses of the Koran were written, hold it in the palm of his hand and allow a red-hot ploughshare to be dropped on it and walk ten paces with it. If he did so, the case was taken as proven.

'The water oath was in this way. In the Marri country, in a river bed, was a pool some fifteen feet deep. In the centre was erected a pole. One party in a dispute was challenged to swim out to the pole, climb down it, pick up a handful of gravel and swim to the surface. If he held his hand aloft with the gravel his case was held to be genuine. If he was making a false claim it was felt that his guilty conscience would prevent him from holding his breath long enough to perform the act.'

In 1926, when Heb became Political Agent for Kalat, he continued to make his long tours on horseback through the tribal lands and to hold jirgas. The then Khan of Kalat was a somewhat decrepit individual, rarely emerging from his tumbledown though picturesque eyrie of a fort, with its round towers and containing some good Persian carpets and ceramics. The federal tribes looked upon him as their head, but he actually wielded little authority, his great hobby being to collect walking sticks. He did however have a wicked uncle who was always interfering in state affairs, and Heb had to have this man banished to Quetta, where he was given a pension. 'You would see him riding around Quetta streets, a fine figure of a man, on a beautiful Hirzai Baluch pony – such a different figure to his nephew.'

After his appointment in Gilgit ended, Heb went as Political Agent at Quetta, and was still briefly there when Walter and Olive arrived in 1934.

Fort Salop

Walter's spell at Fort Salop, as second-in-command of the 5/8th Punjab, lasted officially from November 1935 until he retired from the Army early in 1937. 'Officially', because he seems to have had plenty of leave; duck shooting at Bharatpur in Rajputana and tiger shooting in Bombay province. Olive would have returned to England earlier than she did, had she not had to undergo a series of anti-rabies injections: 'Utter hell, I can tell you,' she wrote to me. But that was nothing compared with her distress over the death of our golden retriever Amber, which had caught rabies. 'It was all so sudden, and awful seeing her suffer so much.'

Amber had been with us all during the Gilgit years. Olive, seeing that she was not well, had allowed her to lick her hand at the back of the car. The next day the rabies was obvious. At least the poor animal was spared the ordeal of being brought back to England with the obligatory six months' quarantine. I have known several dogs, including one of my own, which have had to have this quarantine, and they were never the same afterwards.

Women were barred from Fort Salop, so Olive stayed with friends in the Peshawar cantonment. She had refused point-blank to live in 'Holmes Flats', some dank and 'common' furnished rooms where regimental wives were usually sent. Peshawar in the winter was always gay, but the injections subdued her. There was plenty of bridge though, and she also played the new craze mah-jong.

So at last, after five years' separation, except for her summer visits, I was reunited with my mother and brother. But the 'P.G.' life continued while she house-hunted in Essex. 'I'm worried stiff about Walter,' I would hear her say, and no wonder when one reads John Masters's *Bugles and a Tiger*. Masters, in the Gurkhas, was much younger than Walter, and stationed further south in Waziristan. All the same, the conditions and dangers were much the same as around Fort Salop, which was in Afridi country. According to Masters, castration and beheading were the usual fate of anyone taken prisoner, unless women were to hand, in which case you were more likely to be flayed alive and have your skin stretched out on rocks or bushes. Death by a thousand cuts, with grass pushed into the wounds, was another variation in torture. Heads and hands might be cut off and stuck on poles.

The tribes were restive, but as it happened, and fortunately for Walter, bad trouble only really sprouted on the Frontier as he was leaving India. It was the period of the 'Modified Forward Policy'. By 1929 Waziristan had been considered pacified, but in the year before, rebellion had broken out in Afghanistan against King Amanullah's policy of Westernization. He had had to abdicate in favour of his brother Inayatullah, who after three days had had to be evacuated with his wives by air; it was their plane that I had been taken to see when we were stationed at Nowshera. As the British Minister in Kabul said, it all showed 'what this new thing, the aeroplane, can really do'.

A ridiculous rumour had circulated in India that T. E. Lawrence – when as Aircraftman Shaw he was trying, or pretending, to lead an anonymous life in the desert outpost of Miramshah in Waziristan – was behind the rebellion. It had actually been claimed that Lawrence had dared to disguise himself as a holy man. I remember Walter saying he had been in Lahore at the time and a real holy man there had been lynched because word had got around that he was Lawrence.

(Actually Walter despised Lawrence as a show-off and a 'pseudo', another of his favourite words of disparagement, just as for the same reasons later he was furious with the behaviour of Lady Mountbatten during the war, when she insisted on taking up a vital seat on a plane to Chungking.) In the event Lawrence was sent back to England.

In 1930, whilst we were in Gilgit, there had been the Red Shirts riots in Peshawar, which although quelled after six weeks stirred up both the Afridis and the Mohmands. The trouble that was brewing when Walter reached Fort Salop was mostly in Waziristan and due to an episode known as the Bibi abduction case: a Hindu girl had been abducted by a Muslim and converted to Islam, but a court had ruled that she should be returned to her family. A Wazir holy man who became famous as the Fakir Ipi had proclaimed that this was an example of British interference in religious matters, and so yet another jehad was proclaimed.

I had always visualized Fort Salop as a kind of Beau Geste fort, or at least a lesser version of Miramshah, the 'dust-hole' that Lawrence spoke of in his letters home. It was, as I eventually discovered, some eight miles to the south of Jamrud, on the Kajuri Plain, but reached by winding tracks through a pass. It had been established, with some small outlying posts, in 1930. By a lucky chance I came upon a 5/8th Punjab newsletter of 1936, and found that I was not far wrong in my vision of Fort Salop. 'We had imagined previously,' I read in this, 'that Baluchistan was unequalled for its stony wastes, but we found, on arrival, that Fort Salop can hold its own in that connection.' A description of Miramshah by Lawrence, in a more literary style, also seems to fit Walter's photographs of Fort Salop exactly:

> We are in a brick and earth fort behind barbed wire complete with searchlights and machine guns. Round us, a few miles off, in a ring are low porcelain-coloured hills, with chipped edges and a broken-bottle skyline ... The quietness of the place is uncanny – ominous, I was nearly saying.

At 10 pm the searchlights would flicker over the plains around Miramshah, and all the jackals would begin to howl. One was not allowed outside the fort at night, so the only 'temptations', until reveille, were 'boredom and idleness'.

At Miramshah there were twenty-six British officers and men in the camp, with seven hundred Scouts. In the 5/8th Punjab there were nine British officers and five Indian officers, and all the other ranks were Indian. The battalion was also holding Jamrud, which – so the

5/8th newsletter ran – one of the three companies would take its turn in rotation.

Walter had different interests to Lawrence. He loved going on 'ghast', or patrol, and in spite of possible perils managed also to go on chukor shoots. Never a gregarious person, he liked mess life when faced with it, and could hold his drink, though I cannot see him joining in those sing-songs I have heard at 5/8th regimental reunions. He told me that one night he heard a plop above his head, and in the morning saw a scar in the plaster wall and a bullet under his bed. Meetings with Pathans tended to be a lengthy business, what with exchanges such as 'May your shadow never grow less'; 'May you never grow weary'; 'May God bless you.' Sometimes the hospitality could be embarrassing. In Mahsud country the headman might offer you a local delicacy made of apricots that looked like hide and smelt appalling. It seemed that local women trampled it on stones and then slapped it on their bare thighs. Hence the distinctive flavour.

When Walter took his turn at Jamrud, he could go into Peshawar for his polo and the jackal drag hunts, and the quail, teal and snipe shooting. In spite of all the hardships and dangers whilst on duty at Fort Salop, Walter – I now see – enjoyed the challenge and comradeship, the stimulus of being always ready for emergencies. It was a demanding life, a whole man's life, exhilarating, a test. In larger outposts of the Empire, like Bannu, where women were allowed, life became claustrophobic, hardly tolerable after the trouble in Waziristan worsened. There was an electric wire fence, and at night tribesmen would shoot regularly and at random into the cantonment.

But in less organized places, such as Kalakhar, in the totally flat Salt Lakes area south of 'Pindi, you might have to sleep in tents, specially deep-dug, again because of the sniping at nights. (It was at Kalakhar that a friend of mine, who was commanding officer of a Muslim Transport Company in 1941, had his own private thunder box. When he sat on it, he could see over the top of the canvas surround. One morning the guard came marching past and gave him the eyes right.)

An effort was made by the 5/8th to plant trees and create a garden in the monastic wilderness of Fort Salop. Before their arrival there had only been a dusty hockey ground, but now the stones were cleared away and two more hockey grounds and a running track were made. In previous years a battalion had stayed only six months at Fort Salop, but the 5/8th were to be there for two years. 'We are not in the position,' ran the newsletter, 'to boast about the number of Ceremonial Parades we have attended, but we have certainly manned one of the outposts of Empire.'

From the letters we received from Walter during the house-hunting in Essex, I realized that the mention of a certain Maggie did not please Olive. In his albums there are a few photographs of this Maggie on picnics and bathing parties, taken presumably on bouts of leave. She was indeed a beautiful woman, very feminine and chic, on special occasions with a fox fur, head and all, round her neck, and always with rather a dreamy expression. It seemed that her husband had gone to Japan at some stage. Some years later, when Walter read out to us the first pages of his novel, I was amused to hear that his heroine was also called Maggie. No wonder Olive fidgeted as we sat there listening in our Essex drawing-room.

When Walter was in retirement in 1938 he was annoyed by criticisms of British policy in the NWFP, which he felt was playing into the hands of the German and Japanese propaganda. He began writing to the press, particularly about the bombing of tribal areas. He pointed out that bombings only took place after warnings, and then where tribesmen were in action against our troops. 'The Pathan tribesmen of the Frontier have lived for centuries by banditry and looting at the expense of the more peaceful people of the plains. They have steadfastly refused to accept roads, schools, hospitals, irrigation schemes and all other civilising influences, and quite openly prefer their lives of pillage at the expense of their less warlike neighbours... As one example, the Afridis, south of the Khyber, recently burnt a school, and built and manned a picquet overlooking our territory to prevent a road being built.'

But it was not of course just the civilizing influences of the British that the Pathans objected to...

The fighting classes

British officers and soldiers before proceeding to India in the 1920s and 30s might be handed a useful little official booklet called *The Indian Empire*. Here it was explained that the Indian Army units were organized on either the 'class regiment' or on the 'class squadron or company' system. In the former case all the men were of one particular class, such as Gurkhas, Sikhs, Baluchis and Dogras. In the latter several classes were recruited together in the same unit, though all the men in each squadron or company were of the same class.

Reading the potted descriptions of those 'fighting classes' I could see why people like Walter admired them almost to the exclusion of other races in British India. Take his favourites, the Sikhs:

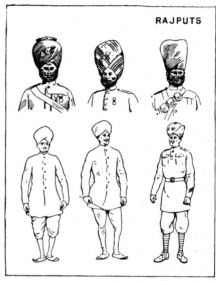

Some fighting classes of India. From *The Indian Empire*, HMSO, 1921

Since the Sikhs came under our rule in 1849, they have made our quarrels their own; in every campaign and minor expedition they have fought side by side with the British soldier.... Two traits – a love of military adventure and the desire to save money – combine to lead them to accept service in distant lands... They are fond of running, jumping, wielding large clubs, lifting heavy weights, wrestling and quoit throwing, and join readily in hockey or football... They are very handy, obedient to discipline, faithful and trustworthy, though sometimes given to intrigue among themselves.

Then the Rajputs, second in his esteem:

In appearance they are fine muscular men who carry themselves like soldiers. Their complexions are fair when compared with those of Indians generally and they often give their moustaches or beards a fierce upward twirl. They are particular about their clothing and spend much money on it... In all their habits they are scrupulously clean and are frugal livers. They are fond of all sorts of athletic exercises and sport and many of them are splendid horsemen. Very proud, they are particularly sensitive to an affront and are jealous about their women.

As for the Pathans, the booklet summed them up thus:

Though they make bad enemies, they can also be very good friends, and the Pathan is, in every sense of the word, a man.

And Walter would have agreed with that too.

On our fifth and last afternoon in Peshawar, John having got over his gout, we decided to visit the public gardens in the old British cantonment area. The cantonment bungalows were more opulent and with leafier gardens than those that I had dimly remembered at Nowshera: like a semi-tropical Bournemouth suburb. We spotted several 'manly' characters, in English-style suits – the modern brand of Pathan? We passed along the neat 'Mall' which, like the 'Circular Road', was a common feature of most cantonments. It was all so quiet. No Studebakers.

In the public gardens there was a number of strange shrubs that even John, the expert on plant names, could not identify. Soon we were surrounded by small boys, who pointed out to us an enormous swarm of bees at the top of a jacaranda; it looked about five foot long. As we wandered on the boys began throwing stones at the swarm.

We had walked about a hundred yards: John in front, then me, then Raúl. I heard running and turned round. The boys were dashing towards us, frantically brushing their hair and faces with their hands. Then Raúl started to run, doing the same thing. I realized that the bees were on the attack. I had, as it happened, not long before been reading about Indian bees in *Bugles and a Tiger*. Bees were 'lords of the province', said Masters. Not even snakes or man-eaters were so dangerous. Even the echo of a shot in the jungle could annoy them. 'Caught helpless in the open, the hunter would get a thousand stings into him and die before he could reach help.' Admittedly Raúl had only one sting, but the boys looked worried. Then someone took out a penknife and squeezed the already malignant swelling, out of which the sting duly popped.

Raúl is one of those who refuse any sort of medicine or pill, and who clamp up when you start worrying about their health. I noticed that we had emerged from the gardens into 'Hospital Road', and suggested that we might therefore look for the building after which this street had been named. But the idea was met with complete blankness, and it was difficult later to get any modicum of response when every now and then John and I asked how he was feeling.

However by evening he did seem recovered, and we celebrated with a dinner at the Salteena, said to be the best restaurant 'downtown'. Salteena! To fans of *The Young Visiters* the name was unbelievable, and the place turned out to be suitably quirky, with tables inside cubicles across which you could draw curtains in deference to lady guests who might be in purdah. There were a lot of coloured tiles, as in a Turkish bath. Indeed there was a decidedly sexual atmosphere, with curtains constantly being dragged open and shut, feminine squeals, and young men dashing past us excitedly, their shouts echoing. The food we chose arrived in gargantuan piles and was – we soon realized – a mistake for European stomachs, being too rich and spicy, and we had to leave most of it.

We walked back through half illuminated streets. There was music from the tea-houses, and people were sleeping outside on charpoys. We had forgotten the warnings about muggings. We bought a bottle of mango juice, in case there was none at Kabul, and when we got back to Dean's the stephanotis in the dark was in full scent outside our rooms.

Yes, to use the well-worn guidebook cliché, Peshawar was well worth a visit.

But looking at an old guidebook on my return to London I was sorry that we had not made a search for the tomb of a Rev. Isidore Löwenthal, who had been at the American Presbyterian Mission. A well-meaning colleague had caused these words to be written in the register: 'Murdered April 27 1864. Shot by his own chowkidar. Well done, thou good and faithful servant.' For some reason recent books attribute these words to the gravestone of Captain Ernest Bloomfield, 'shot by his orderly March 2 1879'. Geoffrey Moorhouse in *To the Frontier* writes how on 'one fiery morning' he went to look for Captain Bloomfield's grave, but without success, and not surprisingly. At any rate, the Indian who did the engraving of the Rev. Löwenthal's stone added a comment of his own in Persian at the bottom, and this was 'Don't laugh.'

At Peshawar airport we were frisked by young self-important soldiers. Raúl's three lapis stones were discovered in an inner pocket. A smuggler! During the argument that followed the soldier offered to let Raúl go if he would give him one. Raúl, furious, at once threatened to report him to his superior, and so ended up as the victor.

It was an extraordinary flight over the barren mountains, with the Hindu Kush black in the distance, though still with snow streaks like guano. There was hardly any green below, but occasionally we saw a lake itself almost lapis-coloured. Kabul lay in a plain ringed by mountains topped by heavy cumulus, and elsewhere the sky was cloudless. We could see the tents of nomads and grazing flocks on the outskirts. The mighty Moghul Babur had loved this city and had beautified it, but we were prepared for twentieth-century Kabul to be dull architecturally – and so it was. As with the Khyber, the excitement of going there was mainly to do with its history. The chief site of archaeological interest, the fort of the Bala Hissar, had been destroyed by the British after Cavagnari's murder in 1879, and its ruins had been abandoned.

We had been warned by Allen Drury, who had gone to Afghanistan after Gilgit with his Californian ladies, that the Kabul Inter-Continental was the most expensive hotel he'd ever come across. In any case we were feeling so hard up that it never entered our heads to stay there. We chose the Yama, which overlooked an old clothes market – the largest in the world we were told – in the so-called park of Timur Shah. The actual tomb of Timur Shah appeared to be derelict; he had been the father of the unfortunate Amir Shah Shuja, whom the British had championed in the First Afghan War. John's room at the Yama had a view of a stack of lavatory pans.

Kabul being 6,000 feet up was much cooler than Peshawar, and we thought it cleaner, even if the open drains were filthier and smellier. The Kabul River was the colour of chocolate. There was an absurdly flimsy footbridge near us, with some of its slats missing as in the wilder areas round Gilgit. In our search for the tourist office and maps, we found ourselves in the diplomatic quarter, with much smarter buildings and some government offices: a sort of garden city, along the lines of what Islamabad presumably hoped to be. Raúl said that Kabul reminded him of Ankara.

We came upon an ex-royal palace, inhabited by Daoud Khan, who although styled the first President of Afghanistan was nevertheless royal, being the first cousin of King Zahir Shah, whom he had ousted in 1973. The gates were guarded by ferocious sentries, evidently Turkomen of small intelligence, with fixed bayonets. When we paused to look up the drive towards the palace, the sentries menaced us. Our first inclination was to pretend to take no notice, but we soon realized that these louts were dangerous. It was humiliating, but we had to move on.

Within a year Daoud, his family and closest advisers, mostly relatives, were to be butchered one by one in those very grounds, possibly by these very sentries, or carbon copies of them, in a Soviet-led coup d'état. That would be the end of the Baraksai royal family in Afghanistan. In familiar Kabul style their bodies would be dragged through the streets as a 'warning'.

And eighteen months later, in October 1979, Daoud's successor Nur Mohammed Taraki would in his turn be murdered in the same palace after a shoot-out with the followers of his deputy Hafizullah Amin, who would himself be sliced down only three months later as the Russians invaded Afghanistan. (Some say Amin strangled Taraki with his own hands.) It was Taraki who in December 1978 had signed the fatal treaty of 'good neighbourliness' in Moscow with the ominous clause that allowed either of the contracting parties to take 'appropriate measures' if it felt that the security of the other was threatened. So in theory Afghanistan could send its troops into Russia if it were considered in Kabul that Nato was being too aggressive in Western Europe.

The river near our hotel reminded me of the Lungarno at Florence, with low walls covered with rugs for sale, some of them very tempting. As at Peshawar there were huge mounds of fruit and vegetables: peaches, tomatoes, plums, radishes, chilis. There were also big open sacks of grain. We noticed quite a mixture of races. The more Mongoloid you were, the more liable you seemed to be for the heavy tasks. We saw men – Turkomen again, Uzbeks – staggering with refrigerators on their backs. Not all the women were veiled either; but we did not dare respond to some meaning looks.

We had Russians staying at the Yama. In contrast to the Chinese in our Islamabad motel, they were polite, always saying 'Good morning' in English, even at night. Empty half-bottles of vodka accumulated outside their bedroom doors. They all had the physiques of boxers gone to seed. We were glad not to be staying at the Hotel Astor, where we had seen a girl washing a lettuce in the open drain outside.

The next day we hired a car, with a driver whose name was Azmadin, and went to look at the camel market, which also turned out to be a dromedary and sheep market. We were horrified by the emaciated state of many of the camels. Poor old oonts, the 'floppin' droppin' oonts'. One of them expired while we were there, and was at once disembowelled and had its throat slit in front of the other wretched beasts. The sheep were of the fat-tailed variety, some black, but the white ones were smeared with crimson dye. The gutted camel appeared to distress the sheep, and they huddled together, heads inwards. Small boys posed for photographs on the backs of camels that were too exhausted to stand up.

Next we went to the mausoleum of the Amir Nadir Shah, who had ruled from 1929 until the inevitable assassination in 1933. He was descended from one of the fifty sons of Dost Mohammed's brother. The tomb was plain, of blue and white crisscrossed marble, with a low copper dome; it looked rather Fascist in conception. There were a great many wild white hollyhocks on the way up. We stood under the crumbly bastions of the Bala Hissar. Pottery shards had been found on the site dating from pre-Greek days, though it has not been established whether Kabul was ever occupied by the Greeks. The original castle is presumed to have been built by the Emperor Babur, who took Kabul in 1504. The British Residency where Cavagnari had died had only been of mud-brick within a foetid rabbit-warren of alleys. I thought of the description of bluff old 'Bobs' Roberts, later the great Field-Marshal, arriving there with his army of retribution, written in his typical style:

It may be imagined how British soldiers' hearts burned within them at such a sight, and how difficult it was to suppress feelings of hatred and animosity towards the perpetrators of such a dastardly crime. I had a careful but unsuccessful search made for the bodies of our ill-fated friends.

Babur's tomb, in its sloping garden, where he used to sit and admire the view, was rather sad. Some of it had been built by his illustrious descendant Shah Jehan, but it had in the last decades been over-restored and mucked about. The chinars and mulberries did look as if they had been planted in Babur's time, but the gardens, we were told, were to be used for some municipal club, and two swimming-pools were to be built. We thought there were too many beds of petunias, French marigolds and love-lies-bleeding. Suddenly there was a big fuss and the guards insisted that we must leave. Some very important Russians were about to arrive. Once more we felt humiliated, but once more there was really no option but to retreat.

We asked Azmadin how many Russians there were in Afghanistan. About twenty thousand. Sensing our irritated mood after the episode in the Babur gardens, he whisked us up to the Inter-Continental Hotel, which he seemed to regard as the chief wonder of Kabul. He was surprised when we did not want to go inside.

We spent the afternoon in the bazaars, mainly in the Char Chattar, once covered over and where the heads of Cavagnari and Macnaghten had been put on display. It seemed as though no attempt had been made to rebuild the upper storeys of the Char Chattar since the British had set fire to it in 1842. The antiques, or more strictly the bric-à-brac, were more interesting than at Peshawar, and the owners of the shops and stalls were friendly though mercifully not persistent.

We decided that Kabul was only beautiful as night fell.

The Macnaghtens

My dreams were all about Sir William Macnaghten. I should never have brought with me a history of the First Afghan War. But it was Emily Eden's description of him that did it: 'A dry sensible man, who wears an enormous pair of blue spectacles, and speaks Persian, Arabic and Hindustani rather more fluently than he does English.'

Macnaghten had been recognized as perhaps the most brilliant scholar to have emerged from the college of Fort William in Calcutta, Charles Trevelyan being close behind him in reputation. He had been Auckland's Secretary when it was decided to invade Afghanistan. Perhaps it was his wife who pushed him into applying for the post of Envoy in Kabul: a lady whom Emily Eden had found 'without exquisite taste or tact'.

Sir William had always worn a large emerald ring with an Arabic inscription on it. The tradition in the Macnaghten clan is that the first his wife knew of his death was when the hand with the ring on it was thrown into her tent. The ring has been preserved, and the inscription has been deciphered as a quotation from the Prophet Jonah in the Koran, something that might have appealed to the Afghans: 'Verily I have been an evil-doer. There is no God but thou.'

Lady Macnaghten was among the small group of hostages retained by the Amir. She succeeded in saving many of her belongings, including her jewels and her husband's cat, but nearly all the other hostages had only the clothes they wore. It is clear that she behaved selfishly throughout the hostages' subsequent and lengthy ordeals, demanding special comforts and privileges. Fortunately for the ladies, the Afghans considered it bad luck to kill a woman, but some of the male hostages died. A hideous journey through freezing landscape followed, and there were some bad earthquakes. The indestructible Macnaghten cat, originally from Calcutta and transported to Simla and then to Kabul, was buried in an earthquake and dug out again.

Afterwards Lady Macnaghten was not at all satisfied with the British Government's pension. However her money troubles ended when she married the second Marquis of Headfort. It was her third marriage. There is a tradition that she said that she had married ''igher and 'igher and 'igher'. In 1858 Edward Lear was in Corfu and told his sister that nothing else was talked about except the Marchioness of Headfort's diamonds, 'which cover her up so much, that few people have seen the wearer'. 'I sat next to her at dinner yesterday, but she hadn't got no diamonds; only about 200 big turquoises and emeralds & bangles & chains & griggly-miggly dazzling messes.'

I found myself being woken by an earthquake. My bed rocked for about five seconds. On drawing back the bedroom curtains, I realized that nobody outside was at all concerned about it. Earthquakes happened three or four times a month in Kabul, so they told us downstairs.

Azmadin, dignified in a new grey astrakhan cap, took us on a drive to Istalif. After Kabul the countryside opened up, and there were large tented encampments. Far away we saw the line of the eternal snows of the Hindu Kush, purplish now; the cumulus had disappeared, the air was so clear, the temperature just right. The road was lined with acacias, mulberries and chinars. It was a superb view. This time the wild roses were white, quite a galaxy. We reached vineyards, and the landscape became more luxuriant at every turn. We left the metalled road and bumped up to Istalif. We saw several big farms, Khyber style, like mud fortresses, each with a watchtower, and there were little turrets on the rocky ridges.

At the Istalif hotel we drank Castellino wine, apparently made in Afghanistan under the direction of Italians. The village, clustered on a hillside, in the form of a pyramid, was very clean, with new wooden arcades and vines over the main street for shade. Glazed turquoise pottery, thick turquoise glass, furs, skins and turquoise and silver jewellery were on sale everywhere. The place was in danger of becoming touristy, but we were the only tourists. We made friends with a startlingly handsome baker wearing an immense striped turban, and sat for a while on steps with him and his kohl-painted little son whom he loved with a passion. The whole experience of Istalif was a bit of a dream, and in 1980 I read that it had been bombed by Russian planes, with many civilian casualties, in retaliation for some attack by mujahiddin rebels. But then one has to admit that Istalif was stormed and destroyed by a British force in September 1842, as a punishment for its inhabitants' assistance in a massacre at Charifar the year before, and for harbouring the murderers of Sir Alexander Burnes.

Our next destination was Paghman, closer to Kabul, and this time the route was through wheat fields edged with closely planted poplars. There were the usual fortified farms, and towers with balconies at the top like fringes. A marble 'arch of triumph' stood at the entrance to Paghman, and here garlands of yellow petals were being sold by children. It being Friday there was a holiday, and Paghman was a great place for picnics. Its gardens, on the grand scale, had been laid out originally by the Moghuls: a series of cool scented terraces, watercourses, fountains, shrubberies and the inevitable flowerbeds of love-lies-bleeding etc. The place was packed with people having fun.

We watched some dancing to drums. A dozen Afghan soldiers appeared, and everyone drew back. This was to be a special performance. The drums beat a slow march, and the soldiers walked round slowly in time, singing in falsetto. Presently the drums increased in tempo, and the soldiers moved faster, and then faster. The crowd began to clap in time with the drums. The men threw off their caps and shoes, became ever more excited giving out sharp cries like cranes. When they reached a point of frenzy, the drums suddenly stopped.

On the spur of the moment we called at the Bagh-i-Bala restaurant, once the summer palace of the Amir Abdur Rahman – it was he who had agreed on the Durand Line between Afghanistan and British India in 1893. The view was huge. Inside it was rather Turkish, with much use of mirrors and some rather inferior European-style mantelpieces. The Amir had loved birds and flowers, but had a reputation for cruelty and harsh justice, as I found corroborated in a book that I owned called *At the Court of the Amir* by John Alfred Gray, a surgeon:

> The Amir punishes the crimes of robbery and murder most severely. For robbery and theft the hand of the criminal is amputated in a rough and ready way. It is done in this manner. The local butcher is called in. He knots the rope above the wrist of the criminal, and with a short sharp knife he severs the hand at the joint, plunging the raw stump into boiling oil. Then the criminal becomes a patient and is sent to the hospital to be cured. No flap of skin has been made to cover the end of the bone . . . A priest one day suggested to the Amir that operations of this and other kinds on criminals should be done by the European doctor. The Amir negatived the suggestion with a sharp reprimand.

Abdur Rahman was a man of colossal strength but suffered much from gout (so John's attack, which had seemed peculiar at the time, was not all that unusual). Partly because of this gout Gray was summoned out to Paghman. Some soldiers were brought in before the Amir; they were in chains for 'conspiring' against their captain. They threw themselves down at their sovereign's feet, but he was tired or bored and they were ordered to be taken to a room apart. 'There you shall sit,' Abdur Rahman said, 'and debate among yourselves what your punishment shall be, and tomorrow you shall be brought before me.' Then the soldiers were hurried away. However Gray continued:

> What the choice of each one was I do not know, but I had occasion to learn the choice of some of them. A few days afterwards on visiting the Sherpur hospital I saw four or five of the men. They each greeted me with a warm smile and held up the left arm – the hand had been severed at the wrist joint.

In the Char Chattar bazaar we found occasional relics of the British, including Victorian medals. Nobody we met in the Char Chattar seemed to resent that we were 'feringhis', foreigners; in the old days we would have been met presumably with hatred and suspicion. One jeweller, who said he was really a schoolteacher, told us – indiscreetly we thought – that Daoud's regime had merely produced a power vacuum in Afghanistan and was doomed. There was no real authority in the country, he said. Too many people were trying to grab money, and there were quarrels among tribes. Daoud was trying too hard to bring the country close to Iran, which as everyone knew was supported by the Americans. Then he began to tell us about the splendid new roads the Russians were making in the north... All this was told to us with a portrait of President Daoud smiling down on us from his wall.

A dust storm blew up, so we hurried back to the Yama. There I found that my traveller's cheques were missing from my pocket. Could it have been the schoolteacher-jeweller? On the other hand I did remember being jostled in the Char Chattar as I leant over a tray of oddments. A truly Kafkaesque afternoon followed, dashing by taxi from one frowsty police station to another, and not helped by the dust storm and the fact that it was Friday. I suddenly began to find the Afghan music terribly monotonous and irritating. I rang the British consulate to find that its staff was on a 'prolonged' holiday because of Queen Elizabeth II's Jubilee. And so, perforce, the next day I had to spend much time in the vicinity of the American Express office. There was a map in this office, showing how most of Pakistan was really Pakhtunistan. A score of American hippies were hanging about in great anxiety, waiting for the mail with the hoped for cheques from Poppa or Momma in Philadelphia or Cincinnati. Every now and then, I was told, some of these hippies would be arrested for drugs, having been selected according to the apparent wealth of their parents, who would then have to bail them out of prison: a useful way of earning dollars for Afghanistan.

John was determined to return to the Char Chattar, to continue bargaining for yet another Victorian ring. On the way there we fell in with two chemistry students. They were appalled that we were actually venturing into the Char Chattar unescorted – it was far too dangerous for foreigners they said. No wonder my cheques had been pinched. So they accompanied us there, and afterwards invited us to their 'living room'. We accepted, but John did so reluctantly. 'We're going into a trap,' he whispered to me.

We were not much encouraged when we were made to follow the students down back alleys, where fresh shit was bulging from drain-pipes into the gutter. They took us to a modern block, with an inner courtyard or well, around which were balconies on several floors with single rooms leading off. The students' room was pathetic, smelling strongly of feet and decorated with chemistry diagrams and the presumably obligatory photograph of the smiling Daoud. We sat on mats. One of the students rushed out and bought a cucumber which was sliced up for us with a penknife. They were both so polite, and so poor, and both aged twenty-two. One, who said his name when translated meant Flower of Summer, came from Jallalabad, where he had a wife and child. We tried to talk politics, but it alarmed them, and we knew nothing about chemistry. When we left they embraced each of us three times, which they said was Afghan fashion. We promised to send postcards.

Perhaps these two students are now mujahiddin, soldiers of God, freedom fighters. Are they followers of the new leader, the latter-day equivalent of the Fakir of Ipi, the Sirdar of Ghazni, who has called the jehad against the Russians? Are they even alive? Is our baker of Istalif alive? Is Azmadin ferrying around Russian soldiers? As we flew from Kabul to Rawalpindi, we imagined that one day we would return to Afghanistan, and we would see the fabled Bamiyan with its giant Buddha in its notch carved out of the escarpment, and Balkh 'the mother of cities' where Zoroaster preached, and Herat, and the Arch of Bost. Instead, as I write these words, I receive an invitation for the pleasure of my company at the 'Afghan Ball', black tie, to be held at the Café Royal in London and organized by the Afghan Support Committee as an appeal for funds to supply medical centres at refugee camps in Quetta and around Jamrud.

Were charity balls arranged at St Petersburg when the British invaded Afghanistan in 1839 and 1878? In those wars three million Afghans did not have to leave their country. And the British did withdraw from Afghanistan, though admittedly not entirely by choice.

I hope and believe that the British would never have contemplated attacking villages with phosphorus and napalm from helicopter gunships.

The heat bulldozed us as soon as we returned to Pakistan. At Rawalpindi we headed straight for Flashman's Hotel, noting that the thermometer in our taxi registered 125°. Flashman's was the Dean's of 'Pindi, a must for anyone on a nostalgic jaunt, but unlike Dean's it had been much modernized and added to. It was therefore quite expensive. Still, it was our last night in Pakistan before returning to London, and we found we could afford the splash. Not that the hotel was anything like the jackets of George Macdonald Fraser's books, showing that splendid cad of Victoria's wars, Brigadier Harry Paget Flashman VC, lounging on cushions with a goblet in one hand and a semi-naked houri at his knee.

Rawalpindi had a strongly British atmosphere. The centre of the town was well laid out, and rather dull. We spent a great deal of time by the Flashman's pool, while flocks of slim jade-green parrots screeched overhead under the blinding sky, in and out of the banana trees. In the evening there was cricket on the Maidan outside, and hoopoes were popping about with their fantastic cockades and long curved bills on the hotel lawn. We visited St Paul's Anglican Church nearby, red brick Gothic. The Raj association here was very frail. The windows were broken, the organ broken, the fans had been stolen. The old man acting as caretaker had not been paid for three years. The congregation consisted of some fourteen to sixteen persons, and the service was in Urdu.

By the pool we met an Army lieutenant who was on leave from Gilgit. He was keen on developing his physique, and did handsprings and pressups even in that heat.

He knew all about John's arrest in Gilgit. 'The Tourist Ministry is not pleased with you,' he said, noting with particular disapproval that John had the gin bottle concealed under his bathing towel. This remark completely ruined the rest of John's time in Rawalpindi, but we promised to send him food parcels in Karachi jail if he got bored with chapattis.

We asked the lieutenant about General Zia, who was being tipped in Peshawar as a kind of Guy Fawkes of Pakistan. 'He is a soldier of Islam,' he said sternly. 'He is not interested in politics.' Zia ul-Haq had been made chief of staff by Bhutto in 1976, to succeed General Tikka Khan, and in the same year had made the pilgrimage to Mecca. 'He has given us soldiers a slogan, and we are proud of it,' said the lieutenant. 'Iman, Taqwa, Jehad: Faith, Abstinence and Readiness for Holy War.' Then he added, glaring at the shape of the gin bottle: 'He has no vices.' Next we heard a great deal about how Bhutto was to blame for the break-up of Pakistan in 1971, and of course about the alleged vote rigging in March. But hadn't Bhutto agreed to new elections, we asked? The lieutenant was scornful. 'That will never happen.'

It seemed that we were leaving Pakistan at the most explosive moment in its short history. Out of the slaughter of 1947 a democracy eventually had been born, and Bhutto for a time had appeared to be bringing to a reality Jinnah's and the poet Mohammed Iqbal's dream of a strong, independent Muslim state. Whatever the Army lieutenant and his like thought, Bhutto had given Pakistan a confidence and a respectability after the disastrous war of 1971 which had resulted in the creation of the separate state of Bangladesh. He had been idolized by the poor.

But by 1977 Bhutto was no longer the idol of the poor, partly – to be fair – because of the economic crisis. Nests had been feathered, political opponents had been incarcerated without trial. And the Army lieutenant said that some of the things Bhutto had done were an affront to Islam.

Later I was to read that Bhutto's supporters said that all the ills were due to the greedy sycophants around him. So he was a bad judge of men? He thought he was indispensable. 'If I go, the Himalayas will weep,' he had said. Perhaps, in any case, in that fractious country, with its impulsive population, democracy on British lines will never be possible.

To many of those British who gave their careers to the old India, and worked loyally for it, such a thing as a Pakistan separate from India had appeared potentially a strategic disaster; and with the Chinese road through the Karakoram and the Russian road from Kabul up to the Khyber their fears appeared to me to have been justified absolutely. Pakistan had become the cockpit of Asia.

John left Pakistan with some relief. For Raúl our journey had been the beginning of a kind of entrancement with the whole subcontinent. As for me, my feelings were mixed. I could only fear for Pakistan's future, but I was also happy because a childhood vision of Gilgit had at last turned into a reality. If I had gone to Gilgit three years earlier, as I had originally planned, Olive would still have been alive and we could have discussed and joked about it. But Olive had died in 1976, so the reality was in some measure also a relief from that pain, and a reaching out.

On July 5 1977, within a month of our return to London, there was a military coup in Pakistan. Both Zulfikar Ali Bhutto and General Tikka Khan, with other top rankers, were taken into custody, and General Zia ul-Haq became the country's new leader, he said only temporarily. There would be new elections in ninety days. Zia called it 'Operation Fairplay'. Bhutto was kept incommunicado in a Murree resthouse, and his family – including his beautiful daughter Benazir, who had just arrived from England where she had been President of the Oxford Union – had been put under 'light restriction' in their home in Karachi. British newspapers seemed to think Bhutto's interests would be best served if he boycotted the new elections.

On the same day, July 5, I read a small article on a quite different matter, but with some bearing on our journey, that had unexpectedly brought up so many grim associations. The article was headed 'Yorkshire Girl Shot Dead by Afghan Tribesman'. Two English girls had been swimming in a lake near Bamiyan, and on their way back to a camp site one had been killed. The murderer could not be traced, but it was assumed that he must have regarded the exposure of their naked limbs 'as an affront to Islam'.

The Second Journey

I

1979. Now it was the turn of the Vale of Kashmir: Srinagar of course, but Gulmarg especially, and if possible some of the country south of the Burzil and the cease-fire line between India and Pakistan. I hardly expected that Hut 46a, our home in Gulmarg with that incredible view over the fir trees to the Himalayan ranges, would still be standing after the tribesmen's raids in 1947 and the fighting of 1965.

Bhutto was hanged at 2 am on April 4 1979. Like a thief in the night, so said the *Guardian*, which had been critical of him in his years of power; it was a 'deed done shamefully'. Throughout the democratic world there had been outrage when he had been condemned to death, and General Zia was said to have been annoyed by the many pleas for clemency. The Turkish Prime Minister had offered to let Bhutto live in exile in Turkey, with a guarantee to prevent him from taking any part in politics; but this offer had been refused.

Bhutto had been kept, it was reported, in filthy conditions, with hardly any medical treatment during his nineteen months of solitary confinement. In his last weeks he had hardly been able to eat because of a gum infection. If he had been no White Knight, that was no excuse for killing him. His ostensible crime had been complicity in the murder of a political opponent, and he had also been accused of bribery and corruption, as well as vote rigging. Three out of the seven judges had said that he should have been acquitted. The traditions of common law, which the British had thought were at least their legacy, were collapsing.

Zia's proposed elections for October 1977 had been postponed indefinitely. A new puritanical regime descended upon Pakistan. There were public floggings and hangings. The cutting off of hands for theft now became a common punishment. I was to read of the case of a young, blind, unmarried woman who was sentenced in the Punjab to three years' imprisonment and fifteen lashes for having had illicit sexual relations with a man by whom she had had a baby; the accused man was given the 'benefit of the doubt' and set free. A leading Pakistani journalist was arrested and photographed in chains. Bhutto's daughter, Benazir, came to be regarded as the leader of the Opposition. So, like her mother, she was kept under house arrest. She denied the vote rigging. 'My father believed in history,' she said. 'He wanted his place in history.' But not in the way he found it.

In Rawalpindi I had met a chief executive of the Murree Breweries, quite a humorist. He was accepting the laws against alcohol philosophically. Under the Zia regime all Muslims faced the lash or imprisonment if they drank alcohol, but non-Muslims were permitted it on feast-days. According to him the Buddhists had pleadèd that to them every day was a feast-day, but this was overruled. Tourists could have drink taken to their hotel rooms, but only under plain covers. A large bottle of beer cost about £20. 'Eat, drink and be Murree' had been the slogan in British times. 'As you say in England,' my friend remarked, 'we have a great past in front of us.'

Kashmir since Independence has been the root of most evil between India and Pakistan, though I do not think that any Indian seriously believes that the old Gilgit Agency will gravitate to them. It is the fertile south, the Vale, where the majority is Muslim, that the Pakistanis want. The Indians say that all Indians are Indian, irrespective of religion, customs or even shade of skin.

Pondering in due course on such worrying matters as whether British rule in what is now Pakistan was any more successful than under Zia or Bhutto, I remembered a letter that Walter wrote to me when I was a soldier in Italy in 1946. He was horrified by my enthusiasm about the Labour victory in Britain, and sent me a copy of a paragraph written by my ex-headmaster at Winchester, Spencer Leeson. In Walter's typical way he had put at the top, 'Worth learning by heart I think':

> By democracy is presumably meant something of this kind: a polity in which the government is held accountable to an assembly elected in the widest possible franchise; in which the sovereign legislative power rests in that assembly; in which there is equality of all before the same law; in which the elementary rights of freedom of person, discussion and meeting are carefully safeguarded by this same uniform law; and in which the independence of the judges who administer that law is adequately guaranteed.

With all of which I could not but agree. These were at any rate the *ideas* that the British had hoped to leave behind.

Raúl and I – he was to accompany me again – decided this time to experiment with a 'package', in order to avoid further dramas and anxieties about overspending, and above all the wearisome haggling and cheating. We chose a tour that would include ten days on a houseboat in Kashmir, as well as some time at Delhi, Agra and Simla. And it turned out to be very much an à la recherche tour for nearly everyone accompanying us. About three-quarters of our companions had had connections of some sort with British India, and a good many were ex-Indian Army widows or daughters. Our leaders were Major Ted Blessington and his wife Scottie.

In retrospect I realize that we had among us people who could well have been cast for roles in the TV serial *The Jewel in the Crown*, especially as friends of 'Mildred'. We certainly had a potential Daphne Manners and a Lady Manners, and a possible Barbie Batchelor. I thought that one lady would have looked well as a heroine in a film about the Mutiny (at the Siege of Lucknow?), except that she smoked a lot and was rather fond of gin and tonics.

At this stage, however, only the often harassed Ted Blessington – in blue blazer and occasionally addressing us collectively as 'chaps' – and his consort took on any definite character. 'I advise you to ease springs before we board the aircraft,' Ted warned us confidentially. He told us that for a bet he had once stood on his head on the top of the Qutab Minar tower at Delhi, and had in return been awarded a case of whisky. This encouraged us, though we felt that Indians might not have been much amused. Scottie, as befitting her name, had a delightful Scottish accent, and was soothing in times of crisis, which were not infrequent with so many elderly people among us. The Blessingtons had two sons, they told me, both also called Major Blessington. Ted had been born in Simla.

It was by the pool the first morning at the Imperial Hotel in Delhi that I noticed someone who was out of a different mould to the other females, and decidedly non-ex-Raj. She was rather handsome, with shortish grey hair, and wore an old-fashioned bathing suit. It was hot and we were all jet-lagged. Kites called mournfully overhead. 'This is what I need,' she said loudly to nobody in particular, and then spread her arms and did a perfect old-fashioned dive. After four or five swift lengths, she climbed out and went straight back into the hotel. No lounging about or sunbathing in deckchairs for her. Her name was somehow appropriate for someone who could dive so well: Delphine Flash. She was travelling with her husband, a Lieutenant-Colonel ex-Royal Artillery, Monty Flash, also out of a different mould to the rest – and to Delphine, various people came to think, as the two of them seemed to like doing different things, and separately. Not many of our companions could understand these independent-minded eccentric Flashes. For instance, on coach trips Monty sat at the back, Delphine at the front. I felt at times that if we were in a poultry yard they would have been pecked. Monty liked singing opera in the swimming-pool. As Raúl and I were oddities too – Raúl simply for being a Spaniard, and because we refused to wear ties at dinner – we soon became friends of Delphine and Monty Flash, though we saw much more of them at the end of the tour.

Every evening, on our travels, we would get an invitation: Mrs So-and-so is giving a party in her room, bring your own drink. We discovered that many of the ladies had brought long dresses and jewellery with them. Raúl dared to ask one of them why she had done this. 'Well, you see, we lead such quiet lives,' was the answer.

The pool at the Imperial Hotel, with its lush garden of cannas and frangipani, is – so I discovered later – well known as a cruising spot and for assignations. Looking back, I do remember a pudgy Sikh in a bathing cap, with a lot of hair on his back, being interested in a couple of European women in minimal bikinis; and that the interest was reciprocal. Most of the ladies in our group were perhaps not of the right age for this game. We did however get an appeal for help from one of them, who was being bored by the attention of three Iranian students.

The oldest of these students, who said his name was Ahmad, had been in the Shah's army, but was now anti-Shah. 'Ahmad's shot six people!' What fun! 'Now we must shoot Ahmad!' Ahmad was hoping to go to New Zealand, where he heard that Maori girls went about topless. Two little girls, possibly French, breastless and aged about ten, leapt squealing into the pool. The Iranians immediately followed them. We thought the girls' parents could cope, even in that debauching sun.

I was particularly glad to meet the managing director of the Imperial, Major-General Naranjin Singh, since at that time I was in the throes of writing a book about the Italian campaign in the first months of 1944. He, as a lieutenant, had then been with the 2nd Punjab Regiment at Cassino.

I was just at the point in my book of dealing with the immediate aftermath of the bombing of the Monastery, when troops of the 4th Indian Division, Rajputs and Gurkhas, had attempted to capture its ruins, with frightful casualties. The General, who had won the

Military Cross, told me some stories which I eventually used, and one of which I shall repeat here.

He had to requisition a house in a newly·captured village. The woman inside, primed by German propaganda, was terrified by the sight of this great turbaned man with the curled moustache. 'Mangiare bambini?' she quavered in childish Italian. 'Do you eat children?' 'No,' Naranjin Singh replied. 'Mangio soltanto uomini. I only eat grown-ups.'

On to Agra. It is impossible, even if I do not write of Fatehpur Sikri, not to make a passing reference to the Taj Mahal. Murray's *Handbook for the Bengal Presidency* for 1882 says: 'As the Taj is the most beautiful building in India, perhaps in the world, and cannot be seen too often, the first thing the traveller must do after locating himself is to pay it a visit.' And this is what we did, after duly locating ourselves. And, yes, we did also see it by moonlight: il sogno delle zitelle inglesi, the dream of English spinsters, Pier Paolo Pasolini once said. No photograph, no model, no watercolour by a zitella can adequately prepare one for the real thing. It shimmers, it has an aura, its proportions are perfect. It is sublimely sad, but also a celebration of the beauty of death. One revelation for me was the view *from* it along the Jumna, which at the time because of the inadequate monsoon looked as if it was at low tide; on the banks, far below us, were little temples, and there were black boats like floating carob beans and black water buffaloes bathing, and in the fields opposite – in la cadaverica sensualità del paesaggio indiano, the corpselike sensuality of the Indian landscape – I could see camels and elephants being herded. How dramatic black is in bright sun, and how dramatic Shah Jehan's proposed twin black Taj Mahal would have been, if such a thing had been contemplated – which it hadn't, contrary to what guidebooks say. (Another total falsity, often repeated, is that Lord William Bentinck wanted either to demolish the Taj Mahal or remove it to England – though it is true that his officers held quadrille and tiffin parties there.)

A further revelation for me was the romantic view of the Taj from Agra Fort, from the marble pavilion where the imprisoned Shah Jehan had sat and gazed at his immortal creation. From that same spot, in happier days, he had watched captured elephants fighting on the plot of ground between the Fort and the river.

Pietra dura

I had particularly wanted to see the pietra dura work in Shah Jehan's audience rooms in the Delhi and Agra palaces and at the Taj Mahal. A book on pietra dura by Antonio Zobi was published in Florence in 1841, and here it is mentioned that in 1608 Grand Duke Ferdinand I of Tuscany decided to send four workers 'to the Moghuls' because of the abundance of especially good silica to be found in northern India. Zobi thought it possible that the workers decided it was more profitable for them to stay in India, and that they might have taught their craft to the natives.

Pietra dura was an innovation in Shah Jehan's reign, though inlay work, in coloured and semi-precious stones, in geometrical patterns, had been used much earlier. Shah Jehan was proclaimed emperor in 1627, and work on the Taj began soon after. It at once struck me – as it has others – that the pietra dura flowers looked very like European medieval herbals, though the scrolls and arabesques were typically Indian. The effect of the brilliant stones on the pure white marble and in conjunction with the carvings in relief was superb.

Zobi in his book goes on to say that Charles Trevelyan had written to a Miss Loke, an Englishwoman living in Florence, telling her about this pietra dura in India and how similar it was to what he had seen in Florence. Early in 1838 Charles, his wife Hannah and brother-in-law Macaulay had travelled together from Calcutta on their way back to England. Hannah, in a memoir of Macaulay, tells how Charles went to Italy with his sisters in 1839 whilst she stayed behind with Macaulay to settle him into his new home.

The Indian pietra dura, Charles pointed out in his letter, was not so concentrated in design as the Florentine examples, but this was because it was used for wall decoration on a much larger scale. He mentioned 'Etruscan' vases, in addition to flowers, birds and butterflies, as being used as motifs in India, and remarked on the panel of Orpheus and his lute 'with various beasts and birds listening to the music' behind the marble throne in the Diwan-I-Am hall of public audience in Delhi. He thought the Orpheus the 'richest and most perfect specimen I have ever seen in the East' and surely proof of European influence (I myself thought it more odd than beautiful, even rather crude, and preferred the birds and floral designs). Charles also considered Indian pietra dura 'superior in taste and execution' to anything he had seen in Italy. After Florence he had gone to Pavia and in the Certosa had been even more impressed by the similarities between Indian and Italian styles. Indian craftsmen, he said in his letter, were still producing exquisite pietra dura work, and he had seen remarkable chess tables made for Lord Combermere and Lady William Bentinck.

Later at Charles's instance, Thomas Metcalfe, Collector at Delhi and brother of the more famous Sir Charles Metcalfe who had been

Resident there, wrote to Zobi with suggestions about the provenance of the so-called Orpheus. If the figures were the work of a native artist, he thought it could be 'Tanseim the Oriental Mozart' (i.e. Tan Sem, *c.* 1506–89) or even Solomon. It does however seem generally now agreed that the Orpheus is Orpheus and of Florentine origin, possibly imported ready-made. After all, he is shown as blond, and his instrument is not at all oriental, and not even a lute – more likely it is a cremona, the early form of the violin.

Once there was a theory that the Taj itself was designed by an Italian, a Venetian jeweller called Geronimo Veroneo, but this has been disallowed, and it is thought that the design could mostly have been Shah Jehan's own, inspired by the tomb of Humayun in Delhi. Shah Jehan's last building before his imprisonment was the Jami Masjid mosque in Delhi, with proportions almost as breathtaking as the Taj, and no one could claim an Italian influence there.

The most elaborate example of pietra dura in Agra is the tomb of I'timad-ud-Daula, built in 1628. Here the marble front is entirely covered with geometric designs and floral traceries in cornelian, lapis, onyx and topaz.

'Everything [at the Taj],' Bishop Heber quaintly said in 1824, 'is finished like an ornament for a drawing-room chimney-piece' – but at least he did find the general effect 'solemn and impressive' rather than 'gaudy'.

I saw the dome of the Taj at dawn from my window at Agra, having been kept awake all night by a wedding party seven hundred people strong. Hundreds of green parakeets flew out of their roosting places into the coral sky.

On the subject of colours, and thinking of Walter, I have always felt that inhabitants of Delhi must have found the sun-reddened faces of British soldiers would have been indistinguishable from the sandstone walls of the Red Fort. The view of the Jami Masjid from the Fort is like an illustration to Omar Khayyam, with its three bulbous domes and four minarets. At first I rather agreed with the French botanist-traveller Jacquemont who in 1830 found the red sandstone too harsh, 'though the grandeur, elegance and simplicity make one forget this'. But the red is really rather splendid against an Indian sky, and the warm white of the marble stripes and of the pavilions on the minarets give just the right contrast. Five thousand workmen were employed for six years in its construction, and it was finished in 1658, the year that Shah Jehan was deposed by his son Aurangzeb.

I had been told by an Indian friend that Chandni Chowk, the main street of Delhi that runs opposite the Fort, meant Place of Silver, but others have said that it means Canal of Paradise. Either version is in any case derived from the fact that there used to be a canal, lined with trees, that ran down the centre of the street. Personally I cannot imagine any canal in the centre of an Indian town, especially before the days of proper drainage, looking paradisaical, though I concede that the Chandni Chowk might have seemed silver by moonlight . . .

At the time of the Mutiny Charles Trevelyan, then in London, wrote a series of letters to *The Times* in resounding mid-Victorian prose, but under the pseudonym of 'Indophilus'. In the first letter, which he headed 'Retribution in Delhi', he made quite reasonable suggestions about how to deal with mutineers and reward faithful sepoys. But he also said this:

> The Palace of Delhi, the sink of iniquity, and rallying point of every hostile influence, should be razed to the ground, and a new strong citadel erected on its site, called Fort Victoria. The carved blocks of marble from the halls of audience should be transported to Europe.

It would seem that some of this advice was heeded. In the frenzy of hate that followed the Mutiny, British troops did occupy the Palace within the Red Fort, and buildings were destroyed to make way for some hideous barracks, now looking like dismal versions of London's Peabody Buildings, and which quite ruin the atmosphere of the place. The hall of public audience was used as a hospital, troops were billeted in the harem quarters to the south Gardens and fountains were cleared away. The Lahore Gate, the main entrance to the Fort, was renamed Victoria Gate, while soldiers prised out stones from the marble with their bayonets and stole gold from the Pearl Mosque, whose copper gilt domes were sold at auction. The Orpheus and other panels from the hall of private audience were removed in 1857 by Captain, afterwards Sir John, Jones, who had two table-tops made from them. These were eventually sold to the British Government for £500 and deposited in the South Kensington Museum. They were retrieved in 1903 by Lord Curzon at his own expense, and reinstalled by a Florentine expert, though too late to be shown at the Delhi Durbar. (A ball was held in the hall of private audience in 1876, in honour of the Prince of Wales.)

At the time of the Mutiny a holy war against the British was preached from the Jami Masjid, so some people were all for destroying that too. Instead it was turned into a warehouse.

The glories of Lutyens's Viceregal House, now called the Rashtrapati

Bhawan, obviously revivified the older members of our group, on our return from Agra. It was like visiting some stately home where we could all claim grand relations. As so many of us were ex-Army wallahs we had also to see the Mutiny memorial. After passing at some speed the Skinner Church and the chaos where the Kashmir Gate had once been, we went to the famous Ridge to which the British troops had clung in 1857.

My feelings at the Ridge were rather as they had been at the Khyber Pass. One could almost smell the cordite and see the guns spitting. One part of the Ridge had indeed been nicknamed the Khyber Pass. We saw the memorial, made of the usual red sandstone and much defaced by Indian visitors who regarded the Mutiny as India's first war of independence. Around the base one could still occasionally descry names of officers who had died and, more clearly, lists of actions fought. I saw that Delhi was given as Dilhí, a favoured version in the late nineteenth century, just as Lucknow was Lakhnau for a while and Jaipur Yájpúr. (Delhi for Muslims used mostly to be known as Shahjehanabad.)

Then I noticed:

Attack on the Sabzi Mandi	June 30
Action of Alipur	July 4
Attack on the British Camp	July 9
Actions of the Sabzi Mandi	July 14 and 18
Affair of Trevelyanganj	July 20
Action of Metcalfe House	July 23

Trevelyanganj and Metcalfe House

Ganj means quarter or area. The Sabzi Mandi was once a picturesque suburb of Delhi; from the description I visualize it as a Daniell aquatint, peaceful and exotic, with palms, domes, bullock carts and vegetable sellers. During the Mutiny it was a key point in the assaults on the British. Trevelyanganj was to the south of the Sabzi Mandi, which was across the Grand Trunk Road, and in the direction of the Lahore Gate. It was called this because early in 1830 Charles Trevelyan acquired a piece of waste land, about 300 acres, for poor people and had a road laid out down the centre at his own cost.

Charles had strong, indeed passionate, ideas about improving the lot of the native population. On the other hand one cannot help feeling that the creation of Trevelyanganj may have been a dramatic, if not defiant gesture, because of his recent unpopularity among most of the British residents of Delhi. As Macaulay said later, Charles at the time had been 'almost everywhere abused and generally cut', and this was because of an episode known as the Colebrooke Affair, which had raised a 'perfect storm'.

It would seem that Charles lived in the Shalimar Gardens further north of the Ridge, and if they had been anything like the Shalimar Gardens at Lahore or Srinagar, with their traceried pavilions, small mosques and waterfall terraces, it must have been a delight. Here the Emperor Aurangzeb had been crowned on the Peacock Throne. Charles used to be known as the 'fellow of the Shish Mahal', and the Shish Mahal was the central pavilion in the gardens.

When Charles went first to Delhi in February 1827 it was as assistant to Sir Charles Metcalfe. Originally most of the British houses, like the Residency, had been within the walls of Delhi, between the Red Fort and the Kashmir Gate, but as Delhi had become less of a frontier town so the British were beginning to feel safe enough to have their mansions in the countryside beyond, some on the Ridge, with its lovely leafy view over to Delhi's domes and minarets. Sir Charles Metcalfe had an Indian family, and preferred the seclusion of the gardens, with its turtle-doves and peacocks; he was probably glad therefore to have the company of Charles Trevelyan, who believed in the mingling of the races – not that this straitlaced young man would ever have dreamt of keeping a bibi or Indian mistress. Sir Charles Metcalfe used to travel out at weekends by elephant, as he found it easier for reading.

The Metcalfe House shown on the Mutiny Memorial belonged to Thomas Metcalfe, Sir Charles's younger brother and who had corresponded about pietra dura. His house was built in 1830, and he lived in Delhi for forty years. Metcalfe House, on the banks of the Jumna, was one of the sights of British India, with its thirty-foot verandah, stone pillars, sumptuous marble and rosewood furniture, Napoleonic relics, silver, clocks and engravings.

Thomas Metcalfe was said to have been full of fun, and a lover of puns. (It is also believed that he could not bear to see ladies eating cheese – the reason unexplained.) In a sense he was lucky – although said to have been poisoned (not by cheese one hopes) – to have died in 1853 before the Mutiny. His house was one of the first to be looted, and 25,000 books, mostly bound in Russian leather, were lost. For some decades its bullet-spattered and blackened shell was a different sort of sight for tourists. Few however ventured to the Shalimar

Gardens, which became a wilderness of creepers, banyans, banana trees and snake-infested pools.

Raúl and I went in search of Trevelyanganj, but if we ever found the site it had become submerged in railway yards and the kind of slums from which Charles would have wanted to rescue his poor people. As for the Shalimar Gardens, we were told it was being turned into a residential estate. The only conceivable transport for getting back to our hotel was a bicycle taxi, with a pathetic straining old boy doing the pedalling, and we two lumps felt ashamed to be his passengers. He didn't really understand English, and took us to a hotel near a railway siding that certainly was not *our* Imperial. He was exhausted. Luckily there wer real taxis about, so we paid him off and seized one . . .

Charles Trevelyan arrives in Delhi, *1827*

Charles Trevelyan had been brought up in a Somerset parsonage, according to strict Evangelical principles. His father was Archdeacon of Taunton and a Canon of Wells, and through him there was a descent from a Huguenot banker. The senior branch of the Trevelyan family in the nineteenth century, to which he belonged (and I do not, alas) has been bracketed with the Aclands and the Howards as 'radical, plain living, high thinking, generally considered eccentric by their neighbours'. A. L. Rowse once summed them up like this:

> Integrity to the point of eccentricity, honesty to the point of rudeness, tactless and rough-handed but of an indubitably aristocratic distinction, devoted public spirit with an equal ability to carry it into action; a marked idiosyncrasy held in check by strong common sense; not much sense of humour. That distinguished family was apt to think that there were Trevelyans – and then the rest of the human race.

Charles's maternal grandfather was a Governor of the Bank of England. On his mother's side (the Neaves, a family similar in tastes and ideas to those Trevelyans) he had an uncle who was a judge at Benares and another who was deputy paymaster to the forces. He was educated at Charterhouse and the East India Company college at

Haileybury,★ where he showed an amazing flair for oriental languages. He was also influenced by the philosophies of Bentham, Mill and Malthus, and by the rising creeds of Utilitarianism and laissez faire. In 1826, at the age of nineteen, he was appointed as a writer or clerk to the Bengal Civil Service.

Portraits of him vary. In the romanticized ones his features might be described as clear-cut, but always what Macaulay described as ardent. Later portraits made him look hawklike with a long Trevelyan nose. He was dark-haired and awkwardly mannered, fond of sport – as a result of those 'boyhood rambles in Somerset springs', as G. M. Trevelyan put it. 'Nobody could call him handsome,' Macaulay later said, but he had a fine figure, looked well on horseback and was 'very active and athletic'.

It was typical of Charles that he should have wanted to ride to India cross-country from Europe by way of Constantinople, Persia and Afghanistan, but the Company would not allow this. He arrived therefore by ship in Bombay in June 1826, the hottest month in a city that as a child I used to dread for its sweaty humidity. He was met by his elder brother Henry, a Lieutenant in the Bombay artillery, and not surprisingly transported to the coolness of the local hill station, Poona.

Of Charles's five brothers Henry was the only one not either in or destined for the Church. A future Major-General, he looks a good sort in his pictures, but the face, with its fluffy whiskers, certainly does not have the strength of Charles's. When their father died the following year it seemed to be assumed automatically that the brilliant Charles, the fourth son, would take the lead in that large family, and certainly from Charles's own letters to his mother, so full of filial piety and concern, it is obvious that he accepted this role by right: 'I thank you for what you have done already and for the sake of the whole family as well as myself. For I shall always consider the interests of my brothers and sisters the same as my own and serve them at any sacrifice.'

No doubt he found the British inhabitants of Poona as boring as did Victor Jacquemont, the French botanist-traveller, when he arrived there in 1832: 'They go out riding and driving, breakfast, dine, dress, shave and undress, or meet on committees for settling the affairs of a public library where I have never seen anybody but

---

★ This was founded in 1806 as a training school for the East India Company's civil service and the higher rungs of commerce. It was dissolved in 1858, but reestablished as a public school in 1862, still retaining a great pride in its origin. Now a house at Haileybury is called Trevelyan after Charles. The equivalent College for young men to be trained for military service was at Addiscombe, and this survived the changes of 1858.

myself. They sleep, sleep a great deal and snore hard, digest as best as they can, sin, no doubt, as much as they can and read their newspapers from Bombay; and that is their whole life.' These people were completely incurious about Indian habits and traditions, or what was going on elsewhere in India. Charles must have horrified them by deciding to ride 800 miles through the monsoons by way of the great ruined city of Vijayanagar, otherwise known as Hampi, nine miles square. From Madras he took the ship for Calcutta, the 'city of palaces', of porticoes, colonnades, piazzas, palms and banyans, described by Bishop Heber as smelling like a greenhouse. Not for him the balls and amateur theatricals, or the evening drives round the 'Course' in some spanking equipage, let alone (God forbid!) 'nautches' by local dancing girls. Apart from visits to St John's Cathedral on the sabbath, he spent twelve hours a day studying at the East India College of Fort William, only occasionally allowing himself a glance at the Hooghly River, bristling with the masts of European shipping, and with native budgerows (houseboats, painted green), bolios and other strange craft shimmering over the water, among which floated the garlanded bodies of dead Hindus, with fat vultures perched on them. In less than two months he had passed his final examinations, with two gold medals and a rave 'eulogium' in the *Gazette*, including special praise for his grasp of Sanskrit, Persian and other oriental languages: a contrast to the behaviour of some other students at Fort William, where there were complaints of idleness and indiscipline.

So in February 1827 this formidable and, it must be confessed, rather priggish young man was sent as assistant to Sir Charles Metcalfe in Delhi, a post regarded as giving some of the best chances of promotion for an ambitious and clever junior, especially one with liberal ideas. Sir Charles was Resident for the second time, and had a reputation as an administrator of unimpeachable integrity. When first in Delhi he had prohibited suttee and had abolished corporal punishment. Delhi, still a strategic centre, was regarded by Europeans as one of the pleasantest and, unlike Calcutta, healthiest places in which to live in India, with a cool, sometimes even cold, climate for half the year, and plenty of good pig-sticking and tiger-hunting in the neighbourhood. Then for studious people like Charles there was the attraction of an intellectual and literary tradition.

Delhi, however, did not by any means escape the great heat of summer, which most assumed meant changing your clothes four times a day. The dust could be fearful. When the ice-pits were used up, and the country was panting for rain, and the mosquitoes were at their worst, drinks had to be 'cooled' with saltpetre, and tatties, blinds of dampened grass and bamboo, had to be fixed to doors and windows to keep out the dust. Samuel Sneade-Brown, who became Charles's colleague and friend at the Residency, wrote home in the month of June:

> The weather is now in its glory; the only time in the day in which it is possible to stir out of one's house is between five and six in the morning, and at seven in the evening, when it is almost dark. All nature languishes. Imagine yourself placed in front of a huge oven, and a large bellows introduced at the opposite end, so as to puff the heated vapour in your face ... I am obliged to have the punkah, or large fan fixed to the ceiling, moving night and day.

But such heat, as Charles said to his mother, was 'nothing' to him, and did not interfere with his work. Like Sneade-Brown he also had plenty of servants to wait on him: a valet to dress and undress him, bathe him and rub him down, a butler, two men to wait at table, a water-carrier, a sweeper or 'menial servant' for the thunder box, six grooms, and six bearers for the palanquin. Delhi for Europeans had a reputation for being very hospitable, though there was a dearth of young women. The wives of the Delhi officers were unkindly known as the Painted Corpses. Charles, however, had decided that, as it would be some years before he would want to marry, the society of ladies was mostly a waste of time.

A Moghul descendant of Shah Jehan still reigned in a shabby dream-world behind the walls of the Red Fort, on a salary provided by the British, while the grander Europeans lived in the usual Anglo-Indian Palladian splendour. The population of Delhi was about 150,000, about half of them Hindus, who were generally the poorest. The grandest inhabitant, who had a palace overlooking the Chandni Chowk, was the Begum Sumroo, about whom Bishop Heber had severe reservations, and with good reasons – to Macaulay, later, she was an 'old hag'. Travellers remarked on the gaily coloured and graceful attire of the locals; and in one's palanquin, chaise or buggy, one would constantly be encountering performing bears and monkeys, and 'gentlemen of rank' with large sawaris or retinues on horseback, jingling camels, and sometimes royal elephants with cloths of gold and gilded howdahs. In the streets and alleys off the Chandni Chowk there was a babel of coffee houses and small shops, especially jewellers, ivory workers, sword and shawl makers; also dreadful poverty. There was one great advantage about the Delhi bazaar for British travellers, as one of them said: 'Elephant and camel trappings are obtainable in any quantity and at reasonable prices.'

Charles had just arrived in Delhi when the then Governor-General Lord Amherst and his wife came for a durbar. He was in charge of some of the arrangements. In her diary Lady Amherst was impressed by the size of Delhi's streets, 'wider than any in London, not excepting Portland Place'. Their palanquins were greeted by a cacophony of Indian music and the bellowing of a 'vast concourse of elephants'. At the durbar inside the royal palace the venerable King, Akbar II, permitted Amherst to sit at right-angles to him, which was a slight sensation since no one except a royal prince was permitted to do this, and presented him with a pearl necklace, while the heir-apparent offered to change clothes with the Governor-General, 'an honour which it required some ingenuity to escape'.

Amherst did not in return give a nazr, or gift, which would have counted as a token of submission. The other British, including Charles, not only had to bow three times to the King but present nazrs of money. In return, as Lady Amherst sarcastically remarked, they received some 'trumpery dresses, only fit for chimney sweeps'. 'So much pride and ostentation combined with so much meanness, dirt and poverty is incredible. How is the race of Timur sunk!'

Actually the ritual of nazrs, which discreetly ended in a large net gain for the royal family, was a form of bonus on the normal stipend the King received from the Government. By the Company's rules all Indians' nazrs to British officials over a certain value, and not only those from the palace, had to be handed to the Treasury, whereupon they would either be auctioned or bought by the original recipient at valuation price. The nazrs given by the British were out of Government funds. When Bishop Heber visited the palace in December 1824, even the 'Queen', the first lady of the harem, never seen by him, though she kept strict watch behind some marble tracing, insisted on her nazr, and courtiers brazenly asked for presents.

Lady Amherst noticed how the once beautiful gardens in the palace were all overgrown. The marble walls of the audience rooms were stained with the dung of bats, pigeons and sparrows. Nine years later Emily Eden was with her brother, the new Governor-General, Lord Auckland, at a similar ceremony, and she wrote:

> The natives all look upon the King of Delhi as their rightful lord, and so he is, I suppose. In some of the pavilions belonging to the princes there were such beautiful inlaid floors, any square of which would have been an enviable table top for a palace in London, but the stones are constantly stolen; and in some of the finest baths there were dirty charpoys spread, with dirtier guards sleeping on them. In short, Delhi is a very suggestive and moralising place –

such stupendous remains of power and wealth passed and passing away – and somehow I feel that we horrid English have just 'gone and done it', merchandised it, revenued it, and spoiled it all.

The Colebrooke Affair

Disappointingly for Charles, Metcalfe was summoned from Delhi to serve on the Supreme Council in Calcutta. The new Resident was a very different type, Sir Edward Colebrooke, an urbane and sociable baronet, aged sixty-five, at the climax of a long career in India and brother of Henry Colebrooke, the famous Sanskritist.

Sir Edward wrote to Amherst saying how delighted he was to have such an exceptional young man as Charles Trevelyan to work with him. He did not realize then that he was nursing someone who would prove to him a viper.

Lord Amherst was also replaced, by Lord William Bentinck, like Colebrooke known to many of Charles's mother's family. Charles, who later professed a strong aversion to string-pulling, at once wrote to his mother asking for the strongest possible recommendations on his behalf to be sent urgently and personally to Bentinck.

'Sir Edward,' wrote Charles's colleague Samuel Sneade-Brown in June 1828, 'is a frank and pleasant old gentleman; I like him much. We call his lady the *Bore Constrictor*.' Indeed it would seem that Louisa Ann Colebrooke, very much the burra memsahib, was the cause of many of Sir Edward's subsequent troubles. Sneade-Brown also called her a termagant and said that her husband 'stood in awe of her'. She was his second wife, the widow of a Captain Henry Stuart. On their arrival in Delhi, so Charles said, they brought with them a large number of relatives and dependants.

The troubles revolved mostly round the matter of nazrs, about which Colebrooke had already been in slight trouble when at Allahabad. The system of handing over gifts, whether in cash or kind, to the Treasury had been instituted by Lord Cornwallis, as a way of dealing with the corruption and scandals that had so enriched the eighteenth-century 'nabobs'. It would have been offensive actually to refuse nazrs, and as Charles was to say: 'It is natural for an Indian to endeavour to secure by presents the favourable disposition of his rulers.' Officials were also forbidden to trade privately, or to accept loans from Indian bankers.

But the easy-going Colebrooke was not going to be bothered by all this. When he received nazrs in cash, he kept half and gave the rest to underlings, really as hush money, although such a thing would never have been said openly. Nazrs in kind were deliberately undervalued so that he could buy them back at very nominal rates. He asked for entertainment allowances when he visited chiefs on tour, so that each time he ended up with a profit. In due course he began to accept bribes, which were accounted for in the books by fake sales of Residency furniture, which in any case had been paid for by Sir Charles Metcalfe and was still his property. He received loans, which ended up by not being loans at all. To his horror, Charles found he was expected to help in what he began to regard as a 'putrefying mass of corruption', which most other British residents looked upon with indulgence.

It was to be revealed that Colebrooke was paying into his bank account in Calcutta sums far larger than his actual salary. He built himself a mansion, and it has been suggested that it could have been on the Ridge, the one eventually bought by Hindoo Rao, the scene of much hand-to-hand fighting during the Mutiny. Charles found out that Colebrooke's son, who had been put in charge of the Treasury, pocketed the difference when banks' rates were increased.

Ultimately, however, it was a clash of personalities, of old and new values. The twenty-one-year-old Charles, as part of the official 'family', had meals at the Residency table. It was said that he had no small talk. He sat and listened in silence to Lady Colebrooke proclaiming that she was not bound by Company rules and would certainly not hand in nazrs. When she openly made some money out of fake sales of jewellery, Charles dared to remonstrate, pointing out the harm he was doing to her husband's reputation. She then rounded on him, using 'furious invective'. He therefore absented himself from the table, and managed to get himself some missions outside Delhi. On being recalled, he withdrew himself altogether from the Residency, and began a private investigation.

When Charles found out that Colebrooke's babu or private agent, a Bengali called Ram Gopal, was actually forging the Resident's signature, he decided he must act and brought a suit against the babu. Colebrooke tried to stop this, on the grounds that Charles had not the authority, but Charles pointed out that he was now a private citizen.

Colebrooke began writing angry notes about Charles's 'underhand and dishonourable' proceedings. 'I shall not stand much longer to be made the laughing stock of the whole town. The very chaprassis [messengers] are whispering and tittering at my forbearance.' At last Colebrooke saw the wisdom of having Charles permanently transferred from Delhi, and picked on Kotah, some two hundred and fifty miles to the south; as Charles himself said it was like being sent by the

Emperor of Russia to Siberia. But, as luck would have it, Charles had a bad fall from a horse and could not travel. Colebrooke next took the counter-step of prosecuting Bakhtawar Singh, Treasurer of the Residency, who had been obtaining details from bankers' account books for Charles, for 'conspiracy, perjury, disturbance and holding an illegal court', and for appointing himself both prosecutor and judge. If Bakhtawar Singh were to be convicted, he would be branded on the forehead. Colebrooke said that he would arrange to have him 'mounted on an ass, to have his face blackened, and in that state have him conducted through the streets of the city'. He also announced that he was intending to prosecute Charles himself for conspiracy.

Lady Colebrooke now played her part, and sent a round robin about Charles to the officers of three regiments and to officials at Delhi, declaring: 'Lady Colebrooke cannot but think that *liar* and *villain* are the mildest terms which can be applied to such an act of depravity in so young a man.'

Charles now found himself being ostracized not only by almost the entire European community, but by the Indian nobility and traders. The royal family and the chieftains outside Delhi 'took the greatest possible exception to the exposure of these corrupt dealings'. Some 'honourable men' among the Europeans felt it was wrong to expose 'so gross a system of corruption' because it would 'cast a stain on the entire civil service', and demean it in the estimation of Indians. 'I shall never forget,' Charles wrote, 'the many solitary hours which I passed with only an occasional visit from Bakhtawar Singh whose constant theme was the dreaded anticipation of his seemingly inevitable fate.' Charles faced the ruin of his career, and guided only by 'an approving conscience', on June 9 1829 he wrote to the Chief Secretary at Calcutta formally charging the Resident at Delhi with corruption.

At once Colebrooke was suspended, and his place taken temporarily by his friend William Fraser, the next senior officer. Charles had to apply for Fraser's suspension too, and this was granted. Insults flew backwards and forwards, but Colebrooke realized he was losing. He accused Charles of having been jealous of visits by important Indians to Lady Colebrooke: 'The inveterate hostility, the infuriated hatred, with which he is presenting his revenge would disgrace a Nero . . . I never met with so infamous a character in my whole life, and I do not recollect that I ever read of one.'

Colebrooke turned to self-pity and pleading. The merit of forty years' service had been blown away in a moment by the 'clandestine whisper of a stripling': 'Let me only retire where the sound of his name may never insult my ears. I may say, with the frogs pelted by boys, what is sport to you is death to me.' His final and desperate ploy was to attack his predecessor, Sir Charles Metcalfe, whom he described as 'puny', suggesting that what he had done had also been done by him. This was not quite so foolish, as investigations did reveal that the great Metcalfe's servants had received bribes.

By now Bentinck was fully on the side of Charles. The result was inevitable: on December 29 1829 Colebrooke was dismissed from the Residency, suspended from the Service, and convicted of violating his oath of office and of countenancing corruption among his dependants. All this was in due course confirmed by the East India Company directors.

Bentinck wrote to Charles in his own hand:

> Your successful endeavours in rescuing the character of the service at large, and the fair name of our country, from the disgrace, which the base conduct of so high a functionary would otherwise have for ever entailed upon it, are entitled to my very best thanks.

And this was by no means the only flattering communication Charles had from him. Colebrooke was allowed to stay in Delhi for a while, and took the opportunity of attacking Bentinck himself, accusing him of abetting the 'Delhi spy office' and of bringing British rule into contempt. Here again he could do this with some confidence, knowing that both Bentinck and Metcalfe were unpopular in Calcutta for many reasons – partly because of bringing in economies (Bentinck was known as the Clipping Dutchman), partly because of their disdain for ceremonial ('he thinks and acts like a Pennsylvanian Quaker'); partly because they favoured the advancement in public life of educated Indians and Eurasians, partly also perhaps because of lingering criticism as a result of his recall twenty years before as Governor of Madras. There was also great discontent in the Army because of the rescinding of the 'half batta', an allowance drawn in cantonments – the Bentincks were snubbed by the Army and deliberately insulted when they visited Cawnpore and Meerut. It was said 'that Bentinck's unpopularity swept before him like a pestilence', and that the very Commander in Chief, Sir Edward Barnes, was the 'encourager of general disaffection'. He also had to have the Residents of Lucknow and Hyderabad dismissed.

In Delhi Samuel Sneade-Brown could not but feel sorry for Colebrooke, remembering past kindnesses and the old man's 'amiable disposition'. He had occasionally been to see him during the eight months when the 'eyes of the European community were turned on Delhi':

But he knew me too well to invite me to dinner again, where I should have encountered her ladyship and been exposed to a pointed insult. How strange that a man possessed of a most handsome competence – I should say rather a splendid fortune, of good birth, and of liberal education, should descend so low! . . . On my friend Trevelyan's conduct the highest encomiums have been passed by the Government . . .

Sneade-Brown also recorded that when the time came for the Colebrookes to leave Delhi, Lady Colebrooke did receive him kindly.

Charles piously summoned it all up: 'God befriended me and supported my conscience.'

Hunting from elephants

The cherub-faced naturalist Victor Jacquemont, friend of Prosper Mérimée and Stendhal, arrived in Delhi in March 1830. Whilst in Calcutta he had enchanted the Bentincks, who had obviously praised Charles Trevelyan to him. Then Jacquemont on meeting Charles described him as being marked out for a great career in India.

Thomas Metcalfe, Sir Charles Metcalfe's brother, took Jacquemont to the King of Delhi, the 'most adorable of princes', with a 'fine white beard' and the expression of someone who had suffered much. Jacquemont was amused by the system of the King conferring titles on Europeans, by which they would be introduced. Jacquemont was 'Sahib Bahadur'. Charles Trevelyan, however, he said, had 'formally' refused to accept any title whatsoever.

Jacquemont wanted to go to the Himalayas, by way of Simla. His route took him through the southern Punjab, and at his camp some 150 miles from Delhi he was joined by Charles 'with a huge train of men, horses and elephants'. Charles intended to hunt wild boar and tigers, and was spending a sixth of his year's salary on this ambitious expedition. His horse was a 'superb Arab', whereas Jacquemont, who always worried about money, only had a 'Persian nag'.

In some ways Jacquemont and Charles could not have had much in common. Together they 'galloped hard' for three days, until they reached a group of tents with seventeen of the Rajah of Patiala's elephants and four hundred of his horsemen waiting for them. An elegant luncheon had been prepared, and then they mounted on elephants. Jacquemont was given the Rajah's own beast, complete with a chair covered with velvet and tinsel. Charles, because of his official rank, had on each side of him various vakils or ministers of the Rajah, also on elephants.

Our cavalry was deployed on the flanks of this imposing line and, with the Rajah's two drummers rolling out the royal march before us, we entered the desert.

It consists of vast sandy plains covered with stunted thorny shrubs and scattered here and there with tall trees; in other places there are grassy steppes. It presents no obstacles for the elephants, which laboriously uproot trees between which they cannot pass and tear off the branches which might touch the rider.

The horsemen formed a semicircle, driving the game ahead. Hundreds of hares and partridges were killed, and some wild boars and a hyena were wounded, but there was not a shadow of a tiger. Nevertheless Jacquemont was 'enchanted by the strangeness of this novel scene', and he felt he had seen more of the Orient in that one day than during the whole year since his arrival in India.

Baths consisted of having cold water squirted over you from a goatskin. The guests put on the 'lightest of cotton garments' and had dinner in a huge tent, illuminated like a ballroom. There was a champagne, followed by claret and port, with entertainments by Persian mimes and nautch girls. For once Charles let himself unbend; Jacquemont said that they threw themselves on the carpet with laughing.

The hunts continued for about a week in the same style, though pig-sticking of course was on horseback. A surgeon was to hand in case of broken bones in the particularly dangerous sport. But hunting lions and tigers was always from elephants.

Every huntsman is perched up like a witness in an English court of justice, in a very high box strapped on the animal's back ... It sometimes happens, though very rarely, that when the tiger is brought to bay it leaps on the head of the elephant; but that is nothing to do with the likes of us: it is the business of the mahout who is paid to put up with this sort of accident. If he is killed, he at least has the satisfaction of being thoroughly avenged, for the elephant does not calmly play the clarinet with its trunk when he feels a tiger on his head ... There is another poor devil behind you, whose business it is to hold a parasol over your head. His state is even worse than that of the mahout; when the elephant is scared and flees from the charging tiger, as the latter leaps on its hind quarters, the true function of that man is to be eaten instead of the gentleman.

Some tiger hunters had a worse experience than this. Emily Eden wrote of a friend being attacked by a swarm of hornets as his elephant was being charged by tigers (fifty stings had to be extracted from his face); then the elephant rolled down the bank among the tigers, which were 'happily too badly wounded to do any harm'.

The following month Charles was in Kotah as Political Agent, the post to which Colebrooke had originally assigned to him. It was good pig-sticking country, and there were plenty of tigers. Almost at once he found himself having to deal with some serious trouble in the neighbouring town of Bundi, which was under his control. Thanks to his decisiveness and real bravery an invasion and sacking of Bundi by men from Jodhpur was just in time prevented.

But Charles was restless. He felt cut off in Kotah, and was also worried by reports that Colebrooke meant to lash back as soon as he reached England. Such a thing could well damage or distress his family. So he had all the official documents on the case printed, with his comments, and sent a copy to Bentinck, suggesting that they should be sent to the press. Bentinck however advised against. So other copies only went to relations and close friends in India.

But even privately printed documents have a way of getting to newspapers . . . Bentinck was not altogether pleased about this. A report on the case was also published in the *East India Magazine* of October 1832. Lady Colebrooke at once had her own disdainful comments printed and circulated. Sir Edward died in 1838. Because of his rank, it was deemed the honourable thing for a long time thereafter not to refer to the matter or his name. Charles features in the *Dictionary of National Biography*, but the Colebrooke Affair is not mentioned.

Simla. What did I expect of Simla, our group's next stop after Delhi? I suppose I mostly had in mind Emily Eden's descriptions, and – inevitably – Kipling's stories. I did rather hope, since everyone must mention her when writing of Simla, that I might still find that most famous character in *Plain Tales from the Hills*, Mrs Hauksbee, of the 'rolling violet eyes' and 'many devils of malice and mischievousness'. Even more would I have liked to have found Mrs James, for it was she who in the 1830s kicked over the traces and fled back to Europe, there to become a dancer and change her name to Lola Montes.

'I love those Himalayas, good old things,' Emily had written. 'The hills were *really* beautiful tonight, a sea of pinkish white clouds over them, and some of their purple heads peering through like islands.' Over those same hills her brother would have gazed and agonized, deciding whether or not to invade Afghanistan. And when that invasion had happened, Emily cheerfully was writing home: 'We have been uncommonly gay at Simla this year, and have had some beautiful tableaux with music, and one or two well acted farces, which are a happy change from the everlasting quadrilles.' She was no doubt being discreet, avoiding politics in letters. Rightly or wrongly, Sir John Kaye blamed her as one of those who influenced Auckland in his decision. 'That pleasant hill sanatorium at Simla,' Kaye wrote, had been the 'cradle of more political insanity than any place within the limits of Hindustan'.

As for the renowned 'Scandal Point', an old Army friend had said to me: 'Well, I suppose there was a lot of silly female chatter and gossip, and Kipling upset people over Mrs Hauksbee, but Simla was quite the most difficult place to be naughty in. We all lived on top of one another. Everybody knew what everybody else did. Anyone who succeeded in carrying out a clandestine love affair must have been a genius.' He did, however, concede that there had been fleas in Simla. Emily Eden had complained that the more you had your house cleaned the more the fleas multiplied.

I alarmed my companions in our coach, on the climb up to Simla, by talking about fleas. We were arriving at the end of a late monsoon, so we hardly had a glimpse of the far Himalayas. It also being September, we missed the rhododendrons in flower. The first impression, indeed, was of darkness, low clouds, dripping leaves and ferns, and rusty corrugated iron roofs over collapsing wooden fretwork. Even the top of the celebrated fir-clad Jakko Hill was in mist. The town of Simla clung to the hillside, like an avalanche of corrugated iron, though in tiers. Here and there one did notice massive late Victorian structures: all as far away as possible from the traditional colonial architecture, the temples and mosques of the plains. The only memorial of the Raj era that had any grace was the yellow-painted Betjemanesque church, begun in 1844, but it really had nothing to do with the landscape.

Maybe I was hoping for a sort of Gulmarg, but the places were totally unlike. Gulmarg was on a plateau, its name meaning meadow of flowers. The houses there were more scattered, more primitive, not trying to look like Surrey in olden times.

We had been travelling from Delhi since 4.30 am in spite of some of our party being quite ill. It had been noticeable that fewer people found it necessary to bring down their plastic bags of bran for breakfast. On enquiring later, I found that all those who had cracked up from stomach complaints admitted to having put their toothbrushes under the tap: the same old story. On top of this, Scottie Blessington had cut her leg quite badly after a suitcase had fallen on her from the top of our coach. Ted was hectically trying to work out who was getting on with whom, with a view to pairing off couples to share houseboats when we reached our next destination after Simla, Srinagar. It seemed that there were four 'problem' people among us: two singles and one couple, with whom nobody wanted to share.

By now our companions were beginning to take on identities for Raúl and me. The most distinguished were without any doubt Sir Cyril and Lady Pickard. He, among other things, had been High Commissioner in Pakistan, and both were concerned with the Tibetan Society – there were many Tibetan refugees at Simla. Douglas Orgill I had met before, rooting in a second-hand bookshop in Naples. He was a feature writer on the *Daily Express* and had come on this trip to collect material for a novel set in Kashmir. Butterflies as well as rare books and prints were among his interests. We found that Ted Blessington – happily – had decided that we would share our houseboat with Douglas and his wife Margaret. Like the Flashes, the Orgills were the kind we knew could be friends for life.

On that steep drive from Kalka to Simla I thought again of Kipling, but this time once more of *Kim*, and of the wonderful description of that 'wandering' road, climbing, dipping and sweeping among the deodars and pines, and of the sound of a 'thousand water channels'. We saw the branched cacti and the huge precipices, where there were some signs of avalanches. An early nineteenth-century traveller had written of houses like seabirds' nests, and how every ridge was cultivated. It was still like that. Horns of cars were being mercilessly honked, like Kipling's twanging of tonga-horns, but now there were no strings of ponies or carts, only lorries. In Kipling's day, however, the little narrow-gauge railway had not yet been built.

The sight of the railway line produced a frisson of gloom in one section of our coach. The whisper went round that in June 1942 dacoits had attacked the Kalka–Simla train, and that Major Baxter's brother-in-law and father-in-law had both been murdered. What was more, we also had with us Mrs Permain, and she had actually been on that same train. She had hidden under a seat when the attack came. 'You see, I was tiny then,' she sweetly told me afterwards.

In 1942 the train had consisted of a diesel rail car only. Shortly after dinner had been served, the driver saw a boulder on the line. He stopped and two men leapt down the embankment out of the darkness and shot him dead. With handkerchiefs round their faces, they then thrust their guns through the windows and began firing indiscriminately at passengers, three of whom died at once, including Wing-Commander H. W. Hogg, the Chief Commissioner of the Boy Scouts in India, and his son Lieutenant H. R. H. Hogg of the Gurkhas, Major Baxter's relatives. Two others died of wounds later. The dead and the wounded were searched for money and valuables, and some of the passengers were ordered outside. Three Englishmen managed to escape and reached Kalka on foot, where the alarm was raised.

The dacoits turned out to have been brothers. One died soon afterwards, but the other, Abdul Rahman, was caught and sentenced to death. The verdict was that the motive had been highway robbery, and had not been political.

Ted Blessington told us that he had travelled to Simla in the same train the very next day. He had sat next to an American who had a revolver on his lap. 'Gee, Major,' the American had said, 'if there is going to be any shooting around here, it's going to be by me.'

Our hotel might have had bandicoots in the roof, but we did not come across fleas – though the monkeys outside obviously suffered from them. The bazaar area swarmed with monkeys. Up on the Ridge, the famous and fashionable Simla Ridge, they were quite a menace, and males tried to charge you. We imagined that in the heyday of the British the monkeys must surely have been kept well away from the Ridge, lest they alarmed the 'fair sex' under their parasols or in their jampans, or frightened the steeds that bore those dashing young aides-de-camp in their tight uniforms and white kid gloves. (Ted Blessington told us of the chaos when in his day a swarm of locusts once descended on the promenaders, 'all over everyone, up skirts, up knickers'.)

On the whole, watching the monkeys was a delight. They were outrageously sexy as well as cantankerous and quarrelsome. It was difficult to see how the babies could still hang on to their mothers' chests during the vicious fights and quarrels. There were monkeys scampering all over the bazaar roofs, darting into houses to steal food if anyone was foolish enough to leave a window unbarred. All were presumably related to the ones up at the temple at Jakko, and this meant that they were holy and thus inviolate. For the temple was dedicated to Hanuman, the monkey god, who had dropped a sandal there on his way to Ceylon.

Having failed to find anyone who resembled Mrs Hauksbee on the Ridge, Raúl and I set off south-east, past gnomish ex-British houses, nearly all with corrugated roofs, some painted red, and with names such as Edgeworth. Emerging from Simla's suburbia we found ourselves at Barnes Court, half-timbered baronial on an enormous scale, on a spur with a view to match the house's grandeur.

The original Barnes Court had been built by Sir Edward Barnes, Commander-in-Chief under Bentinck but recalled in 1834 for insubordination. For a while it had remained the summer residence of Commanders-in-Chief; then in the 1880s Sir Louis Dane, the hospitable Lieutenant-Governor of the Punjab, had lived there. He had been an apiarist, but had to give up his hobby when owners of shops below in Chota Simla complained that the bees were raiding their sweet counters. Barnes Court was now the State guest house, so we had to obtain a pretence of a permit at the gate.

The house was half-timbered, with a tiled roof, and the garden was ablaze with potted fuchsias, cosmos, dahlias and agapanthus. There was a weeping willow, and the enormous wistarias looked as if they had been planted by Sir Edward Barnes himself. We were shown the ballroom, decorated with swords, chain mail and helmets, also the room in which the Indo-Pak summit of 1972 had been held. Mr Bhutto, his valet and fifteen others had stayed in the house. There were eighteen bedrooms. Some rooms were panelled, and some had moulded ceilings with vines, rising suns and the like. We saw the billiard room, so essential for Victorian grandeur, and the dining-room with a vulgar carved mantelpiece surmounted by a coat of arms (the Barnes arms?).

We continued our walk, and found ourselves on what had been known as the Jakko Round, a three-mile road skirting Jakko Hill that once had been as fashionable as Rotten Row. It was so quiet, apart from the wind in the pines and the crickets. Then the monsoon caught us. A schoolteacher offered us a share of his umbrella, which didn't help anybody much. During a short lull we dashed into an unlocked shed. Another lull, and we ventured on. The next downpour was like standing under a waterfall. We crouched among ferns in a low grotto, and were joined by three roadmen. Then a stream began suddenly to swirl around our ankles, and we clung like the monkeys of Jakko to some overhanging roots. It soon became obvious, as earth showered on us, that five people doing this was very dangerous; Raúl and I were soaked anyway, so we struggled back to the hotel through the blinding rain, past Emily Eden's Elysium Hill. But, looking back, we knew we had enjoyed it all.

The sky clearing in the afternoon, we went in a party organized by the Pickards to visit Kasumpti, where there was a Tibetan handicrafts centre, on land bought by the United Nations. We were met at the top of a calm and beautiful valley by a young man called Kansong, who spoke very good English. It is hard to think of any word to describe that afternoon's experience except 'heart-rending': the Tibetans were such courageous, hard-working, resigned people, calm as the landscape around them, a hundred and two of them altogether. Kansong said that he had left Lhasa with his family when he was seven, with only enough food for the journey. His father had been told that he would have been arrested the next morning. They had got into Bhutan, but could not proceed until His Holiness – the Dalai Lama – had safely reached India. The family worked on roads in north-east India, but were expelled at the time of the Sino-Indian war and had had to start life over again. Most of the monasteries in Tibet, Kansong said, had been turned into barracks by the Chinese.

We all bought things. The Tibetans were touchingly grateful. They gave us rancid butter tea – an acquired taste obviously, even if out of politeness we all had to accept second cups. The atmosphere of our visit was however suddenly spoilt when a pi-dog bit a lady in our party. Everyone seemed far more alarmed than she was. She explained that she was a nurse, and therefore knew that there would be plenty of time before she would need anti-rabies treatment, which she would 'see about' when she got back to England. The dog, realizing that it was doomed, whether it had rabies or not, had wisely fled, and was never found again.

That evening the Blessingtons gave a bring your own drinks party. The men wore suits and ties, the women long dresses, with new hairdos, as if in deference to our being in the summer capital of British India. Raúl and I as usual were in shirt-sleeves, and were thought exotic because we had brought vodka. The view of Simla by night, glittering, pointilliste, with low wisps of cloud floating above it, was something that Emily Eden could not have dreamed of, but I think she would have approved.

Ted Blessington's family had been the von Goldsteins, the owners of Wild Flower Hall, where Lord Kitchener had also lived. Felix von Goldstein, Ted's grandfather, had been bandmaster to the Viceroy. We saw a little house called Eheu, which seemed appropriate for Simla. Eheu Wild Flower Hall; and Bentinck Castle, and Peterhof, Elysium Hill, Benmore and Viceregal Lodge. Eheu too Emily Eden; eheu Lady Dalhousie, Lady Reading and her Moonlight Revels; eheu even the boring Lady Willingdon whose favourite colour was mauve. Eheu Kipling's Venus Annodomini, and his Wittiest Woman in India to whom *Plain Tales of the Hills* was dedicated: fugaces all these ladies, not in spirit though.

Still discernible were Poletti's Coffee House, the Gaiety Theatre and the Club. Simla is now the capital of Himachal Pradesh, and there was a row of quite grand shops. But Simla was continuing its pretence, holding on to its past. Douglas Orgill – trust him – had ferreted out the best booksellers, who were also antique dealers. The shop was run by Mr O. C. Sud, an author, quite a character, though certainly not at all like Kipling's Lurgan Sahib, and as far as we knew not a Russian spy. We liked visiting his shop as much as anything in Simla; that, and a picnic with the Orgills and the Flashes at a place called Fagu, when for a change the monsoon spared us, and we did get a sight of the Himalayan range, behind which lay Tibet.

'Are you bloody Britishers?' an old man in 'Congress' style dress said to the Pickards whilst they were walking in the Mall. They stiffened, expecting trouble, but agreed that was the case. 'Then why don't you bloody well come back? Simla's never been the same.'

Charles at Simla

In August 1832 Charles wrote to his mother from Simla about meeting 'old friends' such as the honeysuckle, the dog rose, the daisy and even the dock, and of the extraordinary number of cuckoos and woodpeckers calling to one another. He and others, he said, were enjoying the great treat of listening to the lectures of that 'highly interesting missionary Mr Wolff, the converted Jew', just arrived from an adventurous journey overland that had included Bokhara and Kabul. Wolff's adventures had indeed been more than just adventurous, and had included being captured by slave-dealers and having to travel stark naked for six months through deserts and over mountains. His particular obsessions were to win over other Jews to Christianity, and to track the descendants of the lost tribes of Israel, sometimes associated with the Afghans. Whilst in Bokhara he had actually had a vision of Christ, 'surrounded by little children', and had been told that the original Garden of Eden had been in Kashmir, and that there he would find one of the lost tribes. Wolff was also convinced that the Second Coming was nigh: in 1847, to be precise. In Cairo he had 'cast out a devil'. Charles said that he was being lent a copy of Wolff's journal, which he would copy and send home – no doubt this was the journal later published as *Researches and Missionary*

Labours among the Jews, Mohammedans and other Sects.

The Rev. Joseph Wolff was already a celebrity in England, after publishing accounts of other travels. He had been born the son of a Bohemian rabbi, and had been fired to travel east by the example of St Francis Xavier. Deeply pock-marked, pasty-faced, double-chinned and habitually dirty, he had nevertheless won the love of Lady Georgiana Walpole, whom he had married and left behind him in Alexandria before setting out on this recent trip. It would seem that his escapes from persecution and even death had been largely due to his powers of argument and gift of the gab. When he had reached Lahore, he had met Maharajah Ranjit Singh, who had been bemused by this apparition and finally not impressed, so that no permission had been given for him to enter Kashmir.

The Bentincks were at Simla. Because of Wolff being married into the aristocracy, they naturally gave him special attention, and indeed they both, especially Lady William, fell under his spell. As a result Wolff did finally get his permit to go to Kashmir. Unfortunately, though, his four days in Srinagar were a dire disappointment. 'Instead of the splendid palaces described so enchantingly by the poets,' he wrote, 'one sees only ruined and miserable cottages; instead of the far-famed beauties of Kashmir one meets only the most ugly, half-starved, blind and dirty-looking females.'

The meeting with Wolff was useful to Charles Trevelyan in other ways. On returning to Delhi from Kotah the year before Charles had first met the ill-fated Arthur Conolly, who was to be beheaded later at Bokhara. It was then, in 1830, that they had jointly compiled the reports already mentioned on the dangers of a Russian invasion.

In due course, after Delhi, Conolly had gone back to his regiment, which was stationed at Cawnpore, and Wolff went to stay with him. Wolff seems to have been a tease and Conolly high-spirited; nevertheless we learn that they 'took sweet counsel together, and walked in the House of the Lord as friends'. Because of this deep spiritual bond, Wolff all those years afterwards went back to Bokhara to try to save Conolly's life. But he arrived too late, and was nearly executed himself before returning.

Even if, as is likely, Charles had met Bentinck face to face before the summer of 1832, the weeks with him in Simla were important consolidating the extraordinary influence that the young man's ideas had on the Governor-General. Already in April that year Bentinck had been writing of Charles's 'powerful mind', and he was to describe Charles to Macaulay as the 'ablest young man in the service' and the 'most noble-minded man' he had ever seen. The Bentincks were childless and attracted to clever and articulate young men, two others being Victor Jacquemont and Alexander Burnes.

Reports from Burnes on the navigation possibilities of the Indus, for so long to be an obsession of Charles, had been received in 1831. During 1832 Burnes was travelling in Turkestan, including Bokhara, and he did not return to India until the following spring, when he submitted his sensational report which among other things convinced Bentinck, and Charles, of the pressing necessity of setting up a 'commercial agent' (namely Burnes himself) in Kabul to counteract growing Russian influence in the region.

But Charles at Simla was working on another, more personal matter. He arranged for his elder brother Henry, then adjutant of the 2nd Battalion of the Bombay Artillery, to join him there on leave. The ruse worked and Bentinck sent Henry as assistant to the Resident at Ajmer. Again Charles received a highly flattering letter from the Governor-General, written from Gwalior on December 4 1832: 'Throughout your zeal for the service, your honorable principles, and your real usefulness . . . will entitle you for ever to my sincere respect and esteem.'

One cannot of course blame Charles for being ambitious. His mother had asked him why he could not come back to England on leave, and he had replied: 'The real state of the case is this – my career has been rather a stormy one for a civilian and after much tossing I find myself settled down in a position of considerable influence.' To which he had added, with a certain smugness: 'I have a great talent entrusted to me which it is my duty neither to bury in the earth, nor to resign into the hands of Him who gave it to me until He Himself thinks fit to take it from me but to employ it to the best advantage for the benefit of His people.'

It was also true that Sir Charles Metcalfe had a high opinion of Charles, who came to be regarded as his favourite political officer. Metcalfe wrote to Bentinck: 'I perfectly agree with Your Lordship in thinking Mr Trevelyan a very uncommon and superior young man who, if he keeps his health and has not bad luck, must be one of the most distinguished men in our Indian Service.'

But Charles still had enemies and was to create many more.

All this while he was in a state of immense excitement over the progress of the Reform Bill in England, as his colleague Samuel Sneade-Brown recorded in a letter home:

Some newspapers arrived . . . I was compelled to put your letter in my pocket while Mr. Trevelyan was reading aloud details of the present contests in England . . . I was eager to read your letter . . . Still Mr. T. continued to read in a sonorous tone of exultation the newspaper details about the successes of the Polls and the progress of the Reform Bill till my companions chimed in with 'bravo' and 'excellent', so that even I caught a portion of their enthusiasm.

Travelling in the Himalayahs.

II

JUST AFTER DAWN at Chandigarh airport we were startled by five or six vicious-looking Russian-made jets streaking overhead at an astonishing speed. At Jammu airport there was even more of a military atmosphere. And here we were greeted by a placard which said: 'Wel Come to Joint Conference Cardiological Society and Association to Cardio-Vascular Surgeons of India.' Hardly tactful for a mainly elderly group.

We old Indian hands, the 'koi-hais' – that is, not including the Orgills and Raúl – knew that Srinagar must be pronounced more approximately Sirri-nugger, or if you like Shri-nugger; just as Gulmarg is really Goolmurg, and Nanga Parbat is Nunger Purbut. The name Srinagar according to some means city of the sun, though others claim it means city of knowledge, since the place was once a seat of learning.

The moment we crossed the bridge in Srinagar, and had seen what had been Maharajah Hari Singh's palace, a hotch-potch of styles, and the tottering gabled houses with the thatched boats – doongas – on the Jhelum River, I felt again that old nostalgic twang. But as in Gilgit it was the smell that got me: a mixture of spices, curry, horse, and cooking smoke from the doongas' stovepipe funnels.

We drove straight to the Nagin Lake, where a fleet of curtained shikaras, loaded with coloured cushions, awaited us. Their names were fun – 'Prince Charles Super De Luxe', 'Dryfly Love Me', 'Newfriend Ship Ta Ta', 'Heaven Lotus Three Star'. Raúl and I were allocated 'New York Ha Ha Special Spring Seats'.

There was a great lifting of spirits through the group. It had become obvious that only those who had known Simla in prewar days had really enjoyed our visit there. The weather had been to blame mostly. Now in idyllic Technicolour we skimmed across placid waters, green instead of Jhelum brown and so clear considering what must have constantly been pouring into it. The houseboats were lined up on the far bank with plank bridges to the servants' quarters and cookhouse. The Orgills, Raúl and I were in the 'Helal', with three double bedrooms, and our host was Sobra Sultan Wangnoo. We discovered that practically all the more up-market houseboats on Nagin Lake were owned by branches of the Wangnoo family. The décor in our saloon was what Douglas Orgill called stockbrokers' Kashmir, leaping stags instead of flying ducks. But did stockbrokers go in for flying ducks? 'This is the sort of furniture you find in Haslemere,' Monty Flash said to the elegant couple who shared his and Delphine's boat, only to find that they lived in Haslemere. 'Let's talk about folding tables,' was Monty's effort to change the subject. Our predecessors in the 'Helal' had left some lotuses in a vase. I now appreciated the lotus's renown as among the most perfect flowers in the world.

But it was not Englishness any more, even with leaping stags or flying ducks. There was no feeling either of clinging on to a musty past. Houseboat living was a culture on its own, and had become big business. The Wangnoos could almost have painted the reflections of the mountains, poplars and willows on the lake for us, have sprinkled around a few lemon-scented waterlilies, let loose a flock of kingfishers and artistically placed the Hari Parbat fort in just the right spot.

A soft dipping of oars announced more shikaras, selling flowers and postcards. Then a shikara post office appeared, and a shikara tailor who said he could run up a suit overnight if we paid in advance. On some neighbouring houseboats there were mild complaints about mouse droppings under the pillow, but otherwise everyone was delighted. A Colonel on leave from Singapore invited us all to his boat for drinks, but few could be prised away from their fretwork verandahs hung with flower baskets and the contemplation of a pink and blue Kashmir sunset.

In the days of early travellers one would have been offered nautch girls instead of postcards. Jacquemont said that every day forty or so 'public women' presented themselves at his gate. Perhaps that was why, there being no houseboats in 1831, he removed himself to the Isle of Chinars in the Dal Lake.

Four years after Jacquemont's visit Baron Hügel came to Srinagar, and was as little impressed by its dirt as the Rev. Joseph Wolff had been – or for that matter as V. S. Naipaul was to be in the 1960s. 'All that I saw,' Hügel wrote, 'during my first day's stay in Kashmir, were the ruins of what had been palaces, old dilapidated houses, streets of unexampled filthiness.' Naipaul called Srinagar 'a town of bodies and picturesque costumes discoloured and acrid with grime, of black, open drains, of exposed fried food and exposed filth; a town of prolific pariah dogs of disregarded beauty below shop platforms, of starved puppies shivering in the damp caked blackness below butchers' stalls hung with bleeding flesh.'

In due course Hügel turned his 'disappointed gaze' to the mountains, and there saw what every traveller to Kashmir expects to find: a 'thousand peaks' of 'snowy whiteness', gracefully outlined, 'their harmony and repose seeming to characterize the calm, motionless valley'. He too decamped to the little Isle of Chinar, and there, in the white pavilion with its garden of roses and stocks – too far from Shalimar to hear its nightingales – he met another traveller, Godfrey Vigne, whose book about Kashmir is to this day among the best of any.

I can understand Naipaul not feeling sufficiently English to want to try out a houseboat, but I think even so he would have preferred Wangnoo hospitality to his Mr Butt's hotel. There are flush systems on houseboats too! Maybe, though, he also had kingfishers on his windowsill and visits from the ubiquitous 'Mr Marvellous', who every morning rushed round the lakes delivering bunches of cosmos whether you wanted them or not.

The Vale of Kashmir, and especially its lakes in the time of the Raj, will forever be immortalized for us 'Anglo-Indians' by quantities of loving little books, not very literary and usually by ladies. One of the earliest of these is Mrs J. C. Murray-Aynsley's *Our Visit to Hindoostan, Kashmir and Ladakh* (1897). In Margaret Cotter Morison's *A Lonely Summer in Kashmir* (1904) some typical dramas and embarrassments are when she finds that she has to ride astride instead of side-saddle in front of the coolies, and when her mare stops to suckle its foal outside, of all places, the British Residency. Often these books are illustrated with reproductions of watercolours – plenty of shikaras and kingfishers on windowsills – that would seem absurdly prettified if one did not know them to be true.

The gentle, possibly pale hands of these ladies must have been at least subconsciously in all our minds when we visited the Shalimar, the Nishat Bagh and the Floating Gardens. All the hundred and forty-four fountains of the Shalimar were in full play, just as when Vigne went there, and just as he had said they were 'imparting a delicious coolness to the air'. The scale of the gardens was quite different, grander, than the Generalife's in Granada, but as our Spaniard remarked, nothing is more beautiful than water in the sun. Water is life. Both the Shalimar and the Generalife derive from the Muslim concept of the heavenly garden.

A transistor was playing in the central pavilion with its famous octagonal pillars of black marble. Vigne had been entertained there by the Sikh Governor, who had worn a heron's feather in his turban. Needless to say, he had been entertained by 'warbling' nautch girls, in addition to being offered too much of the 'strong spirit' of the country, made from fermented grapes. 'Orientals have no idea of drinking unless they can drink too much.' He would have preferred some quiet in order to contemplate the past splendour of the Moghuls, and the love of the Emperor Jehangir for the fair Nurmahal.

In the end, many of us were not sure if we did not prefer the Nishat Bagh. The view was certainly more spectacular, and then there was the 'shawl' water, sliding from terrace to terrace. Nishat Bagh, our guide told us, meant 'garden of gladness', but Vigne gave its definition as 'garden for the indulgence in the pleasure of drinking to intoxication'.

The Floating Gardens are less romantic than they sound. They are merely curious. We took a shikara to see them, Raúl taking over the paddling. We had a bit of a demonstration of how they were made. First find your reed-bed, then cut a trench of about twenty yards, at whatever distance from the water you prefer. Dig down underneath about three or four feet, slicing away the roots of the rushes. Push the whole thing into the lake, and it will float, rising upwards. Heap with mud and dung, and it will be ready for your melons, tomatoes and cucumbers.

Childhood summers

From the age of two onwards I spent my summers at Gulmarg: that is, apart from the year 1926, a dramatic one for my parents, when we were on leave in England. We only acquired Hut 46a during the Gilgit period. Before that we stayed with friends, or at Nedou's Hotel, or at boarding houses, such as Miss Christie's or Mrs Barnes's, each capable of taking some hundred guests. Europeans were not allowed to own property in Kashmir, so these huts – chalets really – were rented on an eight-year basis, renewable, from the State. The ban on owning property was also the reason for the houseboats at Srinagar.

There are names of people that I still find instantly forgettable. Others intrigue me at once, women's especially, I don't know why, and in that mostly female and infants' society in Gulmarg the names of Olive's friends have remained in my mind always: Violet Mc-Clenaghan, Madge Biddy, Joy Latham, Marion Walker, Peggy Wagstaffe. As for me, I can only remember a few friends of my own at Gulmarg. I loved my brother John, even though he was so small, and I loved Multana, who took me on rides as in Gilgit; I tolerated a boy named Bun and was especially fond of a girl called Ann, who however lived in a houseboat overlooking a smelly canal at Srinagar and rarely came to Gulmarg.

I didn't much like having to go to Srinagar, chiefly because of the heat and the glare. Gulmarg is 8,500 feet above sea-level, Srinagar 5,000. Once there, however, there were some happy picnics with Ann, at Shalimar or the trout hatcheries, and there were excursions to watch potters making bowls and flowerpots. I can almost to this day smell the clay from those potters' wheels. Smells again... But it is the scent of irises that still evokes the essence of the Vale of Kashmir. There were fields, knee-deep, of tall purple irises; sometimes one also saw them growing on temple roofs.

Between Srinagar and Tangmarg, which is at the beginning of the ascent to Gulmarg, there is a raised highway, dead straight and lined with poplars, across the rice and maize fields. There must have been at least a thousand of those poplars. We had to travel along this road in the cool of the night, but it was impossible to sleep in a tonga. I would lie on the cushions looking up at the tops of the poplars against the stars.

When I was old enough, I rode down the khud from Gulmarg to Tangmarg, where ponies would be left until our return. And it was a relief, after hot noisy Srinagar, to inhale yet another familiar scent, that of pine-needles, and to hear woodmen's saws and the forest birds, especially the golden oriole.

Ann's houseboat had an upper floor that looked top-heavy. We once saw a cat swimming across her canal. At Srinagar Olive had a friend who was quite different to any of the others up at Gulmarg: Mrs Roween, a strange, exceedingly rich, red-lipped, slinky, cocktail-drinking person, an organizer of other people's lives. I recognized that she had 'marvellous furniture' but always felt uneasy in her dimly lit house – *not* a houseboat for some reason – which was full of grand furniture, unlike the rough locally made stuff I was used to at Gulmarg and Gilgit. I see her now as a kind of Circe. All the same, she did give me very nice presents, though usually to please Olive I thought. There were two quiet pale spoilt Roween girls, I believe adopted, called Minny and Mona. 'We're off to see Minnyanmona!' Nanny Spicer would say brightly, because she too was impressed by Mrs Roween. One year at Gulmarg Olive went to a fancy dress dance (were there enough men to go round?) as a Norwegian Hardanger bride, copied from a picture in the *Geographical*

Magazine. It was an exceedingly elaborate dress covered with buttons and braids, which won her the prize. When I was told that it was a present from Mrs Roween I found myself hating it. I made things worse by saying, quite innocently, that the headdress reminded me of Ganesha, the Hindu elephant god.

The earlier summers, when I was aged three and four, included long fishing and shooting treks to Budwan to the north of the Vale and over the Tragbal Pass, where Nanny Spicer and I had to be carried through the snow on coolies' shoulders. Walter was not often at Hut 46a, but when he was with us we usually went to fish at the glorious Ferozepur nullah, which again is always brought back to me by a special smell: freshly caught trout.

We were always going on picnics, even in the rain, and there was plenty of that at Gulmarg. Olive's ciné films also show me, in an oversized topee, hacking away at a golf ball on what was known as the Rabbits' Course. In Gulmarg there was, inevitably, a polo field, but only three and a half chukkas were usual instead of seven because of the altitude. Hari Singh, who had a summer palace at Gulmarg, liked playing polo, and also came to Gulmarg for the skiing. I don't think my parents went to the palace much, even though it was close to our hut. It stood on a hill among pines, hardly visible, like a mysterious Grimms' castle where no children dared venture. Olive and Walter did however go to the one in Srinagar. 'Absolutely lovely carpets,' Olive used to say. She didn't like Hari Singh, because he danced with her too closely. She said he had a 'moon face'. Everyone referred to him as 'Mr A'; this was because of a humiliating court case after he had been blackmailed for being found in bed with a Mrs Robinson in a Paris hotel. His own women were kept in purdah. 'He treated them badly.'

The Club House was the great social centre at Gulmarg, with a membership of four thousand. The ballroom at Nedou's was separated from the hotel by three hundred steps: very trying for children at the time of big parties, such as those organized by Mrs Roween, who would arrive from Srinagar like an apparition out of a whirlwind. I used to be fascinated by the advertisements in the bazaar, for Pond's Cold Cream and Gibbs Dentifrice, shown as fighting 'Giant Decay'. One poster advertised an eye-lotion, with the picture of two huge eyes and the words: 'Whose eyes are these?' After a while I said to Nanny Spicer: 'Whose eyes *are* these?' She thought for a while, then said: 'The Duchess of York's.' Another poster announced: 'Virol. Anaemic girls need it.' When I asked Nanny Spicer why girls not boys became anaemic, all she said, with great finality, was 'Hush.'

For grown-ups at Gulmarg all was enjoyment. 'We played golf madly, we danced madly,' an old friend from those days has said. 'You did absolutely nothing except enjoy yourself. What a life!'

But part of the enjoyment was also the flowers, perhaps the grandest wonder of all, especially the alpines and bulbs. When we arrived in June there were still wild tulips, crocuses and gentians. Later there would be monkshoods, anemones, rock-roses, saxifrages, orchids, thrift, potentillas, columbines, and above all three which were my favourites: androsace, primula denticulata and meconopsis. Now, except in the highest regions, many of these Himalayan flowers are scarce, thanks to heavy grazing.

The night before our group's departure for Gulmarg the rain came down on the houseboat roof like bath taps turned full on. In the morning it was calm again, and we saw through the seraglio frills of our curtains that there was snow quite low on the mountains. Then as we boarded the coach for Gulmarg, we noticed that the locals were dressed for winter.

At last: that poplar avenue, and by daylight. It was still impressive, still beautiful, but I suddenly realized that by turning it into a reality I had killed a dream. We sped along at such an unromantic speed. We stopped at Tangmarg, which was muddy, and as in the past just the staging point before Gulmarg with a bit of a bazaar. An old pi-dog with a fearsomely diseased bottom, making it look like a baboon, followed me around when we halted for tea. Then we began the ascent of the khud and found ourselves in a gradually thickening mist. The pine trunks were like chilly phantoms, hostile. This was not oriole country any more. I even began to dread seeing Gulmarg again. I was convinced that our hut would have been destroyed by the tribesmen in 1947.

By the time we reached the plateau we might have been in a November fog of the densest kind in England. Somehow our bus crept to a hotel, which we found consisted of a series of chalets, each – mercifully – with a stove, already lit. Dimly through the fog outside we could see a bank of dahlias making a pretence of colour. But in spite of the weather, in spite of the cold, I had to start at once on my hunt for Hut 46a. Raúl, evidently alarmed by my obsession, insisted on coming too. We hired ponies – I think even their owners, boys aged about sixteen, thought we were mad. The only directions I could give were that I knew our hut was near the Maharajah's palace.

The cloud lifted slightly, and I saw that we were skirting the golf course. The boys steered us to a tourist office, but it was a useless place; there were no maps or plans of Gulmarg available, because the

Pakistani frontier was so close, 'just over those hills' a man said, pointing at the white blankness. We plunged on, and I was irritated by the way one boy kept clutching at my reins; I might not have done much riding since the age of eight, but I did like to think that being on a Gulmarg pony, however bony, however uncomfortable its saddle, was second nature to me. We met some huddled figures who pointed the way to the Maharajah's palace; Hut 46a meant nothing to them.

And there, on a steep hill among dripping pines and firs, was the silent mysterious palace – once to me the great inaccessible. Now we two scruffy tourists on our miserable little ponies were allowed into its precincts without question.

The palace hardly deserved such a name. It was a jumble of gables, with the usual fretwork and a wooden verandah overlooking the khud (if we could see it). Part of the roof was corrugated iron. A caretaker appeared, and explained that the palace had been looted in 1947. It was a hundred and two years old and was now used as a rest house for government VIPs. But how did the VIPs manage if there was no furniture? Question unanswered. We wandered through the empty rooms, the bedrooms small, the reception rooms panelled in walnut and suitable for grand entertainments. I had a strong and encouraging feeling that people had been happy there, had enjoyed the privacy. We were taken into the pantry and in a cupboard I found five Coalport plates, a Coalport butterdish, a silver-plated pepperpot and a coffeepot that had escaped the looters.

So on with the search for Hut 46a. We called at various derelict ex-Raj houses, all of wood and bark-covered. In one of them – could it have been Joy Latham's, or the Resident's hut? – we chanced upon five shivering woodcutters, who at once began complaining about their low wages. I could just make out some new brick houses on hills which could or could not have been the site of our hut. I was beginning to despair when an old man said he knew exactly where 46a was. The two boys were delighted. Good tips! I felt a terrible need to turn round and escape.

Then, through the mist, it was there before us: a muddy track that had once been our drive leading to a hill, whose shape to me was unmistakable. I hardly needed to look higher. I knew what I would see at the top of that hill, and I was right. Hut 46a was just a jagged pile of ruins. Even the pine trees that I had known had become naked, like fish skeletons. A telegraph pole seemed about to heel over. Among the scant and withered plants where once had been our garden, never up to the standard of the one in Gilgit, I saw something that was at least unexpected: a notice with the – under the circumstances – bizarre words: 'City View Hotel and Restaurant'.

The hut had been burnt. I could still see the sockets of fireplaces, an alcove with shelves. Where my schoolroom had been I stepped in human shit. Then I saw a thing which I think affected me as much as anything in my life.

I have said that Olive died in 1976. She was buried in Cornwall. Before leaving on this journey to India I had, to my amazement, noticed that a tall yellow verbascum was growing in the centre of her grave. It must have been self-sown, even though there had been no other verbascums visible in the churchyard. Now as I navigated the blackened bricks, old tins, bottles and more shit, I found what had been Olive's and Walter's bedroom, and there right in the middle of this disgusting debris another verbascum was growing.

My greatest wish on coming to Gulmarg had been to see not so much the hut but its view, across the khud to the great expanse of the Himalayan range. More especially I wanted to see Nanga Parbat. All that was now denied to me because of the mist and clouds. Then a crow landed on one of the dead trees above me, and began to caw. It was an absurd Gothick climax, and I might almost have laughed.

I could just see the shape of a new house some yards off. Perhaps that was the City View Hotel, but I didn't feel like investigating. So we descended into the 'city', the bazaar. The buildings there were modern, as the old bazaar had been burnt down in 1947.

After a night of restless dreams, at 7 am there was a furious banging on our door. Our neighbour from the next chalet was shouting: 'Quick! Nanga Parbat!' We stumbled out into an almost cloudless morning, and sure enough there was the miraculous vision, not only of the symbolic, lonely mountain, but of the whole line of the lesser Himalayan peaks, still gold from the sunrise. To our right we saw that the so-called Pakistani frontier was only just above our hotel, and that the snowline had nearly reached us. People were crowding on to verandahs, some with fieldglasses, all wrapped in blankets. Nanga Parbat might have had an evil reputation as a place of death, but now it was our Holy Grail. Then, as if the Almighty had said: 'Well, that's enough, you poor old koi-hais, you've seen what you've come to see,' the distant clouds came down and all was blotted out, like a curtain in a theatre. We were left staring at the silly pom-pom dahlias in the hotel garden.

Heartened, or at least reassured, by the sight of Nanga Parbat I determined to visit the City View Hotel. By 8.45 we were off again on our ponies, this time accompanied by Monty and Delphine Flash, who were interested to see Maharajah Hari Singh's palace. Delphine was the sort who could make the sorriest nag into a prancing steed. We (especially Monty) could hardly get our animals to trot, but she made hers canter across the meadows and through the streams. I had forgotten the delight of splashing through a mountain stream on horseback.

After a while we had to part from the Flashes. Delphine outpaced us, and Monty's pony seemed reluctant even to walk. In any case I felt that the City View Hotel was something private.

I could not bear to reenter the ruins of the hut, so Raúl and I rode straight up to the hotel. Then I had another shock. In Walter's albums there had been photographs of interiors of various rooms. Now I saw a few chairs and a table or two rotting on the grass, and I recognized them at once as having been ours. As in the case of Gilgit, furniture had been passed on to each new resident of a house. The proprietor of the City View emerged and offered us coffee. His name was Mohammed Khan. He had a sad, dignified face, which did not brighten when I told him that I had lived here. We sat on the chairs, and he told me that Hut 46a had *not* been burnt down by tribesmen but in a forest fire just over two years before. I felt a great relief on hearing this. At least it had not been destroyed maliciously. Mohammed Khan confirmed that he had been able to rescue some furniture, including these chairs, and that it had mostly dated from the British period.

The City View was a humble building. Two Australians and a French couple were staying in it, all students, all disillusioned by the weather. Heavy cloud was swirling over the khud, and they had missed the 7 am view of Nanga Parbat. The husk of Hut 46a did not make the atmosphere any more cheerful.

The ruins of the room nearest to the hotel I recognized as having been our spare room. Once, when Olive's friend Marion Walker had been staying, I had heard cries and groans coming from it, and had opened the door. Olive and Nanny Spicer were bending over Marion on the bed. 'Get out, Raleigh, get out,' Olive had cried in a way that startled and hurt me. But Marion saw me and smiled, though her face was frightening.

For a long time afterwards I confused this episode with another of Olive's friends dying of appendicitis. She had had an operation on the kitchen table, I always used to be told, but too late. Now, looking back, I realize that Marion must have been suffering from prenatal pains. Whether her baby was eventually born in Hut 46a I cannot now be certain, but the yells of an infant called Vanda did upset our peace for some while during that summer.

The possibility of being afflicted by appendicitis when travelling in some remote part of the world has always haunted me since that story of the death of Olive's friend.

A name suddenly came into my head, as I was remembering poor Marion Walker moaning: Dr Antony Craig-Jones. He was a Captain, rather good-looking in a military way, with a red face ('weak' Olive said), a yellow moustache and yellow eyebrows. He came first to visit Marion and Vanda, and then to take Nanny Spicer out riding. Olive was not particularly keen on this burgeoning love-affair – I suppose it was to do with differences in class, but Nanny was 'far too old' and he was a 'confirmed bachelor'. Anyway, one night Nanny Spicer came into my room in tears because Dr Craig-Jones was being posted to Calcutta. I was sorry for her but I am afraid not especially moved, more annoyed because she kept me awake with her sobbing.

I felt I could give no comfort to the owner of the City View Hotel, and was glad to leave. There was just one place left I was determined to see, and that was the prosaically named Outer Circular Road, which ran, out of sight, below Hut 46a. I used often to ride along there with Multana. Really, it was only a forest bridle path, and in my memory it conjured up more of the real Gulmarg – its silence, its scents, its glimpses through the trees of the silver Ferozepur River and the great plains of Srinagar – than fancy dress parties, Wolf Cub outings and golf lessons.

And yes, the Outer Circular Road was still there. Many pines had been cut down, and the road, although still full of pot-holes, was being turned into what Italians call a strada panoramica. Perhaps if there had been sun it would have had some of its old magic; but I had killed another dream.

End of a dynasty

Hari Singh succeeded his uncle Pratab Singh as Maharajah of Kashmir in 1925. There had been serious rumbles of discontent at the end of Pratab Singh's reign, particularly among the repressed Muslims who formed the majority of the population. A demonstration in the important state-owned silk factory had been especially ominous. The Maharajah had been annoyed when a deputation of Muslims delivered a memorandum to the Viceroy asking for his help in the improvement of their rights.

As an individual Pratab Singh was respected and popular in Kashmir. He was pious and generous with his alms-giving. Unfortunately he was addicted to opium, and therefore found himself signing orders which he afterwards had to countermand. Early in his reign he had virtually been deposed by the British for some alleged flirtations with the Russians. Then for a period the British had been able to bring about some improvements in a country where the conditions of the population were notoriously abject, thanks to the rapacity of previous Maharajahs. In particular there was a reform of land tenure and forced labour was abolished. Hospitals and roads were built. Schools were created, among the most famous being the mission school for boys run by Canon C. E. Tyndale-Biscoe and still in existence. (If I misbehaved, I would be threatened with being sent to the Tyndale-Biscoe school in Srinagar, where I was told dunces were made to sit on parrot perches – quite true, as I have since found out.)

When the Russian 'menace' began to recede after the turn of the century, Pratab Singh was restored to his autocratic powers. The British have since been blamed for not having previously concentrated enough on alleviating the frustration of the Muslims, though in fairness it should also be said that there had been opposition to modern education from Muslim religious leaders.

On the accession of Hari Singh there was great hope for social improvements among educated classes in Kashmir. In a polygamist society the Mr A indiscretion was not of much account. But whether Hari Singh was a weak and selfish character, addicted to 'cheap pleasures', or cultivated, charming and able, depends in part whether you back Muslims or Hindus. The British made him a Major-General and loaded him with decorations. They encouraged his interests in horse racing and breeding. Nevertheless politically they found him far less amenable than his predecessor. He spoke up strongly and quite movingly, for freedom and self-rule in India on behalf of the Princes at the Round Table Conferences in London. He removed some of the privileges of the British Resident in Srinagar, and demanded to have the Political Agency in Gilgit abolished.

But those original golden hopes for the new reign began soon to evaporate, what with Hari Singh's personal extravagances and the patent rottenness of some of his personal advisers. Although the British were now regarded as encouraging Muslim agitation, there was also a general anti-British feeling, encouraged by the example of the Congress movement in the rest of India. The news of Gandhi's renowned salt-march resulted in strikes and demonstrations, and there was a bonfire of foreign cloth in Srinagar's main bazaar. The serious floods of 1929 and 1931 increased the economic discontent. At the same time the Muslim press outside Kashmir began attacking the Maharajah's totally Hindu-dominated regime.

A crucial date for Hari Singh was July 13 1931, when a mob stormed the Central Jail at Srinagar. I remember the repercussions, though not the details, because it happened during my last summer in Gulmarg and a belated birthday party had to be cancelled. Walter had expected to accompany Olive, my brother John and me on the train journey to Bombay, to see us safely on board the P & O liner *Cathay*, but instead had to hurry back to Gilgit.

The riots at Srinagar spread, and twenty-one people died. Hindu shops were looted. A prominent part in creating the unrest had been played by a young Muslim who was to dominate Kashmir politics long after the British had left India: Sheikh Mohammed Abdullah, son of a shawl-maker and who had recently left university in the Punjab. He was at once arrested, and it was then that he gained the nickname of 'the Lion of Kashmir'.

The British insisted on an inquiry, and the Maharajah agreed to set up a commission to investigate questions of constitutional reform and the raising of standards for the Muslims. Sheikh Abdullah was released and a People's Assembly created, although only six per cent of the population were entitled to vote. Among the Muslims in the Assembly Sheikh Abdullah's party was dominant. The press was freed, possibilities for education were improved. Marriage for girls under fourteen was forbidden, Hindu widows were allowed to remarry, the killing of daughters at birth by Rajputs was prohibited. The reduction of the seven-year sentence for killing a cow was however violently resisted by the Dogras.

As a result of the 1931 agitations, the negotiations over the future of the Gilgit Agency changed course, and it was thus that in 1935 the Wazarat – the parts hitherto directly governed by the Kashmir state – was leased to the British for sixty years. Now the British relaxed their pressure on the Maharajah, and he was left free to deal with political agitators as he liked.

Sheikh Abdullah was not a 'communalist', or believer in the political separation of religious groups. 'We must open our doors,' he said in 1938, 'to all such Hindus and Sikhs who like ourselves believe in the freedom of their country from the shackles of an irresponsible ruler.' He visualized a secular, independent Kashmir, headed by a Maharajah as a constitutional monarch. In this he was to some degree influenced by his friend Pandit Nehru, himself of Kashmiri descent. The Sheikh had little sympathy for Jinnah and the Muslim League, who in 1940 saw Kashmir ethnically and geographically as part of their concept of the future Pakistan – the letter k in the word was meant to signify Kashmir (Punjab or Panjab, Kashmir and Baluchistan). There was therefore a split among the Muslims of Kashmir, the more conservative group being attracted towards Jinnah's ideals.

In the Second World War Hari Singh gave as much support as he could to the British. Kashmiri troops fought with distinction in East Africa, also in Italy. During this period there was, naturally enough, even less interference in Kashmiri affairs by the British-Indian Government.

By 1946, with the approach of Independence, there was a change of heart as far as Sheikh Abdullah's view of the Dogra dynasty was concerned. He was foremost in the 'Quit Kashmir' campaign against the Maharajah, and as a result was sentenced to a fine and nine years imprisonment. Other colleagues and Muslim leaders were also arrested. He was freed however just over a year later, by which time he found himself in a very different political world: partition of British India had already occurred, and the Hindu Maharajah of Kashmir had not yet decided whether to turn towards India or Pakistan. To Jinnah the release of Sheikh Abdullah, who was known to favour India, was sinister, when other pro-Pakistan Muslims were still in jail.

Every official account of those crucial months in Kashmir between June and November 1947 is unclear and biased. It seems probable that at first Hari Singh really hoped that he might emerge as a ruler of an independent state: a strategically placed buffer, like Nepal or Bhutan, with all the advantages. It has even been suggested that a guru told him that one day he would rule from Lahore like a new Ranjit Singh. Certainly there were advisers, such as his Prime Minister, who thought he would have a better chance of survival if he joined Pakistan. The evidence on the whole appears to be that he inclined towards India; either the same guru or another seems to have urged this, and there were strong rumours that he had agreed with Nehru that he would join India at the right moment. But both Mountbatten and Gandhi visited Hari Singh, and each found him evasive, as did Lord Ismay. It was a case of Hamlet.

According to the Indian Independence Act of 1947 the rulers of the Princely States had a legal right to opt for either Pakistan or India. It was made obvious that they could expect no further assistance from the British: a blatant repudiation of previous guarantees. At the time of the lapse of paramountcy of the British Crown, there were 562 Princely States, large and small, but in nearly every case there was very little option for the Princes, who were now faced with losing handsome stipends.

Poonch province in Kashmir had been an important recruiting ground during the Second World War. Now some 40,000 ex-servicemen became the nucleus of a 'Free Kashmir' movement. Arms were reaching them from Pathan workshops in the North-West Frontier. There were scattered revolts in Poonch, which always had had a reputation for being independently-minded, and the Kashmir government responded with the burning of some villages. Then came the even more serious incursions by Hindus and Sikhs into Jammu province, when at least 200,000 Muslims were massacred or died; in Pakistan it was and is still claimed that this atrocity was condoned by the Maharajah. At the same time Muslims were being murdered in horrible circumstances in Delhi. Immediately a jehad was proclaimed in the North-West Frontier and on October 19 1947 some 900 Mahsud tribesmen left for Kashmir. Within three days they had been joined by many other Pathans: Afridis, Swatis, Mohmands, Wazirs. No doubt the new Pakistan government was powerless to prevent this frenzied march of hate. Perhaps it also feared that to oppose the Pathans might lead to secession. Even so it must to some extent have abetted the invasion.

The Kashmiri border town of Muzaffarabad was sacked. As the tribesmen advanced, they found it difficult to distinguish between Hindu, Muslim or Christian: villagers were slaughtered indiscriminately. They reached Baramulla, a few miles from Gulmarg and thirty-five miles from Srinagar. This was the scene of the greatest terror. A convent was burnt down, and nuns and Europeans were killed. Perhaps 3,000 people died altogether.

The invaders lost four valuable days looting and murdering at Baramulla. Meanwhile the Maharajah and his family, on the advice of a delegate from the Indian Government, fled from Srinagar, and on October 2 Hari Singh signed the Instrument of Accession to India. He really had little option. The Indians were ready with troops – a fact which has always seemed suspicious to Pakistan. On the next day an airlift began from Delhi to Srinagar. The tribesmen were already near the outskirts of Srinagar.

When Mountbatten, Governor-General of India now instead of Viceroy, accepted the Instrument of Accession, he wrote a personal letter to Hari Singh insisting 'that as soon as law and order have been restored in Kashmir and her soil cleared of the invader the question of the State's accession should be settled by reference to the people.' But, to this day (1987), there has been no reference to the people on that matter, no plebiscite or referendum.

The situation for the British was made urgent because of the number of Europeans still living in Srinagar, and complicated because British officers were still at least nominally commanding both the Indian and Pakistani armies. For this latter reason outright war was averted, though localized fighting continued until the cease-fire of December 1948, cutting the old Kashmir into two zones: the Gilgit Agency, Skardu, Poonch and some western strips of territories being held by Pakistan. On a spectacular occasion Gilgit Scouts had reached one of the main entrances to the Vale of Kashmir, but had been beaten back as a result of the Indians' feat of bringing tanks to a height of 10,000 feet. On March 5 1948 Sheikh Abdullah became Prime Minister of an interim government.

After the cease-fire (to last until the three weeks' war of 1965) Hari Singh went into voluntary exile, and his son Karan Singh became Regent while the sore question of Kashmir was placed before the Security Council of the United Nations. Dogra rule was formally ended by the Kashmir Constituent Assembly in October 1951. In an election, hardly 'free', Sheikh Abdullah's party won all the seats. By that time Delhi saw with some dismay that the Lion of Kashmir was moving away from his original pro-Indian attitude . . .

We were recovering from a day of Gulmarg saddle when there was a knock on our chalet door. An impeccable Indian Captain was there, inviting us to a party in the mess of the 2nd Maratha Light Infantry.

About twelve of our group had had those invitations, plus Raúl, who found himself considered as part of the old 8th Punjab Regiment. It was starlight when we arrived, the sky having completely cleared, and we were greeted by Gurkhas playing Scottish bagpipes. The party was extremely elegant, with curry puffs and an everflowing supply of very large whiskies and water. Wives were present, all superbly dressed, and I heard from one how the fire at the City View Hotel had been caused by an electrical fault, and what a devastating loss it had been to the owner. She spoke of her escape by train from Lahore in 1947, and how like Mrs Permain at Simla she had hidden under the seat when other Hindus were being murdered. Her brother-in-law had been shot dead on a plane at about the same time, for possessing a revolver.

The guests of honour in our group were inescapably Brigadier and Mrs Baines; he, aged eighty-four, had been in the 2nd Gurkhas, and she had been born at Gulmarg. The Brigadier therefore made a speech of thanks, and our host General Mehta replied, welcoming us each by name in turn, including the mysterious Mr Raúl Balín. He spoke of India's debt to the British, of past differences now healed, of the imperishable bond . . . Suddenly there was a great sob, and Mrs Baines began to weep.

Afterwards an orderly brought round presents of a little head and shoulders effigy of Kali-Panchwin, a martial god who was also a god of anger. Then we went out on to the by now moonlit verandah, and the Gurkhas played 'The British Grenadiers' and 'Bluebells of Scotland'. I could see, like woodcuts in the stark cold night, the hills and forests of Gulmarg where I used to ride with Multana.

The next day I was invited to tea by Benjie Nedou, grandson of the original Nedou, an Austrian, who had built the hotel where sometimes my family used to stay. Benjie's grandmother had been Scots, but his father had married a Kashmiri. His sister was married to Sheikh Abdullah. He himself had been educated at Charterhouse, and now he ran the new big hotel at Gulmarg, the Highland Park.

In 1947, he said, it had been the caretakers not the tribesmen who had looted the British homes, and they had mostly stolen blankets, curtains and tea-cosies (to wear as hats). These things had been taken to be sold in Peshawar. He did not believe the story I had heard (from a good source) about the ransacking of the English church. Gulmarg had died a sudden death then, and had been closed to the outside world for five years.

The reason why the Maharajah's palace was hidden away among trees was because of women having been kept in purdah. It was an impractical building, difficult to heat. We spoke of Colonel Phillimore, famous because of *The Survey of India*, and whose large hut with bay windows I had been to see. Colonel Phillimore had been 'tough as old boots', the first Englishman to come to live in Gulmarg, and the last to go. Right until his death in 1964 aged ninety-two he had been 'fit as a fiddle', always 'prancing up mountains'. On his eightieth birthday he had climbed Mount Apawhat. Where I had seen monkeys digging up newly planted potatoes he had had a magnificent garden, entirely of wild Kashmir plants. After his death his wife had had to be sent home to England because she was 'off her rocker'.

We then spoke of other colonels, boarding-houses, riding-schools, golf and of course picnics.

Regimental murders

And now I must write of the murders of two of Walter's brother officers in the 5/8th. One I have already mentioned early on, that of Major Billy Haycraft at Nowshera in April 1929. The other was of Captain Peter McClenaghan, husband of Olive's friend Violet McClenaghan, and this happened at Lahore in December 1930. Both men were killed by Indian soldiers, and their deaths in different ways had a considerable effect on me.

I see now why I was hustled up to Gulmarg so soon after Billy Haycraft's murder, particularly as I have now – all these years later – learnt that the mysterious disappearance of the two Pemberton children, à la *Mary Rose*, happened only a few days after that event. It was the year my parents acquired Hut 46a, before Walter took up his posting to Gilgit.

Billy Haycraft was slightly older than Walter. In 1915 he was already in Mesopotamia with the battalion, then known as the 93rd Burma Infantry, at the time that Walter arrived there at the age of twenty-one. They were in the relief force when Townshend was besieged at Kut, and in the subsequent retreat. Billy was wounded at the battle of Beit Aeissa, and was awarded the Military Cross. The horrors of that campaign are almost blandly described in the battalion's official history, although the writer's nausea in recollection sometimes breaks through. Sodden trenches in winter, parching thirst in summer, lack of cover from snipers and artillery fire, cholera, jaundice, dysentery, scandalous hospital arrangements, lice, flies, sandflies: all these make their brief appearances in the narrative. 'Water of a slimy green colour was obtained from the wells, which were afterwards found to be full of corpses. However most men's stomachs were tin-lined in those days.' The stigma of defeat and the ensuing depression were the worst aspects of the campaign. Lieutenant Trevelyan received a mention in despatches and became adjutant of the battalion. Soon afterwards he was promoted to Captain. When Townshend capitulated to the Turks on April 29 1916, the fighting strength of the 93rd had been temporarily reduced from 735 to 96.

In Walter's lifetime I knew almost nothing of his experiences in Mesopotamia. He never wanted to speak of them, and I never asked about them. Now my lack of interest makes me feel a little ashamed, and I also feel humbled. But my ignorance was also to do with the lack of communication between us, and I do not think that this was altogether my fault.

Percy McClenaghan makes his appearance in the battalion history of the Middle Eastern Campaign as a company commander at the Battle of Brown Hill near Samaria in Palestine. At that time Colonel W. H. (Rufus) Ralston, seconded from the 47th Sikhs, was in command. Percy won his MC there, Billy a bar to his; I am not sure whether Rufus, who was to play such an important part in the lives of our family, got his DSO or his MC then or earlier on in France, where he had been wounded three times; he was also mentioned in despatches five times. The battalion arrived in Damascus two days after the Armistice. 'The rain ceased at daybreak, and it was a cold, crisp morning, whilst Mount Hermon, to our left, had taken on its first covering of snow during the night.'

The total deaths in the battalion whilst in Mesopotamia and Palestine had been 235, including twelve British and nine Indian officers. Seventeen British and twenty-seven Indian officers had been wounded.

By April 1921, when Walter and Olive were married in Rangoon Cathedral, the 93rd was back in Burma still under the command of Rufus. It reached Nowshera in 1926, by which time it was known as the 5th (Burma) Battalion of the 8th Punjab Regiment. Rufus was also in Nowshera then, but in command of the 11th Sikhs, though at the time of Billy's death he was stationed at Poona, some 1,200 miles away – an important detail to which I shall later have to refer.

My nanny had told me that Billy Haycraft had 'gone to heaven', but did not say why. The idea of this rather gruff and to me hazy character floating around up there was intriguing, like Father Christmas coming down chimneys with stockings of toys. Twice I asked Olive why Major Haycraft had left us. The first time she didn't answer, but the next time she was angry and said: 'I want you to promise never to mention that name again.'

As I now know, Billy was commanding the Sikh company. A bugler in it had applied to join a training cadre, which would have meant his eventual promotion. Both Billy and the adjutant turned this down. Some months later Billy took the company down to the shooting range. The bugler drew his ammunition, then swung round and shot Billy dead. He was immediately overpowered and taken to Nowshera jail. At the court martial it had to be decided whether he should be hanged or shot. It was decided that he should be shot. The bugler said that his only regret was that he had not shot the bloody adjutant as well. It was a matter of honour.

Billy Haycraft's murder was quickly followed by half a dozen others, all apparently unconnected, in different parts of India. These included a garrison engineer who was shot in his sleep on the North-West Frontier, and both the Inspector-Generals of Police and Prisons for Bengal. Bombs were thrown in the Legislative Assembly in New Delhi, and in December 1929 a bomb exploded under the Viceroy's train. The Governor of the Punjab, Sir Geoffrey de Montmorency, was shot at and wounded in Lahore. Memories of the murders of British civilians leading up to the Amritsar massacre of 1919, and of the Moplah rebellion of 1921, the most serious since the great Mutiny of 1857, were still vivid for the British, and there was now a fear of a general uprising. Perhaps most worrying of all was the recent murder of a junior superintendent of police in the so-called Lahore Conspiracy Case, in revenge for the death of a Congress party leader, Lala Rajpat Rai, who had been beaten by police when leading a procession. Many Europeans at Nowshera and Lahore slept with revolvers under their pillows.

I know now that the years 1929 and 1930 were crucial in the independence movement, especially in the attitude of Gandhi. It was also the time of the great Depression, which hit the Indian peasant. Following his salt march Gandhi and several hundred others, including Jawaharlal Nehru, were arrested. In May 1930 there was the horrific incident at the Dharasana Salt Works, when an unarmed crowd of peaceful Gandhian demonstrators were methodically beaten down by the waiting Indian police under the command of six British officers.

The news of the death of Percy McClenaghan had a much more upsetting effect on me than that of Billy Haycraft. It was a hard blow for my parents, since our families used to go up to Gulmarg together in the summer, as Walter's albums show. Percy was killed whilst we were in Gilgit, so the news took a while to reach us. Nanny Spicer came rushing into my room to tell me. 'I can't believe it! I can't believe it!' This was the first time that I had heard of somebody dying whom I had known fairly well, and Nanny's behaviour made the situation all the more real. That evening she even cried a little, but I think it was because Olive was annoyed with her for telling me.

Percy had been killed by a Gujar Sikh sepoy whilst conducting a physical training course. Again it had been due to revenge, or a slight on the sepoy's honour. He had been merely standing by 'supervising some beam work', so ran a report.

By chance, forty-five years after that affair I ran into a General who had been adjutant when it happened. We were at a party. 'Yes,' he told me, 'I took a pot-shot at McClenaghan's murderer myself. Got him in the bottom.' Then a crowd of friends engulfed the General, and I heard no more, on that occasion.

Could this mean that he had taken a pot shot when the sepoy was facing the firing squad? Such a thing seemed outrageous . . .

But it wasn't at all like that. This is what he later told me:

As adjutant of the training battalion at Lahore, I was responsible for all the recruits who came in. I had a group of young instructors, among whom there was this brilliant young sepoy who had suggested that he might be promoted to lance-corporal. For some reason we decided not to promote him. He made the most frightful fuss. Next morning the training battalion went on parade, and when I arrived I found everything completely chaotic. I was told that the young sepoy had shot dead an Indian officer and Percy McClenaghan. He was now shooting at all and sundry. So I had a crack at him at once, and luckily got him in the bottom. The sepoy just leant over his rifle and blew his own head off. Saved an awful lot of trouble, because it meant no court martial. Percy had nothing to do with it. The sepoy had been out to get his own platoon commander. There was a court of enquiry of course. The man had simply run amok.

Three times I had to deal with cases like that. Once in Persia a Mohammedan went on leave and came back wearing a beard, without permission. This beard made him into a holy man, and he became a bit of a nuisance. Then he too ran amok – shot an Indian officer. I, as colonel, was summoned, and was told that the man was hiding in a slit trench. I told him to come out at once. He came out quietly with his rifle. It was lucky he didn't shoot me too, he simply said he had had enough of shooting people.

When a British officer died suddenly in India, it could be a desperate situation for the widow, since there was no immediate official provision for her. Usually she had to clear out of her bungalow at once, to make way for her husband's replacement, and within a matter even of three or four weeks she would have to take the boat home. A subscription would often have to be raised in the mess in order to help her expenses. In Violet McClenaghan's case officers also volunteered to help with the packing. She was not well pleased, when she reached England, to find that plates had just been 'shoved' into packing cases without newspaper wrapping.

Early marriages were also discouraged. There was no marriage allowance until you were twenty-six. Colonels kept a watch on the love lives of their junior officers. It was considered very bad form to have an affair with the wife of someone in your own unit. Members of regiments from Britain which were not part of the Indian Army considered themselves a caste apart. When Violet McClenaghan's sister arrived in India and an officer of the Rifle Brigade fell for her, the Colonel intervened and told him that it was not done for a Rifle officer to marry someone connected with the Indian Army.

As has been remarked so often in books on British India, those girls who arrived from home were known as the Fishing Fleet. They were like Elizabeth in Orwell's *Burmese Days*, looking forward to the clubs with punkahs flapping and barefooted white-turbaned boys reverently salaaming, and above all to bronzed Englishmen with clipped moustaches playing polo on the maidan. If they were not married or engaged by the time they returned, they were called the Returned Empties. I had a godmother who was perhaps not the marrying type, and who had genuinely come to India to visit her brother and my parents, and to see the country. She was annoyed when she had a proposal from a 'pipsqueak' within two weeks of her arrival. 'I had hardly noticed him,' she said to me. She turned him down, and the next week he proposed to somebody else. 'Then I had another proposal, and was jilted. It was such a bore.' She met somebody called Rob in the Poona Horse whom she rather liked. Olive one day found her in deep contemplation in our garden at Lahore, and asked her what was wrong. 'Rob has just proposed to me,' she said, 'and I'm weighing up the pros and cons.' Olive always thought that remark extraordinary. However my godmother 'left it open', and on her way home decided against. Many years later I questioned her about this romance. 'Rob pursued me quite hard,' she said, 'and I took pity on him because he kept failing his exams. I suppose I was twenty-four, and he was ten years older. He had a way of saying "When I was young", and that put me off.'

'I sincerely hope that Bill has at last got India out of his system,' said one of the bossier memsahibs in our group as we left Gulmarg.

Poor Bill, he was forced at this stage to return to England with some of the others – anyhow it was Mrs Bill who was paying for his trip. The rest of us stayed on for our 'optional' week, being paddled around in shikaras or making expeditions to the mountains. The Orgills, Raúl and I were now in a new Wangnoo houseboat, the 'Iraq', and our host was a glamorous Omar Sharif character called Mohammed. The fringe, or scarf, of poplars and willows on the far side of the lake had turned a pale yellow. The weather was warm again, due – Mohammed said – to people having gone up to a temple to pray for the rain to stop, on account of the rice crop in the process of being cut. Kingfishers and wagtails were surprisingly tame, paradise fly-catchers flitted past with long tails like ribbons. There were moorhens and dabchicks. Mr Marvellous brought cosmos and perhaps a late lotus, Mr Delicious brought macaroons, Mr Melody played 'gazals'. Water-skiing would have been a disturbance, but for the fun of seeing nymphs doing it in flowing crimson saris. In the evenings the houseboat chintz was flung aside and barefoot tradesmen would leap in hoping to sell us turquoises, shawls or sables. 'I don't think I can stand the strain much longer,' Douglas Orgill said.

Not everybody was enjoying this idyll though. Tensions were growing on the houseboat 'Monarch', which two elderly ladies shared with the Flashes. One of these ladies, the more feminine Kitty, was deaf, and the other, Peggy, was a compulsive raconteur. Peggy complained that Delphine avoided her, and both said that Monty asked too many personal question like 'How old are you?' and 'What is your income?' Because the Flashes joined us on journeys that would have been too arduous for the other two, Peggy said she had been 'shelved'. 'Too absurd for women like you to act like schoolgirls,' Monty had said, which did not help much.

Douglas felt that we were in the right setting for a *Death on the Nile*-type murder. I had already known that living in one of the world's greatest beauty spots did not necessarily mean sweetness and light. Only the year before I had heard how, on this very lake, two literary editors from London had battled for the favours of one of their girl friends. 'It must have been sheer Grand Guignol,' a friend of theirs had said to me with glee...

Mohammed, on learning that I was interested in buying an old Kashmiri rug, said he would take Raúl and me to just the place in Srinagar. In due course we followed him up a staircase, dingy enough to make us feel hopeful about bargains. But as soon as we reached the top we realized that we had made a mistake. We found ourselves in an Arabian Nights hall, full of brass trays, cushions and divans.

I had not revealed to Mohammed how much I had wanted to pay for a rug – actually I had set aside a hundred pounds. After we had been settled and offered tea and pink cakes, perhaps thirty carpets were unrolled for us, one after the other. The starting price was fifteen hundred pounds. Soon we had reached two thousand, then three, then four. Still we did not appear to be satisfied. Many of these rugs were indeed beautiful; they had come from Maharajahs' palaces, we were told. One after another glorious ruby reds, emerald greens, fantastic indigo and saffron designs, peacocks, crouching tigers, startled deer were unrolled for us. The last rug was a tree of life, superb, rather William Morris in design. It cost six thousand eight hundred pounds. Our appreciation of it was noted. 'Rather a lot of money?' I ventured. 'How much will you give for it then?' 'Not as much as that.' 'Doesn't matter, doesn't matter. You send cheque from London. What you want to pay?' The men went to look for more rugs.

We had a quick consultation. How to escape? The only thing, I decided, was to say that we had set our hearts on the most expensive rug, and would have to think it over. Nearly every day thereafter we had a visitor asking if we had made our minds up.

There was a contrast to this experience when on a walk near the mooring place of the 'Iraq' we met a child who invited us to his father's house. He said that his name was Zulfikar Ali. It was a one-roomed house with an earth floor, and the father made papier-mâché boxes. In a corner the sick mother lay on a bed, staring at us with eyes like a frightened squirrel. We were shown her medical report, which mentioned headaches and vomiting. The hospital said nothing more could be done for her, and she had had to be sent home. The previous night there had been a party for her return. She was aged twenty-five, and already had had five daughters and this one son, aged ten.

Mice darted across the floor, and we noticed that because of them food had to be hung from the rafters. There were pictures of Baghdad, Zulfikar Ali's father and Bhutto – of course, *Zulfikar Ali* Bhutto! The boxes were pathetically cheap, so we bought several, mostly with little red foxes painted on them. We were asked not to tell Mohammed about our purchases in case he asked for a cut.

We didn't spend much time in Srinagar itself, though we paid the obligatory visit to the emporium known as 'Suffering Moses', after its founder Suffdur Mogul and which had been in existence in Raj days, at least since 1900. We also went to look at what has been claimed by some cranks as the real tomb of Jesus, and on the way there we also underwent Naipaul's 'overwhelming' impression of muddiness in the slatternly, tumbledown medieval city. How did Jesus get to Srinagar, you may well ask? Even if he did survive the Cross, it seems unlikely that he would have been so cowardly as to have fled so many thousands of miles from Palestine; and on reaching Kashmir not to have attempted to spread the Gospel. Anyway, there was a complete lack of any feeling of 'presence' in that banal, dismal place. We were made to circumnavigate a plain stone sarcophagus, apparently for a giant, and we were shown a crudely carved foot-mark, again supposedly of Jesus. Promoters of this cult should go on an Exploitation Course at Fátima or Lourdes.

It was more amusing to be told that all Kashmiri boatmen are de-scended from Noah (but aren't we all?). With the Orgills and the Flashes we paddled off in a procession of shikaras to Lake Anwar, for the first of various wonderful picnics in good Kashmir-Raj tradition. Out of the haze low punts emerged so laden with sheaves of rice they seemed bound to sink. We passed along canals and waterways lined with willows, exotic versions of a Sisley or Pissarro landscape. In some places the water chestnuts were so dense we could hardly push our way through. Typically, Monty, when all was settled on one side of a river, our picnic laid out by the servants, announced grandly: 'I think we'd be much better off on the other side.' So everything had to be packed up again, and we had to be ferried across.

Then to Pahalgam, past the saffron fields, and past Anantnag, where I found there were still as in my memory holy fish in a holy well, still guarded by a holy man with a white-smeared face and a hennaed beard. ('We prefer to do our sight-seeing in silence,' Monty firmly told an annoying guide.) Pahalgam was where pilgrims as-sembled for the climb to the cave of Amarnath, abode of Lord Shiva. It was clear that Delphine was casting her eye on the unusually frisky ponies for hire, but we outmanoeuvred her and settled on an appar-ently unfrequented walk along the mountain stream. We found some outsize mushrooms, and were appalled – except for Monty, who took it calmly – when Delphine ate some of them raw.

Sonamarg, nearly 9,000 feet up, was the nearest I could get to the dream landscape of that childhood trek to Gilgit, given the by now uncertain weather and the prevalence of military zones. The autumn shadows and colours, the exhilaration of the air, the snow among the pines where there were bear droppings, the scent of resin from sawn wood, even red-billed choughs; all these brought back strongly my first journey from Srinagar in September 1929. I felt that coming to Sonamarg had made the whole trip worthwhile. We spent the night in a hideously chilly rest-house. Monty had discarded his red hat for a white fur one, Cossack style, but was no more successful with his pony than he had been at Gulmarg. Delphine of course was up and away at once, reaching the local glacier before any of us. But then we males did not want to be castrated by the saddles, and it was Margaret's first time on ponyback. Dear old Douglas, he was not built to be an equestrian either. Monty's pony, Bulbul, kept wanting to go home and turning his back on us.

At night Mohammed made a bonfire, and Delphine insisted that we all danced round it – including Mohammed – while she sang children's rhymes. But my most enduring memory of Sonamarg will always be seeing Monty and Delphine next day, arms round one another in the early morning sun, watching the clouds drift up the valley to the snow peaks above the dark green forests.

Rufus

I only found out after the war, in 1949.

My parents were worrying about John's future. He was twenty-one, just finished with National Service, and could not bear the thought of working in London. He only wanted to be a farmer, but Walter and Olive could not possibly set him up with a farm. Indeed they were in a financial crisis. Walter was not well, with a virus disease that affected his sense of balance; the house in Essex was too large, and they were struggling with a hardly economic market garden that Olive had originally started as her war effort. I had recently joined a publishing firm, and used to be irked by Walter telling me that I was now the rich one of the family, at a salary of £300 a year. I did however take an author to an expense account lunch at Prunier's, once Olive's favourite restaurant, and foolishly thought she might be pleased at hearing what we had had to eat. She burst into tears and said things that made me feel I was gloating over their new poverty. I found out afterwards that the day before she had sold her mink coat to help over the mortgage.

When, eventually, we again discussed the problem of John, I suggested that perhaps he ought to emigrate, to Australia or New Zealand. The idea seemed to sink in. Then I had a brainwave. Why not Southern Rhodesia? Rufus Ralston was there. He had been Walter's Colonel and was my godfather. I knew he was well off and influential in that country, having been Minister of Defence and Air at the end of the war. There was no reaction. I became annoyed by their obtuseness, and kept hammering away with Rufus's name.

Nanny Spicer had meanwhile returned to her native Liverpool, where she had a job as a housekeeper to a widower, whom – she had confided to me in a letter – she was plotting to marry. I made my annual journey to see her, and we met as usual at the Adelphi Hotel. I told her about what I thought was a brilliant proposal, that John should go out to Rufus Ralston. By her attitude I realized that she disapproved of Rufus. 'You know,' she said, 'Captain Trevelyan should never have left us alone with that man when we went fishing at Budwan. Your mother thought I didn't know, but I did.' This seemed like an old woman's tittle-tattle, and I changed the subject.

At home again I brought up Rufus. I saw Olive give Walter a peculiar look. She got up and left the room. Walter lit his pipe, and told me to sit. I thought I was in for what at my prep school we called a pi-jaw: perhaps about the desert boots which I had brought back from the Army and Italy and he disliked, or my speaking in what he thought was too exaggerated a manner, or – much more hurtful – making me put down my mongrel Bobby which I had also brought from Italy. But it was to tell me to shut up about Rufus. Then, quite flatly, he told me something for which I suppose I should have been prepared after seeing Nanny Spicer. He said that in the 1920s Rufus had been in love with Olive. 'I had to go and speak to him. He had the cheek to say that it was up to Olive to make the choice between us.' Apparently Olive had decided that a broken marriage was disastrous for a child, and it was therefore because of me that she had not left Walter. I of course at once realized that she would have been influenced by Walter having had a miserable childhood on account of his own parents being divorced. All the same, I was astounded. I had never doubted Olive's total affection for Walter. It was true that we often teased her about George Clark, her 'admirer' from Gilgit days, but that was always a joke, in the same way as we had laughed about an old widower known to us as Flash Alf who kept calling on her unexpectedly whilst Walter was away during the war. 'It was when Olive became pregnant with John,' Walter said, 'that Rufus realized he had no hope and decided to leave the Army. He had come into some money I believe, so went to Southern Rhodesia.'

Over the next years more fragments of the story emerged, but mainly from Olive herself. It had been another family joke that when Walter had come on leave in 1920, before joining the battalion in Burma, he was out to find a wife, and Olive had been one of three possibilities. Walter had tossed for which girl to take out; Olive had won, and he had proposed to her in a taxi going round Trafalgar Square that evening. She had been considered a good catch, her father not yet having ruined himself, and she had had several proposals before, which had made people say she was 'fast'. All those parties we used to hear about, all those extravagant dresses (newspapers reported that she had spent the then ludicrous sum of a hundred pounds on a dress for Ascot) – it was surprising that she had thrown it all up for the jungles of Burma. 'I had to get away from my mother,' she said to me. 'She was such a snob, trying to make me meet the right young men. Besides, I thought Walter very good-looking.'

So Walter and Olive were married in Rangoon on April 6 1921. Rufus was still acting Colonel of the battalion, and was aged thirty-eight. She was twenty-one and Walter twenty-seven. When Rufus saw her coming down the stairs at the wedding reception, he immediately fell in love.

Olive at first had no inkling of this. After a year Rufus could not endure having her in his sight, so he took the opportunity of posting Walter to the Andaman Islands, where the battalion had to keep a company for garrisoning the penal settlement. Thus it was that in July 1923, at Port Blair in the Andaman Islands, I was born.

Early in 1924 Walter again had home leave. Whilst we were with my grandparents near Chester, Rufus suddenly turned up. He was immediately invited to come fishing with my grandfather, Walter and Olive on the island of Skye. It was at Skye that Rufus told Olive that he loved her. Olive then realized that she loved him too.

Judging from Walter's and Nanny's albums this must have been kept secret for about two years. There are so many photographs of Rufus on what look like blissful holidays in the mountains around Gulmarg, often with me and Nanny there too. I find it really extraordinary now if Walter did not have some suspicions. Rufus even gave Olive a diamond and sapphire ring (which, so she was to tell me, she lost down the plug-hole of a wash-basin). As for me, I have only a hazy memory of him then, as a pleasant adjunct to our picnics. Oddly enough, Rufus and Walter looked rather alike. Both had ginger hair, though Rufus was not bald on top, and both had military moustaches. They were about the same height. 'Rufus made me spark,' Olive said. He was more cosmopolitan; although Scottish, he had been brought up in France.

Then came the Budwan trip in 1926. Walter photographed Olive, Rufus, Nanny and me, all smiling and happy, on the rest-house steps. After that he disappeared to look for markhor.

The great confrontation would have been in Nowshera, where Rufus was by now commanding the 5/11th Sikhs. In April the following year Walter had home leave, taking Olive and me with him. By the autumn Olive was pregnant, and John was born in Srinagar in June 1928. The 5/11th had been sent to Poona. In 1930 Rufus retired.

'I cried a lot,' Olive said about her parting from Rufus. 'Walter and I had been perfectly happy together. I couldn't bear the thought of his being left alone. Then there was you. But I did love Rufus.'

Rufus invested the money he had inherited in a small gold-mine in Rhodesia. It did quite well for a while, then 'fizzled out'. He did not marry. Before the outbreak of the Second World War he visited London, and Walter gave permission to Olive to see him. She knew then that she still loved him, and did something that was fairly spectacular for those days: she flew to Paris for the day, unknown to Walter, to get her elder sister's advice on what to do. Her sister told her that she ought not to leave Walter, who in any case had just retired from the Army prematurely at Olive's own insistence. The argument about children being upset by a broken marriage could still apply, at least as far as John was concerned, as he was ten.

In 1953 Walter died in Cornwall after some weeks' illness, when he was fifty-nine. Olive was near a breakdown, and it was my job to open letters of condolence. A cable arrived from Rufus. I showed it to her, and by the way she just said 'Oh dear' I knew that for the first time she understood that she was now free. I sent her off to her sister, who was in Madrid. Olive's letters always had an inconsequential, even naïve quality. In one of them she wrote about some Spanish relative's marriage, and then in the next sentence mentioned Rufus. I guessed what lay ahead.

Our solicitor in London had warned me that Olive would be extremely hard up after my father's death. She might not be able to afford a car. But she came back from Madrid, not looking like a distraught widow but radiant. What she had to say was no surprise either to me or John. Rufus was now seventy, and he had suggested that they should get married as soon as possible.

She married him five months after Walter's death. I think local people in Cornwall were shocked, but John and I were delighted for her (and I must admit relieved for those financial reasons). She was to claim that in their ten years of marriage she and Rufus had never had the proverbial cross word, and it could have been true. Given the inevitable unease one feels at the beginning when confronted with a step-parent who is also in effect a stranger, I felt I had more interests in common with Rufus than with Walter. To me, though, he always had the stamp of the Army. He had been living so simply hitherto, even using whisky packing cases for tables, that everyone in Rhodesia thought he must have married a millionairess. Olive's talents for interior and garden design – the cherry-red drawing-room curtains, the satinwood furniture brought out from England, the long avenue of different coloured bougainvillaeas – were quite a sensation. Once again she was in a remote place, miles from the nearest neighbour and with huge views, but this time in luxury. Rufus let her do whatever she wanted. He gave her more diamonds and sapphires, as well as jewellery specially designed in Paris. Walter had liked staying at home, but Rufus enjoyed travelling. 'Your father had humility, but not so much humour and breadth as Rufus,' someone who knew them all said to me. Every year Rufus and Olive motored around France, Spain or the British Isles. John, who had been working as little more than a farm labourer in Devon, came out to Rhodesia with his wife and child and was settled as a manager on an estate.

In 1963, when he was nearly eighty, Rufus died. He had gone out at night in his pyjamas to call in the dogs which were barking at some animal in a tree, and had caught pneumonia. After a few years Olive returned to Cornwall, and life in a small cottage, plunging into community work and playing her bridge – I don't think she ever spent a single day 'doing nothing'.

The Haycraft murder again

As I have said, Billy Haycraft was shot at Nowshera in April 1929. It was when John left for Rhodesia that Walter's albums were given to me. In one of them I saw a photograph with the title 'The Haycrafts' – Billy tall with a topee, but in civilian clothes with baggy trousers, and his wife much smaller and in a cloche hat and a low-waisted dress, with pointed shoes.

I showed this picture to Sylvia May King, aunt of the writer Francis King and who I knew had some family connection with the Haycrafts. 'Are these your relations?' I asked. 'Yes,' Sylvia May replied, 'they are my sister and brother-in-law.' She immediately became gloomy, which surprised me a little, seeing that Billy had been dead some thirty years. But then Sylvia May was always eccentric.

I began to realize that Sylvia May was behaving differently to me whenever we met, and I became worried. Eventually I decided to ask Francis's sister what was wrong. 'Don't you know?' she said. 'She thinks that it was the fault of the Colonel, and that *he* should have been shot. She also thinks the Colonel was either your father or step-father.'

At least I could say that Walter, although a Major when he left the Army for good, had only been a Captain, and therefore not a battalion commander, at Nowshera in that fatal year of 1929. I could not, however, at that particular moment, answer for Rufus's position, although I did indeed know that he had been a Colonel.

The years passed. After Rufus's death, Olive on a brief visit to England suggested that she and I might go somewhere together quietly for Easter, and we decided on Aldeburgh in Suffolk. Whilst we were there, I told her about Sylvia May's suspicions, and at once Olive flared up angrily. It was totally absurd. Rufus had left the 5/8th Punjab long before, and in 1929 was stationed far away with the 5/11th Sikhs at Poona. She and another woman had actually gone to break the news to Mrs Haycraft (whose Christian name was also Olive) up in the hill station of Murree.

It had been a long hot journey. 'Olive Haycraft was always very highly strung, so we decided to have a doctor waiting. But we never even had to open our mouths. The moment she saw us she had hysterics.'

She added: 'It was Colonel Pemberton who was in command then.' Then she had an idea. 'I know, the Pembertons are living at Southwold, not far from here. Let's look them up.'

The Pembertons were so pleased to see us. They had recently moved into a new house in a kind of superior housing estate – Olive and I both felt that we were also back in a cantonment atmosphere. At length I mentioned, casually, that I had been seeing relations of Billy Haycraft. Colonel Pemberton became distraught and pale. He told me, after being pressed for the details, that the Sikh bugler had come to see him because both Billy and the adjutant had turned him down for promotion. 'I said that if Major Haycraft and the adjutant were not in favour of his promotion, then there was nothing I could do about it.'

He seemed so upset that I did not like to ask about the 'Mary Rose' disappearance of his two children, in the next-door garden to ours at Nowshera. I concluded that this must have happened quite soon after Billy's death, and now, having checked with Army records, I see that Colonel Pemberton went on home leave not long afterwards, taking his children with him. He retired in 1931. Later I discovered that after the court martial the bugler's family had sworn to be revenged on Colonel Pemberton. I also was to find out that neither the Pemberton son or daughter, in their middle age, could remember a thing about their reputed disappearance. 'I seem to think,' one of them said to me, 'that there was a maize field nearby which we used to go and play in sometimes.' Rather dangerous, considering that there were cobras about? 'Yes, a cobra was killed on our verandah, where we used to sleep.' They had never been told anything about the Haycraft murder.

Mrs Haycraft was luckier than Violet McLenaghan, whose husband was murdered the year afterwards. Olive Haycraft was at least able to go and stay with relations. 'The poor thing's two boys had very bad dysentery,' I was told. 'She was with us for five months, doing nothing but play tennis, sleep and eat.'

After Sylvia May's death I asked the Kings for more information as to why anyone should have considered that either Walter or Rufus was to blame for the death. 'Olive Haycraft thought that your mother came to Murree out of guilt.' This made me understand: the gossip must have been buzzing around the Nowshera cantonments over the Rufus affair. It made me wonder too whether that was why Walter had been tactfully removed by the authorities to Gilgit for four years.

The story of Sylvia May's reaction to the photograph of the Haycrafts has intrigued some novelist friends. Beryl Bainbridge has invented a wonderful theory about my father 'having it off' with the Sikh's wife at Peshawar, and that the Sikh shot Billy Haycraft thinking he was Walter.

Mrs Roween again

I would never have dreamed of asking Olive how far the affair went between her and Rufus – I can't bear to use Beryl's phrase! I would not have wanted to know. I believe that Olive did try once to reassure me, but as with Nanny Spicer at the Adelphi I felt slightly embarrassed and changed the subject.

Flash Alf was not the only one to have shown that he was attracted by Olive when Walter was back in India during the war, and I had been amused about this. What did surprise me much later, when she was in her seventies, was the way that women also seemed to be drawn to her. She used to go and stay in Devon with a contemporary who had lived in Gulmarg, and then suddenly stopped. 'I think —— is dotty. She has somehow fallen in love with me,' she said. People have claimed that Olive was an 'unconscious flirt', but I think her elegance and style had something to do with it. She continued to like having her own way in Cornwall, and in her old age could sometimes be quite fierce, organizing lives (including attempts at mine), but she always remained feminine, even an ingénue, and ultimately warm.

Nevertheless I was taken aback when talking to somebody who had been a young woman in Kashmir when we were there around 1930.

'Do you remember Mrs Roween?' she asked.

Certainly I did, and I told her about my unease when going to her house at Srinagar.

'*Fascinating* you should have felt like that. You know she tried to seduce your mother? Everyone was talking about it.'

There was little I could say to this, so she went on: 'Mrs Roween was a very rich and very sinister woman. She was also very beautiful, and had very good taste.'

'Very good taste.' Well, that would have appealed to Olive, after having to live in roughish conditions both at Gulmarg and Gilgit. As I had seen for myself, Mrs Roween was far from being the cantonment type.

But where did Mrs Roween's wealth come from? 'Oh, that was a mystery. From Calcutta, we were told. I think her husband was half Bengali half Armenian. An ugly little man. We hardly ever saw him.'

It was all my friend could tell me, and is probably all I shall ever know, or again want to know. At least there was a reason for my instinctive annoyance over Mrs Roween's spell over Olive. I do not feel disloyal in recording this conversation, because I also now understood why Mrs Roween suddenly dropped out of our lives in 1931, and why John and I were not allowed to go to the children's fancy dress party Mrs Roween gave at Nedou's Hotel, after all the expense of having costermongers' suits made for us.

The Third Journey
I

1982. DESTINATION PORT BLAIR, Andaman Islands. Also Calcutta, because of Macaulay, Hannah, and Charles Trevelyan. Also Rangoon.

Although geographically closer to Burma, the Andaman Islands remained part of India in the share-out of the Empire. Port Blair has one of the great harbours of the world, but there are other smaller and useful harbours in an archipelago about 250 miles long – Port Cornwallis for instance, where it was rumoured that Russian submarines might be seen. All of which were reasons for the Andamans being designated a 'restricted zone'. The annoyances over getting permits were far worse than when we were planning to go to Gilgit.

There were boats from Madras or Calcutta to Port Blair, and twice weekly planes from Calcutta. We reckoned that the whole process of obtaining those permits took us fourteen months, taking into account that we wanted to avoid the time of monsoons. The Orgills were to have joined us, but – fed up – they switched their plans to Kenya. We intended to fly. It was typical that we should be told, after what seemed like a hundred and one visits to the Indian High Commission, that in any case 'Delhi' had finally decided that permits could now be issued at Calcutta airport. Our rage at this was softened a little when we found that, if we had relied on what seemed a highly suspect concession, our passports would have been stamped 'Bazaar and Jail only'.

'¡NO VAYAS A CALCUTA! ¡PROMETEME QUE NO IRAS NUNCA A CALCUTA! Don't go to Calcutta! Promise me you'll never go to Calcutta!', a rich girl friend of Raúl's had once written to him whilst she stopped for the night at Calcutta on her wild round-the-world trip. A single look at the beggars outside the Grand Hotel had decided her to keep indoors.

We too found ourselves temporarily staying at the Grand, which is on the old Chowringhee Road, now renamed Jawaharlal Nehru

Road. We had long ago become accustomed to seeing poverty, not only in the sub-continent but in North Africa. I had also experienced it, possibly to a worse degree, in Naples during the war.

For most people poverty and chaos are synonymous with Calcutta. It is difficult to write about them without feeling sanctimonious, hard-hearted or guilty. There are those who refer to Calcutta as 'my favourite city', a kind of travel snobbery one suspects, and its more well-heeled inhabitants fiercely defend it – and I am sure genuinely love it. We did not penetrate beyond Tolly's Nullah, on the other side of which are Alipur and the fashionable areas. Perhaps there were fewer beggars on Chowringhee Road than we expected. Nearly all of them were professionals, chasing you down the street like horse-flies, clutching at your arm with cries of 'Allah, Pappa, Mamma'. The deliberate display of mutilated limbs and deformities simply made me turn my face away; the people who did this were pro-fessionals too, even the man without arms or legs who moved by rolling over and over on the pavement.

I think most travellers would now hardly dare to wander on foot outside the Chowringhee area, and not just for squeamish reasons. They would also be mad to drive their own cars, because at Calcutta there is no rule of the road. What's more, any accident would mean immediate lynching of the driver by even casual passers-by. We saw a bus burnt out because the driver had knocked somebody down. This possibility of a sudden eruption into violence, and the stories in newspapers of unwanted daughters-in-law being set on fire, are a frightening side of Calcutta. 'Five members of the Ananda Marga spiritual-political group,' I read, 'were burned alive and another eight stoned or stabbed to death by a frenzied mob that accused them of stealing children.' Calcutta is still a city of dreadful night. And yet, and yet, you find yourself loving the people for their cheerfulness, their doggedness – and indeed, paradoxically, their gentle manners. Calcutta is full of male and female Mother Courages. It is bigger than London now, a terrible apocalyptic vision of any great city of the future in decay, where public order and public services barely hold their own. Refugees from the country camp on the pavements, give birth there, wash their bodies (but not their nether parts, it seems) from street-pumps, puddles or in the Hooghly River among the floating ashes of the dead. The real non-professional poor scavenge among the rubbish heaps, like the jackals and adjutant birds a hundred and fifty years before. There are a lot of rats. Coming from Dum-Dum airport, we saw a cart full of carcasses of meat over which sacks had been thrown; about thirty crows were pecking at the meat through the sacking.

An Indian whom I met in our hotel and who lived in north London said to me: 'In England you can be poor but you can fight your way up. Here in India if you are born poor there is no escape.'

Mother Teresa. You notice her face on calendars, competing with Hindu gods. I was surprised to learn that she had missions in over a hundred and fifty cities throughout the world. Many foreigners coming to Calcutta would like to visit her, but she doesn't want to see them, and rightly: she is not a tourist attraction. Neither does she like being called a social worker. 'All the time we are touching Christ's body in the poor,' I read.

We were not quite so prepared for all the pimps. No sooner had we managed to shake off the beggars and one-armed dwarfs than these pimps took up the pursuit. 'Hey, you want student girl?' At first some of these offers were almost amusing, but by the second day they were a bore. 'Girls! Girls! Fresh from Bangladesh!' 'Big strong boys do French jobs!' 'Come on, what you want? You say. Anything you like. Massage in your hotel!'

A metro was being built, at the suggestion originally of the Russians. The work was spasmodic, and like so much else at Calcutta subject to bureaucratic rivalries and inefficiency. No project could surely have been crazier, what with all the power-cuts, the floods during the monsoons, the possibility of invasion by pavement dwellers. The mess made by the excavations was hideous too. In places like Alipur most people have to have their own generators because of the endless power-cuts.

The Raj had meant nothing to Raúl's girl friend, and one couldn't blame her. For the British the palimpsest side of Calcutta is its real fascination, however melancholy: the pleasure of ruins. Here once were riches unimaginable. Here were high fashions, pomp – and some kind of orderliness. Calcutta is quite different to other British inventions like Simla, Ooty, or even New Delhi. Ideally you should arrive at Calcutta having read your William Hickey, Macaulay's letters, Emily Eden or Fanny Parks, and be familiar with the aquatints or watercolours by the Daniells or Charles D'Oyly. You must be ready to visualize the palanquins (otherwise known as palkis) and carriages along the Esplanade and Chowringhee Road, the barouches and the buggies, the grooms in laced turbans and sashes, the Governor-General's bodyguards with their drawn swords and 'blazing uniforms', as Macaulay saw them. New arrivals in the 1830s compared the magnificence of the buildings along Chowringhee Road and at 'Garden Reach', next to Fort William, with St Petersburg. Macaulay landed in September 1834, to be greeted soon after by a seventeen-gun salute. It was the same year in which an enterprising American had brought a load of forty tons of ice from Boston: a great advance in modern progress. He stayed first at Government House, a copy of sorts of Kedleston Hall with a gateway inspired by that at Syon House. The view of the Maidan, he thought, was like looking across Hyde Park from Park Lane.

Fanny Parks was more impressed by the British 'palaces' than he was. At that time there were no shops in Chowringhee Road, nearly two miles long. 'The houses,' Macaulay wrote, 'are all of stone or white plaster, with numerous windows, with a great display of green Venetian blinds, and generally with porticos and verandahs. Considered as architectural compositions, they have no claims to admiration. But the size, the loftiness, the brilliant whiteness, and, above all, the immense number of those large mansions, and the immense profusion of columns, though not always happily disposed, give a certain splendour to the general effect.' The so-called Black Town, or native quarter, mainly of thatched houses, ran northwards behind Government House, 'with a population of nearly a million souls, spreading for miles up the river'.

The Esplanade now runs into Lenin Street. There is also a Karl Marx Street. I was however relieved to find that Bentinck Street and Shakespeare Street remained, not to mention Queen's Way. Macaulay went to live in No. 33 Chowringhee Road, facing Fort William. I knew that some while after he had left it had been taken over by the Bengal Club, and later demolished. Still, it was nice to find on its successor a plaque recording that Thomas Babington Macaulay as Law Member of the Supreme Council had lived on this site between 1834 and 1838 (actually he had already left it for England by January 15 1838). Lord Combermere, the Commander-in-Chief, had occupied No. 33 up to 1830. Its dining-room could hold a table for forty, and the drawing-room had been fifty feet long, with fine sofas, gilded punkahs and a shiny floor. There had been a pretty garden too, with a gravel path, many flowerbeds and plenty of shade. Now a mean building stood in its place, and there was no garden.

Cricket was almost the most visible legacy of the British. The enormous Maidan was dotted with groups playing the game, and near the Eden Gardens (named after Emily and her sister) was the amphitheatre so familiar now on television sports programmes.

We hunted out several ex-British palaces, très lépreux as a Frenchman at the Grand expressively said, their stucco falling from the brick and blotched like vaccination marks. Often these once grand houses still had a single top-heavy palm growing by the ruins of their porticoes – a forlorn, humbled thing. And most of these houses had been turned into tenements. They nearly all had had large compounds in front, but now these compounds have blocks of flats or offices built in them, as if to shield whatever spectral memories remain from the nightmare of Calcutta traffic.

The refugees from wars with Pakistan and from Assam have made the plight of Calcutta much worse; all the same there is no need for a modern Briton to take the smug line that things have become automatically worse since the departure of the Raj. A guidebook for 1854 describes how a visitor on arriving by river would be astounded by the enchanting beauty of the palaces and the verdure of Garden Reach sloping down to the water. But, on coming closer, the eyes would soon be offended by the 'admixture of mean and dirty huts which abound in some of the finest streets, and come almost into contact with the colonnaded mansions'. There might once have been smart barouches and cavalry officers cantering on Arab stallions across the Maidan, but there were also ox carts, camels and elephants 'with their accompanying excrement' on Chowringhee Road, which at night was 'most wretchedly lighted by means of sordid oil-lamps'. The city was not watched, paved or efficiently regulated, and everywhere there were 'unemployed men lounging or lying about the streets'. As for the India Bazaar just behind Chowringhee Road, it was a 'scene of riot, knavery, prostitution and filthiness'. People living in Garden Reach had to employ a special man to push away floating dead bodies.

A palanquin always sounds a particularly glamorous form of transport, but there were complaints that it was often like travelling in a flea-infested sea-chest with holes for windows, borne by four long-suffering, jog-trotting, almost naked, sweating men. Most Europeans preferred to lie flat in a palanquin, but Indians would sit cross-legged, which was far more sensible in that 'abominable shaking'. Another writer, in 1844, listed an exotic variety of means of locomotion: britzkas, landaulets, palki-gharries, brown-berries and crahanchys.

I was sorry to see that so many trees on the Maidan had been cut down. Sorry too that the adjutant birds, a species of crane, had apparently abandoned Calcutta. In the pictures by the Daniells and others you see them standing incongruously among the traffic or on arches and parapets like a detachment of well-drilled soldiers. Sometimes these majestic things stood on two legs, sometimes on only one. Old Calcutta hands would speak of their 'philosophic calm' and 'impassive self-content'. When the birds took off, it was with difficulty and a hop, skip and jump. Good scavengers, they were able even to swallow bones, and took an unseemly interest in the goings on at the cemeteries.

The tombs of some of the first owners of the palaces are still to be seen in the South Park Street Cemetery, rescued from dereliction, desecration, rabid dogs and snakes, thanks to Dr Maurice Shellim: a small cramped town of domed temples, pyramids, obelisks, urns on pedestals, and broken columns, among bougainvillaeas, poinsettias and other exotic plants which would probably have amazed swells like Lady Anne Monson and Sir Elijah Impey, the first Chief Justice of Bengal in the great days of the Nabobs. Ideally on a visit you should bring William Hickey's Memoirs with you, for checking the names of the mausolea against the index. Charlotte Hickey's tomb is still there, and with a most un-Christian inscription, in contrast to all the other pious verses and epitaphs: 'Leaving a truly disconsolate husband bitterly and, incessantly to deplore the loss of her' – no acceptance of Divine Will here, nothing of the 'shuffled off this mortal coil' sentiments. (I was glad to learn from Maurice Shellim that a Charlotte Hickey Cup is still run every year at the Calcutta races.) Charlotte died on Christmas Day 1783, not yet twenty-one.

Lucia Palk's 'stately tomb' was singled out by Kipling: the 'fair Kentish maid', who died aged twenty-three of 'putrid fever' in 1772, long before the arrival of William and Charlotte Hickey. She was the 'toast far up the river', was painted by Tilly Kettle, and had danced with Warren Hastings. Captain Jacob Sarly, 'citizen of New York, America', died in 1793. The Eurasian poet, Henry Derozio, whose dress 'went to the extreme of foppery' and who is regarded as a forerunner of Indian nationalism, is buried here: he died of cholera in 1831, aged twenty-two. The North Park Street Cemetery, where Thackeray's father was buried, has gone now. Somewhere there used to be the grave of the second baby of Charles and Hannah Trevelyan; she died in 1837.

So many, especially women, died before the age of thirty. Two monsoons, so it used to be said in early colonial days, were the average expectancy of life. No wonder eighteenth-century sailors called Calcutta Golgotha. And so many infant deaths are recorded. In one grave there are four children, dying between 1820 and 1827, and none of them reaching the age of two. I saw the grave of little James Siddons, born in April 1818, died in August. He was the grandson of Sarah Siddons, who had acted in the Calcutta Theatre. His father became a colleague of Charles Trevelyan's, and his mother was said to have had the blood of Moghul emperors in her veins. Late August and September were the dangerous times, when the 'reek of this deadly marsh', as Macaulay called it, caused the greatest havoc:

We are annually baked four months, boiled four more, and allowed the remaining four to become cool if we can. At this moment the sun is blazing like a furnace. The earth, soaked with oceans of rain, is steaming like a wet blanket. Vegetation is rotting all round us. Insects and undertakers are the only living creatures which seem to enjoy the climate.

In those months razors lost their edge, thread decayed, clothes fell to pieces, books mouldered away and dropped out of their bindings, plaster cracked, and timber rotted. Then there were the 'infinite armies of white ants'. By November the blessed cool returned, with 'morning fogs, cloth coats, green peas and new potatoes'.

Rose Aylmer

Out of loyalty to my friend Leila, my old Wolf Cub leader at Gilgit, I wanted to see the tomb of her kinswoman Rose Aylmer. There was also a connection between Rose and General Aylmer, hero of the Hunza Campaign of 1891.

Rose had died on March 2 1800, aged twenty, and is of course remembered because of Walter Savage Landor's lines, 'carved as it were in ivory or gems' during the vigil of the night: 'Ah, what avails the sceptred race!/Ah what the form divine!... A night of memories and of sighs/I consecrate to thee.' To some the beauty of the name Rose Aylmer was the most expressive of all. Charles Lamb found that the ode had a 'charm I cannot explain', and Crabbe wrote to Landor in 1831 that he had been to see Lamb, who 'both tipsy and sober is ever muttering Rose Aylmer'. Landor wrote of her afterwards in another poem, *Abertavy*: 'Where is she now? Call'd far away ... Where Ganges rolls his widest wave/She dropt her blossom in the grave.'

Rose's tomb at South Park Street has a fluted tapering column, wreathed with drooping roses between inverted torches, and stands on a sarcophagus reached by steps. It has been vandalized, but repaired and the inscription restored, again due to Maurice Shellim.

It seems that Rose met Landor at Southsea when she was seventeen and he was twenty-two. Whatever their feelings really were towards one another, Landor then was living fairly openly with a mistress. Rose lent him a copy of *The Progress of Romance* by Clara Reeve, and this inspired him to write his epic poem *Gebir*. Landor himself died in 1864, having lived much in Italy. He had a hot temper, which often got him into trouble. 'Whatever he may profess,' Browning said, 'the thing he really loves is a pretty girl to talk nonsense with.'

Rose was the sister of the fifth Lord Aylmer. Obviously she had a delightful character. When her mother remarried she was sent out to Calcutta in 1798 with her aunt Lady Russell, a friend of William Hickey and wife of Sir Henry Russell, later Chief Justice. Hickey said that Rose had several professed admirers, one being a Charles Ricketts and another her cousin Henry Russell, who was the most favoured, to his parents' alarm. Rose seems to have died of cholera, but Hickey gives a different reason for her 'sinking into the grave':

> She was attacked with a most severe bowel complaint, brought on entirely by indulging too much with that mischievous and dangerous fruit, the pineapple, against eating so much of which I had frequently cautioned her, but instead of my remonstrances being attended to they only excited her mirth, and she laughed at me for my grave sermons, as she termed what I said upon the subject. The disease made a most rapid progress, baffling the skill and exertions of the physicians. At the end of a few days this lovely young girl fell a martyr to the obstinacy of the malady, leaving poor Henry Russell truly miserable. As for her other lover, Mr. Ricketts, he very shortly after her premature death sought comfort for himself in the arms of a vulgar, huge, coarse Irish slammerkin, Miss Prendergast.

Devoted sisters

Thomas Babington Macaulay was not quite thirty-four when he reached Calcutta. He and his sister Hannah had left England on board the *Asia* on March 1 1834. By June 10 the ship lay off Madras, an exceptionally quick journey. It was at Madras that he received 'tidings the reverse of welcome': the Governor-General was detained by ill-health at Ootacamund – Ooty to us – in the Nilgiri hills above Mysore, a distance overland of some 400 miles. This would mean that Hannah would have to continue the voyage in the *Asia* alone, at the hottest time of the year. Luckily, however, another letter arrived. It was from the Bishop of Calcutta, whom they both already knew, insisting that she should begin her life in India 'nowhere except under his roof'. They were therefore separated for four months. After a while Hannah moved to Government House, where Lady William treated her 'quite as a mother'.

Hannah, born in 1810, was ten years younger than Tom Macaulay, in a family of five girls and four boys. As children of the great anti-slavery agitator, Zachary Macaulay, they were brought up in the aura of the Clapham Sect, 'the chosen home of the Low Church [Evangelical] party in its golden age', a party which included the Wilberforces and the Thorntons, and by association Hannah More, after whom Hannah More Macaulay was named.

Their mother was completely absorbed by the family, 'really disliking Society'. Hannah was to write a memoir of her brother Tom for her own children, and in this she said: 'I think some of the wants in your uncle's life were owing to the far too exclusive manner in which he was brought up.' He used to cry for joy at seeing his mother after a few hours' absence. This 'power of exciting his feelings' became a kind of show for visitors, until it was stopped by Zachary. 'My father had no patience with your uncle's faults'; he was annoyed by the boy's eager impatience, his carelessness of dress, the way he was always forgetting to wash his hands or brush his hair, his execrable handwriting, and the way he contradicted elders at table. Nevertheless it was a rumbustious household, dominated by Tom's brilliance.

> I think my father's strictness was a good counterpoise to the perfect worship of your uncle by the rest of the family. To us he was an object of passionate love and devotion. To us he could do no wrong. His unruffled sweetness of temper, his unfailing flow of spirits, his amusing talk, all made his presence so delightful that his wishes and his tastes were our law. He hated strangers; and his notion of perfect happiness was to see us all working round him while he read aloud a novel, and then to walk around the Common, or, if it rained to have a frightfully noisy game of hide-and-seek.

After dinner he would pace up and down the drawing-room talking and making 'wretched puns, so many a minute'. They also sang, 'none of us having any voice, he least of all'. 'He could never pack or arrange anything. Lighting a candle or a fire was a difficulty. When he began to shave he cut himself awfully indeed [some of his surviving books are still marked with his blood mixed with soap].'

By the age of twelve Hannah knew that her 'whole heart was completely wrapped up' in her brother. Her youngest sister Margaret also adored him, and he adored them both, drawing even closer after the death of the mother. As the girls grew older, it seemed that all three accepted that they would live together as a ménage à trois. Because of his love for them we have some of the most brilliant and sparkling letters in the language.

Macaulay's article on Milton in the *Edinburgh Review* in 1825 marked the real beginning of his fame as a writer; it was described as 'bristling with point and glowing with eloquence, with an oriental wealth of imagery and illustration, and evidencing a superior judgement presiding over vast stores of erudition'. From then onwards his articles became an eagerly awaited feature of the journal. In 1826 he was called to the bar, and in 1830 he became a Member of Parliament. His speech in favour of the Reform Bill was a sensation. An American journalist wrote how he had watched a 'little man of small voice' get up, with an 'affected utterance, clipping his words, and hissing like a serpent'. He soon learnt that this was Mr Macaulay. Then, 'never did Bonaparte gain a field of battle in a style more brilliant, or with a suddenness more astounding to his enemies'.

Macaulay was now often to be seen at Holland House. Some of his fellow guests such as Creevey thought him vulgar and ungainly, and were taken aback by that great flow of talk, anecdote and quotation. He had the most extraordinary memory. Disraeli was to say that the 'intellectual expression of Macaulay's countenance was magnificent – never was a nobler forehead piled up with sagacity and depth'. Bulwer-Lytton, while remarking on the 'full forehead, the firm lips, the large, cloven chin, the massive bold brow that overlays an eye small but full of deep, quiet light', said that he had hardly ever seen a 'head so expressive of intellectual grandeur'.

Fanny Kemble wrote how she would be amazed by his torrent of loud, even declamatory talk. He stood on the hearthrug at Bowood, always in the same position, from morning until evening, 'like a knight in the lists, challenging and accepting the challenge of all comers . . . I used to listen to him till I was breathless with what I thought to have been *his* exhaustion.'

Hannah also had a strong and intelligent face, rather masculine, longer than her brother's. Margaret told her that she had been compared to Jane Austen's Emma, but considered that Hannah had a 'more restless and irritable frame', with an 'excitability impervious to medicine'. Hannah was certainly inclined to be nervous, and like her mother had a dread of society. She does not seem quite to have shared her brother's sense of humour. In a letter to Margaret she admitted that she idolized Tom almost more than God: 'I cannot endure the thought of ever loving him less than I do at the moment, though I feel how criminal it is.' Margaret was a more commanding character, and in her diary looked forward to the time when the three would be drawn even closer in a 'oneness of interest'.

Then came the stunning blow for Macaulay. In December 1832 Margaret married a Liverpool Quaker, Edward Cropper. He saw this as an 'impossible gulf'. He even wrote to Hannah that Margaret was now dead to him, 'what I see is only her ghost'. But that was a temporary exaggeration, as his long and loving letters show, particularly after his arrival in India. Meanwhile he leant more than ever on Hannah, whom he called Nancy.

He scored an electoral victory at Leeds, and made an outstanding speech in the Reformed Parliament on the renewal of the charter of the East India Company. Early in 1833 he was appointed to the Board of Control for India. Hannah received almost daily letters from him as if they were journals: 'The House is sitting; Peel is just down; Lord Palmerston is speaking; the heat is tremendous; the crowd stifling; and so I am in the smoking-room with three Repealers making chimneys of their mouths under my very nose.' Sometimes these letters were addressed to 'Dearest Love' or 'My Darling'. It was a relationship part fraternal, part paternal, almost a marriage of the spirit.

On August 17 1833 he wrote a letter, which even he did not realize would upset Hannah quite so deeply. It was to announce that almost certainly he was to be offered a 'post of the highest dignity and consideration' on the Governor-General's Council at Calcutta.★ The salary would be ten thousand pounds a year. 'I am not fond of money, or anxious about it. But, though every day makes me less and less eager for wealth, every day shews me more and more strongly how necessary a competence is to a man who desires to be either great or useful.' He went on to explain the difficulties ahead in his political career. If he lost his seat in Parliament he would have to rely on his writing, which at present only brought him in two hundred a year. The family's financial prospects were 'if possible darker than ever', and he would inevitably have to make some provision.

Whether the period of my exile shall be one of misery, or of comfort, and, after the first shock, even of happiness, depends on you, my dear, dear Nancy. I can scarcely see the words which I am writing through the tears that force themselves through my eyes. Will you, my own darling, if, as I expect, this offer shall be made to me, will you go with me? Will you entrust to me a few years the care of your happiness? I call God to witness that it is as dear to me as my own – that I love the very ground you tread on – that, if I shrink from poverty, it is more for your own sake than my own. I know what a sacrifice I ask of you. I know how many dear and precious ties you must, for a time, sunder. I know that the splen-

★ This was a result of the new Charter Act, which made the Governor-General the law-making authority for India. Law reform was much needed, and the post involved was 'Law Member' of the Council.

The Haardt-Citroën Expedition, 1931; an awkward moment on the road to Gilgit

Olive and M. Haardt,
Srinagar

The Mir of Hunza's castle at Baltit

Polo Gilgit style

Leila Backwell on the Outer Circular Road, Gulmarg

John and Raleigh in fancy dress as costermongers, Gulmarg

Hut 46a, Gulmarg 1930

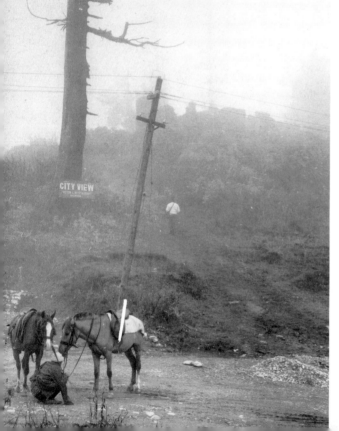

Hut 46a, Gulmarg 1979

The Nagin Lake, Srinagar

The Taj Mahal: the obligatory 'snap'

His Highness Lieut-General the Maharajah of Kashmir and Jammu, Hari Singh Bahadur, rides in state through Srinagar

The Haycrafts

Picnic at Bundipur, Kashmir:
Nanny Spicer, Raleigh, Rufus
Ralston

The Cellular Jail, Port Blair, Andaman Islands

Andamanese, 1923

dour of the Indian court and the gaieties of that brilliant society of which you would be one of the most conspicuous ornaments have no temptation for you. I can bribe you only by telling you that, if you will go with me, I will love you better than I love you now, if I can . . . Farewell, my dear, dear Nancy. You cannot tell how impatiently I shall wait for your answer. TBM

Hannah replied at once. She said that she had a horror of India as a region of disease and death. The thought of leaving her friends, and especially Margaret (whose baby she was helping to look after), was dreadful for her. She sent him an 'agonised appeal', she said in her memoir, entreating him to give up the very idea. He wrote back, leaving it open still. He explained that he principally wanted to 'have a home for my Nancy, that I may surround her with comforts, and be assured of leaving her safe from poverty'. But if 'on mature reflection' she still felt they should both remain in England, 'I will, at once and without a moment's regret, give up the scheme, and forget every thing connected with it, except your generous and confiding affection'.

Within a few days he was up at Liverpool with Hannah and Margaret, and had persuaded her to change her mind – though the prospect was a nightmare for her. The post in India was confirmed. Lady Holland warned Macaulay that within six months his sister would be engaged to some rich nabob. Margaret, aged twenty, gave Hannah the advice of a married woman: 'Beware of men . . . Above all, do not become a flirt. I have no doubt that is your tendency and therefore I honestly warn against this.' Macaulay told her that he would want her to 'appear among the dancing, pianoforte-playing, opera-going damsels at Calcutta as one who has seen society better than any thing they ever approached'. Another sister, Fanny Macaulay, evidently concerned about Hannah's state of mind, offered to come out to Calcutta too. Tom Macaulay turned this down. He only wanted Hannah, and in any case Fanny's duty was to look after their father, who was in poor health.

'One word about your maid,' he wrote to Hannah:

You really must chuse with great caution. Hitherto the Company has required that all the ladies who take maid servants with them from this country to India should give security to send them back within two years. The reason was that no class of people misconduct themselves so much in the East as female servants from this country. They generally treat the natives with gross insolence . . . The state of society is that they are very likely to become mistresses of the wealthy Europeans, – and to flaunt about in magnificent palanquins, bringing discredit on their country by the immorality of their lives and the vulgarity of their manners.

A household of probably sixty or seventy people could easily be destroyed by such a woman if she were ill-tempered and arrogant.

They must, he said, find very large and very fine dinner and tea sets for Calcutta. He was bringing twelve dozen shirts for the voyage, and listed the authors whose books he was taking with him – Richardson, Voltaire, Gibbon, Cervantes, Homer, Horace, Ariosto.

Still, Hannah's heart was 'almost broken'. The last evening she spent 'in the arms' of another brother, Charles, before leaving at 5 am for Gravesend. She was utterly exhausted, 'worn out by the distress which I laboured to control'. When she reached the *Asia* she could only collapse on the sofa in her cabin. 'I feel,' she wrote to Fanny, 'I most deeply feel, that I have not counted the cost when I consented to this dreadful separation . . . I have taken leave of almost everything I care for on earth and given up all chance of happiness . . . Forgive my selfishness but I cannot restrain my pen . . . I have sealed my destiny for the next six years and after that what will be left.'

In the English Channel the ship ran into a storm, 'tossing, pitching, rolling'. 'Dear Nancy suffered terribly – thought she was dying – and seemed to care very little whether she died or lived.' They had to put in at Falmouth. Then, after a fortnight's delay, they were off. Hannah wrote more miserable letters: 'I am obliged to conceal what I really feel.' Macaulay himself kept in good humour and stayed mostly in his cabin, reading ten hours a day. 'Except at meal times I hardly exchanged a word with any human being.' Hannah enjoyed walking around the deck in the tropical evening, and wrote of the brilliancy of the stars, the lights and the shadows – 'the ship's white sail is a beautiful object itself by moonlight.' She began to revive, took some dancing lessons, and read aloud novels and sermons with some other ladies on board . . .

Macaulay made a profound impression on the Governor-General at Ooty. Lady William, at Calcutta, would read from letters that were full of praise for his talents and powers – 'several of them I remember,' said Hannah, 'ended "E un miracolo".' Macaulay for his part regarded Bentinck as the greatest man he had ever known, and liked to trace a resemblance between him and King William III.

In that year, 1834, it was estimated that there were about 24,000 British civil servants, military officers and soldiers in India, ruling directly over a population of 90 million and 'protecting' another 140 million. The native armies on whose loyalty the British relied, numbered about 120,000 men.

Feelings of warmest interest, we are told, had been aroused in Macaulay's favour at Calcutta. 'Excitement was on tiptoe.' Before his arrival people had been refreshing their memories about his speeches, essays and poems. They awaited a modern Lycurgus. A great ball was given in his honour by Sir Charles Metcalfe, the ladies being requested to wear fancy dress. There was a dinner for two hundred people on St Andrew's Day, at which Macaulay – Scottish by descent, though not by birth or education, as he pointed out – was asked to preside. But such festivities were not to his taste.

Hannah described the routine to which he soon settled. He attended Council two days a week, otherwise worked at home. He rose early, walked about the garden and read till breakfast at nine. 'I did not see him again until tiffin when he always joined me except on Council days when he returned at five. After tiffin he sat with me talking and reading till our drive at 6 p.m.' All the while, during the day, the punkah would be swinging. 'The afternoon airing,' Macaulay himself said, 'was never omitted by anyone who could afford a carriage.' So the Course (the road round the Maidan) was always very crowded, and the lack of places to trot around became monotonous.

'Then,' Hannah went on to write, 'came the greatest trial of his life. My marriage.'

> This is a period I could never speak of or think of without exquisite pain. But for the elucidation of his character I must recall it, not that he disapproved of my choice. From the first he warmly and cordially liked and esteemed my husband, and afterwards they became brothers indeed. But strange to say, he had never contemplated the possibility of my marriage and leaving him. When at the Nilgherries [Nilgiris] Lady William wrote to her Lord that a certain person wanted to marry me. Lord William replied that he had spoken to Mr Macaulay, who had treated the whole thing with scorn, and Lord William added that with a simplicity unworthy of his sense Mr Macaulay asserted he was certain his sister would never marry.

Presumably by that certain person she meant Charles, though Macaulay said she had had other suitors. It evidently took some while for Tom Macaulay, when he got to Calcutta in September, to appreciate what was happening. Hannah and Charles would have met often at Government House, Charles being such a favourite of both Bentincks and at that time Deputy Secretary in the Political Department. According to Macaulay Charles was struck by Hannah at once. 'But she could not bear him', evidently put off by his awkward manners, lack of small talk and his obsession with what we now call 'shop'. One day Macaulay noticed her reading the account of the inquiry into Charles's battle with Sir Edward Colebrooke at Delhi. Then she began learning Hindustani by means of Roman characters, which was one of Charles's many crusades. 'Her eyes looked bright whenever we met him on the Course, and her cheeks extremely red whenever he spoke to her. In short she became as much in love as he.'

'Trevelyan is a most stirring reformer,' Macaulay continued in a letter to Margaret. 'He is quite at the head of that active party among the younger servants of the Company who take the side of improvement. In particular he is the soul of every scheme for diffusing education among the natives of this country.' Whilst up at Ooty, Macaulay had read some of Charles's correspondence and reports, and had been impressed. Lord William, though quite aware of Charles's faults ('rash and uncompromising in public matters'), had spoken of him as being 'noble-minded' and one of the ablest young men in the Service. On coming to Calcutta Macaulay had completely approved of Charles's ideas – if sometimes too impetuously expressed in print – about native education, and had put all his influence into backing him. He only regretted that Charles's reading had been so confined – probably he had never read a novel in his life. Perhaps also Charles was too fervently religious for his taste. 'He has a very good figure and looks like a gentleman everywhere, but particularly on horse-back. He is very active and athletic and is renowned as a great master in the most exciting and perilous of field-sports, the spearing of boars.' 'Lover enough to be a knight of the Round Table,' Macaulay wrote to his friend Thomas Flower Ellis, his 'love-making, though very ardent and sincere, is as awkward and odd as you would wish to see.' He summed Charles up as 'a man of genius, a man of rigid integrity and of a very kind heart'.

Then in that letter to Margaret, he let go his pent-up distress. Hannah, as mistress of his house, had been second only to Lady William Bentinck in Indian society:

> My parting from you almost broke my heart. But when I parted from you I had Nancy – I had all my other relations – I had my friends – I had my country. Now I have nothing except the resources of my own mind . . . I have been unable, even at Church or in the Council-room – to command my voice or to restrain my tears. I have known poverty. I have known exile. But I never knew unhappiness before.

He realized though that he was reaping what he had sown. He was alone in the world now. But that world was after all a tragi-comedy; for he saw that Hannah was frightened out of her wits at the prospect of being married.

But she was frightened because of *him* – Tom. When Lady William heard that Hannah had accepted Charles, she came to 33 Chowringhee Road and seemed transported with joy, kissing her over and over again. Then Hannah decided to break off the engagement. Finally Charles agreed that after the honeymoon all three could live together. At least that would save some money, as his salary was only £1,800 a year. Charles also said that he would postpone his furlough, which was nearly due, so that they could all travel back to England when Macaulay's term of office ended in 1838. So the engagement was on again. The Bentincks were still alarmed about Macaulay's 'tone of mind' and insisted that the marriage should take place at once.

'But,' wrote Hannah:

he never while we were in India at all recovered his spirits, nor do I think his former light-hearted vivacity ever returned. A certain amount of depression remained and to his last day there are entries in his journals referring to this unhealed wound which were exquisitely painful to me to read, and most of which I have erased.

The wedding was at that 'Regency building so full of architectural blunders', (according to Heber), St John's Cathedral, on December 23. She wore white with a lace veil lent by Lady William. Macaulay, who gave her away, thought she looked very pretty and very frightened. Charles was suffering from a swollen face. After the ceremony the couple drove to the Governor-General's park at Barrackpore, where Bentinck had lent them a cottage. Hannah in her memoir continued:

In the evening the Bentincks went to see him, and wrote to us to return as soon as we could as they were frightened about him. I am sure his mind was disturbed, for he wrote me the most fearful letter of misery and reproach, followed the next day by one begging me to forgive it.

On that next day Macaulay wrote another letter to Margaret, and in this he said:

Every thing is dark. The world is a desert before me. I have nothing to love – I have nothing to live for – I do not care how soon I am carried to the Cathedral on a very different occasion from that of yesterday. I have nobody but myself to blame. I have indulged in a foolish dream ... A love like that which I bore to my two youngest sisters, and which, since I lost my Margaret, I felt with concentrated strength for Nancy, I shall never feel again.

Soon after he had despatched this letter, news came that Margaret had died in the summer, from scarlet fever. So she had been dead when he was still at Ooty. He had been addressing all his hugely long letters, so full of amusement, gaiety and wonder, to the grave. The calamity, Hannah said, was so terrible as to 'annihilate all other thought'. She and Charles returned instantly from Barrackpore. 'Oh, I shall never forget our meeting.'

The stirring reformer

'I felt very unhappy and desolate for some time before I married,' Charles wrote to his mother, 'owing to my having with me no kindred heart united to me in love.' In addition he said that two friends, Awdry and Blake, had been killed, 'the latter in a very horrible way in a popular tumult'. They were the 'only two persons out of my own family for whom I felt <u>very</u> <u>warm</u> <u>affection</u>, and to have them both cut off almost at the same time was a severe trial to my feelings'.

However self-assured and strong-principled he might have been, and however fervent his religious beliefs, he must indeed at times have felt isolated and lonely at Calcutta. Half his waking life would have been spent in writing or planning official reports, or in pouring out articles and letters of huge length to the newspapers. He therefore would have had very little time for social life, even if he had wanted it, and even if the more conventional Calcutta hostesses would have dreamt of inviting such a strange and brusque young man to their tables. As Macaulay said, Charles had little tact, and he was also still unpopular with some members of the old guard because of the Colebrooke affair at Delhi. The fact that he had the protection of the somewhat radically minded Bentinck made the same people uneasy. In his public, and usually controversial, writings he expressed himself with the passionate zeal of a crusader and with such a display of moral superiority that he easily made enemies, and was therefore satirized and mocked. He was not the sort of person to laugh at himself.

But Charles could lash back. His gift of sarcasm makes one wonder now at that 'very sweet temper' and 'tolerance' of other people's views that Macaulay made such a point of, let alone at his 'boyish gusts of laughter' remembered in future years. It was conceded by all that he had an astonishing memory for detail. He was also extremely ambitious, which to some was equated with mere ruthlessness, and he had an annoying habit of giving opinions on matters which were thought not to have been his business. Lord William Bentinck said to Hannah before her wedding: 'That man is almost always on the right side in every question; and it is well that he is so; for he gives a most confounded deal of trouble when he happens to ask the wrong one.'

It is no wonder therefore that Charles was impressed by the serious-minded, intelligent, reserved, unsocial Miss Macaulay, brought up as an Evangelical of the Evangelicals. Maybe the fact that she was the sister of the great man – whose eloquence and Utilitarian views in his Charter speech of 1833 Charles had so much admired – had its bearing; but Charles certainly did fall deeply in love with her.

For all his faults, there were those at Calcutta who saw Charles as a shining paragon of correct behaviour. John Milford, for instance, in *A Few Parting Hints to my Dear Boy on his Leaving Home for India*, urged his son to emulate Charles's studies of twelve hours a day at Fort William. Charles, he said, had distinguished himself by his 'activity of mind and high integrity of character more than any other man of his time', disdaining those time-wasting 'billiard-room frequenting, drinking, smoking, racing gallants'. Milford then told a story of how 'a fellow came into Charles Trevelyan's room with a bag of gold coins under his cloak, and placing it on the table, said his master had long wished to make him a present, but not knowing what article to fix upon, had sent him the money, begging he should purchase with it anything he liked best.' Needless to say the former scourge of the Colebrookes was 'almost bursting with indignation at this insult to his honour'. Charles said nothing at first, but 'calling his servant, gave the man into custody and at once sent him before the magistrate'.

Ordinary mortals felt 'positively battered' by the amazingly wide range of schemes for moral and political improvements to which Charles was able to apply his mind between 1831 and 1834; and young though he was there is no question but that his views had an influence on Bentinck's thinking. Charles at the time was at the height of his Evangelical fervour and as Bentinck's biographer, John Rosselli, has pointed out, the Governor-General's own Evangelical convictions noticeably deepened during this period. Thoby Prinsep, an Under-Secretary to the Government, became one of the main opponents of both Charles's and Macaulay's views on education in India. He was not particularly fond of Bentinck either: 'I never saw a man who had such a love of work, and such an incessant desire to meddle with everything, small or great. Wherever he went, he called for reports.' In a period of general gloom, when many mercantile houses at Calcutta were failing, Bentinck was always writing minutes, looking for economies, 'something to be dispensed with or obtained at a cheaper rate'. A decade later this could very well have been an assessment of Charles.

Prinsep also spoke of Bentinck's suspicious temper, his inordinate love of power, and his overweening estimate of his own abilities; 'everything had to be referred to him'. Bentinck's measures were made even 'more grating by his ungracious manner' and his 'unfeeling remarks'. To Charles, on the other hand, he was the 'most honest man I ever saw'. Quite simply, he was the 'first Governor-General to place our dominion in India on its proper foundation, in the recognition of the great principle that India is to be governed for the benefit of the Indians'.

The highly important reports on the defence of India, mentioned earlier in this book, by Arthur Conolly and Charles Trevelyan were written mostly at Delhi early in 1831. Conolly was the more concerned with the politics of central Asia and Russian invasion routes, the Utilitarian Charles with trade, which he saw as the only way of bringing a stable balance of power beyond the frontier of the north-west. And that vital frontier, he was convinced, should be the River Indus.

Whilst the first report was being written, Lieutenant Alexander Burnes was on a spying mission up the Indus, bringing with him as a present for Maharajah Ranjit Singh a curious gift from the British Government in the form of five Suffolk Punch carthorses – a stallion and four mares. (Prinsep said that, thereafter: 'The stallion always on state occasions was bedizened with gold and jewels outside Ranjit Singh's tent. The mares the Rajah would never look at, and I never heard what became of them.') By the end of 1831 Charles was at Calcutta, ready in due course to receive Burnes's 'grave' and, to Bentinck, unreadably long report, following his second epic – and, famous – journey to Lahore, Peshawar, Kabul, Bokhara and elsewhere. Burnes spoke of the need to unify Afghanistan, and of the enlightened character of the Amir Dost Mohammed, anxious to cultivate relations with the British. Afghanistan and the states of Tartary, not to mention the amirates of Sind, were crying out for British goods, it was revealed. To Charles promotion of British trade would automatically mean the introduction of British ideas of social justice and moral values – the all-important catchwords – to those benighted areas. In this way Russian influence would be peacefully superseded, friendly buffer states and settled frontiers created. And to satisfy the Sindians in particular, the free navigation of the Indus would be essential. In his report Burnes had sought to prove that the Indus was highly suitable for navigation, especially by the new discovery, steam.

In 1833 Charles began to bombard the Calcutta papers with his lengthy letters, mostly hard going for readers today, under the pseudonym of 'Indophilus'. The navigation of the Indus was an often recurring theme; it was his 'beau ideal'. Bentinck went further than Charles in his vision of the importance of the Indus. He saw it not only in commercial terms but as a useful place of rendezvous for an invading army, should the need arise. As it turned out, Burnes had been over-optimistic: the Indus was not quite so suitable for steam navigation – there were too many shallows, and it was too swift-flowing when the Himalayan snows melted. There was also the problem of tariffs imposed by the amirs of Sind; and this was something that Charles, imbued with the principles of free trade and laissez faire, also inveighed against.

Nine years later, after the military disasters in Afghanistan, when Charles was in London, he was still harping on the importance of the Indus, now recommending to the Government a return to the policies of Lord William Bentinck, even that a steam flotilla should be assembled at the river's mouth. And in 1843 Sind was annexed by the British, neatly cancelling out the problem of the tariffs: a piece of unprovoked aggression.

When Charles fought his lone battle against Colebrooke and produced his reports with Conolly, his writings and letters had a certain youthful freshness which now seem almost endearing. He was so convinced that time would prove him right, and of the great future that lay before him.

Such adulation from on high and from lesser sources had its effect on Charles, as one sees from the oracular tone of his 'Indophilus' letters. In his attacks on the 'Ultra-Tories' at Calcutta he became ever more formidable and stern, not hesitating to call in the Scriptures or the Old Testament to reinforce his arguments. His *Report on the Inland Customs and Town Duties of the Bengal Presidency*, completed in March 1832 and printed privately, was an Utilitarian masterpiece – one might say manifesto: Macaulay, writing in 1834, was quite sincere when he said: 'Accustomed as I have been to public offices, I have never read an abler state-paper: and I do not believe that there is – I will not say in India, – but in England – another man of twenty-seven who could have written it.' (Actually in March 1832 Charles was still twenty-four.)

Whilst Charles had been leading what he called his vagabond life at Kotah in 1830, he had brooded on the abolition of those transit duties, which he saw as the greatest impediment to economic incentive and social reform in the Presidency – he had originally become 'vexatiously aware' of them in the laying out of Trevelyanganj at Delhi. He had also, incidentally, become convinced that by granting full scope to the individual's potential for self-improvement, and to the expression of the market for British manufactures, it would eventually help to lead the way to that ultimate dream of his, the Christianization of India. Bentinck, very impressed, put Charles on the Customs Committee, and it took three years before victory could be achieved, after some hot debates in the press.

'Indophilus' also campaigned for more freedom for Europeans to buy land in India and an equalization of the sugar duties: in other words that the duties should be no more than those charged on West Indian sugar. He wanted the local press to be freed, and the state to assist in the distribution of English language newspapers to remoter areas. He wanted details of the Government's annual Budget and a selection of its more important papers to be published and thus be available to all. He wanted a committee that would produce a digest of English laws, to be translated into the colloquial languages of India. He wanted a revision of the laws of deportation for criminal offences. He wanted the abolition of discriminating duties on the importation of American books.

Several subjects had been put forward in James Mill's *History of British India* and thus automatically had the support of Bentinck – who on assuming his post in 1828 had told Mill that it would be he who would really be the Governor-General of India. Charles's position was that he was at the head of the shock-troops, even if his schemes had little to do with his official position in the Political Department. Since he was convinced that any opposition to his views could only come from those with selfish or vested interests, or for reasons of monopoly or patronage, he believed that by resorting to the 'Parliament of the Press' he would reach the true heart of the public. He also felt that in this way pressure could be brought on the Government, whose process of discussion on important matters he found frustratingly lengthy. Again, one might, at this remove, fairly think it odd behaviour for a civil servant, even when writing pseudonymously. And Charles's dashing into print without a by-your-leave was, in years to come, to get him into severe trouble.

Thoby Prinsep and other 'Ultra Tories' counter-attacked in the press on some issues. Prinsep also objected to the report on Transit Duties, where it was considered that permission should have been sought before publication. No doubt Bentinck took his indulgent attitude towards 'Indophilus' because he saw Charles as a useful publicist in his not always popular drive for economies and the improvement of efficiency and integrity in the Service. Charles, in the *Bengal Hurkaru*, even attacked individual Collectors by name, accusing them of being responsible for the ruin of entire districts through self-interest. This form of 'public trial' naturally caused outrage, particularly since one of the Collectors was William Fraser, under whom Charles had once served at Delhi.

Charles was put on the Prison Discipline Committee. He became Secretary of the Native Medical Education Committee. He had long learnt to despise the descendants of the Moghuls at Delhi, even if he admired Moghul architecture. For him there was no romance in their fallen grandeur, and he considered the whole system of nazrs humiliating. He had little sympathy for the King's stipendiary wangles, and supported Bentinck's decision not to see him, after the King's insistence that they should meet on equal terms.

When on March 18 1832 Charles posted a copy of his Transit Duties report to Bentinck, he disclosed his scheme for another project which he had also been working on during his Kotah days. Like some prophet inspired, he wrote to his protector:

It is now my intention to apply myself seriously to what I have for a long time past considered the great enterprise of my life. I mean the moral and intellectual renovation of the people of India. I long to see established under your Lordship's auspices a system of education so comprehensive as to embrace every class of public teachers, so elastic as to admit of its being gradually extended to every village in the country, and so interwoven with the constitution of the State by affording a ready access to its honours and emoluments to the most distinguished servants, as to furnish the highest motives to intellectual exertion to the whole body of the people which this world can afford. In short, I long to see such a system of education established in India as already exists in the state of New York, in the New England states and in Russia and such as it is now proposed to establish in France and England. This would form the crowning measure of your Lordship's administration. In 25 years it would entirely change the moral face of the country, and countless millions in their successive generations would bless the memory of the man who has called them to a higher and better state of existence . . . The whole country is craving for a system of education . . .

Charles on the warpath

Charles had been working on other grand ideas for the 'regeneration' of India, that would bring to its people not only the blessings of Western learning but of British constitutional liberty. A first essential, he had become convinced, was that Indians should be taught to write their own languages (of which there were many) in the Roman alphabet. This in turn would help them to learn English, which must replace Persian as the language of official business, commerce and the law. Inevitably the spread of knowledge would follow, and this would surely go hand in hand with the spread of Christianity, preferably of the Protestant variety.

The British public was already accustomed to hearing of the 'errors' and 'darkness' of Hinduism. Few cared or bothered about its basic philosophy, or about India's 'eternal truths'. Centuries of despotic rule, so it was understood from the works of Charles Grant and James Mill, and latterly from the posthumously published *Narrative* of Bishop Heber, had deprived Indians of any sense of independence or security. The practice of suttee, or sati, had been held among the foulest examples of Hindu barbarism. Bishop Heber had vividly described how the widow might be tied under the corpse and then soaked in ghee, the better to make her burn; as the flames leapt up relatives threw on more of the stuff. Years later, after the death of Ranjit Singh, who was of course a Sikh, his four ranees and seven of his concubines were burnt with him. But Bentinck had abolished suttee in 1829, and was also aiming to eradicate thuggee, which involved the strangulation and robbing of travellers in the name of the goddess Kali. Missionaries were also complaining about other 'bestial vices' such as the juggernaut at Puri. Slavery was still prevalent. Then there were purdah, Muslim as well as Hindu, and, especially, the caste system, which Charles hoped in due course would be totally broken down through contact with Western liberal ideas. Both he and Bentinck also wanted to adapt the strictures of the Hindu law of inheritance, so that Eurasians would not be victimized.

Bentinck's great aim was to found 'British greatness on Indian happiness', but he did not go so far – at least publicly – as to believe that the Hindu and Muslim religions should actually be replaced by Christianity, even in that age of high missionary fervour. Hindus and

Muslims might learn the English language, but their institutions, customs and 'harmless rites' (as distinct from blood-letting, murder and all forms of 'brutalising excitement') would have to be respected. As it happened, Bentinck's abolition of suttee was criticized by some of the British Orientalists at Calcutta; Hindus looked on suttee as an act of heroism and loyalty by the widow (as in the case of Ranjit Singh's ranees, done willingly), and certainly such a peremptory abolition caused a shock in some places.

Charles had arrived at Calcutta at the time of the 'Bengal renaissance'. There was a real demand among Indians for modernization. Wealthy Hindus had at their own expense established the Hindu College precisely in order to study European literature and science. The great Bengali reformer Rammohan Roy had just gone to England, and had left many disciples at Calcutta. Then there was the meteoric and foppish Henry Derozio, an Eurasian of some genius but who carried his desire for Westernization to extremes.

The dramatic battles between the Orientalists, headed by Thoby Prinsep, his brother James, Henry Shakespear and John Tytler, and the Anglicists, of whom Charles was the driving force, have been well charted in a book by David Kopf. Charles's typically obsessional behaviour, as recorded in his various manifestos, makes one understand only too well why Calcutta hostesses shied away from inviting him to their dinner-tables. In a sense the clash was between traditionalists and modernists, with Charles and his allies, such as his fervent admirer John Colvin (who was to die at Agra during the Mutiny of 1857) and the Presbyterian minister Alexander Duff, campaigning against the 'redundant' Sanskrit and 'alien' Persian and Arabic. Charles was convinced of the necessity of building up a new literature in the vernacular language – the 'real' languages of India – and this could only be done through a familiarity with Western ideas. There was also the essential question of Indian medicine, which was considered antediluvian and dominated by quacks, who 'preyed' on the people.

Like Bentinck, Charles foresaw a time when India must inevitably regain its independence. 'In the nature of things,' he was to say, 'our rule cannot be permanent.' He compared the future of India with the then situation in America, where Britain reaped the advantages of trade and investments, thanks to a common language and a common 'morality'. Bentinck looked forward to the time when Indians would become responsible advisers and partners in the government of their country, even on the Supreme Council. He and Charles wanted equal treatment in schools, whether the pupils were Christian, Hindu or Muslim. There would be no distinction except in merit. Bentinck gave 'native parties' at Government House – the problems of the right food and caste always being difficulties. Both he and Charles respected and had esteem for Eurasians, or 'Indi-Britons', finding – in the words of Charles – that the 'amicability, quickness and tact of the natives' mingled well with the 'high moral quality of Europeans'. Quite apart from all this idealism, there was a practical aspect: employing Indians and Eurasians in places of trust and responsibility saved money.

So far so good – at least for some. And so far Utilitarian, in the tradition of the precepts of Jeremy Bentham and James Mill, even if Bentinck seems to have been hazy about the actual meaning of the word Utilitarian. Macaulay, when he wrote to his sister Margaret on December 7 1834, said that on reaching Calcutta he had found Charles 'engaged in a furious contest against half a dozen of the oldest and most powerful men in India on the subject of native education'.

Charles Trevelyan at Calcutta, by James Siddons.
From the collection of W. B. Clowes

If the Anglicists were attacked as 'dangerous Utopians', with schemes that were a 'visionary absurdity' which would simply provoke unrest and possibly bloodshed, Charles flayed the Orientalists for their 'ivory towerism' and 'mania'. The Orientalists, he said, could not change a civilization that was already a corpse. India's past must of course continue to be studied, but for antiquarian reasons only. Yet Hindus were a literary people, 'capable of every virtue' and eager to learn. Indeed they had been literary 'when we were barbarians'. As for the Muslims in Calcutta, compared to Delhi their education was being disgracefully neglected.

The Orientalists, while being forced to agree that there was a period of 'exhaustion' or even 'stagnation' in Indian culture, saw themselves as the heirs of men like Sir William Jones, the eminent founder of the Asiatic Society, who were prepared to assimilate themselves as much as possible to their Indian surroundings and learn about the customs and heritage of the Indian 'golden age'. The aim of the Orientalists was to help the Indians to find the roots of their civilization, and many of these men made highly important contributions to archaeology and the study of ancient literature. Charles's superior at the Political Department, William Macnaghten, eventually murdered at Kabul, also joined the Orientalists, and this probably later had an effect on Charles's career.

Charles blazed with indignation after a jibe from James Prinsep about 'ultra-radicalism' in connection with support for a proposed Urdu-English dictionary. He retaliated with 'ultra-Toryism' and published Prinsep's views without permission. He then wrote a paper of many thousands of words, showing how the Education Committee had actually provided money for the printing of erotic Sanskrit dramas, epics and poems about *prostitutes* and *lechery*. Touché! As he said over and over again, what must be taught in schools was a *living* language like English. 'How desirable it would be to engraft upon the popular languages of the East such words as virtue, honour, gratitude, patriotism, public spirit!'

Tytler countered all this with a warning against teaching French, which 'should be strictly prohibited, as that language contains an abundance of immoral books'.

Always the enemy of academics, Charles accused members of the Committee of being more interested in their own careers and reputations, and in having books written by themselves published at Government expense, than in the beneficial instruction of the Indian people. It was his tone of moral superiority that was so much resented. He had seized on the word 'engraft' because it had become a favourite of the Orientalists; they had said that English must be 'engrafted' gradually and peacefully on the Indians, not superimposed on them by 'uncompromising guerrillas'. As the polemics increased, particularly after the return from England to Calcutta of Thoby Prinsep, it became clear that Charles was also advocating the abolition of the Fort William college. 'Men who had been remarkable for their self-restraint completely lost their tempers.' In many ways it was difficult to defend Fort William, originally founded to train civil servants who had been grounded as boys at Haileybury in England. It had become expensive to maintain, and the idleness among students there, especially among those 'billiard-room frequenting gallants', had become notorious. Nevertheless it was still an important link with the intelligentsia of Calcutta.

Thoby Prinsep was not everyone's idea of an asset at the dinner-table either, at any rate at Calcutta. Emily Eden was to write of him: '*The* Prinsep – the greatest bore Providence ever created, and so contradictory that he will not let anybody agree or differ with him.' On the other hand some thought of him as 'large and philosophic in mind, grand in his stature, his learning, his memory, his everything, even to his sneeze (once received with an encore from the gallery in a theatre)'. His wife Sara was the 'kind of woman who would have turned a convent into a tumult'.

When the Thoby Prinseps finally retired to London, they created a salon at Little Holland House, where they entertained G. F. Watts, the Thackerays, the Tennysons, Ruskin, Browning etc. Their son was Val Prinsep the Pre-Raphaelite painter. One of Sara's sisters was Julia Margaret Cameron, the pioneer in photography. Another was Maria Jackson, grandmother of Virginia Woolf.★

On April 9 1834 Charles reported on the grand education debate to Bentinck, who was then at Ooty. Because of the efforts of Thoby Prinsep, he had to admit that what he described as the 'anti-popular course' was having a temporary ascendancy. However he launched into another tremendous paean:

> It cannot be concealed that India is on the eve of a great moral change. The indications of it are perceptible in every part of the country. Everywhere the same decided rejection of antiquated

---

★ According to Virginia Woolf, her great-grandfather Jim Pattle (known as Jemmy Blazes) was a 'gentleman of marked, but doubtful, reputation, who after living a riotous life and earning the title of "the biggest liar in India", finally drank himself to death.' The Pattles lived at Garden Reach, overlooking the Hooghly. Jim Pattle and James Prinsep saw to the construction of the Calcutta Ice House, ready for the first importation of ice from Boston, Massachusetts, an event which caused all business to be suspended until noon. Everybody, it was said, invited everybody to dinner, to taste claret and beer iced by the American importation. Another Pattle girl was baptized Louisa Colebrooke Pattle, after Charles's arch-enemy at the Delhi Residency. I have often wondered whether the name Pattle derives from Patel, which is common among Hindus, and would like to float the idea that Virginia Woolf's genius in part derives from her Eurasian ancestry.

systems prevails, everywhere the same craving for instruction in a better system is to be perceived and the abolition of the exclusive privileges which the Persian language has in the courts and affairs of court will form the crowning stroke which will shake Hinduism and Mohammedanism to their centre and firmly establish our language, our learning and ultimately our religion in India.

Your Lordship's situation is the most solemn and responsible that ever fell to the lot of any individual in any age of the world... It is a glorious privilege, which I trust in God is reserved for your Lordship, to become the regenerator of more than 100 millions of your fellow creatures in all their successive generations. Nay, India is merely the stepping stone to the rest of Asia...

All this while the 'Indophilus' letters, on a variety of other proposed reforms, were still pouring out. The *Hurkaru* now went into the attack, resenting his over-confident manner. When he started producing a monthly list of recommended books of a suitably 'high moral tone', he was accused by the *Calcutta Courier* of creating a self-installed censorship.

As always, he seemed incapable of laughing at himself. Macaulay joked that Charles had never sufficiently studied Sanskrit because his dictionary had fallen overboard during the voyage to India. Charles now took it upon himself to write open letters to 'Dear Bengalee children' about why they should learn English, and produced a book for them called *The Polyglot Fables*. He was not pleased when a nonsensical lampoon appeared, first in a Meerut paper, then as a booklet, entitled *Polyglot Baby's Own Book*, 'edited by Bartolozzi Brown, Gent' and dedicated to 'THE BIGGEST BABY IN INDIA'. It began:

A new era is dawning upon this hitherto unenlightened land. Knowledge, as Lord William Bentinck says, is generated by Steam Navigation, the capital of the late Agency Houses, and has acted as an insensible and invisible agent in the formation of Indian schools; little Bengalee girls take in plain needle work, little Bengalee boys study Lindley Murray [English Grammar etc.]; and Telunga women, under the influence of the missionaries, have achieved the important reform of bearing their water pots on their heads' antipodes ... Yes, it was the great Trevelyan who first pointed out to me under how great a mistake our instructors of youth have hitherto laboured ... [I have been] animated to this understanding by Mr. Trevelyan's assurance that 'English is the ocean of knowledge, and translations the rivers flowing from it'.

The 'author' then proved how 'Hey diddle diddle, the cat and the fiddle' could be changed so as not to offend Hindus, by making a horse instead of a cow jump over the moon.

The Polyglot Fables were not among the papers which Charles so carefully preserved after leaving India.

The Minute

Macaulay may have thought in 1834 that Charles looked like a gentle-man, but there were many at Calcutta who certainly did not think that he behaved like one. Bentinck was due to retire in the first half of 1835. His decision on education was therefore pressing, but even Charles's letters had not convinced him that the correct moment had been reached.

Macaulay, as he had commented in his letter to Margaret of December 7 1834, arrived at Calcutta already predisposed in favour of Charles, after having read at Ooty his correspondence to Bentinck and the transit duties report. He did admit though to finding some of Charles's papers on education 'rather too vehement'. Nevertheless, 'I joined him, threw all my influence into his scale, brought over Lord William – or rather induced Lord William to declare himself . . . We now consider the victory as gained.' Shakespear had resigned from the presidency of the Education Committee, and Macaulay was to take his place. 'Lord William,' Macaulay said, 'intends, very speed-ily, to pronounce a decision in our favour.'

The letter shows that Bentinck's mind had already been made up before receiving Macaulay's famous Minute on education of February 2 1835. 'When all this was going on,' Macaulay wrote, 'I was constantly with Trevelyan: and he was constantly becoming more and more in love with Nancy.' Meeting Macaulay had made Charles aware of one great lack in his own education, and this was Greek and Latin literature, and indeed English classics. He now re-garded Macaulay as an oracle of wisdom. His thirst for literary knowledge of this sort became 'insatiable'. Macaulay gave him his Homer which he read with 'perfect rapture'.

The news of Margaret's death was assuaged a little for Macaulay by his own rereading of Pindar, Thucydides and Demosthenes. He was also preparing the Minute. As Bentinck said, he and Thoby Prinsep 'butted one another like wild bulls'. Both Charles and Macaulay loved provocation. Macnaghten said Charles had become 'perfectly rabid'.

The Minute is still being lambasted for such things as its chauvinism, insensitiveness, arrogance, legal weaknesses, 'colossal ignorance' of the 'rich store of Oriental learning', and as being a supreme example of how demagogic brilliance and polemical eloquence can win the day. At the same time one has to admit that Macaulay's vision of English as the world language was prophetic.

Although the Minute was not officially published for many years, extracts appeared in Charles Trevelyan's *On the Education of the People of India*, but without referring to Macaulay's authorship (at Macaulay's request). Its thesis may well be summed up by a remark, chauvinist indeed, in an essay that Macaulay wrote on Thornton that year: 'The English have become the greatest and most highly civilized people the world ever saw.' In effect the Minute centred on the interpretation of the Charter Act of 1813, which vaguely stipulated that a sum was to be set apart 'for the revival and promotion of literature, and the encouragement of the learned natives of India, and for the introduction and promotion of the science among the inhabitants of the British territories'.

It is enough to quote three of the passages which still cause outrage all these years later:

Suppose that the pasha of Egypt, a country once superior in knowledge to the nations of Europe, but now sunk far below them, were to appropriate a sum for ... the study of hieroglyphics, to search into all the doctrines disguised under the fable of Osiris, and to ascertain with all possible accuracy the ritual with which cats and onions were anciently adored?

I have never found one among them [the Orientalists] who could deny that a single shelf of a good European library was worth the whole native literature of India and Arabia.

[Shall we] countenance, at the public expense, medical doctrines which would disgrace an English farrier, astronomy which would move laughter in girls at an English boarding school, history abounding with kings thirty feet high and reigns thirty thousand years long, and geography made of seas of treacle and seas of butter.

He compared the situation in India to that of England in the fifteenth century, and of Russia in the eighteenth, both periods of literary awakening.

He brought up the Anglicists' favourite 'downward filtration'

theory – concentrating on the upper classes and the intelligentsia –
and followed this with a resounding piece of Macaulay rhetoric that is
often quoted:

> We must at present do our best to form ... a class of persons
> Indian in blood and colour, but English in tastes, in opinions, in
> morals and in intellect. To that class we may leave it to refine the
> vernacular dialects from the western nomenclature, and to render
> them by degrees fit vehicles for conveying knowledge to the great
> mass of the population.

He proposed that the Muslim Madrassa College and the Sanskrit
College at Calcutta should be closed down. If his proposals were not
accepted, he said, he would resign from the Committee.

On reading Macaulay's Minute, Bentinck wrote at its foot: 'I give
my entire concurrence to the statements expressed.' Some of the contents leaked out (thanks to the over-enthusiastic John Colvin), and as
a result thousands of petitions were gathered against the abolition of
the two colleges. Prinsep attacked Macaulay in a minute of his own,
only to be somewhat harshly told by Bentinck that it was an 'irregu-
larity'.

The new educational policy of the Governor-General was finally
put forward in the 'Resolution' of March 7 1835: 'The great object of
the British Government ought to be the promotion of European
literature and science among the natives of India, and ... all the
funds appropriated for the purpose of education would be best
employed in English education alone.' This was almost identical
with Macaulay's original draft, except that the Madrassa and Sanskrit
Colleges had a stay of execution.

Bentinck was by now a sick man. There was a possibility of a
'morbid condition of the brain' as well as an 'impaired state of the
digestive organs'. It had not yet been decided in London who should
take his place. By the end of the month Sir Charles Metcalfe, who had
recently been nominated Governor of Agra, was hurriedly recalled
and became Acting Governor-General. Before he left, Bentinck instituted another reform: the abolition of flogging in the East India
Company's army.

The Orientalists were in retreat, but they had not surrendered.
Their spirit, so Charles said, had indeed been stirred to its 'innermost
depths'. If more money had been available, perhaps the battle would
not have been quite so desperate. At least it can be said that the British
would have been much criticized if they had *not* provided oppor-
tunities for learning English and Western ideas. Macaulay, Charles

and Bentinck underestimated the strength of Indian religion and culture. They could not have foreseen the decline of Christianity, let alone the decline of Britain as a world power. They underestimated British colour prejudice and the memsahib factor. It has also been pointed out that embedded in the Minute were not just Macaulay's views on education in India, but on education generally in Britain.

Ironically, as many have pointed out, Indian nationalism was one of the by-products of the new educational policy, with its infusion of Western liberal ideas. Macaulay's biographer, Professor John Clive, has shown how those crude and contemptuous remarks of his merely led to an increased consciousness among Indians of the value of their cultural and spiritual heritage. The educational policy also helped to create a social divergence between Hindus and Muslims, since the Muslims tended to be opposed to the introduction of the teaching of English and thus in due course found themselves falling behind in obtaining the more lucrative and influential jobs.

Whatever immediate struggles remained, whatever amendments were likely to be made by subsequent Governors-General, Charles rejoiced, and he wrote this in his book *On the Education of the People of India*:

> The English language, not many generations hence, will be spoken by millions in all the four quarters of the globe; and our learning, our morals, our principles of constitutional liberty, and our religion embodied in the established literature, and diffused through the genius of the vernacular languages, will spread far and wide among the nations . . . Whether we govern India ten or a thousand years, we will do our duty by it. We will look not at the profitable duration of our trust, but to the satisfactory discharge of it . . . But interest and duty in this case are indissolubly divided . . . The existing connection, between the two such distant countries as England and India, cannot, in the nature of things be permanent: no effort of policy can prevent the natives from ultimately regaining their independence. But there are two ways of arriving at this point. One of these is, through the medium of revolution; the other, through that of reform. In one, the forward movement is sudden and violent; in the other, it is gradual and peaceable . . . The political education of a nation must be a work of time; and while it is in progress, we shall be as safe as it will be possible for us to be. The natives will not rise against us, because we shall stoop to raise them . . . Trained by us to happiness and independence, and endowed with our learning and our political institutions, India will remain the proudest monument of British benevolence; and we

shall long continue to reap, in the affectionate attachment of the people, and in a great commercial intercourse with their splendid country, the fruit of that liberal and enlightened policy which suggested to us this line of conduct ... By governing well, and promoting to the utmost of our power the growth of wealth, intelligence, and enterprise in its vast population, we shall be able to make India a source of wealth and strength, with which nothing in our past history furnishes any parallel.

Three well-known gentlemen in Calcutta

II

'Have you ever seen Kanchinjunga from Darjeeling?' an Indian Army wallah once asked me at a party.

I hadn't, and hardly expected to do so. But faced with several days' stay at Calcutta before our plane left for the Andamans, I decided that now was my chance. We could fly to Bagdogra from Calcutta, so I learnt in London, then either climb by the renowned Toy Railway for eight hours to Darjeeling, or – rather more swiftly – share a taxi with somebody.

'But Darjeeling's like Wimbledon!', José, a Filipino friend living in London, had laughed at us. When he said this, my mind went back to a favourite film, the Merchant-Ivory *Autobiography of a Princess*, when Madhur Jaffrey placed a teapot near the shy James Mason, not at Wimbledon but in her South Ken. flat: 'Good Darjeeling tea,' she had said with an encouraging smile.

José couldn't I suppose have read his Sir Joseph Hooker, *Himalayan Journals* vol. 1, with all the glorious descriptions of the peaks around Darjeeling which were nevertheless 'too aerial to be chained to the memory', or those books about the adventures and perils of the old plant-hunters: 'Here are great scandent trees, twisting round the trunks of others and strangling them. Leeches swarm up to seven thousand feet, and have been known to live for days in the jaws, nostrils and stomachs of human beings, causing dreadful suffering and death.' Sir Joseph Hooker during his travels in the mountains had frequently fifty or sixty leeches stuck to his ankles. We braced ourselves therefore for the perils of this Wimbledon of the South.

January, I had been warned, was a bad time at Darjeeling for views and flowers. So I would miss two more of my favourite shrubs in bloom, *Magnolia Campbellii* and *Rhododendron falconeri*, both of which I had tried to grow in Cornwall but which had been cut down in a severe winter. And I could not pretend that Darjeeling had links with my family, even if the indefatigable Charles Trevelyan had been an enthusiast for starting up the tea industry in north-east India. Why go to Darjeeling at all then? I think chiefly – Hookers and Kanchinjunga apart – Darjeeling meant my friend Barbara Milne, aged ten running away from her convent school with nine other little girls, looking for 'Peggy's aunt'. . . .

We had to show passports at Bagdogra, and as usual Raúl's caused some perplexities, this time because of his profession, Abogado, lawyer. A file marked 'Spain' was solemnly brought down, and Avocado inscribed in it, the first and only entry.

The Toy Train had left on its long climb, so we shared a taxi with two Nepalese girls and a doctor, guarding his cardiac equipment from jolts in a box marked White Heather Laundry, Thornton Heath, Surrey. But I'll have to skip over that dramatic drive, far more spectacular than the one up to Simla, and with rather more close shaves from other cars and lorries. Eventually in giant tree-fern and bamboo country we caught up the little train (Glasgow 1925), just like the old Emett cartoons, indeed an Emett itself, with a great black spout of coal smoke. After Kurseong there were notices, to comfort us no doubt in case we tumbled down a precipice: 'To give joy is to receive joy', 'The greatest truths are the simplest', 'Like a tree we must find a place to grow and branch out' – put there, our doctor guessed, by some 'guru set-up where Europeans go'. Then we drove into the setting sun, among the scandent trees into the dusk, and finally the mist. 'You won't see Kanchinjunga tomorrow you know,' the doctor said sternly.

The enormous, nearly empty Mount Everest Hotel at Darjeeling was like last year in Marienbad: a score of round tables each with a complement of chairs and ashtrays, and upstairs a musty place for a band and dancing. If we really meant to try for Kanchinjunga at sunrise, we were told, it would entail a jeep ride to Tiger Hill at 5 am. We were advised to take with us the blankets off our beds.

At 5 am Darjeeling was still invisible to us, but we could see that there was a hoar frost. Stars, and a clear sky; so we were going to be in luck. But we had an hour's wait on that icy pinnacle, conscious of the huge unseen black chasm, thousands of feet deep, between us and the mountain ranges.

Then it began to happen.

In the early morning the valleys are filled with mist, so that all the lower ground looks like an icy ocean; then the top of Kinchin, and those of its neighbouring giants, flame with a pink or ruby light, while the gloomy shades lower down seem to give increased loftiness to those stupendous peaks.

Murray's *Hand-Book*, 1882. But in the gradualness of dawn there were other colours: citrine, gold, orange; and the dark of the sky became a pale zircon, then pearl, then aquamarine; with of course some purple patches.

When at last it was nearly day, I noticed that on a terrace just below our watchtower there were hundreds of prayer-flags hung between trees, and moving among them were people dressed in scarlet or brilliant blue. I thought at first these people were priests, but they were only sightseers like us, wrapped in blankets.

Our Gurkha driver in a woolly hat tried to point out Everest to us – he worked with Tenzing, who was then Darjeeling's resident hero. I remembered something about Tenzing attempting to show Everest to several American ladies from this very spot on Tiger Hill. 'No, not that peak,' he had said. 'Everest's the small one.' And if we now understood our driver properly, Everest from Tiger Hill looked like a tiny piece of chalk.

When I got back home, I looked up the touching last paragraph in Tenzing's autobiography:

'The small one' . . . Perhaps that is a strange name for the biggest mountain on earth, but not so wrong, for what is Everest without the eye that sees it? It is the heart of man that makes it big or small.

Now I had to decide which peak was the fairest of them all: Kanchinjunga, Nanga Parbat or Rakaposhi. Kanchinjunga is officially 1,508 feet higher than Nanga Parbat, 2,618 feet more than Rakaposhi. It was like choosing which English cathedral you prefer. I have always loved Winchester, because I know it best, and after that Salisbury and York Minster. Nanga Parbat is part of my childhood, so I would never dare offend its ghosts by preferring another peak; I must admit though that the experience on Tiger Hill on that January 13 1982 was a good match for October 2 1929, when I first saw Nanga Parbat from Bunji on our way to Gilgit. But Rakaposhi . . . perhaps she does have a perfection in common with the spire of Salisbury Cathedral . . .

We found ourselves unexpectedly deposited at the Buddhist monastery of Ghoom. There we were shown all the sights: the library, the pure water, the Buddha with two thousand hands and twenty faces. As a result we gave the monk ten rupees and all our change. On emerging we were beckoned at by a younger monk who showed us a prayer wheel and then asked for money. He became hysterical when we said we had nothing else to spare. The guilty satisfaction of his rival did not escape us.

At last the view of Darjeeling. Built round a ridge like Simla, it was an alive town, a working town, a town with a purpose someone remarked. Kanchinjunga from down there seemed to loom, and the odd thing was that it appeared cut in two, because of a vast granite wall, always completely bare of snow. We could imagine how homesick little English girls would have felt trapped or overpowered. And in the afternoon, as Edward Lear had said in 1874, Kanchinjunga became a wonderful hash of Turneresque colour and mist and snow.

We liked Darjeeling/Wimbledon, and we liked the ropeway over the tea-gardens, and the gigantic fangs of the Siberian tigers which were given by Khrushchev to Mrs Gandhi; and the mahonias, and all the little Tibetan dogs (Lhasa Lapsos) running about. No leeches, but we did glimpse some of those 'short, thick, rosy-cheeked women' mentioned by Murray, who liked dealing 'tremendous thumps on the men' though 'in a good-humoured way'. Good old Wimbledon.

A tea-grower from Kurseong told us he had come to sack a hundred and fifty men out of a workforce of a thousand. Mrs Gandhi just would not allow his firm to close down. On the way to Darjeeling his car had been stoned. Under the circumstances we declined his offer of a lift the next day to Bagdogra.

Back in Calcutta we called at the Fairlawn Hotel to book rooms for later, after the Andamans, and after Burma, where a visa for only one week was permitted. We had decided that we were in the wrong financial bracket for the Grand; anyway the English were in some disgrace at that hotel because of recent bad behaviour there by our cricket team. The Fairlawn was complete Somerset Maugham, my ideal of a hotel; perhaps once a small 'palace', open to the garden without any doors from outside to the entrance lobby, it was owned by Mrs Smith, a small and elegant Armenian. 'Mamma mia. Olé,' she said to Raúl, pointing to posters of bull-fighters above the desk. The waiters seemed aged about eighty-five, very courteous, in white gold-threaded pugrees and barefoot. The garden, mostly red-tiled, had bicoloured umbrellas, protecting you from the droppings of roosting crows in the banyan tree. The Fairlawn was to be one of my great experiences at Calcutta.

We met Mrs Smith's English husband, Ted, about to take the two snow-white poodles for an airing in the car. He had been an officer in Burma, a major in the Northamptons. 'If you're going to the Andamans,' he said, 'then you've got to meet my friend Captain Dennis Beale.'

This was the third time I'd come across the name of Dennis Beale.

The first had been in one of those awful queues at the Indian High Commission in London, when I had heard a young woman ahead of me complaining about the frustration over permits for the Andamans. Her name was Dolly Sancho she had told me, and she was half Burmese. She had urged me on arrival at Port Blair in the Andamans to call on her brother, who was none other than Dennis Beale. 'Ask for Junglighat. That's where he lives. Beale's Marine Service.' Junglighat! From Somerset Maugham back to Edward Lear. Dolly was trying to get a permit for their mother, who was wholly Burmese, and could not speak English although travelling round the world visiting her scattered family.

The second time I encountered the name Dennis Beale had been in Gavin Young's *Slow Boats to China*, where there is a chapter about him. Beale had 'opened a magic door to the Andamans' for Gavin; he lived in a house on stilts and listened to Sinatra and Vera Lynn on the hi-fi. He had a boat, also called *Gavin*, in which he sailed round the coral islands, fishing and towing logs.

It was thrilling, at last, to see the Andamans below us, thick with apparently virgin forest, and with long white beaches, creeks and bays, the water turquoise in the shallows and greenish beyond: like brochures of the West Indies without the houses or people. Although there were said to be two hundred and four islands altogether, there were four main ones, running north to south, never more than thirty miles wide. They with the Nicobars were part of a submerged mountain chain running from the Arakan peninsula in Burma to Sumatra. Between the Andamans and the Nicobars there is the Ten Degree Channel, always regarded as treacherous. Ptolemy had called the Andamans the islands of the cannibals, and Marco Polo perpetuated this legend about cannibalism, adding that the inhabitants had 'heads like dogs'. Fanny Parks, in her *Wanderings of a Pilgrim*, when she sailed past them in 1822, still believed that there were cannibals who ate shipwrecked sailors. I found that 'Port Blair' really encompassed one large area, and that the main town is Aberdeen, where there is also the great jail. The British had chiefly lived on a small island half a mile to the east, Ross Island.

We landed on an airfield that is now part of a naval air station and built originally by the Japanese during the occupation. As soon as I decently could, I asked our hotel manager about Dennis Beale. 'Of course you must meet him,' he said. 'He's a great friend of mine.' The hotel was on Corbyn's Cove, which I knew to have been the favourite spot for 'bathing picnics' in my parents' day – you used to reach it by launch from Ross or in victorias through the palm groves from

Aberdeen. It was also where the Japs had landed in March 1942.

'A crescent-shaped white sandy beach, five hundred yards long,' I had read, and had indeed seen in Walter's photographs. The fringe of coconut palms was exactly the same age as me, planted in 1923, though I regret to say that some trees already had reached the stage of bending over at right angles. From the hotel windows local people, bicyclists and cattle made silhouettes under those palms against the dazzle of the sea, The manager, Vijay, late of the Indian navy, came from Lucknow originally, his wife, Sheila, from Bombay. Her parents had been born at different ends of India, and could only speak to one another in English. That would have pleased Charles Trevelyan. To our delight – after so many mediocre meals in India – we discovered that she was intensely interested in food. She also had an amazing wardrobe of beautiful sarees, and was keen on Chopin and Mozart, softly piped in the hotel. Almost at once she began discussing the works of James Baldwin, as we sat together in the Cecil Beaton-type wicker chairs in front of a curtain made from shells. Her husband gave me two booklets on the Andamans. One was on the Cellular Jail, and I had a shock.

This 'Indian Bastille' was now a national monument, I found, 'a mute witness to the indescribable sufferings of the patriots who were incarcerated in the cells of the Jail by the align [sic] Government. Some of the prisoners lodged in the Jail even had to lay down their lives as victims of tyranny and brutalities of the foreign Government.' Every brick had a 'heart-rending story to tell'.

Had I now to be ashamed of having been born at Port Blair?

I was relieved, however, to find that the High Commissioner at the time of my birth, Colonel Ferrar, was still remembered with respect. Indeed part of Port Blair is known as Ferrarganj.

Life on Ross Island

Lieutenant-Colonel M. L. Ferrar had been forty-six when he took office at Port Blair as Chief Commissioner for the Andamans and Nicobars. Olive always used to speak of his kindness, and the first ever picture of me, on her lap, is in the garden of Government House on Ross Island. Ferrar had been at Sandhurst with Winston Churchill, and during the First War had worked in Censorship at Bombay. In 1919, on the very day before he had been due to sail for England, he had been urgently summoned to Lahore as Assistant Commissioner, after the Amritsar massacre at the Jallianwala Bagh.

He was slightly built and 'butterfly mad', infecting Olive with the craze. His collection of butterflies is now in the Natural History Museum, South Kensington, but Olive's became progressively more battered as we later moved about India – for a while afterwards, in England, they were part of my 'museum'. Colonel Ferrar walked or 'cantered' everywhere, with his wife Nancy usually following on a pony. If you asked him to lunch, he would only want water biscuits with milk and soda. This regime, with whisky at sundown, 'kept a man going', and he did keep going until he was ninety-six. He was so highly thought of by the 'powers that be' that his tenure of office was extended twice, and he stayed on at Port Blair until 1931.

The main garrison, which in 1923 consisted of Walter's company of the 93rd Burma, was on Ross with the food store – convenient in case of a mass uprising by the convicts. Ross also had the advantage of being free from malarial mosquitoes. On arriving in April 1923 Ferrar wrote to his mother:

> Ross Island is very small, half a mile long at most and two hundred feet high. On the top is Government House, and the whole place is well covered with bungalows and barracks. The house is very attractive – downstairs a large hall, my office and miscellaneous godowns – a fine staircase with a wooden gallery all round the top and upstairs a very fine ballroom; drawing room and most spacious verandahs forming rooms in themselves – some seven or eight bedrooms – the whole thing in wood, brown teak panelling and above that yellow colour washed (!) – much good furniture but much also v. bad, wooden floors with rugs and mats strewn about.

This furniture was mostly made from the red padauk wood of the Andamans. Years after Ferrar's departure, and not long before the Japanese invasion, Lady Diana Cooper stayed at Government House and had a different view on it: 'Indescribable,' she wrote in *Trumpets from the Steep*: 'Very large and wandering and shapeless, with strange devil-carvings mixed with suburban taste.' Her bedroom was huge and haunted, without nets, though she said she had a miserable night from mosquitoes. There were the 'inevitable plumbing horrors of India, and an impossible trickle from a cold tap into a pan-bath'. The garden was flowerless, which was indeed a shame as the Ferrars had taken such pains with it, planting flame of the forest trees, casuarinas, plumbago bushes and hibiscus and making rockeries and shrubberies. The Ferrars had also built a pergola, and had made a terrace with a view across the sea, and steps lined with cannas; the paths had been of loose coral gravel, and two cannons had stood guard over the lawn. The 'devil-carving' had been done by Burmese convicts.

In 1923 Government House had forty servants and ten gardeners, nearly all convicts. The Ferrars' English nanny had been horrified to know that a murderer was looking after their little son's pony. In order to polish the ballroom floor, two men would hold another by the arms and legs and swing him up and down. Entertaining was very formal, 'Lahore manner', but the Ferrars really preferred informality. During the rains the ballroom was used for deck-tennis.

The Club, down by the landing stage, was of course the social centre. It had three grass tennis courts and a salt water swimming pool, wired against sharks. Gin and bitters were the 'favourite tipple', and meals usually began with rock oysters, of giant size. Lobsters were also plentiful – the 'locals' wouldn't eat them; and there was a little hut where turtles were kept. In 1923 thirty-six Europeans were on the Ferrars' 'list', nine of them women; if this figure included children, there were thirty-seven when I came along.

Ross was kept in 'perfect condition', thanks to convict labour. Olive used to speak of the perpetual clanking of chains from road gangs. All our ten Burmese servants were murderers, including, as I have said, my ayah Mimi, who had murdered her husband at Pegu. Olive drew the line at poisoners however. In a photograph our house looks buried in tropical foliage. You slept upstairs, and there was always a police orderly on guard below.

I had it in my mind that I had been born in the hospital at Aberdeen, but it was only after my return to England in the spring of 1982, when I met Mrs Theo Robertson, whose husband had been Assistant Commissioner of Police from 1923, that I discovered that Ross Island had been my place of birth. The Chief Commissioner's hot-weather residence was at Mount Harriet, 1,200 feet high, beyond Aberdeen, and as I was born in July, nearly the worst month for heat, Olive spent the last weeks of her pregnancy up there.

The convicts on Ross had their own barracks, and the troops' barracks were a miniature copy of Windsor Castle. Ticks, giant centipedes and snakes were a nuisance. Dogs were always getting eczema and pneumonia, and one of Olive's dogs died from snake-bite. In monsoon time you took out your mattresses to dry when there was sun. Theo Robertson once found a snake in her bed, brought in with the mattress. As for sharks, it was supposed to be safe to swim out as far as seven feet. ('Yes, there are sharks here,' someone told me, 'but it's not infested.') On picnic parties the servants would beat the water to frighten them away. Sharks of course congregated round the slaughterhouse, waiting for offal, and if you went round there by boat you could find them bumping against the bottom. Some Japanese pearl-fishers, who everyone thought were spies, came once, and a few lost limbs, so they never returned. Then a young soldier swam from Ross to Aberdeen and was bitten to death by barracudas. 'The bleeding just wouldn't stop.'

The convict population

The Andamans were formally annexed by the British in January 1858, during the great Mutiny, specifically as a penal settlement. Men with good records were allowed jobs such as boatmen or merchants, and earned money. But to Hindus in particular the journey across the Kala Pani, or black water, to Port Blair was regarded with the utmost fear and terror: a separation from families and villages probably for ever, and a loss of caste.

Lord Mayo, as Viceroy, came to inspect the settlement in January 1872. At dusk, after visiting Mount Harriet, he was about to step into his steam launch when a convict leapt on him 'like a tiger' and stabbed him to death. It has always been known that the murderer, Sher Ali, was a Pathan, but on reading a book published in 1880 by one L. R. Trevelyan (a woman, no relation this time), called *A Year in Peshawur*, I found points which I had not come across elsewhere. He had been, she said, the Commissioner's orderly. His family had had a blood feud with another of the same tribe, which she inferred was the Afridis. Whilst at home on a month's leave, he had murdered a man belonging to that other family. So he had been brought to Peshawar, tried by the civil court, and sentenced to be hanged. The Viceroy, taking into consideration the customs of these tribes, had commuted the sentence to transportation for life. But Sher Ali had been insulted by the alteration of the sentence, and had sworn to be revenged by murdering an Englishman, preferably the Viceroy.

The sad sequel, as L. R. Trevelyan said, we all know. It seems that Sher Ali had been sharpening his daggers for months at Port Blair and had been employed as a barber.

The convicts were greatly harassed by the indigenous tribes of the islands, and the tribe which mostly attacked them was the Jarawas. This was quite different from the more pacific tribe known as the Great Andamanese, who were semi-pygmies. A chaplain, the Rev. H. Corbyn, introduced a scheme of Jungle Homes for the Andamanese. In 1875 it was noticed that most of the inhabitants in the Homes had syphilis. The source was traced eventually to the convict in charge. Other diseases were picked up by Andamanese through contact with convicts and Europeans, particularly ophthalmia and measles, which reduced their original number of about 4,000 by two-thirds.

Jungle clearance continued. Coconut and banana groves were planted, rice-fields made. Then in 1896 the massive prison, known as the Cellular Jail, was begun on the promontory above Aberdeen and facing Ross. The original plans, though later altered, were based on the jail in Pennsylvania (Quaker, therefore 'humane'). The structure was like an octopus with seven legs radiating from a central tower. There were 698 cells, each measuring thirteen feet by nine.

In 1910, the year of the Jail's completion, a decision was taken to transport political prisoners to the Andamans. Among the best-known names at this time, in the long process towards India's independence, were the Savenkar brothers and Barindra Kumar Ghosh, brother of Sri Aurobindo who – as a fugitive from the British – founded an ashram at French Pondicherry and became revered almost as a saint. Vinayak Damadar Savenkar was sentenced to fifty years' transportation for complicity in the Nasik conspiracy case (which included an attempt on the life of another Viceroy, Lord Minto). He was later to be accused of being in the plot to murder Gandhi, but acquitted. He also wrote a book on his experience in the Andamans, and these tally with the outcries about the treatment of political prisoners that appeared in the Bengal newspapers. Some of the main complaints were that 'politicos' were treated in the same way as common felons, with the same degrading and often exhausting tasks, such as working the oil-mill, and the same punishments for offences committed whilst in prison, and that sanitary arrangements were revolting. The Irish prison superintendent, Barrie, sounds in these accounts like a caricature of the old style Brigade of Guards sergeant-major. There was a suicide, and there were hunger-strikes and a plot disclosed to murder all the British and blow up the Chief Commissioner's house.

By 1921 the convict population at Port Blair was officially recorded as numbering 11,532, of whom 1,168 were self-supporters. Of these about 3,000 were prisoners convicted of crimes of passion, about 6,000 were prisoners convicted of serious offences but not habituals, and the remaining 2,500 were professional criminals. Under the system in force up to that year the convict would spend his first six months after arrival at the Cellular Jail, and thereafter for nine and a half years would live in barracks as a member of a labour corps, earning a small gratuity. After this convicts could be given their ticket-of-leave, involving a life of near independence, doing work as cultivators or in service, from which they could gain a livelihood; wives could be sent for, and local marriages were allowed. Release came after twenty years, subject to good conduct, or twenty-five in the case of dacoits or professional criminals.

Alarm grew in Britain about conditions in the penal settlement following an article in the *Daily Telegraph* headed 'Hell on Earth', written by an MP after he had met a 'soft-spoken' man on a train who had spent five years in the Andamans. The settlement, it was claimed, was being run for a profit – pure slave-labour. Malaria and dysentery were rife, and the death-rate was twice what it was in other jails. Ruffians were bullying weaker prisoners, and a third of the Burmese prisoners were male prostitutes.

The Government announced that it had been decided to abandon the Andaman Islands altogether as a penal settlement. Soon other kinds of difficulties were revealed. For one thing, there was now a permanent population of 3,000 which was 'local born', descendants of convicts. Some people preferred to be self-supporters on the Andamans rather than to be incarcerated in mainland jails. There were not enough jails on the mainland to take so many convicts if they were returned. Then, in the summer of 1921, there was the serious Moplah rebellion on the Malabar coast, the Moplahs being Sunni Muslims, descendants of Arab traders and sailors who had married low-caste Hindus – they had become convinced that the British were against Islam. So 5,000 Moplahs were sent to the Andamans.

In the following year, 1922, there was the Chauni Chaura riot when twenty-two police constables were killed. It was also the year in which Gandhi was first arrested.

Walter and Olive arrived at Port Blair in November 1922. The political situation was considered so dangerous that Olive and other women were at first not allowed off Ross, except on heavily guarded picnic parties at Corbyn's Cove.

Two elderly and rather reserved Italians from Rome, a gynaecologist and his wife, were the only other guests in our hotel. Every winter they went to some southern spot: Tahiti, Fiji, Madagascar. We all visited Aberdeen, which turned out to be a collection of small houses and booths with corrugated and thatched roofs and a little painted temple, surrounded by begonias in old kerosene tins. It was near this spot that some say the supply officer to the Commissioner, A. G. Bird, was killed by the Japanese. The noise of cars hooting was cacophonous. Beyond the village-like atmosphere there were suburbs where the serious work was done, such as boat-building and the sawmills. We glimpsed the Cellular Jail on high, reduced now to only three wings – after an earthquake the Japanese had demolished the rest. The cinema, I noticed, was called 'Mountbatten'.

On the beach at Corbyn's Cove we watched a group of very black-

skinned fishermen and some children light a fire and then begin praying before it. Afterwards they covered themselves with grease and
plunged into the sea. The oldest man was very severe with the rest.
They then left, leaving behind a pile of what seemed like rubbish.

Raúl and I went to have a look at this pile and found that it was a
carefully laid out sacrificial offering, including two coconuts, a half
medicine bottle of milk, some coins, flowers, biscuits, bananas and
loose grain. We were told that it was an offering to a god, and that
somebody's ashes would have been scattered in the sea. The tide
would eventually wash everything away. Some boys and men
arrived, and one of them, because apparently of our interest which he
mistook for amusement, took out a machete and slashed at the coconuts. I shouted at him to stop, which he did, though reluctantly. We
decided to stay on guard until the tide came up, and it did quite soon.
I settled down under the shade of a palm to read *The Book of Sand* by
Borges, but the youth of the machete had the cheek to ask if he could
see the book, though not understanding a word of English – afterwards it had to be handed round a growing crowd of spectators.

There were baby lobsters and barracuda in mayonnaise for lunch.
That evening it was announced that the four of us were invited to
drinks at Dennis Beale's. The great moment! '7.15. For half an hour
only,' were our instructions.

Dennis Beale was younger than I expected, and decidedly
Burmese-looking. He was a character, without doubt, and we soon
realized that if we wished we could have stayed drinking rum with
him until morning (he despised vodka, and would not accept the
bottle we had brought). His house was built above a workshop where
a small houseboat was being built. The living-rooms were large and
bare, and he sat beneath a photograph of Prince Charles and Lady
Diana. The hi-fi, playing Tchaikovsky mostly, made him difficult to
hear sometimes, and the Italians obviously felt out of it. His old
mother, aged eighty-one, sat in the far room with her back to us,
first eating bits of fish, then fanning herself with a red fan. She had
had ten children, and her husband had been a well-to-do Englishman with a rubber plantation near Moulmein. Dennis was now
staunchly Indian. His family lived in Calcutta, because of the better
schools.

There were two things I longed for: to see elephants doing lumber
work, and to visit coral reefs. Dennis could easily arrange both of
these. The Nicobars were out of bounds to tourists, and anyway it
would be a question of spending some nights there. We spoke of the
aborigine tribes in the Andamans, of which there are four, all negrito,
without body hair. It was absolutely taboo to visit their villages,

Dennis said. The so-called Great Andamanese, who are actually the smallest, rarely more than four feet tall, have been reduced now to a pathetic twenty-four. Their blood is to some extent mixed with Burmese and Indian, and they live on Strait Island. A baby had been born recently, a cause for excitement.

The Jarawas are usually about five feet tall, and are still in a primitive state, numbering about three hundred. They inhabit the jungle in the remoter parts of the west coast of the three main northerly islands, moving from kitchen midden to kitchen midden in the manner of our Stone Age ancestors. They are dangerous to approach, although the Indian Government tries to make friends. In 1977, for instance, two farmers had been killed by them. Generally they are naked, but they like decorating themselves with fillets of red cloth and necklaces of shells. Sometimes the men wear cuirasses of bark, wound round their stomachs three times. Their weapons are arrows, often poisonous, not blow-pipes as in Conan Doyle's *The Sign of Four*. Dennis said that the Jarawas are not cannibals either, though I have since found out that there is a suggestion that they eat, or have eaten, the brains of enemies, to obtain their intelligence. Widows sometimes go around with their husband's skulls tied round their necks.

'Mark that, Watson,' as Sherlock Holmes said. 'Now listen to this.' On North Sentinel Island there is an offshoot of the Jarawas, about a hundred and fifty people, therefore known as the North Sentinelese. The island is only about eighteen square miles. There people are completely untamed, naked and ferocious. It would be courting suicide for any intruder to set foot on that island, though some officials have dared to do so recently, bringing gifts – only to be showered with arrows as they departed.

'One night,' Dennis said, 'I was out fishing late, and had to anchor not far from North Sentinel Island. In the morning you should have seen those buggers screaming and waving their arms up and down on the beach, and shaking spears.' A yacht had been once wrecked near there, and the crew had been rescued by helicopter, just in time.

Then there are the Onges, officially numbering a hundred and twelve. Like the Great Andamanese, they are now quite pacifically-minded. They wear minimal clothing, the men sometimes nothing at all, the women with bunches of coconut fibre in front; they are very amorous among themselves, and there is a certain amount of homosexuality among unmarried young men. They are hunters and fishermen, like painting their bodies and never wash, apart from swimming in the sea or getting wet from the rain. They love honey and before climbing trees chew the leaves of a plant called tanjohge which makes their breath smell so frightful that even bees flee in terror.

Colonel Ferrar and the Jarawas

Colonel Ferrar's letters are full of his dealings with the Jarawas, with whom there was running warfare all during his time. In January 1925 he was at Delhi and found the Home Department 'very alarmed about my Jarawa campaign', since a military appreciation had given as its object, 'to hunt down and exterminate the tribe'. He had to explain that thirteen convicts had been murdered in lurid ways by Jarawas within the past year. So the word 'exterminate' had had to be toned down.

A year later he was telling his mother that twenty convicts and three Great Andamanese, two of them women, had been murdered by Jarawas since his arrival.

> They had no concerted plan and seem to act almost out of wantonness and blood lust. I think they objected very much to our restarting the village of Alipur, and for that they certainly attacked three times in the last two years ... Recently they crossed into the Middle Andaman which is *not* in any way their tribal area and killed a convict in a forest camp. Poor man. His wife had been persuaded by us to join her husband and arrived in Port Blair from India to find her husband had been killed two days before. Then making targets of buffaloes and leaving them to wander about the roads with six or seven arrows in the livers and stomachs. Convicts cutting fuel in mangrove swamps, where no [wild] pig can live and where accordingly no Jarawa can pretend to have game rights, are murdered and laid on their back with their throats cut. There are two thousand square miles of country teeming with food for the Jarawas and unoccupied by any human being. Why must they keep coming in to our hundred square miles of settlement and keep killing our wretched convicts? Because it is a sport and a pastime... There is plenty of room for the Jarawas *and* us, and we would be only too pleased to be left alone, and to leave them alone.

The old familiar story. Incas. Aztecs. Red Indians. Maoris. And now Jarawas. About that time a proposal was put about for settling destitute Eurasians in the Andamans, which would thus become a kind of Promised Land for them. But this scheme collapsed.

In October 1926 Ferrar said that Jarawas had come into a settlement and had shot a man 'with great barbarity', digging the arrows out of his body and leaving huge gashes. A Bush Police naik or corporal (a Burmese convict) had sent out three parties of three men (all convicts), each with twelve-bore guns. The Jarawas had walked into their ambush; two had been killed, and many wounded.

We have never before had such luck to interrupt a raiding party in this way. The pity is that we killed only two. Some of the others must die miserably. The failure of this raid and the loss of so many iron-tipped arrows must, we think, stop further raids unless the Js have determined to kill all they can.

Nevertheless within days two more Jarawas were killed in return for the man 'dismally done to death':

A piece of his spine is going home with a *wooden* arrow *piercing* it through. Imagine the strength of their bows!

The Jarawa raids continued spasmodically. Theo Robertson told me how a Captain West went to hunt Jarawas and came back with two heads hanging from the yardarm, along with the Jolly Roger. Ferrar was furious and sent him back to Burma.

A year before Ferrar left the Andamans for good, he wrote to his mother, on May 18 1930:

The monsoon came in very violently this year. The Jarawas have at last had their go at Ferrarganj and killed a man at about midnight in his sugarcane machan, full moon and fairly bright . . . I have sent out a party of some six rifles and forty slug guns to beat up their rains quarters and kill as many as possible during a week's hunting. It is the only thing to do. They are implacable and their outrages are without reason or shame.

The Japanese method of subduing the Jarawas was to bomb them.
Ferrar actually landed on North Sentinel Island, which – impossible to contemplate now – he explored for six hours. He reckoned then that there were only about sixty natives, 'the most remote and most unalterably primitive of all races on the face of the earth'. Only three were glimpsed, but Ferrar was able to enter two of their camps, which had been hastily abandoned at his party's approach.

We left presents in the shape of iron, files, enamelled mugs, plates, red cloth and so on, and took in their place some bows, arrows, a paddle and a complete skeleton, the first from this tribe, for Sir William Keith, a leading anthropologist. This tribe alone among the Andamanese shoots birds with four-pronged arrows with barbs made from birds' bones. The arrows had numerous feathers sticking to them. The plain wooden tipped arrow was nearly six foot long.

Two months or so after I was born Olive and Walter went on a tour round South Sentinel Island, Little Andaman and the Nicobars. In Walter's pictures the Nicobar Islands look even more beautiful than the Andamans: a Gauguin landscape with Gauguin people, but completely naked (at least on Car Nicobar) and, unlike the poor Great Andamanese, with cheerful faces.

South Sentinel had no humans but was inhabited by countless thousands of land crabs. One wondered what they could eat besides each other. Robber crabs, *Birgus latro*, were also to be found there: as big as cabbages, purple, with legs fifteen to eighteen inches long, and 'almighty strong claws'. The shore of the island was a mass of deep pits dug out by turtles and redug by five-foot long monitor lizards which ate the turtles' eggs. The dense jungle was full of flying foxes, which left the island at dusk and flew some eighteen miles away to Little Andaman.

The party encountered about sixty Onges on Little Andaman, all without a stitch of clothing, and a little lighter in colour than the kitchen-range coloured Great Andamanese. Men and women were smoking out of crabs' claw pipes. They loved their dogs, which the Jarawas would not have in case their barking gave away the camps.

I remember quite well Olive telling me about the dreamlike Nicobars. What she saw was very like what Fanny Parks described in her *Wanderings of a Pilgrim*, though I don't think *she* could have been quite so modest.

The island where we landed was covered to the edge of the shore with beautiful trees, scarcely an uncovered or open spot was to be seen. Off the ship the village appeared to consist of six or eight enormous bee-hives, erected on poles and surrounded by high trees; among these, the cocoa-nut, to an English eye was the most remarkable.

The ship was soon surrounded by canoes filled with natives; two came on board. The ladies hastened on deck, but quickly scudded away, not a little startled at beholding men like Adam when he tasted the forbidden fruit; they knew not that they were naked, and they were not ashamed . . .

One of the canoes which came from a distant part of the island was the most beautiful and picturesque boat I ever saw; it contained twenty-one men, was paddled with amazing swiftness, and gaily decorated.

The Nicobars were annexed by the British in 1869, having been occupied previously by Danish pirates, French Jesuits, the Danish East India Company and Malay pirates. In Fanny Parks's day it was customary for ships to sail from Ceylon across the Bay of Bengal to the Nicobars, where fruit, vegetables and fresh meat would be bought, before proceeding to Calcutta. And in 1779 William Hickey was nearly wrecked there, off an uncharted island, with a tremendous sea running.

Walter photographed scare-devils, looking rather, like vultures with outstretched wings, on Car Nicobar. He also went to Nancowrie, to see the monument to the Indian woman trader who had bluffed the German ship *Emden* in the First World War. She had hoisted the Union Jack, causing the captain to assume that there was a large British force on the island. When the *Emden* left Nancowrie, the woman sent a canoe to carry the news to the nearest signal station, as a result of which the ship was caught and destroyed by HMAS *Sydney* off the Cocos Islands, in the South Indian Ocean. In 1947 this Indian woman was still very much alive, very pro-British; Compton Mackenzie met her, and not surprisingly she was known as the Queen of the Nicobars.

The equivalent of the Jarawas in the Nicobars are the Shompens, who are still wild and hostile – notable for their large wooden ear distenders. These inhabit Great Nicobar and because of their bad reputation were avoided by both my parents and Compton Mackenzie.

Dennis Beale took us on expeditions to Jolly Boy Island and Grub Island. Before that, we had plunged into the jungle and had seen those silent, resigned, ragged-eared elephants delicately loading logs on to lorries. The wood was destined for a Swedish match firm, but we also saw padauk and satinwood being cut. We noted the elephants' satisfaction as two bullocks stumbled when unable to drag a load – so easy for an elephant. In the old days when elephants were brought from Rangoon they would be lowered into the sea and made to swim the last hundred yards.

There was something tragic in the sound of crashing forest giants; it was the slow death of a rain forest. We saw the flash of kingfishers and – quite an achievement – the Nicobar Imperial pied pigeon.

There were a few orchids still in flower. This wilderness of naked creepers, tendrilled plants, waist-high grass and ferns was my first sight of real jungle which some say is denser and more luxuriant than Burma's. Almost I expected to see Bagheera the panther, or Hathi the bull elephant chewing up a plantain tree. But there are no panthers in the Andamans, and all the working elephants are female – bull elephants tend to go berserk when randy.

The Jolly Boy trip was special. We all met for tea and betel nuts just after dawn on a muddy landing stage, among corrugated shacks, piles of nets, tarpaulins, ducks and goats. Cumulus clouds and mangrove roots were reflected in the dark translucent blue. One of the Italians dropped a flipper, and I seemed the only person around capable of diving so deep to retrieve it; which was nice for my ego.

Dennis's launch *Gavin* was waiting among the canoes and fishing boats. We chugged along, cutting through the reflections and immense clusters of fawn-coloured fish, Dennis talking all the while: about escaping from the Japs, how he had been in Burmah Oil and then went into the merchant navy, his love of solitude and the sea. Behind the mangroves was a tumbling mass of greenery. Emerging from the creek into the blinding glare of the full sun, we collected oysters, about three times the size of English Colchesters. Then, avoiding sandbanks, we saw the islands coming into view: stark white strips of sand around thick jungle. And the sea so clear and silky. North Sentinel Island was only about three miles away.

'If you see a shark, head for the shallow water,' was Dennis's cheerful farewell as he dumped us on Jolly Boy. We took our chance, and as soon as possible swam in the lukewarm sea to the reef – the sight of which, underwater, was scarcely believable. Not hundreds but myriads of fish, some minute, some the size of salmon, of every imaginable colour, swam in and out of the coral thickets and gorgonians. Most were extraordinarily tame – you could swim among the shoals – but some, like the ones which were bright red with cobalt spots, darted away into the waving tentacles of giant sea-anemones, emerald or with lavender tips that glowed. There were yellow butterfly-fish, with huge black round eyes, blue and gold angel-fish, bat-fish, cardinal-fish, fish with snouts, fish with trailing fan tails, struggling masses of tiny luminous blue fish feeding among mounds of royal purple. Some corals were like horns, some like toadstools on which you could stand. There were ugly fish too, glaring from dark recesses of brain coral. I also saw a sting-ray. The more edible a fish would seem, the more it kept its distance.

When Dennis returned, we cracked open the oysters with a chisel, and gorged. It was not wise to be on the beach at dusk, he said, because of the sand-flies, as two Dutchmen who had recently camped on Jolly Boy had soon realized. One of these men used to go out windsurfing to feed the sharks.

We left feeling very happy, though under the stern and disapproving observation of a black and white sea-eagle. The reefs round Grub were even better but had fewer fish; the shells were superb. In the far distance, those 'buggers' on North Sentinel were guarding their Stone Age paradise, hating the whole damned world outside, always in fear.

Next it was Ross Island. This involved a new permit, because Army ammunition was stored there.

The Italians had no nostalgia for the Raj and stayed behind. There now began for me another haunted experience.

Only the old Club House was recognizable from the photographs. Otherwise nearly all the British buildings were in ruins. Some were just foundations. The jungle had reclaimed Ross Island, but not so long ago, because there were quite legible notices outside houses that had been rebuilt, notices such as 'Magazine', 'Printing Press', and 'Dancing Club'.

There were conflicting theories about the site of the hospital in my time, and from various enquiries it seems to me that I was born at 'Dancing Club'. I could make out the pseudo neo-classic architecture. We climbed uphill, our feet crunching on dead palm fronds. Along this path Olive had been carried in a dandy by the two murderers. A peacock suddenly flew from the undergrowth, then another, and another. These were descendants of birds that had inhabited the grounds of Government House. We also disturbed a spotted deer: another descendant. Every now and then a ripe coconut dropped in the silence. There were banyan trees with roots like giant spider webs. Birds sang, but it was too dark for butterflies, unless Colonel Ferrar and Olive had wiped out the whole population. I had hoped to see his yellow swallow-tail, seven inches across.

We reached the brick church. It was roofless. The windows were gone and there was an anthill in the nave. Once there had been railings outside, but these had disappeared too. The tower and spire were separate, nearly intact, but entwined in the roots of a banyan. Through the undergrowth we could make out broken terraces and stairways. By now I had forgotten about snakes and I fought my way up to the mound of rubble, rafters and wooden slats that had been Government House.

I stood on the terrace where a convict band used to play on the King's birthday, and I could see the very tree, now a giant, under which my mother and I had been photographed over half a century ago; but a branch had fallen just where we had been. The views of the sea were blocked off. I saw a mango tree, a sprawl of bougainvillaea, and some acacias. We stumbled on, to the southern end of the island, disturbing peacocks and deer, and perhaps snakes. We discovered the lake: stagnant. Then we passed more foundations, and some Japanese blockhouses, and pushing through a tangle of creepers and thorns came upon the graveyard. It was like finding a shipwreck under water.

Nearly everybody in the graveyard had died in the 1860s and 1870s. 'Alison, much beloved wife of the apothecary A. S. Xavier, died – 1863. Also their daughter Laura, died 6 April 1862.' 'Percy Brett Esq, Commander in the Bengal Marine, departed this life while in command of H. M. Steamer Lady Canning, 15 January 1862.' 'James Pratt A.B., H.M. Indian Naval Brigade. Who was killed by the natives of this island 28 January 1863.' 'Katie, beloved child of Hall and Julia Hilton, died – April 1871 aged 2 years 3 months.'

That night Dennis played *The Sleeping Beauty* on his hi-fi, which seemed appropriate.

Reluctantly, I went to see the Cellular Jail. It was grim, but not claustrophobic like other jails I have been to see, such as Wormwood Scrubs in London and Regina Coeli in Rome. The names of some hundreds of freedom fighters were inscribed in the central tower: an aspect which came as a shock. We went along a long row of cells and saw the solitary confinement cell. They could have been worse, I thought, but maybe they had been squalid in the 1930s, which had been the decade of the freedom fighters.

Then we saw the hideous gallows, with its trap door, and the room next to it where the condemned had their last breakfast. Inevitably I thought of the George Orwell story, of that hooded prisoner calling to his god: 'Ram! Ram! Ram!' There was a museum, with the original flogging block and a model of a black man strapped to it and with red weals painted on his back. We looked at fetters, prison uniforms, and a modern artist's impressions of a sort of Belsen concentration camp: 'relics of ignoble past', the guidebook said. I never hope to go back in there.

The ignoble past

Colonel Ferrar insisted that there should be only a gradual running

down in the convict population. At the same time, given the Andamans' inherent wealth in agriculture and forestry, his dream was to
create an even longer, free, permanent settlement. This could partly
be done by improving the quality of living and thus making working
conditions so attractive that convicts would prefer to remain in the
islands at the end of their sentences, rather than return to the mainland, and partly through enticing across non-convict settlers. So
grants of land were made, usually with the bonus of a buffalo or two.

On June 20 1925 he told his mother that twenty-five Moplahs had
been sent to Malabar to search for convicts' families. So far, he said,
three hundred women and children were expected to arrive. He
spoke of a sawmill in the north, where seven hundred tons of wood
were cut a month, and of plantations of tea, coffee, rubber, sugarcane, maize and turmeric. Two months later he was writing again to
say that four hundred convicts from Bellary, north of Bangalore, had
actually applied to be transferred to the Andamans with their families. By September a hundred of these volunteer convicts were arriving every month; 'bad hats' were sent to replace them in mainland
jails.

Ferrar himself would play hockey with the convicts in the compound of the Cellular Jail. He told his mother about a wrestling
match in a natural amphitheatre, watched by 3,000 convicts, 'all in
clean civilian clothes' and 'looking and sounding well and happy'. It
was not surprising that he was irritated when the Indian press persisted in articles about 'hell on earth'.

The village of Ferrarganj was, in the first instance, created for
Bhantus from the Lucknow area. In March 1929 he was able to say:
'Ferrarganj is going strong. There are now 530 people in the village,
and 200 in India wanting to come.'

I had asked Theo Robertson about the whippings. She told me that
in her husband's time only two convicts had been whipped, both
Sikhs. It was a sickening business. Leather had been put over the kid-
neys, and the top of the back covered with muslin soaked in disinfec-
tant. The men got ten lashes each.

She also said that her husband used to go to the mainland to recruit
wives. The women would then be paraded so that men could choose
them. She remembered the delight of one man who was confronted
with a woman whom he already knew from his own village.

Any death penalty had to be approved by Delhi. There was the case
of the murder of the Trenoweths' orderly, again a convict and who
was known as the Assistant Post Officer. The man was extremely efficient, wrote Ferrar; 'He wanted work out of everyone too, and was
for ever getting servants and even police orderlies charged.' A victim

rebelled against this martinet, and drove a sharp file into his skull, 'Sisera-wise'.

Theo Robertson could only recall three hangings. One was of a woman who poisoned her husband by giving him the liver of a pufferfish. Another was of Mrs D'Oyly's murderer, a Muslim bheesti or water-carrier. Mrs D'Oyly had insulted the man by calling him son of a pig, so he had rushed outside and seized the axe for chopping wood. Then, flinging aside her baby, he had slashed at her face – the ayah bravely trying to stop him.

One day Theo and her husband were on a picnic and smelt the dead body of someone who they realized had been murdered. They went to the nearest village and immediately found the culprit. This was the third case.

On June 1 1929 Ferrar wrote:

In the last two days I have had to reject appeals from two policemen sentenced to death for murder. One of them was stroke in our boat and was a fine young fellow gone wrong. Then yesterday I began and finished two separate murder trials, very clear cases, and sentenced the accused, Burman convicts, to death. One brute for no disclosed reason suddenly during a Pwe (nautch) stuck a pocket knife into his friend's back and killed him dead. The other, a nice-looking young man in the Bush Police, took his weapon and cruelly shot a young woman at six yards in the groin and shattered her to pieces. She died in twenty minutes. This was a strange case, for if the youth's appearance and story and the several letters he wrote (all Burmans are literate) before and after the occurrence are to be trusted, he acted as a sort of protesting and avenging Providence in the interests of his alleged friend, the deceased's husband. The woman, he said, was a bad lot and intended to take up with another man, her friend. Whatever the real motive, he plastered the woman with seven big slugs in a five inch circle and she died after great suffering. This is the first convict Bush Policeman to abuse our trust, and I thought of swinging him and the other brute straight up – but am not doing so. I have this power if I can certify that it was necessary for the tranquillity and safety of the settlement. In practice I have never heard of it being done.

Political unrest in India was again becoming serious. Gandhi's salt march was in 1929, and once more he was arrested. The authorities had to decide that there would be no alternative to temporary transportation for those convicted of terrorism. 1930 was the year of mass civil disobedience, and in particular of the Chittagong armoury raid, when some guards and a British officer were killed – it took place on April 18, deliberately chosen because it had been the date of the Easter Rising in Ireland. However the first political prisoners did not arrive until 1932, after Ferrar had left, and more came in 1933. They were kept in the Cellular Jail, isolated as much as possible from the other convicts. Immediately there were complaints about inadequate conditions. After a hunger strike some concessions were made about better bedding, special food and the provision of books and magazines. Then, after the Tharwaddy Rebellion, 535 Burmese political prisoners arrived.

There are, as usual in such circumstances, conflicting accounts of the next three years. It was claimed that prisoners were being flogged for any 'slight violation of the rules', but this certainly does not tally with memories of police officers of the time. The cells were described as 'dingy', and no doubt they were. 'Worthless' books were provided, not what prisoners had asked for; but then Bengali prisoners had been demanding Marxist literature. Really the complaints were mainly due to an intense frustration. The medical officer in charge, Captain Chaudhari, was an exceptionally benevolent individual and responsible for several improvements, including more recreation and exercise.

Sir Mohammed Yamin Khan visited the Jail, and wrote a reassuring report about conditions. No doubt this was why the Government was slow to make up its mind about repatriation, which the prisoners had understood he was going to press for urgently. So on July 24 1937 a mass hunger-strike began, the number of strikers soon rising to 225. There was force-feeding, including one or two deaths from starvation, and the strike only ended after fifty-six days, as a result of a joint appeal by telegram from Gandhi, Nehru, Rabindranath Tagore and others in Congress.

The strikers had achieved their point however, and repatriation of 'politicos' began in September that year. Their presence had always been an upsetting influence on the convicts, so the prison authorities were anxious to see them go. Meanwhile conditions for convicts were much as they had been in the time of Colonel Ferrar. A visitor to Port Blair in 1939 said that it was hard to tell who was a convict and who wasn't. There was a convict agricultural and crafts show, even a convict baby show. By the time war broke out there were about 6,000 convicts in the Andamans.

The Japanese occupation

At a spot called Humphreyganj on the way to the elephants we had seen the Martyrs' Memorial, commemorating a common grave of forty-four people who had been executed by the Japanese.

We heard terrible stories about the Japanese occupation of the Andamans, some of them by a man aged a hundred and three who said that he knew my parents (but could tell me nothing about them): stories corroborated in *All Over the Place* by Compton Mackenzie. The population of the Andamans was 34,000 at the time of the British evacuation. When the British returned at the end of the war it was 18,000.

Early in 1942 the Japanese began their bombing raids on Port Blair, 'leaving their cards' as the supply officer A. G. Bird – a quiet little man known to all as 'Chirri', Chiriya being Hindi for bird – described it to his wife. 'Non-essential' Europeans were evacuated to Calcutta. The others began packing up their belongings, in the hope of being able to have them shipped home somehow.

There are several mysteries about what happened next. It is said now at Port Blair that in the middle of the night news suddenly came that the Japanese invasion was on its way. There was panic, and not enough time was given for five of the British, including Chirri Bird and the Chief Commissioner, Sir Francis Waterfall, to reach a motor boat for Madras, that only waited fifteen minutes.

The Japanese, naturally enough, on arrival proclaimed themselves the liberators of their fellow Asians. All the prisoners in the Cellular Jail were released. Dr Diwan Singh, a medical officer, acted as liaison between the Japanese and the local people.

Another, more sinister, character was meanwhile coming to the forefront. This was an ex-convict named Bagchi, who supplied 'comfort girls' for the Japanese. From British days he had a particular grudge against Bird and his Indian storeman, Harup Singh, and now decided to have his revenge. He did this by planting some bits of wireless transmitter in Bird's house, and then denouncing them both as spies. Although the Japanese admiral in command is now said to have been 'fairly decent as those chaps went', on April 30 1942 Bird and Harup Singh, after having been kept without food or drink, were paraded round Aberdeen; a large crowd was rounded up to watch. Bird had a placard with the word 'Traitor' put about his neck. Then he was beaten. Several of his bones were broken. It is said that he never cried out until the end when he moaned for water. A child came forward with a jug, but a Japanese guard took it and poured the liquid over his sword in front of Bird and then beheaded him. The blood 'rushed up high into the sky'. People still weep when they tell this story, for Bird was extremely popular and had been supply officer ever since the days of Colonel Ferrar.

To everybody's amazement Harup Singh was reprieved. In the English-language newspaper there was a headline: 'Execution of Worst British War Criminal'. Whether Waterfall and the three other British were sent to Rangoon jail before or after Bird's execution is not at all clear. Quite likely it was before.

For the first months the Japanese behaved tolerably well towards the Indians. Anyone of mixed blood took the precaution of dressing in Indian clothes. Nobody dared speak in English. The use of forced labour for building the airstrip, as well as roads and blockhouse, was not at all popular, and there was growing outrage about the kidnapping of women by Bagchi. A Swede called Cato, manager of the match factory, was taken to Ross Island and executed, because he 'showed contempt'. The Allies bombed Port Blair, and the Japanese began to suspect that there were secret contacts with the enemy – rightly as it happened. So there were indiscriminate arrests for spying, particularly among educated people, and eventually Diwan Singh was put in the Cellular Jail. Bagchi meanwhile had over-reached himself – in his arrogance he had struck the representative of the Japanese-sponsored Indian Independence League and had broken the man's arm. He also went to the Cellular Jail and was still there when Compton Mackenzie saw him: 'a small young man with the face of a weasel and eyes of a viper . . . he deserves to be stamped out like a cockroach'.

The Allies had secretly begun to land on a series of small reconnaissance patrols by submarine; this was known as Operation Baldhead. The first was headed by Major Denis McCarthy, who had been Superintendent of Police at Port Blair from 1936. In January he and five others landed at Flat Island on the west coast, in the heart of Jarawa country and seventy miles from Port Blair. With two men he travelled by folboat through jungle creeks and mangrove swamps until they reached Ferrarganj, where they were taken in by the head-man. Here they heard stories about Bird's death and other summary executions. It was estimated that there were about 5,000 troops on the islands, though this figure was soon to grow. There was a near escape from capture. Thanks to their radio directions Flying Fortresses were able to bomb strategic targets. After nearly three months McCarthy and his men returned to base, where there had been a little trouble from Jarawas. The leeches had been dreadful and McCarthy was ill with anaemia. Then the rescuing submarine (Dutch) was slightly damaged on a coral reef. But before the journey back to Colombo it was decided that the stores brought for future Baldheads would have to be moved to a more secluded place further south. The dump could not be buried, so a wall had to be built around it as a protection against wild pigs, and primed hand grenades were laid on top to scare away any marauding Jarawas.

Compton Mackenzie has said that the kindest way to account for the Japanese atrocities is to attribute them to panic. Diwan Singh's tortures were particularly nauseous. He was hung up by the hair, then upside-down, his genitals were burnt, he was electrocuted and his eyes were gouged. All this to make him confess to something he knew nothing about. Just about then there was an announcement in Tokyo that the Andamans and Nicobars, as the first bits of Indian territory to be liberated, were to be handed to the new Provisional Indian Government, formed by Subhas Chandra Bose.

The name of Subhas Chandra Bose continues to provoke strong feelings among the British, though to many Indians he is a national hero. His story is dramatic and indeed courageous – escape to Germany at the beginning of the war via Afghanistan disguised as a Pathan, then a journey by submarine around the Cape to Japan, and finally dying after a crash in a plane bound for Formosa, just at the time of the Japanese surrender. The ignoble side of Imperial rule can be recognized, the deficiencies in the British character, their stupidities and blunders, acknowledged; there can be sympathy for the Indian revolutionary movement. But alliance with the Axis powers is for many in Britain a matter of disgust, beyond sufferance. Bose liked quoting the proverb, 'The enemy of my enemy is my friend'. Rejecting Gandhi's principle of non-violence, he wanted 'not the spinning-wheel but a springing tiger'. He had charisma and vision, but power went to his head and he was ruthless. Perhaps in the long run he was even naive. As for the Indian National Army, which he created, chiefly out of prisoners of war in the East, I think this is now mostly viewed with sadness, and with a degree of understanding, though it was not at all the case during the war. My father was no Teddie Bingham of *The Jewel in the Crown*, but I can almost hear him exploding, like Teddie, about Indian officers in the INA: 'I find the idea of King's commissioned officers leading their men – our men – utterly unspeakable.' A matter of honour again. The regimental mystique.

The INA certainly did contain some fervent nationalists as well as opportunists. But there were others, simple men, demoralized, puzzled, threatened and cajoled, who believed what they were told, that the British were about to be defeated, and this was therefore the quickest way of getting home, as well as an opportunity of avoiding degrading jobs in prisoner of war camps. Nevertheless out of the 60,000 Indian troops who surrendered in Malaya more than half remained firm in their old allegiance, and several of the Jiffs, as the turncoats were called, took the chance of deserting or surrendering as soon as they were sent into the line in Burma and found themselves faced with their former comrades.

Bose arrived at Port Blair on December 29 1943 and spent three nights at Government House on Ross, where the Japanese admiral in command was living. There were some fine speeches, and he was taken to see the 'Indian Bastille'. It has been said that he was told about the plight of Diwan Singh and others who had been tortured; if so, he must have thought it politic not to ask to see them. On his return to Singapore, he arranged for a Commission, under Colonel Loganadhan, to go to Port Blair in order to investigate supposed cases of espionage. But this Commission arrived after Diwan Singh was dead. Loganadhan was supposed to be the new Chief Commissioner, but the Japanese prevaricated and this never came to pass. At least he may have been able to intercede on behalf of a very few new victims. By December, disillusioned, he was in Singapore, telling Bose that up to September fifty-five Indians had been executed and thirty-three imprisoned as British spies, and that a further two hundred had been arrested in October and were being 'investigated'. This was only a small beginning to the horrors however. And some of the original prewar police were now acting as informers and taking part in the tortures.

According to the booklet now on sale for tourists at the Cellular Jail museum, 'the atrocities of Japanese towards Indian prisoners came to a close when Netaji [Bose] visited the Islands ... He also visited the Cellular Jail and stopped punishing prisoners without proper trial. There were no executions after Netaji's visit to the Islands.'

A British submarine appeared off Ross and shelled Port Blair. There were more air-raids, and patrol dumps were fired. All this increased the Japanese spy panic. As it happened, Mountbatten had been planning an amphibious landing on the Andamans, to be known as Operation Pigstick. By the end of 1943, much to his disappointment, it had had to be abandoned – or Pigstuck, as Churchill put it. This was because the landing craft needed to be transferred to the Mediterranean theatre. The plan for a landing was revived and renamed Operation Buccaneer, scheduled for March 1944, but this again had to be scrapped, partly due to lack of enthusiasm by the Americans.

The burning of a victim's genitalia with candles was a favourite method of torture. A typical case was that of Dr Nawab Ali, who had been particularly friendly with the British before the war. He was tortured, and eventually died, but before his death he had had to sign a 'confession'. And this is how, according to his friend Arfat Ahmed Khan, he came to do so:

> Two of his daughters, both very beautiful, Saira and Sofia, were brought before the father stark naked, and their legs forcibly stretched. Then the Japanese lit newspapers and placed them under their open thighs. The father covered his eyes. The girls shrieked. They cried, 'Abba Jan, bol do han! Abba Jan, bol do han. [Please dear father say yes.]' So he said, 'Yes, I am a spy,' and signed the paper.

In July 1944, during a monsoon, six hundred prisoners from the Cellular Jail were herded into small boats. They had no idea where they were going, and were without shelter or food. Suddenly, in the middle of the night, they were ordered to jump into the sea. About half were drowned or killed by sharks. The rest managed to reach Havelock Island, which was found to be ruled by ten strange and vicious Burmans, who set about murdering survivors for any jewellery that they might have with them. Some hundred people were killed in this way. Then the Burmans as mysteriously disappeared. There was nothing to eat except grass and roots on Havelock Island. As more died, through starvation, or were dying, there was cannibalism. Eventually only two men survived.

Another notorious case I heard of took place at the village of Gurachana, where the Japanese had a lot of troops in barracks. This happened only two days before the Japanese surrender. Three hundred men, women and children were taken to a small island and machinegunned.

The reason given to me for the massacres was shortage of food. I was also told that people used to be taken to Ross one by one on the pretence of providing them with treatment at a clinic, but instead they would be given fatal injections. Interview Island was another place where unwanted people were marooned, and left to die of starvation. I was shown a monument to a young man who had fled into the jungle after firing on Japanese for molesting women; he was told that all his family would be killed unless he returned – so he did return, was made to dig his own grave, and was shot.

When Compton Mackenzie went to the Nicobars, he heard more stories of atrocities and torture. On Car Nicobar seventy-five people had been tortured to death. It had been customary as a punishment to make men climb up a tree and stay all day on a precarious branch.

Compton Mackenzie also met Bishop Richardson, a Nicobarese who had been ordained into the Anglican Church and whom my parents had met as a young man. The bishop's son, son-in-law, brother-in-law and nephew had all been murdered, but news that the war had ended came just in time to save Bishop Richardson from execution.

It was pathetic to read what Compton Mackenzie had to say about the island of Chowra in the Nicobars. When Walter and Olive went there in 1923 it had been inhabited by beautiful, naked, friendly people. In 1947 they were riddled with syphilis, elephantiasis and tuberculosis. The villages were littered with refuse, and flies were thick everywhere.

The inhabitants of Port Blair at the end of the war looked like 'so many Rip Van Winkles', my 103-year-old friend said. They all wore rags or clothes made from gunny bags. The Cellular Jail had been damaged by an earthquake in 1941, and then by bombing, so four of its wings had to be demolished. One of the remaining wings is now used as the District Jail, and another is a hospital. The third is mostly 'for show', part of the National Memorial.

Ex-convicts were offered repatriation in 1945, and 4,200 took advantage of this. The penal settlement was thus officially abolished. In subsequent years the population of the Andamans was increased by refugees or migrants from Burma, Sri Lanka and East Pakistan. Ross Island was left uninhabited, partly because it had developed an evil reputation during the Japanese occupation, partly because it was rumoured to be sinking.

As so many of the present-day inhabitants of the Andamans are drawn from all over the sub-continent, there is something of a cosmopolitan atmosphere. There is no caste system, and a variety of creeds: all of which is a matter of local pride. The lingua franca is Hindustani. One Sunday Raúl and I went with Babu José, from our hotel, to a Roman Catholic mass, in a plain wooden church which was completely packed. Babu said that there were 8,000 Catholics in the Andamans.

The topic of the moment at Port Blair we found, was monkey malaria, which had been discovered in the Nicobars. It seemed that a crab-eating monkey called *Macca umbrosus* carried a strain of malaria that could also affect human beings.

There was also some stir about the possibility of oil and natural gas being found off the Andamans and Nicobars. Which is probably why in 1986 I heard that groups of Russian naval engineers were to be seen at Port Blair.

Nearly every time we had to catch a plane anywhere in India there was some major drama about delays. It had happened at Bagdogra and Calcutta, and now here we were going through the usual routine at Port Blair airport. Our plane might not arrive at all, we were told, either because of a fog at Calcutta, or because of an earthquake in the Nicobars – which seemed more likely. This was serious news for us, because we had tickets for Rangoon from Calcutta the next day.

'Jetty tumbles, many hurt,' we read in a paper. 'The naval jetty at Campbell Bay gave way and several civilian buildings collapsed or suffered heavy damage in a series of earth tremors of severe intensity which hit the south-eastern Nicobar Island in the Bay of Bengal yesterday morning ... Several people were injured as twenty-seven tremors rocked the region ... Ships and aircraft rushed to the assistance ... People spoke of panic as they were hit by a shock wave which swept the island.'

The rumour was that a hundred and fifteen people had died, but as in the case of the monkey malaria we were soon told that this was 'just a load of bullshit'.

A few days before we had taken some shells, which looked like huge striped icecream whips, to be polished professionally, but every time we went to the 'factory', in a kind of shanty-town dealing in poultry, the place was shut. We had given up hope of ever seeing them again, but now, to calm our nerves, Babu José offered to drive us there yet again.

Amazingly the place was open, but the shell polishing had not started. Babu began to rage at the young Bengali polisher, who sulked and muttered something. 'What is he saying?' I asked. 'He says that if I speak to him with love he will do anything we want.' So we begged Babu to oblige, which he did. The polishing would only take ten minutes, we were told, but of course it took forty-five minutes. We began pacing restlessly up and down among the chicken-crates, listening for aircraft arriving.

Babu as always was cheerful and calm. He suggested afterwards that we should go back to the hotel for coffee, but we insisted on returning to the airport. And it was lucky we did do this, because we found that our aeroplane was due to arrive in fifteen minutes.

Generally speaking, I rather hate having to share tables with strangers at hotels. At the Fairlawn, where we stayed briefly before moving on to Rangoon, it was one of the fascinations. At breakfast, for instance, we met three dour-faced American 'students', two male, black-haired, bearded, vegetarian, from New York, and one female, frizzy blonde, rather grubby, from Baltimore, who had come – so they said – looking for babies to take back to be adopted by childless couples at

Seattle. So they said, because we became suspicious about their motives. Were they a kind of mafia? They were determined to see nothing but horror in India. The more we teased them, the more grim they became – as if our behaviour was typical of heartless Europeans. 'Would *you* recommend Calcutta for a holiday?' the girl snapped. We had to admit that we wouldn't. And later we had to climb down further, for we found that Mother Teresa was running a child adoption scheme, in place of abortions.

Then there was an Australian girl, rather fey, who said her name was Miss Moppet. She was working on a thesis in cholera. She told us about her train journey from Katmandu. Swarms of people had been on the roof. When the train stopped at a station after dark, several men forced their way into her compartment. 'We tried to fight them off, but it was hopeless. Some of them slept on the floor and under the bottom bunks. When I woke up three black faces were staring at me.' She had a further, and worse, battle when she got on a bus; some boys had jumped on top of it and had begun slitting the ropes that held the luggage.

Another exceedingly humourless student from Sydney, bleary and bearded, had been travelling for two weeks second class by train from Delhi, stopping at Lucknow, Benares etc. His story made it all seem like a penance, and now he was off, by train again, to Madras. 'Are you writing a book?' I asked. He was embarrassed and mumbled something that sounded like: 'I'm no Paul Theroux.' Two New Zealanders were on the contrary lively and naughty, making passes at the Australian girl. They gave us some good tips about travelling in Burma, in particular recommending buying duty-free cartons of State Express 555 cigarettes (that brand only) and Johnny Walker Red Label whisky (nothing else). 'You'll treble your money on the black market, and from then on it's lobster every night for dinner.' It seemed that the Burmese were also very short of ballpoint pens, which therefore had a black market value.

Up the Irrawaddy

Walter was stationed at Bhamo when he married Olive on April 6 1921. Bhamo is six hundred miles up the Irrawaddy from Rangoon, under the Sinlunkaba hills and near the road to Chungking, which was of such great importance in the last war. The area, like so many others in Burma, is forbidden to tourists, because of spasmodic forays from various tribes, in this case the Kachens. An Australian at the Fairlawn had claimed to have penetrated into Kachen territories regardless, but we felt too old for that. In any case there is the overriding problem of only a week's visa being allowed in Burma.

I had always imagined that the fatal wedding reception, when Rufus saw Olive coming down the stairs and instantly fell in love with her, would have been at the Strand Hotel at Rangoon. So I determined to stay at the Strand. The wedding had been in the Anglican cathedral, where I had also been christened, and the honeymoon was spent on the long journey up the river to Bhamo in a steamer of the Irrawaddy Flotilla.

I find the photographs of Olive on that trip a little pathetic, but perhaps that is because I know she was feeling homesick. Usually she is shown holding one of the three dogs she had brought out with her from England. On arrival at Rangoon she had at once met someone who was to become a lifelong friend, her 'nearest and dearest', Una Nimmo. As with so many of Olive's real friends, Una had 'marvellous taste'; and she had a remarkable address: 2 Tiger Alley, Pineapple Jungle, Rangoon.

Una's husband Harry was Electrical Adviser to the Governor of Burma. He and the Governor, she told me, were the only people who were allowed to go round the Shwedagon pagoda with their shoes on. Harry always remembered Olive with a bandeau round her head, and a bunch of flowers made of shells hanging down at the side. 'Your mother would really have liked to have been married in England,' Una said. 'She had a nice dress, but not a wedding dress. She wore a big round hat with ostrich feathers over the brim, and a long amber necklace to her waist.' Olive had stayed with Bishop Fyffe on arrival, and Mrs Fyffe went to 'endless pains' explaining the marriage service to her. The Fyffes were very old-fashioned. There was a joke, Una said, about the bishop not allowing his sons to say jam because it was too like damn.

The first British steamer from Mandalay to Bhamo had sailed in 1867. This was in the days of King Mindon, who had also allowed a British consul at Bhamo. No doubt the British were becoming agitated by the presence of French missionaries. Bhamo had always been an important staging post for traders, and Marco Polo may have visited it in the late thirteenth century. The Kachens, great dealers in jade, had originally come from Tibet, and did not feel at all Burmese, like the Shans further south in the now notorious heroin smuggling area known as the Golden Triangle.

Flocks of flamingoes on the Irrawaddy, eyes glaring from the jungle when the steamer's searchlight was switched on at night (to avoid sandbanks), white pagodas like follies on hilltops, sunsets, gibbons swinging in the trees, fireflies: I remember Olive telling me about these. A lot of chickens travelled with them in crates, and every now and then they would be let loose on dry land, but not the rooster, which would remain crowing on the masthead. The steamer passed through the second and third defiles, when the huge river narrowed to about two hundred yards and swirled past spectacular dark green and red cliffs. At Katha Olive and Walter went to look at the ruby mines.

The house at Bhamo was called No. 1 Paradise Alley. It was quite large, wooden, with sixteen windows along the front upstairs and fretwork under the eaves. Bhamo was a purely Burmese town, and the Kachens, many of whom were Christians, lived in bamboo villages outside. Further north, in the area of the Myitkyina and Mogaung, the Kachens were to be generous with help and hospitality to Allied troops during the war, suffering terrible reprisals when their settlements were captured by the Japanese or pro-Japanese Burmese troops. But in 1921 there was a certain danger from dacoity locally, so Olive usually had to have a guard. It was in any case a time of political tension all over Burma, which was still a province of India, and there was talk of boycotting the Prince of Wales's visit in December. However a few nationalist leaders were neatly put into detention for a while, and the visit was considered a splendid success, politically and socially.

Walter took Olive to see the Kachen and Shan entertainments laid on for the Prince at Mandalay. There were dragons thirty feet long, birds twice as tall as men, fabulous bulls, elephants, tigers and peacocks, 'all let loose on a fiery night' according to a local newspaper. And of course on display were the giraffe-necked women, each with at least fourteen brass rings and wearing little spiked brass pagodas as head-dresses.

At Christmas it was 'Mandalay week', with parties at the Club and the Military Police Ball, a white tie affair. Walter had some polo and snipe shooting.

The dear old Strand, built in 1901, let us in. The plumbing was haywire, the lift boy had to jump to make the lift work, there was a giant cockroach under our table in the dining-room. By the reception desk there was a lost property case, full of things that seemed to date from before the Japanese occupation: fans, ear-rings, cuff-links, yellowed Sherlock Holmes books; and of course dust and rat droppings. And there was the great teak staircase, one of my reasons for wanting to come to Burma: rather ordinary really, but then I hardly expected something out of Hollywood. I stood where Walter would have been waiting, in his Sam Browne belt, breeches and boots – waiting for Olive with her amber beads, ostrich feathers and the bouquet with its long trail of frangipani flowers. Around me were piles of bedding rolls and sweaty knapsacks belonging to 'cheapies', young Australians who had opted for the train ride to Mandalay. It was hard to switch on the 1921 nostalgia.

At the airport I had been asked by a customs officer if I would sell him my Johnny Walker whisky, but I decided to hold off. Rangoon, after Calcutta, was amazingly sedate, with big plain office buildings laid out on the grid system. The people, men and women, in their longyis or sarongs, looked so neat and clean. But for the Shwedagon and the Sule pagodas, and such peculiarities as the Scots market and the Karawaik, a concrete restaurant in the shape of the old royal barge, it would be a dull city to look at. I could not help thinking of the terrible Japanese air-raid on the port of Rangoon on December 23 1941, when 2,750 died and 1,700 were wounded. The people had in their innocence walked out on Strand Road to watch the dogfights, and then the anti-personnel bombs had come down . . .

Theroux had wisely avoided even a mention of the Shwedagon in his book. It is difficult, I admit, to avoid the clichés. We saw it at sunset, the golden stupa ablaze. It was superb. With the temple bells, the lights, the sparkling mirrors, the jumbled shrines, the chanting and general air of enjoyment, it was like a magic fairground of fantastic richness. I hope that Diana Cooper, 'breathless with excitement', was exaggerating when she claimed that she had been dissuaded from going in, even if people like Harry Nimmo had special privileges. 'You have to enter barefoot,' she had been warned. 'An Englishman can't do that. Full of lepers.' Certainly Walter had taken some photographs in there. But then Una has said that she never walked round it, and – come to think of it – I can't imagine Olive, with her often proclaimed 'horror' of feet, walking barefoot in a Burmese pagoda, however beautiful and famous. There is something sensual in the feel of the still warm marble after dark.

Needless to say I wanted to see the Anglican cathedral, which turned out to be in Bogyoke Aung San Street, and an austere contrast to the Shwedagon. Officially a 'modified form of Early English architecture', it was red brick picked out in white; the foundation stone had been laid on February 24 1886, and the architect had been 'Mr Chisholm of Madras'. The font was painted red, white and blue. Much damage had been done to the building by the Japanese, who had used it as a storehouse. We met the Rev. David Than Lwin, and had coffee followed by tea and bananas with him at the Vicarage. Inevitably there was a tale of a dwindling congregation, but the Archbishop of Canterbury had been there for the New Year and morale had been boosted.

That same evening we went in search of 6 Cheape Road, where my parents and I had lived after the Andamans. To my annoyance, our driver picked up a friend who travelled with us, but this friend, whose name was Mynt Thint, alias Uncle, alias Mint Tea, soon won us over with his Burmese charm. By the time we reached Cheape Road, which had changed its name, the light was dwindling. All the British houses had gone, because they had been built of wood no doubt, and there was no number 6 any more. The place had become a backwater, anonymous; the road was rough and stony, and lined with a few straggly palms like ink scratches against the dusk. We turned into a grander, more suburban area, full of houses that seemed to be embassies. It had become dark. Mynt Thint was now fully in charge, and stopped the taxi to speak to somebody. We were told that an old Anglo-Indian lived in a house nearby.

So we found ourselves outside a great Charles Addams mansion, with lattice windows and a drive. There was one small light upstairs. Mynt Thint began ringing the bell at the gate, and immediately this set off an uproar of Alsatians barking. It was like the beginning of a Daphne du Maurier story.

Eventually an old man appeared briefly above the portico, and we saw lights switching on and off as he descended the stairs. By this time the dogs were hysterical. He came to the gate, quietened the dogs only a little, and began telling us all about his hernia and cataract operations. Yes, he had lived here since 1939, having bought the house from Mr Justice Sem. He had been in Rangoon all during the Japanese occupation: 'quite a grind'. At this stage an enraged woman appeared at a side door and screamed at him. He turned, and then came back nervously. 'I say, old chap, you haven't got an *English* cigarette, have you?' I gave him part of our black market supply. 'Ta awfully.' Once more he came back, and this time said with an arch smile: 'See you later, alligator.' The dogs seemed to hate this familiarity, and began barking even more wildly.

The profits from our Johnny Walker whisky enabled us to have our first, and rather disappointing, lobster thermidor that evening at the Strand. The longing for ballpoint pens in Burma had turned out to be a myth. A group of Japanese war veterans had arrived with their wives: they looked just like wartime caricatures – prominent teeth, spectacles, snub noses. We were to find that they were the cause of our being stuck for yet another day in Rangoon: they had pre-booked all the accommodation in the only plane north. Visions of Army friends who had died on the Burma railway surged up before me and had to be suppressed. After all the Japs had been *defeated*. We tried losing our tempers at 'Tourist Bureau', then cajoling, then bribing, then offering dollars, but the clerk, Mr U Thoung Sen, just laughed. Everybody in Rangoon laughed when things went wrong. We sat rather miserably drinking beer in the huge bare lobby of the hotel until quite late, with the occasional Strand rat scampering past.

It was Mynt Thint who suggested we should drive to Pegu, and I was glad to do so because my ayah Mimi had come from there. We were able to do this on the black market profits from our remaining 555s. Our new driver was Chimon, half Indian, half Burmese, a Muslim, and we went in a rattling 1947 Chevrolet, which broke down seven times. The city of the Mons turned out to be rather a shanty town, though with some nice banyan trees. Having seen the glories of the Shwedagon we were scornful about Pegu's Shwemawdaw, but then it had been completely rebuilt after the earthquake of 1930. I felt like dashing up to every cheroot-smoking biddy with her grey hair bunched under a plastic comb, and asking: 'Are you Mimi?' The girls of Pegu, however, must surely be the most beautiful of any in Burma, and that's saying something.

The Shwethalyaung, a reclining Buddha a hundred and eighty feet long, a little outside Pegu, is a sensation. It had been submerged by jungle, and rediscovered by British engineers when laying out the railway. The smiling face on the glittering pillow, with the enormous ear-lobes and thick arched eyebrows, was full of a gentle humour. Several young Chinese were celebrating their New Year around it, playing noisy games with transistors blaring. The iron canopy over the Buddha was hideous, we thought.

Next we bumped down a bullock track to another wonder, quite different, deep in a country like the Zimbabwean bush. This was the Kyaik Pun, four Buddhas back to back, about a hundred feet high, one crumbled away, with greenery sprouting out here and there. It dated from 1476.

We were the only visitors. Mynt Thint told us the legend of the four Mon sisters who had built the Kyaik Pun: It had been said that if any of them married, her own particular Buddha would collapse – and one sister did marry, which is why the fourth Buddha is nearly gone. As we left, an old monk looking like Harold Macmillan in tangerine robes beat a gong to make sure we gave him his tip.

We also went to the British war cemetery, where there are 27,000 graves. Several Burmese in bright longyis were wandering round it, light-hearted as always but not at all disrespectful, merely enjoying the beauty of the arrangement of the cemetery and the flowers.

When I read about the Chindits and the US force known as the Marauders, it always seems to me that the conditions in those drenched, leech-ridden, muddy northern jungles must have been as wretched as anywhere during the war – and malaria, jaundice, jungle sores and dysentery were the least of the nightmare. John Masters, as I know from a mutual friend, was far too modest about himself in *The Road Past Mandalay*. It was that friend who also told me about the loyalty of the Kachens, and how in one ghastly retreat our own wounded soldiers, too bad to be moved, had had to be finished off with the pistol rather than let them fall into Japanese hands. A 'devil's palette of mud and blood', that bit of the war has been called. I have some good Japanese friends, and certainly do not hold the war against *them*. But there are things in such recent history that are hard to forget.

I left the cemetery feeling humbled, smelling the smell of suffering among the honeysuckle and roses, and thinking of sacrifices and comradeship and being pushed to the limit of endurance.

It was depressing to have to drive afterwards past various military zones between Pegu and Rangoon. One of our breakdowns was near a place where peasants were bringing in cartloads of rice, watched by soldiers. There were flags and music, to keep up the pretence that all drudgery is happiness, so long as one is working for the common good and the nation. Here we had the contrast between the Communist ideal and the intense devotion in the pagodas, where we had been amazed by the piles of offerings from poor people – bank notes and gold leaf.

The four of us were hungry, because Mynt Thint had not allowed us to eat: 'Pegu rice no good. Rangoon rice good.' So on our return Chimon took us to a Chinese Muslim restaurant, where we had a rather suspicious-looking communal soup into which all had to dip. But the fried chicken rice with prawns, coconut milk and ginger was good.

At last we flew from Rangoon, to Pagan, under the guidance of a Burmese beauty, Darleen, whom we had all to ourselves. Kubla Khan is said to have devastated the city in 1287, though apparently he spared five thousand out of the once 'four million' pagodas and temples. So now, if you stand on the tower, say, of the Thatlyinnyu Temple, the highest of them all, you see laid out before you an immense plain with any number of buildings that could have been models for his stately pleasure-dome: some of them huge and still in use, some merely stupas, some in ruins. It all reminded me a little of the old wilderness around Paestum, where great monuments have also survived not only ancient sackings but the shells and bombs of the Second World War. 'I never want to see Pagan again,' Mr Smith of the Fairlawn Hotel had said to us. I could appreciate that, but all the same, Pagan must be one of the most extraordinary sights in the whole of south-east Asia, not excepting Angkor.

Strictly speaking, the Buddhist religion does not recognize the need for prayer. Pagodas and temples are places for meditation and spiritual refreshment. But we did see a lot of praying in Burma. Darleen, who was inclined to spoil her looks by smearing her face with yellow, was forever sinking on her knees and praying for several minutes on end. We came to the conclusion that she was in love. She had a great awe for the Nats, which are spirits or souls of the dead who have not yet found peace and come to plague the living. Nats are demons rather worse than gremlins or poltergeists. Some live in trees, but other established ones have their own images. 'You must be very very careful to please them,' Darleen told us. 'They can do you terrible harm.' I began to doubt whether my camera was working, and suggested I might ask the help of one of thirty-seven Nats in the Shwezigon Pagoda. Darleen agreed rather doubtfully. I chose Nat number twenty-seven, the Master of the White Elephants, and knelt on a stone. She was horrified. 'No, no! That's no good! Not *there!*' All was ruined. I had upset the Nat. Sure enough, on my return to England, I found my photographs of Pagan were blank.

I know my parents stopped at Pagan on their honeymoon journey, because there is a picture of Olive with her parasol on the shore of the Irrawaddy by the little white Bupaya pagoda. This pagoda, the most ancient of them all, slipped into the river in the 1975 earthquake, but has not been completely restored (as have other damaged pagodas at Pagan). Raúl and I went at sunset to that same spot where she had been photographed. Children were bathing, and a group of sampans were setting out, perhaps to fish. An ox cart sent up a pink cloud of dust. There were a lot of swifts. Lights began to appear in the town opposite, and the sun's last rays caught the pagoda's tapering dome.

Our guide at Mandalay was a Nepalese this time, and she was certainly in love. Her boy friend, aged forty-two, was in Rangoon and half English. 'He loves me too much. He calls me Baby.' She was very interested in Charles and Diana (we had noticed several pictures of their wedding in Rangoon). The girls dreaded having to work at Pagan: 'so dull'.

> Tho' I walks with fifty 'ousemaids outer Chelsea to the Strand,
> An' they talks a lot o' lovin', but wot do they understand? . . .
> I've a neater, sweeter maiden in a cleaner, greener land!
> On the road to . . .

Mandalay is not nearly so romantic as its name, and it's not Mandalay's fault. The royal palace, which had been made of wood, was destroyed when the British drove out the Japanese in 1945. All that is left of the palace of wicked Queen Supalayat (known as Soup-plate to the British) and King Thibaw are the walls, the lotus-filled moat and some tombs. It is not surprising that after the war the Burmese opted for a long period of isolation from the rest of the world.

We found that only eight months before our visit to Mandalay a great fire had burnt over 6,000 buildings near the Irrawaddy's waterfront, leaving 35,000 people homeless. The aftermath of this did not add to the gaiety of Mandalay. In the Atumashi Kyaung monastery we had a serious talk with two handsome bare-shouldered monks, brothers, about the meaning of Nirvana, where self-consciousness ceases and the misery of living is no more; in this way one escapes the endless round of reincarnation and suffering. The bestowal of alms is one of the ways in which merit is gained in this world. We got that gentle message . . .

Mandalay, like Rangoon, is planned on the grid system. I am afraid it mostly conjured up for me the sweat, dust and boredom of Victorian parade grounds and cantonments. But we did cross the Irrawaddy by the Ava bridge – destroyed by the retreating British in 1942 (with the oil derricks at Chauk), and restored thanks to the Japanese in 1954 – to Sagaing, one of the 'four deserted cities', where the wooded hills are dotted with scores of white pagodas, like an Edmund Dulac landscape. Young monks and nuns with shaved heads were bathing and washing clothes, laughing and splashing one another. We took a boat and rowed among the bathers, and were splashed too. Along the shore were Italianate villas used as monasteries or for pilgrims. The dome of the Kaunghmidan pagoda, we were told, was modelled on the exact shape of the breast of some nubile seventeenth-century Burmese queen. And once more, at the same pagoda, we met a hundred or more images of our ugly little friends the Nats. 'Don't be fooled by those silly splashing nuns,' they seemed to be telling us. We took no notice. It had been our happiest afternoon in a happy country. In the now blue-green mistiness of the approaching dusk a hundred domes glittered in the setting sun, and we heard temple bells, gongs and cymbals.

We were back at Calcutta, and at the Fairlawn Hotel. Our room, with its curtained door, opened on to 'el gran salon', as Mrs Smith called it, full of potted plants and curios from all over the world. Over our beds, instead of a Bleeding Heart or a Virgin Enthroned, such as one might see in Spain, we had posters, 'Science in the Ukrainian SSR' and 'Energomachexport USSR Moscow'. Mrs Smith explained that Russians on business often stayed at the Fairlawn.

Sure enough, on our descending for breakfast, she pointed out two Russians, alone at a table for four. We rushed to join them. One was surly, with big biceps, evidently the boss, but the other – better-looking, younger, with filthy nails and tattooed – smiled just a little. The ancient waiters in their white pugrees now padded up with porridge, scrambled eggs and tea.

I could see Raúl casting round for an opening question. Eventually he came out with: 'Do you like Indian food?' Surly seemed even surlier at this intrusion, but Smiley said after a while: 'This is Scottish food.' Another silence, then Raúl was daring. 'What are you doing in Calcutta?' Surly answered this time. 'Helping,' he snapped. That shut us up. Mrs Smith, observing some tension, came up and spoke to them in Russian. She told us that Surly often came to Calcutta and had once, at her request, brought her a samovar. Both Russians seemed glad to escape from this inquisitive Spaniard.

It was different in the evening, Smiley opened the conversation. I was rubbing an old Burmese mosquito bite. 'Is something wrong with your heart?' he suddenly asked me with a wink.

Soon we were hearing how they were setting up some printing press at Calcutta, and had done the same thing in Brazil and Poland. They both came from a town on the Volga. Smiley spent his summer holidays canoeing, Surly only liked motoring. Smiley surprised us by being a fan of Yves Montand. Both had watched Spanish corridas on television.

Next morning they were uncommunicative again. Perhaps they had hangovers. We were however joined by a bright-eyed, dark young man in an emerald shirt, just arrived by train from Bombay. He looked Mediterranean, but to our surprise was also Russian. He said he had some Arab blood in him, and was an interpreter at a steel plant. Being a member of the Party, he had his own flat in Moscow. We asked if he had a religion. 'Young people in the Soviet Union do not go to church any more,' he said. 'That is for grandparents.' After I had gone from the table, leaving Raúl alone with him, he felt able to attack the Iron Lady. 'At least the British can criticize Mrs Thatcher,' Raúl said. 'Would you criticize Mr Brezhnev?' Our friend laughed. 'I would be very foolish if I did.'

A mysterious French writer, M. Pélissard, who dressed in a sarong and was off soon to Bangladesh, was fascinated by the Russians, but did not have Raúl's knack of drawing them out. Mrs Smith guided us next to an Iranian tea merchant with a beautiful Assamese wife and a squinty baby. They had been allowed out of Iran in order to visit her parents, but now the husband had been told that he must have a special permit for Assam and could only get this in person at Delhi. By the time Indian bureaucracy had taken its course, it would be time for them to fly back to Tehran. . .

We had arrived in Calcutta for the festival of the goddess Sarasvati, representing the cult of the earth mother. We heard some singing down a side alley, decorated with flags and coloured lights, and found ourselves invited to sit before an improvised shrine containing the four-armed seated goddess, painted white. We were given tea, in the usual small earthenware cups, and some sweet yellow rice wrapped in newspaper. On joining the procession round the shrine, I noticed that Sarasvati had a book and a large pen in her two left hands. This was because she is the goddess of learning (also of music). Some of the effigies elsewhere were made of salt, a man said. At the end of the festival they would be thrown into the Hooghly.

It was also evident that Sarasvati was a kind of Ceres, associated with agriculture and fertility. At another shrine, in the entrance-hall of a bank, she was holding a plough. Here, among some old men performing their puja, we were given small green fruits to eat.

On the next day the atmosphere of the festival was quite different. Trucks carrying the effigies to the ghats for dumping in the river, and full of students, shouting and waving, raced at a crazy speed through the streets. We were inclined to join in, but I decided against, having been at school at Winchester where one was brought up to have a horror of making a fool of oneself.

We had been to the ghats by the Eden Gardens, not quite sure whether we were intruding on holy ground or whether we would be lynched for daring to be near females ceremonially washing themselves. There were scores of people knee-deep in the murky water, not bothering at all about the floating garlands and presumably ashes, from the recently cremated dead. Steps led up to what must have been customs halls in British times, and here in dank recesses there were small shrines lit by candles and presided over by priests in loin-cloths. In other corners such activities as hair-cutting were taking place. Outside, in blessed sunlight, were quantities of shacks for pilgrims. I thought we had wandered into the heartland of Calcutta's beggars, but instead we had offers of ghee and chapattis, or were ignored.

I confess it was a relief to turn into the Eden Gardens, the creation originally of Emily Eden and her sister Fanny, and once a sanctuary for British society at Calcutta. The Burmese pagoda, brought from Prome in 1854 after the Second Burmese War, was still in good order, but I was sorry that Lord Auckland's statue had disappeared.

On our last day we decided to drive to Barrackpore, not because of the cantonment, nor yet because of Emily Eden, who so vividly described staying there, but because of Lady Canning, who loved it so much and was buried in the park.

Barrackpore is fifteen miles upstream from Calcutta. It was to the vast but not very impressive country house on the banks of the Hooghly that Governors-General and their families would escape as often as possible from the burning climate of the city. Emily Eden was the sharpest, wittiest and the most brilliant of Governors-General's ladies, but Charlotte Canning has been remembered as the one with the most charm and the most aristocratic grace and modesty – there had been engravings of her when young as a 'keepsake beauty', the equivalent of a pin-up. She caught jungle fever on her way down from Darjeeling, and died in her husband's arms after a week's illness.

Virginia Surtees, when she was writing Charlotte Canning's biography, went to visit the tomb. She quoted in her book from the desolated Lord Canning's letter of November 22 1861 to Queen Victoria:

> Lord Canning presents his humble duty to Your Majesty... The Funeral is over. It took place quite privately at sunrise on the 19th. There is no burial place for the Governor-General or his Family, and the Cemeteries at Calcutta are odious in many ways. Lord Canning has therefore set a portion of the garden at Barrackpore apart for the purpose. It is a beautiful spot; – looking upon the reach of the grand river which she was so fond of drawing, – shaded from the glare of the sun by high trees, – and amongst the bright shrubs and flowers in which she had so much pleasure.

In due course he read Charlotte's journals; and when he realized the extent of her devotion and self-sacrifice he appears to have broken down. He was in bad health, worn out from the nightmare of being Governor-General during the Mutiny years, and returned to England, where he died seven months after his wife.

We knew that what had been the old Governor-General's house was now a police hospital. Our taxi driver was a Sikh, without a word of English, and after many complications we reached a guard post at a side entrance to the park, only to be told that it was absolutely prohibited to enter. We looked longingly across to the trees, across a pretty eighteenth-century bridge, and drove miserably on. But there, suddenly on a high mound, stood a Grecian temple, surrounded by Corinthian columns, and we realized at once that this was none other than the Temple of Fame, originally put up by Lord Minto in memory of men who had died during the conquest of Mauritius and Java in 1810 and 1811. From a distance it looked in perfect condition.

Unfortunately the temple was within the garden of the official country retreat of the present Governor of Bengal, and he was not at home. I now saw what had happened to the statues of eminent men that had been removed from their plinths at Independence. They were here, ranged round the Governor's garden, and two equestrian statues were outside the Temple of Fame. The effect was like the forum of a provincial Roman town.

Without a permit we were again absolutely forbidden to put a toe inside the gates. We were directed to the local kindergarten, where a kindly memsahib had an idea. Why not go straight to the main entrance to the park and then boldly tell the guards that we had an appointment with the Commandant? We did this, and to our surprise soon found our ancient taxi, driven by its bewildered Sikh, trundling along an immense drive with an escort of outriders and a jeep.

It was like being in the epilogue of *Brideshead Revisited*; for among the glades and coppices, so obviously laid out in the traditional manner of Kent or Capability Brown, were Army blocks and corrugated huts. 'The Park,' Charlotte Canning had indeed told Queen Victoria, 'is carefully planted with round-headed trees to look as English as possible.' But, whatever her homesick predecessors had contrived to produce, the result was inescapably Indian, with its palms, mango trees and bamboos. 'The luxuriant growth in the jungly ground outside, of dazzling green during the rains, is more beautiful than I can describe, and I always think of the Palm House of Kew.' She in point of fact had deliberately added exotic touches, like a double bank of poinsettias.

We halted at a large Regency bungalow and were ushered into the rather dark but newly painted central room, typical of its period, and here we saw English books, a cushion from Fiji and some leather armchairs that might well have been transported from the Travellers' Club in London. At last the Commandant, in his late thirties, arrived, but wearing pyjamas, with a shawl round his shoulders. He was suffering from diarrhoea, he explained. On the spur of the moment I made up the story that Raúl was related to the Spanish branch of Lady Canning's family, and was therefore especially anxious to see her tomb. The Commandant said that he would arrange for an officer to accompany us, and called for tea.

All was very leisurely. He had read some G. M. Trevelyan and my mention of Macaulay seemed a help. He told us that the bungalow, originally thatched, had been used as a guest-house by the Governors-General, and that Wellington was said to have stayed in it. It dawned on me then that this might have been the very house lent by the Bentincks to Charles and Hannah Trevelyan on their truncated honeymoon. The whole area was haunted, the Commandant said. Sometimes at night people heard the sounds of marching and a brass band – he had actually heard drums. The park was infested with snakes. They were even in the house, and his wife had caught a poisonous one when closing a door. 'They drop from the ceiling,' he said.

A telephone rang. He gave sharp commands. We waited, and waited, thinking of our Fairlawn lunch, always so punctual. The Commandant showed us the antiquated water system. At last there was the noise of a motorbike arriving, and a subaltern in a crash helmet appeared.

As we passed the certainly rather plain ex-Governor-General's house, I began now to remember scraps from Emily Eden's letters. She and Lord Auckland had ridden together about the park on elephants; she had had to use a ladder when mounting or dismounting. There had been a menagerie, to which creatures had been added such as giraffe, porcupines and sloths. Jackals had been a nuisance, and one had even snatched a little screaming greyhound called Fairy by the throat. The servants had been brought from Calcutta, and had been dressed in loose muslin robes, with scarlet and gold sashes and scarlet and gold turbans.

Lord Auckland had been succeeded by Lord Dalhousie, under whose regime the drawing-rooms had been redecorated with red damask and velvet. Charlotte Canning had set about making the place cosier, with armchairs, small round tables, framed sketches, recollections of Balmoral and Osborne, and four hundred and fifty yards of rose-chintz.

At last we came to the tomb in its quiet spot near a tamarind tree and overlooking the Hooghly. It had a guard, and we were told that this was always the case. Facing the grave, within the Gothic enclosure, was the bronze equestrian statue of Lord Canning, which had been removed with the others from its original place at Calcutta. So husband and wife were reunited.

The tomb had obviously become a kind of holy place, a shrine. The white marble headstone was a replacement, so I had read in Virginia's book. The original had had Italian mosaics, and had been designed by Charlotte's sister, Lady Waterford, friend of Ruskin, and had been removed to St John's Cathedral. All the while, as we wandered round, the officer and guard stood at attention.

The park at Barrackpore, drawn by Bishop Reginald Heber, 1824

Although it was daylight, I was sure I heard a jackal howl.

While packing up our things at the Fairlawn, we worried about the Andaman Islands shells, which were now stinking. Ants were supposed to have cleaned them out on the hotel roof while we were in Burma, but they had not done their job. We would have to carry them on the plane with our hand luggage. What would the customs man say on unwrapping them at Heathrow? We tried pouring in Jeyes Fluid and stuffing them with loo paper.

Once aboard our Jumbo, we stowed the packet of shells in an overhead locker. All was well until somebody opened the locker to look for blankets... Here the story had better end.

Tom, Hannah and Charles 1835–8

There were months of great unhappiness, Hannah said, after she and Charles had joined Tom Macaulay in the great house on Chowringhee Road. 'I seem not to belong to the world here,' she wrote. 'All my feelings are given to home.' Macaulay continued to respect his new brother-in-law for his youthful ardour, extraordinary drive and perseverance, even for his simplicity of manner, but that did not prevent him from telling Charles's brother John, a naval chaplain visiting Calcutta, that he thought 'death a less trial than the living death of a marriage'.

'The tremendous blow which fell upon me at the beginning of the year,' Macaulay wrote on August 25 1835 to his great friend Thomas Ellis, 'has left marks behind it which I shall carry to my grave. Even now I dare not, in the intervals of business, remain alone for a minute without a book in my hand.' He would get up early at about four or five, so as to be sure of some cool solitary hours before breakfast. 'I really hope that, by the time of my leaving this country, I shall have completely gone through all that is valuable in Greek and Latin literature – not in a childish way, or in a cramming way – but understanding, judging, reperusing what is good again and again, skipping what I perceive to be worthless.'

As soon as Bentinck had left India, the Orientalists returned to the attack against the 'Anglomania and Russophobia of Trevelyan', who as William Macnaghten said, 'was becoming perfectly rabid' and had 'infected' Macaulay. However the acting Governor-General, Sir Charles Metcalfe, was not one to go back on a predecessor's decision. Metcalfe also went ahead with that other violently controversial measure, the freeing of the press, in which Macaulay played a leading part.

As each new problem loomed following the official acceptance of his Minute on Education, Macaulay rose up to the occasion with enjoyment, delighting his supporters with his 'strong sterling commonsense' and the way in which he dealt with 'irritable colleagues and subordinates', cutting through the knots and sweeping aside mediocrity. It was difficult for his opponents to compete with his style and wit, let alone his command of the language.

In May 1835 Metcalfe asked Macaulay to head the Law Commission. According to George Otto Trevelyan this offer was accepted eagerly; among other things the complicated and detailed work would be yet another form of therapy after his bereavement. By a resolution of the Council a draft of any new law proposed had to be printed and published. As each one appeared there arose among the European residents of Calcutta 'unpleasant indications of a heated state of feeling', which before long turned into fury and vilification, and not only from defeated Orientalists of the education debate. Hannah was to say that 'cheat, swindler and charlatan' were among the least of the insults. It was noted that Macaulay was a bachelor and 'inhumanly insensible' to female beauty and fashion. He was accused of being malicious and wilful; many of his proposals were said to be in breach of his duties as Councillor and 'contrary to the unwritten law and constitution of the United Kingdom and Ireland'. Everyone knew that he had a salary of ten thousand a year. This huge sum was to many a monstrous waste of public money and received by Macaulay under false pretences. He was unsociable and mean, and so were his sister and brother-in-law who shared his house.

It was true of course that Macaulay had come to India in order to give himself financial security, and he had no intention, if he could avoid it, of wasting it on people who did not interest him. He found himself surrounded by gossiping women and snobbery. 'Circles of fashion', for instance, avoided mingling with civil servants. A Mrs Butler had pointed out that in England newspaper journalists were never admitted to 'good society', and they were thus by inference also a lesser breed at Calcutta. It became clear that journalists were not only jealous of Macaulay's literary standing, but resentful that he did not attempt – as 'one of their own order' – to have them admitted to 'that society from which they were uncharitably excluded'.

A series of financial crashes and bankruptcies had made Calcutta a much more subdued place than, say, in Bishop Heber's day: all the more reason, it was thought, for Macaulay and the Trevelyans to try to brighten the scene. There were plenty of performances of Italian opera and French vaudeville, as well as amateur theatricals, but they were mostly despised by the inhabitants of 33 Chowringhee Road. There seemed to be little sympathy in the outside world for the possibility that both Macaulay and Charles could be very hard-worked.

Macaulay wrote to his sisters Selina and Fanny in England:

The public diversions are of a miserable sort, – vile acting, viler opera-singing, – and things which they call reunions, – a sort of subscription balls. These and great dinners of between thirty and forty people constitute the dissipation of Calcutta ...

I am forced now and then to be a guest, and now and then to be a host. Last week we had a party of 36, and next month we must have another. Nobody speaks except to the person next to him. The conversation is the most deplorable twaddle that can be conceived; and, as I always sit next to the lady of highest rank – or in other words next to the oldest, ugliest, proudest, and dullest woman in the company – I am worse off than my neighbours.

The British civilian population of Calcutta, apart from the civil servants, was an ephemeral thing. People tended to be either on their way somewhere inland or on their way back, and they would try to confine themselves to the cold weather period, from October to early March. New arrivals were usually criticized as 'coarse' or 'vulgar' until their skins had lost their healthy glow from the sea voyage and had turned a pale primrose, transmogrified into orange after a few fevers.

There were plenty of occasions when Macaulay was good company. At one house the lady he was accompanying into dinner was laughing so loudly at his jokes that the host – in holy orders – was unable to say grace and had to sit down.

Among the male residents of Calcutta whose intellects he approved of were his opponent in educational matters, Macnaghten, and Charles's special ally and contemporary, John Colvin.

> I often ask some of them to a quiet dinner, and should do so oftener, but that one or two of them, between ourselves, have most particularly disagreeable wives, who must be asked with them.

And Macaulay did at least attend parties given by the wealthy Hindu merchant and philanthropist Dwarkanath Tagore, who had been a friend and follower of Rammohan Roy, and was the grandfather of Rabindranath Tagore. The rooms in Dwarkanath Tagore's house were a spectacle indeed: 'rich in more than the fabled magnificence of the East, combined with the statuary and decorations of Western Art'. At his parties there would be music, ices, plenty of champagne, dancing and 'all the luxurious adjuncts of an oriental factory'; and 'coloured lights, then recently imported from Europe, illumined the dark masses of foliage in the garden'. 'Prince Tagore' had cooperated in the campaign for the freedom for the press and the abolition of suttee, also in the reorganization of the Hindu and Medical Colleges and the Fever Hospital. He was the first Indian Justice of the Peace.

As for Charles, married life appears to have quietened him a little. At least he seemed less anxious to pontificate in the press – no doubt Hannah was restraining him. He might have been Metcalfe's 'favourite civil servant', but there was not the same filial bond he had had with the Bentincks. He now had to concentrate on consolidating and defending the educational policy he had worked so hard to procure. And, after all that campaigning in 1833–4, he was on quite a number of committees. Obviously, from remarks by Macaulay, his manners were still considered odd and unpolished.

His religious fervour was as strong as ever, and in this Hannah supported him. 'We see a great many Americans here,' she wrote, 'and my husband corresponds with some of the most influential Americans at home, but I never saw anything like their immoveable bigotry on the subject of slavery. Religion seems to have no effect.' On the other hand there were also several American missionaries, of whom she and Charles approved. The English missionaries had become lax and worldly. 'My husband gives all his assistance to the Americans.'

Charles was always an admirer of the United States, the question of slavery apart. In his *Town Duties Report*, an out-and-out tract in favour of laissez faire, advocating self-help in towns in place of the ponderous wastefulness resulting from central government intervention, he had written in 1835:

England and the United States, let who gainsay it, are the favoured instruments of God's providence in the establishment of His kingdom of peace and love. These are the two western nations whose religion is purest – whose government is finest – whose fleets command the oceans, and whose commerce pervades the whole world; and they have at once the greatest amount of temporal and eternal benefits to communicate, and the most extensive and effectual means of communicating them.

When Emily Eden arrived, she found the Americans 'valuable creatures' in other ways. 'They send us novels, ice and apples – three things that, as you guess, are not indigenous to our soil... The first freight of apples the Americans sent covered the whole expense of the ship's passage out.'

English ladies had perforce to spend many hours shut up in their darkened houses under the punkahs with nothing to do, and, as Emily also said, with no strength to do it with. Hannah kept herself busy with planning good works and worrying about 'raising the moral condition of Hindu women' and 'all the cruel rites'. She helped with the founding of asylums for orphans. So she had 'very little occasion to complain, as most ladies do here, of the long dull days of India'. Then on October 14 1835 her baby Margaret, always known as Baba, was born, and life for the whole household became much more cheerful. The child also proved a great solace for Uncle Tom, especially when she began to walk. 'I am becoming every day fonder of my little niece,' he told Ellis. 'It is long since I have minutely observed the gradual development of intelligence in a child.' Baba and her ayah would come to disturb him in his reading, still dressed in his slippers and dressing-gown, in the early morning, and she would want to feed the crows with pieces of the dry toast that accompanied his cup of tea, 'a ceremony during which', said G. O Trevelyan, 'he had much ado to protect the child from the advances of a multitude of birds, each about as big as herself, which hopped and fluttered round her as she stood on the steps of the verandah.'

On May 9 1836 Macaulay gave his sisters Selina and Fanny this résumé of life at Chowringhee Road:

Towards evening a fresh breeze springs up; and we take an airing in an open carriage along the banks of the Hoogley. We come home by starlight a little before 8 o'clock, and sit down almost immediately to dinner. After finishing our mango-fish, our curry, our asparagus, and our snipes (these are now chief articles at table), we fall on a very fine Stilton-cheese which my aunt has sent us.

273

Hannah and Trevelyan generally indulge in ale and porter. I more aristocratically confine myself to sherry or hock and soda and water.

A most 'unIndian' existence, as Hannah said, and very different to the cosmopolitan brilliance that Macaulay had enjoyed at Holland House in London. They would go to bed by a quarter to nine. Before six the barber would come to shave him, and when the sun drove him in from the garden he would 'luxuriate' in an enormous tub. He would always dress himself, without the help of servants, unlike most other Europeans who came to India. Then he would have breakfast, which would consist of eggs, mango-fish, snipe pie, hot beefsteak, coffee and toast. After that the business of the day would begin.

Lord Auckland, as the new Governor-General, disembarked at Calcutta with his two sisters on March 4 1836. Macaulay already knew and liked Auckland, a fellow Whig, though he thought him a little shy and not very dignified in his bearing – nobody in his estimation could compare with Bentinck. Of all people at Calcutta in the mid-1830s Emily Eden's sophisticated and penetrating wit would have been a match for his, which is probably why they did not get on. Emily was also a good artist and a keen gardener, and Macaulay was a bit of a philistine. Hannah said later to her children about the Edens: 'Though they were always good friends I do not think they were especially suited, or that your Uncle ever cared for their society.' Emily evidently did not take to Hannah either. When she was asked if there were any pleasing or accomplished women at Calcutta, she answered: 'Not one – not the sixth part of one; there is not anybody I can prefer to any other body.' In one letter she spoke rather tersely of going out after breakfast, 'awfully hot though it was', to Mrs Trevelyan 'to get her to arrange with some embroiderers from Dacca to embroider a gown in coloured silk'. However this was probably because of Hannah's efforts to set up 'work rooms for the poor'. Hannah also managed to get Emily to support 'our reforming efforts' at the orphan asylum.

Nearly three weeks after her arrival at Government House, Emily – known as the Burra Memsahib, First Lady – wrote:

We had another dinner of forty-six people today. Mr Macaulay came to my share at dinner. Just as we were assembling for dinner there came on what they call a 'north-wester' – a most violent storm of thunder, lightening, and wind, which is at its height in a moment. There were hundreds of white-muslined servants rushing about the house, catching at the blinds and shutters, but everything was blown off the table in an instant. I never heard such a row. It cools the air for three or four days; half our guests were shivering, and borrowing shawls; I thought it charming.

On one occasion Macaulay and Emily were seen bidding against one another at an auction, going up to absurd sums, for a popular novel. When at last the time came for Auckland and his sisters to depart 'up the country', leaving Calcutta in a barge pulled by a steamer, they were seen off by all the celebrities – 'Even Mr Macaulay turned out for it,' said Emily.

Years later, when everyone was back in England, some sort of quarrel erupted. For on July 4 1844 Macaulay wrote to his sister Fanny: 'Yesterday I dined at Lord Westminster's . . . Miss Eden was there, and very civil to me; – but I was as distant as possible. They have asked me to dinner. But I sent an excuse. I will never enter their house again till she makes an apology for her insolence to Hannah.'

Auckland had been instructed by the President of the Board of Control in London, John Cam Hobhouse, to restrain Macaulay's reforming ardour, and presumably Charles's as well. He arrived almost at the height of the great row about what was scathingly known as Macaulay's Black Act, which in civil cases would subject Europeans living outside Calcutta, in areas known as the Mofussil, the provinces, to the jurisdiction of the Company's courts, where Indian judges might preside. To Macaulay equality under the law, irrespective of race, rank or colour, was as axiomatic as freedom of the press. He was determined not to legalize the existence of a specially privileged European class in India. When he was threatened with a lynching and a duel, he was amused, and retorted: 'I must own I am unable to comprehend this solicitude for the welfare of the few, and this indifference to the welfare of the many.' If British settlers were to be encouraged in Bengal, and if the old system were to pre-vail, it would simply mean a tyranny of race over race, 'a tyranny of the worst sort'.

He wrote to Ellis:

To a person accustomed to the hurricanes of English faction this sort of tempest in a horsepond is merely ridiculous . . . The lawyers of the Supreme Court have set up a yelp which they think terrible, and which has infinitely diverted me. They have selected me as the object of their invectives; and I am generally the theme of five or six columns of prose and verse daily. I have not patience to read a tenth of what they put forth. The last ode in my praise which

I perused began 'Soon we hope they will recall ye, Tom Macaulay, Tom Macaulay'.

The Black Act was passed into law in 1837. A petition against it was sent to the British Parliament. There was a parliamentary inquiry, but the petition had to be withdrawn.

Macaulay completed the draft of his new Penal Code a little before he left for England in January 1838. It included the abolition of the death penalty, except for treason and premeditated murder, and of flogging and the pillory. Some other aims were the abolition of slavery in India, the improvement of prisons and the right of a woman to have reparation in cases of rape and to own her own property. As he said, once more to Ellis: 'It has cost me very intense labour, and whatever its faults may be, is certainly not a slovenly performance. It is full of defects which I see, and has no doubt many which I do not see. Yet I think that it is, on a whole, better than the French Code or Livingston's Code of Louisiana.'

Macaulay, November 1847. Caricature by John Doyle

'A miserable legislative abortion, which, before he reaches England, will be put upon a shelf, and like himself forgotten'; that was the reaction of the Calcutta press to Macaulay's Code. But for twenty-two years it continued to be discussed by his successors.

During that period there were wars and rumours of wars, followed by the Mutiny: all of which made domestic matters seem less urgent. The Code, with some amendments, only came into operation on January 1 1862, but was still in effect Macaulay's creation. It has of course been criticized for attempting to superimpose alien ideas from the West. Macaulay may have been condescending and arrogant about Indian history and culture, and his knowledge of the huge and diverse country might have been limited, but it is not altogether far-fetched to say that it is in at least a small part thanks to him that India emerged after 1947 as the world's largest democracy and has remained as such. John Clive, in his biography of Macaulay, quoted Whitley Stokes in 1887:

> Translated into almost all the written languages of India, it [the Code] has familiarised the native mind with ideas of justice and humanity, the maintenance of public order and public morality, the rights of the individual to life, health, freedom, honour and property, the possibility of expressing a law with clearness and authority, and of dealing systematically with a vast and complicated subject.

Meanwhile Macaulay had not relaxed his reading of the classics. On December 18 1837 he told Ellis that during that year he had read again all Livy and all Cicero, and was now going through all Tacitus again. He had read Homer twice, the greater part of Plato, Aristotle's Politics, Thucydides, all Xenophon's works, Philostratus's Life of Apollonius – 'a heap of impudent lies' – and much else. He also wrote an extremely long article on Bacon for the *Edinburgh Review*. It had even crossed his mind that he might abandon politics altogether and give himself wholly to letters; he would be able to undertake 'some great historical work which may at once be the business and amusement of my life, and to leave the pleasure of pestiferous rooms, sleepless nights, aching heads, and diseased stomachs, to greater men'. He did not give up politics, but his private reading in India, followed by the leisure of his long journey home by sea, gave him the basis of inspiration for the *History of England*, which he began in 1839, and the *Lays of Ancient Rome*. India had certainly not dulled his faculties, as he had feared it might.

'Reproachfully fat', he also returned to England in his own (and others') estimation a rich man, and this was not only because of the money he had saved but because of a legacy of £10,000 from his father's brother General Colin Macaulay, who many years before had served in India at Seringapatam and Travancore.

Now some Calcutta papers were actually angry because he was leaving. Just when he had amassed a fortune in India, it was said, and had gained some real experience, he was going to play the deserter. Macaulay never bothered to answer back. He had arrived to great acclaim, but now there were only a few insulting paragraphs to see him off. 'He leaves us,' was one comment, 'not amid sighs and tears, but curses, not loud but deep.'

Macaulay had persuaded Charles Trevelyan to write an article for the *Edinburgh Review* on the suppression of the Thugs, a hot subject at the time, some thousands of them having already been rounded up, executed or deported. He described the result as an unpretending article, but it was not very inspired, which is why one suspects that Macaulay must have had a hand in composing the literary flights of *The Education of the People of India*.

Charles was called upon to write his dramatic memoranda on the Afghan frontier and the defence of India against the Russian menace soon after Auckland's arrival. His recommendations obviously had an effect, and it therefore – at this distance – seems odd that he should have been so swiftly transferred from the Political Department to the Sudder Board of Revenue, though it marked a step up in his career. Perhaps Macnaghten, who now became Auckland's Secretary, saw it as a way of keeping Charles out of controversy. It was a job with much more routine work than hitherto. But then Charles was a first-rate administrator, and his successes over the abolition of transit duties and questions of land reform certainly more than qualified him for the Revenue. Needless to say, in his new office he at once found fresh hobby-horses, such as the reform of postal charges. He was also able to use his authority to push forward other educational ideas.

It is clear, nevertheless, that once back in England Charles regarded himself – and was officially regarded – as an authority on matters concerning the 'Great Game'. Certainly for a while he was kept in touch about confidential foreign policies in India through John Colvin, who became one of Macnaghten's two assistants and consequently in due course close to Auckland.

Like Macaulay, Charles rose early at Calcutta, but one imagines that he spent the cool hours working on office papers rather than the works of Tacitus or Thucydides. Macaulay was amazed that Charles kept his 'florid' health after ten years in India. As for himself, he said, he was like Napoleon after the retreat from Russia, 'J'ai le diable au corps.' Then suddenly during the hot weather and monsoons Charles began to crack, chiefly because of overwork, and little Baba started ailing.

Calcutta is some hundred miles from the sea. In the 1830s the usual rest-cure for someone suffering from strain or needing convalescence was to send him or her on a steamer trip to the mouth of the Hooghly. Although Charles's return to England was so close, he had to make two of these journeys, in October and November 1837. It being too dangerous to navigate at night, a ship would have to anchor at places such as Kedgeree or Sagar Island, which in spite of being a great pilgrimage centre was terribly infested, so Charles wrote to Hannah, by man-eating tigers. There were also crocodiles of a prodigious size. At Dowdeswell Island a crocodile when killed was found to have forty pounds' weight of women's bangles in its stomach. On these trips Charles tried to catch up on Tom's recommended reading, including *Tom Jones* and *Robinson Crusoe*, which he was 'surprised to find a religious book'. From one letter it seems that some unspecified setback, causing him 'great bitterness', had caused a nervous collapse. Perhaps there had also been cruel remarks about his imminent departure from Calcutta from enemies in the newspapers. But, as he said: 'God educates us for another life in the school of affliction...'

In the midst of these strains and illnesses Charles's elder brother Henry, now a Captain, had come to stay at 33 Chowringhee Road. He had risen to be Second Assistant Agent in Rajputana, and Charles had duly passed on laudatory comments from friends and officials to their mother, which however reflected far more in his own favour and would have compensated for the hostility in the Calcutta press: Captain Trevelyan, for instance, was 'a man, who though perchance he may never emulate that extraordinary man and truly great ornament to India, his brother Charles, may still be regarded a man of sound judgement...'

Henry had won praise for rounding up Thugs and for settling some tricky disputes between local rajahs and chiefs. He had written saying that he was looking forward to leave at Calcutta, 'though the rattle of a large city and the Anglicized natives (or Trevelyanized I might rather say) will scarcely suit me so well as the unsophisticated and primitive denizens of those parts. I have not beheld an European lady for upwards of half a year, neither do I wish to see one till I have beheld my sister Hannah.' This last sentence must have alerted Charles to danger, for he wrote home: 'my wife and I would equally lament to see him united to one of the class of ladies who came out here entirely for the sake of being married and whose families are often anything but respectable.' The sequel is given in a letter from Macaulay to Selina and Fanny:

The Captain had long been promising us a visit. At last ill-health compelled him to go to the Cape, and he came to Calcutta for that purpose. His brother promised that we should find him a most delightful man. But when he came, though a very good sort of man, he bored me a little, Hannah a good deal, his brother almost to death. Hannah and Trevelyan accordingly took to match-making, and got rid of the Captain by marrying him to a bouncing Scotch girl at the next house. It is just a month since we escorted the happy pair to the Cathedral: and since that time the bridegroom has been boring his wife's relations instead of his own.

The bride was Emilia Anne Greig, slim-waisted and ringleted. It would seem that Charles and Hannah eventually regretted their match-making. Possibly her parentage on her mother's side had not been all that they had expected. The father, long dead, had been a merchant at Madras, with some grand connections including an admiral in the Russian navy under Catherine the Great. On the other hand, it appears that Mr Greig had had some illegitimate progeny before Emilia, and that a certain lady with the intriguing name of Lucille Due Bue engaged his affections after his wife's death – and that this lady had previously had other attachments.

Just after the wedding Charles set out on one of his steamer excursions. 'I watched Henry and Emily through a telescope,' he told Hannah in a letter written on board before sailing, 'as they were taking their evening walk. On returning from that walk they went to the steps at the water side, and the ayah who was standing there with two of the servants came up and spoke to them. Henry had a stick in his hand and had his usual fashionable stoop. Emily was bolt upright.' All this was affectionate enough, but the harmony was not to bear the brunt of time. For on November 26 1848 Macaulay was to write in his journal:

Would not go to Clapham where Charles and Hannah were living because that execrable Mrs Henry Trevelyan is there. I do not choose to insult a woman, but I cannot be civil to one whom I believe to be capable of any excess of wickedness. I therefore deny myself the pleasure of visiting Clapham while she is, much against my advice, received as a guest by those whom she hates, whom she calumniates [illegible], if she could she would murder.

The *Lord Hungerford* sailed from Calcutta on January 21 with Macaulay and the Trevelyans on board. At the Cape they saw Henry and Emily, who had preceded them. The ship had a reputation for being a bad sailer, and was delayed. It became known in London that there had been some very rough weather, and the rumour went about that all on board had been lost. A succession of Whig politicians, as G. O. Trevelyan has related, went to the City to enquire at Lloyd's about the safety of the ship's precious freight.

She docked at Dartmouth on June 1. Charles and Hannah, who was in her eighth month of pregnancy, went to his mother in Somerset, and Macaulay went to London, where he learnt that his father, Zachary Macaulay, had died on May 13.

III

ALTHOUGH CHARLES WOULD proclaim that India was his 'first and last love', and it was of course assumed that his career out there was by no means over, Hannah recorded that her brother was in a state of misery at the prospect of her and Charles returning to Calcutta. It was an 'hourly trial' for him. Macaulay took a house in Great George Street, opposite the Treasury in Whitehall, and invited the Trevelyans once more to share expenses there. By this time he was MP for Edinburgh and Secretary of War in Melbourne's Cabinet.

The house proved to be conveniently located, for in January 1840 Charles was offered and accepted the post of Assistant Secretary at the Treasury, in effect head of the department. So the Trevelyans would not be going to India after all. Friends in Calcutta must have smiled at the news. Everyone believed that Macaulay had arranged it, and Hannah said that he could never speak of it without emotion. Charles himself was always to say that the Chancellor of the Exchequer, Sir Francis Baring, had been the real 'sponsor' of his career in the Treasury, which was to last for nineteen years, and it is true that Sir Francis had been impressed by the record of his energy and power of organization whilst at Calcutta.

The Trevelyans eventually moved to a house in Clapham – where else? one might ask – next to the Thorntons, doyens of the Clapham Sect, and Macaulay went to Albany in Piccadilly. Macaulay enjoyed walking out to Clapham, and a bed would always be ready for him there. The child who had been born in July 1838 was George Otto. Another baby, a girl called Alice, followed in 1842. The visits from Uncle Tom were always a delight for the children, and for Hannah it was like old times. 'The jokes, the puns, the laughter turned on familiar figures in fiction and history or in the public life of the day', and there was a 'daily loving familiarity with an unseen world'. He would also read from the *Lays of Ancient Rome*, which was published in 1842.

By contrast Charles would – as G. M. Trevelyan has written –

'read the Bible and family prayers in his deep sonorous voice'; he 'loved reading them, and the rest loved to hear him', and he also particularly relished the 'religious controversies of history'. Every morning he rode to the office from Clapham, having spent a couple of hours at his papers before breakfast.

In 1846 Charles became 'virtual dictator' of relief work during the great disaster of the Irish Potato Famine. His huge correspondence in the Trevelyan family papers clearly shows that a lot could be said in his defence, since Cecil Woodham-Smith, author of the standard book on the Famine, *The Great Hunger*, and before her Jenifer Hart have cast him so unfairly in the role of chief scapegoat for the disasters during the governments of Sir Robert Peel and Lord John Russell, by quoting him out of context.

In 1848, when the Famine was nearing its last stage, Charles published a long article called 'The Irish Crisis' in the *Edinburgh Review*, and had it republished as a booklet. It was on the whole (for him) modestly written, and he was proud of it, sending copies to the King of Prussia and the Pope, among others. Some of his ideas were followed during the Bengal Famine of 1873 by Lord Northbrook, the then Viceroy of India, and Charles had the booklet published once more in 1880.

Because of the huge sums involved in the relief work, the ultimate control of day-to-day expense necessarily had to rest with the Treasury. The catastrophe of the Irish Famine occurred at a time of great public alarm over public expenditure in Britain. There was a general scarcity of food all over the British Isles and in Europe, with famine also in Scotland. The cotton crops had failed, threatening unemployment in Lancashire. Then, in Charles's words, there was 'pecuniary exhaustion consequent upon the vast expenditure for the construction of railways'. An entire army had been lost in Afghanistan. There was also fear of a possible invasion from France.

To be sure both writers emphasized his reputation for 'rigid integrity', and that great achievements in other aspects of his career lay ahead. It is also true that some of Charles's attributes, in this age of different standards and easy communication, and of different dogmas about economics, are not immediately endearing: his 'inconsiderate rashness', for example, his moral rectitude, and reluctance to delegate. Peel and Russell had divergent policies in very different phases of the Famine, and it was Charles's duty loyally to carry out both. A Government servant is supposed not to have politics, but Charles was at heart a Whig and felt more at home with Russell's policies. His views were bound to influence the Prime Minister and the Chancellor of the Exchequer, and this became much more noticeable when his great friend and admirer Sir Charles Wood, the future Lord Halifax, became Chancellor. Nevertheless, it is only too easy to transfer the 'guilt' of a Government to a single civil servant. Peel was furious with Charles in 1843, when he first visited Ireland and wrote letters – in his usual tactless manner – for the *Morning Chronicle* about the possibility of rebellion, under his then favourite pseudonym 'Philalethes' (lover of truth). By February 1847 however when Peel was in Opposition he spoke of the Irish Board of Works as having been 'inspired by the untiring activity, the integrity and the devotedness of Mr. Trevelyan'.

At the time of greatest stress Charles sometimes worked until 3 am, 'dead beat', even on Sundays, and returned at 6 am. His family life suffered; the 'sonorous' readings were over. He drove his team in Ireland as hard as himself. When Sir Randolph Routh, the Commissioner General, complained of overwork and said he was having to spend the rest of the day resting, Charles at once wrote back: 'I hope to hear you have got rid of your indisposition – we have no time to be ill nowadays.'

In April 1847 he was made a Knight Commander of the Bath. At the end of the same year he was awarded the gratuity of a year's salary (£2,500), but, according to a family tradition, after being hurt by objections in Parliament he contemplated returning the money.

Even after the Irish Famine Charles – now Sir Charles – was accustomed to work at the Treasury until his strength was 'completely exhausted'. He used to spend three hours before breakfast going through papers that he would not have time to read at the office. Macaulay came to the Trevelyans one evening and read them part of his *History*, noticing that Hannah cried and Charles managed to stay awake. Not surprisingly at that time Charles seems to have had few personal friends outside his work and family. He did have a weakness though: he loved champagne. He also told a teetotal cousin that he could testify 'from my own personal experience' that a 'glass of pale ale does me more good when I come home of an evening than anything else I can eat or drink.'

In 1848 and 1849 he was on commissions investigating the administration of the Home Office and the Treasury, checking efficiency, estimates and audits. Not surprisingly long and bitter battles developed. Charles then moved on to the investigation of no less than thirteen other Government departments. Because of his relentless pursuit of economies and his outspoken denunciations he made enemies. If some people admired Charles for his fearlessness, others considered him an incorrigible meddler. Now he was the most prominent Government official; his public façade was austere. 'Some scribbler in the *Morning Post*,' Macaulay wrote in his journal in July 1849, 'has just now a spite to Trevelyan, and writes several absurd papers against him every week. He will never hear of them probably, and will certainly not care for them ... yet I, who am never moved by such attacks on myself ... cannot help being irritated by this low, dirty wickedness.'

Nobody could deny Charles's tremendously high sense of public duty, or his amazing capacity for work. It is recognized that it was he who laid the basis of modern Treasury practice. Disraeli, after the defeat of his Budget of 1852, wrote to thank him for his zealous, efficient and friendly manner, but Gladstone was the Chancellor after Charles's own heart.

Charles was called upon to give evidence before a Select Committee of the House of Lords at the time of the renewal of the East India Company's charter in 1853. He spoke dramatically and with supreme self-confidence, glad to be able to restate his many ideas and ideals about India, especially on education. He pressed for the employment of Indians in positions of responsibility, and for equal rights for Christians, Hindus and Muslims. He warned that British prejudices against colour and religion could arouse a spirit of dangerous patriotism in the Indian Army. 'In reading his evidence before this committee,' Humphrey Trevelyan wrote nearly a hundred and thirty years later, 'I have been astonished by the breadth of his vision and of his understanding of the reality behind the Indian scene.'

He still disapproved of Hinduism, but felt that Christianity would gradually and naturally spread throughout the country as the Indians learnt more of Western ways. If the British Government took the proper course, he said, India like Australia and Canada would eventually make its way towards independence. At this point Lord Ellenborough, an ex-Viceroy, interjected: 'Why should we ever leave it [India] at all?' To which Charles replied: 'I hold that is the way to keep it as long as possible.' If and when the time came for India to be independent, he said, she would be so highly 'improved' that trade conditions for Britain would have become much more advantageous; and he pointed to the example of the United States, where Britain now had more trade advantages than before.

Sir Charles Wood was President of the Board of Control and immediately turned to Charles (among others) for advice on Indian reforms. Wood's 'Education Despatch' has been called the Magna Carta of English Education in India. It was a dissemination and adaptation of the old Orientalist–Anglicist debates. Macaulay's influence and persuasive pen were enlisted in a new, and triumphant, attempt to liberalize the Indian Civil Service on the occasion of the renewal of the Charter, by opening the ICS to university graduates and abolishing patronage. Thus in high hopes, and in the false dawn before the Mutiny, the 'competition wallahs' came about, and Haileybury, the East Indian Company's training college, was closed.

By the time Wood's Indian Bill had passed the Commons the so-called Northcote–Trevelyan Report was ready. Commissioned by Gladstone, it was only twenty-three foolscap pages long, but it is still regarded as a key document in the history of the modern British Civil Service. Once again the main proposals were for entry by competitive examination and for the abolition of the patronage of aristocratic and other influential families; also promotion by merit, division of labour and uniform conditions of service. The report was solely the work of Charles and his colleague, Sir Stafford Northcote, and based to a great extent on Charles's investigation of the various government offices; he had found 'the same evils and circumstances pointing to the same remedies, with reference to every department'. Blistering in tone, attacking incompetence, indolence, narrowness of views and extravagance, it was submitted to Parliament on February 24 1854. There followed an immediate and furious debate. When Macaulay went to Brooks's Club he found everybody there 'open-mouthed' about Charles's proposals: 'He has been far too sanguine. The pear is not ripe.'

Charles though had been indefatigable in his canvassing, and as always had looked upon the press as a means of preparing the public, as a forum for discussion. He kept feeding material to Delane, the editor of *The Times*. 'There is no doubt,' he told him, 'that our High Aristocracy have been accustomed to employ the Civil Establishments as a means for providing for the Waifs and Strays of their families,' thus ensuring them pensions for life at the expense of the public; 'the Dukes of Norfolk provided for their illegitimate children in this manner, generation after generation.'

As in the Calcutta days the counter-attack was furious. Charles had underestimated the opposition. He had indeed been tactless, and often unfair on colleagues. Queen Victoria had misgivings, and summed up what his opponents feared: that public offices would henceforward be filled with 'low people without the breeding or feelings of gentlemen'. Trollope in *The Three Clerks* satirized Charles as Sir Gregory Hardlines, 'something of a Civil Service Pharisee', who wore on his forehead a 'broad phylactery, stamped with the mark Crown Property'. Later, however, Trollope said that he came to know and like both Charles and Hannah, though he continued to hate the whole scheme for competitive examinations. 'We always call him [Charles] Sir Gregory in the family,' Hannah told Trollope.

Even Lord John Russell disapproved of this throwing open of the Civil Service to 'all sorts and conditions of men'. James Wilson of the *Economist*, now at the Treasury as Financial Secretary and never a friend of Charles, thought the proposed reform would encourage 'cramming' and be 'productive of an enormous amount of mischief'.

In 1855 a Civil Service Commission was set up under the chairmanship of Sir Edward Ryan, Macaulay's friend, lately Chief Justice of Bengal. But twenty years were to pass before the recommendation of the Northcote–Trevelyan Report really came into force. This was frustrating for Charles, and Gladstone had to ask him to refrain from writing to the press without consulting him. Charles, said Gladstone, was 'not an unmanageable man, though he is one who requires to be managed', needing a 'strong man over him'.

For the first year of the Crimean War Charles was responsible for the commissariat, which has generally been regarded as a disastrous failure. All the same, Charles does not seem to have been directly criticized, though he hotly defended his officers against an 'immense crop of lies' before a Select Committee. His association with the army in Crimea led to a long friendship with Florence Nightingale.

Meanwhile his brother Henry was still in India, and the great Mutiny was about to break.

Henry

Doubtless it was through Charles's efforts (in spite of the attacks on patronage) that in 1842 Henry had become Political Agent at Bhopal – the scene of the terrible chemical gas disaster of 1984. A dozen years later Henry was posted to Bhuj in Kutch, which before the conquest of Sind had been of great strategic importance, lying to the south of Sind and the Indus. Kutch in effect is an island, bounded on the land side by the Rann, a grim, salt-encrusted desert of 9,000 square miles, a place of mirages and a breeding ground for flamingoes, impassable during the monsoon months. Inland are fertile pastures and ranges of hills, the Black Hills of legend and song. In Henry's day it was full of wild game: panthers, lions, black buck, sand-grouse, quails, and herds of wild asses. The capital, Bhuj, famous for its silversmiths and enamellers, was a walled city, its five gates locked at sunset and opened at dawn. The Raos of Kutch were descended from the Moon. Alexander 'Bokhara' Burnes had been stationed at Bhuj in the 1820s and had collected together bits of the history, later embroidered by

Marianne Postans. He had related how the recent Rao, in spite of his celestial ancestry, had 'rendered himself very odious by the most wanton cruelty'. Such behaviour, in addition to complaints of marauders from Sind, had been an excuse for the British to move in.

Henry fell under the spell of this strange place and enjoyed his patrols by camel along the edge of the Rann. He became a particular friend of the young Prince Pragmal in a time of tension between the ruling Rao and the British. Nevertheless, feeling himself to be more of a man of action, he asked to be returned to his regiment at Karachi.

In October 1856 the Persians seized Herat in Afghanistan. Lord Dalhousie, the Governor-General, then declared war, and in November an expedition of 6,000 set out for the Gulf. Henry was in command of the artillery.

This was to be the East India Company's last war. The target was Bushire, Persia's chief seaport, with a good anchorage. The British force landed at Hallilah Bay and pushed up to the old Dutch fort of Reshire. 'No quarter was given or asked,' but there were few British dead. Bushire was easily captured, with the help of a naval barrage. It was at once renamed 'Victoria City': two Protestant churches were built and a racecourse made. Loot was disappointing.

The new commander was Lieutenant-General Sir James Outram, a self-publicist par excellence but to become one of the great figures during the Indian Mutiny. He decided to take the bulk of his forces forty-six miles inland to Borasjoon, beneath the high mountains, where the Persian commander-in-chief was entrenched. The journey was hell, vilely cold and over rough country. When the attack came, Henry's guns decisively routed the enemy in a few hours. But the British troops were exhausted and short of food, and Henry was in command of the withdrawal, in remorseless rain and with mud knee-deep. He was mentioned three times in despatches.

Another figure to be associated with the Mutiny arrived: Brigadier-General Henry Havelock, a very different character to Outram, 'pure gold through and through'. He was in command of the 2nd Division. Outram had also summoned from Sind one of the most extraordinary soldiers and administrators of his time, Colonel, now Brigadier-General, John Jacob of the Sind Irregular Horse, the founder of the town of Jacobabad, a man of immense physical and moral courage, a bachelor and a bit of a mystic.

Jacob arrived in March 1857, and was horrified by the state of confusion and low morale at Bushire, blaming it all on Outram. Then General Stalker, commander of the 1st Division, blew his own brains out. A few days later the Commodore of the Gulf Squadron, Ethersey, also shot himself. Both men had apparently felt unequal to their responsibilities and had been oppressed by the witch-hunting of generals in England after the scandals of the Crimean War. Outram was fearful lest his overbearing nature would be regarded as responsible for the suicides – which it probably was in part. Now he left with the main force for Mohammederah at the head of the Gulf near Abadan, leaving Jacob in charge at Bushire. He was in Baghdad when he heard that there was a mutiny in Bengal and that Europeans had been massacred at Delhi. Both he and Havelock hurried back to India. Jacob had to remain at Bushire, with 5,500 men, 200 of them Europeans, and with Henry Trevelyan still in command of artillery.

It was immensely frustrating to be stuck in the Gulf with Bengal in flames. A strong friendship grew up between Henry and Jacob, who both were sons of Somerset clergymen.

Jacob had an amazing way of inspiring esprit de corps; as Outram himself had said, 'All ranks, officers and men, white forces or black, regard General Jacob with equal devotion, and his influence with Troops is such as I have never seen surpassed in the thirty-three years I have served in the Army.' Jacob sent Henry on a diplomatic mission to Borasjoon to meet the Persian commander-in-chief: a considerable success it would seem, and as a result Henry was awarded the CB. There are so many references to his 'kind gentle disposition' and the like – probably why Macaulay found him so boring.

In spite of Henry's preference for active service, he had shown that he had a particular talent for diplomacy. Therefore, when he returned to India in October 1857 he was sent again to Bhuj as Political Agent in Kutch, and he remained there until 1861.

Pragmal succeeded as Rao in 1860. A portrait shows the young man loaded with more pearls and jewels than ever was Queen Elizabeth I of England. Jacob went back to his Jacobabad, and both Henry and Charles kept in touch with him over matters of Army reform, which became Charles's next hobby-horse after the Mutiny.

Rao Pragmal wrote affectionate letters to Henry when he returned to England, keeping him informed of Kutch affairs, describing his new palace – in the Gothic style and 'designed by Colonel Wilkins of the Bombay Engineers'. In due course Henry was promoted to Major-General, and at the end of his life he was Colonel Commandant of his regiment.

The outbreak

The sparking off point for the Mutiny had been the arrest on May 9 of ninety sepoys at Meerut, about forty miles from Delhi, for refusing to accept cartridges greased as they supposed in pork and beef fat.

The men had been sentenced to ten years' imprisonment and had been stripped of their uniforms. On the next day their comrades had broken out in fury, murdering European officers and their families and looting houses and shops. In the small hours of May 12 the mutineers began their march on Delhi.

Charles Trevelyan, as soon as he heard of this in England, rushed off a letter under the name of 'Indophilus' to his old stamping ground, the *Bengal Hurkaru* of Calcutta. His theme was meant partly as reassurance, and he wrote of the mutiny at Vellore in 1802, when Lord William Bentinck, then Governor of Madras, had to be recalled. Charles saw parallels, in that the ostensible cause of that other mutiny had been the enforced change in the uniform of the sepoys, which – as with the greased cartridges of 1857 – had been regarded as an insult to their religion. There had been some panic then, but no catastrophe. The real cause had been a 'total want of kindly feeling between the Europeans and native officers, which still after all these years lingers on'.

Catastrophes did follow very quickly in 1857, and 'Indophilus' became silenced. The appalling news day after day must have seemed the negation of all that he had been working for. Delhi fell to the rebels, and every European there was either murdered or had to escape. Mutinies flared at one place after another throughout the north, at Bareilly, Shahjahanpur, Neemuch; and sometimes the civil population was the first to attack, burning churches, mission schools and British-owned factories. The Europeans in the key military station of Cawnpore were under siege and among them were several of Charles's family connections. From all over the north of India there were fearful tales of atrocities, with women and children murdered.

The Punjab was saved by the prompt and resolute action of the Chief Commissioner, Sir John Lawrence. But now was the time for revenge. Villages were burnt down by the British, and anyone seeming at all suspicious would often be hanged after a trial that was a mere formality. Newspapers reported 'every tree covered with scoundrels hanging from every branch'. Another form of punishment was the blowing of prisoners from the mouths of cannons, a method familiar in the time of the Moghuls and indeed used by the mutineers themselves. A prisoner would be lashed to a gun, his stomach or the small of his back against the muzzle; and in the case of a sepoy if possible his face would also be smeared with the blood of a murdered European. Vultures became accustomed to these executions, and would hover overhead, skilfully catching lumps of flesh as they flew into the air, 'like bears taking buns at the zoo'.

The letters of Macaulay show the dilemmas of liberal-minded people in England. On August 10 he wrote to Hannah:

There is a terrible cry for revenge. The account of that dreadful military execution at Peshawar [in *The Times*] – forty men blown from the mouths of cannons, their heads, legs, arms flying in all directions – was read with delight by people who three weeks ago, were against capital punishment. [John] Bright himself, Quaker as he is, declares for the vigorous suppression of the mutiny. The almost universal feeling is that not a single Sepoy, within the walls of Delhi, should be spared, and I own that is a feeling with which I cannot help sympathising.

Across the Atlantic there were similar reactions, even among the philanthropists. At Boston Oliver Wendell Holmes, writing of the 'baby-killers of Delhi', wrote: 'Delhi, *Dele* [destroy]. The civilized world say, Amen!' And even two months later Macaulay admitted that until then he had not known what real vindictive hatred meant. Normally he could not bear to see a 'bird or beast in pain', but now reading of the devilries of such persons as Nana Sahib of Cawnpore he could look on 'without winking' if such people underwent 'all the tortures of Ravaillac'. He feared for the eventual effect on the national character.

Charles's son George Otto was at Trinity College, Cambridge. He was at the Cambridge Union and heard an undergraduate declaim: 'When every bayonet is red with blood; when every gibbet creaks beneath its ghastly burden; when the ground in front of every cannon is strewn with rags and flesh and shattered bone – then talk of mercy.' This peroration, George Otto was to say, was received with 'tumultuous applause' (though not by him).

The Fourth Journey

I

'YOU WERE CONCEIVED in Ceylon.'

Olive told me this in Cornwall in the last year of her life, with a funny, rather wicked smile. We were having an evening gin, and she – as usual – was lying on her sofa, her legs covered with a lavender and brown plaid rug.

I had become accustomed to such 'frank' remarks from her. In some ways she was changing in her old age. She was still something of a leader in the village, still elegantly dressed but never pretentious, though she obviously gave people the impression of being rather grand, with an exotic past. I was secretly amused, too, by the way she had been converted to Victorian clutter in her cottage. She said exactly what was in her mind, and I was surprised, and a little annoyed, when I heard a young neighbour call her 'the old alligator'.

I had merely been saying that I always wanted to go to Sri Lanka. Her new revelation delighted me, but I still felt I could only ask: 'Where exactly?'

'The Galle Face Hotel.'

I later found that this unlikely sounding place did exist, and had been the superior establishment at Colombo for tea-planters on leave. When I glanced at Walter's albums, sure enough there were two 'snaps' of the Galle Face, a massive plain two-storeyed mid-Victorian structure, with a balcony all round and little striped blinds over the upper windows. It was right on the sea, looking over the breakers and a long narrow beach, but what I liked particularly were the spindly palms, higher than the hotel and bent from the wind.

Calculating backwards from my date of birth, Olive and Walter would have been there on leave in November 1922, before the Andamans. She had had a miscarriage that summer. Come to think of it, I remember now some talk of a 'ghastly' sea journey from Burma – Olive was always a 'rotten' sailor. Walter's other photographs were mostly of conventional sites: the Temple of the Tooth at Kandy, tea-gardens, ruins at Anuradhapura, and romantic palms over lashing waves at Mount Lavinia.

I had been undecided in 1983 whether to opt for Sri Lanka and the south of India for my fourth journey, or to visit some Mutiny sites in the north, especially Cawnpore.

I needed to go to Madras, because Charles Trevelyan had been Governor there from 1859 to 1860: another stormy episode in his career. And I wanted to go to Ooty because of Macaulay, and because Ooty was Ooty. Ootacamund, Titicaca, Popocatepetl, Antananarivo, Pondicherry: these had all been places that had intrigued me in my school geography days. Mysore would give me some idea of the India of the Maharajahs.

I had come across about a hundred letters from an Emma Halliday, whose mother had been a Trevelyan. These date from her first arrival in India in 1853, when she was twenty-one, right up until the outbreak at Cawnpore in June 1857. I found out that she, her husband and their baby all had died at Cawnpore. It was obvious that those letters had been circulated among the family, and very likely Charles and Hannah would have seen the final ones, especially when the details of the massacres at Cawnpore became known in England.

Nevertheless I decided on Sri Lanka and then Madras.

Real travellers like Colin Thubron or Dervla Murphy would scorn the idea of hiring a car *with chauffeur* to drive round Sri Lanka. But I think even they would find it madness to attempt to drive themselves in a country where there is hardly more road sense than at Calcutta. We were lucky in having Sunil as our chauffeur, and occasionally cicerone, and he has remained a pen friend ever since. Unlike most Sri Lankans he was large; and he was discreet, with a musical voice and rather prominent teeth. We had been told in advance that he was an 'exceptional being', and so he was.

The Galle Face Hotel was exactly like Walter's photographs, even to the palms, and was as grand as the Grand Hotel at Calcutta. I wasn't quite sure what I was trying to conjure up for myself there. Music from the ballroom drifting out among the Chinese lanterns? Planters and their lady wives dancing the Charleston? A scene from Noel Coward? Hot passion to the rustle of palm fronds? Perhaps I should have been musing on the creation of life itself. What actually transpired for me was rage, over a matter to do with a sponge-bag; but I won't elaborate because nobody could have been more courteous than the people who ran the hotel. Our 'butler' left frangipani flowers on our pillows, and there was a basket of fruit inscribed 'For Master'.

We were off early the next day. Having noted street names such as 'Kensington Gardens', I was not surprised to pass a Methodist Chapel. Suddenly the word Ouspensky flashed into my head. His Buddha with the sapphire eyes must surely be near here. Along the narrow lane to the left, so my instructions had been. Subodharama Temple. Sunil had never heard of it, but we did find such a lane and took the chance.

There it was, just as Ouspensky had seen in 1914, a white stone enclosure, small white buildings, a belfry, and an ancient bo-tree. Some saffron-coloured monks' robes were drying on a trellised balustrade. A few diseased dogs lurked around. We ascended some steps to the shrine and were shown a garish painting representing scenes in the life of Gautama. In the second room, very dark, was the great reclining Buddha. His face and body were painted yellow, the lines of his features strongly marked. He lay with his hand under his head on a lotus flower pillow. A monk lit some candles for us, and at once Raúl and I were caught in that strange gaze of the deep blue sapphire eyes – not actually looking at us but seeing us, into us.

This Buddha, so completely in repose in that quiet place, made more impression on me than any other I had seen, or was to see. His lips and nostrils were an unnatural pale pink, his ear lobes reached as far as his chin; it was not a human face, but it was strangely alive. I felt that those eyes knew why I had come to Sri Lanka, and why I had also been to Gilgit, Gulmarg and Port Blair. Almost I could go home now.

The monk said that the Buddha was a thousand years old, and that each eye was worth a million rupees. It was pointed out that one big toe was discoloured. This was to show that it was putrefying. That was how it was known that the Buddha was dead.

The mosaic floor seemed in part to represent a beast like an unicorn. The wooden ceiling was shaped like a lotus. In the monks' 'lecture room' there were paintings of men with cobra head-dresses, and of a ceremonial band with drummers and pipers. A prize object was a blue finger-bowl of Bristol glass: a dull blue, not at all like the sapphires. When we left they gave us fruits from the bo-tree, like pink plastic, covered in ants but as we later found thirst-quenching.

We drove through thousands of palm trees, shading what seemed like a jungle of house-plants, hibiscus, bougainvillaea, frangipani, banana trees; past lemon-yellow almost empty beaches, lagoons, catamarans, iron bridges. Some months before Sunil had driven Sir Hugh Casson, at that time still President of the Royal Academy in London, and Lady Casson on this route. 'Sir Hugh drew that tree. Sir Hugh liked that roof,' we used to be told. Sunil had also driven Mrs

Pattrick, a friend of ours and an architect like Sir Hugh. We kept hearing about her likes and dislikes. 'I don't know if Sunil is more in love with Sir Hugh or Jo Pattrick,' Raúl said.

Past clients had sent Sunil presents for his car. We liked the thought of the orange plastic bird dangling in front of the Cassons all round Sri Lanka, and of their having 'Mafia Staff Car' stuck on the car's boot.

We stopped to bathe at Bentota. 'Please sir be careful,' Sunil said. 'Don't leave things on beach.' We wouldn't have anyhow. As soon as we were settled on the sand, two dusky figures sat down nearby, gradually edging closer. One of them was exceedingly ugly, with a tongue like a dog's, lolling out through missing top teeth. Raúl could not resist some bantering conversation. He and I had to take turns to swim. 'I have a sister,' said the ugly one predictably. 'Is she as beautiful as you?' I asked. We soon got fed up, and the men became a little frantic. As we walked to a restaurant, the ugly one shouted: 'You can have *me* for a Coca Cola.'

At Dodanduwa we went up to the Gangarama Viharaya monastery, overlooking a lake. Here our guide was the Theko Premarathana. He had once been a high court judge, but after sentencing nineteen people to be hanged had felt remorse and had become a monk. He was on a visit, as he was now living near Trincomalee, alone with just once acolyte. They were twelve miles from the town and had to go on foot for all provisions. He seemed well nourished however, and was a jolly, civilized man, with a colloquial knowledge of English. 'Let me shake your paw,' he said on introducing himself.

At the back of the shrine there was a long series of identical praying figures of monks with acolytes in multi-coloured turbans. They were nearly three hundred years old but repainted every two years. There were also some gruesome setpieces. In one a man goes to war for ten months, returning to find that his wife has just had a baby, so he orders the baby to be dismembered; the baby's torso ascends to heaven and a voice comes down telling the man that it was his own child; so the man goes to hell. In another a greedy drunken man orders his baby to be cut up and made into a curry; when he is sober again he calls for the child, to discover what he has done; he gives up drink.

We saw an iguana swimming in the lake. The Premarathana told us that fifteen German monks were living in seclusion on the other side. They got very annoyed if any tourists, especially women, came across in a boat.

Then a crowd of schoolchildren arrived, clamouring for 'school-pens'. Luckily we had been forewarned in England of this craze for ballpoint pens and had brought a supply of about fifty with us. We couldn't oblige with 'bons-bons' though, for which there were also insistent demands.

We arrived at the New Oriental Hotel at Galle when it was nearly sunset, roosting time for crows. This was another of my ideals of a hotel, where I would have preferred to have been conceived. Nothing could have been more Dutch colonial, and it was run by old Nesta Brohier, a grandmother in pink, fourth generation and born in the hotel. Pictures of the Dutch and British royal families were on the walls. A huge fan whirled from the ceiling. Our room had tall beds hung with mosquito nets, a washstand with jug, and a bat. The garden was full of dramatically luxuriant shrubs, with a notice: 'Do not spit in the pool.'

Point de Galle used to be the port of call for vessels to the Far East, after Aden or Mauritius, though in the days of the windjammer the reefs were sometimes considered too unsafe and ships used to go on to Trincomalee. On 'passenger days' balls would be given in the hotel's dining-room. Until the breakwater at Colombo was built, you had to travel north by coach, which took a full day. Galle is also supposed to have been Tarshish, whence Solomon obtained his apes, ivory and peacocks.

In the morning we walked under tulip trees past the old Dutch houses to the Fort, through the gateway with its cypher VOC (initials of the Dutch East India Company) 1669. The sea washed against the ramparts and the dangerous rocks. There were loopholes for cannons, and bastions for sentries.

Sunil told us about the promontory to the east of Galle. Rama, the seventh incarnation of Vishnu, sent Hanuman the monkey god to the Himalayas to fetch a herb that would cure him. But Hanuman forgot which herb he was supposed to find, so he brought the whole promontory rock.

On we went, calling on Sunil's sweet shy grandmother, a great honour, in her new bungalow, with its cinnamon, coconut and rice plantations. Nearby was the village of Weligama. Hereabouts were fishermen standing on stilts, motionless as herons, waiting to spear fish. Only a few yards from the Weligama beach was the island of Taprobane: a magic view – rocks and palms like jade, a sparkling sea; the pavilion-house just visible, a fantasy, a daydream, impractical. Paul Bowles had lived there. As he had once said, there was nothing between Taprobane and the South Pole.

At the temple of Rasamukhandra, Sunil told us, the dead priests were worshipped by cobras.

Then, at last, very tired, we reached Nuwara Eliya, Sri Lanka's answer to Ooty and Gulmarg. We had booked at the Hill Club, naturally, and were at once put in a temper by having to wear ties and jackets at dinner, though both could be borrowed at the bar. Two working-class Englishmen, possibly from Yorkshire, came storming out of the dining-room, ripping off ties and muttering 'crap'.

Yes, the place did 'cry England', but perhaps we weren't in the mood for it. The billiard-room was dated 1876, and there were paintings of outsize rainbow trout caught by members in the good old days. There were even Constance Spry flower arrangements of agapanthus, lilies and arums.

Not being golfers, we were not as thrilled as we ought to have been by the golf course, 'a real beauty for Asia' a visiting pukka sahib remarked. The landscape reminded me of the lower foothills of the Dolomites. Leeks and carrots were being grown on the racecourse: great luxuries. We walked in the bazaar, mostly Tamil-owned – four months later we were to read that it had been looted and burnt.

Decisions had now to be made. Our time being short, should we now head for the game reserve to look at elephants, and should we also go in search of two graves, one being of my special heroine Julia Margaret Cameron, the photographer-aunt of Virginia Woolf? The other grave that interested me was that of a clergyman named Tribe, the brother of the Flying Duchess of Bedford and son of an Archdeacon of Lahore. Much as I loved the story of the Camerons travelling out to Ceylon with their own coffins, packed with glass and silver, we decided to be sensible and stick to the tourist round. As for the Rev. Tribe, I had heard about him on the family grapevine. His grave had once been desecrated and his jawbone stolen as a talisman, something which only happens in the case of a twin. The matter was reported to the Bedfords, who were amazed, because Tribe's twin brother had died as a baby. How did the vandals know?

I had never seen such a rich glow of vegetable green as the Sri Lankan tea-gardens. Our visit to a factory however turned me off tea-bags for good.

It was to be expected that Olive and Walter, as fanatical gardeners, would spend much time at the Peradeniya Gardens outside Kandy, and the album confirmed this. I am not sure whether, à la Murray's Guide, I would rank the Gardens among the Seven Wonders of the World, but they are superb nevertheless. When we saw an elephant bathing in the river below, Sunil said: 'Sir, this is our lucky day.' He might have been wrong, because soon afterwards I was charged by a large humped white ox. The bignonias, the pitcher plants, the orchids and the sealing wax palms possibly thrilled me the most. The giant bamboos were capable of growing two feet in a night, a gardener told me. We walked down the Bat Drive, so-called because of the hundreds of flying foxes, hanging head-downwards in the branches above, squealing and quarrelling. Sunil said that the rather maddening bird which never stopped singing was called the barbet, alias the 'brain-fever' bird. A cannon-ball or sal tree, planted by the future George V, was dead. Just as we were about to leave, there was a flash among the palms. A golden oriole. So it was my lucky day after all.

We went to the fourteenth-century Lankatilika temple, the 'Crown of Sri Lanka' because of its beautiful high position. We could hear chanting, and two orange-robed monks carrying parasols wandered out of the woods below. People have said that the temple looks Norwegian. So be it. The golden Buddha with his pink tattooed hand upraised – meaning 'I know everything' – had an impersonal, flat stare. We gathered a few flowers fallen from the sal tree: the colour of dried blood, with stamens like stupas and a fringe of purple and white.

On our leaving we met a good-looking young monk, shaven-headed and with one shoulder bare in the usual manner. He was carrying a black umbrella, and seemed anxious to be photographed. He was surprisingly well-travelled for a presumably Theravada monk with no personal possessions.

'Of course I prefer Paris to Rome, don't you?' he said.

Apparently he had recently been teaching meditation to businessmen at Geneva. Two Englishmen were meditating at his monastery at this moment: 'Maybe you heard their chanting.' They would be staying until Wesak, the high point in the Buddhist calendar, celebrated on the day of full moon in May.

We admired the stylish way with which he used his umbrella. On our parting, he opened it with a twirl, and then with his back turned fluttered his fingers in farewell.

You arrive in Sri Lanka, and find a sort of paradise: sensuous, full of beautiful people, jungly. Then you meet the Buddhist religion, teaching the transience of all pleasure in face of pain, grief and suffering; and the need to escape from the earthly fetters of hate, lust, ignorance and covetousness. And you meet a very sinister racial tension.

We were at Sigiriya, one of the most exciting and mysterious places in all Sri Lanka. We were climbing the rusty iron ladders and up the grooves that passed as steps to that dizzy rock, and were behind a party of Italians. 'Adagio, adagio, Marcello!' screeched an anxious mother. Maybe we were all mad to attempt such a thing, seeing that monsoon clouds were swirling away over to the east. In Sri Lanka the monsoon hits the east coast early in the year, and the west coast in the summer. As Sigiriya was plumb centre, we thought we were going to be spared.

From afar Sigiriya looks like a red- and black-streaked Portuguese man-of-war floating in jungle of a powdery blue. Now it has a new immortality, because of Arthur C. Clarke's *The Fountains of Paradise*. For eighteen years at the end of the fifth century AD the rock – three acres on top, 200 metres high – was a fortress-palace. Some Buddhists apparently believe that the design of its buildings signified initiation into absolute truth, but it did not strike me as an especially holy place, *pace* Clarke. At Dambulla, that other outcrop, there were at least Buddhas to be seen, but I felt there that Buddhism had been too adulterated with Brahminism.

We were introduced to Claude, a friend of Sunil, and he told us how in the sixth century King Dhatusena had been walled up alive by his son Kasyapa, the son of a concubine, and how another son, Moggallana, born of the Queen, had fled to India, vowing vengeance. Kasyapa had lived in fear, but he had the soul of an artist, so on the very summit of this impregnable rock had created his marvellous citadel of white marble with burnished roofs whose flashes were visible for sixty miles. At last Moggallana had arrived from the mainland with his army. For some unexplained reason Kasyapa had gone out to meet him in battle – so all that was lavished on Sigiriya had been in vain. He had ridden on an elephant and on coming to a swamp had turned round to avoid it. This had been taken as a signal for retreat, and his men had fled in panic. Kasyapa, rather than fall into his brother's hands, had cut his own throat.

Two small boys, Lalanka and Padma, joined our party, and insisted on holding on to our arms as if we were tottering octogenarians. We reached the giant lion's claws carved out of the rock, and then came to the famous frescoes of topless damsels in head-dresses like miniature Hindu temples, and carrying bowls of fruit and flowers. Some vandal from a rival archaeological site had fifteen years before thrown tar over a few of them. What had happened to this monster, I asked? 'He is no longer with us,' Claude said with satisfaction. A soldier stopped Lalanka and Padma. It transpired that the boys were playing truant from school. Lalanka was terrified and wet his pants, making even the soldier laugh.

We were quite pleased to learn that neither Sir Hugh, Lady Casson nor Jo Pattrick had dared make the final ascent. Up on the summit we clearly saw what had been a large cistern or swimming-pool. Claude showed us the couch where the King used to watch his girls dancing naked: an unlikely story, since Kasyapa, out of shame for being a parricide, had turned to a life of asceticism. We saw some niches which had been for sentries, so small that a man would hurtle to his death if he fell asleep. As we tried to conjure up a picture of this castle in the air, three helicopters appeared out of the distance and flew round us, and we were back with Arthur C. Clarke.

We joined the Italians on the King's couch. Even at that height we got the hot smell of the jungle. The Italians told us that on their way back from Polonnaruwa their car had been charged by a wild elephant. Before we could hear the end of this alarming story, the Signora leapt up screaming: 'Marcello! Marcello!' Some fearsome black clouds were sweeping down on us from the east. There was a flash of lightning. 'O Dio, Dio, Dio. Marcello – DOV'È MARCELLO?' But wicked Marcello was halfway down the iron ladder. In the downpour that swiftly followed it was impossible for any of us to follow him. We were all drenched. The frantic Signora began to pray. But to whom? To Sinha the lion after whom the rock was named? She had lost her hat too. Perhaps she was really Cora in Clarke's book, sending out radio distress bleeps: 'Help! Will anyone who hears me please come at once! This is a Cora emergency!' The sacred mountain – if it was indeed sacred – was having its revenge.

In a matter of minutes the shower was over, and there far below on the platform by the lion's claws Marcello was waving to us. 'Sir, I do not think it is this lady's lucky day,' Sunil said.

Negombo, north of Colombo, was important in Dutch days, chiefly because of cinnamon, but if Dutch means all things neat and clean we certainly didn't get an impression of that from where we were staying on our last night in Sri Lanka. The beach couldn't remotely compare with those in the south, though the lagoon when you got there was picturesque enough. We came across a boat for hire called *Lady Chatterley*, available for deep-sea fishing: 'Ladies fifty per cent off.'

Negombo was a great place for crows and mosquitoes. We walked on the island among open drains. The villagers were Karavas from South India and fished from outrigger canoes. Among some foetid piles of drying sprats we found a monkey tethered to a post. It had a piglet tightly clasped in its arms. 'You've no idea how I love her,' its eyes seemed to be saying to us. The piglet, trapped, showed no emotion in return, and when eventually released darted off, without any gratitude or pity for its captive admirer.

Later in July of 1983 I read the account of a British holidaymaker, a week after the race riots had broken out. Three hundred people had possibly been killed, including fifty-two in Colombo jail. 'A taxi driver took us into Negombo just before the curfew and the whole town was smouldering. All the Tamil property in the centre of the town had been burnt down. The cigarette factory had gone together with a cinema and a garage. There was smoke everywhere and the whole area was a burnt out mess. The houses of rich Tamils had been burnt to the ground, and there were no signs of Tamils anywhere. We were told that Tamils were being grabbed off buses by groups of people wielding iron bars. We also saw young Sinhalese stopping cars to siphon out the petrol so that they could use it to start fires.'

Sunil had from the beginning of our tour advised us not to travel in the north, where the Tamils wanted to establish their separate state, Elam. Indeed I had already read in England about tourists being stoned at Jaffna. The riots in July started after thirteen soldiers had been shot dead by guerrillas, well educated young men calling themselves Tamil Tigers. This in turn could have been a reprisal for soldiers raping girls.

The murders, arson and looting spread not only to Nuwara Eliya but to Kandy and villages where there were Tamil workers on tea estates. We worried about an extraordinarily bright little girl called Chamindra Kumara whom we had photographed at a Tamil village near Nuwara Eliya. All these stories seemed inconceivable after meeting such friendly, quiet people, both Sinhalese and Tamil, and especially after experiencing the tranquillity of Buddhist shrines.

A number of hippies smelling of pot were flying with us to Madras. 'Smoking or non-smoking?' the girl at the airport desk asked. What a question.

II

Emma Halliday

Before moving on to Charles Trevelyan at Madras, it is necessary to describe some events of the Mutiny, particularly as they affected his young cousin Emma Halliday and some other relations.

Emma's early letters were too girlish and flippant to be of interest to Charles and Hannah. They were filled with comic drawings and comments on birds, flowers and such things as rock formations, which she knew would appeal to certain natural history-minded Trevelyans and, on her paternal side, Wyndhams.

An aged relative whom I consulted about the Hallidays had said: 'All I know about Emma is that she braided her hair and flung her arms about when she was asleep.' Then she thought for a moment and added: 'Those Wyndham girls were underhung and didn't like being photographed. I suppose you know that Emma's sister Ida was the first person to die under gas in the dentist's chair?'

Well, I didn't. I then learnt that Emma's eldest brother went to Australia where he had lived with aborigines in Queensland, had tied up his beard with a purple bow, and had had an aborigine family. Emma took after her mother, who was an erudite blue stocking, a good artist and 'quite a wit'. I was also shown a cutting from the *Poona Observer* of November 1857 which said that her husband Captain Willie Halliday of the 56th Bengal Native Infantry had been 'among England's most glorious sons' and that his name 'should be remembered by all who respect great deeds'.

I also discovered that there was a close link between the Hallidays and a family called Vibart, and it soon became clear to me that a number of Vibarts had also died at Cawnpore. So I started on a quest for Vibarts, and soon found that name repeated in all sorts of unexpected places. For instance, Shane Leslie in his autobiography mentioned that the 'Demon' in Vachell's famous novel of Harrow school-days, *The Hill*, had been a Vibart. And this was confirmed to me by someone whose father had been a contemporary at Harrow. She said that this Vibart had been a 'black sheep' and had come to a 'sticky end', possibly in Argentina. Why 'black sheep'? Because he had brought over a lot of polo ponies from Argentina, and they had all died on the way, and because he 'broke women's hearts'.

In George Otto's book *Cawnpore* there are quite a number of Vibart entries, and I could see that they were very different people to the 'Demon'. Indeed Major Vibart of the 2nd Cavalry had been one of the heroes of the Entrenchments.

Emma Halliday's Indian letters began at Ambala in the Punjab; the nearest military station to Simla. That same Major Vibart and his family were also at Ambala. There the homesick Emma began to collect pets – three parrots, a spaniel and a monkey – a typical family habit. Later a spotted deer was added to the 'menagerie'.

The cantonments at Ambala covered some thirty square miles, and had been laid out in the 1840s. As the church, in the Gothic style though not consecrated until 1857 (and bombed in the India–Pakistan war of 1956), was the work of Captain G. F. Atkinson, author of that delightful book *Curry and Rice*, one must assume that it had affinities with his mythical Kabob; in which case it is not surprising that Emma felt homesick. 'Everything is so dull,' she said, and the Army officers were a 'horrid set of snobs'. At least she and Willie had Major Vibart and his wife Emily for company. 'I often nurse their baby. Their children are pretty on average.'

Ambala, January 2 1854

You ask why the pigs are not eaten in this country. The reason is that they are unclean animals, i.e. there are no Uncles in this country, so in passing a village you see what I have drawn. Now don't show anyone this letter as to an unIndian eye it looks most disgusting, though the natives think nothing of it, but squat close by the roads and the pigs only live on that sort of thing, so do you wonder at their not being eaten.

A visit to Simla followed, packed with botanical excitements. En route to Barrackpore, Willie's next posting, they stopped briefly at

Cawnpore, which in some parts they thought 'very pretty'. 'A peep at the Ganges quite refreshed me.' Emma was pregnant.

The baby, Edith Mabel, was born at Barrackpore on March 10 1854, after 'great pain and suffering', according to Willie. Emma had to ask for chloroform. She became obsessed by Mabel and filled her letters with drawings of her.

Soon they were on the move again.

> *Bancoorah, September 3 1855*
> Major Cooke put me in a carriage with two half-caste ladies who were very much powdered and covered with chains and bracelets.

Early in 1857 she told her mother that they would be posted to Cawnpore. At last she would be able to see a dentist! Even in 1803 Cawnpore had been the largest up-country British cantonment in India. It had been regarded in those days as a frontier post between Oude and the Mahrattas. By the 1850s it was a major emporium, and after the annexation of Oude its military importance increased. Once it had a reputation for being 'bleak, dreary, sandy and dusty', but now it was an oasis of beautifully planted gardens, with assembly rooms, a theatre, a racquets court, a racecourse, schools and a church.

Emma and the baby arrived in advance of Willie, and on the very day that news reached Cawnpore of the fall of Delhi. It was also known that the Vibarts' eldest boy, aged nineteen and stationed at Delhi, had managed to escape, but there was no further news of him. She wrote at once:

> *Cawnpore, May 22 1857*
>
> So far so safe. My darling Mother, though you may never see Willie, baby or me you can still remember us as we shall only have left this world of care and gone to our last home. It won't be so like dying as going home, as we have always been moving about, so it will only be rest at last and there we will meet again, so please Mama be ready for it as I try to be, but at any rate I will sell my life dearly. I have two 6 barreled revolvers loaded under my pillow every night . . . We got to Cawnpore in the middle of the night. I went to the Vibarts who were sitting up or rather not gone to sleep . . . There are reports that there will be a rising here. We were the *only* people who did not sleep in the Barracks last night. 1,000 Mahratta horse came in last night and 50 Europeans from Lucknow. The guns are all ready and everything is prepared, Willie will not be in before Saturday week. Last night I awoke at every little noise. At every hour of the day reports of a most alarming nature are spread about . . . Now my darling Mother goodbye. You see that there is real cause for danger but don't be very frightened. I remain your affectionate and dutiful child, Emmie.

If she but knew, her mother had already died earlier that month.

It was rumoured that the Muslims had decided to rise up on May 24, the day of their festival of Id, and had 'sworn to destroy every European in the station'. But the night before went off quietly. Emma wrote to Willie, still in camp miles away, to tell him that the telegraph line between Cawnpore and Agra had been cut; Agra was the headquarters of the North-Western Provinces. She had also received the grisly news that a friend at Meerut, Mrs Chambers, had had her throat cut by a butcher.

The weather was 'boiling hot'. On that afternoon of the 24th Emma went to the church with Mrs Vibart, but found the gates shut. So they called at the clergyman's house, only to discover that he had taken refuge in the barracks, round which the Entrenchments were being dug. They drove round in the carriage to the barracks and forced him to come out. Afterwards they went inside to inspect the place. 'Every room was crowded with beds. In front of the verandah were groups of ladies and gentlemen. The guns were ranged round, sentries posted and Mahrattas picketed beyond.' After chatting with friends and being reassured, they were startled by Mr Larkins dashing in to say that 'an attack was decidedly going to be made during the night, no time was to be lost, as it may have begun already, and everyone had left their houses, General Wheeler and all.' So Emma and Mrs Vibart tore back home in the great heat. She told Willie:

I lifted Baby out of her bed. Edward [Major Vibart] took me in a buggy. She never woke. I laid her on Mrs. Bowling's iron chair. Next morning all had been quiet, so we returned home. Just after breakfast in rushed Edward. 'Everyone running from the Bazaar, the whole station risen. Rush off whilst you can.' Well, we sat in the barracks, and at half past twelve it was so quiet that we returned, and I have determined never to believe a report without ocular demonstration. All is perfectly quiet, and I really think there is nothing to fear.

That stifling night of May 24 had indeed been one of shameful confusion and fright. She sent home hurried drawings of the scenes within those fateful Entrenchments.

'Night at Cawnpore, May 24 1857', by Emma Halliday.
Her key to the drawing reads: '1 Mrs Bowling, 2 Myself and Baby, 3 Ayah, 4 Punkah collie, 5 Mrs Larkins, 6 Young Lady.'

Willie Halliday, by Emma Halliday

Willie arrived on May 30, and on the next day wrote his last letter home. Emma and Emily Vibart were the only European women not sleeping in the Entrenchments. The Vibarts had four young children with them, and were still without news of their elder boy. Until Delhi was retaken, said Willie, the country could not be settled. If the Home Government did not send out at least 20,000 British troops within the next six months, it would be 'all up with India'. 'God bless you all and if we shall not meet again in this world God grant a happy meeting in Heaven. Goodbye.'

'Scene at Cawnpore, May 24 1857', by Emma Halliday

Escape from Delhi

In my search for relics of the Vibarts, I found letters written by this elder boy, whose first name like his father's was Edward. Some years after the Mutiny he married a daughter of Henry Trevelyan, therefore a niece of Charles.

Young Vibart described his escape from Delhi to his sister in England, Henrietta, otherwise known as Mipsie. As the theme of Charles's first 'Indophilus' article was 'Retribution – Delhi', it is very likely that Charles would also have been shown this letter and accounts of the boy's subsequent ordeals.

On May 11, Vibart said, being unaware of what had happened at Meerut, he and his fellow officers had repaired to the coffee house in the Mess, 'laughing and chatting as was our wont' until nearly eight o'clock. Afterwards, whilst he had been having his usual bath before breakfast, a havildar (sergeant) of his company had come rushing to the bungalow to say that the whole regiment had been ordered to the city immediately. Vibart learnt then that some troopers from the 3rd Light Cavalry had arrived from Meerut and were 'creating disturbances'. 'Hurrying on my clothes therefore as quickly as possible and ordering my horse to be saddled, I without loss of time, galloped down to the parade ground, where I found the regiment falling in by companies and ready to start.'

The nearest point to the city, about two miles from the cantonment, was the Kashmir Gate, on the other side of which was the Main Guard, a fortified enclosure. Vibart and others had been told to wait for the guns of the artillery, so the Colonel had gone ahead with the rest of the regiment. Soon firing had been heard from the direction of the Kashmir Gate. 'By Jove,' Vibart had thought to himself, 'our chaps are at it and we shall be too late for the fun.' He pushed on, looking forward to a 'good scrap', but was met by Captain Wallace of the 74th who begged him for 'God's sake' to hurry, 'as all our officers were being shot down by the cavalry troopers, and our men are making no effort to defend them'. After such startling news Vibart had the guns loaded, and advanced through the Gate. 'At this moment the body of our poor Colonel was carried out literally hacked to pieces. Such a fearful sight I never beheld in my life. The unfortunate man was still alive though frightfully mutilated. One arm appeared almost severed. I went up and spoke to him, but I don't think he recognized me.'

At the sight of the guns mutineers had 'scampered' back towards the city. The British decided to stay in the Main Guard until reinforcements arrived. Meanwhile, parties were sent out to bring in the bodies of officers lying about the Kashmir Gate. 'I myself brought in poor Burrowes. I had *never* before seen a dead body.' Throughout the day they were joined by several Europeans who had managed to escape from their houses in the city. Some of them had hidden in their servants' quarters whilst their bungalows were being rifled and burnt. Many civilians had been murdered, among them Mr Fraser the Commissioner and Mr Jennings the clergyman and his daughter.

A screaming horde had plundered the church of St James (Skinner's Church), and its bells had been rung in mockery before they were cut down. Suddenly there was a terrific explosion, making people in the Main Guard start to their feet. 'All was confusion and dismay, everybody rushing here and there, some pacifying the ladies, none of us knowing what to make of it.' Then a dense column of smoke ascended from the direction of the Magazine, which they realized must have been blown up. On the arrival of Lieutenants Forrest and Willoughby, bleeding and grimy, it was learnt that this had been done deliberately and with great gallantry, whilst on the orders of the King – the octogenarian Bahadur Shah II, now the figurehead of the revolt – mutineers had actually been scaling the walls. Hundreds of men had been buried in the rubble or blown into the air. 'All this time we saw fires blazing in the city,' Mipsie was told.

'Amid a storm of bullets' Vibart made his way to one of the embrasures of the bastion. He was about to leap down into the ditch below – 'one would have thought it madness at any other time' – and to scramble up the other side, when he heard screams from 'a lot of unfortunate women who were in the officers' quarters imploring for help'.

Some of these women, he found, had been wounded by bullets, which were whistling like hail and hitting the walls with a 'frightful hiss'. The Misses Forrest were weeping over their mother who had been shot in the shoulder. Then a gun went off in the courtyard, its shot passing over their heads 'with a horrible screech'. 'Quick as lightning' Vibart and other officers tied their sword-belts together to act as ropes, and some jumped into the ditch to break the fall of the ladies, as one by one they came over the parapet.

One very stout lady, Mrs Forster, commenced to scream and refused to jump. At this instant another shot from the gun crashed into the parapet a little to the right, covering us with splinters. It was madness to waste time in expostulation; somebody gave her a push and she tumbled headlong into the ditch beneath. And now an almost perpendicular bank rose before us, to scale which with delicate ladies appeared a hopeless task indeed. Meanwhile a few sepoys were observed peering over the rampart ... After a short while of extreme suspense their heads disappeared, and we surmised they must have gone with the rest of their comrades to join in plundering the Treasury. With beating hearts we commenced the ascent of the counterscarp. Again and again did the ladies almost reach the top, when the earth, crumbling away beneath their feet, sent them rolling back into the ditch. Despair, however, gave me superhuman energy till at length we all succeeded in gaining the summit. We now quickly ran down the short glacis, and plunged into some dense shrubbery that grew at the bottom.

Here they stopped to take breath, but the sound of voices coming from the road close by made them hurry on. Then:

I must relate a most painful incident, the thought of which still sickens me. The poor old lady I have before mentioned, Mrs Forster, had now become utterly helpless, and unable to proceed any further: a musket ball moreover had grazed her temple, and it was with difficulty we could get her on. Two of us then attempted to carry her, but the jungle had become so thick, that it was all we could do to make our way ourselves; and to carry her through this was quite impossible. Every little delay too might hasten our capture and preclude the possibility of escape; to have remained behind would only have been to sacrifice the lives of the whole party as well as hers. What then did we do? Alas! we left her behind! May God rest her soul!

Her daughter was in the party, for a long while believing that Mrs Forster was following. On reaching the bank of the River Jumna they realized to their dismay that they were being silently tracked by about a dozen men. They knew that they were nearing Metcalfe House and began to run towards it, scrambling over rough and uneven ground, covered with thorny bushes that tore at the women's dresses. Sweat streamed down their faces and their lips parched, but they dared not stop or look back. After ten minutes they reached the great house, but saw to their alarm that it was surrounded by a crowd of suspicious-looking persons. But nobody molested them, and a khitmadgar (butler) took them down to some pitch-dark underground rooms, where he eventually brought candles and beer. After three hours, spent 'in the greatest state of suspense', they were advised to move on, since when the sepoys came, as they must, to plunder the house they would be sure to be discovered and killed.

The khitmadgar gave them some bits of meat and bread, and his own turban to Vibart. On they trudged through the darkness for half an hour, when suddenly a bright streak of fire rose up behind them. It was Metcalfe House in flames – that fabulous mansion full of treasures. At once they imagined that the servants would have betrayed them, and have disclosed the direction of their flight. They tried desperately to hurry on, also noticing in the direction of the cantonment a 'lurid glare' in the sky; the whole place was burning. At last, after wading a deep stream, they felt able to rest in a sandy defile, 'weary, dispirited and bereft of all hope of succour'.

Many more perils were to lie ahead. Vibart summed them up in his letter to Mipsie, describing how for three days and nights they wandered in the jungles, sometimes being fed by villagers, sometimes robbed. They fell in with some other British refugees, and became a party of fifteen. At last they were able to shelter in a hut for four days, where they heard that Meerut was once more under British control. They managed to send a note, and an escort of cavalry was despatched to rescue them:

Oh! Great Heaven! to think of the privations we endured and the narrow escapes we had. We used to ford streams at night, and then walk on slowly, in our dripping clothes, lying down to rest every half hour; for you must remember that some of the ladies were wounded and all so fatigued and worn out, that they could scarcely move. Of course had we been by ourselves we would have made a dash for Meerut at once, which is about forty miles from Delhi, but having these unfortunate women with us, what could we do?

At Meerut Vibart was told of the fate of some friends. Lieutenant Willoughby, who had blown up the Magazine at Delhi, had been murdered whilst trying to reach Meerut. Osborn, whom he had last seen shot through the thigh at the Main Guard, had been with Willoughby, and had collapsed because of his wound; villagers had stripped him of all his clothing except his pith helmet, but a woman had taken pity on him and had fed him for three days; after 'enduring incredible sufferings' he had eventually been carried into Meerut on a charpoy.

Vibart was given some clothes – 'otherwise I have not a thing to my name, and am a perfect beggar' – and for a while put on picquet duties. He had no news from their parents, he told Mipsie, and now the telegraph wires to Cawnpore had been cut. 'God grant they may be safe and well,' and he added hopefully: 'We have reason to suppose that troops *there* are quiet.'

The date of that letter was June 1.

Siege and treachery at Cawnpore

The mutiny at Cawnpore finally broke on June 5. By the middle of August it became known that there had only been four survivors out of the thousand who had originally taken refuge in the Entrenchments. Edward Vibart must by then have had some details of the way his father had died, but was mercifully unclear about the hideous fate of his mother. For a long while he vainly hoped that the 'little ones' might have been saved by friendly Indians.

As for the Hallidays, according to George Otto, Willie was sniped whilst carrying a bowl of soup, made from a horse's head, to his wife Emma who was 'sick unto death of the smallpox'. The fate of the baby Mabel was never known. As she had always been considered delicate, very likely she did not long survive the ordeal of the siege.

. . . Actually from my researches, it is clear that Emma Halliday – certainly suffering from smallpox – died of wounds, and *after* leaving the Entrenchments.

The leader of the rebels at Cawnpore was Dhondu Pant, otherwise known as Nana Sahib or Nana Rao, the Maharajah of Bithur. Efforts have been made to exonerate him from some of the responsibility for the horrors that occurred in June and July. It is true that essentially he was a weak character, and that some Englishmen in times of peace had been impressed by his charm. Nevertheless by contemporary writers such as George Otto he was justifiably regarded as one of the most loathed figures in the whole history of the Mutiny.

It is also true that Nana Sahib had as his chief aide Ramchandra Pandenanga, a man of mysterious origins who preferred to be known as Tatya Tope. According to most accounts Tatya Tope was the organizer of the final great treachery at Cawnpore. But in subsequent months he was to prove himself a brilliant leader, a born general.

The siege of the Entrenchments lasted three weeks. Nana Sahib had expected a surrender after the first day. The heat was tremendous, and the temperature reached 138°. The first cannonades caused women and children to scream and to cry out in terror, but 'time and habit taught them to suffer and fear in silence'. Major Vibart was put in charge of the northern outpost known as the Redan. At some stage one of his four children, Johnny, ran out to greet him, and like Willie Halliday was sniped. The Vibart baby died of exposure or sunstroke.

'Some ladies,' wrote George Otto, 'were slain outright by grape or round shot. Some were struck down by bullets. Many were crushed beneath falling brickwork.' A second well lay outside the earthworks (only four feet high), and this was used as a cemetery for about 250 corpses, dragged there by night. The stench of corrupting flesh, gangrenous wounds and excrement was fearful, and flies swarmed everywhere. Babies were born. Food was very short. On the night of June 13 there was a disaster when the thatch of the hospital building caught fire. Emma Halliday was dragged to safety. All the medicines were lost. After this the majority of the women and children had to exist by lying in trenches only eighteen inches deep, without any covering by day or night.

The son of General Wheeler was badly hurt, and whilst he was being fanned by his sister a round shot came over the wall and sliced his head off. The shock so severely affected the General that Vibart seems virtually to have taken over the command.

At last a message came from Nana Sahib offering free passages down the Ganges to Allahabad. The monsoon was late, and it was realized by those inside the Entrenchments that their position would be hopeless once the rains came flooding down. So surrender was agreed upon, but on condition that the British would be allowed to march out under arms, and that carriages or elephants would be available for the wounded.

The spot chosen for the embarkation was the Satichaura Ghat, about a mile from the Entrenchments at the head of a small dried up ravine. Early that day a great crowd of local people swarmed round this normally desolate spot to watch the final departure of the sahibs from Cawnpore. George Otto wrote how Tatya Tope arranged for armed sepoys to be concealed behind some derelict huts, and for guns to be placed in bushes so as to cover the Ghat. Tatya Tope himself watched from the platform of a small fishermen's temple.

Slowly the long ragged cavalcade descended into the valley of the shadow of death, preceded by some two hundred sick and wounded persons, including Emma Halliday – with or without Mabel. Vibart was the last to leave. The boatmen made no attempt to help people aboard the little thatched boats. The water of the river was at a very low level, with mud banks visible.

The silence was sinister, George Otto wrote. Women and children were still being lifted into the boats when at a blast from a bugle all the boatmen leapt out and splashed to the shore. This at any rate is one version of events. Immediately the sepoys of Major Vibart's own regiment, the 2nd Cavalry, opened fire. The Europeans retaliated. Several straw roofs caught fire. In the panic to get away most of the boats became stuck on the mud banks. The sepoys then went in with their bayonets and swords.

Only one boat managed to get away, and this included the four Vibarts and no doubt Emma Halliday – unless she had been among those survivors of the massacre, mostly wounded, who had been dragged out of the by then crimson water and taken to Nana Sahib's headquarters, the Savada House.

There was no food on the boat, with about eighty people on board, and bits of plank and stretcher had to be used for oars. Sepoys continued to fire at them at a range of some 100 yards. The boat kept running on to the mud banks. The rudder snapped. Dead and wounded were tangled up at the bottom of the boat: because of the great heat, and to lighten the craft, the corpses had to be thrown out quickly. At last there was a shower of rain – the monsoon was about to break. Major Vibart was wounded in both arms, and probably dying.

The next day the boat ran aground near a village full of hostile sepoys, who opened up at once, causing several deaths. Luckily a hurricane set the boat free, sweeping it into a backwater where it again grounded. The attacks of the sepoys began once more. Vibart ordered some of the officers and men on board to wade ashore and drive the sepoys away while he tried to get the boat afloat. After a hard fight they returned to find the boat gone. They dashed along the bank, but never saw it again. After various encounters with other mutineers, only four survivors were able to take refuge with an Indian landowner.

The boat of course had been captured. It seems certain that up till then Emily Vibart and at any rate one child had been unhurt. All were taken to the Savada House, and Nana Sahib ordered that the men should be lined up and shot. 'What ensued,' George Otto has said rather sententiously, 'an Englishman would willingly tell in phrases not his own'; and in his book he quoted the account 'from the lips of a native spy':

'Then said one of the Memsahibs, the doctor's wife [Mrs Boyes]: "I will not leave my husband. If he must die, I will die with him." So she ran and sat down behind her husband, clasping him round the waist. Directly she said this, the other Memsahibs said: "We also will die with our husbands." And they all sat down, each by her husband. Then their husbands said: "Go back," but they would not.'

So the soldiers pulled them apart forcibly. But they could not separate the doctor's wife. The Padre (Captain Seppings, with a broken arm) asked leave to read prayers; this was granted and his hands were loosened.

'After the Padre had read a few prayers, he shut the book and the Sahibs shook hands all round. Then the sepoys fired. One Sahib rolled one way, one another as they sat. But they were not dead: only wounded. So they went in and finished them off with swords.'

The fate of General Wheeler's younger daughter became the subject for innumerable plays and magazine articles throughout the world. She was supposed to have been rescued by a trooper at the Satichaura Ghat, though it was not certain if she was then 'dishonoured'. At any rate he took her to his house, and one story is that she got up during the night, took his sword, and beheaded not only him but all the other members of his family. Then she threw herself into a well. Another story is that she married the trooper, and was discovered years later as an old woman living in the bazaars of Cawnpore.

Fatehgarh

Fatehgarh was about eighty miles upstream from Cawnpore, a centre for indigo-planters and containing a small garrison. It is strange that George Otto did not mention that here yet another Vibart was the inspiration of the white community. This was Teddy, a captain and a nephew not only of Major Vibart but of Sir William Macnaghten, who had been murdered at Kabul in January 1842. For good measure, he was also the uncle of the 'Demon' of Harrow, not yet born.

Teddy had been very popular with the Vibart children of Cawnpore, and happened to be at Fatehgarh just as news broke about the mutinies at Meerut and Delhi. Some civilians, including two American missionaries and their families, decided to take a boat to somewhere they thought would be safer: Cawnpore. Needless to say, they sailed straight into a trap. They were sent to the Savada House, where all were slaughtered, including women and children. Their bodies were thrown into the Ganges and floated down to the vicinity of the Satichaura Ghat, where they were still to be seen, with vultures perched on them, when the survivors of the Entrenchments reached that place some days later.

The remaining Europeans at Fatehgarh shut themselves in the fort, and it was then that the 'inevitable and invaluable' Teddy Vibart so distinguished himself. At last they too decided to take to the boats,

'Johnny who died in the Entrenchments.'
By his cousin Edmund Vibart, December 1853

and as George Otto said, 'the rest is soon told'. On arrival at Cawnpore they were herded into the Savada House; but this time only men were killed, Teddy included, though three were thought worth preserving by Nana Sahib as possibly useful hostages. The remnants of the party were taken to the house known as the Bibighar, where 160 people originally from the Entrenchments had now been sent, most of them wounded – and these including Emma Halliday, Emily Vibart and two of her children.

None were to survive. As the atrocities of the Bibighar, also known as the House of the Ladies, were to inflame the attitude of the British more than any other episode during the Mutiny, I shall give some details of what happened in that place in a separate context later in the book. It was fortunate for Emma that she died before the general holocaust – only a day or two before the British entered Cawnpore under General Havelock.

Revenge and 'Indophilus'

By the time Charles felt able to continue with his 'Indophilus' articles for *The Times* the famous siege of the Lucknow Residency was in its

'Emmie who was taken to the boats, and never heard of again.'
Also by Edmund Vibart

second month. He knew by then that Emma was dead. Delhi had at last been retaken after bloody attacks. The Red Fort of Agra was crowded with refugees, and there Charles's great friend from Calcutta days, John Colvin, the Lieutenant-Governor of the North-West Provinces, had died from a stroke brought on – so it was said – by sheer despair and helplessness. The place had thus been left rudderless, with its terrified and squabbling cargo, in the marble pavilions and arcades of that once royal palace, with its sublime view of the Taj Mahal.

Throughout his article Charles avoided the theme of punishment. A reassessment of attitudes had set in, for some people at least, when the sickening behaviour of British troops at the retaking of Cawnpore and Delhi, and the cavalier attitude towards the taking of life, became known. But when 'Clemency' Canning the Governor-General passed a resolution that sepoys should not be punished without reference to the gravity of their offences, there were furious reactions especially at Calcutta, and demands for his recall. The sense of betrayal had been too great, the slaughter of defenceless women and children, and possible tortures, had been a crime too monstrous to be forgiven, the frenzied panic too recent. 'There is a rabid and indiscriminate vindictiveness abroad,' Canning wrote to Queen Victoria. Even *The Times* criticized his resolution as 'silly'. There was also outrage at Calcutta about the so-called Gagging Act, which required all printers of newspapers to obtain licences from the Government, and a further resolution that licences would have to be acquired by anyone wishing to carry arms.

Charles Trevelyan's friends kept him apprised about the military progress of the Mutiny, and these friends included Sir John Lawrence and his Secretary from the beginning of 1858, Richard Temple. By December Lawrence was saying to Charles: 'I see every danger of justice degenerating into revenge of a savage character. Already it looks too like a general war of white man against black.' Charles asked him about the truth regarding atrocities towards Englishwomen at Delhi. Lawrence replied that he had made many enquiries. One young girl, a Miss Hunt, had been 'extremely maltreated' by a Delhi badmash, as had the wife of an officer by several Muslim villagers. Another young woman had been publicly put to death on the courtyard of the Royal Palace, and it was possible that there had been a few similar cases. But the 'stories of girls being crucified, hanging by their hair and the like are not true'. At the Kashmir Gate the body of one European soldier had been found, naked, with marks of chains around him. And at Cawnpore, Temple said, there was absolutely no truth in stories that ladies were tortured or raped before the final slaughter: 'The rebels at most places were thirsty for blood and murdered quick'. As Lady Canning told Queen Victoria: 'Only the massacres are real.'

Temple was able to confirm that there had been no cases of rape of Indian women when the British entered Delhi. He found the city 'thoroughly sacked, gutted and cleared'. At least the great monuments were all safe. When Lawrence took over at Delhi and stopped the wholesale executions, there were again many complaints about leniency:

The fact is these people whatever their sins have been terribly punished already. They suffered (Mohammedans and Hindus) throughout the siege both from the rebel army and from the King's myrmidons. Constantly forced aids and loans were demanded of them. After the storming they were well plundered by the victors, European and native. After that they were kept out in all the cold weather half starved and suffering from cold and distress. Surely we cannot punish for ever.

While some said in England that it was God's punishment for a hundred years of maladministration, it was everywhere agreed that the affair of the greased cartridges had been the immediate cause of the Mutiny. Charles as 'Indophilus' wrote that 'to bite a cartridge greased with cow's or pig's fat was more to the Hindus, and the Indian Mohammedans, than eating pork to a Jew, spitting on the Host to the Roman Catholic, or trampling on the Cross to a Protestant.' The 'atrocious' arrest of the ninety sepoys at Meerut had made the men into martyrs. In fact the grease had been made of five parts tallow, five parts stearin and one part wax. Later it was claimed that only vegetable oils were used in the tallow, but this is still questionable. At any rate no attempt had been made to disabuse the sepoys of the conviction that their religion was being tampered with, 'whether through blindness, ignorance, folly or recklessness'.

But then, as Lawrence wrote to him, the Bengal Army had for a long time been in an unsatisfactory state. It had become one great brotherhood, 'feeling and acting in unison'. The Mutiny was an affair of caste, of 'personal impurity'. 'Both Hindus and Mohammedans believe that we meant by a bit of legerdemain to make them Christians.' The Muslims took advantage of the revolt to convert it into a religious and political war – political because of disaffection over the recent British annexation of Oude, of which Lucknow was the capital. Maybe it was true, as George Otto also said, that the rapid growth had been in part due to the 'violence and greed' of the sepoys, and the lack of discipline. The sepoys knew well enough that European troops were thin on the ground throughout – indeed to a ridiculous degree. There was a widely spread rumour among them that the entire British nation numbered scarcely more than a hundred thousand (the population of India then was nearing two hundred million): all the more reason for wiping out all white persons – they could never be replaced. The prestige of the British had never recovered in India after the First Afghan War, which Charles likened to the Romans leaving Germany at the time of Varus.

Whilst Charles and Lawrence were still convinced that Christian truths would eventually pervade India, Charles warned against too much haste in abolishing Hindu practices that were repugnant to Europeans, such as exposing the sick on the banks of the Ganges, polygamy, obscenities in temples, and swinging from hooks pierced through the muscles of the back. Smaller matters like shaving one's head after a death were important to a sepoy. It had even become plain that the abolition of the practice of suttee in the late 1820s had caused grave unease among Hindus, since it had been a practice embedded in their religion.

319

As for that notorious aloofness of the English, this had also been resented by many landowners, nobles and princes, who also feared for their future after recent British annexations. Charles even tried to show that Nana Sahib, the most execrated figure of the whole Mutiny, had some reason for his grievances.

The ninth letter from 'Indophilus' was his obituary of John Colvin, whom Charles regarded as the last of those statesmen who had derived their inspiration from giants such as Malcolm, Munro, Metcalfe and Bentinck. These wise master builders had completed the edifice of our Indian Empire on the solid foundation of 'good faith, justice and respect.' Since their time 'habitual success' had led to over-confidence and indifference, 'a disposition to undervalue the natives'. It had been, in short, a case of pride before the fall.

Incredible as it may seem, a practice has arisen of late of designating the natives – not the mutinous sepoys, but the natives generally – as 'niggers'. This is passing strange to those nourished in the spirit of Sir John Malcolm's instructions to his assistants. ['I am quite satisfied in my own mind, that, if there is one cause more than another that will impede our progress to the general improvement of India, it is a belief formed by its population, from the manner of their English superiors, that they are viewed by them as an inferior or degraded race', 1821]; – and it is stranger still to observe such practices are suffered to grow up without rebuke by the Indian Government . . . If these things are true, and we do not speedily mend our ways, the knell of our Indian Empire has sounded; and this insurrection, horrible though it is, will be followed at no distant period by another in comparison with which this will seem limited and harmless.

But ways were not to be mended in the future, or not much, though there was not to be another mutiny on such a scale. All the same, hundreds, if not thousands, of English, Scots, Welsh and Irish did over the next ninety years or so devote their lives to India, occasionally with a sad lack of intelligence, but following the precepts of Sir John Malcolm, even if unconsciously.

The Mutiny was the great watershed in attitudes towards India. The memories of what happened are still painful to both British and Indians. The 'Indophilus' letters ended on a characteristic note of hope, with a comparison of lessons learnt in Ireland, where until the Famine the country's social state had been a mystery to England, even though she had been 'connected with us for centuries'. He saw the Mutiny as a social convulsion, which like the Famine and the French Revolution had introduced a new order of things and had precipitated a change for which long years might otherwise have been required. But the 'question really is whether our public morality – that is our justice, our disinterestedness, our sense of duty – is strong enough to bear such a burden.' Would Christian England be able to stand the test, he asked?

So that Evangelical fervour, which seems suspiciously like racial arrogance, had softened. Now there were doubts about the famous 'moral integrity' of the British character. His original Calcutta opponents, such as Thoby Prinsep, must have read the letters of 'Indophilus' in London with a certain *Schadenfreude*.

Delhi, dele

Young Edward Vibart had been at the retaking of Delhi, and had to report home the death of a neighbour's son, Edward Speke, brother of the explorer, Speke of the Nile. He fought under the extraordinary General John Nicholson, 'a man cast in giant mould', in a battle that routed a rebel brigade trying to intercept a vital siege train. 'We drove them out at the point of the bayonet,' he told his sister Mipsie. 'Oh! I can't tell you what a maddening feeling came over me as I rushed on, and I thought of our beloved Parents, and burning for vengeance.'

Yet after his entry into the city, he had a different reaction:

I have seen many bloody and awful sights lately, but such a one as I witnessed yesterday, please God, I may never see again. The Regiment was ordered to clear out the houses between the Delhi and the Turkman Gates, which are the two gates we have to hold. The orders were to shoot every soul, and I think I must have seen some forty or fifty defenceless people shot down before me. It was literally *murder*, and I was perfectly horrified, the women were all spared, but their screams on seeing their husbands and sons butchered were frightful, as you may suppose. I went to see the King's sons lying dead in the Chandni Chowk. They were allowed to remain there until they stank, in one of them I recognized one who used to come and shoot pigeons with us at picnics and tiffins. The old King is still a prisoner, and I suppose they will spare his life.

The King had been captured in the tomb of his ancestor, the

Emperor Humayun. His sons and a grandson had also been shot in cold blood.

'I do feel a shudder at seeing these black creatures killed,' Vibart wrote, 'but it is only momentary. I think of my parents night and day.' He admitted that he had spat on the corpses of the princes.

He went to have a look at the King, the last of the Moghuls, in the wretched little house where he was confined.

> There I saw, sitting cross-legged on a native bedstead, on which he was rocking himself to and fro, a small and attenuated old man apparently between eighty and ninety years of age, with a long white beard, and almost totally blind. He was repeating to himself, in a low but audible murmur, some verses of the Koran, or it may be of some of his own pastoral compositions – for he aspired to be a poet – and he certainly looked an object of pity and compassion ... I merely stood and gazed for a while in silence on this woe-begone picture of fallen greatness, and then left the poor old man still mumbling to himself in the solitude of his dreary apartment.

The King and some of his entourage were, after a trial, exiled to Rangoon, where he soon died.

Delhi was described as looking like a deserted charnel-house. Nearly all the able-bodied inhabitants fled, leaving the streets to looters and marauders. Vultures settled in the Chandni Chowk and gorged on corpses until unable to move. Other bodies were crunched and torn by growling pi-dogs; some lay with arms outstretched, as if beckoning to passers-by. In order to check the looting, Prize Agents were appointed, with orders to hand over any valuables to a Prize Committee. A few officers were given permits to help in this search for buried treasures, and most retained some perks, including Vibart.

Vibart returned to Meerut, and soon found himself marching against the Jodhpur mutineers. In January 1858 his regiment was posted to Cawnpore.

Forbes and a prince

On November 1 1858 a proclamation by Queen Victoria was read out in all the stations of India, announcing the abolition of the Honourable East India Company. There were fireworks and military salutes. Henceforward all the powers of the Company and of the Board of Control would be exercised by a Secretary of State for India in London, and he would be acting in concert, in certain cases, with a Council headed by the Governor-General, who was also the Sovereign's Viceroy and usually known as such. Treaties with native princes would be honoured, and there would be an amnesty for all rebels who had not taken part in the massacres. Religions and ancient customs would be respected and tolerated.

The fighting was by no means over, and certainly was now less of a mutiny than a genuine, though localized war of liberation – fear of reprisal also being an important factor in avoiding surrender. As Richard Temple also said to Charles Trevelyan, during 1858 it developed into a great game of hide and seek. British power was still weak – 'We are like a schoolboy fighting a nest of hornets.' In May there was hardly a safe district between Allahabad and Delhi. Then in June Gwalior fell briefly to the rebels. News of its capture had an 'electric effect upon the whole of Central India'. It had looked like Delhi all over again, and there was new panic among Europeans.

The rebels, said Temple, had the 'nine lives of ninety cats'. There was no destroying them outright. Leaders of considerable courage and great organizing powers had come to the fore, notably Tatya Tope, the man who was said to have sat in the temple at the Satichaura Ghat at Cawnpore and gloated over the massacre. Other leaders included Rao Sahib, the Rani of Jhansi and Prince Firuz Shah. Tatya Tope's main military success was beating the British at the second battle of Cawnpore in November 1857, though soon afterwards he was defeated by Colin Campbell.

Rao Sahib's father, like Nana Sahib, had been an adopted son of the previous Peshwa of Cawnpore; it was he who had captured Gwalior and had forced its pro-British Maharajah to flee to Agra. The Rani of Jhansi was to her followers a kind of Joan of Arc, but to the British she was more like a Jezebel. It is possible that she found herself swept along by the flood of the Mutiny; initially reluctant to fight the British, she had to escape disguised in male dress, joining Tatya Tope at Kalpi. She died a soldier's death outside Gwalior, some say still dressed as a man and wielding a sabre, while holding her horse's reins in her mouth.

Firuz Shah was a Moghul prince and in his mid-twenties. In the summer of 1857 he had only just returned from Mecca, and had not therefore been at Delhi during the siege. He had been seen at Lucknow, as had Nana Sahib, and then at Jhansi. He reappeared at Mandisore, where he declared a jehad, and soon gathered round him an army of 18,000 men. In 1858 he was near Bareilly, but was thrown back, and then again repulsed at Shahjehanabad.

Nana Sahib remained always a shadowy figure; the threat that never was, the arch-monster for whom no punishment would have been adequate. He had been at Cawnpore with Tatya Tope at the defeat by Campbell. At Gwalior he had had a vision of setting himself up as a ruler of vast tracts of country, receiving tribute and honours from beyond his boundaries. Early in December 1858 he was reported to be advancing on Etawa, but it turned out that the rebels were under the command of Firuz Shah, who had cleverly slipped out of a trap prepared by Campbell, by then known as Lord Clyde. This battle against Firuz Shah was the moment of glory in the life of someone who would have been Emma Halliday's future brother-in-law, Lieutenant Lachlan Forbes.

Forbes was accompanied on the thirty-five-mile night march by Allan Hume, the Commissioner of Etawa, a man noted for his conspicuous leniency towards captured rebels and who eventually was regarded as the 'father' of the Indian National Congress party. Firuz was waiting for them at the fort of Hurchundpore, with an army that was no 'unskilled village-rabble, but a body of trained soldiers, whose business was to cut their way through all opposition, or perish in the attempt'.

It was a gory battle, lasting three hours, and at last Firuz was forced to withdraw, in his usual wraithlike manner disappearing once more. Lord Canning sent Forbes a special commendation. The battle was in its way important, and as Temple said, especially in its effect on popular goodwill: 'That old John Bull confidence is returning.'

Firuz joined up with Tatya Tope, who had had some bad reverses. They were defeated at Deosa between Jaipur and Bharatpur on January 14 1859. The rebel leadership broke up, and Firuz went to hide in the Sironj jungle – but when it was combed by British troops, he could not be found. Tatya Tope and Rao Sahib were however both caught and executed, while Nana Sahib was reported to be safely in Nepal. In the following year Firuz turned up at Kandahar, and in 1861 he was at Bokhara. Later he was at Swat, dangerously close to British territories, then at Samarkand, and in 1872 he was sighted at Constantinople. Eventually he tried unsuccessfully to gain support from Muslim rulers for a new jehad. He died, destitute, at Mecca in 1877, but remembered as a romantic if not saintly figure; moreover he was one of the few leaders during the Mutiny who had publicly condemned the killing of helpless women, old people and children.

As for Forbes, the last entry in his diary read: 'LEFT INDIA December 14 1861 after serving there since November 10 1848 or 13 years and nearly 2 months. Hurrah – and may I never see it again.'

Return to Cawnpore

Emma Halliday's younger brother, Spencer Wyndham, arrived in India in 1858 and joined the 88th Foot (the Connaught Rangers). He then to his dismay found himself sent to Cawnpore. The poor boy knew that he would be expected to write to his family something of what he had seen, but obviously found it a hard duty. He still believed that Emma had died of smallpox and that her body had been dumped in the well outside the Entrenchments. All he could bring himself to say in his letter about that doomed place was that the Entrenchments were the 'most miserable attempt at fortification imaginable, the trenches only waist high and then not ball proof'. Hating everything about India, he soon developed chronic diarrhoea, and was thankful to be invalided back to England.

When Edward Vibart reached Cawnpore his reactions were – understandably – far more emotional. He went to the blackened ruins of his parents' home and the desolation of the garden, almost hearing – he said – his mother's voice. He could scarcely tear himself away. Then to the 'fearful Entrenchments':

Oh! my God what a sight met my eyes. There were two long and narrow trenches close to each other, and round this you could see that at one time there had been a small ditch and bank. There is scarcely a *square yard* in the barracks that has not been struck by a round shot – even right *down* to the ground. And *there* for two and twenty days my Parents were shut up, and fired at night and day . . . How I cursed those *fiends* who besieged them. Aye! cursed them from my very heart. I felt driven to madness and despair . . .

He had heard that 'Uncle Willie' Halliday had been shot through the heart and could not have lived long. One can almost see the tears falling on that letter as he wrote of the Satichaura Ghat and the boat's eventual capture. 'Our darling Mother – she could not have survived that last awful day. *God in his mercy grant that she may have died.*'

It was well that he did not know the truth about the Bibighar.

III

Despair at Holly Lodge

Charles was offered the post of Governor of Madras on January 6 1859. It would, incidentally, make him third in order of precedence in India. Macaulay was thrown into a state of fearful alarm. He could not bear the prospect of being separated from his sister Hannah. 'If she were to go,' he wrote in his journal, 'I should die of a broken heart I think.' Two days later Charles had made up his mind. 'All is over. Go he will. A madman. I can hardly command my indignation. Yet what good can I do by expressing it?' At least it had been settled that Hannah should stay behind and look after Macaulay at his new house, Holly Lodge on Camden Hill.

Macaulay's health had been failing for some years. Hannah in her memoir told how in 1853 he had particularly wanted to give his views in the House of Commons on the throwing open of the Indian Civil Service to public competition. 'Owing to the oppression of his breath he could not speak after eating for some hours'; and it was settled therefore that he should speak early. Unfortunately he was forestalled by another Member and was not able to rise until 9 pm, by which time he was exhausted. After a while, his voice failed him and he had to sit down abruptly. His infirmities decided him soon afterwards to give up his seat as Member for Edinburgh. But in 1856 he was given a peerage. Only once did he attempt to speak in the House of Lords, and this was on the new India Bill of 1858; but on the very day he found himself too weak even to go to the House. For all that, he enjoyed Holly Lodge, and was able to continue his work on his *History of England*. His beloved Baba, his niece Margaret Trevelyan, married Harry Holland, a barrister and son of an old friend, one of Queen Victoria's doctors, and incidentally a kinsman of the family of the future Cecily Fairfield, better known as Rebecca West; but although this was 'not without a large mixture of pain' he looked forward to a new home where he would always be welcome.

326

This obvious distress to Macaulay at Charles's decision, and his declining state of health, were not the only reasons for Charles saying that he had gone through some 'tremendous' personal heart-searching. George Otto was midway through his term at Trinity, Cambridge, where he had won a scholarship, and was evidently set for a glittering future, probably in politics. Alice, the youngest of the family, was just growing up and needed help. As Macaulay said to his sister Fanny, what added to his own bitterness was the 'utter want of sympathy' from friends. 'Everyone fancies that we must be in raptures, and pesters us with congratulations.' He had never seen Hannah so unhappy. Baba was miserable, Alice shocked. Admittedly George Otto was not so upset, except on their account. Indeed his reaction was typical of a very ambitious young man. 'He is sorry to part with his father, but glad to see his father gratified and promoted.'

> I am satisfied that Trevelyan does not know what sacrifice he is making on quitting his family. He is now under a delusion. All his virtues and all his faults are strongly brought out; and, between ambition and public spirit, he is as much excited, and as unfit to be reasoned with, as if he had drunk three bottles of champagne.

He probably knew that Charles had already written out to Madras to make sure that there would be a proper supply of champagne of good quality.

At least Macaulay could agree that from a financial point of view the new appointment was a great achievement. Charles's salary would be £12,800, half of which he would be able to send home to Hannah.

Charles set off for India on February 18. 'I took leave of Trevelyan,' Macaulay put in the journal. 'He said, "You have always been a most kind brother to me." I certainly tried to be so. Shall we ever meet again? I do not expect it. My health is better; but another sharp winter will probably finish me.'

'It was a very sad year,' Hannah wrote. 'His spirits never rallied at all.'

The new Governor arrives

There were suggestions that Charles had been feeling frustrated at the Treasury for lack of scope for his talents. If this were so, his restlessness must have been increased by the flow of long, intimate and sometimes desperate letters from Sir John Lawrence about the questions he felt were crying out for solutions. Lawrence for many people had emerged from the trauma of 1857 as 'India's Saviour', a man of action who was almost a saint. Some compared him to Cromwell. He himself said privately to Charles that Delhi would not have been recaptured but for his own foresight. He had on the whole approved of the 'Indophilus' letters, and as his first biographer was to remark, Charles was a man entirely after his own heart. (Another relevant point must have been the fact that Charles was sympathetic to giving Government aid to the Lawrence Asylums, founded by the late Sir Henry Lawrence for orphans, and to a new scheme for helping widows.)

The reformers and Evangelicals of the 1830s had found themselves having to be on the defensive as a result of the Mutiny. All the same there were those who persisted in seeing the whole affair as the visitation of Jehovah's displeasure, and some of these men were in India itself. Edwards at Peshawar looked on the Mutiny as a 'national chastisement' because of the very failure in withholding essential Christian truths from the people of India. There should be more not less missionary work, even compulsory Bible teaching in schools. Lawrence did not go as far as this, and Charles certainly did not, but on Lawrence's return to England his much publicized religious views annoyed Canning at Calcutta so much that he exclaimed: 'Really Sir John Lawrence ought to shut up, and Edwards have his head shaved. The latter is exactly what Mahomet would have been if born at Clapham instead of Mecca.'

Even in 1853 Charles had prophesied that basing education on Christian instruction would only lead to violent reaction. He remained convinced, however, that English ideas and principles taught in schools would eventually lighten the way to the Gospel. In any case the Queen's proclamation at the end of the Mutiny had unambiguously stated: 'We do charge and enjoin all those who may be in authority under us that they abstain from all interference with the religious belief or worship of any of our subjects, on pain of our highest displeasure.'

Lawrence had also poured out his ideas on the reorganization of the Army to Charles, and Charles was one of those called to give his views on the subject to a Royal Commission. Both of them believed in the competitive spirit; men should be allowed to rise from the ranks – though, and needless to say, 'these should be exceptional cases'.

Charles's appointment to Madras prompted a leading article in *The Times*, congratulating the Tories and Disraeli, who had recommended it to Lord Stanley, the Secretary of State.

The appointment of an eminent civil servant to a post of dignity generally one of the perquisites of the Peerage, is a graceful act of homage to the spirit of administrative reform, and an encouragement to the class from which Sir Charles is drawn . . . Sir Charles goes forth in his prime of life to a station which he has earned by a life of most energetic activity, and to duties which are congenial with his tastes and studies . . .

Stanley had told Charles that the Governorship offered 'one of the wider fields of usefulness that man could devise' – as if, one might say, Charles needed to know that! Charles had replied to him: 'I would willingly devote my life to her [India].' He also wrote round to various relatives modestly explaining that he had at once realized that it was his *duty* to accept, in spite of the domestic complications. Few of them, however, could really have believed that he was not intending, as he said, to launch out on an 'avowed course of reform' at Madras. He also wrote to Canning saying that he hoped the Viceroy would find him helpful and obedient. Perhaps it was as well that Canning did not know that Stanley had expressly asked Charles to look into the question of too much supervision of provincial governments by Calcutta. In any case Canning never replied to Charles, nor was there a letter of welcome when Charles arrived at Madras. One gets the impression that there was not much affinity between the Trevelyans and those urbane aristocrats of the old school . . . Charles also wrote to the outgoing Governor of Madras, Lord Harris, for confidential reports on the merits of his future subordinates.

For the voyage he took a good store of Parliamentary Blue Books, which he 'devoured with avidity'. Hannah gave him a book of hymns and he had a Hindustani Bible. Florence Nightingale sent him a flattering farewell letter: 'You are going to Madras but all India is what you are going for . . . I could not let you leave England without saying God bless you for all you have done for us.'

'Do not feel anxiety,' he wrote to Hannah from on board the *Ceylon*. 'I feel sure God will have me in His holy keeping. I have committed myself to Him, believing that I have been prepared and called for what is before me, and I do not doubt that strength and grace will be given me.'

The journey to India via the overland route at Suez now took only six weeks. Charles approved of his fellow passengers, many being missionaries or 'sensible and thoughtful' young ladies going out to get married, to whom he could safely talk without fear of 'committing myself to anything questionable or disagreeable'. Was this remark meant to reassure Hannah, with some previous compromising incident in mind? Or was he thinking of seductive creatures like his sister-in-law Emily Trevelyan's so-called stepmother, Lucille Due Bue of Madras, in the 1820s? The new ship, the *Nubia*, called at Galle. Here Charles landed by catamaran or 'spider-boat', bouncing through the surf. He did not have his brother-in-law's gift of letter-writing, but among the various pious sentiments and exhortations to the children one flippancy was allowed. Charles had wanted to bathe but had been worried about sharks. 'Don't you bother yourself,' an Irishman had said to him. 'There are so many sharks here, they only eat each other.'

A little later Sir Bartle Frere, ex-Commissioner of Sind, with a rather more vivid pen, also landed at Galle on his way to stay with Charles before joining the Viceroy's Council. He thought that the costume of the local males, with their little black silk coats over petticoats, and their hair tied in knots at the back, made them look like respectable Portuguese pretending to be women. The deep blue water of the sea, the perfection of the tropical scenery, the neat cottages with so many children running about made him think of *Paul and Virginia*, of which – being a mere novel – Charles would probably have never heard.

Charles's last day on board the *Nubia* was a Sunday, so he devoted himself entirely to his 'religious exercises' and to his thoughts of his family. 'My voyage only now really begins. May I have grace given me to steer me through all the rocks and shoals which will surround my course.'

An iron pier was to be built at Madras, but as at Galle it was still a question of braving the often quite considerable waves, this time in masula boats made of mango wood sewn together with coconut fibre. Ships would be anchored half a mile out; ladies would be put in chairs and lowered into the boats. Catamarans would follow close by, in case passengers were tipped into the water and were snatched by sharks. It was exactly the same in 1777 when William Hickey had landed at Madras, and again in 1834 when Macaulay and Hannah had arrived there. Macaulay had written then how the first Indian he met was a little black boatman from a catamaran. 'He came on board with nothing on him but a pointed yellow cap, and walked among us with a self-possession and civility which, coupled with his colour and nakedness, nearly made me die with laughing.' And when the masula boats had arrived, 'a dozen half-naked bodies, howling all the way the most dissonant song you ever heard, rowed us with great skill to the shore.'

Rao Pragmal of Kutch, c. 1860

Inner court of the Palace of the Rao of Kutch at Bhuj

Olive with Raleigh, Government House, Ross Island, July 1923 Inset: the same view, 1985

Ross Island, 1923

Calcutta from Garden House Reach, by William Daniell

Sir Charles Edward Trevelyan, after his return from Madras

Macaulay in his prime; a portrait
by J. Partridge, 1849

Madras, by William Daniell

Emma Halliday

Captain Edmund Vibart

Victims at Cawnpore

Major Edward Vibart

Emily Vibart and her daughter Emmie

Shot from the cannon, from *Memories of the Mutiny* by F. C. Maude

Massacre (Satichaura) Ghat, Cawnpore: an imaginative reconstruction, from
The History of the India Mutiny by Charles Ball

Elephant fights at Lucknow, from *Wanderings of a Pilgrim* by Fanny Parks, 1831

The Salaam, by William Daniell

George Francis Train of Boston, Mass., was not so amused by the experience. Whereas boatmen at Calcutta wore nothing but a pocket handkerchief in front, the 'savages' of Madras contented themselves with a twine string. 'The day was perfectly calm,' he wrote in 1857, 'yet the surf washed over our boat once or twice; and ultimately the black, beggarly natives – I hate the sight of them! – took us on their shoulders to dry land.' Women were taken ashore like so many bags of clothing, to be assailed by the incomprehensible clamour of people wanting to be their servant or tradesman, and then pursued by the same folk all the way to their new residences.

Macaulay had said that from the sea Madras looked like Brighton: great white masses of buildings scattered under a rich profusion of deep dark varnished green. He had been greeted with a salute of guns, and so was Charles. Charles was sworn in at Fort St George, and he drove in a carriage to Government House – boys in scarlet and gold uniforms trotting alongside with the fly whisks.

Government House was an enormous palace, rebuilt in 1800, with the usual portico and colonnade, and attached to it was a beautiful banqueting hall, eighty by sixty feet and of a slightly later date – Bishop Heber had thought it in 'vile taste'. Inside Government House the rooms were as 'high as a church', the walls like marble, being plastered with chunan, a mixture of shell-lime and sea-sand. It was a very airy building, open to all the sea-breezes, Charles said. His office was over the main portico. All round was a so-called pleasure ground, dried up and in a terrible state of neglect, with a herd of about a hundred starving spotted deer. Indeed the whole house was in bad repair, previous Governors having been more attracted to their other residence, Guindy Park, six miles away in the country.

Not far from Government House was the Black Town. The Europeans had their offices in the White Town but lived in spacious villas outside Madras. Sometimes these villas were very showy, but, as Macaulay said, 'you may see at a glance that they are the residences of people who do not mean to leave them to their children or even to end their days in them' – there was such a want of repair, such a slovenliness. Each of them had compounds of several acres. The roads, as usual, were thronged with natives, walking or riding or in hackeries, carts drawn by bullocks. The noise was prodigious.

The Governor also had available a Marine Villa near the sea. This was usually at the disposal of distinguished visitors, and had once been the bathing pavilion of the Nawabs of the Carnatic.

Charles at once applied himself to the two things on which he was a past if not notorious expert: the eradication of inefficiency and patronage. Within four days of his arrival he had produced a Minute on the former. There were also instant sackings. George Otto was to write that Lord Harris had apparently a bevy of incapables; his father had come down on them like a hawk on a flock of pigeons. No wonder Harris had never sent Charles that confidential report on subordinates. As for patronage, this included the sweeping away of racial distinctions. Charles began planning a series of At Homes which would include Anglo-Indians, Muslims and Hindus – something unheard of hitherto. The other three most pressing matters at Madras, he decided, were water supplies, sanitation and sewage.

Zeal for good

It was refreshing for me – having so recently seen a Woodham-Smith-type version of the Irish Famine on television – to be able to meet Mr Thiro Sundaram, a leading businessman and philanthropist of Madras.

Mr Sundaram, like the late Mr Baliqa of the Madras Record Office, was an enthusiast for Charles's achievements during his fourteen months as Governor. His office was in a great Palladian mansion, once the residence of Sir Patrick Grant, Charles's Commander-in-Chief, with some beautiful early Victorian stained glass. He kindly provided me with a specially written 'office memo' listing all those familiar virtues of Charles: boldness, energy, vigour, liberal outlook; masterful grasp and knowledge of detail, robust style; immense capacity for hard work. Charles, I read, had left behind him a reputation at Madras for 'suave and amiable manners' (showing, it would seem, how much Hannah had tamed him since the Calcutta days!). 'There was hardly any important branch of the administration,' Mr Sundaram added, 'which he did not improve or seem to improve. He had that ability to select officers, and to encourage them to turn out the best of what work would give. He infused strength into all branches.'

Mr Sundaram was pained when I told him that I met students who had actually turned against Charles Trevelyan whilst writing on aspects of his work. I could understand, though, their feeling of exhaustion, of being 'battered', when trying to see him in the context of his whole extraordinary career. Equality before the law, freedom of the press, Bentinck's humanitarian reforms: I trust that I would have supported Charles and Macaulay in matters such as these if I had lived at Calcutta in the 1830s. I would certainly have favoured the *encouragement* of education in English, but I am not sure whether I wouldn't have been an Orientalist at heart. I certainly would have hated to find myself as one of Charles's opponents, and anyway I would never have fitted into all these resounding Victorian battles. But maybe my attitude now is simply due to my having been educated at Winchester, where the rather dim unspoken philosophy of life had been keep yourself to yourself, never show off, 'do your very best and in the end you will be rewarded'. To be fair to Mr Sundaram, he was only really conversant with Charles's achievements at Madras.

'The exercise of power seems to suit me,' Charles told Hannah, and indeed the year 1859 was a peak in his life. He preferred the climate of Madras to London's, he said; he would even like to retire to the village of San Thomé, among the palms at the mouth of the River Adyar, and 'by the tomb of St. Thomas the Apostle'. But when he began to talk about his great popularity, and how the papers did nothing but praise him, Hannah must have felt very uneasy.

As soon as Lord Harris was well out of the way, Charles gave a grand public fête for all races. In the words again of Mr Sundaram, he won the hearts of citizens by inviting the élite of the city to frequent Government House durbars, which hitherto had only been held occasionally and had been confined to a handful of British officials. He took on an Indian aide. And in due course he wrote to Hannah:

> The high-minded insolence of a dominant race is the greatest danger to which a power like ours in India is liable. I shall take immediate and decisive action in any case of personal abuse or ill-treatment of Natives by Europeans, and I shall hold such conduct as an offence and shall punish it as such.

He abolished the exclusion of Indians from public balls given for special celebrations such as the Queen's birthday (rescinded fifteen years later by Lord Hobart). His entertaining was indeed on a fantastic scale. Between March 29 and July 31 he had 1,955 people to breakfast, 836 to tiffin, 2,090 to dinner, 1,793 to At Homes, and 550 children to tea. His letters mention magnificent arrangements of flowers in Government House, 'far exceeding anything in colour or style that London can produce', with creepers entwined round the staircase, and 'delicate nosegays' provided for the ladies. There were alfresco entertainments by night, with coloured lanterns hung from trees, and dances in the moonlight. He threw open the park at Guindy to the 'beauty and fashion' of Madras, and had a band playing in front of the house; gardeners were in attendance to present cut flowers to ladies.

The cost of all this, out of the Privy Purse, was £600 a month. In addition he bought for himself two Arab stallions and had his coat of arms painted on his carriage.

In 1855 the last Nawab of the Carnatic had died, so Charles arranged for the park of Chepauk Palace to be joined to that of Government House, employing eleven hundred men to clear away the undergrowth, so that both could be opened together to the public. He visualized a 'picturesque wilderness laid out according to the most approved principles of landscape gardening', with ornamental lakes like those in St James's Park, and a palmetum with 'all kinds of rare flowering trees, graceful bamboos and creepers along the waterside'. He built an aviary for peacocks and jungle fowl. Forage was bought to fatten the poor spotted deer.

He pulled down the Black Town rampart which had shut off the suburb from the rest of the city; and beyond the Cooum canal he turned 115 acres into the People's Park and Zoo. In due course, once the zoo was established, a very large rhino got loose, causing it was said terror and confusion. There was also a lion, whose tail had been bitten off by a tiger in the next cage; it was thought to be unwise to approach this animal any closer than ten yards, since it had a habit of turning its back and squirting urine at you.

Hannah knew that tiffins and At Homes could only be a fraction of Charles's activities. Not surprisingly she was becoming very concerned about the possibility of his overworking, and by April had decided she would have to come out to India. There was even a chance that Macaulay would join her – 'a new *grand* and most agreeable feature', Charles wrote back. Tom could have the Marine Villa all to himself, he said; from there he would be able to see the Great Bear and the Southern Cross on opposite sides of the heavens, and admire the glorious sheets of white foam thrown up on the Madras shore.

For his youngest daughter Alice Charles collected huge shells on the beach. He described to her how he loved walking with the surf breaking at his feet: 'At this moment as I write before daybreak I hear the clear voice of the Muezzin calling the Mohammedans to prayer. This is even more impressive than our English church bells. I wish I could show you my wilderness of palm and orange trees, and the natural lakes and meandering streams among the perfumed thickets out of which an antelope followed by her fawn occasionally springs.' He was looked upon at Madras as a sort of Capability Brown of gardening, and was having to teach the natives how to use the wheelbarrow and pickaxe. The local navvies, he said, were called Wuddies. They brought their wives with them, and babies would be slung in baskets from branches of trees.

Among the reforms into which he immediately plunged, main

drainage and the improvement of the drinking water supplies were of course priorities. He swept away unnecessary correspondence with the Home Government and Calcutta, and one notices with amusement – remembering those past obsessions – how he immediately set about standardizing native words in English. Great figures of the Madras Presidency establishment such as Sir Henry Davison and Sir Adam Brittlestone had his displeasure made plain to them, for daring to 'malinger' in the hills. His accountant general Mr Prendergast was sacked for making money out of confidential information (purchasing Tanjore Bonds in anticipation of a rise), and a Mr Reade was exposed for forcing a rajah to give him on permanent loan horses, carriages, tents and money. So there was some washing of Lord Harris's dirty clothes to be done, seeing that Mr Prendergast was Lord Harris's relation.

Charles instituted a civil police force, reduced military expenditure, improved barracks and opened an Army school of dentistry. He abolished the scandal of impressment of labour for the Army.

The reform of the judiciary was however one of his main concerns, and within a month of arriving he had formed a commission to consider the amalgamation of the two systems of Courts then existing. He objected strongly to a High Court Bench composed exclusively of Europeans. He was furious when a certain James Smith was acquitted for the murder of an Indian, against overwhelming evidence. He insisted that there must now be an increase in Indian jurors. Characteristically he published his views on the judiciary in the Madras *Athenaeum*, which annoyed the Supreme Council at Calcutta and led Canning to send him an official rebuke. But he regarded the settlement of the inam question as his greatest achievement – the inams being grants of land for religious purposes. Charles converted the inams into freeholds, thus affecting 3,000 small landed properties. Visitors to Government House in future years would be confronted by a large (and badly painted) oil of Sir Charles Trevelyan in proud oratorial attitude and holding a fat volume on which was written 'The Settlement of the Malabar Inam Lands, 1859'.

There were further clashes with Calcutta over the floating of loans, and on a proposed tobacco tax and an increase in the salt tax. Charles had in any case left England with a preconceived contempt for the 'do-nothing administration' of Calcutta and what he considered to be its utter ignorance of finance. Often Hannah, on receiving his letters from Madras, felt obliged to ink out his 'slanders' before passing them round the family. But one of these embarrassing sentences is still decipherable: in which Charles told her that Canning had 'neither knowledge nor ability nor strength of will·for his post'. She became upset by spiteful press reports circulating at home, particularly in the *Economist*, about her husband's lack of due regard for his subordinate position. But Charles firmly denied it all. 'My position at first,' he said, 'no doubt was an embarrassing one both for Lord Canning and myself. I found the Government in a state of torpor – of absolute paralysis for everything except the most ordinary routine – not only for *action*, but the *habit of action*.'

He continued at length about the 'mesmeric' state of Bengal, due he claimed to a total misapprehension of what had been laid down in 1853, when the East India Company's Charter had been renewed.

In June 1859 the Derby–Disraeli administration in England fell, and Palmerston was again Prime Minister, with Wood at the India Office. Charles was delighted. 'With you I have no reserve,' he wrote to Wood. 'Your cordial letter reminded me of the time when we helped to bring Ireland round. May we be equally successful with India! You may rely upon my hearty support, and as you seem to think that the most useful assistance I can give you is by writing to you fully on every branch of Indian affairs, that I will do. To begin with, we are *all right at Madras*. If ever there was a country developing and improving in a wholesome, natural manner, it is the Madras Presidency.' But he groaned at the continued deterioration of the financial system of India. 'I entreat you to protect the south of India against the consequences of the incapacity of those who administer affairs at Calcutta.' And this applied not only to finance. For instance Lord Canning still persisted in an 'obstinate opposition' to his Police Bill.

Wood's reply was just what Charles would have wanted: 'I am well pleased that you have written so fully and unreservedly on all matters. It is the only way to ensure full and cordial co-operation, and I shall write in the same spirit to you.' He agreed that the Government at Calcutta was overloaded with work and that the local governments were thereby 'too much crippled'. But he did add a warning: 'Pray, my good Trevelyan, do not let your zeal for good run ahead of your discretion.'

Nevertheless one is hardly surprised to find Charles soon defending himself: 'You seem to think I am too much inclined to do things off my own bat. I have been accustomed to be snubbed and discouraged all my life that I do not care . . .' There was an inevitable discussion in their letters about education. Charles disagreed with Wood's scheme for compulsory elementary education, and felt that the time had not yet come in India for extending education to females.

He asked Wood to send out a portrait of Queen Victoria to be hung in the 'noble interior of our banqueting hall' – at present for many citizens at Madras there was merely a government 'by abstraction'. He kept urging that the capital of India should be moved from Calcutta to Delhi, with a railway connection to Mussoorie instead of Simla. To this Wood replied that the advantage of Calcutta was surely that it was 'beyond the reach of war and disturbance', and 'as accessible to succour from sea as possible'. Had not events of the Mutiny shown this to be self-evident?

One gets a slight feeling on reading these old letters that Wood was pushing Charles to commit himself to rather too many indiscretions about the Central Government. Then, suddenly, in the middle of another long letter, Wood in an almost sly manner dropped the news that Charles's old opponent and superior, James Wilson, whose son-in-law Walter Bagehot was now editor of the *Economist*, was to be the new Finance Member at Calcutta. At least Charles would no longer be able to complain of inactivity at Calcutta; and he did not like it. Wilson, until then Vice-President of the Board of Trade, had great ability and was a vigorous character. Wood must have known how Charles would react. 'This is a *very serious* thing for me,' Charles wrote to Hannah. 'I had hoped that I had escaped that trial, but I will endeavour to act wisely and rightly.' Once, indeed, at the Treasury Charles had managed to reduce Wilson to tears.

Nevertheless the finances of India, as a result of the Mutiny, were in an alarming state. During 1859–60 expenditure had exceeded income by nine million pounds and seemed likely to increase.

By this time Macaulay's health was weakening further. He would not after all be coming to Madras. But Hannah had decided finally to leave in February, accompanied by her younger daughter Alice. Macaulay had forebodings about Wilson's appointment: Wilson, he told Hannah, would not rest until he had procured Charles's recall, since he knew that Charles was the only man in India who could act as a check on him. Hannah loyally decided not to pass on this comment, in case as she put it her husband's mind would be 'stained or lowered'.

Before arriving at Madras I had had a letter from my friend there, Prem:

South India is as usual hot and humid – water and power shortage, inflation, a by-election in Tamil Nadu, a proposed state election in Andhra, the induction of yet another filmstar (female) into Tamil Nadu politics, and for the rest of the sub-continent there is corruption in Bihar, dacoits in Madya Pradesh, and plenty of exciting things like the priests in Bombay arranging a mass wedding for frogs to appease the Rain God and bring on the monsoons immediately.

He asked if we wanted to stay with the Theosophists, but I declined the idea, much as I had always been intrigued in a mild way by Madame Blavatsky, and fascinated by that dynamic woman Annie Besant. I felt that on our first short stay we would find ourselves too much on a tangent, when I ought to be trying to evoke a different sort of Madras for myself. Somehow Theosophism did not fit in with Charles Trevelyan, any more than it did with William and Charlotte Hickey, or their friends Bob Pott and the lovely Emily Warren, or the even more exotic Lucille Due Bue.

We began, unexpectedly, by rather hating Madras. The telephone system was terrible, with crossed line after crossed line. There was no reply from Prem – it turned out that he had had to go to Hyderabad, and his letter about this never reached us. So we were going to miss all his exciting gossip. And since we had expected the climate to be hot and humid (which it wasn't) we had decided to stay at the Connemara Hotel on account of its swimming-pool. We had also been attracted by the name of the Connemara's bookshop, Giggles. Giggles was impressive, a connoisseur's shop, but we were banned from the swimming-pool because of a buffet lunch party on the verandah overlooking it, for the International Family Planning Congress, many of the planners being nuns.

Our opinion of Madras luckily soon changed. The city seemed reassuringly appreciative of its past British associations, and of the affection once bestowed upon it. Statues, for instance, of Queen Victoria, George V and Sir Thomas Munro (Munrolappa to Madrasis) had been allowed to remain among all the lurid film posters in that film-mad place. Unlike at Calcutta you felt you could probably wander around the back streets with a certain degree of safety.

The hotel was off Mount Road, on either side of which had been the celebrated garden houses of the old days, leading from the Fort to the place where St Thomas the Apostle had traditionally been martyred. But Mount Road, now Anna Salai Road, was a whirl of traffic. Suddenly into the maelstrom there wandered a sweet-faced skeletal cow, and all the traffic stopped for it. We followed closely behind her, and out of gratitude on reaching the other side gave her a biscuit. She led us past a St Pancras-type building to a back area, where to our delight we found a great Palladian mansion, quite derelict but obviously once a garden house. In the front compound were the familiar palms, their heads bowed with age or shame, also a shack made of boards and sacking, outside which two prostitutes were clattering some cooking pans. The prostitutes were evidently old friends of the cow and gave her some food. We found a caretaker who complained that he was only paid two rupees a day. The house was rescuable, and I hope it wasn't just the cow's friends who made me visualize Charlotte and Emily being welcomed here by some Nabob as they descended from their palanquins. Hickey said that his 'dear girl' never spent much time on her toilette, but I fancied Emily in full fashion, like a Downman portrait I knew, with a saucy muslin bow, gold-striped and blue, round a pile of lightly powdered hair, with another bow to match round her upper arm.

Emerging from the shuttered depths of the house we found our cow waiting for another biscuit. 'Come,' she appeared to say, and trotted off. And there before us was something I had longed to find; the Doric columns and Grecian pediment of the old Madras Club, on a truly majestic scale. This was the Ace of Clubs – which in this century had boasted the longest bar in India; the Headquarters of Headquarters.

Now the whole area seemed to belong to 'Express Estates'. I averted my eyes from such buildings as the Goethe Institute and the Yoga Brotherhood of Madras, and tried to conjure up an engraving of the 1840s; phaetons drawn up on a weedless drive, syces in livery holding sleek horses, stovepipe hats and frockcoats descending the grand balustraded steps.

The Madras Club had been founded in 1832, and considered itself to be on an equal footing with any club at St James's in London. By the 1850s its membership had been well over two thousand.

George Otto Trevelyan, who – at least when young – had been more of a wag than his father, had stayed at Madras in 1863 and had written to him about some local characters:

I went up to Holloway [a judge] as he was sitting with his cigar in the passage which joins the dining-room and card-room of the Club, and in three minutes were as thick – as the subordinate officials of the DPW [Department of Public Works]. After an obstreperous and excessively amusing conversation (Mayne was there) of more than an hour, we separated, and Holloway asked me to dinner for the morrow. We had the noisiest party I ever was present at. Good meat and drink, and a perfect roar of talk and laughter. Stokes was there and Norton (a coarse, very coarse, clever, good-natured man), and deaf Powell, and Robinson, who was silent, and looked vulgar, but I dare say takes dacoits very well. I was very much struck by your description of Holloway, 'a coarse Macaulay'. I picked him out of a roomful of 50 diners by it.'

Mayne was the President of the Club, to be followed in 1864 by the 'coarse' Norton.

We wandered among the immense and silent rooms, washed pink or yellow. 'You can lose yourself in the Madras Club,' I had read somewhere, 'and parts are still believed to be unexplored.' On the great front balcony George Otto had stood criticizing one Peachey, whom Mayne also disliked. Peachey was a good underling, George Otto had said. 'Yes,' Mayne had replied, 'but he always tries to be an upperling.' At which the 'whole neighbourhood roared with laughter'.

We saw where punkahs and chandeliers had been. In the 1860s the rooms had been lit by coconut oil lamps. At the back was the expanse of the bedroom quarters, and beyond that was a bridge decorated with green glazed tiles leading to a gazebo, where no doubt you could have glimpsed the sea over the roofs of the quarter known as Triplicane.

Women had been 'rigorously excluded' from the Club, though by the twentieth century there had been a Ladies' Pavilion. Humphrey Trevelyan, reminiscing in 1972, wrote how they had not even been allowed to watch men playing tennis.

Our cow had gone. We continued to the South Beach Road, which crossed the Cooum by the iron Napier bridge. Out there were the Madras Roads, and the famous surf, hissing and foaming, over which passengers from England had been tossed, their heavy trunks and bales of stores soaked in sea-water.

The promenade ran for about seven miles, as far as the San Thomé basilica. Now I thought of a story about Lady Willingdon in 1921. 'Game for anything', the old girl had leapt on somebody's motor scooter and had gone buzzing off down the Marina. According to Sir Richard Tottenham, then the ADC, she 'hadn't the foggiest notion how to stop the thing'. A car chased after her, until the petrol ran out.

Beyond San Thomé were the Theosophists. Richard Tottenham, sent by her ladyship to fetch Lord Willingdon, had found him in an apparently complicated conversation with Mrs Besant about Indian nationalism. As he approached he heard Lord Willingdon say: 'Can you tickle trout?'

I shall avoid any disquisitions on Fort St George, Elihu Yale etc. I was impatient that day to get on to Government House; but those very words 'Government House' baffled all taxi-drivers until I learnt that the place was now called Rajaji Hall. We were staggered by what we saw. I knew it would be vast, but Charles's letters had given no inkling of its real size. The banqueting hall, a pink and white temple, with a ceremonial staircase, was however not absolutely as he had known it: a front verandah with seven arches had been added, and the trophies of arms, commemorating Plassey and Seringapatam, had been replaced with the arms of modern India. All in all Mr John Goldingham's architecture was something for an Englishman to be proud of. The second Lord Clive had celebrated the Peace of Amiens with a ball there in 1802. I was not surprised to discover that the East India Company had grumbled about the cost.

The main house, yellow and white, was less cared for, indeed unoccupied. It was connected with the banqueting hall by a post-Charles Trevelyan rotunda, covered with variously coloured bougainvillaeas. I could easily make out the alterations he had made for Hannah's arrival, ruining the proportions. In late 1859 he also had been attacked about the expense, which had involved adding a new floor to one wing as well as a verandah. Inside he had reduced the height of the drawing-room, and – it seems – redecorated in dark mid-Victorian colours. Two cannons, perhaps the very ones he had placed there, were still outside the portico. The floor of the front hall was black and white marble; there were some beautiful friezes. Ahead of us was the grand double staircase round the banisters of which he had arranged for flowering creepers to be entwined at his At Homes. Halfway up we saw the recess where he had placed a statue of Aphrodite, 'in more decorous habiliments than hitherto'. I looked in vain for the once much-praised Lawrence portrait of Lady Munro – let alone the picture of Charles himself.

That vast 'wilderness' of tamarinds, palms and bamboo, sweeping down to the 'sounding sea', was no more. Instead there were typically municipal flowerbeds of love-lies-bleeding and marigolds – and some 'sleeping trees' as our taxi-driver called them. The view was blocked by a skyscraper, and there were no spotted deer. I looked back, visualizing this time not phaetons but the 'swarms' of butlers and footmen in liveries and turbans that had stood in two rows on the steps waiting to greet the new Governor.

That evening Raúl and I went for a long walk in the dark hoping to find a more economical hotel for when we returned to Madras. We failed. One hotel, which had for some mad reason been recommended to us in England, was a ghastly frowsy place, and whilst we were waiting at the desk someone came down carrying a dead baby that had been found in a room upstairs. At last, getting hungry, we went into a vegetarian restaurant, hoping for some local delicacy, but instead found a sort of unappetizing tavola caldissima that would have played havoc with Raúl's stomach. So we bought more biscuits and some bananas and ate them in our room at the Connemara. Underneath our window the planners were having another banquet around the swimming-pool. Those who were not nuns were dressed in gorgeous saris. There was soft Western music, and reflected lights twinkled on the forbidden water. We were back in a grumpy mood.

Prem in his letters had kept on emphasizing that on our travels in South India we should be 'absolutely ruthless in NOT TRYING TO DO TOO MUCH'. I knew this already of course, but his tempting suggestions for further travels only made things more complicated: Cochin, 'old Jewish quarter very spooky indeed'; Pondicherry, 'large white females lolloping round the shrines'; Madura, 'most famous temple in S. India though fearfully touristy'; Madras, 'fascinating Ruler's Palace – Glasgow built, 1912, pre-fab cast-iron (Walter Mac-Farland & Co, Harrison Foundry), art nouveau glass (we couldn't make it now), and Jesuit horror cathedral'; Coimbatore, 'steer clear, harsh, horrid'. Then there was Hampi, 'an absolute must, stay at the power station not Bellary or Hospet – Hampi was the centre of the Byzantine-type Vijayanagar Kingdom (14–16 cents) covering all S. India.'

'You must go to Hampi', at least three other people whose taste we trusted had said. Cochin, Pondicherry, Madura and other rec-ommendations by Prem, such as Tranquebar and Pulekat were, in spite of their alluring names, all problematical for us, but Hampi was decidedly off on a limb, two hundred and fifty miles north of Mysore. It would mean having to stay at Bangalore first, and Prem had said: 'Don't waste time there unless you have business. Banga-lore is Boomsville for S. India now – science, Jaguar aircraft etc.' What really decided me about going to Hampi was meeting George Michell, the Australian authority described with reason in a Hampi handout as 'the dynamic interpreter of sacred art', and who would be doing archaeological work there at the time.

I did also have a particular reason for seeing Bangalore, as one of the few letters I had received, or kept, from Walter during the Second World War had been written from there, in March 1941. His bat-talion had had the temporary job of guarding the many thousands of Italian prisoners arriving from Ethiopia.

'Oh I don't care for Bangalore,' a girl student from Bombay had said at the Connemara. 'The people are *dead*.' But we were immedi-ately impressed at its airport by the unusual efficiency, regularity and tidiness. We found ourselves liking Bangalore, Boomsville or no.

The policemen wore pointed Victorian helmets. Perhaps after all we were just a couple of old bourgeois fogies, 'dead'.

Above our names in the visitors' book at the hotel we saw in bold confident letters 'Sir Angus Wilson' and 'Anthony Garrett'. But they had just left. 'You have their room, sir,' I was told.

Even the beggars at Bangalore were better dressed. One particularly intelligent little girl, holding the inevitable baby, kept clutching at our arms in a maddening way outside our hotel. We realized that she was also a mimic. Whenever we shook her off, she would make a face and say in Angus's voice: 'Go away', 'Next time', or 'Tomorrow'.

What did alarm us was the news that there were no trains to Hampi-Hospet; the gauges were being changed from narrow to wide, or vice versa. We would have to travel overnight by 'non-luxury bus'.

Prisoners of war and the Bengal Famine

Generally Walter's letters to me from India were full of what he admitted was 'heavy father stuff', about how I must work for a new and fair society after the war, and warning me against rich friends at Winchester or in the Rifle Brigade I was to join in 1942, who might lead me into extravagant habits. I do remember feeling awed by the letters' admonitory tone, even though I see that he was pleased with my school reports. I must have felt the letters were important, otherwise I would not have kept them. At that time I was aged seventeen.

He rightly said that he could not give any 'real' news because it would be censorable. The letter written from Bangalore early in 1941 was quite an exception however.

I should explain first that he had been given, as a Lieutenant-Colonel, the command of a new battalion which he would raise himself when he returned to Lahore in May. This would be the 8/8th Punjab, and he hoped to take it overseas. Meanwhile he was coping with the Italian prisoners of war at camps eight miles outside Bangalore. Conditions were 'pretty chaotic', as nothing had been ready for them, and the camps had to be started at short notice. 'We almost put the wire round the prisoners as they arrived.' There were about 23,000 prisoners all told, and his present battalion had to guard about 3,000 and 6,000 men.

> The men give no trouble, but the officers gave us a good deal, and some tried to escape the very first night. I was going round with my second-in-command, a Major Fitzpatrick, and we found big

343

gaps in the wire where some had broken into the pen next door to them (they were the first to arrive) and had then gone in through several wire fences and empty pens until they came to the sentry cordon on the perimeter where they thought the better of it. We hastily collected a dozen men or so and searched all the empty pens and also sounded the alarm, and the whole camp turned out.

Walter had been armed only with a bayonet. As it happened, the Italians – on seeing the line of sentries – had decided not to venture further and had gone back to their tents. Several officers had escaped from other camps, Walter said. Some had also tried to bribe the sentries and others had thrown bits of wire over the electric cables to fuse the lights.

Water mains kept breaking in the camps. Conditions were very dirty, and it was difficult to keep good sanitation. 'The Indian cooks, sweepers etc, desert in hundreds,' he wrote. 'I am sorry for the wretched prisoners, but of course one can't blame the Indian government for not being ready.'

In due course prisoners were made responsible for their own welfare, and did their own cooking (no doubt to their relief), cleaning and policing; the British and Indian troops only did guard duties. There were workshops for making violins and furniture, and there was an orchestra. Paper money was issued, so that extra rations could be bought, and 'responsible' prisoners, especially priests, were allowed passes. A few prisoners worked as orderlies in staff quarters and in the hospital, but otherwise there was no compulsory work. A friend who was also at Bangalore then has remembered:

At the beginning it was terrible. As an example, outside the wires there was one tap for four to five hundred staff. Inside the wires there were eight taps. Hardly anyone knew what they were doing, it was indescribable. I worked sometimes sixteen–eighteen hours a day, on constant call. Eventually it became a little easier, especially when the prisoners realized they were in the best place possible and were being well fed and clothed.

Shortly after its formation, the 8/8th Punjab was sent to Landikotal in the Khyber Pass, to dig trenches along the Afghan border. Transport was scarce, so journeys up and down the Pass had to be in rickety local buses. Early in the spring of 1942 the battalion was transferred to Bengal. First it camped at Jessore (now in Bangladesh), and later at Jikargacha Ghat.

The battalion was in the Midnapore area when it was hit by a great cyclone. As one of Walter's colleagues has told me: 'We were on Internal Security duties, chasing the subversive Congress wallahs. It was quite an experience.' All I in effect know about the rest of Walter's wartime career in India is that he became very ill with an ulcer through overwork during the subsequent floods and famine in Bengal, and that he later developed a disease which affected his sense of balance. He went into hospital and had to hand over the command of the battalion, which was sent to Arakan.

Burma had been overrun by the Japanese. On August 8 there had been Congress's Quit India resolution, followed by the arrest of Gandhi and others, and then by riots. It was not surprising that Walter had no time for letters to me. The stories of starving people in the streets of Calcutta during the summer of 1943 are as horrific as any about the tribespeople of Central Africa in the 1980s. Nobody knows how many perished in the Bengal Famine, possibly two million. Even so, the famine of 1770 is said to have been worse, a third of the population of Bengal having died then. The British are still blamed by Indians for what happened in 1943, but one has only to read the pronouncements of the Bengal Prime Minister, Mr Fazlul Haq, to realize that this is not entirely just. It was said to be the worst breakdown in civil administration since the Mutiny in 1857. Walter kept a cutting from the Calcutta *Statesman*, dated September 23 1943:

> To blame the bureaucracy alone would be injustice; file-flattened, racially mixed, having little experience of trade, and with undiminished belief in its own wisdom, it is the prisoner of its accumulated defects, containing many fine men who strive whole-heartedly amidst confusion for the people's good. In Indian public life are elements at least as causative of disaster. The unbridled greed of the mercantile classes, the hatreds among politicians, the widespread lack of civic sense. But India not yet being self-governing, disproportionately many of her people inevitably lack the tradition of public service. Under the present system, responsibility for breakdown rests in the last resort upon Authority in Britain and its representatives here. Every British citizen is necessarily shamed and sullied when his Indian fellow-subjects die of starvation.

Walter was bitter about the attitude of Congress, which he considered a betrayal and inconceivable in the face of Hitler's racial policies. This was before the cyclones had destroyed the winter rice crops, and with the loss of Burma, all the rice usually imported from there had gone. I do also remember his saying that Bengali peasants would not or could not eat wheat instead of rice (reminiscent of the starving Irish in 1846 unable to eat maize flour). For a while in 1943 it had also even been back to the doctrine of free trade and laissez faire; and grain was actually being exported when Bengal was on the brink of catastrophe (again one thinks of Ireland).

The effects of the Bengal Famine eventually killed Walter, so I find it a little hard to sympathize with the claim that the British 'did nothing' until Wavell arrived as Viceroy in October 1943. It was typical of Olive that she should have pulled strings at the War Office to get him invalided home. She always had her way, whether dealing with civil servants at Whitehall or organizing farmers' wives in Cornwall! It was typical of her too that she should have arranged for my own embarkation leave to be postponed so that father and son should have a few days together.

It had been four years since I had last seen Walter, on an exceedingly hot September day in 1939 just before the declaration of war. As he had been on the reserve list, he had been summoned to York in anticipation of hostilities, and Olive, John and I had driven up there with him. The hotels in York had been packed with army families, and John and I had had to share a single sweaty bed. Walter had not wanted us to see him off at the station. I had thought, just for a few seconds, that Olive would faint when the train moved out.

But now he was returning. In twelve years he had spent less than three in England. I think we all realized that what should have been an emotional reunion between him and me had somehow failed.

After ten days I was sent to North Africa, and then to Italy. Three more years were to pass before I came home.

I suppose if anyone wants a clear idea of what a British cantonment used to look like in the Twenties and Thirties, then Bangalore must provide a nearly perfect example, even if some of the original roads have been widened and trees cut down. The grandest bungalows are neo-classical, dating from the early nineteenth century, but the majority were built from the 1860s onwards. A great number of these later bungalows, as at Simla, had steeply pitched roofs (mercifully with less corrugated iron) and 'monkey tops' – pointed hoods over windows, decorated with fretwork and with the upper parts screened by wooden slats usually painted green.

Richmond Road, Cressington Crescent, Alexander Street, Lady Curzon's Women's Hospital, the Sapper Lines, St Andrew's Kirk, the Grand Parade-Ground ... I especially wanted to see St Mark's Cathedral, which although completed in 1812 had gone through many rebuildings and troubles. Someone once and rudely compared its architecture to a Bryant and May's matchbox, but that certainly does seem inappropriate now. The tower kept falling down, so instead there is a small disproportionate dome. Prem had told me to look out particularly for a certain memorial in the cathedral: 'To the memory of Lieut. Col. Sir Walter Scott, of Abbotsford, Bart, 15th King's Hussars, who died at sea on the 8th February 1847 aged 46 'years.' But I searched in vain for one to Frank Ryan – Walter for some reason had kept a cutting about him from the *Pioneer*, date-marked 'Bangalore February 25 1928'. Ryan had been a keen shikari, and whilst out near Kumi had fired at a tiger. The beast had appeared to drop dead, so Ryan had walked over and kicked it with his boot. Immediately the tiger had been aroused. It had seized his foot, ripped off the boot and most of the flesh, then had struck him on the thigh, making a big gash and 'reducing his knee to pulp'. Then it had fallen dead. Ryan had been taken to hospital and had died of shock, aged sixty-five.

Macaulay had approved of Bangalore too. In 1834 he too had found it 'clean and orderly'. He thought the bungalows were like very neat almshouses. He had been the guest of the Resident, Colonel – later Sir Mark – Cubbon, to this day commemorated at Bangalore by the park named after him and by a mounted statue. Clearly both men had admired one another. Cubbon had already been thirty years in the East, without returning to England. Nevertheless he was 'perfectly familiar with European literature and politics ... his eager curiosity, his earnest comprehension was delightful.' Cubbon's relationship with Macaulay's brother-in-law twenty-five years later was not so harmonious.

Hampi was almost unreal, so unlike anything else I had so far seen in India. Perhaps we were permanently in a daze there after the ordeal of our bus journey. It was a good thing we had reached our seats early, as there had been much overbooking. Night was the time when the lorries of South India were on the move, and we had traffic jams in what had seemed the remotest countryside. Every time we stopped at a village Raúl or I had to leap out to make sure our suitcases were not being nicked off the bus's roof.

I couldn't resist the chance of staying somewhere that called itself the Power Station Inspection Bungalow – right in the baking heart of India, miles it seemed from anywhere. And it was a great success: such luxury, all for a pittance. Carved elephants adorned the verandahs. We had our own dressing-rooms, and because we were next to the power station there was always hot water. Hampi had been wiped out as a city in 1565. It had once covered twenty-six square kilometres. The power station was in what had been one of the suburban areas, so there were no ruins of consequence nearby. There was a gypsy encampment not far off. Since gypsies are supposed to be descended from Indians carried off to Turkestan by Tamerlane, it was odd now to find *Indian* gypsies. I photographed some women carrying brushwood on their heads; they were furious and cursed me.

The immense churned landscape of boulders at first produced a sense of turmoil, of underlying convulsions. It had an extraordinary desolate beauty. Beyond the crags and ranges – grey, ochre and pink – were the hazy hills of the Deccan. Sugar cane was being burnt. We passed along a goat track, through palm groves and banana plantations, and there below was a fertile valley of deep lush green, through which ran the River Tungabhadra, originally full of crocodiles and where the goddess Pampa had performed her penance in order to obtain the favour of Shiva, who had married her. Thus Hampi, also because of the Ramayana epic, is a holy place, a place of pilgrimages. The huge white gopura tower of the Virupaksha temple, with its complex of sanctuaries and courtyards, the ceremonial street for chariots, the tourist buses arriving, the Pompeian-like houses filled with squatters, and the monkeys are a contrast to the fantastic wealth of remotely placed ruins of palaces, temples and watchtowers, some of them carved out of the rock. Not surprisingly Hampi is on the hippies' trail, especially as one of them told me you could stay in the Virupaksha temple for only three rupees.

Away at last from hippy-land, on the long haunted walk to the Vitthala temple, walking on pavements on which idols were carved, we chanced on a lone Englishwoman, probably aged about seventy-five, shampooing her hair in the river. 'I hope the crocodiles have had their breakfast!' she yelled at us. Another, younger Englishwoman with pale grey eyes was staring entranced at the elaborately carved stone chariot in the temple enclosure. She came visibly down to earth as we stood near her, and explained to us that the chariot had been conceived as a sanctuary for Garuda, the eagle vehicle of the god Vishnu to whom the temple was dedicated.

George Michell was living in a tent near the palace zone, on a plateau that was evidently too far off for most hippies. He was supervising architectural drawings by Indian students. We ate with them and felt ashamed at not wanting to scoop up the rice and gravy with our fingers. George showed us beautiful friezes of musicians, dancers, warriors and animals, and explained the synthesis of Hindu and Muslim architecture in the Zenana and the famous Lotus Mahal or pleasure-pavilion, and how the upper chambers above the elephant stables could have been used by the drummers who accompanied processions of royal elephants.

We thought we were dropping enough hints to the students about cadging a lift back to our Inspection Bungalow. Instead for the fifth time that day we trailed over the red desolation in a cloud of flies as vicious and angry as bees. The curse of the gypsies no doubt.

The bus journey south was far worse than previously. Dust came up through the floor, and even with a handkerchief over my face I still choked.

After two such trips we thought we deserved the Lalitha Mahal Hotel outside Mysore. We arrived exhausted and looking like members of the cast in *Les Misérables*. Grand American ladies descending the double staircase gazed askance at us. Only a suite was available, we were told. On our being appalled by the price, the man said: 'But this is a royal palace.' 'But we are not royal,' said Raúl, the arch bargainer, but also arch cajoler, and then proceeded to discover that we could have a superb room with four-posters and a twenty-foot-high ceiling at under half the price, because there was no air-conditioning.

On the road, 1834

'I travelled the whole four hundred miles on men's shoulders,' Macaulay wrote when at last he reached Ooty, via Bangalore and Mysore. 'I went in one palanquin, my native servant in another.' His train all told consisted of thirty-eight persons, and he mostly went by night because of the heat. All the while his bearers had kept up strange chants which he found had a lulling effect on him. Later on he learnt that these chants were supposed to be extemporaneous eulogies, though interspersed with 'grunting and howling'. Sir John Malcolm, knowing the language, had understood the gist of the song of his own men: 'There is a fat hog – a great fat hog – how heavy he is – hum – shake him – hum – shake him well – hum – shake the fat hog – hum.'

Macaulay had passed through Arcot. Although the landscape there had disappointed him, the memory of it was of use when he came to write one of his most popular essays, on Lord Clive. Speaking again retrospectively, he said of Bangalore that he did not find the mortality there any less than in other parts of India. 'Indeed in this country caution is everything. The care which people take of themselves in unhealthy places and seasons compensates for the superior salubrity of other places and seasons. Everybody at Calcutta leads the life of a valetudinarian, eats, drinks and sleeps by rule, notes all the smallest variations in the state of the body, and would as soon cut his throat as expose himself to the heat of the sun at noon. At Bangalore a man feels himself as healthful and active as in England. He takes liberties. He drinks his two bottles at night, walks two miles at twelve o'clock in the day, has a coup-de-soleil – and is in the church-yard in twenty-four hours.'

He had told Colonel Cubbon at Bangalore that he very much wanted to see Seringapatam, having remembered as a boy staring at a 'daub' of its capture in a shop-window. It was at Seringapatam that his uncle Colin Macaulay had been imprisoned by Hyder Ali and Tipu Sultan for three years, and had afterwards distinguished himself at its final siege. Cubbon had therefore arranged for an officer to take him there before going on to Mysore.

The town, he found, was depopulated, but the fortress was intact. Everything was silent and desolate. The mosque and its white minarets were kept up but Tipu's palace was 'fallen into utter ruin'. 'I saw, however, with no small interest the airholes of the dungeon, in which the English prisoners were confined, and the water-gate leading down to the river where the body of Tippoo was found still warm by the Duke of Wellington, then Colonel Wellesley. The exact spot through which the English fought their way into the fort is still perfectly discernible. But, though only thirty-five years have elapsed since the fall of the city, the palace is in a state of as utter ruin as Tintern Abbey or Melrose Abbey.'

The courts were overgrown with weeds, the great audience hall only retained some very faint traces of its old magnificence and in a few years would be no more. Macaulay also went to the mausoleum which the 'Tiger of Mysore' had raised for his father Hyder Ali. This the British Government had carefully kept up, and he found its rich carvings and the gardens with its cypress walk very beautiful. 'Within are three tombs, all covered with magnificent palls embroidered in gold with verses from the Koran. In the centre lies Hyder, on his right his wife and mother of Tippoo, and Tippoo himself on the left.'

Then Macaulay proceeded to Mysore, observing that the country-side was the most thriving he had yet seen in India.

Uncle Colin

It was General Colin Macaulay who left his nephew the very welcome sum of ten thousand pounds. In a sense Colin remains shadowy, with many unanswered questions concerning his career. There is no doubt however that he was a strong-minded individual, overbearing sometimes though genial and sociable. George Otto seemed a little hazy about his achievements, but maybe he was being discreet. He admitted that Colin was 'generous to a high degree' and gave his brother's children the sort of books and treats which would not otherwise have come their way. Like his nephew Tom he taught himself many languages, 'from Hebrew to Dutch'. The Duke of Wellington was a friend, and 'earnestly desired' him to join him in the Peninsula, but Colin declined, having by then retired. Indeed in due course Colin settled down to a life of travel on the Continent, saying that his carriage was his only freehold. It must be added though that at least one recent Indian historian has bracketed Colin with the 'arch-imperialist Marquess Wellesley', the Iron Duke's brother.

Colin Macaulay was born in 1760 and enlisted in 1777. One can only conjecture about some of his movements. Perhaps he sailed to India in the same ship as the 71st Highland Regiment and the better documented David Baird, with whom his early career was inescapably connected: a year-long voyage. Baird landed at Madras in 1780, a few months before Hyder Ali, furious at a breach of faith by the British, 'like a menacing meteor' sent his cavalry to within nine miles of Madras – the beginning of the Second Mysore War. Baird was under the command of Colonel Baillie, but Ensign Macaulay, who was in the Madras Army, was at Gingee, one of the most famous forts of the Carnatic, which had been held by the French for many years in the 1750s and 60s.

At Perambakam Baillie's two companies were attacked by a much larger force under Hyder's son Tipu, aided by a French contingent. The slaughter of the British was tremendous, and Baillie decided he had no option but to put up a flag of truce and order his men to lay down their arms. Colin was lucky not to have been there, for Tipu, true to his reputation for ruthlessness and cruelty, simply charged in with his cavalry, chopping men down right and left. Only a few were taken prisoner unscathed, and this was thanks to the intervention of the French commander, Lally. Baird was badly wounded several times, but amazingly did not die, even after tigers, attracted by the scent of blood, had come in by night, and elephants in the morning had been sent to trample over the survivors.

Those who were not wounded were despatched, at least temporarily, to Bangalore or Mysore. Baird and others were for some while kept in a tent near Arcot, and in dreadful heat they lay 'languishing in agony, their wounds literally crawling with maggots', before being moved to 'hideous' dungeons at Seringapatam. More wounded turned up, and on January 29 1781 two more officers appeared: Colin Macaulay and Captain Lucas, Baird's great friend. This brought the number of prisoners to twenty-seven. Soon they were also joined by Colonel Baillie, various other officers and some civilians.

The four dungeons were meant to accommodate sixteen prisoners, and were at each corner of a courtyard. The newcomers had to live on the verandahs or in the old cook-room. Everyone slept on mats. The whole prison was demolished after the capture of Seringapatam, so the air-holes that Macaulay's nephew saw must have been connected to some other building where the ordinary soldiers and captured sepoys were kept. In March all the officers were put in heavy irons, chained together in pairs, except for Baird who was still suffering from a leg wound. Baird was eventually put in irons in November. There is a story, often repeated, about the news of his plight being broken to his old mother in Scotland. She merely turned up her eyes and said: 'God help the puir lad that's chained to my Davie!' A sentiment that the Duke of Wellington would have appreciated in later years.

Meanwhile Sir Eyre Coote, the stalwart victor over the French of two decades before, and the captor of Pondicherry, had arrived at Madras and taken the offensive. In spite of his three victories over Hyder, yet more prisoners reached Seringapatam, many having been forcibly converted to the Muslim faith, involving circumcision. As time went on, more circumcisions took place, the youngest and handsomest soldiers usually being chosen.

Reading the diary of one of Colin's companions, Thomson, one is surprised by the number of European boys who were brought in. Some were drummer boys, but others came from ships. On December 11 1782 forty-seven seamen were mentioned as having arrived, sixteen of them not more than twelve or thirteen, all being immediately circumcised.

Colin and his companions were given the chance of joining Hyder's staff, with the bait of as many horses and wives as they liked, but this was disdainfully refused. Soon it was hinted that they too would have to be circumcised.

At my public school in the 1940s to see anybody uncircumcised at the swimming-pool, where we bathed naked, was a matter for curiosity. In the eighteenth century the 'vile' practice of circumcision was regarded, according to Thomson's diary, as something that 'every Christian of the universe abhors'. A captive sergeant, writing to Captain Lucas, told how he and some other soldiers had been dragged out, stripped and shaved all over, then left lying in a state of 'cruel uncertainty'. At last they had been given doses of the drug majum, and a dark-skinned surgeon had come in to do the deed, while some 'caffres', presumably rough workmen, had held them down. The drug had 'wrought differently', some men becoming 'insensible', others not at all. The eventual pain in any case was dreadful. They had remained 'under cure' for a month, and afterwards had been compelled to give drill instruction to Tipu's battalion of captured Carnatic boys. A silver pearl was put in the right ear as a badge of servitude. Sometimes Colin and the rest would see the European boys on a rooftop; the boys would make signals, and in 'floods of tears' remove their turbans.

There was a terrible lack of medicines, particularly tartar emetic. During 1782 some prisoners died, mostly of dysentery and including Captain Lucas, who had kept up his comrades' spirits with 'lively songs and facetious sallies'. At the end of the year Colonel Baillie died. Hopes were raised when news came of Hyder's death, but Tipu proved even more bigoted and vindictive. General Matthews, who was captured that year, was starved and then given poisoned food. There were accounts of several other officers having been poisoned at Mysore. When Tipu had received a reverse at sea, it was rumoured that everyone in the Seringapatam prison would be burnt alive.

Some women prisoners even turned up. Colin tried to sell his shoe buckles, but these were merely confiscated. Thomson wrote how holes had been bored in a wall, through which Tipu's small son could be seen taking an airing on a beautiful Arab horse, 'finely caparisoned', with a man holding an umbrella over him. Two elephants were trained to kneel at the boy's approach and wave fans with their trunks.

In March 1784 a Lieutenant Stringer went mad, and began accusing his brother officers of trying to poison him. As he spoke the native language well, there was a fear that he might betray all sorts of secrets, and there was discussion as to whether he should be smothered during the night. When morning came, Stringer produced a piece of bread out of his pocket which he told an official was poisoned. Baird immediately snatched the bread out of his hand and ate it, so successfully closing the incident.

At last, at the end of that same month, the prisoners were told that peace had been made. After the irons had been knocked off, they were able to swim in the river, 'a most delicious as well as salutary refreshment'. For a long while they could not get used to walking without fetters, which everyone thought very comic.

Colin, David Baird, and one supposes the other ex-captives went home on leave. Colin is mentioned as having been at the siege of

Valenciennes in 1792. He was promoted to Captain in 1796. Baird, as a Colonel, took an active part in the Third Mysore War, in the army of Lord Cornwallis 'of Yorktown', who as Governor-General had taken personal command. He longed to be the first into Seringapatam, but on attempting to wade the river outside the walls his men sank up to their necks and all their ammunition became wet. Nevertheless, on a night of monsoon, Seringapatam at last fell to the British, who had lost a great number of men. Tipu had to surrender half his dominions and hand over two sons as hostages to Cornwallis: a favourite subject for contemporary artists.

Tipu had secretly kept about a hundred British men and boys in his service in 1784, but now only nineteen had survived, the rest having 'perished through ill-usage'. Those nineteen had been trained to sing and dance, but were put to death in case they would be discovered.

The Fourth Mysore War broke out in 1799, the Commander-in-Chief this time being another veteran of the American War, General, later Lord, Harris, grandfather of Charles Trevelyan's predecessor as Governor of Madras. It would seem that throughout the campaign Colin was Harris's private secretary, particularly concerned with 'regulating and managing supplies'. Previously he had been attached in some capacity to Josiah Webbe, who was now the Governor-General's secretary, and Colonel Barry Close, later Resident at Seringapatam. There is also a mention of his having 'exposed illegal money transactions' down at the fort of Peramkottah, near the southernmost point of India.

The future Duke of Wellington, Colonel Arthur Wellesley, brother of the Governor-General, was placed in command of the army of the Nizam of Hyderabad, who was only too glad to march against his old enemy Tipu. Baird, now a Brigadier-General, wrote furious letters about the appointment to Harris, since he considered that it should rightfully have gone to him and not to a mere Colonel. But Baird had earlier proved himself tactless and a trouble-maker in a political matter at Tanjore; he did not get on well with Indians, and besides the Nizam's Prime Minister preferred to deal with the Governor-General's brother.

At any rate Baird did achieve his great wish: he was allowed by Harris to lead the assault on Seringapatam. Within two hours the resistance ended.

The story of the storming of Seringapatam by Baird and the death of Tipu is a favourite among children's histories of Britain's Glorious Empire. The hour chosen was 1 pm, being the hottest time of day when an attack would be least expected. 'Men, are you ready?' cried Baird. 'Yes!' 'Then forward my lads!' The river was two hundred and fifty yards wide, but luckily this time the water was only waist-deep. There was a hundred yards' stretch between the river and the breach in the ramparts, besides other obstacles. Tipu, woken from his siesta, had ridden out of his palace to rally his already fleeing troops, and was wearing a jewelled turban and a rich sword-belt for his sabre. He personally shot down several of Baird's men as they clambered over the ruins. Gradually beaten back, fighting all the way, he was wounded in the side by a musket-ball, and his horse fell under him. He was placed in a palanquin at the Water Gate, and there found by a British soldier who grabbed at the sword-belt. Tipu was still able to slash back, cutting the man's knee; whereupon the soldier shot him at short range through the temples. Whether it was Baird or Wellesley who found the still warm but jewel-less body is a contested point. And here, no doubt, we also have the inspiration for the beginning of Wilkie Collins's novel *The Moonstone*.

The next day, during a thunderstorm, Tipu's corpse was buried by his father's grave. Baird also learnt that Colonel Wellesley had been appointed by Harris as Military Governor of Seringapatam. 'Before the sweat was dry on my brow I was superseded by a junior officer!' There followed another spate of bitter and outraged letters.

If Baird felt in any way betrayed by Colin, as Harris's secretary, it would have been understandable. Colin however had troubles of his own, which were to pursue him for many years ahead, though once again the exact nature of them is obscure.

In 1816 Colin felt compelled to publish two long letters to Harris because of the 'years of obloquy' he had been suffering ever since that time. Supplies for the Army had been running dangerously short before the storming of Tipu's city. It would seem that Colin had denounced a Major Hart for concealing a large amount of rice, and perhaps later for selling grain in a kind of black market manner in the bazaar. There was an inquiry; Hart was suspended but later exonerated. Colin had to retract and was censured by the Board of Control 'in terms which I dare say they have long since regretted'. In 1815 Hart turned up at Colin's lodgings in London, declaring he had been ruined, threatening Colin in 'very coarse language' and trying to provoke a duel. He also insinuated that Colin had deliberately made these false accusations so that he could be removed and Colin would then take over a regiment and the fort at Peramkottah.

Harris left for Madras in July 1799, and Colin, by then a Major, would seem to have been Wellesley's secretary. For a while he was acting as Resident at Mysore, and in September he was Resident to the Rajah of Travancore – and that did involve having a garden-house at Peramkottah. Colin was also Barrack Master of the Southern

District and expressly allowed to continue in this office when he took up the new appointment.

From Cape Cormorin to Coimbatore the whole area was simmering with danger. The Poligars, a 'race of rude warriors', encouraged like Tipu by the false hopes of French aid after Bonaparte had landed in Egypt, had begun a guerrilla campaign, and many were imprisoned in the fort of Peramkottah. Colin was giving a dinner party for twenty people at his garden-house on February 2 1801, when news came that a great number of prisoners had escaped. A new war soon developed, lasting several months. Colin had 3,000 men under his command, and 'shared every danger' with them. He was joined by Colonel Agnew, who had been military secretary to Harris. Their great moment of triumph was the assault on Punjalumcoady, commanded by a character known as the Cat. At last the elusive leader of the rebels, Marudu, with his brother and several others were caught and hanged in chains. Many of the neighbouring rajahs had helped the British, and to some extent the campaign has parallels with the battles of the elusive Tatya Tope during the Mutiny in 1858. If we read with admiration of Colin's gallantry, firmness and amazing endurance, an Indian writer has a different view. Colin again was behaving like an imperialist, and the 'patriotic acts' of Marudu, 'one of the most colourful personalities of the early anti-British resistance movements', will be a 'source of inspiration for the rebels of all time'.

Serious troubles were to pursue Colin at Travancore, which had the reputation of being one of the most scandalously misgoverned of Indian states. The Dewan, roughly equivalent of Prime Minister and by name Velu Tampi, took a violent aversion to Colin because of his strong Christian principles and his attitude about a subsidy, which the Rajah of Travancore was slow in paying. Some traders in Ceylon also objected to Colin blocking their illicit tobacco trade.

At last any 'intimacy' between Velu Tampi and Colin broke down, and it would seem that London had already decided to have Colin recalled. But Velu Tampi was secretly in touch with his disaffected neighbour, the Dewan of Cochin, about a general uprising throughout southern India with the help of some Americans recently arrived from Persia. Not only that but preparations were being made to receive French and Russian soldiers.

A little after midnight on December 29 1808 Colin was woken by a lot of noise outside the house. He arose and saw a great crowd of men there. On opening the lattice several shots were fired, fortunately missing him. Colin was all for rushing out with his sword, but was dissuaded by his clerk. According to his brother Zachary Macaulay, he was chased from room to room. 'He got at last into his bathing room through which he got out into a ditch, where he lay concealed till morning, and where he must have been found had it not been for the accidental arrival at the place about the dawn of day of two Companies of Seapoys who landed, unconscious of what was passing, and rescued him from his perilous situation. He then got on board a frigate.'

This ship was one of several bringing reinforcements to Travancore. Another vessel anchored at the port of Aleppey; thirty-three English soldiers and a surgeon were lured into a trap by officers of the Rajah's Carnatic Brigade, then surrounded and overpowered, tied back to back with stones round their necks and thrown into the sea.

This meant war. Thirty thousand men rallied to Velu Tampi. A fierce battle was fought at Quilon, with many natives killed. The Rajah of Travancore appointed a new Dewan, who at the instigation of Colin Macaulay offered fifty thousand rupees as a reward for the head of Velu Tampi. Meanwhile the Dewan of Cochin gave in. Velu Tampi was caught and hanged, and Colin had his body sent by express bearers to Trivandrum, where it was left hanging on a gibbet. The Governor-General found this exposure repugnant and 'adverse to the common feelings of humanity and to the principles of civilized government', but Colin rather surprisingly defended himself by referring to the 'heads of noblemen on pikes in the most civilized city of the world', meaning revolutionary Paris. According to the aforementioned Indian historian, Velu Tampi's indomitable courage and matchless spirit of patriotism still enthuse the people of Travancore.

All the same Colin's recall was cancelled. He also received compensation for his losses, since his house had been thoroughly looted. Among the items listed as stolen were 302 shirts, 140 waistcoats, 126 sleeves, 170 pairs of nankeen pantaloons, 180 pairs of white cloth pantaloons, 126 pairs of stockings, 60 pairs of silk stockings, 20 flannel shirts, as well as curtains, pillow cases, a chintz bedcover, guns, swords, razors, spurs, silver, glass, liquors and a great deal of money.

There were more rows, notably with a character called the Linguist of Anjengo, whom Colin accused of having been in treasonable correspondence with Velu Tampi. At Rome in 1828, after his retirement, Colin was challenged to a duel by a Scottish doctor. His relationship with Zachary, however, in spite of some strain during the Indian years, remained close.

He was promoted to General. In his travels round Europe he worked on behalf of the Anti-Slavery Commission and the British and Foreign Bible Society. The family admired his cosmopolitan disposition, and at Geneva he was regarded as an 'universal favourite'.

In 1833 under the pseudonym of 'Investigator' he wrote a long criticism of Theodore Hook's life of Baird. By then he was Member of Parliament for Saltash. He died at Clifton in 1836.

Tom Macaulay, with the legacy added to the savings accumulated at Calcutta, felt that he was now richer than 'I ever wish to be as a single man'. As he told his friend Ellis, 'every day renders it more unlikely that I should marry'.

When at last I saw the walls of Seringapatam across the River Cauvery it was almost as if I had reached some city of the imagination evoked in a novel by Italo Calvino. Seringapatam is on an island, and if you realize that all supplies had to be brought up by oxen, the achievement of its capture is all the more amazing.

The British found that living there was too unhealthy, so they moved the capital to Mysore. (And the surroundings of Seringapatam, beautiful as they are, certainly do look malarial.) Eight thousand of Tipu's troops and sixteen European and native soldiers are supposed to have died within two hours on that day of May in 1799. Being essentially, I suppose, a squeamish (or morbid?) person, I found it easier to conjure up the ghastliness of the slaughter than the vanished glory of the palaces and minarets of the old city – or even the mighty Hyder Ali in his enormous scarlet turban, satin tunic embroidered with gold, and yellow boots, as he rode on his white elephant among adoring crowds. As I walked among the battlements near the Water Gate, where Tipu's body had been found, I suddenly felt I was almost retching from the thought of the stink of spilled guts under the hot sun, and of dungeons reeking of dysentery; I couldn't get away quick enough.

The Lalbagh mausoleum, with its perfect little dome, is at the other end of the island. There death, as at the Taj, has quite a different meaning. We had approached a holy spot. We removed our shoes. Tipu lay there next to his parents, and outside were other graves, including that of his ayah. After seeing a place like that, and especially after visiting Tipu's summer palace at the Darya Daulat Bagh, I almost felt ready to forgive his cruelty and treachery. He was a brave soldier – though not as great as Hyder Ali – and he was fighting for his country. But only a sadist could have enjoyed that horrid toy now in the Victoria and Albert museum: the lifesize tiger feasting on the throat of an European civilian (still wearing his hat), to simulated growls and screams. And, of course, if *we* hadn't conquered southern India, the French would have done the job instead.

Tipu's palace, so delicate and light, adorned with arabesques, so purely eighteenth-century, was like an authentic Indian miniature.

All credit therefore to Colonel Arthur Wellesley for choosing to live there – I couldn't somehow associate it with David Baird. Hyder had usurped rule from the then Hindu Rajah in 1761, and in 1786 Tipu had proclaimed himself Padshah, or King. In 1799 Wellesley reinstated the Hindu Wodejar dynasty in the person of a five-year-old child, Krishnaraja III, who in June 1834 received Macaulay (Tom) at his palace.

Macaulay felt that the British should have paid more attention to educating the little Rajah, growing up as he did only interested in fine clothes, toys, betel-nut and dancing girls. There was an inevitable rebellion in 1831, and the civil administration was taken on by the bachelor Colonel Mark Cubbon, living at Bangalore. Cubbon's powers seem to have been quite despotic, and he was accustomed to 'reign' – Macaulay's word – with hardly any control from the Government of India. Not surprisingly the Rajah was full of moans to Macaulay about his loss of power, and implored him to intercede with the Governor-General when he reached Ooty.

Macaulay, received no doubt with garlands and sprinkled water, found His Highness squatting like a tailor before a magnificent throne blazing with gold and covered with embroidered cushions. The whole room, he said, was covered with little knobs, cups and points. 'Whatever was not painted and carved wood was pier glass, and the glass reflected the room backward and forward in such a way as to make it seem a perfect universe of knick knackeries.' The fat Rajah chewed his betel-nut perpetually. 'He keeps such a quantity of it in his cheek that his face looks quite distorted, and the juice of it makes his mouth a very unpleasant object.'

I was reminded of that visit to the Rajah when we were escorted round the sights of Mysore by a kindly, talkative businessman from Cooch Behar whom we had met at the Lalitha Mahal Hotel. After viewing the inescapable sandalwood oil factory, the new St Philomena's RC church, and an orang-utan at the Zoo, we went with him to the Museum and Art Gallery. There, as Macaulay would have said, we could hardly command our countenances. The building outside was indeed marvellous kitsch, with an embarrassing fountain of two waifish children sheltering under an umbrella. Inside we were made to inspect a jumble of English boarding-house crockery, mostly chipped or cracked, some flimsy furniture and collections of worm-eaten prints which had captions such as 'Old Etchings pertaining to Roman culture' – things that most dealers in the Portobello Road would scorn to show. Some of these objects, we thought, could even have belonged to Krishnaraja III, who lived on until 1868.

It is easy of course to be patronizing. In our museums we are quite happy to display cooking pots of battered brass, the odd bead ornament, or some earthenware shard. But we do, I submit, have a better sense of display.

'The Rajah insisted,' Macaulay wrote:

> on shewing me his pictures, and, if he had been master of the Vatican or of the Florentine Gallery, he could not have been vainer of his collection. It consisted of about a dozen coloured prints, exactly like those which are hung around the parlours of country inns in England, 'Going to Cover' – 'In at the Death' – 'The Battle of Waterloo', and so on. After I had expressed proper admiration of his taste and magnificence ... I followed his highness into his closet, a little room which had more of an English look than any I had seen in India. It was crowded with English furniture, carpets, sofas, chairs, glasses, tables, and a dozen clocks of ivory and gilt metal. It was not much unlike the drawing room of a rich, vulgar, Cockney cheesemonger who has taken a villa at Clapton or Walworth.

The collection of portraits, however, delighted me, especially one of Krishnaraja himself, holding a flower, with Mark Cubbon, looking very dapper, in a frock coat with a cockade in his hat. I also liked the musical gallery, and its wallpaper of grapes and animals.

Humphrey

Krishnaraja III at last had his powers restored to him in 1862. He adopted an heir, whose descendants remained at Mysore until December 28 1970 when the President of the Republic of India signed the ordinance 'derecognizing' the princely order throughout the country. Mysore, famous for its spectacular processions and lavish durbars – always much enjoyed by the guests of the various Maharajahs – was also the last princely state to join the new India. And certainly by the late 1930s, as Humphrey Trevelyan, Charles's great-nephew, was to say, Mysore state was all that the tourist expected from the Orient, with its jungles teeming with tigers, bison, elephants, its monuments such as the giant effigy of the bull Nandi on the Chamundi Hill, and – above all – excursions to the marvellous temples of Somnathpur, Belur and Halebid.

Humphrey, newly married, went to Mysore as secretary to the Resident in 1937. In that twilight time of the Raj he thus belonged to the last generation of British administrators, and now found himself having an agreeable and not very onerous time. He lived in the

Bangalore cantonment, and one particularly enjoyable part of the job was to visit Coorg, separately administered by the British, all hill forest and a place famous for its natural beauty.

Not very onerous – so he has said. In point of fact Humphrey was a man whom *The Times* described as having a daemonic energy, always preferring to overwork and do his best. This might well sound an inherited trait, but as *The Times* also said he had a sardonic sense of humour, which certainly was not the case with Great-Uncle Charles. Nor could Charles have been described as a good diplomat. Humphrey was generally reckoned as one of the most brilliant diplomats of his generation. He was ambassador to Egypt at the time of the Suez crisis, and the last High Commissioner in Aden – thus closing a long chapter in Anglo-Indian history, for Aden had been part of the British Indian Empire until 1937 when it became a Crown Colony.

Humphrey went to India first in 1929. It was typical that he should have denigrated himself as having been 'rude, precocious, arrogant and insecure', unwilling to adjust himself to his new surroundings which were at Coimbatore, regarded even then as a dreary town in Tamil country to the south of Mysore. No doubt he did, as he has said, keep himself apart from the pettiness of local British society; he found people of mixed descent easily the most snobbish.

An interlude at the Secretariat at Madras cheered him up after Coimbatore, but he was glad to be given the post of Assistant Collector at Dindigul, a small country town in the plains of the Madura district. Dindigul had been much fought over during the wars against Hyder Ali and Tipu; and it was noted for its tobacco factories and tanneries, and for the great rock from which Hyder flung his British prisoners. In this rather more socially isolated place Humphrey led a life that was typical of so many young district officers. Not only did he act as magistrate and revenue officer, but he was responsible for law and order and the control of the police. It was a tricky time politically, Gandhi's civil disobedience campaign being at its height. Although the troubles in the south were not nearly so alarming for the British as they were in the north, the National Congress party took full advantage of their foreign government's tradition of free speech. Nevertheless one of Humphrey's special friends was the old ex-President of Congress, C. Vijayaraghavachariar; they used to meet at the hill station of Kodaikanal, to most people much more beautiful than Ooty, and go rowing together on the lake, among the wild nutmeg trees, pepper-vines and sago plantations.

Soon Humphrey achieved his real ambition, which was to be transferred to the Indian Political Service, with a range of posts that were more glamorous and exciting. The Political Service, it should now be explained, was divided into two: the Political Department, which dealt with the princely states that were not part of British territory, and the External Affairs Department, which was concerned with the North-West Frontier, agencies in frontier states such as Gilgit, relations with Afghanistan, Nepal and Tibet, and consulates in Central Asia and the Gulf. In the princely states the Residents, who represented the Viceroy, lived in a very grand way indeed. Humphrey started his new life in the 'Political'.

No doubt in his own writings Humphrey said as much about himself as he wanted to be said. He ended his career by being something of an expert on the princely states, and in his typically succinct way he explained them thus:

> There were several hundred States, ranging from Hyderabad, with an area of eighty-three thousand square miles and a population of fourteen and a half million, to tiny village States of a few square miles. Britain was the protecting power by virtue of a network of treaties and engagements. The Rulers were responsible for internal administration of their States, but Britain, as paramount power, reserved the right to depose a Ruler for gross maladministration. In the larger States there was little need for interference in their internal affairs, though by no means all the Rulers of the largest States had been immune from British intervention. In the smallest States the political officer was often required to intervene. When the Ruler was a minor or had been deposed, the political officer took over the administration until the new Ruler was old enough to be put in charge.

The Indian princes loved titles, honours, medals, ceremonials and of course jewels. Precedence was of great importance, and was fixed by the number of gun-salutes, twenty-one downwards, and you were only allowed to be designated 'Highness' if you had eleven or more. The Nizam of Hyderabad was 'His Exalted Highness'. He qualified for twenty-one salutes, as did the Maharajahs of Mysore, Baroda, Gwalior and Kashmir. Needless to say, in the 'jungle' capitals there was a vast amount of jealousy and intrigues, especially when the time came for a childless Ruler to adopt an heir. To people like Humphrey, one of the great advantages of being in the 'Political' was to be on natural terms with Indians.

His first posting was to Indore, where the Maharajah (nineteen guns), looking 'as if he would break in two in a strong wind', had like his father an American wife or two. At Gwalior he was the young Maharajah's guardian till he came of age. This Maharajah was called

George Jivaji Rao Scindia, after King George V, who had been his father's friend. Humphrey's diplomatic gifts were sorely needed when dealing with the Maharani, or Queen Mother, and the palace – designed by a Neapolitan after the 1857 Mutiny – was full of unhappiness. The Maharajah's great moment came at the spring festival of Holi when he could squirt his ministers with coloured water mixed with oil to make it stick – though even grown-up maharajahs had their tricks at Holi, such as the Maharajah of Bharatpur who would turn a hosepipe of coloured water on the subjects from the top of his elephant.

As the time of the Maharajah of Gwalior's investiture approached, so his attitude changed and he eagerly looked forward to wielding power. His relations with his mother therefore became exceedingly strained. She threatened to throw herself off the palace roof – which everyone knew would never happen.

In 1936 Humphrey was in the External Affairs Department at Delhi, among other things watching the progress of the civil war in Sinkiang. He was in charge of arrangements for the reception of the Maharajah of Nepal, when British officials in dress uniform had to walk hand-in-hand with the Nepalese, in their plumed hats ornamented with uncut emeralds. In 1937 he was back in the Political, and in that year married Peggie Bartholomew, daughter of the Chief of General Staff in India.

And so he came to Bangalore, and by association Mysore. Bangalore was administered by the British, a little state within a state and passionately wanted back by the Mysore Government. Humphrey spent many hours concocting a 700-page document setting out terms for an agreement. 'It was my child, and I loved it dearly,' he later said. But he sent it to 'that amorphous and impersonal institution', the Government of India, and it was never heard of again.

Mysore was regarded as the model state, much of this due to the foundations laid by Cubbon and a succession of efficient Brahmin ministers. 'The Maharajah, gentle, dignified and wrapped in religion, had achieved the peace of contemplative life. He was as near to a constitutional monarch as India has ever seen.'

For the great European Durbars the Maharajah sat graciously impassive, on his throne overlooking the courtyard, surrounded by his courtiers, while a dense crowd packed the square below, all mixed up with the State elephants in their best uniforms, the cavalry and infantry in full dress, pikes, lances, pennons and all, the jugglers and jesters performing their tricks. The Resident and his staff in uniform drove up in a carriage and pair and passed before the Maharajah, followed by the European guests.

At night the fantastic and vast Indo-Saracenic façade of the palace was illuminated by hundreds of light bulbs, like Harrods now in winter, as was the Chamundi Hill, where stood Nandi's sacred effigy. There was also a brass band, supervised by a German. At the festival of Dassera on the tenth day there would be a procession of the Mysore Lancers, in their navy blue and white uniforms, with leopard skins on their black horses imported from Australia; and the Maharajah rode behind, stiff as a statue, in his magnificent howdah on an enormous elephant, gently swaying.

The Hall of Public Audience, the Diwan-i-Am, where Humphrey and others would be received, was ostensibly in Southern Indian temple style, with crenellated arches and sturdy cast-iron columns. The 'Glasgow-built' palace, for which my Madrasi friend Prem had prepared me, and which I explored, was a flamboyant and delicious jumble of styles, all in gilt and peacock colours under scores of massive chandeliers hanging from octagonal stained-glass ceilings: art nouveau, Pompeian, baroque, Saracenic.

But when the Viceroy of Humphrey's day, Lord Linlithgow, came to Mysore, he was entertained to a banquet in the turquoise and gold dining-hall of the Lalitha Mahal (where we tourists in shirt sleeves ate our curries) to the music of sitars and drums. One of Humphrey's jobs was to draft His Excellency's speech of thanks.

The Viceroy, when the Dassera was over, expressed a wish to shoot a tiger. It was suggested to him that this might be too 'strenuous', but he insisted – not realizing perhaps that it might involve hours or even days of tracking. So a semi-tame animal was duly rounded up and placed before the Viceroy's gun.

Some consternation was caused when it was learnt that the Viceroy's son had caught the fish that had been specially kept in reserve for the Viceregal rod. Again it was Humphrey's job to smooth things over.

Tigers

I have written of my mother's aversion to animal heads on walls. She also hated skins on floors. Sometimes I felt she was being a little unkind to Walter about this.

Walter was never stationed in tiger country, at least not before the war, but in 1936, as a sort of Parthian shot before retiring from the Army, he went on an expedition to Rajputana and there at last shot

his beast: the macho symbol for any sportsman. He also shot a crocodile. Olive would only allow the tiger's head to be displayed in our
house in Essex, and then in the tiny room where I practised the flute.
This immense snarling face with the pink plaster tongue stared down
at me as I struggled with tunes such as 'On Wings of Song'. 'What a
stupid waste of time,' it seemed to be saying, 'You've no ear for
music.'

The tiger's skin and some pelts of black bears from Gilgit were
relegated to the box-room, and the horned skulls of ibex and markhor were put in the barn where we kept the car – at least *they* were visible. The crocodile was transformed into a blotter. But as soon as
Walter had gone back to India in 1939, all the skins (except that snow
leopard) were transferred to open tea chests and put in that same barn.
By the time Walter returned from the wars they were so filthy and
moth-eaten that they had to be thrown away, and the ibex and markhor heads were thick with pigeon shit. As for the tiger's head, I suppose Olive must have persuaded him to sell it when we moved from
Essex to Cornwall.

Mysore and Bangalore were good tiger-hunting country. Now
tigers are becoming scarce throughout India and can only be shot by
licence and for a good reason. Man-eaters are usually aged or crippled
animals, which find catching humans easier than a buck or deer, and
quite often are tigresses. Humphrey has written of an attempt to
introduce African lions near Gwalior, but they never settled down
and had to be got rid of when it was realized that they had a taste for
old women fetching water from wells.

If one believes Colonel Walter Campbell, writing in 1864, in one
district near Bangalore 350 men and 2,400 head of cattle were killed
within four years. Sometimes tigers would leap on a team of four bullocks pulling a cart and kill them one by one, apparently just for the
fun of it.

Although Campbell thought tigers 'cowardly, treacherous and
bloodthirsty animals', he had plenty of descriptions of enraged and
courageous creatures charging screaming elephants on which their
persecutors were seated. 'Never attack a tiger on foot,' was his
advice, which seems sensible enough. But if you must do so, 'face
him like a Briton.' Novices were advised to perch in trees and let the
beaters take the risk. Campbell boasted of having shot especially
savage tigers from a branch only ten feet up. Apparently tigers don't
often look up when they are wounded, and in any case their bodies
are too heavy to allow them to climb trees.

Now there are people like Arjan Singh at Tiger Haven near the
Nepalese border who would convince us that tigers can really be very

cuddly and affectionate. For myself, after having seen the fangs of Mrs Gandhi's Siberian tigers at Darjeeling, I prefer a Cornish farmyard pussycat.

Campbell also told a tale of a Resident at Mysore – could it *really* have been Cubbon? – who now and then would loose captured tigers and leopards on the racecourse at Bangalore, and then spear them in the company of 'two other gentlemen on horseback'.

I dare say Walter whilst at Bangalore in 1942 was too busy with his Italian prisoners to be able to go after tigers. Humphrey, rather reluctantly, shot a half-grown male when near Gwalior. At that period, in the princely states, the sport was usually reserved for Maharajahs and their guests. One imagines that in that well-known picture of Lord Curzon after a Viceregal shoot all the dead tigers laid out in a row must have been drugged before they were shooed in front of him. Humphrey used to go tiger-hunting with the Maharajah of Mysore and his nephew, the heir; rope nets would be put up by beaters to prevent the tigers from escaping.

Sometimes Humphrey and Peggie would stay with an elderly coffee-planter between Ooty and Mysore. They would always carry a gun in the car in case en route they met an elephant or tiger. The old boy would shoot specimens for the New York Natural History Museum. Humphrey was allocated a bison.

On one occasion they all met at 5 pm in the jungle, and were to spend the night in a leafy hut on poles. As the light faded, the monkeys, peacocks and birds gradually stopped chattering and screeching. Then came more sinister noises: grunts, growls, rustles. Peggie was so terrified that she had to keep on going down to relieve herself – but she was frightened, above all, she said, not so much of tigers as of snakes. Each time she descended she picked up a few leeches. Her bed in the morning was full of blood. The leeches had to be burnt off with cigarettes.

Then at first light, the birds woke up, and the day started. It was like, Humphrey said, early morning in a big city when you hear milk-floats or people going to work in trains. There had been no sign of a tiger that night, even if they had been aware of one lurking nearby. But Humphrey did get his bison – and it had not been drugged either.

And so to Ooty, dear old Ooty. Lovely Ooty, Queen of Hill Stations, Queen of the Nilgiri Hills – the Blue Hills.

We left the Lalitha Mahal in a right rage: not unusual at the start of our Indian journey. Somebody else, at 5.30 am, had pinched our taxi for Mysore.

We reached our mini-bus just in time. It was called 'Matador', which as Raúl pointed out means the one who does the killing at a bullfight. Macaulay (Tom) had written of the vast jungle that lay at the foot of the Nilgiris. He could give no notion, he had said, of the beauty of the scene, and certainly we thought the approach far more spectacular than going up to Simla or even Darjeeling – fumes of buses ahead of us notwithstanding. We saw peacocks and monkeys, but did not meet any wild elephants, which Macaulay had said could have squashed you to the shape of a half-crown. All the way up we were entertained in the bus by piped Hindu music, some of it not unlike the cante jondo of Granada gypsies.

Our friend Prem had urged us to stay at the Ooty Club, which – in spite of being full of 'nouveaux riches from Coimbatore' – was irresistible to us after reading Mollie Panter-Downes's *Ooty Preserved*. Lord William Bentinck had been living in that very same building when Macaulay was at Ooty in 1834.

A scene of pastureland, woods and downs made Ooty, at first sight, seem more like Gulmarg than Simla or Darjeeling. Names of houses such as Sedgemoor or Glyngarth were promising, nostalgically speaking. Charles Trevelyan had suggested that the name Ootacamund should be changed to Victoria, but mercifully he had been overruled. All the same, to discover that in the Tamil language Ootacamund had been transmogrified to Udagamandalam seemed a shame.

Charles had however recommended that the barracks at Jakatalla – which once must have looked like a kind of Escorial in that wild country between Ooty and Coonoor – should be called Wellington. The suggestion this time had been taken up, and as Wellington the barracks still remain.

On arriving at the Club I made a few notes. 'Steak and kidney for lunch! Tiger skins, leopard skins, heads of big game and deer on walls. The famous bar with its frieze of jackal heads (c.f. Panter-Downes) where old Major Stuffy Banting told me he used to pick up his grass widows. Not much evidence of the 1830s, apart from the very fine portico (four Ionic columns). Green painted verandah, red tiles. *Country Life, Harper's* in big lounge. Cosy English armchairs, some of shiny worn leather. Lists of names – Ootacamund Hunt Club, Ladies' Point-to-Point. Collar and tie de rigueur at dinner tonight. Ancient waiter in ear-rings and pugree. Portraits of Queen, Churchill and the great Colonel Robert Jago – famed for the mighty blast from his horn, *c.* 1880, when hunting the pack. Snooker *not* invented here, but at Jubbalpore in 1875; invented on a wet afternoon – never much progress until taken up at Ooty. In the billiard-room faded baize on a handsome table. In our apartment some solid furniture, leather-topped desk, separate child's room and dressing-room. Along the drive, below, a stream choked with arums. Roses, delphiniums, acanthus, agapanthus, morning glory and an unEnglish jacaranda. Eucalyptus groves. Club Secretary lives at Rose Cottage where Macaulay stayed (*not* at Woodcock Hall, as sometimes stated): a disappointing little bungalow – maybe only one window and a medallion original 19th cent.'

Macaulay at Ooty

The day after he had arrived at Ooty, Macaulay wrote his six-thousand-word letter to his sister Margaret that the poor woman was never to read. It was mainly about his journey. During the ascent of the Nilgiris he had met the victorious British force returning from a little war in Coorg. The Rajah of Coorg had been in the custody of Colonel Cubbon at Bangalore, and Macaulay had seen him: 'He had been a horrible tyrant, and had murdered every relation he had, and had filled his dominions with noseless and earless people.' Years later, in London, Macaulay was to meet the Rajah once more, as a guest of Lord Ellesmere and still with 'all the vices of an Oriental despot written on his face'. 'Or was it my imagination?' he added.

At last Ootacamund was before him. It had, he thought, very much the look of an English watering-place, the grass green, the climate cool and pretty little houses scattered about. There was a new Gothic church. The hills formed a sort of a basin and there was a small lake in the middle. 'The largest house is occupied by the Governor-General. It is a spacious and handsome building of stone. To this I was carried, and immediately ushered into his Lordship's presence. I found him sitting by a fire in the carpeted library. He received me with the greatest kindness, frankness, and hospitality, insisted on my being his guest, ordered me breakfast, and entered at once into business.'

'I am in a pretty little cottage,' he later told his friend Thomas Ellis, 'buried in laburnums, or something like them', only two minutes walk from Bentinck's house up the hill. 'While London is a perfect gridiron, here am I at 13° North from the Equator by a blazing wood-fire, with my window closed. My bed is heaped with blankets, and my black servants are coughing round me in all directions.' Within two weeks he had lost his half-caste servant, Peter Prim, who died of an abscess of the liver. The Ooty climate, he said, was not at all good for those suffering from liver complaints, or – presumably – for those prone to diarrhoea. (Even in 1921 Sir Richard Tottenham wrote how 'everyone developed chronic tummy trouble up there, which dropped like magic in the plains'.) Although it was often so cold at Ooty, there was never any snow.

> The tigers prefer the situation to the plains for the same reason which takes so many Europeans to India. They·encounter an uncongenial climate for the sake of what they can get. Ootacamund is the only inhabited spot within many miles. Its flocks and herds tempt the wild beasts to leave warmer, if less plentiful situations which lie below. There is no danger to any European who does not wander imprudently into the wilderness, which I am not likely to do.

Apart from Bentinck and his Chief Secretary Macnaghten – 'a very great man in India I can tell you' – there were few people at Ooty whose minds Macaulay really respected. He met Colonel Morison, who had succeeded Colin Macaulay as Resident at Travancore, and who had preceded Cubbon at Mysore, but did not think he was up to his high reputation in India. There were also plenty of persons 'of inferior note' around. 'I meet every day with riding parties, which have also much the look of flirting parties, consisting of smart English damsels escorted by young officers, and with nurseries of fine, chubby, rosy children' accompanied by their ayahs and bearers.

But down came the monsoon. For the first, and probably last, time in his life Macaulay was bored. He found himself for two whole months 'buried' in an immense mass of cloud and moisture. The rain streamed down in floods. He could scarcely go out of doors for more than two hours a day. Then there were no books at Ooty except those he had brought with him. 'As for my companions, their faces only reflected each other's ennui.'

One great excitement, though, was his discovery of the delights of Samuel Richardson's *Clarissa Harlowe*. His enthusiasm for the novel lasted after his return to England, as Thackeray was to describe:

'Not read Clarissa!' he cried out. 'If you have once read Clarissa, and are infected by it, you can't leave it. When I was in India I passed one hot season in the Hills; and there were the Governor-General, and the Secretary of Government and the Commander-in-Chief, and their wives. I had Clarissa with me, and, as soon as they began to read, the whole station was in a passion of excitement about Miss Harlowe, and her misfortunes, and her scoundrelly Lovelace. The Governor's wife seized the book; the Secretary wanted it; the Chief Justice could not read it for tears.' He acted the whole scene: he paced up and down the Atheneum library.

Hannah in her memoir said that Macnaghten used to talk of reading *Clarissa* as an epoch in his life. Dr Turner, a 'harsh' Scotsman, had made a bad impression on Macaulay at their first meeting, being a 'furious Jacobin, and a very noisy and boisterous professor of [religious] infidelity'; but 'after crying and almost howling over the last volumes', he had been 'too ill to appear at dinner'.

Bored Macaulay may have been, but one is not surprised to learn that he dazzled everybody at the Governor-General's with his talk, his immense and wide knowledge and his delight in argument. Whilst at Ooty he began to write what became the *Lays of Ancient Rome*. It is still the tradition at Ooty that whilst there he began taking notes for his Penal Code, which seems likely enough. Certainly within days of his arrival he had written a Minute on his future role as legal member of Council.

At last Bentinck finally released him. But on the very last evening Macaulay found himself face to face with the uncertainties of Indian justice. His servant, a somewhat unsatisfactory successor to Peter Prim, was accused of having seduced or having attempted to seduce the wife of one of Bentinck's under-cooks. A great crowd of jabbering men surrounded Macaulay's bungalow. So an Indian judge was called, and soon the man was pronounced not guilty. The next morning the servant was due to leave three hours ahead of Macaulay, but just as he was setting out in his palanquin that same mob dashed up and attacked him. They dragged him out, stripped him nearly naked and seemed ready to tear him to pieces. Macaulay, looking from his window, snatched up his sword-stick and ran into the middle of the fray. He too began to be menaced, so the police were called, and in due course the rioters were sent to jail. Macaulay considered the attack to have been a case of 'religious malignity', and a 'gross and intolerable' outrage, considering that the man had been acquitted. In point of fact he later admitted to having had doubts about his servant's innocence, and he also found out that the judge had been bribed – 'even if I had known it, such is the state of Indian morality that there would have been nothing uncommon or disgraceful in the transaction.'

The whole drama was twisted to Macaulay's discredit when his unpopularity reached a peak at Calcutta in 1836. Then it was said by his enemies that it was not the servant but Macaulay who had seduced the woman.

I walked with Raúl to the bijou grey and white Gothic church. The door was locked, even though it was Sunday. Richard Burton, famous later as the explorer, who was on sick leave in the 1840s, had hated it: 'an unpraisable erection'. The surrounding graveyard, which seemed charming to us, he had found so well-stocked as to make him shudder. Indeed as a 'demi-Oriental', with his mind perhaps already on the journey to Mecca that was to make his name, he had found Ooty not much to his taste at all, after the first excitement of cool air, good mutton and English fruits and vegetables.

We made for the Reading Room, the heart of the Ooty legend, now renamed the Nilgiri Library: built in 1867, and looking like it, red and white this time, set off by blue hydrangeas. The man at the entrance distrusted us on sight and refused to let us set a foot inside the sanctum without paying a year's subscription. We did manage to glimpse some massive lecterns and a few mounted animals' heads. My mention of *Ooty Preserved* was not appreciated. Where was Kathleen Myers, the Library's Secretary in the Panter-Downes days?, I asked. 'In there,' the man said, pointing to the cemetery.

The original Law Courts were a Betjemanesque gem, but on descending to the bazaar I began to realize that very little of the atmosphere of Victorian Ooty had been preserved at all. Even the Botanical Gardens were a disappointment, admittedly partly due to a frost and drought; it was hard to approve of the fun-fair atmosphere. It was the wrong time of year for the giant heliotropes. We had been told that several light industries had been set up in the Nilgiris. It was reckoned that the population of Ooty was now around 60,000. So the name of Udagamandalam began to seem all the more appropriate.

In Burton's time there had been a hundred and four 'sanatorians', officers on sick leave, and a total of perhaps five or six hundred Europeans altogether. By then Bentinck's house had already become the Club, and it was there that most bachelors stayed. From his descriptions many of those bachelors had tended to be misanthropes or 'worshippers of Bacchus', hating the occasional ball, also held at the Club. After the fair sex had left for home in their creaking palanquins, there had been 'profoundest satisfaction' among the males. Cigars would then be lit, strong spirits mixed, and a sing-song would develop. There might also be a bit of horse-play in odd corners, after which tables would be hammered, glasses rattled and heels drummed. At last Aurora would arrive, 'elbowing her way' through dense waves of smoke. But these sanatorians were in two groups, which did not at all mix: the 'Mulls', and the 'Ducks'. The mulls were from the Madras Presidency (mulligatawny soup), and the Ducks from the Bombay Presidency (Bombay duck).

Raúl and I found that the temperature certainly did drop alarmingly at night. We could have done with Macaulay's blazing log-fire and a few of his blankets. But in the morning, at the hour of 'bed tea', all was freshness and cleanness outside – the sky translucent, the downs really blue. Even the distant crows sounded like English rooks. Firs and eucalyptuses blotted out most of Bentinck's view. A pathetic little squeak from the bazaar followed by chugging indicated the departure of the toy train, on its corkscrew journey southwards to the dreaded Coimbatore.

Macaulay, Burton, Lady Canning: none of them had been enthusiastic about Ooty. But none of them would have enjoyed the company of the likes of Major Stuffy Banting. Edward Lear had been depressed by the weather, but then he was tired of Indian travel and worrying about the health of Giorgio, his Italian servant. By 1900 it would have been far more difficult to have been bored at Ooty. Isabel Savory in *A Sportswoman in India* wrote how one could gallop with the hounds for miles over sound turf in the bracing air, go out on shooting expeditions or fish for trout in the wildest of country, or picnic in some fresh place every day of the week. There were whole hedges of scarlet geraniums and heliotrope, baskets of mushrooms for only a few annas. In May and June there was a constant round of dinners, gymkhanas, polo, tennis and cricket. You could 'dance to your heart's content', and for men there was that convivial billiard-room at the Club.

We saw what had been Lower Walthamstow, the modest house where Lady Canning had stayed briefly in 1858. We decided against going for a row on the artificially created lake, dating back to the 1820s – the notice board of charges certainly needed some deciphering: 'Rowers are available for rowing capacity including rower's rowing cooly charges extra.' We visited Fernhill, the Maharajah of Mysore's palatial ex-hunting lodge and turned into a hotel. Was I being snobbish to be more intrigued by the framed photographs of the Maharajah's family than the beaky Anglo-Saxon faces of huntsmen and masters of the hunt that adorned the Ooty Club? Probably.

It was a delight to meet Mr and Mrs Kariappa, who invited us to the Dunsandle tea plantation. And there was an extra bonus: Mr

Kariappa had been born in the Andamans, at Port Blair. His father had been a vet for the elephants. The idyllic country through which we drove, perhaps looking like the north of Scotland, had at last shown me what had been the attraction of unspoiled Ooty. Dunsandle had been started about a hundred and twenty years before. After the production and growing of tea had been explained to me, we were given the best meal we had had so far in India: lightly spiced in deference to our European stomachs. We were also shown a settlement of Todas, the aborigines of the Nilgiris and believed by some to be a lost tribe of Israel. Mr Kariappa assured us that the Todas' habit of having baby girls trampled to death by buffaloes had now been ended, but the women still practised polyandry, sometimes being shared by all the brothers in one family.

We also had an introduction to the 'Queen of Coonoor', Mrs Sashala Dass. We wanted to visit Coonoor because of Glen View, the cluster of bungalows where during the Mutiny Lady Canning had stayed, writing her letters to Queen Victoria, sketching and going for rides among the rhododendrons and tree-ferns, worrying about her husband, having disagreements with the local clergyman, listening to her companion Mrs Stuart playing Beethoven. Burton had also stayed there – scorning the Travellers' Bungalow, with its reputation for discomfort; Glen View had then been called Tusculum. He could find no fault, if reluctantly, with the view from Coonoor – 'It has beauty, variety and sublimity to recommend it.' We agreed with him about this, but not with Lear, who thought Coonoor looked like Bournemouth. Lady Canning had been the most lyrical of them all, comparing the distant plain seen from a place still known as Lady Canning's seat to a blue sea with islands, with streaks of pink, blue and yellow 'all melted together, like colours of an opal'. If ever *I* venture to the Nilgiris again, I think I would prefer to stay at Coonoor, even if it means risking the whirligig bus-rides on the terrifying roads. Ten English people only, we learned from Mrs Dass, still lived at Coonoor, and seven at Ooty.

The extraordinarily energetic and enthusiastic Mrs Dass was only able to meet us as light was fading. We were nervous about a bus-ride back to Ooty in the dark – our previous driver having tended to use one hand – but she insisted on rushing us round her impressive garden, terrace upon terrace, decorated with gnomes and including aviaries for cockatoos and canaries, among a great variety of mature trees. Glen View had been turned into the 'United Planters' Association of Southern India'. A certain atmosphere of Victorian times still persisted, but Mrs Dass's house, Brook View, in spite of the gathering twilight, was far more interesting to look at.

373

'Pity we didn't meet earlier. We could have had some of the hard stuff together.'

The Club secretary had arranged for us to meet one of the handful of British residents left at Ooty. A chartered accountant from Chester and three timid teenage girls had, for some unexplained reason, joined us, and listened to the ensuing monologue, in bewildered silence.

For example:

In the old days there used to be a lot of suicides at Ooty. People used to get pissed and maudlin. Colonel Maconachie had been one of the last of the old brigade. He was aged ninety-two when he died. Only four people attended the funeral, including Mrs Maconachie and the Maconachies' dog. The grave-diggers had knocked a lot of dirt into the grave before the coffin went in. Angela Maconachie had remarked: 'I bet old Gordon is saying what a clumsy lot of old buggers these wogs are.'

General Penrose had been an objectionable little sod, two and a half thunder boxes high. When he said that he wanted to be buried at Ooty, the answer had been: 'Well, we've fourteen generals buried here. There's room for one more.'

Kathleen Myers, late Secretary of the Library, had been an outspoken character. When somebody on the Library committee talked of a Gallic novel, she had said: 'More likely a phallic one.' Whereupon several ladies walked out of the room.

Old Dick Stoney had been of Irish origin. He had suffered from varicose ulcers, and one of his legs had to be amputated. So he used to take out a piano stool into the marshes when shooting duck.

There had been someone called Mrs Thatcher living at Ooty. She was a 'forceful general's lady', used to bossing groups of coolies.

It was then suggested that we might listen to some Irish drinking songs on tape, whereupon the accountant from Chester quickly gathered up his brood and departed.

'The harbour at Cochin is choked with jellyfish,' they announced at the Club.

That was one excuse for our deciding to head east not west. But we were sorry to miss Cochin and its Jewish ghetto, sorry not even to have glimpsed the Malabar coast. It was sad also having to abandon the idea of leaving Ooty by train, but we wanted to get on to Tiruchirappalli, known to the British as Trichinopoly and now affectionately as Trichy. A train journey would have meant spending the night at poor despised Coimbatore.

After the usual loss of temper, and anxieties about the non-arrival of a taxi, we boarded a Super De Luxe coach. Super De Luxe meant piped music full blast, At the Personal Choice of Your Conductor. So, to Indianized versions of 'Pollywolly-doodle' and 'Maria' from *West Side Story*, we sped steeply down a great mysterious wooded valley. Scores of monkeys watched us from the roadside, as if they too were stunned by the noise. The hills opposite were wilder and rockier, 'full of elks and leopards' a man warned us, realizing no doubt that I was getting frantic, stuffing my ears with Kleenex and looking for emergency doors. There was also another anxiety: Ooty had not been good for Spanish blood, and Raúl felt feverish.

Dazed, slightly ill and very tired, we reached Trichy at midnight. Which is a cue for my returning to Charles Trevelyan.

On tour: bad news

'I am distressed at the pain your absence will give to Tom,' Charles wrote to Hannah, on learning of her final plans to leave with Alice for India. Before their arrival he had decided on a grand tour of the south of the Presidency, lasting two months. He would go to places such as Madura, Trichinopoly and Tanjore, and to the Nilgiri Hills. Bangalore and Seringapatam would be kept until later, so that Hannah and Alice could come with him. He also wanted to visit Ceylon, where there was trouble about Tamil coolies flooding over to work on coffee plantations and not returning.

But Hannah's imminent departure was worse than mere pain to Macaulay. It was a real agony. 'I dread the next four months,' he told Ellis on October 24 1859, 'more than even the months which follow the separation. This prolonged parting – the slow sipping of vinegar and the gall – is terrible.' In his journal he wrote: 'Even if I should live to see them again what can compensate for the many years taken from a life which must be drawing to a close? I wish I were dead.'

Stories about Charles's 'imprudences' continued to reach London. 'Never was anything more unfounded,' he assured Tom and Hannah. As always, the key to everything that he did was 'perfect freedom of discussion'. 'You must make allowances for positive differences of opinion as well as inevitable disturbances of settled habits consequent upon getting the Government into motion after it has been so long paralysed. I stand well with all classes, Native and European.' But Macaulay was still worried, though Hannah did remind him that Charles had been saying and doing rash things all his life, and had always managed to get out of his scrapes.

In mid-November James Wilson, the new Finance Secretary, called at Madras on his way to Calcutta. One detects that there was a big show of friendliness. The visit was only for six hours; Charles met him on the beach, and they then drove to Guindy, where Wilson was given a good breakfast. Presumably Charles, with his usual dogmatic force, then laid out his views on the over-centralized financial administration at Calcutta and its 'clogged and overburdened' machinery, and the need to make economies in the Army; and no doubt the canny shaggy-browed Scotsman listened to his old adversary with gritted teeth. Wilson suggested to Charles that he might himself like to come to Calcutta to air his views before the Council, but Charles neatly replied that, whilst he was always at the disposal of the public service, his place was in his Presidency and he did not wish · to leave it.

Mrs Wilson and the two daughters had not dared to brave the Carnatic surf, so instead Charles went on board their ship, with a present of fresh fruit. The Wilsons narrowly missed one of the notorious Madras hurricanes. Charles wrote a description for Alice of the approach of the storm, when the flagstaff was struck as a signal for all vessels to leave the Roads. Heavy clouds could be seen on the move. Then after a death-like stillness there were mighty gusts of wind, and the horizon was a deep brassy red. The atmosphere thickened like mist, he said, and the wind began to howl. The surf roared. Down came the rain in 'sheeted masses'. Palm trees were bent over almost to the ground. There was vivid lightning and sometimes the heavens seemed a 'vast reservoir of flame', with thunder like gunpowder explosions overhead. But he found it all 'sublime and grand'. Unfortunately the rains were also the signal for all manner of reptiles and insects to take refuge in the house: scorpions, lizards, cockroaches, snakes small and large.

Inevitably, when the Wilsons reached Calcutta, there were spiteful remarks in the Bengal press about Lord Canning not being present to greet them, but the overworked Viceroy had long before arranged to spend the winter touring the northern provinces. Wilson therefore almost at once had to set out to join him at Delhi. Copies of all his letters to Sir Charles Wood at the India Office were sent to his brilliant and formidable son-in-law Walter Bagehot at the *Economist*: which does make one raise one's eyebrows indeed – though Charles when he had been at the Treasury had done much the same sort of thing with Delane of *The Times*.

Earlier that year Charles had been writing personal letters to Canning trying to cajole him into overriding decisions about Madras in the Supreme Council. The result had been a complete failure. Canning feared that any personal encouragement from him would only be a 'lever for impropriety'. It was noticeable that from November 1859 all such correspondence between them ceased. This may of course have been due to Canning's many preoccupations on his tour. It may also have been due to the advice of Wilson.

The strain of the Mutiny years had affected Canning's health. Since his arrival in India he had always been forced to spend the hot weather in the plains. After his tour he would go to Simla for a rest. In 1858 Lady Canning had had to hasten from Coonoor to be with him after a collapse at Allahabad. People noted a 'Hamlet distraction' about him – just like a predecessor, poor Lord Auckland.

The urgent need to reduce military expenditure was a perpetual theme in the letters between Charles and Wood. Because of this Charles railed against India having to send troops on what he considered to be a lamentable expedition to China – the so-called 'friendly pressure' on that country, which was to result in the destruction of the Summer Palace of the Emperors. He was under the painful impression, he complained to Wood, that he was living in an age of unjust wars, the Afghan War of 1840 having led the dance. 'We are more completely in the wrong than ever,' he said.

Again he hammered away at the 'obsolete and mischievous' system of purchasing commissions in the Army. The result was that 'underaged, undersized, often deficient' youths were being sent out in positions of command. He also deplored the calibre of many of the chaplains arriving in India.

Now it was reported to him by Hannah that the Lord Privy Seal, the Duke of Argyll, had told Macaulay that he was unpopular at Calcutta. Charles absolutely refused to believe that this could be true, though he did admit that the *Friend of India* newspaper had pursued him with unrelenting bitterness ever since his arrival at Madras. Indeed on New Year's Day 1860 he was able to tell Hannah, with a certain complacency, that he felt a great ease of mind, as if he had completed a mission: he had laid the foundations, and all that remained was to carry on with 'what has been so well begun'. However, he added, a little more firmness was still needed to fix in the minds of some Europeans that they were not to keep Indian workers in a state of helotism, which in some districts bordered on slavery. He saw the day very soon when natives would be on his Council at Madras. A new generation of remarkable young Madrasis was growing up.

On Christmas Day Wood himself wrote a long letter to Charles, rejoicing at all his successes.

Charles spent Christmas and the New Year at Guindy, with

Lady Canning going out to sketch.
From *Two Noble Lives* by Augustus Hare, 1893

several 'unhappy bachelors' from Madras as his guests in those 'charming' surroundings. Just as he was setting off on his tour he was irritated by an 'objurgatory, captious, sarcastic, *insolent*' letter from Calcutta, which he immediately sent on to Wood, 'so that you can judge for yourself the fitness of the Bengal Secretaries'. Battle clouds were gathering.

On January 8 Charles wrote to his 'Dearest Wife' from Cuddalore, just south of the French territory of Pondicherry. It was his last letter to her in England. His next would be waiting for her at Suez.

The Pondicherry visit was he said an act of self-denial, as he could neither dance nor speak French. At the end of the tour he wrote a long and thorough report, recommending building new houses, hospitals, sewage works, roads, schools wherever he had travelled in the Presidency, but as by that time he was totally out of favour at Calcutta he must have thought he was writing into the blue. He recommended work to preserve old buildings, Hindu or Christian, and was enthusiastic about the beauties and climate of the Palni Hills, which inspired him to write an uncharacteristically elaborate account of their flora – nettles and cowslips of Brobdingnagian proportions. All in all, he felt the Palni Hills would be ideal for European settlements.

Tanjore had a particular interest for him, because of his support for the Princess, the only legitimate heir of the last Rajah who had died five years before. It was a complicated case, involving the claim that, with the lack of a male heir, Tanjore had now escheated to the British.

The Princess was a minor and in love, but her guardians wanted to prevent what they saw as an unsuitable marriage, which would have affected her own claim and therefore any subsidies to the quantities of ex-wives and dependants of the late Rajah. To the Princess love was evidently more important, and Charles was always ready to be on the attack against those who 'sought to fleece ignorant women'. He had therefore secretly arranged not only a date for the wedding, but had promised a grant towards its expenses, to the tune of 35,000 rupees. He then, to the dismay of some of his Council, had publicly announced what he had done. Later, the Government of India, and especially Wilson, seized upon the episode as proof that Charles was being insincere about his vaunted desire to make economies – his addition of an extra floor to Government House at Madras being also held against him. Wood, however, sanctioned Charles's action without comment, and was in due course sent a description of the wedding ceremonies: how the groom's face was plastered with turmeric which he pretended to resist, how a ring was dropped into a basin of the liquid and bride and groom struggled for its possession, how the Princess was for the first time able to call her husband by his real name. The Princess was not beautiful, Charles said, but had one of the most intellectual foreheads he had ever seen.

Charles's championship of the rights of women also came in for criticism when he asked the Resident at Travancore to recommend to the Rajah that he should abolish certain 'degrading and oppressive' restrictions in the dress of low caste females.

He was at Trichinopoly when he heard by telegraph of the death of Macaulay on December 28, and at Ootacamund when he received all the details. George Otto had that day gone to see his uncle in order to propose himself for dinner, but had left on finding him in a 'languid and drowsy reverie', his head sunk on his chest. Hannah, alarmed, had decided to spend the night at Holly Lodge, but just as she had gone from the drawing-room to make preparations a servant had appeared with an urgent summons. 'As we drove up to the porch of my uncle's house,' George Otto wrote, 'the maids came crying out into the darkness to meet us, and we knew that all was over. We found him in the library seated in his easy chair and dressed as usual.'

In her memoir Hannah was to say:

We had lost the light of our home, the most tender, loving, generous, unselfish, devoted of friends. What he was to me for fifty years how can I tell? What a world of love he poured upon me and mine! The blank, the void he had left – filling, as he did, so entirely both heart and intellect, – no one can understand. For who ever knew such a life as mine, passed as the cherished companion of such a man?

A few weeks later she sailed for India, on a journey she had last taken with her beloved brother.

Charles was still at Ooty when on February 18 Wilson brought forward his Budget to the Legislative Council at Calcutta. It had been calculated that Wilson had to clear a net deficit of more than nine million pounds. The Mutiny had cost India over thirty-eight million pounds, and the loans incurred had meant charges of over two millions a year. This was to be a watershed Budget, a cleansing of the stables. Wilson's main proposals therefore were an income tax, a professional tax, a tobacco tax and an increase in the monopoly price of salt.

Charles was appalled. Any form of direct taxation was an anathema to him, especially income tax. He told Wood that this was a '*pure English Gladstonian* Budget, framed with an utter ignorance or recklessness of its applicability to *Indian* circumstances'. Brooding over this iniquity during the next days he became convinced that the Budget was 'more pregnant with portentous results than any which has occurred within the memory of the present generation'. So he cut short his tour, returned to Madras and telegraphed his alarm to Calcutta – though without using cypher, for which he was curtly reprimanded.

And so began what supporters of Wilson described as the Madras Mutiny. To Bagehot, who had of course been supplied with all the details, it was a 'monstrous act of misjudgement and insubordination on the part of Sir Charles Trevelyan', and he said so in the *Economist*.

This was not to be just another 'scrape'.

The Great Pagoda of Tanjore!

Those eighteenth-century aquatints by Thomas Daniell, William Hodges, Henry Salt, Elijah Trepaud ...

The hot sun of the lush delta of the River Cauvery at once drove away the chills of the Nilgiri Hills. It seemed to me, on reaching Trichinopoly/Tiruchirappalli and Tanjore, that we had come to the romantic heart of the Western penetration of southern India. The first missionaries, German Lutherans, had reached the Coromandel coast, where the Danes had established a trading post at Tranquebar and had then come hither.

The very word Coromandel conjures up spices and pirates, palms and idols, gold and peacocks, martyrs and Nabobs. Also war: a game of war between redcoats and bluecoats, between English and French in a wildly remote part of the world; between the 'subtle and ambitious' Dupleix (Macaulay's words), master of Pondicherry, and the raw twenty-five-year-old Clive, defender of Arcot.

The French besieged Trichy between 1753 and 1754, but the Fort and famous Rock, 253 feet high, were impregnable. There is a horrid story about a night attack, when about four hundred Frenchmen fell into a moat thirty feet deep, their screams alerting the garrison.

The saintly C. F. Schwartz became chaplain to the British forces at Trichy in 1767. Later he went to Tanjore, where in his strange apsed double-domed church you can still see his pulpit. Also in the church there is – unexpectedly – a marble memorial by John Flaxman, showing the dying man with his hand clasped by the young Rajah Sarfoji, who had been his pupil and almost foster-son.

The death of Bishop Heber in his bath is inescapably part of the folklore of Trichy. Looking at the slightly squalid site I admit I found it impossible not to start humming 'From Greenland's icy mountains' and those other wonderful ding-dong lines of his: 'Casting down their golden crowns about the glassy sea'.

Trichy also brought to mind Edward Lear. He had told how he had met at dinner a real pukka sahib called Colonel Baker, who had told him that he had lived at Trichy for six years but had never visited the temples. At that same dinner there had also been a 'coffee or tea-planting cove' who had 'talked principally about dogs'.

Trichy and Tanjore brought me a little closer to appreciating – I won't say understanding – Hinduism. Perhaps laziness has stopped me from getting to grips with Hindu philosophy and rituals, but I did at least try to learn a little about its Four Goals of Life: Dharma, Sacred Law; Artha, Polity; Kama, Pleasure; Moksha, Liberation.

The Kapaleeshwara temple at Madras had been a bewildering initiation. After those neat Buddhist shrines and temples in Sri Lanka it had seemed merely a vulgar, if enjoyable, hustle. The half-naked priests had looked bored and sweaty, in contrast to that elegant and sophisticated Buddhist monk twirling his umbrella at Kandy. 'Hurry up. Keep going. Move along'; this had seemed to be the message of the Madrasi priests, after administering a hasty dab of ash on the forehead. The whole experience had been as much of a spectacle as watching the venom being squeezed out of cobras' throats at the neighbouring zoo.

From the point of view of learning to appreciate Southern Indian temple architecture, our trip was working out the wrong way round. We had been to Hampi and Somnathpur, and were heading eventually for Mahabalipuram. But the cave temples and shore temples of Mahabalipuram belonged to the earliest period: to the Pallava dynasty of the seventh to eighth centuries. The Brihadeshvara temple at Tanjore (the Great Pagoda) belonged to the Cholas of the tenth to eleventh centuries, Somnathpur to the Hoysalas of the twelfth and thirteenth centuries, the Virupaksha temple at Hampi to the Vijanagas of the fourteenth to sixteenth century and the Sri Rangam temple complexes at Trichy to the seventeenth century Nayakkas.

It was true that entering the temple at Hampi through its colossal pyramidal gopura or entrance-gate had been a rather more solemn, though still touristy, affair, memorable chiefly for a double wedding, both couples like children, the brides tied by the wrist to their grooms, all four of them smothered in flowers, and parading slowly round and round the temple to music that sounded awfully like the last trump.

As for Somnathpur, I had thought the sanctuaries to Vishnu and the pillared hall among the most beautiful buildings I had seen in India. But the temple was deconsecrated, and so had lost a certain sense of mystery – which was dispelled altogether when three busloads of schoolchildren descended upon us.

At Tanjore I felt that at last I had reached a sacred spot. Alberto Moravia once compared the Great Pagoda to a ship in port: a rather profane comparison but in its way apt. The extraordinary pyramidal gopura, 216 feet high, with its fantastic richness of sculpture, was surmounted by a dome of solid granite, estimated to weigh eighty tons. There was also an enormous and beautiful black Nandi, always kept glistening with oil, and supposed to have been brought from four hundred miles away. But looking back, I wonder now if what first appealed to my Western eye at Tanjore was the sheer relief of seeing muted colours and of having just a few uncluttered spaces.

It was quite a different experience at the temples of Sri Rangam at Trichy: here there was a feeling of participation, even enjoyment of worship, and entertainment, in a different sense to Kapaleeshwara. First, however, we went to the ghats, and watched pilgrims washing themselves and their clothes in the muddy Cauvery, reduced to a trickle because of the drought. Far out, across the flats, men stood with arms outstretched to dry their clothes, looking like white cormorants. About thirty little girls surrounded us, each with her address written on a cigarette packet. We must write to them *all*, we were told. Where from, we asked? Paris of course: where else!

We entered the Srinanganatha temple, having had to walk barefoot through the wildest mêlée of bicycles, black pigs, ancient cars, vegetable and trinket sellers. After passing through a series of gopuras we met the old boss-eyed temple elephant, her face painted in sky-blue whirls in the manner of Aubrey Beardsley. She accepted coins with her trunk, gave them to her keeper, then patted us on the heads. In the hall of a thousand pillars (actually only 960) we were rather too much pestered by Brahmin priests, but the compensation was seeing the marvellous carvings on the front columns, showing warriors on rearing horses.

In the older temple of Jambuhuswar, amid chanting and almost overpowering fragrances, we met a procession led by another elephant, with an exhausted but obedient old cow in tow. Here, I admit, we were involved unwittingly in a fracas, not knowing that non-Hindus were forbidden to enter the sanctum sanctorum ... We had to escape on to the roof from angry Brahmins.

Finally, it was up the Rock, through yet another temple succeeded by smaller temples in caves, dating back to Pallava times. One of these cave-temples was dedicated to the god Ganesha, and here at least we were allowed to enter.

When I was aged about five I was given a little bronze figure of Ganesha, and I had loved him. I loved him because of his elephant head and pot belly, and because he had four arms. Only in later years did I come to know that Ganesha is the God Who Removes Obstacles, and that you should invoke him when building a house, or starting a dance, beginning a book, or seeking knowledge of any sort. So I am especially glad I presented the Ganesha of the Rock with a bunch of marigolds.

There were 290 steps, all told, painted red and white, up the Rock. In 1849, so we heard, there had been a fearful disaster here, when a crowd of pilgrims had panicked and five hundred people had been killed, tumbling down on top of one another. By the time we reached the summit it was the hottest time of the day, and all we could say was, yes, the view was terrific.

With Charles Trevelyan's efforts on behalf of the Princess of Tanjore in mind, we made for the royal palace. Some members of the family still lived there we heard, but they were very poor.

Charles's successor as Governor of Madras, Sir William Denison, had gone to Tanjore in order to distribute some private property among the late Rajah's heirs. He had been met at the door by six or seven great bearded fellows, who had kissed him on both cheeks, and had then led him to a curtain with holes in it, behind which sat the Rajah's sixteen widows. The senior widow, through an interpreter, then tried to persuade Denison that a fat youth by his side was the lawful heir to the throne. Next he was pounced upon by another man, who said that he was the husband of Charles's Princess. After passing through a number of apartments, Denison found himself before another curtain, since the Princess, who spoke English, was too shy to be seen. She addressed Denison as her father and grandfather, and claimed – quite wrongly – that Sir Charles Trevelyan had promised to put her on her father's throne.

To this I was, of course, obliged to make the same sort of evasive answer that I had given to the other princesses. The husband, however, thinking that I might be influenced by the sight of beauty in distress, just as we were taking our leave, pulled up the curtain, and exhibited the princess in the shape of a young girl gorgeously dressed, arms, neck and legs covered with gold and jewels; and my firm conviction is that he wanted me to salute her on both cheeks. I, however, backed out of too much familiarity, and kissing her little henna-tipped fingers very respectfully, took myself off.

The entrance to the palace was spoiled for us by some of the worst of Indian kitsch, but there was a decayed antique grandeur inside.

One hall was used as a museum, with a collection of very good bronze figures but also including a rather startling statue by Flaxman of Rajah Sarfoji with hands joined as though in prayer and wearing a curious three-cornered hat. Upstairs was the skeleton of a whale, reputedly four hundred years old, recently washed up at Tranquebar.

I read that the funeral of Schwartz had been delayed so that the Rajah could gaze on the missionary's face once more 'ere the coffin was closed'. At the sight of the corpse the Rajah had been 'painfully agitated' and he 'bedewed it with tears', covered it with a cloth of gold, and 'in spite of the defilement, according to Hindu belief, followed it to the grave'. Sarfoji had been an accomplished musician, a linguist, read the daily English newspapers and light literature. 'In the management of his revenue he displayed all the prudence, liberality and exactness of the most sagacious English nobleman.'

Alas, in the end, he 'yielded himself to dissipation', became unfriendly to missionaries, and gave immense sums to the Brahmins.

Those royal personages still living in the palace at the time of my visit could not have been the Princess's descendants, as I discovered when eventually I returned to England and found an affectionate little letter written by her to Charles in about 1880. Her two sons had died in infancy, she told him. Her husband's sister had also died, leaving three daughters whom she had cared for. One daughter was now the Maharani of Baroda, another had married the son of the Jung Bahadur of Nepal. The third 'in all probability will go to some equally high place'. The letter ended: 'Your Excellency stood in the place of my father; but unlike my father you have forgotten me. Still I am grateful to you. My consort the Rajah Sahib, my niece and myself are quite well.' It was signed: 'Your Excellency's dutiful daughter the Princess of Tanjore'.

In a book of a later date I read that she ended her life in 'extreme penury', as a recluse 'without any of the luxuries or even comforts befitting her rank'.

Alas, again, I have to report that Macaulay, writing from Ooty in 1834, said that there was a 'perfect scandal' about 'Schwartz's people at Tanjore'. It had all been to do with the fact that missionaries were refusing to recognize any distinction of caste in the administration of the sacrament.

We left the ramshackle palace with a certain sadness. Parakeets and swifts tore madly overhead. The large flat roof must have been wonderful for wandering about on as evening fell.

The sky was blood red on our return journey to Trichy. We saw silhouettes of palms, and a great bright evening star.

Pondicherry (or Pondy) was so fascinating that it was quite painful to have to leave it, and not just because of the French colonial atmosphere. At a wayside café en route from Trichy, where you eat your curries off banana leaves instead of plates, a German couple told us some lovely gossip about the 'war' going on between the Aurobindo ashram at Pondicherry and the ideal dream-city of Auroville.

I already knew about Aurobindo Ghose, who had fled from the British tyrants before the First World War and had taken refuge at Pondicherry, there to establish a yoga centre. As Sri Aurobindo, with a growing reputation for saintliness, he had been joined in 1920 by a Frenchwoman called Mirra Richard, who had been in Japan. She became known as The Mother, and together they formed the Pondicherry ashram, attracting quantities of pilgrims. Sri Aurobindo died in 1950, The Mother in 1973 aged ninety-seven.

The vision of Auroville, the 'City of Dawn', had been The Mother's. She saw it as an eventual place of 50,000 inhabitants, a city 'belonging to nobody in particular, belonging to humanity' – 'somewhere on earth which no nation could claim', where money would no longer be the 'sovereign lord' and where people would have an 'aspiration for a change of human consciousness'. On February 28 1968 young people representing 124 nations came to the chosen site a few kilometres outside Pondicherry, bringing with them handfuls of soil which they threw into an urn. UNESCO backed the project. It was so typical of the 1960s, so touching. Settlements were created with names such as Promesse, Hope, Discipline, Fraternity and Aspiration. A French architect with the inappropriate name of Roger Anger designed a great futuristic dome, as the Matrimandir or Meditation Hall. Wells were dug, plantations created, crafts begun, and a printing press was set up.

Then The Mother died. The Sri Aurobindo Society based in Pondicherry proper claimed ownership of Auroville. This was vehemently contested by Aurovillians. But the Society had the money. Aurovillians were accused of indulgence in free sex and drugs. The police had to intervene after some violence, and the embassies of the United States and other countries had to provide funds for food for starving Aurovillians. Then in 1980 the Indian Government assumed responsibility for Auroville, and an investigation into the financial affairs of the Society produced some highly questionable facts.

As soon as we arrived in Pondicherry, we realized that the Aurobindo Society was very well organized indeed, running all sorts of institutions, not only cultural and educational. There were Auroboutiques, and Aurotravels, an Aurogarage, Auro Electronics, the Ashram Post Office, the Ashram Press and a Hall of Harmony. But we also heard grumbles in Pondicherry bazaars about all this; there was a feeling of being swamped, and a resentment about not being allowed to participate enough in such money-making ventures.

We were glad to be back by the sea at Pondicherry. Standing near a statue of the great Dupleix, we inhaled the ozone, mixed with shit. Nevertheless Pondicherry was a fairly clean city, and much of this could have been due to the Society. As our Madras friend Prem had warned us, there were plenty of ashramites wandering around in flowing white garments, the men usually shaven-headed and bearded. We visited the graves of Sri Aurobindo and The Mother, strewn with flower petals and surrounded by scores of pots of marigolds, dahlias, gladioli, zinneas and coleus. We were impressed by the Society's library, where there were complaints about lack of funds, and noticed works by such unsaintly writers as Tolkien and Henry Miller.

Of course we hastened to Auroville. The Aurovillians disliked being gawped at by tourists, we were told. Soon the effects of the hiatus caused by the 'war' and the shutting off of funds became only too obvious: we saw, here and there, half-finished buildings, rusting girders and concrete-mixers green from abandon and overtaken by jungle. At a place called Bharat Nivas, or the Pavilion of India, we spotted a mass of parked motorcycles and decided to investigate. Twenty or thirty European children under the age of ten ran squealing like parakeets in and out of the shell of a building that reminded me of a smaller, unfinished version of London's National Theatre. We were joined by an elderly man from Allahabad and his wife; they had driven from Pondicherry on a scooter. Wandering with them into another derelict structure we found a meeting of Aurovillian residents in progress. We sensed crisis, and a girl rushed out of the audience and drove us away. She was an Israeli, the only Israeli in the Auroville community, and gave us a long spiel on ecological infrastructure and how Auroville was built on a non-hierarchical and collective order based on real needs and individual self-discipline. What about the education of all these children, we asked? Oh, they were being allowed to grow and develop integrally without losing contact with their souls; education was not for passing exams and so on, but for enriching existing faculties and bringing forth new ones. The community now consisted of some five hundred people, including a hundred children. There were very few English, some Indians, but rather more French, Germans and Americans. The oldest inhabitant was a Dutch woman of seventy-five.

After the conference the Aurovillians emerged, looking mostly like well-heeled, middle-aged denizens of the French Riviera, certainly not starving. Their faces were grim as they mounted their motorcycles.

Off we drove to the Matrimandir and saw the skeleton of its monster concrete sphere, still with a crane on top. This was to have been the 'living symbol of Auroville's aspiration for the Divine', and it was an interesting building. We saw the grassed-over amphitheatre where the 1968 ceremony had taken place. A banyan tree was said to be sacred; beneath it was a 'Garden of Unity'. It was all so forlorn. Our companions from Allahabad were shocked; they had been thinking of retiring to Auroville, and had saved up for the journey.

We called at the Fraternity settlement, which cooperated with local Tamil villagers in reviving handicrafts such as weaving, chair and candle-making. There was also a printing press. It was a pleasant enough place, surrounded by Indian huts. But again the Aurovillians were sour-faced, in contrast to the high-spirited locals, especially the Tamil children, some of whom were totally naked.

So it was back to Pondy, and hotspots such as Le Nid Amical and the Foyer du Soldat, and Vietnamese restaurants like Chez Aziz. One night we dined at the Hotel de l'Europe, totally French in atmosphere with heavy ancien régime furniture. The food was superb, also ancien régime; potage, sole à la délice, veau à la mode de Dupleix, crème caramelle. M. Le Patron, in a green suit, hovered over us as we were served, appreciating our every spoonful.

We left feeling that we had drifted a long way from the Raj 'ethos'. Getting away by bus was more of a scramble than usual, and as we drove along the coast, through salt-pans and thatched villages, more and more people crammed in. To everybody's astonishment Raúl offered his seat to a woman carrying an apparently newborn baby, which we later realized was a wrinkled and slobbering midget with a twisted foot, wagging its head from side to side. A man told Raúl that the woman was going to beg in Madras and hoped to make a lot of money by exhibiting this creature.

I volunteered to take a small girl on my knee. She fell asleep at once, her head – soaked in coconut oil – on my shoulder. After an hour we became very sweaty.

Then it was Mahabalipuram, and once more the romance of old aquatints, except that a breakwater now prevented the Coromandel surf lashing against the Shore temple. I had expected a tourist trap, but instead it was possible even in solitude to enjoy some of the greatest wonders of southern India.

At Mahabalipuram, by Mary Fedden

And so back to Madras and memories of Charles Trevelyan.

Recall

If Hannah Trevelyan had arrived at Madras a few weeks earlier she might have prevented her husband from taking a rash step that nearly caused his ruin.

Charles in his open telegram to Calcutta demanded that the usual three months' grace should be allowed before 'these tremendous taxes' were put before the Legislative Council. This would allow enough time for public discussion about such a 'leap in the dark': a form of taxation entirely new to India and, to him, quite unsuited to her type of economy, undermining his reforms at Madras and typical of the clumsy way in which Calcutta tried to keep the rest of the sub-continent 'in manacles'. More important, the Secretary of State and Parliament in England would have time to have the whole matter, with all the pros and cons, laid before them.

The rebuke he received from the Government of India for such an indiscretion as sending the telegram in plain English was written confidentially, and affirmed the determination to impose the new taxes on the Government's own responsibility. Not only that, but the period of consultation would be reduced from three months to one.

Charles's excuse for the open telegram was that Wilson in his Budget speech had explicitly said that he wanted 'fullest and frank discussion'. But this cutting down to one month was too much. He had no time to lose. Every moment now seemed precious. He had to act at once. He therefore decided to send to the Madras press not only his own Minute of March 20, objecting to these 'obnoxious' taxes, but similar Minutes written by members of his Council. As he was to say later, he knew such a thing was a desperate remedy and that it might involve him in serious consequences.

His colleagues, apart from his Commander-in-Chief, Sir Patrick Grant, were horrified at their Minutes being published without their knowledge. Other newspapers throughout India took up the dramatic story. Lord Elphinstone, Governor of Bombay, also objected to the taxes. A paper at Lucknow prophesied bloodshed, and ladies there who had endured the Siege were said to be in a panic.

Up till then there had been enthusiasm in Bengal, especially among indigo-planters, not only about the contents of the Budget but the confident and authoritative way in which it had been presented. Canning, up at Simla, was pleased. Copies of the speech were sent to England, and Wilson was to receive letters of congratulations from Prince Albert and even Wood, though these arrived after the bombshell of Charles's 'Madras Mutiny'.

In the weeks previous to his speech Wilson had been writing letters to Wood full of criticisms of 'our friend Trevelyan' and the way he automatically would oppose any new proposal about improving the revenue. With obvious glee he had come upon the ingredients of what seemed a real scandal, and had sent all the lurid details both to Canning and Wood, showing that far from Charles making economies in his military expenditure he had been grossly extravagant. Wood, astounded by such a revelation, involving the sum of £1,500,000, wrote an unusually censorious letter to Charles that reached him soon after the publication of the Minute when he was in a state of boiling fury. The letter survives and is scrawled all over with Charles's pencil, including words such as 'Bosh!'

It is impossible to say whether this so-called exposure was a wilful misrepresentation on the part of Wilson. Charles thought it was. Some erroneous figures had indeed been sent to Calcutta by Charles's military auditor as far back as June 1859 but had immediately been corrected. Wilson had either chosen to ignore the correction or it had not been shown to him. Charles wrote to Wood:

> At this distance from home, both public and private duty require that I should speak out to you. Having acted with Wilson for several years I know every inch of him. He has neither *religion* nor *gentlemanly feelings*, but only what he thinks *worldly wisdom*. In working out a cherished object of ambition he is utterly *unscrupulous*. His great object now, upon which he has staked all his fortunes and by means of which he hopes to attain the English Chancellorship of the Exchequer, is to make it appear that the finances of India were in a hopeless state, and that there was nobody in India able to retrieve them, until he, the great Financial Saviour, appeared. To this end not only my hard earned public reputation but, what is of immeasurably more importance, the future of India is to be sacrificed.

Wilson, for his part, complained of the unbecoming and insulting tone of the Minute, which he said was more appropriate to a hostile newspaper article or a political pamphlet. 'Poor Trevelyan,' he wrote to his son-in-law Bagehot, who naturally rose to his defence in the *Economist*, 'is scarcely accountable for his actions.' He wrote of Charles's impulsive ill-balanced mind, his overweening confidence in himself, his dogged obstinacy, his inordinate vanity, and his lack of judgement and discretion.

'We are standing on a brink of a precipice with our eyes turned to England,' Charles dramatically told Wood. The introduction of income tax alone was a 'plunge worse than the Afghan War'. Civilians at Madras were 'standing aghast' at the very idea. In any case why should the people of Madura and Malabar suffer for the offences of Oude and Rohilkand? Income tax would be a tax on honesty. It was the army not the people who had rebelled in 1857. The remedy now was to reduce the native army and 'put it on a proper footing', as he was doing at Madras.

Wilson had his speech translated into Bengali and sent copies to Madras, but Charles refused to distribute them or have them translated into Tamil or Telugu – his argument being that his thirty million 'subjects' would think therefore that he supported the proposals.

At a time of increasing hot weather Canning, who had been suffering from neuralgic pains, had to hurry down from Simla to Calcutta, in order to vindicate his authority, which he felt was also being undermined by the Mysore affair. He had not yet been disabused of Charles's supposed military extravagances, and therefore wrote angrily to Lord Granville, Liberal leader of the House of Lords: 'The outrageous proceedings of that beggar on horseback Trevelyan have made my presence in Calcutta very necessary . . . He is such a liar as I have never met. Even in his figures where most men mind what they say, he is not to be trusted.' Should Charles be 'ten times in the right' about the Budget, his insubordination could not be excused. He must be recalled.

Many people thought Charles would resign, and Hannah even begged him to do so. But Charles said such a thing would be mean and cowardly, a betrayal of the people of Madras.

Canning was also furious with Charles for plotting with Wood to have the state of Mysore absorbed into the Madras Presidency. Old Cubbon's anomalous position did not at all appeal to Charles's tidy mind. Unfortunately Charles did not appeal to old Cubbon. Krishnaraja III had had no legitimate descendants. All the more reason, Charles considered, for the British to move in.

Now Mrs Wilson fell ill, and it was decided that she and her daughter would have to go to the mountain air of Ooty, which meant their having to stay at Madras on the way. Her maid had died at Calcutta. All this was highly embarrassing, and Charles arranged for the ladies to stay at his Marine Villa, a charming building in the Saracenic style, the one which he had earmarked for Macaulay, and on the site of which the modern University buildings now stand. A guarded but polite exchange of letters between Charles and Wilson now became necessary. On May 25 Charles wrote how gratifying it had been to him and Hannah to be of any use to Mrs Wilson. He had been glad to observe her at the Queen's Birthday Parade, and she looked as if she could safely undertake the journey to the Nilgiri Hills. 'We have arranged that a Medical officer should accompany her to Bangalore. We have frequently had the pleasure of seeing Miss Wilson, and she has delighted us and our guests and instructed our daughter by the exercise of her admirable musical talents.'

He then added: 'On the public differences which have unfortunately arisen between us, I feel as certain that you intended no personal disrespect to me as that I did not mean to be needlessly offensive in my first Minute or in any subsequent paper. I entirely repudiate any intention of giving personal offence, and much regret if I have unintentionally done so.'

He did not receive a reply to this. Mrs Wilson told her husband how Charles would ride past the Villa every morning at sunrise, 4.30 am, and that morning his horse had just missed stepping on the largest cobra ever seen.

Scraps from contemporaries' letters show that the arrival of

Hannah and Alice at least brought a little humour into life at Government House, even at such a dramatic time. We learn of people called FitzRoy setting off for Rangoon, and fearing that they would be wrecked on the Andamans en route. 'One consolation,' Charles's military secretary Robert Glover said to Hannah, 'is that if the natives *do* eat Mrs. FitzRoy she will certainly disagree with them as she does with everybody else at Madras.' Then there was the 'Angel of Death', Mrs Sydney Smith, always in and out of her black velvet and jet; she was currently hovering over a Mr Serle, who was in a dangerous state, she felt, on account of no less than nine carbuncles.

It was not known until early June in India that the British Government had decided that it had no option but to recall Charles. The decision had already been published in the London newspapers. *The Times* said it was like a Secretary of State who had been overruled by the Cabinet sitting down to write a letter to the paper quoting secret documents.

On May 10 Wood wrote to Charles that he had not for many years passed such unhappy days as those following the receipt of his letters about the Budget.

There had been a Cabinet meeting, he said, and the unanimous decision had been to recall him. The Minute had been an appeal to the people of India against the course determined by the Government of India. 'I do not see how the Government of any country could be carried out if such conduct is permitted.'

> I cannot tell you how unhappy it has made me . . . I was happy in the thought that we were again working together, as of old, and that in any administration I should have the advantage of your knowledge and advice on Indian affairs. I thought that you had a career of singular usefulness before you, in which you might do as much credit to yourself as to your country, and I am grieved more than I can express to you that these prospects should be cut short, and that the blow, in the execution of my public duty, should come from me. My dear Trevelyan, you do not know how miserable I have been for the last three days. I can never forget the unwearying zeal with which you worked with me in the trying times of the Irish distress, or our cosy and constant friendly intercourse for the last fourteen years . . .
>
> [Sir Henry] Ward [Governor of Ceylon] will be your successor and I hope you will give every information and assistance in your power . . . God bless you, dear Trevelyan, and believe me never more than now your sincere friend.

Charles had asked that all the papers should be placed before Parliament, as a duty to himself, his family and the 'truth of history', and three days later Wood wrote to say that he had done this. Wood meanwhile had received several other letters from Charles, but it was 'too painful' for him to have to answer them.

On June 8 Charles wrote a dignified reply, regretting that he should have been a cause of embarrassment and distress.

> My duty at present is perfect *obedience*. We should, *if we possibly can*, go by the next steamer, but it is doubtful whether we can get passages, and it is still more doubtful whether our daughter, who is suffering from a bad attack of jaundice, can make the voyage without serious risk at the hottest season of the year. While I remain here I shall see only my private friends among Europeans, *and I shall receive no visits from Natives at all*. Without this I could have no certainty of not being misinterpreted.

He left Madras, he said, with the greatest regret, feeling that he had been more usefully employed there than ever before. Hannah also wrote a letter to Wood, possibly without Charles's knowledge and quoting that original warning by Macaulay that Wilson would not rest in India until he had got rid of Charles. She was proud of the achievements Charles had made within only fifteen months.

> When I arrived here, the mischief was done, but my husband related the whole to me – Mr Wilson's begging him to come to Calcutta to consult with him, give his opinion on the financial plans, the entreating [Wilson's] of him to write more frankly and fully all his suggestions and criticisms. Then when the leading on process began to work, and he [Charles] asked for time to comply, the snubbing silencing process was begun; and knowing well who he had to deal with, and that where good was to be done or harm averted, my husband would never think of his own interests, Mr Wilson knew his work was done, his object gained, and he had nothing to do, but to affect alarm and indignation. It was exactly my brother's prophecy put into practice. I never doubted what the end would be, and I am only thankful that he has a good story to tell ... The bullying insulting tone, the determination to throw every obstacle in the way of improvement, which prevails now at Calcutta, make this a very difficult post for any honest man set on doing his duty.

Mrs Wilson, who by this time had reached Bangalore, told how Sir

Mark Cubbon, against doctor's orders, had drunk a glass of champagne on hearing of the news of Charles's recall. The Rajah of Mysore had fired off forty rounds.

But the distress of almost the entire community of Madras at Charles's departure was genuine and lasting. He received a number of addresses of appreciation: signed by five hundred of the European community, a thousand of the Catholic community, fifteen hundred of the East Indian community, two thousand of the Muslim community, and seven thousand five hundred of the Hindu community. Other addresses reached him from the Bombay Association and even the British India Association of Calcutta. The address signed by eight thousand five hundred of the 'general public' of Madras was typical. 'Our belief is that your departure is a public calamity,' it began.

The publication of the Minute had indeed been reckless and was typical of a side of Charles's personality that, related to his undoubtedly overbearing and insensitive behaviour in other contexts, has irritated, some modern writers grappling with the task of encapsulating the whole of his public life. To counter this let me quote from Mr B. G. Baliqa of the Madras Records Office, writing some ninety years after the recall:

> No wonder that all classes of people admired him and regarded him as their champion. They loved him and looked upon him as their friend. And this was because he had certain unique qualities which could not fail to endear him to all those who came to know him. His simple and unassuming manners, his frank and free intercourse with the high and the low, his kind and courteous treatment towards all, irrespective of caste, creed or colour ... There never was a more popular Governor since the days of Bentinck or Munro.

Charles replied to each of the addresses. This was his reply to the Hindu community:

> Qualify yourselves for representative institutions and they will be sure to come in good time. You are united, under the common protection of the British Crown, with a free people, who have never grudged to others a participation in the political advantages which they themselves enjoy. The delay is on your part. Cultivate the literature of England, which is instinct with the spirit of self-government. Learn by our example how to work representative institutions, for this is by no means an easy task, and several

famous nations have failed in the attempt. Above all things, strive to attain a high moral standard. Public morality, without which national self-government is impossible, is only the aggregate of each man's national character. Truth, justice, scrupulous fidelity to engagements, habitual preference of public to private interests, are the qualities which elevate a nation.

It was not a pleasant journey back for the Trevelyans, in the cramped, hot and cockroach-ridden steamer. The temperature on leaving Madras was 107° in the shade, and Alice was still as yellow as a guinea.

On reaching London Charles was able to read in *Hansard* the debate resulting from his recall, which had been announced to the Commons by Wood with tears in his eyes. Every speaker regretted the necessity for the recall, but felt it just. John Bright and Lord Palmerston both spoke of Charles's merits, his ability and integrity. 'On the other hand,' Palmerston said, 'I am quite sure that no one will impute to Sir Charles Trevelyan anything but an exaggerated belief in his own opinions, and a recklessness of consequences which I feel was a great fault occupying so responsible a situation, but a fault which, nevertheless, does not detract in any degree from those eminent qualities which everyone who knows Sir Charles Trevelyan must acknowledge he possesses.' With which, in her heart, even Hannah could not disagree. Canning, who by now had retracted over the 'dishonesty', had decided that 'Vanity is at the bottom of his doings', which made Charles a 'pestilent man to hold authority' – and one must sympathize with him.

Meanwhile at Calcutta even Sir Barnes Peacock, the Chief Justice, was protesting against the taxes, and Wilson's proposals had to be modified. The strain was beginning to affect Wilson, and he spent far too long at his desk each day. The Cannings liked him, but people at Calcutta were beginning to find him overbearing.

Wilson was persuaded to take a rest at Barrackpore. For some while he had been complaining of liver trouble, but on August 2 he was struck down with severe dysentery. With terrifying Calcutta suddenness, he died on the night of the 11th and almost his last faint words were: 'Take care of my Income Tax.'

Very shortly afterwards Sir Henry Ward, the new Governor of Madras, also died, of cholera.

On my return to Madras I gave a talk on Charles Trevelyan at the British Council. Mr Sundaram, whom I had met originally on my first arrival, was also there. At the end of the evening he stood up and quoted from Curzon's resounding farewell speech at the end of his Viceroyalty, a speech which Mr Sundaram felt also summed up Charles's ideals of fifty years before. And he was probably right:

> To fight for the right, to abhor the imperfect, the unjust, or the mean, to swerve neither to the right hand nor to the left, to care nothing for flattery or applause or odium or abuse . . . All the rest is either tinsel or sham. I have worked for no other aim. Let India be my judge.

The Fifth Journey
I

FOR MY LAST and fifth journey in 1984 I would head for a few of those
Mutiny sites, including Cawnpore/Kanpur. I also wanted to go to
Chhatarpur, where Charles Trevelyan's grandson, R. C. Trevelyan
the poet, had travelled with E. M. Forster and Lowes Dickinson in
1912–13 – Chhatarpur also being 'Chhokrapur' in J. R. Ackerley's
semi-novel *Hindoo Holiday*.

We felt it was about time we visited a few of the tourist shrines in
Rajasthan. Then there was Goa. We hadn't been to Goa yet. There
the only slight link with my past had been a Goan cook (you mustn't
say Goanese now, apparently it's too like Portuguese), a rapscallion
with a squint who stole my father's First War medals when we were
at Nowshera. But above all, apart from seeing the churches and the
relics of St Francis Xavier, we longed for some days of beach life –
remembering those wonderful bathes the year before in the south of
Sri Lanka and at Mahabalipuram, where the beaches seem to go on
for eternity.

We arranged to meet Diana Petre and Francis King at certain points
on the journey. Diana was J. R. Ackerley's half-sister, as she revealed
to the world in *The Secret Orchard of Roger Ackerley*. Francis was Ackerley's literary executor as well as an authority on Forster. Our final
rendezvous would be at Khajaraho, only a few miles from Chhatarpur
and giving us a chance of seeing the erotic temple sculptures which
are always considered part of the essential tourist milk-run.

First, Raúl and I would have to fly to Bombay. Ever since childhood days I had a dread of Bombay. My memories were all of arriving half-asleep at night after a hideous, rattling, grimy, hooting train
journey (I find it incredible that people should think those prewar
train journeys in India were so glamorous), followed by dripping
heat, dazzle on the pavements, and noise, frightful noise. My parents
stayed at the 'legendary' Taj Hotel, but Nanny and I went to a
boarding-house run by a nice motherly Eurasian lady called
Marguerite, who had a very grand English accent.

My prejudice against Bombay had not been altered much in modern times by some unhappy sweltering hours I had spent at its airport in 1979, when we arrived shortly after the main building had been burnt down.

Bombay for me as a child also used to be equated with the horror of the Towers of Silence, where Parsees put their dead to be eaten by vultures. I was to learn that there is a crisis now in Bombay about these vultures, as they don't like the surrounding high-rise buildings. So the colony is dwindling.

Not having booked at a luxury hotel, and having as a result to some degree to reorganize our accommodation, we in due course ventured into the Bombay dusk, stumbling over an object like a dead cat near our hotel entrance. But we were soon attracted by the sound of rockets, and this led us to the sea-front.

A great crowd was watching a wedding procession, moving it seemed at about two yards a minute. The excitement and the gaiety of the colour cheered us up immediately.

Acetylene candelabra, with tap, by Mary Fedden

Fireworks and squibs were being exploded in front of three elephants in diminishing sizes, each with fantastically designed canopies in turquoise, canary and emerald green. Behind was a group of about thirty men, all in gold and red, banging drums and blowing trumpets

in an endlessly repetitive tune; some of the men carried acetylene candelabra on their heads. Then came the pathetically weary but obviously grand bride and her bespectacled groom in a glistening gold
tunic, sitting with some junior members of the family, all of them in
one chariot garlanded with flowers and drawn by four white ponies,
also garlanded and in gold tunics. Finally there were eight more men,
again in gold and red, carrying a palanquin in which sat someone
who was evidently the most important person of all, the bride's
mother.

A European kept dashing up and down, master of ceremonies. The
front elephant carried a man in a dark business suit – the groom's
brother? A tiresome blonde, Scandinavian we guessed, but admittedly pretty, wearing pink trousers, selfishly ruined the atmosphere
by climbing on the smallest elephant behind the mahout.

Anyway the calves of her legs were too fat.

At last we walked on to the Taj Hotel, which was as splendiferous
as it was always cracked up to be, with marble floors, a swimming
pool, a jacaranda and that great feature, its tremendous winding staircase going up and up, overlooked by balconies on each floor. To our
surprise we were handed a card which bore the legend: 'Anita weds
Kumar shifted to Crystal Room'. That seemed to indicate that our
bride and groom had at last reached the hotel.

Being so casually dressed we were flattered to be mistaken for
guests. Nevertheless we ascended to the Crystal Room, chiefly in
order to watch the gorgeous saris and jewellery filing up the stairs. It
was like a display of models. Such riches! Obviously this was a major
Bombay social event, quite different to the 'folklore' of the procession. Nobody except photographers could get anywhere near Anita
and Kumar on their dais. We had the impression that very few guests
stayed more than ten minutes. So after guiltily eating some proffered
sugar cakes, we slunk away.

And now, by rights, I should be making some apt comparison
with the beggars outside the hotel entrance... But I think I shall
leave that to the imagination.

Having planned to hurry on the next morning to Goa, I never had a
chance to revise my opinion of Bombay. I did wish though that I
could have gone to hear Salman Rushdie, whose novels I admired
greatly, and whose attacks on the current British nostalgia for the Raj
were being reported in local newspapers. He had found, so I read, the
TV serials of *The Far Pavilions* and *The Jewel in the Crown* respectively
a 'black and white minstrel show' and 'grotesquely over-praised'. If
and when these spectaculars reached India, he advised his listeners to
switch off their sets at once. The film *Gandhi* he called a 'big budget

fantasy'. He also attacked a recent 'alleged documentary' on British TV about Subhas Chandra Bose, which – he said – was billed as 'impartial' even though it described 'India's second most revered Independence leader as a "clown"'.

I was not a fan of *The Far Pavilions* on TV either, but I didn't find the characters in *The Jewel in the Crown* 'pure lead', whether acted by Europeans or Indians. Reading Salman Rushdie's comments made me quite ashamed to admit to myself that I had loved nearly all *The Jewel in the Crown*, even though I knew that some of my parents' generation were, with some justification, horrified by the depiction of the police officer Merrick, which they considered damaging to the reputation of British officers in the Indian Police. Personally, as a now elderly product of the Raj, who as a child had little sense of colonial guilt, I don't think this new nostalgia is really a hankering after an imperial past – 'the phantom twitchings of an amputated limb', as Rushdie so neatly described it; most of us are just amazed that it ever happened, and that is probably all. Most of us are also relieved to be rid of the Empire, and to hand over our unpopularity, anywhere in the world, to the Americans.

Like so many other critics in India Rushdie complained that too many important aspects of Gandhi's life had been left out of Richard Attenborough's film, too many dramatic possibilities had been avoided or sacrificed in the interests of deification. In this way, he said, history was being deliberately distorted.

The Amritsar Jallianwala Bagh incident in the film made him cry. But I think it shocked many British viewers profoundly, and probably made some of them cry too. It certainly upset me so much that I went to see the film a second time, and I looked for books which would tell me about what *really* happened before and afterwards. By an extraordinary piece of luck I came across some original documents about the Jallianwala Bagh massacre, from which I shall be quoting later.

Any drawbacks to the film *Gandhi* seemed to me obvious: they were due to the attempts to please too many different sorts of people, including the American market. Its message, a message, lay in Gandhi's doctrine of non-violence. But this does not mean that we are all today being urged to lie down and let ourselves be methodically bashed by the lathis of policemen. It is true that Attenborough, if he had wished, could have contrasted Gandhi with Subhas Chandra Bose and the Indian National Army; it would have been a subtle point. The snag is that, whatever Bose's standing in India as a 'founding father', his alliance with the Nazis would have made it a little difficult to attract sympathy elsewhere, especially among the backers.

Gandhi was one of the greatest men of the twentieth century, and the film is admirable in the way it brings out his nobility of character, his humour, his courage. But he was not a single-minded leader. There were plenty of complications in his character. One of the most misleading aspects of the film was the way that the British personalities, some of whom had given their lives to the country, were shown as mere bloody-fool caricatures.

In a real tyranny Gandhi would have been obliterated early in his career. And take this remark by the 'Auk' – Field-Marshal Sir Claude Auchinleck, Commander-in-Chief in 1946 – after the trial of some INA men had taken place: 'It is a poor specimen of humanity who doesn't want freedom for his country.' This is a sentiment, believe it or not, on which the British way of life has been built.

The whole truth about Gandhi was too complicated for one film, but important points were made and one gets a vivid impression of India, more perhaps than in any film not made by Indians themselves. Attenborough himself said at the Manila festival: 'There are certain things I care about very deeply. I might not be able to write about them. I make my statements emotionally in dramatic form. If you try to deal with something as emotive as the beginning of the demolition of the British Empire, which was Indian Independence, you can't expect to escape without being clouted here and there.'

Ah those Goan evenings at Prainha under the half moon. Chinese lanterns hung between the coconut palms, and the gentle swish of waves. And those prawns . . .

Most people at our hotel seemed to be British, but kept to themselves, speaking in low voices – except for a lady, of mixed blood she told us, who was quite opposite and very funny about the old prejudices against Anglo-Indians: a young officer at Poona might get suspicious about a girl's origins and demand to see whether her gums were purple, or if she had no moons on her fingernails.

Prainha was next to the fishing village called Dona Paula, which in turn was near the promontory of Cabo on which stood the Lieutenant-Governor's palace and the old British cemetery. Anyone in England interested in the subject of far-flung cemeteries became aware that there was one at Goa at the time of the Commonwealth Conference in November 1983, which had happened not long before our arrival. I had been deputed by a British organization to give a report on this cemetery, about which little was known, and by way of preparation had been sent a cutting from an Indian newspaper describing how 'no less a person than British Prime Minister, Mrs

Margaret Tatcher, accompanied by her husband Denise, visited the cemetery to pay homage to British soldiers'.

Thanks to our host at Prainha, arrangements were made for us to see not only the cemetery but its neighbour Cabo Raj Niwas, the Governor's palace. Until Mrs 'Tatcher's' visit I had not realized that there had ever been a British presence at Goa, but it turned out that we had moved in during Napoleonic times.

We were met at the cemetery by the caretaker, old Maria de Silva. She was wearing all her jewellery (chiefly an object like a large gold bell in her nose) and her best yellow blouse (rather tight-fitting), just as she had done – we were honoured to hear – for Mrs T, for whom the place had been specially cleaned and tidied, and the walls repainted: a very considerable work, apparently, since, to quote again that Indian newspaper, the cemetery had long been 'lying disused and defaced by nature, man and animals'.

I was glad that Mrs T had also given Maria a present. The job of caretaker was hereditary, but the problem now was who would take over after Maria. It was obvious that the grass had been clipped all over again in our honour. For all that, the place was rather a desolate one, with a few straggly mango trees as decoration, though with a nice whitewashed Portuguese gateway. Nearly all the sarcophagi were without names, the marble having been stolen. The marked graves had little to do with soldiers, and the oldest I found was that of Margaret, wife of John William Reed, 'Conductor of the Honble Company's Service', who had died on December 19 1808; 'She was a Virtuous Wife, an Affectionate Mother and a Faithful and Sincere Friend'. Captain James Graham of the 7th Regiment had died April 8 1829 aged forty-four, 'on board the Lady East off Vergola on his passage to England'. There was one American in the cemetery: Thomas J. P. Kennedy, born at Pittsville, Pa, in 1840, and who had died in 1901.

Originally there had been a Franciscan convent at Cabo, with only a small fort, which under the circumstances was surprising for such a strategic spot overlooking the River Mandovi. The sixteenth-century chapel, incorporated now within the blindingly white palace, had also been cleaned and its woodwork regilded for the Commonwealth Conference. There I learnt about the original Dona Paula, after whom our fishing village had been named. A stone in her memory said that she had been Dona Paula de Menezes, wife of Antonio de Santo Major, and had died in 1682. 'Legend has it', the inscription ran, 'that she was the paramour of the Viceroy and was victimized by the vengeful Vicereine to whom she was lady in waiting. Ask for pity and say a Pater Noster and an Ave Maria for her soul.'

For victimized, read poisoned, we were told. Usually Portuguese wives at Goa were shut inside convents when their husbands went abroad. Heat, jealousy, murder and the Inquisition. What scope for a romantic novel!

The view from the nineteenth-century iron verandah reminded me a little of the Amalfi coast, but it was not such a pleasant spot up there apparently in monsoon times. We were allowed upstairs, to see the chandeliers and Canton bowls and vases left behind by the Portuguese. We passed an open door and had the privilege of seeing the Governor himself at his desk. He did not look up, and we crept by like trespassers.

Goa had indeed changed since Graham Greene wrote about it in 1964, three years after the 'bloodless' invasion of 1961 which we have now to call the liberation. For one thing he had stayed at Anjuna, and Anjuna is where the ageing remnants of the hippy colony live, occasionally murdering one another or dropping the odd babies, who have to be adopted by local fishermen's families. Middle-class Indians flock up to Anjuna to stare at the naked Europeans living like animals. We came across a few nudes at Calangate further south, but they were just casual tourists, not necessarily drugged. Ladies with big boobs obviously had more appeal to the Indians than the several naked gays who were also disporting themselves.

Graham Greene, when he went to Mass on Christmas Eve at Old Goa's cathedral, thought it was like attending one of the last ceremonies of Christianity. Although the great religious buildings had been restored since his day, and there were throngs of coaches, that apocalyptic and sinister atmosphere that he had sensed was very noticeable still. Here stood the Inquisition; 'only a small stone like that on a child's grave marks the spot'. The very bell of the cathedral that we heard had been used to announce an auto-da-fé. In the church of Bom Jesus the fearful shrunken mummy of St Francis Xavier (he died in 1552) is still to be seen in a glass case above the richly elaborate alabaster, bronze and pietra dura tomb, presented by Grand Duke Cosimo III of Tuscany. The saint's toe is missing, bitten off by an enthusiastic Portuguese woman in 1554, and part of one hand is now in the Gesù church in Rome and another with the Jesuits in Japan. The body used to be exposed regularly, to show its miraculous state of preservation, but when the Portuguese left Goa it began to disintegrate and the practice had to stop.

Most haunting of all, I thought, was the gallery of portraits of black-garbed Portuguese Viceroys, who it seemed generally stayed en poste only about three years. Several of the pictures were primitives, which made their subjects look even more cruel and unhappy.

At Panaji, the slightly dull capital, I do recommend a glance at the statue of the Abbé Faria, said to be the inventor of hypnotism. Here again I quote Graham Greene: the Abbé is shown as pouncing 'like a great eagle on his mesmerised female patient'. Diana Petre later sent me a postcard of it, and because I knew that Francis was prone to stomach upheavals, wrote underneath the picture: 'Francis is feeling much better after the treatment.'

We coincided with Diana and Francis at Udaipur, but we, not they, were the lucky ones who stayed at the Lake Palace Hotel; due as usual to Raúl's ability to switch on the charm.

We arrived in the early hours at Udaipur, and there before us was the famous floating palace on its rippling Pichola lake, dreaming against a landscape of pink hills, marble pavilions and ochre forts. In some ways the scene reminded me of the Srinagar lakes, except for the huge and extraordinary cream-coloured royal residence on the shore, really a conglomeration of buildings, where the Maharana of Udaipur lived, the grandest of all the Rajput princes and head of the 'Solar' clan. We took the equivalent of a shikara across to the hotel. A few years ago Julian Trevelyan, R. C. Trevelyan's son, and his wife Mary had been to Udaipur and had been told that the ripples were due to alligators and turtles heaving up and down. But our boatmen discounted this, we thought without conviction, and we were reminded of the curt reaction to our asking about sharks off the Andaman Islands.

The hotel was even more 'fairylike' than we had imagined, a confection of arcades, marble, mirror mosaics, courtyards and fountains – with such prospects! But in spite of having paid handsomely in advance for a room, we were still wait-listed, we were told. This was maddening, but Raúl was determined to win so we hung on; at each rebuff he was furious with me whenever (so he said) I let my face 'fall'. We had to make ourselves look cheerful. Finally, after three dogged hours, the hotel management got sick of seeing us in the lobby and gave us the royal suite, for our original price. Diana and Francis were very indignant, and considered that we ought at least to have entertained them with champagne.

Humphrey at Udaipur

Humphrey Trevelyan was Political Agent at Udaipur in the early 1940s. The Maharana in his day was Bhupal Singh, a cripple who could not walk without help. 'Yet,' Humphrey said, 'his natural dignity and presence made his disability appear of little account. Every afternoon he went for a drive round the town in an open Rolls Royce, scarlet inside and out, sitting alone on the back seat, while his aide de camp, himself a noble, squatted on the floor of the car. Behind were three buses with a mixed complement of nobles and servants.' During the Boat Festival, the Maharana sat high in the front of a galley which, as Humphrey said, might have been Cleopatra's barge on the Nile, rowed by banks of oars, with nobles in white robes grouped below him like the chorus in an opera.

Humphrey and his wife Peggie lived in a seventeenth-century palace, with a superb garden. They had six men exclusively employed in cleaning the marble halls. Fifty prisoners in fetters weeded the lawns and the five grass tennis courts. Also at their disposal were a hard tennis court for rainy weather, two swimming pools, a squash court and a stable of horses. A guard of fifty soldiers lived on the premises.

Every Tuesday the Trevelyans gave a tennis party. The nobles and officials arrived first, carrying both swords and tennis racquets. Before playing they would tuck up the skirts of their official dress. Then a whistle would blow; the Maharana was approaching. 'Tennis stopped in the middle of a rally. Tennis racquets were thrown down; swords were picked up, skirts were untucked and the courtiers stood in line in order of precedence to await their Maharana.' Humphrey received the Maharana in his car, from which he was helped by two bearded warriors; he then walked a quarter of a pace behind as they progressed to their seats. 'I sat on one side, my wife on the other. "May we go on with the game, Your Highness?" I asked. He signified assent. Swords were dropped, skirts were tucked up and the game was resumed. After twenty minutes' conversation the Maharana turned to me and said: "May I go now?" So the whistle would be blown and the game once more abruptly stopped.'

Humphrey had a great respect for the Maharana, who in spite of his old-fashioned habits was remarkably liberal in his views and understood the changes that were taking place in his country. His father Fateh Singh had been more of a traditionalist, and so mighty that he had refused to go to the Durbar in 1911 for King George V and Queen Mary: it would have meant admitting that he was a vassal, and no Maharana had ever gone to Delhi in the time of the Moghuls. A chair had been offered him next to the King, but even this had been declined.

Fateh Singh had not been accommodating during the First World War either, and had refused to send troops to help the British. On the other hand his predecessor, Swarup Singh, during the Mutiny in

1857 had given refuge to forty Europeans on the island in the lake, the present hotel.

For Humphrey, inevitably, there were tiger shoots and pig-sticking. He admitted that it could have been the most perfect time of his whole life, but the year was 1942 and he could only feel restless. So he applied to move on, and went to a more active post further east.

Now the British Agent's palace is a girls' school for a thousand pupils, running around like flamingoes in their pink blouses.

Humphrey's immediate predecessor as Political Agent had been Heb Todd, my parents' great friend from Gilgit days. Heb and his family had been torpedoed on the SS *Simla* almost immediately after setting out from Glasgow. While recovering from that experience before sailing out again, they had stayed at our house in Essex. In the Udaipur palace museum I was delighted to find on display not only framed photographs of both Heb and Humphrey but Maharana Bhupal Singh's Rolls Royce.

We had an introduction to an Englishwoman called Caroline Singh, said to be married to a minor Rajah outside the city, but we had too much sightseeing ahead of us and in any case were put off by someone who had tried to ring Caroline from our hotel.

'Hullo, can I speak to the Rani?' our new friend had asked. '*I* am the Rani,' came the answer in a very Indian-sounding voice. Perplexed, our friend tried to explain. 'Oh you mean the concubine,' was the reply. 'Wait a minute, please.' About ten minutes passed, and then the telephone was cut off.

Like Julian and Mary we went shopping in the bazaar for silver rings, an Udaipur speciality. We could imagine Mary – who paints as Mary Fedden – loving all those Rajasthan women in red circular skirts, hectic printed orange veils, gold and silver bangles up their arms, and with great gold nose-rings. Whilst doing our bargaining, again just like Julian and Mary, we were pressed round by about fifty children all saying, 'I love you good night how are you what is your name,' and falling about hysterically whenever we tried to reply.

The only sounds in the mornings from our suite at the hotel were the cooing of pigeons, an occasional motor boat and the slapping of clothes in the ghats. We went to look at those ghats, among onion domes, pagodas and pavilions, but were chased away from the women's area, all draped with vividly coloured saris put out to dry. Diana however was not excluded from the male section, even though everybody there was only in his underpants. Yes, there were a few alligators, we were told, but no one worried. Alligators don't like bright colours.

We parted from Diana and Francis, and drove to Kotah, with a few punctures, not to mention wrong turnings and deviations – deliberate as we discovered, in order to 'earn' our driver more kilometres. Kotah was where Charles Trevelyan had spent some frustrating months as Political Agent in 1830 after the Colebrooke drama at Delhi.

Which brings me back to Charles in the 1860s, and the last lap of his Indian career.

Return to Calcutta

Charles, having published a 'statement' on his recall and being satisfied that he had the support of trusted hands like Sir John Lawrence, made it clear that he looked forward to some new appointment either in India or on the India Council. His loyal ally, Sir Charles Wood, the Secretary of State, also continued to seek his advice on many matters.

Wilson's successor as Finance Member of the Supreme Council of India at Calcutta was Samuel Laing, but he was a failure and in any case forced to retire in the autumn of 1862 because of illness. To the amazement of many, Charles was nominated to succeed him.

At that time the Supreme Council, headed by the Governor-General or Viceroy, had five 'Ordinary' Members appointed by the Secretary of State, with the Commander-in-Chief in India and in certain circumstances the Governors of Madras and Bombay as Extraordinary Members. This was also known as the Viceroy's Executive Council. There was in addition a Legislative Council, mostly consisting of men who had held high office in India for some years and nominated by the Viceroy.

Wood had at last convinced himself that Charles had been 'tamed', and indeed during their discussions he and Charles had found themselves in almost total agreement on Indian financial policy. He also was eager to redress the pain he had been forced to cause Charles eighteen months before. The new Viceroy, Lord Elgin, had however to be reassured. He was told that Charles had the ideal qualifications, being a good organizer and a 'stern economist', with years of experience at the Treasury. Perhaps Charles was apt to be long-winded, but he was no orator and so would not be anxious to become a public figure. He was popular with Indians, and moreover a gentleman with some independent means, and not personally ambitious.

The Queen also had to be calmed. Delane, the Editor of *The Times*, was told that in substance Charles had been nearer the right at Madras than he had been given credit for. As for the thorny matter of income tax, Charles was pledged to retain it until 1865, when it would be abolished.

To friends like Florence Nightingale, the new appointment was a matter of joy and 'gratitude to God'. Even some newspapers in Bengal were optimistic. It was agreed now that Charles had acted in 1860 like a 'Whig of pur sang'. To the family of Wilson, the thing was – needless to say – a matter of pain, and Walter Bagehot wrote a leader on the subject in the *Economist*, raking up that old 'monstrous act of misjudgement and insubordination'; Charles had 'never been a safe man', he said, or willing to 'confine himself to his proper sphere'. His qualities were the opposite to what India required. This prompted a slightly comic, and insincere, correspondence with Wood and Charles himself, who claimed that his private relations with Bagehot's father-in-law had always been 'perfectly friendly'.

Charles was to be accompanied to Calcutta not only by Hannah, her maid Elizabeth, and Alice but by George Otto, who would act as his unpaid private secretary. It was some sacrifice for Hannah, now over fifty and who did not like India, but she was determined never again to be so separated from her husband. Alice was in the middle of a mild love affair, and a year away from her admirer was considered useful. From Charles's own point of view, his new office would be inferior in rank to his last but in other ways more important. Writing to a cousin, Sir Walter Trevelyan, the head of the family, he said: 'As a mark of confidence nothing could be more complete, for it involves the management of the entire finance of India.' To which he ominously added: 'Income tax included.'

George Otto was aged twenty-four. Brimming with confidence and high spirits, and with political aspirations, he had a Macaulay sense of humour, and his rather simian features, adorned with thick black whiskers, and short nose were probably more Macaulay than Trevelyan. He had been head boy at Harrow, winning prizes for poetry. As a scholar at Trinity, Cambridge, he had read and reread the classical authors for pleasure, and had shown a gift for satire not appreciated by the Master, the formidable Dr Whewell. His two 'jeux d'esprit' there, *Horace at the University of Athens* and *The Cambridge Dionisia*, were later published. Among his Trinity friends were the Prince of Wales and future academics and intellectuals such as Henry and Arthur Sidgwick, Montagu Butler and Sir George Young. But he failed to get a Fellowship, which depressed him, and his parents hoped that the experience in India would be some compensation as well as giving him a grounding in public service.

Just before they left England Charles received a letter from his very rich, eccentric and childless cousin, Sir Walter, mainly on matters to do with Sir Walter's pet subject, the evils of alcohol. A brief postscript was added, informing Charles that some years ago Sir Walter had made a will leaving him and George Otto a 20,000-odd-acre estate in Northumberland and a large eighteenth-century country house, Wallington. Charles, overwhelmed at such astonishing news, replied gratefully but told Sir Walter that he had decided it would be a mistake to tell George Otto about his prospects until his return from India: 'He [George Otto] feels now that his future depends on his strenuous exertions at this crisis of his life, and he is braced up to work hard with me and under my guidance. Such an announcement might unsettle him.' Which seems sensible enough.

Be that as it may, George Otto must have had plenty of hints, which resulted in a number of quite lively letters which he wrote from India to Sir Walter and his wife Pauline, the confidante of Ruskin and friend of many in the Pre-Raphaelite circle. The first of these letters, from Calcutta, was written on January 13 1863:

We have arrived here after a sufficiently prosperous journey, all well. We had some very dirty weather in the Bay of Biscay, and between Gibraltar and Malta a real genuine hurricane, which frightened Mamma dreadfully. The voyage on the other side was very safe and and uncommonly dull. The ship in which we were to have sailed, the Colombo, was wrecked on Minnicoy, a coral island halfway between the Maldives and Laccadives. Our steamer stopped there, and my father and I went with the captain to pay the shipwrecked crew a visit. They had been on the island about six weeks, employed in clearing out the wreck, and had grown very ragged and sun-burnt. Poor fellows, they were very proud of their bread, and of a spring of cold water near the encampment. The first sight of coconut trees, the coral reefs, the tents with flags flying, and debris and stones lying about all reminded me of the pictures in old books of travel . . . When we got to Point de Galle it was easy to see what an excitement there was in India on account of my father's appointment. The Governor entertained us most royally, and was very attentive. Unfortunately the horse in the carriage in which the Governor, my father and mother were riding took fright at a snake, and ran away. The driver was knocked off and run over, and the reins trailed to the ground! Providentially the horse stopped after a mile and a half. At Madras the whole business resembled a triumph. The attachment of the natives was really affecting. The sentence most in their mouths was 'This Governor [Sir William Denison] is the Governor of the Sahib people, but Sir Charles was the Governor of our people.'

The sea journey had also prompted some typical light verse from George Otto: 'Fair dames, whose easy-chairs in goodly row/Fringe either bulwark of the P. & O.' etc. But triumph was an understatement. Only a few days before their arrival at Madras there had been a 'Trevelyan meeting' to decide on how Charles should be welcomed, and this had been an occasion for a gala. Now the whole thing was repeated. The new pier, started in Charles's time, was ready, so there was no need to plunge through the surf. In spite of threatening weather, Charles and his family were conveyed in carriages to – where else? – his very own creation, the People's Park, through an archway which among evergreens and flags displayed the words WELCOME TREVELYAN. A crowd had gathered, so it was reported locally, 'as is seldom seen at Madras, with people of all descriptions, men, women and children of all denominations, of all creeds, complexions and castes, assembled at the sound of a name which has become to each and all as familiar as any nursery song'. After a welcoming address from the bandstand, above which were intertwined the initials of Queen Victoria, the Prince of Wales, Charles Trevelyan and the Rajah of Travancore, the band itself played waltzes and gallops. The trees were illuminated with blue lights, and there were fireworks. 'Such an endless diversity of attire, hats, turbans, pugrees, black coats, coloured scarfs, rich uniforms and simple white cloths!' Some of the 'fair ones' saved their crinolines from being crushed by having seats provided, but otherwise everyone, high and low, mixed freely with the 'vast multitude of the unwashed'.

But Charles had only six hours to spend at Madras. His easy-going successor as Governor, Sir William Denison, irritated him slightly, but he admitted to Wood that the man was at least honest and, most important, resentful of those Calcutta 'trammels'.

Macaulay's Penal Code had at last become law, and this had been followed by the Code of Criminal Procedure for India, which meant that legislative rights were restored to Madras and Bombay. All this was very satisfactory to Charles, but whenever he discerned further hint of 'trammels' to be imposed by the central Government, he 'boiled with fury'. Soon he was (predictably) complaining to Wood about Elgin's 'despotism'. For his part Elgin, who admittedly was generally considered vain and a bore, told Wood that he found Charles 'rather a strange person', prone to speak in broad crude terms.

In a run-down of his new colleagues for Wood's benefit Charles wrote approvingly of Henry Maine, the Legal Member, whom he thought 'sensible, able and perspicacious'. But he was suspicious of the Secretary for Public Works, Colonel Richard Strachey (later father of Lytton Strachey), whom he found very clever but 'sanguine, morbidly active, ambitious and strongly disposed to partisanship', needing an 'experienced and sagacious man always over him to keep the effusions of his genius within bounds' (just in effect what Bentinck used to say about Charles himself). In due course the Trevelyans found a house, 9 Elysium Row, next door to the Stracheys. It was not an easy relationship, and Hannah found Richard Strachey 'peppery'.

Charles's first Budget was to be at the end of April, but in February Elgin, with wife and daughter, set off on a lengthy tour, involving durbars at Cawnpore, Agra, Delhi and elsewhere. At this distance it is rather touching to note how Hannah, remembering that headstrong behaviour at Madras, encouraged Charles to confide in her about office matters. Soon, for instance, she was telling her eldest daughter Margaret about his trouble with the Manchester Cotton Lobby in London, which was worried about the drying up of cotton supplies from the United States owing to the Civil War; the Lobby wanted a massive increase in state spending to help the Indian cotton growers, in the way of railways, roads and irrigation. Charles, however, at this stage seemed more interested in spending money on the building of new and better barracks for European soldiers in stations throughout India; no doubt due to his friendship with Florence Nightingale, who was writing to him frequently on her special subject, sanitation reform. Otherwise he believed that all such works should be left to private enterprise.

Broadly speaking his convictions and shibboleths were much as they had always been, particularly in the encouragement of free trade and the training of Indians to take on subsidiary government posts. He was also still urging the removal of the capital from Calcutta to Delhi. 'People forget that Calcutta has become what it is because Job Charnock [in 1690, the 'founder' of Calcutta] had a fancy to pitch his tent under a certain banyan tree on the riverside.' He did not want Wood to think him quarrelsome. 'To you I say exactly what I think. In relation with my colleagues *I am discretion itself*. Even my wife, who is a keen critic in my case, has not yet hinted that I have made a mistake.'

George Otto's duties as secretary to his father were certainly not onerous. In February he was invited by Cecil Beadon, Lieutenant-Governor of Bengal, on a tour of the province, visiting indigo plantations and places of the Mutiny such as the so-called Little House of Arrah, and was sad to discover how memories of its gallant defence were fading away so soon. The diary that the Collector Herwald Wake had written on its wall, 'in full expectation of the siege terminating in the garrison having their throats cut', had been whitewashed. Many Collectors' or Court Houses however still had their old fortifications around them. But, as he wrote to Pauline Trevelyan on February 16 1863,

> The chief traces of the Mutiny are not material but moral. It is no longer the fashion to show the slightest interest in the natives: the 'confounded nigger' style is the thing nowadays. The Englishmen who do not belong to the Government Service behave too much like the Orangemen in Ireland. Every day there is a ferocious article against the natives in one or other of the Calcutta papers, and I fear that there is more chance that this feeling will extend to the Civil Service than that the Civil Service will influence for good the Planters and Merchants. I am going to Nepal today for a fortnight's tiger-shooting. We are to have a line of eighty elephants and shall be about seven sportsmen.

Hannah at Calcutta

Evidently George Otto was not a very great sportsman. He shot a domestic cow by mistake; one hopes that it did not belong to Hindus. However he enjoyed the scenery and especially the joking and the earnest political discussions with his companions. At long last a royal beast did appear, and was slain by combined volley of several rifles, to the accompaniment of much plunging and rolling by the elephants.

On his return to Calcutta he settled down to some half satirical sketches on life in Bengal, for sending to *Macmillan's Magazine* in London. He found that his mother Hannah had slipped and broken a rib.

Hannah had thought the weather at Calcutta delightful during February, but now, being also in pain, she found it exceedingly unpleasant. She wrote to her eldest daughter Margaret Holland on April 8:

> You can form no notion of the anxiety here about health. In the morning perhaps Alice has a pain in her head or is sick, and she has to be doctored. Yesterday Elizabeth was very poorly for some hours. Then George is feverish, or C. is quite prostrated for a time. Till each attack goes off, one feels a quiver and sinking at heart. Not *a dog* passes without some such alarm; ease of mind is a thing one never knows. April 10, Calcutta. We find Charles quite ill

413

when we came back, and I sent for the Doctor. He says it is simply overwork, and that he could do nothing for him until the Budget is over.

She also kept Margaret and her husband Harry fully au fait with the dramas over Charles's first Budget. He was having a big tussle with his colleagues on the Council who wanted it to be a joint enterprise. The Military Member, Sir Robert Napier, later Lord Napier of Magdala, was a 'very ignorant nervous morbid kindhearted prejudiced soldier' who would say at intervals in a trembling voice: 'Why do we need a Budget at all?' It was unfortunate for Charles that the Council members were so 'very sore' after Wood had blamed them for the disastrous 'escapades' of the previous Finance Member, Laing.

Lord Elgin was the only one who knew about finance, but he was on tour. He was 'far from public-spirited', caring for 'nothing and no-one but himself', but a 'sensible man, well acquainted with business and how it ought to be done'. Only Maine could be relied upon as a supporter; he stood by Charles nobly, 'doing yeoman service'. 'I like him more and more,' Hannah predictably said.

Charles had given an undertaking to Wood that he would not abolish the frightful Income Tax until 1865. All the same he did reduce it by one per cent, and as a good free trader also cut down taxes on some imports. He also increased some of the allotments to public works, but not in connection with cotton production, and this caused Wood severe embarrassment when he had to face angry members of his own constituency at Halifax.

Hannah was concerned that Alice was becoming too 'flirty and frivolous'. But, to her relief, it was decided that in August she, Alice, George Otto and Elizabeth should go to the cool of the Nilgiri Hills, and that Charles would follow later.

About this time George Otto wrote a tactful letter to his future benefactor Sir Walter Trevelyan agreeing that alcohol was a bad thing for soldiers in India; seventy-five men out of a thousand died from it each year. He did not dare say that his father had reduced the tax on wine and beer. He added:

My father ... has certainly overworked himself during the past month. Yesterday I was sleepless and began roaming the verandahs at two in the morning, and there he was dressed, and at work. People say that it is sheer madness during the hot weather out here ... Yesterday and the day before three young people of our acquaintance, all under twenty-five, were very dangerously ill, one of them Mamma's maid who is likely to recover. When people have been out here some four or five years they feel the heat more, but do not seem so liable to have dangerous attacks of fever. Perhaps the weak ones have gone home or died.

One of the three sufferers, a recent bride, did die. Hannah had been quite convinced that Elizabeth was going to die too. The doctor diagnosed congestion of the liver with an abscess forming. Leeches had to be applied, and a nurse was called in. 'I cannot tell you how much I have felt it,' Hannah wrote to Margaret. 'Having persuaded her to come, if anything happens to her, it will be most terrible to me. Besides I have got very fond of her, and she is most attached to me.' But Elizabeth did begin to mend, though the doctor felt she would never be quite right again. Then Alice became ill.

Poor child she is terribly fidgety about her health. Last night she called me to see if she had a fever which she had not, but as she had a headache I let more air into the room. Then she thought it might be rheumatism, so it was all shut up again. If she has any uneasiness she thinks straight away she is going to die. In real illness she is very patient. I have had a slight attack but I know exactly what to do and am not in the least nervous. Of all the party George suffers most from the climate. He never sleeps, only occasionally is put to sleep by treatment, and looks *dreadfully white and thin*. His nerves and brain suffer, and sometimes the doctors forbid all work for a day or two . . .

It was now settled that Alice and George Otto would return to England in January, probably with Elizabeth. 'I am glad I came out,' George Otto told Sir Walter, 'glad we are staying a full year: and oh! how uncommonly glad we are going back at the end of it.'

But Hannah was getting worried about her son 'wasting away'. And Alice was looking 'very faded'. 'Oh the heat! No-one can tell what it is to rise every morning languid and nerveless to another day, and to know it must go on getting worse until June 15 when we expect the rains. Want of sleep at night is very trying. The punkahs, the noises in the compound, the screams of the jackals and the crows keep me very wakeful.'

And now Lord Elgin wrote to Charles proposing that the Council should go to him at Lahore in January 1864, and return to Calcutta in April. 'Did you ever in all your life hear anything so brutal and selfish?' Hannah wrote to Margaret. 'Lahore is hundreds of miles from any railroad. The grandees might manage it without fatigue, but several hundred clerks must go, papers, records etc.; all these must march at the rate of a dozen miles a day . . . There we must all live in tents.'

In spite of the unusually hot weather, balls were regularly being held until early June. Hannah, who still disliked dancing, spent the last ball in a corner with Cecil Beadon, 'quaffing champagne in iced water'. Much as she longed for Ooty and the Nilgiris, she felt increasingly wretched at leaving Charles.

> You see he has not a soul here with whom he can talk over his difficulties, and he often comes to me so worn down and worried, and then I show him the bright side and cheer him up. He has not a creature to help him in the Treasury to whom he can trust. Private: a most annoying thing has just occurred. He has discovered that the men employed to manage the accounts were busily cooking them up to conceal a mistake in the estimates sent in for the Budget . . .

Some of the accountants were Indians, and this revelation was a particular blow to Charles, who had been advocating so strongly the advancement of Indians in Government affairs.

Hannah's gloom on her departure for Ooty via Madras was intensified by a letter from Elgin still insisting on having the Council up to Lahore in January. How could Charles possibly get out his next Budget in time for April? It would only add to his load of work, again in the great heat. But Elgin was 'so intensely self-absorbed that he cannot see beyond his own little nose.'

The Competition Wallah

The articles that George Otto wrote for *Macmillan's Magazine* were in the form of letters written by an imaginary Henry Broughton, a 'competition wallah', to an old school pal in England. The competition wallahs were the new breed of 'civilians', or civil servants, who had obtained their posts through competitive examination after the closing of the East India college at Haileybury: something in which Charles, himself a Haileyburian, could truly have claimed to have had a certain responsibility. These men were therefore a kind of phenomenon at Calcutta, considered rather gauche and often, like the Army griffins of old, a bit of a joke.

The first letter was written within a month of George Otto's arrival at Calcutta, and was published as soon as it had reached

England. It was followed in swift succession by five more letters. These were mainly based on his tour in the Mofussil that he had made with Cecil Beadon (also given a pseudonym). The tone was occasionally facetious and a little cocky, but did not detract from the impression of a writer with an alert, witty and highly intelligent and modern young mind. The letters were favourably noticed in other papers, both in Britain and at Calcutta. The piece on Arrah was – and still is – considered historically valuable, and his various strongly topical references were appreciated: for instance on the American Civil War. The present-day reader is naturally able to detect the influence of his father's views, but the approach was George Otto's own and based on first-hand impressions. He was even to admit afterwards that he had begun his tour in the Mofussil by being a rabid 'Anglo-Saxon', by which he meant anti-Indian, or anti-Bengali – the opposite camp, which included his father, being then known as 'Anglo-Indian'.

Not surprisingly his parents had mixed feelings about those first letters. They read them with indulgence, but not with particular enthusiasm. Hannah thought the one on railways rather bad. Perhaps she considered it too flippant, or too condescending towards Indians. Nevertheless there are some typically witty passages in it, for instance on the word 'pucca' (pukka):

An Englishman may keep his ground in Parisian salons, and pass for a very sensible, intelligent fellow, by a copious though judicious use of 'par exemple'. In the same way a man who is a thorough master of the word 'pucka' may hold his own in any society in India. 'Pucka' literally means 'ripe', and is used to express the notion of perfection and completeness ... A permanent barrack is 'pucka', as opposed to a thatched hut. The arrangements for a shooting party are 'pucka' when the pale ale does not run short, and the bore of the station is prevented from coming by an attack of dysentery.

He quoted an 'old civilian' having an argument in a French railway carriage, and saying: 'Ah, monsieur, votre Empereur n'est pas pucka du tout, du tout, du tout!' And here is his impression of an English sahib's arrival at a railway station:

Suddenly, in the rear of the crowd, without the gates, there arises a great hubbub, amidst which, from time to time, may be distinguished an imperious, sharp-cut voice, the owner of which appears to show the most lordly indifference to the remarks and answers around him. A few moments more, after some quarrelling and shoving, the throng divides, and down the lane thus formed stalks the Sahib of the period, in all the glory of an old flannel shirt and trousers, a dirty alpaca coat, no collar, no waistcoat, white canvas shoes, and a vast pith helmet. Behind him comes his chief bearer, with a cash-box, a loading-rod, two copies of the *Saturday Review* of six months back, and three bottles of soda-water. Then follows a long team of coolies, carrying on their heads a huge quantity of shabby and nondescript luggage, including at least one gun-case and a vast shapeless parcel of bedding. On the portmanteau you may still read, in very faint white letters, 'Calcutta. Cabin.' The Sahib, with the freedom and easy insolence of a member of the Imperial race, walks straight into the sacred enclosure of the clerk's office and takes a ticket, at five times the price paid by his native brethren. Meanwhile, the bearer disposes the luggage in a heap, rewards the coolies on a scale which seems to give them profound discontent . . .

Henry Broughton, alias George Otto, then reaches Patna where he visits a government school and an opium factory. Hannah did not think much of this letter either, and there was less scope for witticisms.

Patna had the most important factories for producing opium. The awkward moral issue of exporting opium to China had to be explained away with a great deal of cant by governments both in India and Britain. Wars had been fought with China on the subject, the last 'Opium War' ending only in 1860 with the entry of French and British troops, under the future Viceroy of India Lord Elgin, into Peking. Dutch and Americans had also been involved in the trade, which was now made legal.

India had produced opium for centuries and was considered to produce the best quality. Already in Bentinck's time it was responsible for one eighteenth of British India's gross revenue; soon it was to rise to one seventh. After the first war with China in 1840 Lord Ashley, later Lord Shaftesbury, had without success moved a resolution in Parliament to stop the opium trade, as being among other things 'utterly inconsistent with the honour and duties of a Christian kingdom'. The drive to suppress the trade totally was still strong in Britain twenty years later, and was supported by men like Sir Walter Trevelyan. Charles obviously found himself in a difficult position, not only as a Christian but because of the huge inheritance in Northumberland he expected from Sir Walter. He therefore had to take time off from his work to write soothing letters of reassurance on the subject. The export of the crop to China, he pointed out, was a part of India's revenue that no government would dare lose. As a vice the drug was 'no less harmful' than gin or spirits, and even had a beneficial effect on the 'sluggish, unimaginative Tartar character'. Charles's estimate for revenue from the opium crop in 1863–4 was no less than eight million pounds (actually receipts dropped drastically). It was important, he said, to keep the duty as high as possible – to release opium from taxation would only stimulate it tenfold.

In his own way George Otto backed his father's views in his *Competition Wallah* letter. Now, under that same pseudonym of Henry Broughton, he wrote a satirical play called *The Dawk [i.e. Dak] Bungalow, or Is His Appointment Pucka?* This was performed eventually at Cecil Beadon's magnificent palazzo, Belvedere, in November 1863, by which time no doubt the real identity of its author could no longer have been a secret. Years later when *The Dawk Bungalow* was published he said in his Introduction: 'This play takes its name from the comfortless hostelries of India, in which the larder consists of a live fowl, and the accommodation of three rooms on the ground floor, less than half furnished even according to Oriental notions of furniture; the traveller being supposed to bring with him bread, beer and bedding.' (All of which sounds very like my own experience at Naltar on my journey in 1977.)

Hannah, with good reason, thought the seventh letter, 'About Calcutta', much the best so far. There was much in it about the horrors of the climate: something which she was certainly able to appreciate. Writing of one of those gruesomely 'sticky' balls he said:

> You probably never waltzed in full evening dress round the inner chamber of a Turkish bath, and therefore can have no conception of the peculiar charms of the dance in this climate. Terpsichore is a muse who loves shade, and zephyrs, and running streams; but not shade in which the thermometer stands at 93°, where the zephyrs are artificial, and the only running streams those in the faces of her votaries. The waste of tissue during a gallope, with a partner in high training just landed from England, is truly frightful. The natives understand those things better. They let the ladies do their dancing for them, and content themselves with looking on.

He had come to the sad conclusion that colonization by the white man in India, in the sense that it had happened in America and Australia, was at present an impossibility. There was no such thing as acclimatization for the 'settler', i.e. the planter and the merchant. As the years rolled by, it was a losing battle between the sun and one's constitution. If the European race were to survive in India, there would have to be an infusion of native blood. Most important of all, the seat of the central Government ought to be moved to a new and more salubrious spot, away from Calcutta, the 'city of plague', and George Otto's choice for this was not his father's favourite candidate, Delhi, but Jubbulpore. He cited the deadly effect of Calcutta's climate on Lord Dalhousie, and on both the Cannings and the late Mr Wilson. His letter ended with a typically sarcastic 'Ode to Calcutta', the first lines being as follows:

> Fair city, India's crown and pride,
> Long may'st thou tower o'er Hooghley's tide,
> Whose hallowed, but malarious stream,
> The peasant's god, the poet's theme,
>   Rolls down the dead Hindoo;
> And from whose wave, a stagnant mass
> Replete with sulphuretted gas
>   Our country beer we brew! . . . etc.

The eighth letter concerned 'The Hindoo Character'. Now his mood was changing, thanks to study and increasing knowledge of the country. He had become a 'firm friend of the Hindoo', hating what he called the 'damned nigger' style.

One requires more than a few months to form a correct set of opinions and impressions concerning an ancient and wealthy society, with a singular and complicated organisation . . . He [the Hindu] is not like the North American Indian, a barbarian with a few sound ideas about the bearings of the stars and the habits of deer, and a few crude ideas about the Great Spirit and the future condition of his faithful dog . . . He belongs to a social order, which dates far back into the depths of time, with innumerable well-defined grades and classes; with titles which were borne by his forefathers, when the ancestors of English dukes paddled about in wicker canoes.

But George Otto then proceeded to enumerate some tendencies and faults in the Hindu character which he did *not* like: laziness, no feeling for the sacredness of toil; a thin line between truth and falsehood.

All these letters to date were read with enthusiasm at Calcutta, but

'About Calcutta' and especially the ninth letter, entitled 'British Temper towards India, Before, During and Since the Mutiny', both published after George Otto had left, were received with fury. He had now become an 'ignorant, conceited coxcomb', a stripling whose effusions could only be received 'with silent contempt'. He was also attacked in England, especially by the *Spectator*, which described the ninth letter as spiteful, 'a burst of civilian hate against the independent settler'.

In his travels with Cecil Beadon George Otto had become sickened by the utter contempt that the British indigo-planters in Bengal were showing towards the ryots or peasant workers. Not only that, he became astonished by the 'violence and ferocity of the anti-native journals', which to him was a 'sure symptom of an unjust and unhealthy cause'. He challenged his readers to agree with him that the 'children of the soil' in India were their equals in the eye of the law, and that it was *not* hypocrisy to believe that 'we hold India for the benefit of the inhabitants of India'.

There could not be much humour in such a letter. Starting it with a résumé of the liberal idealism of the 1830s, and mentioning his father's achievements, he described in chilling details how the cry for retribution against the mutineers after 1857 had turned into a deadly hatred, and in so doing went much further than 'Indophilus'.

> The best hope for the miserable natives lay in the justice and moderation of official men. The stern and cold animosity of the civilians, the reckless and unscrupulous retribution dealt out by the military, were as nothing to the rabid ferocity of the non-official community. These men had come to the shores of India for the sole purpose of making money. They were under no professional obligation of providing for the prosperity and happiness of the population, and indeed were too apt to regard their dark fellow-subjects as tools for promoting their own ends.

The philanthropy of the previous generation was now at a discount. 'Have we poured forth our blood like water,' people like the indigo-planters were beginning to ask, 'in order that the children of sepoys might have a better education than they would have obtained in the event of their father having overturned the British supremacy?' And what, pray, was England to gain from India in return for millions of money spent and thousands of lives lost? Did she not merit some more substantial recompense for having recovered the country, than the privilege of 'governing the Indians in a spirit of wisdom and unselfishness'? George Otto then added:

The European settlers in India speedily acquired that contempt for the Bengalese which it is a law of nature that the members of a conquering race should entertain for the subject population among whom they live. As the Norman baron regarded the Saxon churl, as the Dutch boer regarded the Hottentot, so it was inevitable that the English planter should regard the ryot and the cooly. No one can estimate very highly the moral and intellectual qualities of people among whom he resides for the single purpose of turning them to pecuniary account . . .

The tone of the press was horrible . . . The pages of those brutal and grotesque journals published by Hébert and Marat during the agony of the French Revolution contained nothing that was not matched and surpassed in the files of some Calcutta papers.

It was a long, brave and ultimately important letter. He was especially dispirited by the attitude among settlers that if an European happened to murder a 'nigger' he should be excused the death penalty.

'The ravening clamour of the friends of indigo' and the whole Anglo-Saxon party continued to be lambasted in three more letters. But at least the 'Civilians' still hearkened to the voice of equity and humanity. The Indian Civil Service was a fine career (applause from Charles?) with splendid prospects for anyone with honourable ambitions.

He wrote about Christianity and education, quoting in full Macaulay's Minute of 1835. He had come to the conclusion that it was unlikely that India would ever be fully converted to Christianity, and gave several reasons. For one thing, 'the very simplicity which, to the educated mind, constitutes the chief grace and virtue of Protestantism, renders it distasteful to the Oriental'. And here he got himself unexpectedly into trouble with the Roman Catholics when – after making some disparaging remarks about idols and fanatics – he tried to show that Romish pomp and ceremony were likely to have more appeal to Hindus. He pointed out that the missionaries had failed because they insisted on keeping up their European way of life. Could one imagine such a missionary sleeping in a native hut, living on native food, and going on foot from village to village in June? This of course was an exaggeration; but simple souls had to be won, and Jesus had recognized that. The missionaries in India tended to be intellectuals. And how could Christianity, with the doctrine of love and humility, work so long as white Christians regarded dark-skinned Christians as niggers?

Another great problem was that Indian converts to Christianity had to contend with the ugly social consequences of losing caste among their fellows, and were likely to be ostracized by their families and friends. The real business of Europeans was not so much to evangelize, but to educate, enlighten and fight against superstition. There was no need to despair however. 'Though there be differences of administrations, there is the same Lord, and, though there be diversity of operation, it is the same God that worketh all in all.' Which was a point also reached by Rammohan Roy in the early 1830s, and also since by many present-day Christians in India.

George Otto did not attempt to water down Macaulay's sweeping dismissal of Sanskrit learning, but he had concluded that the old Utopian dream of 'amalgamation' between the races – which had once been his father's – was hopeless. There was far too much of an 'incompatibility between sentiment and custom', and the main example was the Hindu and Muslim attitude towards women. Even so, all this did not imply that as time went on the two races should not live side by side with mutual sympathy and self-respect, striving for the same ends. It was unfortunate that the 'intense Anglo-Saxon spirit of self-approbation, which, though dormant at home, is unpleasantly perceptible among vulgar Englishmen on the Continent, becomes rampant in India'.

So what was to be done? 'We cannot exterminate a wealthy and ancient community of a hundred and fifty million of human beings, like so many Maoris or Cherokees; and if we do not exterminate them, we cannot continue to humble and wrong them.' His great hope was that his letters might help to stir up the English at home, lift them out of their apathy towards all things Indian.

The letters of *The Competition Wallah* were published as a book in 1865 under George Otto's own name. It continued to be reprinted over the next decades, though with some judicious omissions, including the paragraph felt offensive by Roman Catholics. Charles, believing still that Christianity was the ultimate benefit that the British would bestow on India, could not have agreed with all that his son had to say. Nevertheless he became intensely proud that his son's mind had matured and developed, and was especially glad that he had made friends with some of the most promising officers of the Civil Service, all older than himself. 'It has given him,' Charles wrote to Margaret on July 19 1863, after the family party had left for the Nilgiris, 'a habit of work such as he has never had before.' In the autumn George Otto would make a grand tour of Delhi and Agra. By then he would have got 'as much as India can give him' and it would greatly help him with his parliamentary career.

But it is time to return for a while to my own travels. The round-about journey from Udaipur to Kotah was through every sort of landscape: desert-like, palm groves, rich cultivation, quarries, romantic castles on crags. Sometimes the dust was like a fog. There were broken-down lorries every few miles, so we did not feel that our own mishaps were out of character. At Bhilwara, a rough town whose outskirts seemed overrun by piglets and cows, our car totally collapsed, and we were delayed for an hour and a half. Raúl had a haircut which made him look like a pineapple.

Perhaps I should have been more prepared for the kind of luxury in which we were about to stay at Kotah. In London I had met Mr S. P. Mehra, who lived at Kanpur/Cawnpore and who with great kindness had arranged for us to stay at the Kamla Retreat, described as a 'good guest house' owned by his friend Dr Gaur Hari Singhania, who he said liked cricket and was a member of the history society, as well as being head of the JK Organization. All this sounded charming and modest, even if the JK Organization was new to me. When I told Mr Mehra that we would earlier be visiting Kotah, he wrote back saying that Dr Singhania would be delighted for us to stay at the guest house of JK Synthetics Ltd there. This offer, needless to say, was very acceptable, if surprising.

We reached Kotah in the dark, and driving through the sprawling town discovered that JK Synthetics was a huge factory, with four plants producing nylon filament yarn and tyre cord, polyester and acrylic fibres. The guest house was the equivalent of a cantonment, and was run on somewhat military lines by Captain Davinder Singh, a Sikh, who had flown down specially from Delhi. I was reminded of Sandhurst. We were overcome by the welcome and offers of a personal servant, cars, chauffeurs, guides. Drink seemed unlimited.

In short, the JK Organization is one of the most important industrial and commercial empires in India, with main interests at Kanpur, but with mills, factories and other establishments at Bombay, Calcutta, Kankoli etc. Not long before our arrival a strike of some months at Kotah had kept the factory's residential area in a state of siege. We felt safe indeed behind the wire fence, and with guards at the entrance.

Duly humbled, ashamed at our ignorance, we asked for information about the Singhania family. We discovered that early in the century Lala Juggilal Singhania and Lala Kamlapati Singhania had been running several textile firms at Kanpur, but it was the latter who was the founder of the house of JK. In a period of non-cooperation with the British and boycott of foreign goods Lala Kamlapati had the vision of turning India into an industrial country in its own right. He was the first to produce calico prints from Indian cotton (what would the Manchester Cotton Lobby have thought of that?) and developed other enterprises such as a hosiery factory and sugar and oil mills. In 1934 he established the JK Iron and Steel Company. Through his inspiration and munificence the great Radhakrishna Temple at Kanpur was built. He was succeeded by his son Sir Padampat Singhania, under whom the organization continued to grow. JK was the first to manufacture television sets in India. JK Synthetics was formed at Kotah in 1962, and was the first to produce fibres and dyeable nylon in India. And much else. Sir Padampat died in 1981, his eldest son only forty days afterwards. This was shattering for the family. Later we were to be taken to the Singhania 'picnic palace', once owned by the Maharajah of Kotah, in the Dara forest; it had a swimming-pool, a squash court and a garden, all well tended but unused by the Singhanias since that year. Our unseen host, Dr Gaur Hari, was the second son and Chairman. Other Singhanias were also directors.

The industrialists of India are the new maharajahs, a fellow guest remarked to us. Kotah, a town of a quarter of a million people, was booming. We saw the dam over the River Chambal (unusually clear for India) and the highly popular public gardens full of scented flowers and with an alligator pool (plus one crocodile) over which a bridge hideously swayed. The palace of Kotah had become mostly a museum, and its outside, surmounted by pavilions, was gleaming white and in good repair, with a superbly decorative gateway, above which were two trumpeting elephant effigies. The door had spikes, originally to repel the elephants of attackers.

We were eager to see the famous Kotah murals. The art of Kotah had originally derived from its neighbour Bundi, for Kotah had been part of Bundi state until the seventeenth century. Whereas the figures in Bundi pictures had by the eighteenth century become heavier and the compositions stiffer, Kotah's best period was between 1720 and 1870, excelling in hunting scenes and the depiction of animals. We found the murals well looked after – the colours brilliant, exciting indeed. There was a tremendous display of weapons, as well as palanquins and chairs of ivory etc., and a silver howdah. Anything in bad taste derived from the British.

In the club at Kotah Humphrey Trevelyan, when based at Gwalior, used to see the old Maharajah every evening, clicking his false teeth and playing a card game called jabbar with state officials – the only important rules, Humphrey has said, being that the Maharajah could look at the neighbour's hand and must always win.

Bundi is twenty-four miles from Kotah. Driving along that road in our JK car I was back with Charles Trevelyan in 1830, galloping alone to stop the advancing Jodhpuris from besieging the nineteen-year-old Maharao of Bundi.

But I also felt a comforting link with my own childhood, for my parents had gone fishing at Bundi with Heb Todd when he had become Political Agent for the East Rajputana States. Not only that, but Robbie Robertson, Assistant Commissioner of Police in the Andamans at the time of my birth, had been acting then as Diwan, in view of the ineptitude of the amiable old Maharao. Robbie and his wife Theo had had the usual difficult time coping with court intrigues, especially between the two Maharanis, one fat and plain, the other thin and bad-tempered: apparently not quite so bad as in the days of the previous Maharao, when there had been no less than ten quarrelling Maharanis.

Queen Mary came to Bundi in 1911 when George V was tiger shooting in Nepal, and had been met with the whole paraphernalia of state elephants and uniformed troops. She had been presented with a katar, the national weapon of Bundi, and there had been a fireworks display. She could hardly fail to admire the fantastic reflection in the artificial lake of the honey-coloured palace and Taragargh fort, which Kipling, inappropriately I think, described as the work of goblins rather than of man, constructed out of 'uneasy dreams'. Certainly he was right in saying that it is 'built into and out of the hillside, in gigantic terrace upon terrace and dominates the whole of the city'.

Bundi town is the opposite to Kotah, provincial, unchanged and unspoilt, ramshackle, but once much grander, and more spectacularly situated. There are fortifications all over the mountains. Looking at the Taragargh fort, I again had the sensation of seeing a castle of Outremer. The great rambling airy interior was in dire need of the help of a benevolent industrialist. Bundi paintings are renowned for court scenes and landscapes with blossoming trees. There were plenty of these, especially in the Queen's quarters, but I photographed only murals of Hindu mythology: Krishna lifting the mountain Goverdhan on his little finger; gopis (female cowherds) imploring Krishna after their bathe to give them back their clothes; Lakshmi having a shower of Ganges water from the trunks of elephants.

I was told that the Maharao was in the palace below with his mother. Anxious to meet a real live Maharao/Maharajah I sent him a note, mentioning Heb Todd, the Robertsons and Charles Trevelyan.

Macaulay, near the end of his life: a favourite photograph in the family, probably taken by Claudet

George Otto and Alice Trevelyan, Calcutta 1863

Hannah Trevelyan, Calcutta 1863

A croquet party at Simla

1. Lord Elgin (Viceroy 1862–3), 2. Lieut.-General Sir James Outram (completed the capture of Lucknow, 1858), 3. Major-General Sir John Inglis (commanded troops in the Lucknow Residency), 4. Lord Canning (Governor-General and Viceroy 1856–62), 5. Sir John Lawrence (Viceroy 1863–9), 6. Sir Charles Trevelyan (Finance Member of the Supreme Council 1863–65), 7. Field-Marshal Lord Clyde (Sir Colin Campbell, Commander-in-Chief 1857–60)

Humphrey Trevelyan and Maharajah Bhawani Singh of Chhatarpur, outside the durbar hall, 1942

Guests at Mysore, 1938: Margaret Nahi Khan, Peggie Trevelyan, the Maharajah of Bikaner, Lady Todhunter

Hindu Temple at Tirutchengodu by William Daniell

Maharao Raghubir Singh of
Bundi, c. 1880

The Prince of Mysore and his bride,
1938

Maharao Ishwari Singh of Bundi, and his
adopted son, the future Maharao, Bahadur
Singh

Government House party, Lahore, 1913. Melicent Wathen seven from right, back row

Gerard Wathen and hockey team, Government College, Lahore c. 1913

Walter and his tiger, Dundshi, 1936

Officers of the 5/8th Punjab on a scheme in the Khyber Pass, overlooking Afghanistan, 1936

Camp picquet at Fort Salop, North West Frontier, 1936

But, understandably, he didn't want to be treated as a sight for tourist, and escaped.

Heb had told me about a tiger shoot that the then Maharao had laid on for him. He and his wife Nancy were put on a machan – a raised platform – facing two cleared paths in the jungle:

> When all was ready a bugle sounded and away in the distance one could hear the beaters starting off in the jungle – beating on trees with their sticks, rattling cans and shouting ... One of the State shikaris – hunters – assured me that there was certainly a tiger in the drive, as he had noted a male tiger's pug marks on a path he had brushed the night before. Suddenly the shikari whispered, 'Get ready Sahib, I hear it coming.' Nancy and I nearly burst out laughing, as the noise he had heard was my excited gurgling tummy!

At any rate Heb bagged two that day. Now there is a shortage of tigers in the district. As the Maharajah of Kotah claims to have shot six hundred it is not surprising. *And* he shot them all from the ground, never from a machan.

The father of the present Maharao of Bundi, Bahadur Singh, won the Military Cross with the Indian Cavalry in Arakan during the Burma campaign. He later became ADC to the President of India – a sign indeed of the new order of things. He was a great friend of Mountbatten and had him to stay at his new Phool Sagar palace outside Bundi.

We visited Phool Sagar and found it tawdry and sad, the swimming-pool and squash court all in ruins: quite a contrast to the Singhanias' picnic palace. We were shown rooms full of stuffed animals, including a tiger which had killed twenty people. Some rooms were done as a 'fun' place, in Thirties style, with a bar, stools covered with leopard skins, and pin-ups.

Afterwards, in the half-light, we went to the cenotaphs of the Bundi Maharaos. Most had chhatris, domed pavilions, over them, and one had been the scene of sixty-five suttees. But Bahadur Singh was not there. We wandered in silence in that shadowy place, with so many generations of illustrious dead packed together. It was very late when we got back to Kotah, and Captain Davinder Singh rushed out to tell us that the Managing Director of JK Synthetics, Mr Misra, and his second-in-command, Mr Agarwala, had arranged a surprise party for us, and everyone was waiting.

Charles, working away in 1830 on his *Report on Inland Customs and Town Duties*, and visualizing India as providing raw materials for British manufacturers, would probably have been shocked to be confronted by JK Synthetics. By 1863, when his attitude had altered, he would I am sure have been delighted.

Ooty, and trouble in the North-West

When Hannah left for Ooty in July 1863 with the children and Elizabeth, Charles was in the midst of many worries: currency reform, a storm over the salt monopoly, which had to be withdrawn, and a looming frontier war in the North-West which was bound to be costly. It could not have been much of a surprise to her when he wrote that after all it was impossible for him to leave his desk and join her.

He was a milder man now, less dogmatic, very different to those Kotah days, steering a path between his own convictions and what he felt Wood expected of him. Towards the end of his time as Finance Secretary he was being violently attacked again in the Calcutta press. The fact that it had been revealed that his son was the author of the *Competition Wallah* letters did not help; not that he cared.

George Otto wrote to Charles that he found Madras an 'uncommonly jolly place' compared to Calcutta, and its people were still 'devotedly attached' to his father. On August 3 he wrote to Sir Walter Trevelyan from Ooty:

> After an extremely troublesome and tiring journey, like all journeys in India, we came here towards the end of last month, and found ourselves in Paradise. We went to sleep in bullock-wagons in the midst of the burnt plains of Madras, and before noon the next day were in a climate resembling an Italian winter ... You cannot imagine the pleasure of drawing a blanket over oneself at night, and awaking in the morning to a tub of cold water, after those long long nights of sleeplessness, and mosquitoes, and prickly heat, and quarrelling with the punkah-puller. My mother enjoys herself intensely, or would enjoy herself intensely if my father was with her, and if the English letters had not to go round by Calcutta. She drives about in a pony-chair ... Alice delights in her pony. We take long rides all over the mountains. Her pleasure is somewhat tempered by the wild buffaloes, which carry on a guerrilla warfare with all Europeans.

There was a rumour of a tiger on Elk Hill, and he found the Ooty Club 'very pleasant' whenever he felt a desire for billiards and the company of bachelors.

Although Hannah enjoyed the change, and thought Ooty's air was like champagne, Charles's 'salt trouble' weighed on her mind and she poured out her worries in a letter to Margaret. She was always fussing about Alice. For instance they had a new friend up there, she said, Sir Victor Brooke, an Anglo-Irish baronet. 'He is a fine handsome fellow as brave as a lion, ignorant and uncultivated, very young even for his age, which is twenty. He is very fond of us and quite lives with us. He has never I believe thought of flirting, falling in love etc. He behaves to Alice just as he does to me. But still of course people talk.' Brooke had proposed going back to Calcutta with them, and then accompanying George Otto to Delhi and Agra. Afterwards he would sail home with George Otto and Alice, and at Marseilles would journey with them through France to England. 'I was a good deal startled at this. To travel together, three such young things, without a chaperone . . . I think it would be placing Alice in such a very uncomfortable position, and exposing her to much unkind gossip.' Eventually Hannah decided on a quiet frank talk with Sir Victor, and said she could not allow such a thing and explained why. At which the poor boy 'coloured crimson'. However the next year he managed to find and marry another Alice, daughter of another Anglo-Irish baronet, Sir Alan Bellingham; and these two were the parents of the future Field-Marshal Lord Alanbrooke.

By mid-October Hannah wrote to say that she was back at Calcutta, 'this most odious place', where the heat was 'intolerably greater' than ever, 104° in the shade. She reported to Margaret that Charles was looking 'fairly', Alice had been quite ill again, and that Lord Elgin was more despised and disliked than ever, 'which is very unfortunate for Charles, because Lord E. really does support him, only it does no good for he has neither authority nor influence.' Every now and then, she said, the Council 'bursts into a sort of jealous attack on Charles.' As for the Lahore business, there would be no end of full dress mornings; an exhibition was to be opened, durbars would be held, and there would be fêtes, races etc. The poor ladies of Calcutta were having to pay £30 and £40 for dresses.

The tone of Wood's letters to Charles could occasionally be sharp, but on the whole was appreciative and affectionate. But Charles had had to warn him that he would probably have to retire in 1865.

The trouble along the frontier in the North-West was one reason why Elgin had wanted to hold his Council at Lahore. The original source of disturbance had been at Sitana, between Saidu in Swat and what was to be the Gilgit Agency, where the Sayyids (holy men) had sheltered mutineers in 1857. Sitana was burned down by the British, but a new base had been formed nearby at Malka on the upper Indus. Alarming stories circulated about an underground Muslim organization which was being built up throughout northern India, with a headquarters as far away as Patna, to recruit Bengali Muslims. So a major expedition under General Sir Neville Chamberlain had been launched in October through the Ambela Pass towards Malkan. Fanatical tribesmen immediately arose, aided by the Akhund of Swat, and Chamberlain's force was pinned down in the pass for six weeks. Charles, always against frontier wars, which he considered a sign of weakness in the central authority, was outraged by accounts of the burning of villages. Worse, he saw the campaign as an indirect attempt to interfere in Afghan affairs at present unsettled by the death of old Dost Mohammed. The new Amir was his son Sher Ali (against whom Lytton was in years to come to launch the Second Afghan War), but his position was being contested by a host of relatives.

Against the background of this crisis George Otto set out on his tour of the Upper Provinces. By the time he had reached Delhi one of the British picquets at the Ambela Pass had been overwhelmed. On November 13 there was a more serious reverse. This was not however the only bad news.

He wrote to his sister Margaret from Delhi, 'the most interesting place in the world, Rome excepted', and told her that Lord Elgin was dying. The Army had also met another and more serious disaster, and people were expecting a retreat during the winter. Meanwhile sedition had 'begun to show itself in our Sikh regiments ... God grant that it may be exaggerated!' (It was not.)

> Everyone here is praying that my father may take the reins; and, as men believe what they wish, it is universally said that he has the appointment [Viceroy] in his pocket. No-one trusts anybody except him and Sir John Lawrence. Unfortunately the Provisional Governor-General is by law the Governor of Madras, poor Sir W. Denison, who knows as much of Northern India, or Southern India for the matter of that, as a pig does of prize-fighting. Lord Elgin might have induced one of the mountain tribes by a bribe of a lac [one hundred thousand] to do what will cost us thousands of lives and millions of money ... So much for the [1863 Budget] surplus alas! Lord Elgin hates India, and knows nothing about it. He only stayed out for the sake of the income: and what a precious mess he has got us into.

He had also been to Lucknow for a week, and compared its siege to Londonderry in 1688 and Hougoumont at Waterloo in 1815. At Cawnpore he had been over all the scenes of the Mutiny with Captain

Mowbray Thomson, one of the four survivors. He was especially moved by the Satichaura Ghat.

The visit to Cawnpore gave him the idea for his famous book, which was published in 1866 and many times reprinted. In that book he recorded that he interviewed sixty-three native and half-caste witnesses. On his return to Calcutta he searched out the original narratives written for the Government by civil officers.

Elgin actually died on November 20 1863. He had known that he was dying, and had even chosen the site for his grave and had telegraphed to Denison to take over. He had had a heart attack when crossing a bridge made of plaited twigs that had swung too violently over the gorge of the Chandra River. The suggestion that Charles would take his place as Viceroy was of course wishful thinking.

Che giorno felice!

George Otto and Alice left Calcutta after Christmas 1863. He looked forward to finding a seat in Parliament, and was secure in the knowledge that one day he would be the owner of twenty thousand acres.

Charles took Hannah to Agra. 'Mamma has had to confess,' he wrote on his return, 'that there *is* a beautiful thing in India – the Taj.' He recalled how, when he was a young man at Delhi, an English officer had committed suicide at the Taj because he wanted to die in the 'loveliest spot on earth'.

Hannah, still low in spirits, nevertheless was relieved that George Otto had left, for he had become seriously changed. 'He has no colour,' she had written to Margaret, 'his cheeks are thin, his eyes look quite large, and his cheek bones are developed. There are some people who cannot live here in India, and he is one.' All the same, until just before his departure, the boy had been working hard, grappling with all his father's papers and Sir Charles Wood's practically illegible scribbled letters, so as to be 'prepared on all topics when he returns'.

She was consoled also in knowing that her presence at Calcutta was essential to her husband:

> I really have a great deal of occupation working with Charles. You see entre nous it is very important for me to keep the threads of everything he does in my hands, or else I should not know enough to be able to interpose a word of caution or opposition at the right time ... I read all the dispatches, negotiations, instructions sent, and I assure you I know a great deal more about it [finance] than

anyone here but C. He feels very strongly that I have to be constantly on the watch that he does not commit himself by interfering beyond giving his advice and opinions as Member of Council. And he is far more willing to hear reason than he used to be.

At the height of the drama over the Ambela campaign she managed to dissuade Charles from sending an 'elaborate epistle' of criticism to Sir Robert Napier, who acted briefly as Viceroy until Sir William Denison arrived from Madras. Charles did not trust the Lieutenant-Governor of the Punjab, Sir Robert Montgomery (grandfather of 'Monty', the Field-Marshal). After all, Afghanistan had been his special subject, and he wrote long letters to Wood insisting that Sher Ali should be recognized as the new Amir.

Denison dreaded having to handle the crisis. In the event the 'petite guerre' suddenly ended, due to the British having burnt down a village or two. As Humphrey Trevelyan wrote in his book *The India We Left*, 'the tribes acquired a new respect for the British army, which kept their part of the border quiet until 1897'.

But what of the effects of the campaign on Charles's Budget? Douglas Forsyth, Montgomery's secretary, breakfasted with the formidable Finance Secretary at Calcutta and 'had to sustain a vigorous onslaught, particularly from Lady Trevelyan', who, as he told his superior, 'evidently made up her mind that somebody or other is to be impeached and crucified for thus wantonly wasting all Sir T's supplies!'

Five weeks after Denison had settled into Government House there was a telegram via Bombay announcing that the new Viceroy was already on his way from England. And he was Charles's old friend, Sir John Lawrence, the saviour of the Punjab during the Mutiny. 'Sir William is greatly discomposed,' Hannah said, 'at being sent back in such a hurry.' The news also unleashed all the niggling spite, pettiness and envy that was so typical of Calcutta society and which she hated:

Sir John's appointment is very unpopular here. They say he is no administrator, knows nothing of India but the Punjab where he has a host of hangers on whom he will bring down and put over them. The ladies say he is not a gentleman, very dirty and ragged. We say he has been in England some years and has emancipated himself from Punjab jobbery, and has learnt to wash and dress. *No one* here likes it but Charles, who really and cordially does.

This last was not really surprising. Lawrence had left for India at ten days' notice, weeping at having to say goodbye to his wife and two-year-old child. He did indeed have a strange dishevelled, craggy appearance, but in England he was a national hero, and at the time of his appointment he seemed the ideal man to cope with the Ambela affair.

As the moment for his arrival approached, so opposition became 'quite ferocious' in the Calcutta newspapers. Hannah was taken aback to learn that he had appointed as his secretary a man whom she particularly disliked, Dr Hathaway, 'who has been horsewhipped over and over again', and certainly one of those Punjab hangers-on.

Back in 1862, when Charles had left for Calcutta, Lawrence had said to him: 'You have lost all your *vice*. Do try and come back as vicious as ever.' Not only did Lawrence find Charles still 'unvicious', but he was alarmed to see him looking so worn, with erysipelas round the eye. Hannah, hearing about his reaction, at the earliest opportunity arranged with the Viceroy for her husband to be divested of some of his minor responsibilities.

An immense ball in Lawrence's honour was given by Cecil Beadon at Belvedere. 'I wore my rose-coloured silk,' Alice was told, 'with a new cape trimmed with real wild roses.' The letters to Alice were full of spicy Calcutta gossip, about the Bishop and the Stracheys, and how Lady Elgin had given her maid all her unopened boxes of dresses which were now being auctioned at great prices. 'Walter Ellis has just been here. Such an object! White cotton mittens cut to the middle of his fingers, and a red sash around his waist!!! He seemed nervous and quite scared of the money market. His appearance was like a mad French cook.' Later he came to lunch, and 'ate his soup with his knife and fork, upon my honour he did'. One is not surprised to learn that he was eventually blackballed from the Bengal Club.

Charles was enchanted by Sir John Lawrence. 'He is the instructor and advisor, instead of the learner, he draws out everybody and is full of action and energy.' On the other hand the snobs of Calcutta thought it wrong for the Viceroy to go *on foot* to church, and the wording of his invitations was not à la mode. He even walked alone on the Maidan and was chased by a buffalo. Knowing the languages, he also 'rambled' in the bazaar in order to hear what the natives were saying about the Europeans. He let it be known that he hated going to the races, not to mention all balls and parties.

Nevertheless, he had to give a ball at Government House on February 9. Hannah wore her new ball dress, which was 'really magnificent', though there was a small tragedy: her cape was 'exquisitely trimmed with seaweed made of wax', which promptly melted. Lawrence was not there to receive guests. This lack of etiquette was considered an affront until a doctor was suddenly sent for.

> Soon Sir John came in looking miserably ill and asked me to walk about with him, which I did. Then we sat down and poor man he was violently sick. I trembled for my dress, but the sofa and floor were a sad sight.

The 'Competition Wallah' article on Calcutta now appeared in *Macmillan's Magazine*. Charles on rereading it liked it even better than before. But for some while local newspapers held back from republishing it, 'the motives for which you can easily guess'. The *Friend of India* soon however went into the attack, linking Charles, Lawrence and Beadon as 'India's greatest curse'. A rival paper mocked at such hysteria: 'Week after week Sir Charles Trevelyan is painted in its columns in colours shocking to good taste and devoid of all good feeling.'

The 1864 Budget was well received by Wood and *The Times*, but Charles's speech annoyed Sir Bartle Frere, now Governor of Bombay, because of an admittedly clumsy comparison with the situation in Ireland in 1847; the point made was that there was a danger in too much state interference in providing public works in connection with the increase in cotton production. Sir Bartle said that a more apt comparison would have been the early days of the gold rushes in California and Australia. The all-important opium revenues were also beginning to crash.

Hannah had hoped they could return to England in the winter, but to her great dismay Wood wrote Charles 'a most urgent letter' begging him to undertake the vast work of currency reform. She knew Charles would never refuse this. As she told Harry Holland: 'In every way it is odious to me, as I have not the confidence in C's management of the currency as I have in him when he thoroughly understands his work. He says himself he feels he is walking on a volcano, that he may make some great mistake, as he has *no one* to consult with. At home the Chancellor can test every stage ... Here there is not a creature who has ever thought about currency.'

But when Charles tried to introduce a gold currency it was disallowed by Wood.

The best news for Hannah was that Lawrence had decided to take the whole Council up to Simla: a move that was to lead to Simla becoming the official summer headquarters of the Government of India. As a result the Trevelyans were up there from late April to the end of October 1864, accompanied by the maid Elizabeth, now in good health, and Charles's secretary, Denzil Onslow.

Hannah at first found the sheer grandeur of the scenery depressing, but certainly preferred Simla to Ooty. To Charles it was a 'noble place', reminding him of a village in the Austrian Alps a hundred times magnified. But their house, The Tendrils, was like a barn: 'great wasty rooms, an enormous table in one, and in another a large torn broken sofa'. There was also an old tattered four-poster bed. 'When we arrived tired to death after twelve days not going to bed, we found not a box had arrived and no linen, nothing. An old muslin curtain and a wrapper or two formed our bedding. Not one door had a fastening of any kind and could not be closed.'

The boxes contained a lot of Hannah's special chintz, so on their arrival she set about buying some 'old wretched wormeaten' furniture in the bazaar and finding a tailor to do the covering. She put fires in every room. Luckily there appeared to be no insects in the house. A bed had to be made specially for Bishop Cotton who was coming to stay with them. But when Hannah saw the 'holes' in which people like her friends the Lushingtons had to endure she was thankful for 'rackety old Tendrils', with the monkeys frisking about on its roof.

Elizabeth thought Simla compared unfavourably with her native Somerset, or for that matter Ooty, where she had dined out 'quite the lady' with captains and majors. At Simla, so Denzil Onslow wrote to George Otto, she had to compete with 'Jezebel and all her daughters', and be content with sergeants. Gradually Hannah began to enjoy herself; she loved her walks round Jakko or to 'some shoulder of the hills, looking on green waves all round me'.

She also found herself caught up in the usual Simla rivalries, 'worse than Calcutta':

Last night we had a grand discussion about the Ball to be given for the Governor-General and the Commander-in-Chief. The question was whether a certain Mrs. Vesey was to be invited or not. *She* is the lady connected so much with the C-in-chief, and *besides* bears a very bad character. Sir John excluded her from the Government House list as did Lord Elgin. Mrs. Strachey, one of the committee [and a friend of Mrs Vesey] ... is vehement she should be asked 'and so give Sir John a lesson'. I say we do not invite Sir John to give him a lesson but to do him an honour, and it would be a perfect insult to invite him to meet a lady he declined to receive in his own house. Mrs. Lushington and Mrs. Bailey quite agree with me ... I am quite determined if Mrs. Vesey is invited to have nothing to do with the Ball, and to tell Sir John my reason. I give no opinion as to the lady. I simply say we should confine our invitations to the Government House list, when we give an entertainment to the Viceroy. Jane Strachey, whose imperiousness and bullying is something awful when excited, is now beside herself because her grandmother was excluded Government House by Lady William, and her mother by Lady Canning, and she is very anxious to prove that *that* is no consequence.

The next day Colonel Strachey sent a 'most bullying and insolent letter' about the ball.

There is another great quarrel going on with which we have nothing to do. *She Stoops to Conquer* is going to be acted, and Mrs. Strachey and Mrs. Innes are fighting for the part of the heroine. I do really think the part suits Mrs. Innes best, though Mrs. Strachey is the best actress, but her despotic and violent behaviour has set the whole corps dramatique up in arms ... I do not think anything seems to stir up more bad blood than theatricals.

Considering that the row about the ball was going on just after the funeral of Sir John's nephew, who had been killed when a bridge collapsed, the squabbles about the ball do seem a bit hard. At any rate the ball was postponed, sine die. The whole business seems now reminiscent of J. G. Farrell's novel *The Hill Station* ...

Lawrence lived at Peterhof, since the monstrous pile of Viceregal Lodge had not yet been built or thought of, and Hannah was often asked to preside there as first lady. Every morning the Viceroy's band would be sent to play outside The Tendrils. Croquet was all the rage, especially down at Annandale.

The Stracheys were living at The Yarrows, which was considered to be the worst of the larger houses at Simla, though it had a vast and wonderful view. Once a leopard leapt on to the verandah and Jane chased it away with a croquet mallet. She was a great one for charades, but could never persuade Hannah to join in.

Just as everyone was about to leave Simla Charles was struck down with his varicose veins. The inflammation was made worse by the shaking of the jampan during the descent, and by the time they reached Calcutta they realized that it was imperative that he should get back to England as soon as possible. But he insisted that he could not leave until at least April 1865, after his Budget.

They arrived in the aftermath of a cyclone. Every house was 'shattered', Hannah reported to Alice. 9 Elysium Row had lost its outside shades, its railings, every tree and shrub; the coach house had gone. Many houses had lost their upper storeys. Trees had been uprooted, the Maidan was littered with dead cows. The cyclone had happened so suddenly that people going to the Opera had their carriages overturned and 'literally had to crawl home in all their finery on hands and knees'. It had been worse at Madras, where Denison reported thirty thousand dead.

The attacks on Charles in the *Friend of India* were now so violent that Hannah began to suspect that Dr Hathaway was passing on confidential information from Council meetings. He was 'such a scoundrel', jealous that Charles's reputation was overshadowing Lawrence's. According to Denzil Onslow, Hathaway's nickname at Calcutta was 'Stinking Jack'. Eventually Hannah was forced to have a confrontation with Lawrence about it, but he 'pretended' not to be convinced. 'I am very uneasy about Sir John,' she told Alice. 'He is too old to bear worry in this country, he looks uncommonly oppressed. He is too fearful about public opinion.' And alas, the verdict of history has generally been that Lawrence did lack 'elasticity', and was too rigid in his views, unable to learn new ways.

Hannah at Simla had written that Charles would not leave India until the doom of Income Tax was sealed, and this even made their departure in April problematical. In spite of many 'quarrels' Wood's letters were still affectionate. 'I hope you may be able to dispense with the Income Tax,' he wrote on January 9, 'but I am very much afraid that you will not be able to spare it.' Opium sales were falling, there was a drought in the Bombay Presidency, more frontier wars were threatening, civil servants were demanding increased pay; for the first time in three years India had a deficit. Charles had hoped that he could compensate for the abolition of Income Tax by economizing on military and naval expenditure. On the other hand, urged by Florence Nightingale, he was determined to go ahead with building new and 'sanitary' barracks for European troops, and proposed to Wood that there should be loans floated for the purpose. Wood however was firmly against such a suggestion.

In spite of Hannah watching over him, Charles could not be restrained from 'interfering' in other departments, mostly too detailed to be described here. He became unpopular with some European diehards for his advocacy of the abolition of whipping criminals, and pressed for an improved prison system, in spite of the enormous cost. He supported Maine's campaign for the abolition of Grand Juries, which discriminated against native indigo-growers. It was noted by his enemies that his policy about financing public works was hardly consistent with his Madras Governorship, when he used to launch into expensive schemes without the consent of the central Government, the excuse being the urgency of the situation.

Lady Lawrence at last arrived at Calcutta. Hannah found her as always 'extremely sweet, intelligent, with plenty of conversation and quite at her ease'. Smart clothes were not Lady Lawrence's interest either, and she was forced to realize that she had not brought sufficiently grand dresses from England.

As the Budget day approached, Charles looked 'totally exhausted', and it was obvious that he had 'greatly diminished energy'. 'Every day,' Hannah wrote, 'brings fresh bad tidings. Yesterday one million additional military estimates for Bombay and Madras, mostly owing to the enormous increase of prices and the scarcity. I do not know how this terrible want of money can be met except by a renewal of the Income Tax. This of course is mortifying to your Father.'

And so up to the very last day, it almost looked as if the Income Tax would have to be retained. Lawrence was totally in favour of doing this, but Charles – looking 'worn and broken' – was able to organize a 'Cabinet revolt' against him, and eventually it was decided to abolish it. As a compromise Lawrence agreed to 'lay on a few export duties' – Charles (ever the disciple of free trade) 'does not like this', said Hannah, 'but thinks it trifling as it only yields a small sum. You have no idea of the excitement of the Committee. They quite raged when Sir John proposed to telegraph Sir Charles Wood.' In his Budget speech Charles tried to be reassuring about the abolition of the tax: 'As a potent but imperfect machine it should be regarded as the great financial reserve of the country; and it will now be laid on the shelf complete in all its gear, ready to be reimposed in case of any new emergency'.

And reimposed it was in 1867. Charles believed that he had left the finances of India in an 'excellent state', and was consequently pained on arrival in England to find the Budget mostly disallowed and regarded by Wood as a 'complication of mistakes'. He had gone ahead regardless of Wood's instructions in arranging for loans to be floated for the barracks. He had increased the Bombay salt tax, again against Wood's wishes, and English industrialists also attacked the new export duties. His enemies called his Budget his Second Rebellion, a Parthian Shot. But he left just before two great disasters which affected subsequent Budgets: the Orissa famine, and a crash of banks mainly at Bombay and particularly that of the Parsee baronet, Sir Jamsetjee Jeejeebhoy, owing to the over-production of cotton 'bubble'. Then as a result of new Russian advances into Turkestan, military expenditure had to be increased.

The Finance Secretaryship was handed over to William Massey. Hannah dreaded the voyage home; 'However it is my last, for I am sure nothing will bring me here again, or Charles either. We leave at daybreak Sunday morning. Che giorno felice!'

But almost immediately after sailing Hannah contracted measles. So it was a wretched journey for her.

In his years of retirement Charles continued to be consulted on Indian affairs, and gave evidence on committees. He also ran various charities. Hannah died in 1873, and in 1874 he was created a baronet. In 1875 he married Eleanora Campbell.

In 1865 George Otto became Liberal MP for Tynemouth. In the following year his book *Cawnpore* was published, and he also wrote *Ladies in Parliament*, 'in the manner of Aristophanes' (though with lines that now seem pure John Betjeman). From 1868 he was an MP in Scotland until his resignation in 1897. The Gladstone ministry of 1868 entered into its great series of reforms, including the reorganization of the Army and the abolition of the purchase system, for which the Trevelyans, father and son, had so long campaigned. In that Government the young George Otto was appointed civil Lord of the Admiralty. In 1869 he married Caroline Philips, an heiress to a Lancashire cotton merchant and daughter of a Liberal MP. It was a great romance. A long and illustrious career in politics and literature lay ahead. His father inherited Wallington in Northumberland in 1879, and after Charles's death in 1886 it passed to George Otto.

During his seven years' tenure of Wallington Charles showed his usual amazing energy and *zest* for improving the estate. Often he would be seen galloping before breakfast with his coat-tails flying on his way to give workmen instructions. He built two schools and improved the church. He is remembered as always having had a kind word for everyone he passed. The last time he left Wallington before his death in London was typical. Ten minutes before rushing to catch the train south, he was clearing undergrowth and hacking down trees.

There is still a strong feeling of Charles's presence at Wallington, which now belongs to the National Trust. The inscription that he had put on a fountain in the local village, Cambo, is an appropriate epitaph to his own career and the careers of his descendants:

'Mindful of future generations'.

A flirtation

Ernest Trevelyan was Charles's nephew, son of Henry. He became a judge at the High Court of Calcutta and a member of the Senate of

Calcutta University. Quiet, unassuming, hardworking, resourceful, old world courtesy: these were descriptions applied to Ernest throughout his life. He was also said to be a 'great tease' where young ladies were concerned.

He retired early because he did not wish his children to endure the same sort of separation from their parents as he had gone through. He went to live at Oxford, and there became Reader in Indian Law and Sub-Warden of All Souls.

In March 1885, whilst he was still a young man at Calcutta, his first wife died, and in the following month on the sea journey to England his baby daughter also died.

Returning on board the *Nizam* he met old Sir William Gregory, nearly seventy, and his vivacious wife Augusta, less than half his age. Lady Gregory was to be famous as the Irish playwright, and it was she who with W. B. Yeats founded the Abbey Theatre in Dublin. Her affair with Wilfrid Scawen Blunt had perforce cooled off, and now she found herself intrigued by Ernest Trevelyan. She lent him Blunt's new book of essays, *Ideas on India*, which was critical of British rule. 'At first,' she recorded, 'his indignation and wrath seemed to overcome his melancholy.' He denounced the book as a 'pack of mis-statements' and one that should be 'burnt by the common hangman'. Yet he also had to admit, she said, that it contained certain truths.

Blunt had been a supporter of the radical ideas of Lord Ripon, now succeeded by Lord Dufferin. In his Introduction he claimed that he had written the 'first complete and fearless apology of Indian home rule which had been published'. Indeed many of his views were not unlike Charles's in the 1830s, though he did also make an attack on the influence of the British memsahib.

One night Lady Gregory inveigled Ernest on deck to watch the moon rise. But it took so long that he left her and went in to play whist. Perhaps she had scared him. In due course she made herself the centre of social activity on board, organizing charades and with the help of Ernest raising money for a sick stewardess.

By the time she met Ernest again at Calcutta she wasn't sure whether she hadn't also fallen in love with Sir Auckland Colvin, an old friend of hers. Sir Auckland was the son of Charles Trevelyan's colleague who had died during the Mutiny at Agra, and was financial adviser to the Viceroy Lord Dufferin, whom Lady Gregory also found fascinating. Ernest was at the state ball at Government House, and the next morning she met him again in the 'park', where deer were romantically 'chasing peacocks over the green grass'.

But soon she was away to Ceylon, in order, as a good wife, to look at a statue of her husband outside the museum at Colombo. Her mind nevertheless went back to that warm night on deck waiting for the moonrise, and she wrote a poem about it, ending:

> I think we just a step above
> That mystic laboratory stand
> Where friendship is transferred to love
> By the chance contact of a hand.
>
> I think the sparks that flash and fly
> From our four eyes, were we alone,
> Would find the mine now guarded by
> The non-conductive looker-on.

The non-conductor was her husband.

As it happened, whilst on his short visit to England, Ernest had already proposed to a young lady, Julia Mark, but the engagement had been broken off after a week. Another cause of the melancholy on board the *Nizam*? However five years later Julia and Ernest did get married, and they had six children. Family tradition has it that whenever he travelled to and from India with his children he would always take a cow to provide milk for the journey. The cow would go dry in the Red Sea.

Ernest's elder sister, Emily Trevelyan, married the Edward Vibart who escaped from Delhi in 1857. She died in 1889, as a result of her horse falling over a precipice at the hill-station of Dalhousie.

II

'SELECT YOUR LIFE partner at Pooja Matrimonial Service'. That and 'Join the Tigers Judo Club' were the slogans that greeted us everywhere at Jaipur, the Pink City, indisputably the loveliest city in India, even if E. M. Forster called it a sham – and I could see what he meant.

Apart from the fact that Heb Todd had been Prime Minister in 1939, I can't claim any special link with Jaipur or its neighbour Amber. So I shall skip writing about the sight-seeing, mostly done in an 'Indian helicopter', Lala Ram's motorbike rickshaw. Lala was in charge of 'fattening' our minds, but he also took us to two weddings: one grand in a marquee, where the bride's hands and arms were so laden with jewellery that she had to be fed, and where the band of the 123rd Grenadiers, mostly Nepalese, wore tartan, and the other humble and noisy, with people again carrying acetylene chandeliers on their heads and where a solemn rather Jewish-looking man in glasses did a solo belly dance. Lala also drove us into the jungle to feed wild langur monkeys with bananas. He knew some good gossip. For instance, an eighteenth-century Maharajah of Jaipur had a penis 'seven measures' long. He would select girls from the bazaar, and they always died from the subsequent ordeal. Afterwards the bodies would be thrown to the crocodiles in the palace tank.

My last image of Jaipur is driving with Lala past the Palace of the Winds, looking like a great piece of stage scenery, and seeing monkeys (rhesus) leaning out of its windows as old women do in Latin countries.

So off to Bharatpur. The ubiquitous Charles had been guardian to its young Maharajah Balwant Singh in 1829. Heb had lived there in 1935 when he was Political Agent for the East Rajputana States, and Olive, Walter and the Berkeleys had stayed with him for the Maharajah of Alwar's shoot.

'Rock bottom day as far as physical comfort is concerned,' I wrote in my diary. We reported to the bus station in Jaipur, at the suspiciously late hour of 11 am, to find our vehicle jam-packed and so filthy that you could barely see out of the windows. It was obvious that over the past weeks a number of people had been sick over the sides. In the *Times of India* we read that somewhere a bus had overturned and thirteen people had been killed: a not unusual state of affairs apparently. Three Germans and one unhappy Japanese student were also on board.

In the heat of the day we shed a few passengers. By then we had decided that we were probably getting too old for this type of travel. At each stop we were mobbed by people selling the drink Limca, rissoles and peanuts. As we jogged over the long straight road we could dimly see that the great industry in those parts was making chapattis out of dried buffalo dung. Occasionally we noticed hills the colour of red Devon earth with forts on them. At Bharatpur it was total uproar, with porters and rickshaw wallahs struggling and fighting round us. Eventually one old man insisted on carrying our two heavy suitcases on his head to the rickshaw of his choice.

We made for the Public Works Circuit Bungalow, which some insane person had recommended to us. The long cream-coloured building with a verandah seemed attractive enough. At first we were told there were no rooms available, but the pleasant manager intervened and said we could have one for five and a half rupees, about thirty pence, each – if I heard him aright. But what a room: dust and hair on the floor, squatter loo stained brown. We won a battle for blankets, another sheet each and some light bulbs.

Bharatpur traditionally was a battle-scarred country, not least because of the siege by the British in 1826, as a result of which Balwant Singh was put on the throne. But our real reason for going there had been to see the bird sanctuary, which in my parents' day had been the scene of some of the best duck shooting in the world.

Walter's photographs of the duck shoot are all of tiny specks flying in formation over reeds and marshland, or distant white blobs representing storks. There had been thirty-five guns at that shoot in 1935, and the bag had been 1,235. At Lord Linlithgow's shoot on February 6 1938 there had been thirty-nine guns, and the bag had been 2,568.

What on earth was done with all those dead things? (When Walter was on leave at Jhansi in 1941 he wrote to me that in his game book he had a total of 592 snipe, 541 duck and teal, and 191 partridge.)

To see the birds properly in the Ghana, you must be up and about before dawn. Even Olive, from her photographs, was more suitably dressed than Raúl, who put on a bright yellow anorak – much to the disapproving scowls of a busload of Japanese, who had brought telescopic cameras – but they wore ties, pin-striped suits and well polished shoes.

We were just in time to see the Siberian cranes before they departed north: huge and white, red-headed, with black tips on their wings in flight, Bharatpur is the only place they migrate to. Through the chilly mist we began to see thousands of strange primeval creatures, at first storks and cranes, some roosting in trees or standing on untidy nests, some creakily flapping their wings, some landing clumsily on the water: raw red necks, scarlet legs, orange beaks of an enormous size, purple wattles. There was an awful lot of quacking and squawking, and as the light improved we began to identify ibises of different sorts, flamingoes, Sarus cranes, spoonbills, pelicans, and for us English the more homely greylags, pintails, wigeons, pochards, coots. Then we saw droves and droves of bright green pigeons, ring doves, hoopoes, bulbuls, parakeets, and jacanas, which are an exotic sort of moorhen. And there were eagles, cormorants, kingfishers, and little dabblers and waders. Such an ammoniac stink from the cormorants' nests!

When light came, and songbirds drowned the squawking, our rickshaw wallah stopped at the Keoladeo temple, and said we would have to walk the next six kilometres round a lake. It became hot. The water was cerulean, the weeds usually reddish or yellow. Then: WARNING – PYTHONS. But we didn't meet any. However we were nearly run down by a couple of sambur, the Indian elk, very Landseer.

And yes, our bill at the Circuit Bungalow was only eleven rupees. Despite the so-called problems the staff had such charm that we forgave all. And we were able to take a taxi to Agra.

At Agra we were reunited with Diana Petre and Francis King, ready for our joint expedition to Chhatarpur. Diana had had laryngitis, and Francis still had the squitters – we heard how on train loos gusts of wind would blow up from underneath.

I saw the Taj at sunrise, which was even better than by moonlight.

Travels with Bob

In October 1912 E. M. Forster set out on his first visit to India. His companions on the voyage out were all also Cambridge men: Goldsworthy Lowes Dickinson, Gordon Luce and Robert Calverley Trevelyan.

Bob, as he was always known in the family and to friends, was the second of George Otto's three sons. The Trevies – the conglomerate name given them at Cambridge – had similarities in features and a considerable physical toughness, and had fully absorbed the intellectual liberalism of their heritage; but in temperament, and indeed eccentricities, they were very different.

The eldest, Charles Philips Trevelyan, has been described as a romantic crusader of the Left, and became a Labour Cabinet Minister. The youngest was George Macaulay Trevelyan, the well-known historian. Bob, born in 1872, was a poet and translator from the Greek. Beatrice Webb, the formidable Fabian, called him the 'highly respectable wastrel of the family', and to Max Beerbohm he was a 'scholar gypsy'. Many leading intellectuals of his generation loved him, and by 1904 he was Forster's most helpful critic.

Forster wanted to go to India to see his Indian friend Masood. He was famous now because of *Howards End* and had enough money to travel. Dickinson, established as an outstanding humanist writer and philosopher, soon to be regarded as the spiritual father of the League of Nations, was travelling on a scholarship, and wanted to visit Indian schools, factories, jails etc. Gordon Luce, also a poet, was taking up a post in Burma. Bob, it would seem, was merely hoping to fall under some exotic Indian spell. He had met the great Bengali poet, Rabindranath Tagore, in London with W. B. Yeats and had had him to stay, which had ensured literary introductions at Calcutta.

The party found the SS *City of Birmingham* packed with Army officers and wives, who were bemused by all its high-brow chit-chat and esoteric literary jokes. Bob used to hold forth at meals on subjects such as the early Greek novelists and Nero as a stage-manager. Eventually one of the passengers could stand it no longer and cried out: 'But what is the use of all these scraps of information?' To which Bob replied: 'Why, to make amusing conversation as we're doing now.'

The difficulty for the 'Professors' as they were known, was how to avoid deck-quoits, shovel-board and other such games, not to mention fancy-dress dances. Forster thought the women 'vile' and 'pretty rotten on the native question'. Everyone agreed that in India you must speak politely to the natives; 'they would despise you if you didn't'. When Forster told a woman passenger that he was going to stay with an Indian, she gave a little gasp and changed the subject.

At Bombay Forster acquired a good servant, but Bob and Dickinson shared a 'deplorable' Madrasi called Samuel, who cheated them and kept wailing: 'This is no proper arrangement' whenever asked to do some work. After two days Forster was off to Masood at Aligarh. The others saw him off, but as the train drew out Bob was too preoccupied with explaining to the 'Byronic' young Kenneth Searight, an Army officer whom they had met on the ship, the complexities and delights of the 'Lake Hunt' – an annual four-day Hare and Hounds event, organized by the Trevies and other Trinity College men over the fells and dales of the Lake District in England.

At Ajanta, by Mary Fedden

Luce had gone on to Burma. Bob and Dickinson set off for the cave-temples of Ellora and Ajanta. Bob thought the paintings at Ajanta the finest example of Indian art he had yet seen, holding their own 'against the best Italian frescoes'. But Forster, finally, only had time for Ellora; he was to go there with a friend of Masood, whose outbursts – as has been pointed out by Forster's editors – are recalled at the end of *A Passage to India*. Bob found a 'wonderful pool at the top of the gorge' at Ajanta to bathe in; and in the cliffs, above a water-fall, eagles were nesting.

Next stop Lahore, where Forster joined them. They all stayed with different friends, Bob with a Harrovian whose name he had muddled. Forster was with Malcolm Darling, the Deputy Commissioner, who had been with him at King's. For a while Darling had also been guardian and tutor to the Rajah of Dewas Senior, with whom Forster was later to stay (*The Hill of Devi*). Dickinson, having a hectic time, took Forster to see schools and colleges at Lahore, and delivered a lecture to a Christian college thinking it was the Brahmo Samaj (the theistic Hindu church to which Rabindranath Tagore belonged and which was founded by Rammohan Roy in Charles Trevelyan's early days); the audience listened, sadly but politely. All three were taken round the Museum by Gerard Wathen, a friend of Darling's and believed to be the model for Fielding in *A Passage to India*.

Forster thought Lahore a 'beastly' place, and Dickinson said it was like an American town with endless broad dusty roads and half-finished buildings in desolate gardens. Later Dickinson, observing the 'twaddle and tea' taking place to the music of Gounod after tennis at the club, likened this Anglo–Indian world to floating on an Atlantic liner – he thought of the *Titanic*. And that made him begin to wonder whether there was more to those men and women than at first would appear. 'They stand for the West, for the energy of the world, in this vast Nature, that is determinate and purposive, not passively repetitionary'. Theirs was a tragic dream, doomed.

The plan now was to go on to Peshawar, where they had been invited to stay in the regimental guest rooms of the Royal West Kents by young Searight. Bob had to be left behind because he thought he had German measles. He was 'very peevish' about it, saying: 'Well, if the whole regiment *did* get it, what would it matter? I feel all right, and why shouldn't I come?' Forster said: 'I'm sure Bob means mischief.' Sure enough, when he and Dickinson reached Peshawar, Searight told them he had had a telegram saying 'No measles coming tomorrow'. Apparently the children's nanny at Bob's hosts at Lahore had assured him that his rash was definitely not German measles.

The first night at Peshawar was guest night. Forster had to change his mind about military people, and found the officers, in their gay mess jackets, charming and hospitable. It was quite a night too. The band played 'The Roast Beef of Old England', and there was dancing 'pas seul'. Everything got 'friskier and friskier'. Searight danced with Forster, and then leapt on the shoulders of Bob, who carried him round the room. Whitewash was thrown, uniforms were torn by spurs. But Dickinson and one elderly officer sat apart, like benign old uncles.

Sightseeing naturally included the Khyber Pass, where they had a picnic. Bob told his mother how they had watched a caravan of 'several thousand' Afghans, and hundreds of camels, donkeys and buffaloes, going south. The men were 'fine looking but dirty'; Forster thought they walked like kings.

To Dickinson these caravans were new proof of the restlessness of the world. Back at Lahore on November 13, Bob wrote to his father:

India has so far shown itself as an ugly country, except Bombay harbour. I can hardly conceive a less attractive country than most of the Punjab. The hills are often impressive, as in Italy. However the people are always interesting and there are lots to see. We dined last night with some Mohammedans, a famous lawyer [Mohammed Shafi] and a famous poet called [Mohammed] Iqbal [both later knighted] and several others ... v. pleasant and cultivated, and the poet was quite a wit. But the lawyer held forth to us on the wickedness of the Hindoos, and one might think it was an Orangeman abusing the Catholics. I suppose the Hindoos are as intolerant as the Moslims, but they could scarcely be more so. However he was no doubt carried away somehow by his eloquence, and probably was less bigoted than he made himself out. The poet, and some of the others, seemed more moderate than the lawyer, who was quite the Carson type [Sir Edward Carson, later Lord Carson, the Ulster Unionist], though a nice man.

In *Appearances*, which was a book of essays, Dickinson also wrote about this gathering. Shafi himself compared the Muslim minority to Ulster. 'The Hindus want to get rid of you,' he said, 'as they want to get rid of us ... for that reason alone I am loyal to British raj.' Bob after a while began to get restive. 'Mr. Trevelyan, you must listen to this ...' But Bob tartly remarked that no doubt there was friction between the two communities, but the worst way to deal with it was by recrimination. Shafi agreed, with tears in his eyes. Muslims had woken up that they were dropping behind in the race for influence and power, and the All-India Muslim League had been founded in 1906. They had started a 'campaign of education and organization', but at every point they found themselves thwarted; and always behind the obstacle lurked a Hindu.

Forster was to say that Dickinson was never very happy with Indians, though he was popular with them because of his great conversational powers and eagerness to learn. As for the English, whether he liked them individually or not, he pitied them for having

448

such an uncongenial job. The party split up again, Forster to Simla, the others to Delhi.

The decision, at long last, to make Delhi the capital of India had been announced by the King–Emperor George V at the great Durbar in December 1911. Naturally there was fierce opposition from Calcutta, especially among Europeans, and the Viceroy, Lord Hardinge of Penshurst, became extremely unpopular with the press. Bob and Dickinson arrived while a Commission was busy choosing a site for New Delhi, one of the Commission's members being Edwin Lutyens, who was to be the architect of the new Government House, to be conceived as a palace to rival Versailles.

At Brindaban on the way to Agra, where Forster reappeared, Bob was enthusiastic about its Red Temple, 'the finest I have seen so far'. As he told his father: 'The place is very sacred to Krishna. It was here that he made love to the gopis. We were shown the place where he stole their clothes while they were bathing in the Jumna; in fact there were clothes (quite new) hanging on a peepul tree. But the Jumna now flows in another bed a mile away, and all the beautiful river front of the town, with its ghats and palaces, looks over cornfields.' The memory of Brindaban and the village of Gokul, where Vishnu first appeared as Krishna, haunted Bob. It was that experience, and another of seeing a mystery play at Chhatarpur, that inspired him to write his play *The Pearl-Tree*, which was set to music as an opera by Edgar Bainton.

After the obligatory Taj ('far exceeded everything I thought possible') they went to Gwalior. Bob was now in one of his 'fidgety moods', feeling that he would never get to China if they didn't hurry up. So poor Dickinson was being 'rather hustled', and had to agree to cutting out Rajputana. They were now to make for Chhatarpur, to visit its Maharajah, Vishwanath Singh, who had been a pupil of Forster's friend Sir Theodore Morison, the distinguished Anglo–Indian official. Bob wrote home from Gwalior on November 27:

Came yesterday. Tomorrow probably Chhatarpur, thirty miles from the railway, where we shall be guests of the Rajah, who is a great reader of Marie Corelli and Herbert Spencer. We shall see a city near his capital where there are some fine Hindu temples [Khajaraho]... Went up to the Fort this morning on an elephant. It is best to take a seasick remedy before starting, at least when the animal is on the level or going downhill... Rock rather like Orvieto, only larger. Country more beautiful than N. India... Hope food [at Chhatarpur] will be good. We have not had very pleasant experiences of Indian dinners so far. A Mohammedan gentleman at Delhi gave me a bad one, and I was quite ill after it.

Bob and Dickinson had arrived late for the ascent to Gwalior Fort, and Dickinson had apologized – to which the solemn reply was that 'elephants sometimes wait for four hours'.

Bob gave a tactful summary of the next days to his parents, describing the Maharajah of Chhatarpur as 'shrewd', though he had 'muddled his head by reading too much European philosophy'. Chhatarpur, he said, was well governed by ministers, though the Maharajah seemed to take very little interest in such work. Tigers were quite near the Guest House, but as Forster said they were too well-mannered to eat men. Monkeys 'of the sweetest sort' sat on trees to watch the newcomers.

They had arrived very late, and Bob's hat had blown off in the dark. Supper took a long time coming, and sheets for the beds only arrived at 1 am. Dickinson was soon struck down with bad diarrhoea – that food again.

The whitewashed palace was half a mile away. The Maharajah was tiny, aged forty-six, very ugly, with a bridgeless nose like a pekinese's and smeared orange, and with a tongue discoloured from chewing betel. He generally wore a dark buff or maroon frock coat buttoned up to the neck, diamond ear-rings and embroidered trousers. Apart from philosophy, he had a passion for pretty boys – though this would not have been a shock to Bob, since many of his closest friends were homosexual, including Dickinson and of course Forster. The three guests would be summoned in the afternoons for literary and philosophical discussions, and he would sit cross-legged in the courtyard of his palace under a huge and flamboyant umbrella, with his private secretary Buddha-like at his feet. Dickinson, often in physical discomfort, had to answer questions such as: 'Tell me, Mr Dickinson, where is God? Can Herbert Spencer lead me to him, or should I prefer George Henry Lewes? Oh when will Krishna come and be my friend, Mr Dickinson?' Books would be sent for, and these would have to be explained. At other times streams of little notes would also arrive at the guest house, asking for advice or elucidations.

Beatrice Webb and her husband Sidney had been to Chhatarpur earlier the same year, and not surprisingly Beatrice had disapproved of the Maharajah, whom she found 'the last word in Hindu decadence and especially repulsive when he asked my husband to save his soul'. Vishwanath Singh was not up to her standards, not a 'refined intellectual companion'. But she had generally admired Hinduism, partly because of its lack of dogma, but mostly because it had an 'almost perfect relation between religious emotion and intellectual life'.

To Forster all was fascinating and amusing, and he wrote: 'Even Bob is calmed and no longer wishes to rush on.' Bob and Forster always breakfasted on the verandah at sunrise, and saw the pinnacles of Jain temples piercing the grey and white mists. Later, while Dickinson remained ill in bed, they would go on excursions with the Maharajah's secretary and perhaps his chief minister, the Diwan, driving in an ancient landau smelling of grease. The elephant trip was to the shrine of the Goddess of Rain. The view was so splendid that Bob wanted to come back with his books of poetry, and lie among the boulders and twisted roots of the huge trees. All the while the 'dear' elephant munched away at reeds in the marsh. They found a tank in which Bob was permitted to bathe.

The British cantonment of Nowgong was a few miles away. Forster was thoroughly irritated and bored by his fellow countrymen living there: 'Polo. Officers' wives with hideous voices. They made dogs beg.' He thought the Padre a bounder and a fool, though the Maharajah tolerated him. Perhaps, he decided, Indians were incapable of distinguishing European bad manners from good. Colonel Pritchard, the Political Agent, was a Theosophist 'of the silliest sort', saying things like 'Everything is all one' and 'You must get rid of Self and not expect a reward.' The Maharajah had some trouble with Pritchard, who did not approve of so much money being spent on boys who were to perform in the mystery plays – and there was such a succession of boys too, all so ungrateful to the Maharajah.

The Khajaraho trip was accomplished 'with endless bungling'. Dickinson came for the day by motor, but Bob and Forster spent the night there in tents, which Forster found comfortable, though Bob could not sleep because of rats, birds and a dripping lamp. Forster thought the temples 'very wonderful but nightmares – all exactly alike and covered with sculptures from head to toe'. Perhaps in any case the erotic contortions of the intensely heterosexual sculpture was something that was unlikely to appeal to him, and Dickinson tended to be shocked by obscenities. (Ackerley's later description of a line of sodomitic soldiers was poetic licence.) And perhaps, therefore, it was here that Forster found Dickinson cowering under the portal of a temple, 'repelled by the monstrosity of its forms'.

By December 16 they were still at Chhatarpur. Bob was now fed up with the Maharajah, and flew into a passion. 'I simply *will* go on Monday. I don't care what he says – we've given in too much already and he thinks he can behave as he likes. You and Dickinson can stop, but I shall go on alone.' At length the Maharajah, regretfully, allowed them to leave on Tuesday, since it was an auspicious day for travel. So now the group broke up for good. Bob and Dickinson went to Benares and then Calcutta, Forster to Dewas Senior via Bhopal, Ujjain and Indore.

Bob found Benares wonderful. Thanks to William Rothenstein they had an introduction to a 'fakir', Narasingh Sharma. Again in *Appearances*, Dickinson wrote of the meeting. He found the fakir the most human of men; 'so human that I thought his religion could not be as inhuman as it sounded'.

> But it [Hinduism] was the religion of the East, not the West. It refused all significance to the temporal world; it took no account of society and its needs; it sought to destroy, not to develop, the sense and the power of Individuality. It did not say, but it implied, that creation was a mistake; and if it did not profess pessimism, pessimism was its logical outcome. I do not know whether it is the religion of a wise race; but I am sure that it could never be that of a strong one.

The Webbs would have disagreed. Bob, for his part, had to bring out his *Oxford Book of English Verse* in order to 'exorcise Hinduism'. Perhaps this was after meeting a friend of Narasingh Sharma who sat stark naked on a bed of nails in one of the ghats.

On the way to Calcutta they stayed three nights with Masood at Bankipore, a suburb of Patna which Bob found 'the most sordid, horrible, slummy place we have yet seen'. Forster described Bankipore as a 'tropical pleasance by a noble river' but all the same 'foul'; and as P. N. Furbank pointed out in his biography, some of the details were recalled in the portrait of 'Chandrapore' in *A Passage to India*.

They stayed at a Raj hotel par excellence, the Great Eastern, at Calcutta. This had originally been opened as the Auckland Hotel in 1841, but had been renamed in 1865 and given a new mid-Victorian frontage, with a row of shops in front. On Christmas Day Bob wrote to his mother:

> Bengalis much more civilized people than the other northern Indians; at least it is only here that we have found any really interesting intellectual society. The family of the Tagores are rather the centre of it, and there are various Chaudhuris and Dr. Bose, an eminent scientist, who are all relations or friends of the Tagores. I am disappointed in the paintings of two Tagore painters [Abanindranath and Gaganendranath] but they are charming people and

great connoisseurs ... Dr. [Jagadis Chandra] Bose showed me
some experiments, proving that plants have heart-beats and circu-
lation of sap. He also took us for a row on the Hooghly.

Everyone at Calcutta, he said, was reading his brother George's
Garibaldi books – 'though I doubt if it will produce a Bengali Garibaldi, Mazzini is more of their kind; and indeed the young men seem
to have a great admiration for him.' (Jawaharlal Nehru was to say that
he was given a copy of one of the Garibaldi volumes by G. M. Trevelyan as a prize at school at Harrow around 1906. It fascinated him.
'Visions of similar deeds in India came before me, and in my mind
India and Italy got strangely mixed together.')

Bob continued: 'Many of them are Cambridge men. They are most
of them inclined to be a little sore about our methods of government,
some of them indeed are really bitter... The trouble is that the
English, with very few exceptions, do dislike and distrust the
Bengalis, and cannot conceal that they do so. The younger men feel
that they have no real career as public men before them except as bar-
risters and judges... Of course the ill-feeling is confined to the rich
and educated classes; it is in no sense a proletarian movement; it is the
lawyers and landowners and the professional classes who are discontented. The trouble is that by giving more power and influence to
those classes as we are doing quite rightly, we are not at the same time
giving more power to the peasants. It makes it all the more necessary
for the English government to protect and legislate for the peasants,
as indeed they have done in the past very effectively on the
whole...'

All this fifty years after the publication of *The Competition Wallah*.

Forster met Dr Bose on his second visit to Lahore in February. At
the same party he talked about Indian music to a Mr Godbole who
sang songs to him. 'What a name!' – but it remained in his memory,
and of course was to reappear in *A Passage to India*. Bob had written to
him to say that there was nothing to see at Calcutta but Tagores and
tapirs at the zoo; and he had replied that though they 'tempted terribly' he had decided that samples of each could be seen in London
and he would not go to Calcutta.

Dickinson now felt a new 'wave of repulsion' against Hinduism,
when they were taken to see a shrine to the goddess Kali, a 'hideous'
idol, 'black and many-armed, decked with tinsel and fed with the
blood of goats'. He and Bob escaped to Darjeeling, and on the way
back spent a night at a Tagore family house on the Ganges. Many of
the Tagores, Bob found, were also fine musicians.

Meanwhile a shocking event had taken place at Delhi. On December 23 the Viceroy and Lady Hardinge had arrived at the station after a long tour. They were to ride in procession for a durbar at the Red Fort. Hardinge wrote afterwards that he had a presentiment of evil ahead, but his wife had reassured him: 'It's only that you are tired and you always dislike ceremonial.'

They rode in a howdah on the usual fantastically garbed Viceregal elephant. When they reached the Chandni Chowk there was a thunderous explosion. The Viceroy's helmet was blown on to the road. 'I'm afraid that was a bomb,' he said to his wife. After a while she glanced round and saw that he was badly hurt. Then he fell unconscious. He was lifted off the elephant, and lying on the pavement recovered enough to order the procession to continue.

The old stiff upper lip... Thus it was the British governed India... Forster heard details of the outrage at Dewas when Darling arrived from Delhi; he was told that several Englishmen, 'of the highest rank' even, had been anxious for Tommies to fire on the crowd, and 'seemed really sorry that the Viceroy had not been killed, because then there would have been a better excuse for doing such a thing'. At any rate the Viceroy recovered, though his nerve and self-confidence were never the same. The bomb had been thrown by a Bengali.

Having had to decide against visiting Luce in Burma, Bob and Dickinson took the train to Madras, where they became very bored at having to meet so many 'second-rate' Anglo–Indians. The Governor's wife took Bob to see the portrait of 'grandpapa', which certainly did not impress him as a work of art.

From Madras to Tanjore to Madura. 'I am not exactly tired of India,' wrote Bob, 'but I am tired of travelling about in it.' They arrived at Trivandrum, the capital of Travancore, where they found the country certainly the most beautiful of all that they had seen, with the population mostly Christian. 'Here at Cape Cormorin,' said Dickinson, 'at India's southernmost point, among the sands and cactuses and the palms rattling in the breeze, comes to us news of the Franchise Bill and of militant suffragettes.' So it was a surprise and a coincidence, in a way, to discover a kind of matriarchate, as Bob put it, at Trivandrum. The women – except the Brahmins – were, and apparently always had been, politically and socially in an equality and 'more than an equality' with men. 'In this respect England lags far behind Travancore.' But had it, then, anything to do with an especially bountiful Nature? How would you or I behave if we were able to live entirely on coconuts, and have nothing to do for most of the year except sit under our own palm trees and listen to the surf of the Arabian Sea under the glorious sun?

After Ceylon, where Bob had bathed in a tank at Anarudhapura that he heard later had crocodiles in it, they set off for China. Forster wrote after Dickinson's death that Dickinson had 'never found in Indian society either the happiness or the peacefulness, which have made my own visits to the country so wonderful'. Bob did not want to return to the Orient. Tuscany became his passion, and as Berenson said he would arrive at Florence every year with the swallows. But he sometimes wrote poems about India, and he kept up with Indian friends, helping them financially.

They went to Singapore, then Java and Sumatra, then Hong Kong and Canton. Now it suddenly dawned on Bob that if he didn't watch out he might miss the Trevy-Trinity Lake Hunt. So off he went on the Trans-Siberian railway, reaching Moscow, where he dashed by taxi from one station to another. He was just in time. Forster said later that Dickinson had told him that although he had found Bob a delightful companion he probably gained by being on his own.

Apart from Bob, Forster and indeed Ackerley, I had another particular interest in going to Chhatarpur. It was in the area known as Bundelkhand, where Kipling had set the Jungle Books, and it was where Humphrey Trevelyan had been Political Agent from 1942 after leaving Udaipur. Humphrey and Peggie had lived at Nowgong, and I had heard that their house was still standing. I had seen a photograph of Humphrey, looking dashing in a white spiked helmet and smiling conspiratorially at the young Maharajah Bhawani Singh of Chhatarpur, son of Forster's and Bob's Maharajah, at his investiture on his coming of age.

I was in touch with a Mr A. N. Mehrotra, whose family used to play bridge with Humphrey at Nowgong and had always recognized him as a 'man of destiny'. He told me that Bhawani Singh now led almost a hermit's life, usually at Brindaba (where there was the temple that Bob had so much admired), but that when he was in Bundelkhand he lived at Khajaraho. The family was now badly off, and there was a son, called Balwant Singh, the Rajah Bahadur as the eldest son was called – but of course, Mr Mehrotra added, such titles were only used nowadays by the older generation.

Diana and Francis were still unwell when we reached Khajaraho. Francis and I had brought presents in case we met the Maharajah. Now Diana became nervous about revealing herself to be Joe Ackerley's half-sister, so we decided not to mention her connection with the author of *Hindoo Holiday*, and to play it by ear. In any case, given the fact that she was a person of exceptional beauty and charm, it seemed inconceivable that anyone would hold such a thing against her. And after all, it had been the great E. M. Forster who in 1923 had recommended Ackerley to Vishwanath Singh, and however cruel some of the book's naughtiness might have seemed at the time, it was brilliantly written – the Aga Khan had even named a racehorse after it.

As soon as we reached the hotel Francis at once let out the secret about Diana's brother having written a book. Horrors! But nobody seemed to care. We telephoned the palace at Khajaraho and later heard that the Prince had called at our hotel to say that his father was away and he expected us at 9 pm 'after the dancing', by which he meant, so we discovered, a music and dance festival.

As it was still morning, we fought our way through a posse of rickshaw boys to pay a preliminary visit to the famous medieval temples. We were shocked at first to find them in a kind of public park, neatly kept up, when I knew that in Humphrey's time they had stood in romantic jungle. But then they had become one of India's greatest tourist sites, rivalling the Taj, so what could you expect...

They reminded me of great encrusted gorgonians, such as might be seen rising from the sea-bed; made of red sandstone, streaked black with age, they seemed almost timeless, rising in layers to tapering points, on which stood little top-knots like something out of *Turandot*. The official handout informed us that they recreated not only the 'glories of the Chandela kings' but 'their spiritual passion'.

'Spiritual passion.' Aha! Passion in the sculpture was what most tourists hoped to see and giggle at: all these voluptuous ladies with melon boobs and twining their legs round the more passive males; often watched by a couple of coy maidservants ready to help them out in the more acrobatic positions (upside-down for instance). Yet the odd thing was, when you were faced with these erotic couplings, all that ecstasy and animal passion seemed to have very little to do with pornography. We were told that young Indians on their honeymoon come specially to look at them – well, I hope the brides learn something useful. The difficulty for us Westerners was to relate all this fun to religion.

But then the sculptures were by no means just erotica. There were all sorts of friezes and groups of battles, domestic and hunting scenes; others were simply heraldic. Francis, like Forster on his first visit, found them repetitive. Only after I came to read Forster's reactions after his second visit to Khajaraho, in 1921, did I feel I had begun to understand a little of the significance of Hindu temple architecture. Forster said that he saw in the Khajaraho sculpture a portrayal of life in its fullness, an admission of pleasure, jokes, love. Each temple had a small dark interior; this, he said, represented the individual's inner life, while outside seethed all the complex panorama of creation.

In contrast to his disappointment in 1912, Khajaraho to Forster was now one of the glories of India. He described how each temple symbolized the world-mountain, Meru, ascending in stages to the heavens, and the 'hat' at the top was the abode of God. He also made the point that the erotic sculptures were confined to *one* transept of the temple only. For all that, he admitted that they were still a puzzle; for instance they had nothing to do with fertility symbols or procreation.

Our guide suggested that all the sexy behaviour could have been to test the will-power of pilgrims, in the same way as Gandhi was supposed to have slept with naked girls. But another man said that whereas you might see Krishna's face in a flight of birds or in the smile of your own child, or in thunder and lightning, so you would also find it in the embrace of your wife. Hindus set great store by 'elemental union', he explained, which was why Allahabad was held to be such a holy place, being at the confluence of two great rivers, the Ganges and the Jumna.

The festival of music and dance was mostly of a sacred nature and against a background of floodlit temples. I remembered Dickinson's account of Maharajah Vishwanath Singh's mystery plays, how he thought the music was not unlike ancient Greek choruses. 'In such dancing the flesh becomes spirit, the body a transparent emblem of the soul.' Raúl and I saw an aspect in it that was quite different. Just as when we had been travelling in the South of India, the singing reminded us of cante jondo, the dancing was almost exactly similar to Andalusian zapateado.

The show was ultimately monotonous, especially for Francis and Diana, who did not know much of Spain and did not share Raúl's excitement. We left early, and in due course found the Prince's palace, which in the dark seemed like a large bungalow. We entered a small room dominated by a stuffed tiger in a glass case. Other decorations consisted of various animals' heads, including an alligator's skull, shooting trophies and photographs. There were also plaster busts of Prince Charles and Princess Diana. Our Prince now made his entrance; well built, jovial, baldish, moustached, perhaps nearly forty, evidently not a scholar like his grandfather. Whisky and beer flowed. I gave him my present originally destined for his father, a photographic book of London, which he appreciated far more than Francis's more expensive nineteenth-century print of Regent Street. He seemed pleased about my connection with Humphrey, and later we found out why; it had been Humphrey who had arranged his parents' marriage, even choosing the bride, and Humphrey and Peggie had attended the wedding in one of the Khajaraho temples. His father, he said, was not quite a sadhu, a holy man, but he liked to meditate, and often went to the Himalayas, where he was now.

Whenever we mentioned the grandfather, there was a tendency to change the subject. Diana, at her request, had been introduced with a fictitious name, but remained very silent nevertheless. Quantities of relatives and friends flooded the room (all male), and Raúl – as usual when things become sticky at a party – did some 'jollying up'. The Prince's maternal uncle told us that he had been in the British Army, and that four years before dacoits had murdered two of his own sons and had thrown their bodies into the river. The country around Chhatarpur always used to be notorious for dacoits, and now was bad again. In Humphrey's day the great scourge had been Man Singh, who had been caught and killed only in the 1950s, his death rating two columns in *The Times*. Thanks to Humphrey putting a price on their heads, Man Singh's number two had been 'bagged' – shot whilst in bed with a girl friend. His body had been laid on the ground, with his armoury all around him, as if he were a dead tiger.

When we left the palace our rickshaw boy kissed the Prince's feet.

Early the next morning, in the hotel swimming-pool, I met again an English judge from Hong Kong whom the Prince had introduced to us as 'my brother'. He told me more about the present Maharajah, who used to drink rather a lot and had been prone to sing 'It's a Long Way to Tipperary' when he'd had a few. The Maharajah had developed diabetes and therefore had been warned off the drink. He used to be a wrestling champion and was very muscular, great fun in the old days. He had been good at squash and hockey, and had preferred to consort with lower-class people.

After much frustration we had acquired a car for the Chhatarpur trip. Raúl had been annoyed over a last-minute demand for sixty rupees more, but Francis and Diana gave in. As a result we left in separate cars, Raúl and I in one driven by a nephew of Mr Mehrotra, who had invited us two to lunch.

On a ridge outside Chhatarpur we spotted the old guest house where Forster and Co. had stayed, with the little temple to Hanuman above. Alberto Moravia and Pier Paolo Pasolini had also stayed there in the 1960s, not knowing or probably caring about Forster or Ackerley. It hadn't been much of a success for the Italians, what with 'ambiguously coloured' mattresses, cupboards the 'kingdoms' of beetles and cobras, and the 'desperate' snarls of the jackals in the penumbra outside. At least, niente dacoits.

Hooting our way through shoals of bicyclists and herds of goats, we reached the palace of Maharajah Vishwanath Singh. Neither Forster nor Ackerley had prepared us for how attractive it was. It was dilapidated of course, perhaps had been even then, but it was still in effect a grand château.

We passed through the crenellated archway, where Humphrey had stood with the little wrestling champion to be – and into the dark cobwebby durbar hall. At the far end was an onion dome loggia at which the Maharajah had presided, and round the sides, high up, were window embrasures, with perforated fronts for the women to look through. This led into the courtyard, cream and ochre, with the most elaborate and charming roof-line, a series of closely built arched domes each with blue spears on top. There was also a big observatory dome. We were welcomed by friendly monks in yellow robes, Buddhist style, and a young acolyte who might have stepped straight out of *Hindoo Holiday*. It was sad to find the Maharajah's wooden throne stacked away in one of the verandahs. We were not allowed inside the palace, but Raúl reported that he had seen a room piled with Victorian furniture.

In the courtyard we had a strong sensation of being watched from above.

Then we drove to the lake of Mau and its diminutive palace, offered as a gift by the Maharajah to Forster, and where 'H. H. would meet Krishna, and is never happy on account of his loneliness'. On a mountain top we had pointed out to us the tomb of the horse of the great Maharajah Chhatershal who had fought against the Moghuls and was the ancestor of all the petty rajahs thereabouts. Chhatershal's palace had become a museum (a good museum too, especially the black basalt Jain sculpture, and with a huge statue of Kitchener in the courtyard, removed from Nowgong barracks). It overlooked the lake where the Cambridge trio and Ackerley went for picnics.

Mr Mehrotra's house was like a wonderful version of a Spanish finca: low, dark red, with an undulating balustrade along the roof, and a portico like a huge coronet on pillars. When we met him we immediately felt we were old and special friends. He gave us an immense meal, and I shall not forget that soup of herbs or the junket with lotus seeds and 'wild' nuts. We spoke of what to us Westerners was the disturbing recent arrival in India of the Russian Defence Minister, Marshal Ustinov; and Mr Mehrotra told us of the current alarm over the 'encirclement' of India by the Americans, now that there was a new rapprochement between them and the Chinese. He was an admirer of Sri Aurobindo and The Mother, and soon we moved to more esoteric matters such as the honouring of ancestors, life the unity of soul and body, and one's eventual goal being the achievement of eternal bliss. Later he took us to Humphrey's old house, tiled now instead of thatched, hardly 'picturesque' as Humphrey had described it, and with a garden that was no longer 'swimming with bougainvillaea full of nesting paradise fly-catchers'. The pool, where some of General Orde Wingate's Chindits had bathed before going on to Burma, was barely recognizable. But the house, packed with desks and files, was in goodish condition, and I was received with respect because of 'Trevelyan Sahib'. I was told that Humphrey used to be known as Hasthi Karn, Elephant's Ears, a sign of wisdom. I also heard that after the wedding of the Maharajah of Chhatarpur Peggie had been given an emerald ring. The British ruling was (as everybody knew) that no present could be accepted that was worth more than fifteen pounds; so she had to return it – though she did wear it for one evening.

Humphrey had introduced a great number of reforms. Within one month he had removed the powers of thirteen petty rulers in his part of Bundelkhand. He created a joint police force, the better to chase dacoits, and a joint agricultural department, and a joint teachers' training school.

Wingate at Nowgong, and a postscript

Humphrey had been told by the authorities that if the Japanese reached Nowgong, he was to give himself up, as his first duty was to protect the civilian population – though, as he said afterwards, he couldn't see how he could have done that whilst in custody. It was perhaps lucky that he didn't know the fate of the wretched Mr Bird in the Andamans.

One day Orde Wingate, then a brigadier, suddenly called on Humphrey, with two officers in attendance. Humphrey was immediately impressed by this strange man, with the gaunt face, rasping voice and piercing blue eyes. 'We gave him,' he has somewhat laconically said, 'the help he wanted for his training, and he disappeared into Burma.' That disappearance was to startle the military world, for it was a raid right into the heart of Japanese-occupied territory.

Humphrey then suggested to Central Command that the Nowgong jungles would make ideal training grounds for other operations in Burma. But this idea was turned down: for one thing, he was told, the nearest railway was fifteen miles away; for another, there were two unbridged rivers to be crossed. He was surprised therefore to be woken one morning by the rumble of Army trucks passing through the village. Apparently Wingate had himself decided that he approved of Bundelkhand and would use it for training his Long Range Penetration units. And those units were the famous Chindits, a word taken from the Burmese Chinthe, the mythical animal that sits at the entrance of pagodas to warn off evil spirits.

Mr Mehrotra said to me that the people of Nowgong were given twenty-four hours to clear an airstrip for Wingate. Eventually 10,000 troops were stationed in the neighbourhood. Wingate's headquarters were at Gwalior, but he caught typhoid and was sent to hospital at Delhi. As Humphrey and Peggie knew that he approved of their house, they invited him to come and convalesce. But Mountbatten had first to be convinced, so a completely untrue story was concocted whereby the Trevelyans were supposed to have a herd of special tubercular-free cows and all the facilities of a modern convalescent home. A stern nurse called Sister McGeary was detailed to accompany Wingate, but even she could not control him. As Peggie has said, you couldn't see him for dust as soon as he arrived – he was dashing off here, there and everywhere, in his private plane. Famous Chindit figures such as Bernard Ferguson and Mike Calvert were constantly 'popping in'.

Wingate ate raw onions and would sit naked in the corner of a room. One day Peggie caught him staring at her baby Kate in her cot. 'What *are* you doing?' she asked. 'Are you interested in babies?' 'Basically no,' he replied, 'but my wife's having one and I want to see what they look like.' He was always a most erratic driver, and would take the Trevelyans' terrified elder child Susan on his knee as he screeched in his jeep along the pot-holes in a fog of dust.

Humphrey has described his guest's unsoldierly figure, with Bible in one hand, and helmet of 1900 vintage in the other, as he recited with great intensity Emily Brontë's 'No coward soul is mine', and explained how no civilian however able could ever think like a soldier. He loved quoting to his men from the poets and the Hebrew prophets. 'Gentlemen, life is fleeting,' he told a group before final departure to the Burmese jungles. 'There are many of you who will never come back from this.' A message of good cheer no doubt . . .

Not all Chindits had happy memories of Nowgong. A number of them arrived during the July monsoons, and for a long while lived in a sea of mud. Otherwise it was just a question of hard route marches, sleeping rough, rock slopes, thick jungle, sweat; all much too far away from any place of entertainment. Yet there was always a sense of excitement, of preparing for one of the great adventures of the war.

Humphrey stayed with Wingate at Gwalior the night before he left

461

for Burma. They walked together round the airport waiting for the take-off. Wingate said:

> Do you know the story of the Italian captain in the first war in the trenches, waiting for the attack, with his eyes intent on his wrist-watch? Five seconds, four, three, two, one, zero. Avanti! He leapt out of the trench and immediately fell under a hail of bullets. His men stayed in the trenches, clapping vigorously and crying, 'Bravo il capitano'. That is how I feel about this campaign.

A month later he was dead, killed in an air-crash.

And now a postscript, about Humphrey. From Nowgong he went to Washington as First Secretary under Sir Girja Shankar Bajpai, in India's first diplomatic mission abroad. In 1946 he was official adviser to the Government of India at the Paris Peace Conference. He then returned to India to work for Jawaharlal Nehru, and with the loom-ing transfer of power carried heavy responsibilities. Nehru asked him to stay on a few months after Independence, but Humphrey had to start a new career and felt that he couldn't do so, even if it were to affect his pension. Nehru wrote on the file: 'I will not stand in his way, but I am sorry to see him go.' Humphrey on seeing this had said: 'It was a good note to end my eighteen years of Indian service.'

I was to have many wonderful letters from Mr Mehrotra, whom I came to know as Ghisoo, on Hindu philosophy and the significance of Hindu gods. As an example I shall quote a few words from one, which was on the death of Humphrey, in February 1985.

> May his soul rest in peace and all of you bear his sorrow. You know one thinks he is born but actually the birth is of DEATH not the person. The very first vow he takes is to achieve the eternal sleep. By our 'Darshan' philosophy the body alone perishes. What is life, it is the unity of Soul and Body. Without this unity we do not realize the existence of the eternal soul, the primeval force, the primordial power.

Aftermath to Chhokrapur

Mr Mehrotra had asked me if I had read *Hindoo Holiday*, and I said yes. He said: 'A very unkind book. I shall not read it. The Maharajah had some weaknesses. There was trouble, but everything was put right.'

Later he said something about Vishwanath Singh getting in a clash with the political department because of his boys in the Rahas Lila, by which he meant the mystery plays that Forster and Co. had admired.

It was Mr Mehrotra who also told me about a book called *Kingdoms of Yesterday* by Sir Arthur Cunningham Lothian, who had been Political Agent at Nowgong in 1921. There Lothian mentions the Maharajah of Chhatarpur, who he said had a 'congenital disease' which marred his features. It was generally believed that the Maharajah was impotent. 'Judge of my astonishment therefore, when once he came to see me he said he wished to marry again in order to beget an heir, and asked if I could not arrange to get him a bride from Bengal.' The upshot finally was that a Colonel Gidney of the Indian Medical Service was called in to examine the Maharajah in order to give him a certificate of potency. 'It was just as well the Maharajah took this precaution, because when, in due course, he married and had a son and heir, the allegation was at once made that the child could not be his, and only Colonel Gidney's certificate enabled the Maharajah to rebut this charge.'

Hindoo Holiday was first published in 1931, the year of the Maharajah's death. Names had been changed, Chhatarpur had become Chhokrapur, and certain passages had been left out. In 1952 the book was to be reissued, with the passages inserted. Ackerley, who at the time was literary editor of the *Listener*, received a review copy of *Kingdoms of Yesterday*, which was due to be published at about the same time as his reissue. He opened it and to his alarm found that Sir Arthur had blown the gaff about Chhokrapur, also describing *Hindoo Holiday* as 'a curious and somewhat cruel book'. Ackerley felt constrained to warn his publishers, particularly as he feared that one of his newly inserted passages could be picked out as libellous. As a result both books were withdrawn and pages in each had to be rewritten. Ackerley's 'missing page' appears in Neville Braybrooke's collection of the *Letters*.

Forster also acknowledged that the letters Ackerley wrote to him from Chhatarpur helped him when he was finishing *A Passage to India*.

We had more rather tipsy meetings with the Prince. His brother-in-law, son of the Maharajah of Panna, joined us during one evening of special muddle and a possible family row.

The rickshaw boys outside our hotel were a pest. They could not understand why any tourist should prefer to walk half a mile to the temples and avoid paying an absurdly high fare. Raúl would bargain fiercely, to Francis's enjoyment, and would end up by walking, with the boys following and arguing until he actually reached the

Khajaraho temples. Francis and Diana always rode, looking very Somerset Maughamish and stiff-backed in cream-coloured clothes and hats.

At the Banduphal Falls we found a dark-skinned hermit, thin and gentle, barefooted and naked from the waist up. He squatted by the pool staring at the reflections and the fish. Did he eat the fish? No! At such a heretical question he dashed up to his damp cave among ferns and trickles of water, and made himself a chapatti. Suddenly we had found ourselves faced with another aspect of Hinduism and to me at that time more easily comprehensible.

We went to Rajgarh, once palace-fortress of the Maharajahs, but now deserted; it was larger and more beautiful than the palace at Chhatarpur, though in the same style of architecture. It was on a hillside, with broad steps up, designed for elephants. There was an enormous spreading view over fields, jungle and hills. Forster had been there on December 9 1912 with his Maharajah, also Colonel Pritchard the Theosophist and presumably Bob.

'Some good paintings,' Forster had noted; but they have all since disappeared. 'Do you meditate?' His Highness had been asked. 'Yes – when I can, for two hours, and when I am busy for forty-five minutes . . . I try to meditate on Krishna. I do not know that he is God, but I love Love and Beauty and Wisdom, and I find them in his history . . .' At which the maddening Pritchard had interposed: 'Oh, Maharajah, because you are alone it is no reason you should be lonely. Everything depends on the life within . . . Oh what a fellow you are, Maharajah.'

Poor ugly Vishwanath Singh, he wanted so much to be loved, and to find love.

I sat with Diana by a weathered pinnacle on the palace roof, listening to the cow-bells and watching the light fade across the jungle. A flock of white unidentifiable birds flew past, with a great whirr of wings. Rajgarh seemed a perfect place in which to meditate on Krishna.

We felt guilty at not going afterwards to see the Prince's animal paintings, copied from the *Reader's Digest*. But then we were to find that others had also played truant.

A German group the next morning was leaving the hotel at the same time as us, and at the desk I spotted a postcard addressed to 'The Maharajah of Chhatarpur', expressing regret about precisely the same thing. The card was signed 'Prince and Princess von Thurn und Taxis'. Which name once more jolted me back to Andalusia and another favourite hotel, the Hotel Reina Victoria at Ronda, where another Princess von Thurn und Taxis's friend, Rainer Maria Rilke, had stayed, and had worked in a little room with a view very like the one from the roof of the palace of Rajgarh.

After the luxury of Kotah we knew that the Singhanias' Kamla Retreat at Kanpur could not be some cosy little place run by nuns. But we were not prepared for such magnificence.

At the lodge gates, on our approach, two ancient chowkidars in uniform and carrying spears jumped to attention. The drive had lamps all the way up, and ahead lay a long but deceptively plain white building. Half a dozen peacocks flapped from its roof. Originally the house, as we were to hear, had been built in 1905 in Scottish baronial style by George Allen of Cooper Allen, the leather manufacturers. The Singhanias had acquired it in 1935.

We were led into a series of saloons lit by pink or green chandeliers. Some of the furniture was in the style of Louis Quinze. Around the walls were many glazed cupboards, packed with cut glass, china and ornaments, mostly Victorian or art nouveau, but some recognizable as hailing from Goode's in South Audley Street in London. There was also an excellent collection of Chinese porcelain. Busts included Wagner and Beethoven, and there was a bronze copy of Laocoön. The many other bronze statuettes seemed to be French, of the Piccadilly 'Eros' period. Most amazing of all was the Chinese room, the size of a ballroom, lit by twelve differently coloured chandeliers under a red Chinese ceiling. The collection of porcelain here was even more impressive. In the centre of the room was a games table, and next to it was a sheeted area, with white cushions, for sitting on the floor. There was also a large JK television set.

Then the garden. This was vast and luxuriant, with flowering creepers, clipped trees and a path a hundred metres long entirely lined with violas and ending at a triumphal arch by a lake. There must have been hundreds of potted plants along other walks – cannas, petunias, lobelias, candytuft, stocks, among others. We were shown an aviary, a pagoda and fountains which produced rainbows, and a very big rose-garden. There was also a swimming-pool, twelve feet deep, that had the only artificial waves in India.

All this, and forty-one servants (admittedly twenty-four were gardeners), we had for ourselves, for we were the only guests. It was no surprise to learn that the Singhanias were probably the fifth richest family in India.

Mrs Gandhi had been at the Kamla Retreat not long before us. We were shown an impressive list of previous guests, including her father and sundry ambassadors, as well as members of the Soviet circus team. We still were not able to meet our most generous host,

Dr Gaur Hari Singhania, because – we were told later – he had been in a severe road accident.

I was due to give a lecture (again on Charles Trevelyan) to Mr Mehra's History Society. Mr Mehra, who had been born in 1911, was a journalist of long experience, having worked for the *Pioneer* of Lucknow and the *Statesman* of New Delhi. He had founded and edited until 1973 the *Citizen Weekly* of Kanpur, and because of his fearless criticism of civic injustices had sometimes been in trouble. He was also a co-founder of the Central Citizen's Forum, dealing with litigation in the public interest and the protection of the consumer. At the time of our arrival he was especially concerned with the question of Kanpur's sanitation. That was something on which he and Charles Trevelyan would have seen eye to eye.

By and large much of our conversation with his friends was on local and historical matters, though we avoided the Mutiny. We would discuss for instance who was the greatest man, Churchill or Nehru; Mr Mehra doubted Churchill's 'genius'. For the first time in India at one of these gatherings I heard someone making a criticism of Mahatma Gandhi – it was in connection with mixing politics and religion, seen by the speaker as being now the great curse for India. 'Pandit Jawaharlal Nehru found it impossible to get rid of this legacy for electioneering reasons,' I was told. 'He personally was one of the most secular of politicians but had to cultivate the goodwill of various religious minorities by visiting Durgahs [shrines of Muslim saints] and getting the Government to organize Kumbh Melas [religious festivals at Allahabad]. As a result of many years of politics based on religion, regionalism and languages, we have more communal tensions and strife than ever before since Independence.' This last remark was by no means meant to flatter me as an Englishman, as my friend had been an ardent critic of the Raj and lucky not to have been imprisoned.

Somebody else asked me whether I had come across records of rapes of European women at Cawnpore/Kanpur in 1857. I was able to repeat Lady Canning's assurances of 'no dishonouring' to Queen Victoria (who seemed to have taken an unhealthy interest in the subject). Rapes, I heard, and dowry deaths – murders of brides without sufficient dowries (TV sets and the like), usually by mothers-in-law – were reported in Indian papers day after day.

Salman Rushdie's books I found were appreciated by the young but not so much by the old. I pointed out that he was one of the few successful innovators writing in England at present. This seemed to be a surprise.

Everyone spoke perfect English of course, but I did hear complaints about English having had to become the lingua franca – people I met were too polite to criticize Charles Trevelyan about that. Under the British, English had been a passport to higher ranks; and it still applied. But the English language was far too difficult for simple folk to cope with..

There was certainly not much 'nostalgia' for the old Raj days, which was understandable; but I sensed a strong regret that the old idealism and sincerity of nationalist times had disappeared.

Several of Mr Mehra's friends were Sikhs, and Raúl and I warmed immediately to the considerable and splendidly jovial figure of Kripal Singh, who wore a large blue turban. We were invited to Kripal's son's birthday party, where I was whirled from one guest to another, usually with some tongue in cheek introduction: 'And now here is an especially dynamic/engrossing/sparkling character.' It was a fashionable gathering, including the family of Nasiruddin Shah, one of the finest character actors in India. Raúl was able to talk for some while to a distinguished old Sikh gentleman, Sardool Singh, who said that as a boy he had survived the Jallianwala Bagh massacre at Amritsar in 1919 because he had been near the dais and had been covered by fallen bodies. Later he had been a student at the Khalsa College, where Malcolm Darling's friend Gerard Wathen, whom Forster had met at Lahore, had been Principal. Wathen had been very popular, and when trouble started at Amritsar the students had mounted a guard to protect him. Later, when Wathen was forced to resign from the College, Sardool Singh and others had gone on strike, as a result of which they had been rusticated for two years.

Whilst travelling around India we had of course been aware that we were in a period of unrest. Indeed 1984 was to prove one of the most shameful years since the country's Independence. I kept hearing about the incompetence of the 'overpoliticized' Government at Delhi. There were riots and murders in Assam, because of unrest over too many 'foreigners' coming in from Bangladesh. Most sinister of all were the incidents of terrorism, resulting from Sikh unrest, in the Punjab. It was reported that some terrorists, including the fundamentalist leader, Sant Jarnail Bhindranwale, had taken refuge in the Golden Temple of Amritsar, the Sikhs' most holy place, and were fortifying it. January 26 had been India's Republic Day, and the flag of Khalistan, of Sikh separatism, had been flown over the Golden Temple. Then in February there had been anti-Sikh violence in the neighbouring state of Haryana: temples had been burnt, and Sikhs' beards shaved off. We had been warned that more anti-Sikh demonstrations were likely in Bombay (and this did come to pass). By the time we arrived at Kanpur Bhindranwale had increased his campaign of terrorism. During March and April eighty-eight people were killed, and a hundred and seven people injured; thirty-eight railway stations were burnt.

Perhaps a bolder spirit than I would have plunged into political discussion with our new Sikh friends, but I felt after such hospitality it would be tactless. Besides, the British seemed to be going through a period of unpopularity, as a result of some television feature I had not seen, to do with the Kashmir problem. The Bombay *Free Press Journal* absurdly claimed that there was an 'active India lobby in Britain which seizes on any opportunity to show India in a bad light'. It was obvious however that the attitude in India towards the United States was becoming increasingly suspicious and sour, mainly because of American support in arms for Pakistan and their rapprochement with China, and there was scepticism about the imminent arrival of Vice-President George Bush.

But I had primarily come to Kanpur to see Mutiny places. Mr Mehra, who drove us around the city, admitted that he had hardly ever been to the site of the Entrenchments or to the Satichaura Ghat. As I already knew, the British had built a memorial park where the Bibighar, or House of the Ladies, had been. This park still existed, Mr Mehra told me, but the Gothic screen and Baron Marochetti's marble angel (designed by Lady Canning) had been removed to the Church of All Souls, begun in 1862 and consecrated in 1875.

The House of the Ladies: I

I have said earlier that Emma Halliday, Mrs Vibart with her daughter Emmie, aged about eight, and probably her next child William spent their last days in the Bibighar, crammed with about two hundred people, some of them slowly dying. It is not known whether the Vibart children, like Emma, were wounded. Among the males in that house only four were grown men.

The Bibighar had originally been built by an Englishman for his bibi or Indian mistress. It had two rooms, each twenty feet by ten, some with windowless cubicles, originally servants' quarters. As George Otto gently pointed out, some of the ladies now had come to realize what 'foul holes' their domestics had had to endure. There was also a small courtyard, fifteen yards square. No furniture or any sort of bedding had been provided. Everyone had slept on the bare floor. Food had consisted of one meal a day of dal and chapattis, served by sweepers, a deliberate insult.

A fearful virago nicknamed the Begum had been put in charge. She had been a prostitute's maid. Every day she would take two of the ladies to grind corn in the stables attached to a yellow-washed hotel, where the Nana now held court, just a few hundred yards away. At night music and singing from the hotel could be heard by the captives.

In those stinking and stifling rooms, full of the moans of the delirious, dysentery and cholera had broken out. Therefore a Bengali doctor, himself a prisoner of the Nana, had been put in charge. When the deaths had reached three or four a day, the Nana began to worry about losing all his hostages. It had been decided that some fresh air might help, so twice a day the Begum had driven such of her charges as could walk on to the verandah for a few minutes: a source of curiosity for the spectators who gathered there.

The doctor had kept a list of the deaths. On July 12 he had recorded the death of Emma Halliday.

The Kamla Retreat was on the western edge of what had been the old Civil Station, the scale of which amazed me – it stretched over three miles along the Ganges. The Entrenchments had been two miles further east, and to reach them meant skirting the whole of what had been known as the Native City. It was only too easy to imagine the panic of that long last-minute dash to an imagined safety.

The large church of All Souls was in conventional red brick. It stood at one end of the original Entrenchments area. Behind were the Gothic screen and Marochetti's marble Angel.

Apart from the graveyard, the rest was open field. It was all so flat, on such a pathetically small scale. You could see where Redan Point had been. I understood why young Spencer Wyndham, visiting this horrific site where his sister had suffered and possibly died, had felt unable even to describe it for the family. I felt far more oppressed there than I had been at the Khyber Pass. I knew too much . . . But cows were grazing peacefully enough under the few scattered trees.

Only about three hundred yards away there were still barracks on the site of those used by Nana Sahib's men. A mysterious culvert or tunnel had recently been discovered. A cow had recently wandered into it and had been asphyxiated by gases.

The most prominent tomb outside the church had a Gothic inscription which began: 'In these grounds within this enclosure are the remains of Major Vibart of the 2nd Bengal Light Infantry and about seventy officers and soldiers who after escaping from the massacre at Cawnpore on June 27 1857 were captured . . .' The bodies, I read, had originally been in the compound of the Savada House but had been brought here in 1861. I also saw the tomb of Judge Thornhill of Fatehgarh and his wife, and another of Francis Whiting, who 'was in command of a boat thirty miles down river and fell while pushing off from a sandbank'. There was another mass grave, of women and children 'of the ill-fated 1st Company 6th Bengal Artillery who were slaughtered on July 18 1857'.

The screen was rather fine, and the angel typically of the period – a sincere effort, but no masterpiece. Inside the church there were many other memorials, including tablets behind the altar, giving lists of all the names of people who had died at Cawnpore in June and July 1857, including the Hallidays and all the Vibarts.

On the way to the Ghat we passed the Racquets Court, which had been used as an assembly point by the mutineers. We looked inside, and found that it had been taken over by squatters. We had a vision of charpoys in the dark. A woman came out with a fearful sore on her face. Leprosy?

Then, at last, we reached the broken dusty path to the place of doom itself. The path ran beside a hideous stinking sewer in which some black buffaloes were happily wallowing. Many of the trees seemed about to collapse, leaning at angles, but a few palms seemed to have been planted in more recent years. The ground on each side looked as if it had been churned up for earthworks of some sort, or tumuli.

On the day of the departure from the Entrenchments, a great crowd had gathered in this normally desolate spot. Palanquins, bullock carts and elephants had assembled gradually near what had been Vibart's Redan. At around 7 am the bedraggled procession had set out, preceded by over 200 wounded and sick persons. Those men able to walk had been mostly barefoot. An elephant with a state howdah had been provided for General Wheeler's wife and daughters. An English memsahib had spotted one of her servants and ordered him to go and find her cook, 'as she wanted him to go down to Allahabad with her'.

I was surprised by the sluggishness and shallowness of the premonsoon Ganges. The sandbanks were very visible. Several shacks had been put up beside the ghat, under the palms: squatters again. Mr Mehra was very angry about this new slum. The original temple, white and red – blood-red – with its five arches above the steps to the murky waters, could have been quite pretty once, in a simple way. Children were bathing and laughing in the shallows, just where the massacre had been. People stared at us, amused at our interest in such a derelict old building, until scared off by Mr Mehra's obvious disapproval. A broken bucket and some cooking things lay on top of the base of the cross put up by the British but thrown away at Independence.

After the Mutiny some imaginative pictures had been published in England of Satichaura Ghat. One at least had shown it as surrounded by fantastic buildings and temples, a kind of Xanadu. Another well-known engraving had given the impression of a deep tropical pool, with overhanging palms and creepers, and with ferns and luscious plants growing out of the bank.

We could easily make out the high ground where the armed men could have hidden. In the midstream of the Ganges we noticed a vulture leisurely tearing away at something. It was a corpse; we could see the white bones and feet sticking up. Other vultures waited their turn on the shore, stretching their wings in the sun.

The far bank had marked the boundary of the old kingdom of Oude. From a distance on that fatal morning the small boats that were to transport the Europeans had looked like moored haystacks. I remembered that description by George Otto, and visualized the ragged officers knee-deep in the water, hoisting in their women and children.

There had been hundreds of watchers, but the silence had been absolute, tense. Then, suddenly, there had been that blast from a bugle, and all the boatmen had leapt into the shallows and waded ashore, having first secreted live coals in the thatch of some boats. Thereupon the very sepoys of the 2nd Cavalry who had helped Major Vibart on his leaving the Entrenchments had opened fire. The Europeans had retaliated immediately. Suddenly several straw roofs had begun to blaze. Ladies up to their chins in water had attempted to avoid the bullets that had been like 'falling rain'. Others had been stabbed or bayoneted . . .

It was a relief and a contrast for us to be taken by Mr Mehra to another ghat at the Bhagwandas temple, which early in the last century had been rescued from decay and restored by a Colonel Stewart. There were small stone statues of the Colonel, on horseback and wearing a top hat, and his Scottish wife and dog. Beneath us the Ganges had silted over and moved course, and the new ground was being illegally cultivated. We noticed by the steps a pile of effigies of Ganesha the elephant god. We asked about them. Oh, said a priest, they had been brought by peasants and would eventually be washed away in the monsoon. Could I have one of them? Of course! So now Ganesha from Bhagwandas sits in my London flat.

We visited the old Cooper Allen leather factory, and were shown photographs of its original British begetters. After the Mutiny

Cawnpore had had an astonishing revival as an industrial centre, as a result in the first place of the cotton boom. Technicians were sent out from Lancashire. By the turn of the century the Elgin Mills were among the most important, financed in part by Indian money, including the Singhanias'.

The apotheosis of the Singhanias at Kanpur is the staggering Shri Radhakrishna Temple, built by the JK Trust. It took nineteen years to complete. The dome-like main steeple, 175 feet high, is in the Orissa style, and there are four smaller steeples. Around the central hall are five shrines, with idols made of a special lustrous alloy, and there are more than eighty inlaid marble murals. Compared to any other Hindu temple we had seen there was a great sense of airiness and light. In the gardens outside were fountains which at night were illuminated in different colours. Such is the richness of the place that armed guards have to be at the doors.

On our last day we went to see the old Memorial Gardens, now de-fiantly called the Nana Rao Park. There was the giant banyan tree, where the British were supposed to have hanged mutineers from the branches – though Mr Mehra said this was untrue. Now people were sleeping in its shade. An ugly swimming-pool had been built, and in front was a bust of Tatya Tope on a pedestal, at the foot of which were two absurd white stone frogs. This bust in turn looked over the site of where Marochetti's angel had once stood. As Tatya Tope was the man usually held responsible for the massacre at the Satichaura Ghat, such an arrangement must have been done deliberately.

The House of the Ladies: II

When the Nana had heard that a strong British army was advancing on Cawnpore, and that the British were in no mood for mercy, it was put to him by his advisers that it might be awkward for him if the prisoners in the Bibighar told their stories. So he had agreed (accord-ing to most versions) to eliminate the lot.

On the afternoon of July 15 the sepoy guard at the Bibighar called out the four men. A merchant, Mr Greenway, was told to bring his fourteen-year-old son, the oldest of the children. Some of the ladies had rushed to the door to see what was happening, but had been pushed back. The little group had been halted outside the gate by a squad of sepoys, who had fired at point-blank range. The bodies had been left lying on the grass for at least two days.

The Begum had told the ladies that they were now going to be ex-ecuted, and had gone to the sepoys to tell them to get on with the deed. But the sepoys had refused to take orders from her. She had disappeared in a rage, returning after a while with five men, two of whom were Hindu peasants, the others being Muslim – two butchers and the third reputed to be her 'sweetheart', Suryar Khan. The sepoys had been told to fire into the house. This time they did so, but had pointed their muskets at the ceiling. So the five men had gone inside. Evening was approaching. In the half-light shrieks of terror and agonized moans and screams had been heard from the Bibighar, to the satisfaction of the Begum. 'Suryar Khan soon emerged with his sword broken off at the hilt,' George Otto wrote.

> He procured another from the Nana's house, and after a few minutes appeared again on the same errand. The third blade was of a better temper: or perhaps the thick of the work was already over. By the time darkness had closed in, the men came forth and locked up the house for the night. Then the screams ceased: but the groans lasted till morning.

After dawn the five had returned with some sweepers to dispose of the bodies. Any clothes worth keeping were removed. Then the bodies had been dragged by the hair to a nearby well and thrown inside. Some of the women were alive and could speak; they had been thrown in regardless.

At least one child had had its head bashed in. An onlooker had reported that three boys, aged between seven and five, had run crying and screaming round and round the well. They had been caught and flung inside, but whether or not they had been killed beforehand was not certain.

The well had been so full that when the British arrived they had seen legs and arms sticking out of it. Other corpses had been thrown into the river. Inside the Bibighar the floor had been thick with congealed gore, and the whole place littered with bloodied clothes, bits of prayer books, hunks of hair, sometimes a yard long. 'The plaster was scored with sword-cuts: not high up, as where men have fought: but low down, and about the corners, as if a creature had crouched to avoid a blow.'

I had to admit that in some respects the park was a pretty place, in spite of the noise of the traffic. On a mound of earth some bits of Victorian Gothic stone tracery had been hurled. I left feeling most upset about the banality of the stone frogs. But now, looking back on that visit, I think I can understand the attitude better. After all Kanpur is a living city, with a present and a future, a place to be *enjoyed*. Life goes on.

We left India before Mrs Gandhi decided to send the Army into the Golden Temple at Amritsar. The operation was successful, but at least three hundred people were killed. The revulsion felt by the Sikhs ended in her own assassination. Then came the reaction: carnage and the destruction of Sikh property. We were very worried about our friends when we heard that after Delhi Kanpur had been the worst affected town. I wrote immediately to Mr Mehra, who replied:

> All the Sikh friends you met, including Mr Kripal Singh and his family, are safe.
>
> Some ruffians tried to loot Kripal Singh's house, but a gun shot drove them away. Kripal Singh and his family also, as a precautionary measure, stayed in the house of their Hindu neighbours for some days.
>
> But for Hindu and also some Muslim neighbours coming to the rescue of the Sikhs, the toll of life and the loss of property would have been greater than is the case. Some of the Sikhs, including a Brigadier, a War hero, and his family, were done to death brutally. It is a blot on the administration. The killers and the looters were not the admirers of Mrs Indira Gandhi, but just ruffians and antisocial elements, who had been nurtured in the last many years by the politicians of all kinds and by the administration under the control of the politicians. Two civil rights groups have blamed Congress politicians for instigating the killers and looters.
>
> According to official figures more than seventy-one Sikhs were brutally massacred, and property worth millions looted and destroyed. Non-official estimates put the figure at near three hundred and seventy.
>
> What we had, cannot be called riots, as the Sikhs were just killed and wounded, and their property looted without any resistance from them. They were taken totally unawares and the administration could give them no assistance for quite some time. They were hunted down and destroyed like Jews in Nazi Germany.

The Wathens at Amritsar

As a child I was unaware of that other massacre at Amritsar, on April 12 1919, but I can now understand why the murders of my father's fellow officers Billy Haycraft and Percy McClenaghan should have caused such intense alarm among the British in the Punjab.

The storming of the Golden Temple by Mrs Gandhi's troops was another – though quite different – watershed in Indian history, and was of course to lead to Mrs Gandhi's assassination. But after 1919 nothing could be quite the same between the British and Indians. There were some Europeans, shocking though it can seem today, who even felt that General Dyer's action in shooting down an unarmed crowd in the Jallianwala Bagh was justified, averting an uprising throughout India similar to the great Mutiny of 1857. Others reacted quite differently, in horror. But, in future years, whenever there was a spate of murders, that old nervousness, especially among the wives and memsahibs, returned.

One of my oldest friends is a son of Gerard Wathen, the possible prototype of Forster's Fielding. He showed me his mother's diaries and letters written from Amritsar at that time. There I found expressed the conflicting attitudes of this intelligent couple. For myself, after seeing that film, I could not conceive of such a thing. But now at least, through Mrs Wathen's accounts, I was able to appreciate some of the panic that led up to that ghastly event – which was not so evident in the film.

When I met Gerard in later years he was running a boys' school at Hampstead, and I found him severe and remote, but that was not at all the reputation that he left behind him at Amritsar or, previously, at Lahore. Nor was it the picture that emerged from the diaries of Melicent Wathen, or Mel as she was known. I found her a much more accessible person. She loved the Himalayas, and now her descriptions and great love for Indian birds and flowers remind me of Olive, though Olive could never have written so vividly. Mel, a keen horsewoman, painted beautiful watercolours of Kashmir scenery such as would have done very well as illustrations to those sentimental books of the period. In some ways there was a counterpart to Walter and Olive in Gerard and Mel.

Mel came out from England with two children in December 1915, during the First World War. About ninety per cent of the students at the Khalsa College at Amritsar were Sikhs. As had been the case at Lahore, Gerard was immensely popular, mixing in their social life, listening to their problems, encouraging them. He extended laboratories, organized new classes, instituted literary and debating societies, cleared ground for playing fields.

The word Khalsa means 'elect' or 'pure'. The tenth and last Sikh guru, Gobind Singh, had in 1699 formed a new order called the Khalsa, in face of religious persecution by the then Muslim rulers of the Punjab. In order that these Sikhs should be distinguishable from other men, he decreed – among other things – that their hair should not be cut or their beards shaved. Originally Sikhism was an offshoot of Hinduism, an attempt at a compromise between Hinduism and Islam. The fifth guru, Arjun, compiled a holy book which he placed in the Sikhs' greatest shrine, the Golden Temple, built in the Sarowar or sacred pool of Amritsar.

Forster would have approved of Mel's opinions of certain of her compatriots. She was furious when at Dalhousie she overheard two young officers airily describing a local rajah of ancient lineage as 'quite a nice sort of fellow for that type of man', after having peremptorily demanded coolies and rifles for a shooting expedition in the Himalayas without even a thank you. And soon after her arrival at Amritsar she and Gerard went to the Club, 'he for the bridge – I to be polite'.

I found one exquisitely robed lady by the fire making that (appalling) sort of heavy crochet lace for table cloths. My heart sank. There were no English papers, owing to the *Persia* [P. & O. ship sunk off Crete]. I sat down and made frantic conversation. Oh yes – she did a lot of work – really had no time to make things for soldiers. 'Oh, what do you do all day?' I said. 'Well, you see, I make this lace, and then there are the dogs, and my pigeons, and of course the club every evening – one really has no time.' 'Wasn't it odd about the earthquake in England?' I began again. 'Earthquake in England? When was that? – Oh, I never read the papers. You see they come just as we're going to the club, and then we don't get home till 9 o'clock, and by that time it is too late to want to read the papers.' 'Have you done much riding lately?' I again started. 'Well, it's been most unfortunate. My horse somehow got two saddle galls. Oh only just lumps under the saddle you know, but still one doesn't like to go on riding, it might hurt the poor thing. So I haven't done much riding. Also the puppies ate a hole in my habit' . . .

In September 1918 there were three days of arson and looting at Calcutta. It was perhaps the first time in British India there had been organized mob violence for political purposes. The alarmed Government decided that it must have special powers, and a commission of inquiry under Mr Justice Rowlatt made certain recommendations dealing with revolutionary conspiracy and political assassination, which in some cases involved internment without any trial at all. His Report was received not just with dismay but fury by Hindus, Muslims and Sikhs alike. To many Indians Rowlatt became the most detested word in English.

The Punjab had been the most strained economically as a result of the war. Prices were rising. Soldiers returning home were discontented. The Muslim element, which was in the majority in the eastern section of the province, was on edge about the fate of the defeated Turkish empire. Nationalist agitators invented provisions in the Rowlatt Report that were untrue and believed in by simple people: such as husbands and wives having to be 'inspected' before being allowed to marry. Early in 1919 Gerard for the first time found politics being discussed by his students; he was always ready to answer questions. His sons also began going to classes with the Sikh boys.

The man who had to deal with the spreading unrest in the Punjab was its Lieutenant-Governor, an Irishman, Sir Michael O'Dwyer. In February 1919 Sir Michael visited the Khalsa College, and Mel told with pride how he 'piled on' the praise for Gerard. Since he was later held by some to be in part responsible for the Jallianwala Bagh tragedy in April, it is worth quoting her first impressions of him: 'He's a tremendous worker – hard as nails – clever – full of imagination – strong – my word he is strong – a man after John Lawrence's heart if you like.' He said that the Government had so much confidence in Gerard that it was giving him twenty thousand pounds to spend as he liked. Whenever Gerard opened his mouth in reply, 'I never heard such cheering and shouting.'

In March 1919 some of the Rowlatt proposals became law. Gandhi, who had always been their strong opponent, was the only nationalist leader to take positive action. He appealed to the Viceroy to refuse these proposals, but when this was disregarded he formed his famous Satyagraha (adherence to truth) Society, an extension of the passive resistance that he had first seen effective in South Africa. Now he decided to call a hartal, or general strike with fasts and mass meetings, throughout India on March 30. At Amritsar on that day there was a meeting of 45,000 in the Jallianwala Bagh, a large piece of waste ground, but otherwise all was quiet. At Delhi, however, there was rioting and more arson. Gandhi called another hartal for April 6, as a protest against those who had been killed by the police.

On April 2 Mel rode into Amritsar:

I pulled up at the shop of a Mohammedan I knew and was greeted with a stare and no answer to my salaam. He continued smoking his hookah. Paying no attention, I got off my horse and was stepping inside his shop when he turned his back on me saying that none of his things were for sale. I saw that things were not right, and remounting I rode on into the city. Instead of being greeted with smiles and salaams I became aware that on all sides I was being stared at. The streets which at that hour were usually untenanted except by those going about their work, now seemed full of men moving restlessly hither and thither with no apparent object. My friends avoided my gaze, and those who did not know me stared in a way that I had never before experienced.

The hartal on April 6 also passed off peacefully at Amritsar, but with another and larger meeting at the Jallianwala Bagh. A notice appeared on the clock tower: 'Prepare yourself to die and kill others'. There were parades at Lahore, carrying black flags. Sir Michael O'Dwyer decided the time had come for strong action. Miles Irving, the Deputy Commissioner, came to believe that the two leading agitators, Kitchlew and Satyapal, were part of a secret organization run by Bolsheviks and Germans. It was known that the Frontier tribes were preparing for an attack, and an Afghan invasion was a possibility. On April 9 O'Dwyer ordered Kitchlew and Satyapal to be detained and deported to Dharmsala, a hundred miles away. On the same day Gandhi was intercepted on his way north and refused permission to enter the Punjab.

Gandhi had been expected at Amritsar on April 16. An Englishman had called on the Wathens to warn them that a plot had been discovered to murder all the Europeans on that day. Mel now realized that she must be prepared to leave with the children, and for the next days always had a small bundle of clothes and food ready that each could easily carry should it be necessary to escape to the villages, where 'with the families of some of our Sikhs we hoped the children at least would be safe'.

Gerard was horrified by the deportation of Kitchlew and Satyapal, furious that Miles Irving had not discussed it with him. It was all the more serious because the annual horse and cattle fair was about to take place, one of the biggest of its kind in the world. Yet more important was the fact that it took place at the time of the Baisakhi Festival, the great religious festival of the Sikhs.

That night the Wathens dined out. Mel wrote:

At that dinner mostly composed of soldiers the attitude was one of optimism. They laughed at the idea of my going away, and Mr Scott, one of the Bank Managers, said to me incredulously: 'Why, with all our aeroplanes and machine guns they will *never* dare to rise!' Alas for his unfounded belief in our strong arm! Within twelve hours he was cruelly and horribly done to death at his bank in the City. No gun was fired, no aeroplane rose to avenge his death, there were none!

On April 10, she said, the storm burst in all its fury. They were sitting in the garden when the Assistant Commissioner galloped up, his horse covered with blood and foam and dust. 'The mob is over the railway bridge!' he cried. 'I have been trying to keep them back with four gunners, mounted, but someone fired at the mob from the back, and it's all up. They've murdered all the white men in the city. Where's my wife?'

That was all we knew, but every moment new fragments of news floated in about the murders, the burning of churches and banks, the pulling up of lines and looting of shops . . . And now the men from the fair were pouring past our house. Wild looking Pathans driving their horses in front of them; men galloping; horse dealers mad to get their valuable charges away before the looting, which they knew must follow. All were making in one rush down the Grand Trunk Road to Lahore, and my husband and I stood and watched them stream past, realizing it was too late to escape ourselves, and that we had now only the loyalty of our Sikhs to save us.

The crowd had forced its way into the National Bank. An old man with an axe went for the manager Mr Steward, who shot him, but before the man died he cut off Mr Steward's head with the axe. The crowd threw the head into the streets. They then beat Mr Scott to death with lathis. The bodies were thrown on a pile of furniture, soaked in kerosene, and set on fire.

Next the Alliance Bank was attacked. Its manager, Mr Thomas, shot three men who attacked them, then ran upstairs to the roof. He was caught and thrown into the street to the people below, who threw kerosene over him whilst still alive and burnt him.

The mob broke into the Zenana Hospital to search for Mrs Easden, the doctor in charge. But she hid in a cupboard, and later escaped. A missionary woman, Miss Marcia Sherwood, was caught on her bicycle as she rode to her schools in order to close them and send her girl students home. She was beaten and kicked, and left for dead. A Hindu family rescued her and cleaned her wounds.

Mel continued:

A roar of voices proceeding from the College broke on our ears. As we turned the corner we found the whole College staff and students coming to meet us. For a second we questioned their meaning, but only for a second. 'Sir, we have come to know,' said their spokesman, 'whether you will grant us permission to form guards round your house so that your family may be safe and need not go to the Fort.' It was indeed a great moment, something to have worked for that in the midst of all this chaos this body of men should have stood loyal to us.

Then came the news that a British sergeant had been 'trampled to death' at the railway station. The manager of the Chartered Bank and his assistant had been saved just in time by the arrival of policemen. A small picquet of British troops had been attacked and had fired back, killing some people.

The Commissioner and the Police Chief from Lahore arrived at the College, to see if any of the Wathens' party were still alive. They were amazed to find them so calm and the students even playing hockey. They asked Gerard if he would come with them on a tour of the city.

At about 6 p.m. Gerard having returned – looking ghastly – with the news that the City was in the hands of the mob, that no troops were likely to arrive before midnight, and that all women and children and non-officials were to go into the Fort. We decided to drive to where everyone was collected and offer what assistance we could. It was a tragic sight. Never did I see horror so grimly written on any face except those who had come from the trenches. There were women with their children all herded together, several not knowing if their husbands were dead or alive. Some knew within an hour that they were dead – others not relieved of their suspense until after midnight. No provision of any kind had been made either in the way of bedding or food; they had left their homes as they were. They were taken in cars, in native carts, in every kind of vehicle. Most of them were weeping, many from sheer fatigue, and no one knew what the future would bring.

About four hundred people eventually gathered there in the Fort, in only four rooms. 'By the luck of the Gods,' a party of Gurkha troops had arrived at Amritsar railway station on their way to the Hills. Their commandant, on finding that a mob was in the process of wrecking the buildings and that Europeans had been murdered, opened fire and cleared the place. Twenty-five rioters were killed. Two aeroplanes, coming from Lahore, flew low over the city. 'Such was the relief, you could see the change on the men's faces.' During the night a company of Baluchis arrived from Jullundur, sent by Brigadier-General Rex Dyer on the order of Sir Michael

480

O'Dwyer. An armoured train also arrived from Lahore. Gerard, on hearing the next morning that there was a council of war at the station, went to find out what was to be done. It had been decided to wait until 2 pm for the dead to be collected and buried; then, if the crowds had not dispersed, aeroplanes would drop bombs and troops would enter the City with orders to shoot on any gathering they might meet. Gerard saw this as a 'frightful blunder', and asked what warning would be given. Eventually he offered to send some of his professors, one a Muslim, as emissaries, and this was agreed.

Mel began to pack away all her favourite things. She lay on the sofa sipping a whisky and soda and could understand how people took to drink.

As 2 pm came nearer, the tension was frightful. At last the hour struck. Three minutes passed. Gerard arrived, then an old professor who had been to the mosques. He had at last managed to get a hearing and people there had listened and gone to their homes. 'Still the planes hovered around, but no bomb was dropped. *Gerard* had saved the city.'

After this Gerard was determined to get Mel, some women friends and the children away as quickly as possible. They heard that a train was likely to get through, so they collected their luggage, and accompanied by a body of students drove two miles to the station. An armoured train was standing there, looking grim but wonderfully comforting.

Their destination was Rawalpindi, but Mel had persuaded Gerard to come with them as far as Lahore. Their own train was four hours late and with only one carriage.

It stopped three times before Lahore, and at every station a dense mob of angry peasants pressed against the windows staring at us, we in the light, they in darkness with our lights shining on their faces. The only thing was not to think, we were absolutely defenceless, and every time the train started on again we breathed a sigh of relief. At Lahore the station was occupied by Sikh troops. As we dined in the station few spoke. The room was full of men in their shirt sleeves, their necks bare, looking as if they had not slept for nights, nor had they. When they did speak, it was only to utter deep forebodings and the impression that it was the Mutiny all over again only worse. At ten o'clock our train [for 'Pindi] came in, somehow nine of us got into a compartment for four. I walked once more with my husband down the platform. He said: 'We may never meet again. Things are as bad as they have ever been in our history. We don't know what we are in for.' And almost with those words we parted, he standing there on that hot platform under its lurid light in which soldiers stood and sat in knots.

Gerard returned safely to Amritsar, and General Dyer also arrived, late on the night of the 11th. The city was now handed over to Dyer by the Deputy Commissioner. On the morning of the 12th General Dyer marched through the streets with about five hundred British and Indian troops, followed by two armoured cars. A crowd was openly hostile, jeering and spitting on the ground. The next day being Baisakhi Day, thousands of Sikh pilgrims were arriving to worship at the Golden Temple. Many had to sleep in the open at the Jallianwala Bagh. Dyer now decided to post proclamations at nineteen different points at Amritsar, to the beat of drums, imposing a curfew and forbidding any processions or gatherings of four men or more – which otherwise would be treated as 'an unlawful assembly and dispersed by force of arms if necessary'. In spite of this, on the afternoon of the 13th he was informed that a large meeting was being held in the Jallianwala Bagh and addressed by 'seditionists'.

The sequel was relentlessly portrayed in the Attenborough *Gandhi* film. As Malcolm Darling was to write to E. M. Forster: 'Enter infuriated general – "I took thirty seconds to make up my mind," said he to Wathen, "and then fifteen hundred rounds." God, it makes one sick.' Nobody is certain about the size of the crowd. Dyer said afterwards he estimated it to be 6,000, but some have said it was up to 50,000. He was accompanied by fifty armed Gurkhas and Baluchis, and forty more Gurkhas carrying only kukris. Dyer ordered the crowd to disperse. It seems possible that he did not know that there were virtually no other exits from the Jallianwala Bagh, and when the crowd did not disperse he panicked. Without any warning, he ordered his men to shoot and to continue shooting until they had used up all their ammunition: 1,650 rounds. There was a rush to a low wall of about five feet, and people were crushed or trampled to death. At first it was reported that 200 people had been killed, but later the official figure was 379. Indians have claimed it was more like 1,000. There were also several hundred wounded. Dyer's armoured cars blocked the entrance and no medical aid could come in.

And this was Mel's immediate reaction: 'The order went out that no meetings were to be held. The blackguard leaders told the mob we should never dare to fire, so a huge meeting collected. They got their deserts this time, for the troops were ready, and fired and killed over 200, and a good thing too.'

It was not however Gerard's view. He was at the time enrolling some students as special constables. A squadron of the 11th Lancers cantered up to the College and ordered him and the two other English professors to leave at once.

'Gerard was furious,' she wrote afterwards:

But it was the General's orders – so he went with them to the General in the cantonments. Gerard attacked him saying India would never forget, but Dyer said he had to decide quickly or his men would have been overpowered. He also said that he meant to strike hard as a lesson.

Gerard discovered that only a cipher telegram stating that 'firing had taken place' was to be sent to the L. G. [O'Dwyer] – and no one was to be sent officially to tell him what had happened. Gerard seeing this was wrong argued the point and induced them to send Mr Jacob, who had come to lecture to the College, in his car – Gerard volunteering to go too. They had a risky drive, well armed, for dacoits were ranging the countryside, but they got through safely ... Gerard roused Sir Michael at 3 a.m. (the first man I should think who has ever dared do this!), to find that the telegram had arrived undecipherable – so that Sir Michael knew nothing of what had happened. Immediately council of war was held, and Sir Michael tried to get in communication with Simla. Of course he failed. Then Gerard (as is his way) spoke his mind and told Sir Michael that unless he wanted trouble in the future with the leaders and to stir up terrible bitter feeling, both immediately and for years to come, he should go at once to Amritsar himself, have Dyer replaced, and admit a mistake had been made – not in the actual firing but in the amount that was done. Sir Michael – probably disliking criticism – refused to listen to what Gerard said. Instead he sent a congratulatory message to Dyer through General Beynen [Divisional Commander] and afterwards sent word through Mr Kitchin [Commissioner] that he did not approve of Gerard speaking to him the way he had.

Martial law was now proclaimed at Amritsar and Lahore. Gerard was at least able to dissuade Dyer from authorizing a bombardment from the air the next day. If anything happened to the Golden Temple, he said, it would permanently alienate the Sikhs, and therefore a large proportion of the Indian Army. However, rioters in the town of Gujanwala, north of Lahore, were bombed and machine-gunned.

The people of Amritsar were stunned and terrified. As Mel said: 'There is now a deathly hush in the city.' And Nehru in his autobiography has written that those who had managed to escape from the inferno and reach the outside world were so terror-struck that they could not even give any clear account. 'Helplessly and impotently, we waited for scraps of news, and bitterness filled our hearts.' These scraps included the infamous 'crawling order': something never forgotten by Indians. Dyer decreed that anyone passing along the alley where Miss Sherwood had been assaulted should go on all fours. All Indians were forced to salaam Europeans. Youths suspected of trouble-making were publicly flogged without trial.

And now Dyer was being hailed by some as the saviour of the Punjab if not of all India. Nehru also has told how later in 1919 he boarded a night train for Delhi and found a vacant upper berth in a sleeper compartment. When he woke in the morning he discovered that all his companions were British military officers, and one was General Dyer, holding forth in an 'aggressive and triumphant' manner about the Jallianwala Bagh affair, and boasting that he could have reduced the whole of Amritsar to ashes if he had so wished. 'I was greatly shocked,' Nehru said, 'to hear his conversation and to observe his callous manner. He descended at Delhi in pyjamas with bright pink stripes, and a dressing gown.'

Many, such as Gerard Wathen, were appalled, comparing the horror and stupidity to the burning of Joan of Arc. But initial support for Dyer was strengthened when the Afghans decided to invade in May, on a day that seemed to be timed to coincide with the start of the Indian Mutiny in 1857. Obviously the Afghans had hoped for a general uprising throughout India. Although this Third Afghan War was swiftly ended, the tribes of Waziristan were aroused and sporadic fighting continued along the Frontier for the next four years. Dyer took a notably valiant part in the fighting in 1919, and was obviously encouraged by the adulation he received.

Gerard's view, according to Mel, was that the original trouble-makers at Amritsar should have been shot or given life sentences. ('They were given the latter,' she wrote in an account later, 'but Sir Edward MacLagan – O'Dwyer's successor – changed the whole lot to two years – really a criminal thing to do. Everyone is furious out here.') The great mistake of the British, she said, had been not sending out agents to explain the truth about the Rowlatt proposals, instead of leaving it to the seditionist leaders; and this was probably correct. The professors at Lahore, unlike Gerard at Khalsa College, had not been allowed to talk politics to their students, many of whom eventually became leaders in the riots.

Mel's attitude, one trusts, softened later, but in October she was still writing this, after a crowd, which had gathered at the railway station in the hope of meeting Gandhi (who never turned up), had fled at the appearance of some British officers:

Fear is the only thing by which you can rule a wild uneducated crowd, and thank heaven Sir Michael and General Dyer acted as they did. I don't care what Gerard says, or any of those other sentimentalists. That shooting was drastic, but it was needed, and it's done more good than a hundred years of soft talk and reasoning – and I *believe* it will carry more weight than all the subtle lies and reasonings of these seditionists – for the people have learnt that after certain limits we do at last turn, and *hurt*, and that is a fact . . . I have also been twice into the city and found the people far more polite than I have known them for more than a year. I am told this is only fear.

The Hunter Commission, set up to inquire into the 'disturbances', only inflamed Indian opinion. Words like 'injudicious' and 'unfortunate' shocked men like Nehru and his father, who had hitherto admired British justice – they both gave up their legal practices in order to devote themselves to the nationalist movement. Mel, hearing of a threat of a railway strike, felt she could bear India no longer and that she must go home to England for a while, to 'compose' herself and put the children in schools. Meanwhile Gerard found himself being consulted for his views at high levels; both British and Indian, which was certainly gratifying after so much hostile opposition in the past.

The effect of Jallianwala Bagh on the Indian mind was comparable to the British reaction on hearing of the Bibighar and Satichaura Ghat atrocities, though in the end more lasting. After Jallianwala Bagh there could be no compromise, no trust. But Gandhi, who had been horrified by the violence that had emerged out of his Satyagraha campaign, shocked Congress delegates at Amritsar when he called for moderation. In this way there was again some – temporary – comparison with 1857 and 'Clemency' Canning.

In November, on the anniversary of the birthday of Guru Nanak, the founder of the Sikh religion, Gerard joined the procession with a turban on his head. This became his regular practice in subsequent years. Every day he would attend the College Gurdwara or temple – which incidentally ensured that all the students would also be present. It was said that 'with folded hands and downcast eyes he used to come in wearing his turban.'

At long last the Hunter Commission reported its findings. As a result Dyer, who had become very ill from the strain, was relieved of his command. Sir Michael O'Dwyer had also come in for heavy attack for his part in the disasters in the Punjab, but the report 'definitely exonerated' him. To Indians it was now clear that the British still regarded them as an inferior race. The clamour in Britain in Dyer's favour, and the hero's welcome that he eventually received on his return, finally changed Gandhi's mind. Gandhi now committed himself to a campaign of non-cooperation, and soon he was the undisputed leader of Congress. Rabindranath Tagore, who had received the Nobel Prize in 1913, wrote to the Viceroy relinquishing his knighthood.

Before Dyer died in 1927 the House of Lords produced a majority vote exonerating him. Previously the *Morning Post*, prompted in part by O'Dwyer, had launched a fund in his support that raised nearly thirty thousand pounds. Kipling had contributed ten pounds.

In 1940 a Sikh called Udham Singh, who had survived Jallianwala Bagh, shot O'Dwyer dead at a meeting at Caxton Hall in London.

By 1920 the British had found themselves in the absurd and eventually dangerous position of protecting the patently corrupt Hinduized priests or mahants who controlled the Golden Temple at Amritsar and other shrines. The cry went up that there was Government interference with religion. The protesters became known as the SGPC, the Shiromani Gurudwara Prabandhak Committee, whose organizers were the Akali, later to become fully political, supporting Gandhi's non-cooperative movement. The mahants, unbelievably, had made General Dyer an 'honorary Sikh' soon after Jallianwala Bagh.

Some of the Akali leaders were professors at the College. There were many awkward times for Gerard, who generally supported the Akalis. When Gandhi advised students to boycott education, Gerard invited him to his house for discussions and convinced him that such an action at Khalsa College would be wrong. The grievances of the Sikhs did not lessen after the Akalis took control of the Golden Temple, and to some extent they are grievances which have their counterparts to this day. For it was the Akali leaders' surrender in 1984 to Bhindranwale that led to the Indian Government's decision to storm the Golden Temple.

As Raúl and I departed for Lucknow we were warned at Kanpur that it was the day before the festival of Holi. 'Don't leave your hotel!' we were begged. That was going to be a bore, because we would only be at Lucknow two nights, and there was a lot of sight-seeing to cram in. After reading *Hindoo Holiday* I could appreciate the possible dangers of Holi.

We were also due to meet an American professor, Dick Swift. It was his first visit to India and we were not at all sure how he was going to react. We could imagine his face when told that he was likely to be squirted with coloured dyes.

Even in your own home you weren't safe from Holi revellers, we were told. They would dash in and hose you all over, never mind the furniture. Mr Mehra's son said that he was telling everyone that he was going to be away that weekend. 'But no need for *you* to worry. They won't dare break into your hotel.' In the old days the bacchanalia went on for days on end, but Mrs Gandhi had ordered that all festivities must stop at midday. So the drinking began at midnight.

Dick, we found, had already arrived at the Carlton Hotel, which we had specially chosen for its Raj associations. He was philosophical about its comforts and bathroom arrangements: 'Plain – rather more Indian than English'. He had already heard about Holi, and someone had placed a vermilion streak on his forehead. An aged fellow guest had also given him a lecture about the mythological origins of the festival – but we decided that it all boiled down to the rites of spring and the joy of sex. In fact Holi was supposed to herald the beginning of harvest, and thus was the equivalent of Baisakhi in the Punjab.

We needed to escape from the mounting Holi excitement around the hotel and face up to more serious matters. If the Rashtrapati Bhawan, the former Viceroy's palace at Delhi, and its approaches, are the most spectacular and abiding reminder of the glories of British India, so the ruins of the Residency at Lucknow are a symbol of the dream that failed: a dream in which some Indians also believed. The red brick skeletons made me think of the Baths of Caracalla in Rome, where – who knows – there might also have been an epic last-ditch stand. The feeling I had at the Residency was quite different to the experience of visiting the Cawnpore/Kanpur sites. Here at least, in spite of over two thousand deaths, there had been a triumph not associated with atrocities and betrayal.

It was like walking in one of those best-selling novels by Maud Diver, who in the 1920s and 1930s did so much to romanticize the British Raj. Any moment I expected to meet her Captain Desmond VC. Here had been Martin Gubbins's house, here the renowned billiard-room with its shattered Gothic window frames, here the Baillie Guard Gate, here Innes's post, here the Redan ... Down in the cellars, black with flies, surgeons had probed and amputated, with the help of chloroform, a new discovery, and ladies had cut up their bombazine dresses for bandages. When people had been killed during the Siege, their effects, especially food, had been auctioned. Henry Lawrence had believed that there were only enough supplies for fifteen days, but the Siege had lasted three months.

I had with me a high-flown account of one of the attacks that had been repulsed in June 1857. '. . . As the rebels poured in, they were mowed down in scores by grape, and their leaders picked off one by one. As the fire grew more and more infernal, even the wounded and sick English rose from their couches, seized muskets and fired as long as their strength allowed . . .' A plaque marked where Lawrence had been fatally hit by shrapnel. It had happened on a day of great heat, July 2 1857, probably the very day on which at Cawnpore the people who had survived the Satichaura Ghat massacre were taken to the Bibighar. 'Sir Henry, are you hurt?', Captain Wilson had called out through the dust and smoke. No answer. Twice the question had been repeated, and at last there was a low murmur: 'I am killed.' Later Lawrence had asked the doctor how long he had to live. 'Forty-eight hours.' And the forecast had been precisely correct.

Henry Lawrence belonged to the pantheon of Victorian giants and demi-saints in India, like his brother John Lawrence, and John Jacob. His greatness shines out in the last photograph – that extraordinary, furrowed, suffering face, with the shaggy brows and ragged beard. The soldiers who carried him to his grave knelt one by one and kissed him on the forehead.

We went to see his tomb with its well-known inscription: 'Here lies Henry Lawrence who tried to do his duty.' The old man in charge of the cemetery was already in a Holi mood, his clothes splashed red and with a black crow's feather in his cap. Perhaps he swayed a little.

Although Bishop Heber had talked of Lucknow as being one of the greatest architectural sights in the world, guidebooks tend to be dismissive of its monuments. But we were impressed by the Great Imambara, and especially by the view from its roof. The Husainabad Imambara I thought very beautiful indeed, in a stagey way, even if it had 'only' been built in 1837. At Lucknow we were back again among Muslim buildings; it seemed more like being in the Middle East than in India.

Raúl decided that Dick must have his first taste of an Indian bazaar, but it was a great mistake, for we were at once sprayed with some bluish water. An elephant passed, loaded with sheaves; it too seemed anxious to get the hell out of there.

We had dinner at Clark's Hotel, which had a rather more Americanized atmosphere. Riding back in our bicycle rickshaw, we saw bonfires being lit, to represent the burning of Holika, the unfortunate lady of legend who was reduced to ashes although her nephew Prahlad was saved because he had prayed to Lord Vishnu.

Dick complained the next morning of having been kept awake by singing and shouting in the streets outside. At the hotel's gates a group of rickshaw wallahs, their clothes soaked emerald green and purple, tried to inveigle us outside for a tour of the city, but we remained sedately in the garden drinking tea. Now and then lorries rattled past full of shrieking and ecstatic mobs. We felt besieged; which seemed appropriate for Lucknow.

Then at last a group of about ten young people, mostly girls, their faces like banshees and their hair and clothes dripping with dyes, caught sight of us through the trees and advanced meaningfully across the lawn. We braced ourselves, but there was no escape. Dick's and my face were smeared violet, Raúl's green. Next we had to embrace everybody three times. The spell was broken. Our clothes were ruined. Never mind. You couldn't tell which was Dick and which the bougainvillaea.

Midday and the witching hour of freedom for tourists. Holi was over. In the afternoon we were therefore able to see La Martinière, where Kim had been to school. Fifty-eight of its boys had died at the Residency in 1857. Today because of Holi there were no boys about, and the Principal was therefore having a presumably well-earned siesta. However, partly due to Raúl's soft talk, partly through flaunting Dick's position at his university, we managed to get inside. The building was a fantastic jumble, architecturally, almost successful but rather sad. Even after nearly two hundred years it was still unfinished. There was a lot of squeaking of bats in the underground chapel.

Dick had to hurry off to Delhi because in his ambassador's absence he was to give a lecture on American foreign strategy, which sounded an unenviable job.

For me it was farewell to India, probably for some years. A curtain had been lifted that was far from any nostalgic memories of childhood. If I did go back, I knew I would want to spend several months there, quietly, without rush. Very likely I would want to revisit some of the places that still had particular associations for me. But first I would want to see the deserts of Bikaner, and Jodhpur, and Trivandrum, and Konarak, and Leh, and the Kulu valley; and Amritsar.

I admit that a certain squeamishness had stopped me from wanting to go to Benares, now called Varanasi. People said that it was very beautiful, 'especially in the early morning', and that there were buildings 'unchanged since the Daniells', but even that did not seem enough of a recommendation.

Pakistan for me had been more like going home, much as I was grieved by the political repression there before and after my visit. It had been nearly fifty years since I was last in Gilgit. I simply wanted to experience again the silences of the evenings, watch the shadows of the mountains like folds in silk, and hear the chukor calling in the cornfields. All this I did find. So Shangri-La had been real. It had been more upsetting than I thought it would be, but not so upsetting as going back to Gulmarg. I shall never want to return to Gulmarg.

I still have a longing to see Hunza, and I would also like to trek up to Yasin and the high Pamirs and Kashgar. I still have a dream of making that journey from Gilgit to Srinagar, through Astor and Bunji, over the Burzil and down to the Wular lake. And I know that I should like just once more to hear the oriole in our chinar tree.

If I went back to Pakistan, I would want to go to Chitral and, for a special reason, Quetta. Now that I have Pathan friends, perhaps I could visit places along the Frontier which would have meant death to Europeans in the time of the Raj. But, as I write, there are different dangers now along the Afghan border. These same friends are convinced that the Russians will never leave Afghanistan, after building all those motorways and airfields. So the last chapter of the Great Game has been reached, just as the Russians always knew it would, over a hundred years ago.

My other travels were partly because of associations with Charles, Macaulay, Humphrey and others. In that way I could visualize more clearly the lives they had led, a hundred and fifty or fifty years ago. In so doing I also found myself beginning to feel the spell of an India that I had never known, that same spell that caught the imagination of so many thousands of British people, pukka sahibs and pukka memsahibs, nabobs and box wallahs: a spell that was India's alone, and nothing to do with the British past. For me this reached a culminating stage at Kanpur/Cawnpore, of all places one might say.

The necessity of having to describe so much violent death surprised me, even more after meeting many gentle people in India, especially Hindus. I have sometimes been asked whether I think the British were a permanent addition to the culture of the subcontinent, providing a 'real set of workable values', or if we were just an episode that crumbled away as some of our monuments are now doing. I could not dare give a positive answer to such a huge question, except to say, and with conviction, that Charles Trevelyan – dogmatic and maddening though he must have been to enemies and even some friends – did help to lay the foundations of India's democracy, as well as some of the ideals towards which many Pakistanis are striving.

Grand Apocalypse

IT MIGHT BE assumed that a book concerned with the British in India, that has also dwelt on the Mutiny and the Amritsar massacre, would end with the holocaust of 1947 in the Punjab, and that the writer would produce conflicting reactions of horror and I-told-you-sos: pro-Mountbatten, anti-Mountbatten, pro-Jinnah, anti-Jinnah, pro-Nehru, anti-Nehru. But as far as my immediate family was concerned, the knell came twelve years before, at precisely 3.03 am on May 31 1935.

The previous autumn Walter and Olive had, with the utmost sadness, left Gilgit for the last time. Walter, now a Major, was to rejoin his battalion at Quetta, where they would have a bungalow in the Cantonment. My brother John was aged six, and he was cared for by an Irish nursery-maid (*not* a nanny – important!) called Elsie, rather pretty with an upturned nose and dark hair Garbo style. First they spent some weeks at Srinagar, 'tidying up' as Olive put it (which meant a new wardrobe for her) and buying things like materials for curtains and covering chairs.

I was then at a school called Horris Hill in Berkshire, and aged eleven. Horris Hill had a high reputation; and many of its pupils went on to Winchester, which Olive was determined should be my destination. It was a Spartan place, cold baths every day, winter and summer, and where objectionable little boys used to be swung by arms and legs by other objectionable little boys into holly bushes. One was liable to be beaten either with a shoe-tree by 'Daddy' Stow, the headmaster, or a fives-bat by 'Twitch' Liddell. At that time I accepted being at Horris Hill as a kind of inevitable turn of the wheel in my existence, but I now know, not that I hated it, but that I disliked it very much and indeed certain nightmares I still have hark back to those days of communal living. The clothes I had to wear were usually cast-offs of older boys in families with whom I boarded during the holidays, and that was something else that upset me – especially an overcoat with a velvet collar. I was taken aback when one of the masters at Horris Hill started nicknaming me 'The Poker'.

This was because I had a habit of sitting very straight, due I now realize to my having spent so much time on ponyback. I am told too that boys were amused by the way I would squat at the end of my bed. (I still find squatting comfortable, when I am gardening for instance.)

Quetta was one of the largest garrison towns in India, with about 12,000 troops, and straggled over five miles. It also possessed the Staff College and a considerable RAF station, and was the capital of Baluchistan. Being near the Khojak Pass, which led to Kandahar, it was strategically placed should the Russians invade Afghanistan. A river-bed ran through the middle. This was the Duranni nullah, to the north of which were most of the barracks and the Army lines; to the south was the Cantonment, which included the Residency and the Club, and the City or Bazaar, which had about 60,000 inhabitants. The climate, except in summer, was considered 'invigorating' for Europeans, in spite of a prevalence of malaria and bowel complaints. The winter was extremely cold, but in the spring there was a certain beauty, with all the apricot and peach blossom and the garden flowers which 'grew like weeds', the fresh green of the willows and the sage green of the tamarisks: all this contrasting with the distant, fawn-coloured mountains, and the stony desert.

'Oh it was enormous fun,' an ex-Army wife has said to me. 'Parties non-stop – white tie, long dresses, that sort of thing – drag hunts, point-to-points, bridge, tennis.' Others described it as 'Aldershot gone septic'. In spite of Olive's often proclaimed dislike of cantonment life, she had a marvellous time, and I really think during six months at Quetta she and Walter had the fullest and most carefree experience in all the years of their marriage. She used to complain about being 'driven mad' by things like brass bands and bugles at dawn and dusk, and being forced to watch boring parades. But she was also able to have her rides before breakfast, she loved going off on shooting expeditions into the remote desert, and she made some lifelong friends. Walter had a horse he was proud of called Toorah, and won a cup on him at the Quetta Hunt Point-to-Point. He also acted in a play, *The Ten Minute Alibi*.

Colonel Bernard Montgomery, who was Chief Instructor at the Staff College, and his wife Betty were also friends. 'Monty' was considered bossy by most people, but Betty was very popular and a good hostess. Their son David was John's age, and every morning John and some other children would go bicycling off in a group to have lessons with the Montgomery governess, Miss Townsend. Betty Montgomery was an artist, and hung her pictures round the house. Olive noticed that the walls of the bedroom were covered with nudes. 'Where did you get your models?' she asked. To which Betty replied: 'I have a *mirror*.' Monty was to become the renowned Field-Marshal.

Then there was Henry Holland, an eye surgeon whom Olive could hardly bear to meet because he kept thousands of cataracts preserved in jars at the hospital.

Olive and Walter got on well with the young Khan of Khalat, who loved motor cars and was trying to evolve a seedless orange. Sometimes they stayed with him at Sibi below the Bolan Pass, and were there for the Shahi Jirga when tribesmen gathered to discuss disputes that could not be settled locally.

The weekend before May 30 they were at Mastung, staying with the Assistant Political Agent. There was alarm locally because the Djinn or spirit of the Bolan Pass had been seen, and this always meant a calamity ahead. There followed a hectic week for Olive and Walter of dances and parties at Quetta. Looking back to May 30, people remember that the crows suddenly disappeared, and that dogs and horses seemed uneasy. John has said that the clouds were in parallel lines. The hot weather had begun, and the night was 'muggy'.

Walter, escaping from a regimental guest night, collected Olive who was playing bridge with friends. They looked forward to an early night for a change. But they were woken by a noise that most people have described as being like an express train underground. The floor was heaving, and plaster and bricks were cascading down. Olive managed to get on Walter's bed, and within moments a wardrobe crashed on hers. He took her in his arms and stood up, but they were thrown down again. He said: 'I think we are going to be killed.' They could only wait. At last the heaving stopped as suddenly as it had begun; and they were unhurt.

Now their immediate alarm was about John, who with Elsie slept in the nursery at the other end of the bungalow. Holding Olive by the elbow, Walter stumbled and groped in total darkness and choking dust over masonry and broken glass and furniture, through the remains of the drawing-room and dining-room. They reached the nursery door, which was fast wedged with debris on both sides. They shouted to Elsie, but there was no answer. As Walter said later: 'My hand found an electric light switch on a still standing wall, and I made a futile attempt to turn it on.' They shouted again and tried to get outside the house, but lost their way in the dark. Olive was frantic, certain now that John had been killed. Suddenly there was the sound of Elsie's hysterical voice somewhere behind them. They couldn't at first understand her: They then heard: 'I'm all right. I'm all right.' 'What about *John*?' they yelled back. 'I'm all right. I'm all right,' she kept on screaming.

At last they got her to say: 'He's here, safe.' And it had been John who had known how to save them both. Typically, always playing with things he was supposed not to touch, he had during his afternoon rest fiddled with the fly-proof gauze frame over his window and discovered how to undo it – nobody else even realized that it was hinged. So when the first shock came, and Elsie started crying out, he simply undid the frame and both of them quickly escaped. Shortly afterwards the whole roof had collapsed into the room, and they would have been buried.

Now the servants began to arrive. All were safe; only the cook was missing, but he slept with his family in the city. Then Olive cried: 'The dogs! Where are the dogs?' Walter's orderly had brought a torch, and eventually they were both found standing by the remains of Walter's bed.

Someone had found a hurricane lamp. With blankets over their night clothes Olive and Walter rushed to their neighbours' house. It was just a pile of rubble, and they couldn't hear a sound. Olive said: 'They're buried!' She knew the direction of the bedroom and clambering over its ruins they found themselves up to the knees in mud from a burst pipe. At last they saw a light, and heard the husband's voice. He had just pulled out his wife, her arm was broken, and she was stunned. They discussed hurriedly what to do next. Presumably the hospital and the rest of Quetta were in the same state. The husband went to look for a doctor, and Olive for bandages. Walter decided that he must get to his regiment.

Back at the garden, they found that their great friends the Stacpooles had just arrived with their nurse and two children. It was discovered that Walter's car, having been left outside on the drive, was undamaged, and as he drove off Olive begged him to find out on his way if various people were alive and unhurt.

The house of other friends, the Wilkinsons, was if anything in a worse shambles. Some men with lanterns were frantically clearing the rubble and had just found the daughter, aged eleven, buried up to her neck. She was alive and speaking sensibly, though very frightened. Mrs Wilkinson had also been buried, and the nurse had been hurt when rescuing the baby. Eventually Walter took the women and children to join Olive and the Stacpooles. Carpets had been dragged out of the bungalow's ruins to make tents.

As Walter drove on northwards he noticed that after about a mile buildings were far less damaged. It seemed that the shock had been local. He found that his men were already dressed and ready, so orders were given for them to make for the civil station at the double.

The earthquake had only lasted thirty seconds. Now there was a new terror. From the direction of the Bazaar huge fires could be seen, and these were spreading quickly. There the houses were jerry-built and the streets narrow, and it was realized that the devastation could have been enormous. Fortunately there was little wind. Walter now took a portion of his men to fight the flames, or at least to confine them. Feeble groans and cries could often be heard beneath the rubble, and it was a desperate and sometimes impossible struggle to free the wounded before the fires reached them. Walter was working near a photographer's shop, which blazed up 'like a scene from hell' and he had to stagger back, nearly suffocated.

Scores of corpses were being dragged out. Some of the adults were completely crushed, their faces unrecognizable as such, but often live babies were found underneath. All the survivors, and the rescuers, became coated with grey mud and dust. Soon after daybreak there was another severe 'quake, and more buildings tumbled down. Thereafter there were shocks about every two hours. 'Piteous appeals for help,' Walter wrote afterwards, 'by stricken parents were difficult to refuse, but our immediate and urgent task was to control the fire, and we often had to harden our hearts to demands outside its area. Occasionally, after a frenzied search for a supposed buried wife or child, we realized that our crafty guide was interested in property only, possibly that of someone else. We could only curse him and continue elsewhere.'

By ten o'clock the sun was hot, and as the fires were mostly controlled, Walter – still in his filthy pyjamas – went back to the bungalow. There he found Elsie, who told him that Olive was working in the hospital, and that she and John were to be taken to the Messervys at the Staff College, which was apparently undamaged. (Frank Messervy, as a General during the Second World War, was twice captured by the Japanese and each time escaped.) She told him that the cook and all his family had been killed, and that among their friends three of the Hengel-Joneses had died and the Severn-Williamses' girl, aged eleven, had been killed.

It turned out that elder children in a family were the ones who usually got killed. The ayah or nanny would rush to save the baby first. Another friend of my parents, B. J. ('Nat') Gould, whose beautiful wife Lorraine had only just died of appendicitis, had been dug out alive, but his colleague Sayce had been killed in the same house. The Residency, the Club, the Jail, the Commanding Officer General Karslake's house, and all the houses along the road known as Snobs' Alley had been flattened. At the Jail it had been total annihilation.

But, amazingly, the area to the north of the Duranni nullah, which included the Staff College, had escaped the earthquake. The shock affecting the Bazaar had been less severe than in the Cantonment – where people said the ground had risen and fallen two feet – but the damage and casualties were far worse. It was eventually estimated that the deaths in the Bazaar were about 30,000, nearly half the population. The most severely hit area was the RAF station at Woodcock Spring to the west of Quetta. There the commander was Wing-Commander Jack Slessor, later to be famous as an Air-Marshal in the Second World War. He and his wife Hermione were both buried and quite badly hurt. Fifty-two British and sixty-six Indian NCOs and airmen were killed, and about two hundred injured, out of five hundred. Only three Wapiti aircraft were left serviceable. Slessor wrote in his book *The Central Blue*:

> Between the years 1939 and 1945 I saw a good many man-made blitzes; one became somewhat of a connoisseur of destruction. But I have never seen anything, even in Germany in 1945, to beat what the earthquake did to Quetta.

At 8.25 Slessor, bandaged and in pyjamas, was watching men digging in the ruins of the barracks in the hope of finding more survivors. All the British dead were laid in a row on one side of the road, the Indians on the other. Suddenly he heard someone say: 'My God, what's this?' It was Monty, accompanied by Colonel de Fonblanque of the Staff College and some students, all of whom had been completely unaware of the disaster.

Walter's battalion had been relieved by gunners and now had the horrid task of burying the dead. He was in charge of the burial party, consisting of a hundred or so sepoys. As mule-carts and lorries began to arrive, piled as high as possible with corpses, the first job was to try to sort them out into Muslims and Hindus. The Muslims and any Christians were buried together, but the Hindus were cremated, usually in batches of fifty. All jewellery and ornaments had to be removed from female corpses, in case villagers came to dig out the graves or rake the pyres, and these were handed over to a civilian of the Political Department. The soldiers vomited frequently because of the grisly sights, and on account of the stench they had to put on gas-masks or cover their noses with first-aid pads. Walter reckoned that they disposed of about five hundred bodies by dark. One woman was discovered alive in a heap about to be burnt.

Two cartloads of bodies arrived too late to be sorted out, and a guard had to be placed over them to scare off the jackals. Walter and the rest of the men bivouacked up-wind. There were rumours now that tribesmen were looking for loot, so cavalry and tanks patrolled all night round the City and the Cantonment. Walter drove into Quetta and found Olive working under Henry Holland at the Military Hospital. She was exhausted, but he managed to persuade her to spend the night with friends in an undamaged area. First, though, she took him to see friends who had been injured and were lying in the hospital.

There was little rest for Walter that night. At every shock his Muslim sepoys would start murmuring prayers. He was of course worrying about the family. At daybreak more corpses arrived, and the work continued. There were soon so many piles that it was impossible to control the great number of people who appeared claiming to search for dead relatives. The sepoys became suspicious of some Pathans, who they were sure were wrenching off ear-rings and stealing rings. They rounded them up and beat them with rifle-butts. When Walter arrived they told him the reason, and he ordered that the prisoners should be stripped of their baggy trousers. Out poured the jewellery.

General Karslake arrived on his horse as this was happening. 'What's going on here?' he asked. Walter explained. 'Flog 'em. Don't mind what you use,' the General said. 'Leave 'em tied up and give 'em another twelve strokes before dark.'

That night Walter was allowed back to the Cantonment and went at once to find Olive. He found that she had been transferred to the Indian Military Hospital:

The number of injured was appalling; they covered every yard in a large area, and it was difficult to thread one's way through the acres of stretchers. There was work for fifty-times the ordinary staff, and even the preliminary organisation and the separation of the various types of cases were very big tasks. It was impossible to dress the wounds of all more than once in the first two days. Operating tents had sprung up ... doctors operated throughout every minute of daylight ... snatching hasty meals when they could, or doing without ... Olive was working in an operating tent, and I waited for her to finish. She would not come away until surgeons could no longer see to work. I had seen some unpleasant sights during the last two days, but her duties were very much worse than my own. One soon becomes comparatively callous to the dead, no matter how unsightly, but not to the appalling suffering of the living. Olive and other volunteers worked for twelve to thirteen hours daily for the first few days, and afterwards for eight hours ... Olive and her friend Mildred remained always in the

497

same tent, pulling fractured limbs, removing those severed, and doing the other gruesome duties of nursing sisters and orderlies. Other British women were cheerfully doing the work of the most menial Indian servants. Olive normally cannot stand the sight of blood. She and Mildred were green in the face when I found them, and ready to drop with exhaustion. I brought them back, and made them drink neat whisky, under protests from Mildred, who is almost a teetotaller.

There was another violent tremor on June 2, and this resulted in an extraordinary, awe-inspiring sight: the whole of the eastern face of the mountain Chiltan, which stood above where the point-to points had taken place, slid down into the plain. A wall of brown dust, hundreds of feet high, hung in the air for several hours. It was discovered that the epicentre of the first earthquake had been at the town of Mach. A fissure had appeared that stretched unbroken for seventy miles. Mastung, where Olive and Walter had stayed, was completely devastated.

Walter continued with the burial work. By the fifth day the flies and stink of death around the Bazaar were so bad that there were fears of an epidemic. It became necessary to clear the place of any remaining inhabitants, and to remove them to refugee camps, mostly on the racecourse. Wire was put on the perimeter, and aeroplanes sprayed quicklime from the air. Still tribesmen and 'all the riff-raff of Karachi and Hyderabad' kept arriving in the hope of plunder, like vultures around a kill – some in the guise of snake-charmers, fakirs, money-lenders or letter-writers. Troops patrolled the roads, moving silently in rubber-soled boots, and ready to pounce.

Walter told how he was most frightened a week after the earthquake had happened:

Olive and I were sleeping at different ends of a small tent. A sharp tremor woke me with a start, and I lived through the first shock again. I thought I was in the house, and grabbed again for Olive on her bed to my left. Of course I found nothing and fell out of bed. For a moment I thought that the earth had opened and swallowed me.

The Indian Government gave free passages to England for women and children, and Elsie and John left after a fortnight. Olive said that she preferred to stay behind. But the experience had decided her that she could not bear to go on living in India any more. Walter became revolted by the attitude of Congress and the Indian press, which claimed that there had been racial discrimination in the relief work. 'The misrepresentation, the calumny and political animosity exceed anything that the Englishman outside India can possibly understand. So much for our legacy of press freedom!' He had arrived in India with ideals, and had felt a real warmth towards the men in his battalion, but he was sick now of the whole anti-British campaign of the last years. Although he would miss an increased pension, he was easily persuaded by Olive to retire.

Olive was given the Kaiser-i-Hind silver medal for her work in the hospital, and had a special cable of congratulations from the Vicereine, the eccentric Lady Willingdon. Various other women received medals, one of the most famous being a nanny, Frances Allen, who threw herself over a cot to protect a child and was kept pinned under the rubble for two days.

Lord Willingdon, looking like a caricature of a pukka sahib in topee and spats, came to congratulate Slessor and the men of his depleted wing for their work in flying out emergency cases. Slessor has told how Her Excellency added to the enjoyment of the occasion by holding on to his hand for some minutes and talking volubly in front of the assembled parade, while the Viceroy and his suite returned to the saluting base. Eventually an ADC had to be sent to fetch her, so that the ceremonies could proceed.

At Horris Hill terrific efforts were made to stop me from seeing any newspapers, and I suppose the same applied to B. J. Gould's son, who was also at school there. I was told that there had been an earthquake, but I don't think I quite understood the implications. I was certainly aware of being regarded by the masters with some awe. My letter afterwards to my parents was often quoted whenever they talked about the Quetta earthquake, and used to make me indignant.

Anyway this is what I said:

Dear Mummy and Daddy, I hear you have had an earthquake. I am third this week. I have two tulips out in my garden and another is in bud.

Walter's Dream

I WRITE THIS in Cornwall. It is February, the day before Olive's birthday as it happens, and from my window I can see the tide creeping in over the creek. The snowdrops are in flower along what is always known as the Monks' Walk. For this house stands on what was a Cluniac cell, and I have dug up several carved stones, including a cresset stone.

The tide comes in. The tide goes out. Every season, every week, has its different beauty. I love the shapes of the old beech trees, which must have been planted here over two hundred and fifty years ago. Just now a flock of curlews has been startled by something, maybe a fox on the escarpment, or a mink, the new peril. The curlews have such an unearthly cry, especially at twilight. Apart from the birds the only sound here is the waterfall, which Olive once had made for me as a surprise: to remind me of the trek to Gilgit, she said.

About a mile from here is the house Trevelyan. How happy Walter had been on that stormswept, but also sunny, hill! As he lay dying, I sat by his bedside, watching him, realizing that it was my father I was losing. I have reread his few remaining and as usual rather didactic letters, and one of them, from near Calcutta in 1942, has unexpectedly moved me. It is about the sacrifices that Olive made to have me educated. So the letters also give me a feeling of guilt, of ingratitude, but towards her, not him; Walter and I were just very different persons. Having written this book has helped me to understand him a little more. He was I think a genuinely good man, and I do not believe that he would have minded that Olive married Rufus so soon after his death.

Olive loved him, but in a different way to Rufus. About two months before he was taken ill, Walter had a strong and disturbing dream, and Olive asked him to write it down – which he did:

You and I were going by car to a local town (I did not recognise it).

We saw a woman, whom we recognised, wife of an Army officer, and gave her a lift. She said her husband had been sent suddenly on a course to the town – there was no accommodation and hotels etc., crowded with Army people on the course, but they had eventually got into the annexe of a hotel. They had all their belongings with them and it was piled up on their verandah.

When we got there we found the husband in shirtsleeves sorting their belongings in a chaos of boxes, luggage etc. We tried to go on but they insisted we should have a drink with them. I offered to get a waiter as the husband was a bit distracted and we decided what we wanted to drink and I went off.

The hotel was huge, full of Army people, wives etc., but no sign of any staff. All the people seemed to be waiting about for something, talking to each other but ignored me. It all seemed queer and unreal. I went up to a man and asked where I could find a waiter but he walked away and didn't seem to hear. I realised that everyone was too occupied with themselves and each other and didn't seem to see me.

At last after going through many rooms I saw a waitress. She was cross and said the annexe wasn't her job but called a waiter and he agreed to bring drinks and I went back.

When I came out of the front of the hotel I couldn't at first recognise the annexe but went in the direction of it and found the husband and wife sitting on the verandah but without the piles of luggage.

The wife seemed surprised to see me and the husband looked puzzled. The wife said 'Hallo' but the husband said, 'I am afraid I don't know who you are, although my wife seems to know you.' She said, 'Don't be silly, it's Walter Trevelyan.' I was looking round for you and suddenly got a feeling of foreboding and panic and said 'Where's Olive?'

They were both gazing at me intently and the wife said, 'I haven't seen her for a long time. The last I heard of her was that she had got a job abroad somewhere.'

I was horrified. They were staring at me in a most peculiar way as if I were a 'social leper' (like George Gillan!).

I said, 'Have I been a long time?' The wife said, 'Years, Walter.'

The tide is nearly in now. After two hours it will begin to recede. The curlews have settled for the night, and now the owls have started calling to one another. The tide comes in. The tide will go out.

Governors-General of India

Warren Hastings	1773–85
Sir John Macpherson (officiating)	1785–6
Earl Cornwallis	1786–93
Sir John Shore (Baron Teignmouth)	1793–8
Lieut-Gen. Sir Alured Clarke (officiating)	1798
Earl of Mornington (Marquess Wellesley)	1798–1805
Marquess (Earl) Cornwallis	1805
Sir George Barlow (officiating)	1805–6
Earl of Minto	1807–13
Earl of Moira (Marquess of Hastings)	1813–23
John Adam (officiating)	1823
Earl of Amherst	1823–8
Butterworth Bayley (officiating)	1828
Lord William Bentinck	1828–35
Sir Charles Metcalfe (officiating)	1835–6
Baron (Earl) Auckland	1836–42
Earl of Ellenborough	1842–4
Sir Henry (Viscount) Hardinge	1844–7
Earl (Marquess) of Dalhousie	1847–56
Viscount (Earl) Canning	1856–8

Governors-General and Viceroys

Earl Canning	1858–62
Earl of Elgin	1862–3
Major-General Sir Robert Napier (Baron Napier of Magdala) (officiating)	1863
Colonel Sir William Denison (officiating)	1863–4
Sir John (Baron) Lawrence	1863–9

Earl of Mayo	1869–72
(Sir) John Strachey (officiating)	1872
Baron Napier of Merchistoun (officiating)	1872
Baron (Earl) Northbrook	1872–6
Baron (Earl) Lytton	1876–80
Marquess of Ripon	1880–4
Marquess of Dufferin and Ava	1884–8
Marquess of Lansdowne	1888–94
Earl of Elgin	1894–9
Baron (Marquess) Curzon of Kedleston	1899–1905
Earl of Minto	1905–10
Baron Hardinge of Penshurst	1910–16
Baron (Viscount) Chelmsford	1916–21
Earl (Marquess) of Reading	1921–6
Baron Irwin (Earl of Halifax)	1926–31
Earl (Marquess) of Willingdon	1931–6
Marquess of Linlithgow	1936–43
Viscount (Earl) Wavell	1943–7
Viscount (Earl) Mountbatten	1947
(after Independence Governor-General of India)	

Glossary

Anglo-Indians	–	originally British persons in India, later a term for Eurasians.
ayah	–	nurse or lady's maid.
baba	–	baby.
babu	–	clerk.
badmash	–	bad character, rogue.
bharal	–	blue sheep of Tibet, but with some characteristics of the goat.
bheesti	–	water carrier.
bibi	–	Indian mistress or wife of European.
bhoosa bag	–	bag for chopped straw in Afghanistan.
Board of Control for India	–	British Government office representing Parliament for India, introduced in 1784 and operating until 1858.
box wallah	–	derogatory term for British businessman; also Indian itinerant pedlar.
burra	–	great, senior.
chapatti	–	unleavened cake of bread.
chapplis	–	sandals.
chaprassi	–	messenger, office servant.
charpoy	–	wooden bedstead with webbing.
chit	–	letter, note.
choga	–	garment worn in Gilgit, like a dressing-gown.
chota	–	little, junior.
chota hasri	–	early morning tea, 'bed tea', little breakfast.
chowkidar	–	guard, night-watchman.
chukor	–	type of partridge.

collector	–	chief administrator of a district, revenue collector; also known as District Officer.
Congress	–	Indian National Congress party founded in 1885 (mostly Hindu) at Poona, with purpose of forming Parliament representative of all Indian people. The Congress party still dominates Indian politics today.
Council of India	–	council in London of the Secretary of State for India, after 1858.
Court of Directors	–	chief officials of East India Company.
dacoit	–	robber, highwayman.
dak bungalow	–	government rest-house or staging point (dak = mail, hence dak runner or dak wallah).
dandy	–	open litter.
dhobi	–	laundry man.
Diwan	–	head financial minister, prime minister.
Diwan-i-Am	–	hall of public audience.
Diwan-i-Khas	–	hall of private audience.
doolie	–	covered litter.
doonga	–	covered craft at Srinagar.
durbar	–	public levee of Indian prince, Viceroy or Political Agent.
East India Company	–	The Honourable East India Company, formed by merchants in 1599; see Court of Directors. Administrative power taken over by the Crown in 1858.
Eurasian	–	of mixed blood.
fakir	–	religious mendicant.
feringhis	–	foreigners.
ganj	–	area; quarter of a town or village.
gazal	–	type of song.
ghast	–	military patrol.
ghat	–	landing place or steps to river or tank.
gopura	–	entrance gate to Hindu temple.
godown	–	storeroom.

Great Game	–	Anglo-Russian rivalry, N.W. of India, in 19th century.
griffin	–	young officer recently arrived in India, 19th century.
gupis	–	cowherd women, symbolizing in Hindu religion souls yearning to merge with the divine.
guru	–	Hindu spiritual teacher.
hackery	–	bullock cart.
hartal	–	strike, including a fast.
havildar	–	equivalent of sergeant.
Hindustani	–	simplified form of Urdu.
howdah	–	palanquin on elephant.
ibex	–	species of wild Himalayan goat with large curved horns.
ICS	–	Indian Civil Service.
jampan	–	type of sedan chair.
jehad	–	Muslim holy war.
jemadar	–	junior rank of commissioned Indian officer.
jezail	–	long Afghan musket.
Jhalsa	–	yearly ceremonial gathering of chiefs at Gilgit.
jirga	–	tribal gathering.
John Company	–	familiar name for East India Company.
khansama	–	cook.
kheddah	–	round up of wild elephants.
khitmadgar	–	butler.
khud	–	steep hillside.
khul	–	water channel in Gilgit.
koi	–	woollen cap, worn in Gilgit.
koi-hai	–	an old hand or character in India, also used for calling a servant.
lac	–	a hundred thousand.
lathi	–	four-foot wooden staff lined with steel used by police.
machan	–	shooting platform.
mahout	–	elephant driver.
maidan	–	public area or park in a town; parade ground.
majum	–	drug made from Indian hemp, nux vomica, poppyseed, etc.

markhor	–	species of wild Himalayan goat with spiral horns.
mehtar	–	Prince; ironic term for sweeper, cleaner of latrines of the Untouchable caste.
memsahib	–	lady, madam.
Mir	–	chieftain in Gilgit area.
Mofussil	–	the provinces, country districts; hence Mofussilites.
mullah	–	preacher, learned in the Koran (not a priest).
Muslim League	–	the All-India Muslim League founded in 1906 at the instigation of the Aga Khan, as a counterpart to Congress.
naik	–	corporal.
nautch girls	–	dancing girls, often prostitutes.
nazr	–	official gift.
nullah	–	valley.
pani	–	water.
peepul	–	Indian fig-tree, much venerated, of very long life; also known as Bo-Tree.
pi-dog	–	pariah dog.
P. & O.	–	Peninsular and Oriental Steam Navigation Company.
Political Agents	–	officers of the Indian Political Service, responsible for relations between the Crown (not the Government of India) and minor Indian princes and the Pathan tribes of the Tribal Territories. See Residents.
pugree	–	turban.
pukka	–	genuine, proper.
punkah	–	fan suspended from ceiling, manually operated.
purdah	–	seclusion for women.
Ram! Ram!	–	Hindu prayer, invocation to god.
Residents	–	senior officers, acting for the Viceroy and responsible for relations with the more important Indian princes. See Political Agents.

sadhu	–	holy man.
sahib	–	European male, sir.
salaam	–	salutation.
sepoy	–	Indian private soldier.
sirdar	–	local chief.
sowar	–	mounted Indian soldier or policeman.
sudder court	–	chief court of appeal from Mofussil district courts until 1862.
shikari	–	hunter (shikar = shooting, hunting).
suttee	–	cremation of Hindu widow on husband's pyre; also known as sati.
Swaraj	–	Home Rule.
syce	–	groom.
tank	–	artificial lake.
Theravada	–	dominant Buddhist sect in Sri Lanka.
thuggee	–	practice of the thugs, members of religious organization of assassins, specializing in robbery and in strangling the victims as 'sacrifices' to the goddess Kali.
thunder box	–	earth closet, commode.
tiffin	–	lunch.
tonga	–	horse carriage with two wheels.
topee	–	pith helmet against sun.
Urdu	–	lingua franca of Upper India.
urial	–	wild sheep of the Punjab and Himalayas.
wallah	–	man.
Wazarat	–	area ruled by a Wazir for a Maharajah.
Wazir	–	high state official.
yakdan	–	wicker boxes covered in hide, originally for yaks to carry, one on each side.
zenana	–	women's quarters in an Indian house, usually Muslim.

Acknowledgments

The Trevelyan family papers, relating to Sir C. E. and Sir G. O. Trevelyan, among others, are in the Library of the University of Newcastle upon Tyne; I am especially grateful to Lesley Gordon of the Special Collections and, at an earlier stage, to Alistair Elliot for their unstinted help and patience, and to Pauline Dower, great-granddaughter of C. E. Trevelyan and main trustee of the Trevelyan manuscripts at Newcastle, for her constant encouragement and enthusiasm. The Macaulay papers, except where stated otherwise below, and the R. C. Trevelyan papers are in the Library of Trinity College, Cambridge; I am grateful to the Master and Fellows for permission to quote, to the Librarian, Dr Philip Gaskell, and to R. C. Trevelyan's son Julian. I must also thank the Huntington Library, San Marino, California, for permission to quote from letters to Margaret Holland, Mrs Cropper and the Macaulay sisters from Hannah Macaulay. My debt to Andrew Webb, for letting me read drafts of his Ph.D. Thesis on C. E. Trevelyan, for providing lists of relevant material, and answering my innumerable questions, is very great indeed.

No one writing about India before Independence can fail to be impressed by the resources, efficiency and courtesy at the Indian Office Library and Records (IOLR); my gratitude goes especially to Dr R. J. Bingle and D. M. Blake. The Centre of South Asian Studies, Cambridge, has a fascinating collection of personal memoirs and letters; here I must thank Dr Lionel Carter. I am also grateful to Philip Reed of the Imperial War Museum, and to Derek Shorrocks of the Somerset Record Office.

I owe a very great debt to Raúl Balín, my companion on the five journeys, for assistance in many essential ways. The following have kindly provided me with diaries or other documents, or have written to me at length about their memories: Colonel George Clark, Mrs Kathleen Dale, Allen Drury, Sir William Dugdale Bart. (for documents concerned with his grandmother Alice Trevelyan), Mary Fedden (Mrs Julian Trevelyan), John Ferrar (for his father Colonel Ferrar's letters from the Andamans), Dr Colin Forbes (for his great-aunt Emma Halliday's letters and Spencer Wyndham's letters, and his grandfather Lachlan Forbes' diary), Angus I. Macnaghten, S. P. Mehra, A. N. Mehrotra, Mrs Leila Phillips (Leila Blackwell in the book), the late Sir Herbert Todd, Carol Vázquez, Dr Philip Warren, Julian Wathen (for his parents' papers at Amritsar). Anthony Verrier lent me the typescript of his long study on the Great Game, which I found invaluable in the early stages of my researches. Bernard Babington-Smith has guided me to material on General Colin Macaulay and I am most grateful to him. Alan Walker and S. M. Vibart have provided valuable genealogical details. Theon and Rosemarie Wilkinson of the British Association for Cemeteries in South Asia have always been ready with help – Rosemarie is the daughter of Captain Percy McLenaghan, my parents' friend murdered at

Lahore in 1930. My deep gratitude goes to Dr Gaur Hari Singhania for his hospi-tality both at Kotah and Kanpur. Mrs Joan Haybittle and her daughter Mrs Julie Pearce have typed, retyped, and retyped, and I thank them both for their fore-bearance; my thanks also to David Charles of the Kirkham Studios for drawing the maps and family trees, to Tony Raven for the index and to Mark Hamilton, my agent.

I can only list names of other friends and relations who have helped me: Major Peter Adams, Stephen Alexander, Professor Ramón Araluce, Ashraf Aman, Mrs Mollie Berkeley, Vere Lady Birdwood, Major Ted and Scottie Blessington, Sue Bradbury, Dr L. W. Brady, Mrs Susan Busse, Elizabeth Claridge, William Clowes, Steve Cox, Barbara Deane, Charlotte Deane, Captain Jack Dixon, Makeshwar Dayal, Major W. G. H. Duglinson, Mrs Evelyn Dyer, Eleanor Ferrar, Kate Forbes, Daniel Frank, P. N. Furbank, Colonel David Gillan, David Godwin, Mrs Sheila Hailey, James Hamilton, Orme Hancock, Major Claude Janitsch, Mrs Faith King, John Lall, Martin Latham, Thérèse Lady MacArthur, Major Denis McCarthy, Mrs Mary Moorman, Kenneth Niggett, Julia Trevelyan Oman, Mrs Anna Permain, Mrs Polly Proudlock, Leslie Rayner, Alec Redpath, Josephine Reid (who helped in the quest for Vibarts), Mrs Theo Robertson (Frances Stewart), Mrs Elizabeth Rosen-berg (niece of Major Billy Haycraft, murdered at Nowshera in 1929), Mrs Barbara Skene, Thiro V. Sundaram, Lady Trevelyan (widow of Humphrey Trevelyan), my brother John Trevelyan, Julian Trevelyan, Mrs Mollie Wade (Mollie Ellis in the book), the late Mrs Betty Waters, the late Major-General D. J. Wilson-Haffenden, the late Colonel Lovell Wooldridge, Lieut-General Sir John Worsley, Dr R. E. Wright, Helen Wythers, and last but not least Mrs Zoë Yalland for answering many questions.

Published and Manuscript Sources

I have only listed the names of authors of my main books of reference, which are given in the Bibliography. References to the Trevelyan MSS at Newcastle and publications by C. E. Trevelyan have not been included.

The First Journey
I   *The Great Game*: By far the most important books are those by Yapp and Alder. Others include Edwardes, Ingram, J. W. Kaye, Keay, Lunt, Maclean, Masson and Wolpert. Private information – Verrier. *Gilgit and Hunza*: Bamzai, Bretherton, Curzon, Duke, Durand, Hassnain, Josty, Kak, Keay, Knight, Le Fèvre (for Haardt–Citroën expedition), Lorimer, Miller, Mirsky (Aurel Stein), Savory, Schomberg, W. R. F. Trevelyan, Younghusband; Private – Berkeley, Clark, Drury, Phillips, Redpath, Norah Spicer's diary (author's collection), Todd. IOLR – Wazarat, Landing Grounds, White Russians R/1/1084/390–1, R/2/1084/88, P&S/12/4010.
II   *North-West Frontier* etc: Barthrop, Chenevix-Trench, Garnett (T. E. Lawrence), Gwynn, HMSO, Mason, Schofield, Singer, Spear, Stephens, Tayyet, Woodruff, Yapp, 5/8th Punjab Regimental magazines. *1st Afghan War*: Alder, Colvin, Fane, Heathcote, J. W. Kaye, Lunt, Colin MacKenzie, Maclean, Masson, Norris, Trotter, Woodruff, Yapp; IOLR – J. R. Colvin's diaries, MSS Eur E 359/1–6. *2nd Afghan War*: Alder, Gopal, Hanna, Heathcote, M. M. Kaye, Lutyens, F.-M. Roberts, Sykes, Trousdale, Woodruff. *Afghanistan*: Adamec, Baker, Curzon, Fraser-Tytler, Gray; Private – Macnaghten, Skene, Todd.

The Second Journey
I   *Pietra Dura*: Gascoigne, Zobi; Private – Dixon, Webb. *Charles Trevelyan at Delhi*: Jacquemont, M. M. Kaye, Parks, Philips, Rosselli, G. Smith, Spear (*Twilight of the Moghuls*), H. Trevelyan, Yapp.
II   *Simla*: Barr, Buck, Eden, Mrs Colin Mackenzie, Sud; Private – Blessington. *Army*: Regt. History 93rd Burma Infantry, Mason. Private – King, Rosenberg, Wilkinson, Wilson-Haffenden. *Kashmir, general*: Bruce, Duke, Hügel, Kaul, Keay, Morison, Naipaul, Wilfred Russell, Stone, Vigne. *Kashmir, history*: Bamzai, Kaul, Korbel, C. E. Roberts.

The Third Journey
I   *Calcutta, general*: Bence-Jones, Boyd, Colvin, H. E. A. Cotton, Eden, Heber, Hickey, Kincaid, Moorhouse, Tayler, Tollygunge Club; IOLR – H. T. Prinsep. *Three Generations in India*, Eur c 97/2 vol. II. *Macaulay Letters*: Trinity Cambridge – Aug. 17 1833, Nov. 22 1833; Aug. 25 1835, Jan. 1 1836, May 9 1836, May 30 1836,

Dec. 13 1837, Aug. 10 1857; C. S. Menell – Feb. 22 1834 (extract); Lady Errington, by kind permission – Dec. 7 1834, Dec. 24 1834; Trinity Cambridge – Hannah Trevelyan's Reminiscences; Huntington Library, San Marino – correspondence of Hannah Trevelyan. *Charles Trevelyan*: J. W. Kaye, Kopf, Panigrahi, Philips, Rosselli, Stokes, Taylor, G. M. Trevelyan, H. Trevelyan, Trotter, Woodruff, Yapp; IOLR – Colvin diaries, Eur E 359/1–6, Bengal Secret Cons. 1826–31, India Secret and Political 1831–38, J. Milford, 'A Few Parting Hints to My dear Boy on His Leaving for India' 1841, Eur A112. School of Oriental and African Studies – Samuel Sneade-Brown, *Home Letters From India*, 1823–41 (1878).

II *Andamans*: Cipriani, Cooper, C. Mackenzie, Parks, Singh, Young. Private – Ferrar, McCarthy, Rayner, Robertson, Worsley. *INA*: Mason, Toye, Tuker; Tuker papers – Imperial War Museum. *Burma*: Orwell. *Canning*: Allen, Hare, Maclagan, Surtees.

III *Charles Trevelyan at Treasury*: Hart, Hughes, McRae, Moore, H. Trevelyan, Woodham-Smith, Wright; re Hart – compare her statements p. 99 (*EHR*) on the 'judgement of God' etc. with the actual wording of the letter of Oct. 6 1846 (Newcastle MSS) when Trevelyan is replying to a letter of Sept. 30 1846 from Father Mathew, the 'Apostle of Temperance': 'Like you, I regard the prospect of Ireland with profound melancholy; but I fear much less from the judgements of God than the aggravation of them owing to the ignorance, the selfishness and evil passion of men.' Here Trevelyan was referring to the selfishness of some Anglo-Irish and Irish landowners and tenant-farmers, and to Dublin and Cork hucksters. Perhaps the 'judgements of God' were Father Mathew's own words, and referred to a previous letter in which he (Mathew) spoke of how 'Divine Providence in its inscrutable ways, has again poured upon us the vial of its wrath'; Senate House, Library, University of London – D. W. Armstrong Ph.D. (1975), 'Sir Charles Trevelyan as Assistant Secretary of the Treasury'. *Henry Trevelyan*: English, Postans; Private – B. Deane, C. Deane, Proudlock, Walker. *Mutiny*: Allen, Ball, Barter, Collier, Coopland, Cosens, Edwardes, Forrest, Gupta, Hibbert, J. W. Kaye, Keene, Maclagan, Malleson, Mason, Maude, Metcalf, Pemble, Perkins, F.-M. Roberts, William Russell, Shepherd, Surtees, Thompson, Mowbray Thomson, Thornhill, G. O. Trevelyan, Vibart, Woodruff; Private – Colin Forbes for Lachlan Forbes, Halliday, Wyndham papers; Kate Forbes, Hancock, Reid, S. M. Vibart; IOLR and R. A. Farmiloe – Edward Vibart letters Eur F 135/21–3.

The Fourth Journey

I *Sri Lanka*: Ouspensky, Zwalf. *Mutiny*, see above.

II *Madras, general*: Bence-Jones, Hickey, Muthiah, Ramaswami, Train, H. Trevelyan; Private – Sundaram, Wright. *Charles Trevelyan as Governor*: Barrington, Wilfrid S. Blunt, Fitzmaurice, Maclagan, McRae, Metcalf, Moore, Sastri, H. B. Smith, Temple, H. Trevelyan, Wright; IOLR – Wood papers Eur F78/55/2–3, 57/2, 59/1–2–3, Lord Lawrence papers Eur F90 13–4–5, *Hansard* May 11 1861 cols 1130–61; Madras Record Office, Chittoor – 'Sir Charles Trevelyan, Governor of Madras' by B. C. Baliqa; Private – Webb. *Macaulay*: Clive, Pinney, G. O. Trevelyan; Trinity Cambridge – Macaulay's Journal, letter July 1 1834, Hannah Trevelyan's Reminiscences; Lady Errington – letters June 27 1834, Oct. 3 1834. *Bangalore*: Mason, Stanley; Private – Janitsch, Niggett. *Hampi, temples*: Anand, Edwardes, Michell, Victoria & Albert Museum. *Colin Macaulay*: Arnold, Chopra *et al.*, Clive, Hook, 'Investigator', C. Macaulay, W. Thomson, Thornton, Weller, Welsh, Ronald Williams; IOLR – Eur 313, F/4/244 – 245 – 337 – 358,8023 bbb 46, 200 30 bb2; Private – Babington-Smith. *Mysore*: Allen, Campbell, H. Trevelyan. *Ooty, Coonoor*: Burton,

Murphy, Panter-Downes, Savory, Surtees. *Tanjore etc*: Denison, Heber, Moravia, Shellim, G. Smith.

The Fifth Journey
I C. E. Trevelyan's letter-books at Newcastle contain a vast quantity of day-to-day correspondence on his activities as Finance Member at Calcutta. *Calcutta*: Campbell, Henry Cotton, Denison, Gwynn, Metcalf, Montgomery, Moorhouse, Mudford, Prinsep, H. B. Smith, Strachey, G. O. Trevelyan, H. Trevelyan, Woodruff; Private – Dugdale, Webb; IOLR – Elgin papers, Eur 586, Lawrence, Eur F901, Temple, Eur F8619; Huntington – Letters to Margaret Holland; Private – Dugdale, Webb. *Udaipur, Bundi, Bharatpur* etc: Allen, Bence-Jones, Pasolini, H. Trevelyan; Private – Fedden, Mehra, *Ernest Trevelyan*: Wilfrid S. Blunt, Kohfeldt (including Lady Gregory's poem); Private – B. Deane, C. Deane, Oman, Proudlock, Walker; author's collection.
II *Forster, R. C. Trevelyan*: Busch, Das, Dickinson, Forster, Furbank, Heine, Islam, Lago R. C. Trevelyan; Trinity Cambridge – R. C. Trevelyan MSS; Private – Furbank, Julian Trevelyan. *Khajaraho, Chhatarpur, Nowgong*; Ackerley, Braybrooke, Edwardes, Lothian, Michell, Mitchell, H. Trevelyan. *Mutiny*: see above; Private – Mehra, Mehrotra. *Amritsar*: Draper, Furneaux, O'Dwyer, Tully; Private – Wathen. *Kanpur*: Mowbray Thomson, G. O. Trevelyan, Yalland; Private – Mehra, Singhania. *Quetta*: Jackson; Private – Hailey, John Trevelyan.

Bibliography

Ackerley, J. R. *Hindoo Holiday* (London, 1952)

Adamec, Ludwig W. *Afghanistan* (Berkeley, 1967)

Aitchison, C. V. *Lord Lawrence* (Oxford, 1892)

Alder, G. J. *British India's Northern Frontier 1865–95* (London, 1963)
  'The "Garbled" Blue Books of 1839', in *The Historical Journal* vol. XV (Cambridge, 1972)

Allen, Charles. *Lives of the Indian Princes* (London, 1984)
  Plain Tales from the Raj (London, 1975)

Anand, Mulk Raj, Michell, George, and Hutt, Antony. 'Homage to Hampi' in *Marg* (Bombay, 1980)

Anon, *Regimental History 1914–1920: 93rd Burma Infantry* (Cardiff, 1920)

Archer, Mildred. *Early Views of India* (London, 1980)

Arnold, Frederick. *The Public Life of Macaulay* (London, 1862)

Atkinson, G. F. *Curry and Rice* (London, 1859)

Baker, Anne, and Ivelaw-Chapman, Air Chief Marshal Sir Ronald. *Wings over Kabul* (London, 1975)

Ball, Charles. *The History of the India Mutiny* (London, c. 1859)

Bamzai, Prithiv Nath Kaul, *A History of Kashmir* (New Delhi, c. 1975)

Barr, Pat, and Desmond, Ray. *Simla: A Hill Station in British India* (London, 1978)

Barrington, E. I. *The Servant of All* (London, 1927)

Barter, Richard. *The Siege of Delhi* (London, 1984)

Barthrop, Michael. *The North-West Frontier* (Poole, 1982)

Bearce, George D. *British Attitudes towards India* (Oxford, 1961)

Bence-Jones, Mark. *Palaces of the Raj* (London, 1973)
  The Viceroys of India (London, 1982)

Blunt, E. A. H. *List of Inscriptions on Christian Tombs and Monuments* (Allahabad, 1911)

Blunt, Wilfrid Scawen. *Ideas about India* (London, 1885)
  India under Ripon (London, 1909)

Boyd, Elizabeth French. *Bloomsbury Heritage* (London, 1976)

Braybrooke, Neville (ed.). *The Letters of J. R. Ackerley* (London, 1975)

Bretherton, G. H. 'Life in Gilgit', in *The Contemporary Review* vol. LXXIV (London, 1898)

Bruce, Hon. Mrs C. G. 'Kashmir', in *Peeps at Many Lands* (London, 1911)

Buck, E. J. *Simla Past and Present* (Bombay, 1925)

Burton, Richard F. *Goa, and the Blue Mountains* (London, 1851)

Bibliography

Busch, Briton Cooper. *Hardinge of Penshurst* (South Bend, 1980)

Cameron, Ian. *Mountains of the Gods* (London, 1984)
Campbell, Sir George. *Memoirs of my Indian Career* (London, 1893)
Chenevix-Trench, Charles. *The Frontier Scouts* (London, 1985)
Cipriani, Linda. *The Andaman Islanders* (London, 1960)
Chopra, P. N., Ravindran, T. K., Subrahmanian, N. *History of South India*, vol. III, *The Modern Period* (New Delhi, 1979)
Clark, John, *Hunza* (London, 1957)
Clarke, Arthur C. *The Fountains of Paradise* (London, 1979)
Clive, John. *Thomas Babington Macaulay* (London, 1973)
Collier, Richard. *The Sound of Fury* (London, 1963)
Colvin, Sir Auckland. *John Russell Colvin* (Oxford, 1895)
Cooper, Diana. *Trumpets from the Steep* (London, 1960)
Coopland, Mrs R. M. *A Lady's Escape from Gwalior* (London, 1859)
Cosens, Lt. Col. F. R., and Wallace, C. L. *Fatehgarh and the Mutiny* (Lucknow, 1933)
Cotton, H. E. A. *Calcutta Old and New* (Calcutta, 1907)
Cotton, Sir Henry. *Indian and Home Memories* (London, 1911)
Curzon of Kedleston, Marquess. *Leaves from a Viceroy's Note-Book* (London, 1926)

Das, G. K. *E. M. Forster's India* (London, 1977)
Das, G. K., and Beer, John (eds). *E. M. Forster: a Human Exploration* (London, 1979)
Denison, Sir William. *Varieties of Vice-Regal Life* (London, 1870)
Dickinson, G. Lowes. *Appearances* (London, 1914)
Draper, Alfred. *The Amritsar Massacre* (London, 1981)
Duke, Joshua. *Kashmir and Jammu* (Calcutta, 1910)
Durand, Colonel Algernon. *The Making of a Frontier* (London, 1899)

Eden, Emily. *Letters from India* 2 vols (London, 1872)
    Miss Eden's Letters (London, 1919)
    Up the Country (Oxford, 1930)
Edwardes, Michael. *Battles of the Indian Mutiny* (London, 1963)
    Indian Temples and Palaces (London, 1969)
    The Necessary Hell (London, 1958)
    Playing the Great Game (London, 1975)
    A Season in Hell (London, 1973)
English, Barbara. *John Company's Last War* (London, 1971)

Fane, H. E. *Five Years in India* (London, 1842)
Farrell, J. G. *The Hill Station* (London, 1981)
Fischer, Louis. *The Life of Mahatma Gandhi* (London, 1951)
Fitzmaurice, Lord Edmond. *The Life of the Second Lord Granville* vol. 1 (London, 1905)
Fleming, Peter. *News from Tartary* (London, 1936)
Forrest, George W. *History of the Indian Mutiny* 3 vols (Edinburgh, 1904–1912)
Forster, E. M. *Abinger Harvest* (London, 1936)
    The Hill of Devi (London, 1953)
    A Passage to India (London, 1924)
Fraser-Tytler, W. K. *Afghanistan* (London, 1967)
Furbank, P. N. *E. M. Forster: A Life* 2 vols (London 1977, 1978)
Furneaux, Rupert. *Massacre at Amritsar* (London, 1983)

Garnett, David (ed.). *The Letters of T. E. Lawrence* (London, 1938)
Gascoigne, Bamber. *The Great Moghuls* (London, 1971)
Gopal, S. *British Policy in India 1858–1905* (Cambridge, 1965)
Grant, Charles. *Observations on the State of Society among the Asiatic Subjects of Great Britain* (London, 1797)
Gray, John Alfred. *My Residence at the Court of the Amir* (London, 1901)
Gupta, Pratul Chandra. *Nana Sahib and the Rising at Cawnpore* (Oxford, 1963)
Gwynn, Sir Charles W. *Imperial Policing* (London, 1934)

Hanna, Colonel H. B. *The Second Afghan War* 3 vols (London, 1899)
Hare, Augustus. *The Story of Two Noble Lives* (London, 1893)
Hart, Jenifer. 'Sir Charles Trevelyan at the Treasury' in *The English Historical Review* vol. LXXV (London, 1960)
Hassnain, F. M. *Gilgit: the Northern Gate of India* (New Delhi, 1978)
Heathcote, T.A. *The Afghan Wars* (London, 1980)
Heber, Reginald. *Narrative of a Journey through the Upper Provinces of India* 2 vols (London, 1844)
Heine, Elizabeth, ed.). *The Hill of Devi and other Indian Writings*, vol. 14 of *The Abinger Edition of E. M. Forster* (London, 1983)
Hibbert, Christopher. *The Great Mutiny* (London, 1978)
Hickey, William. *Memoirs* (ed. Alfred Spencer) 4 vols (London 1913–25)
Hilton, James. *The Lost Horizon* (London, 1933)
His Majesty's Stationery Office. *The Indian Empire* (London, 1921)
Hobson-Jobson, see Yule
Holt, Edgar. *The Opium Wars in China* (London, 1964)
Hook, Theodore. *The Life of Sir David Baird* 2 vols (London, 1833)
Hopkirk, Peter. *Foreign Devils on the Silk Road* (London, 1980)
Hügel, Baron C. von. *Travels in Kashmir and the Punjab* (London, 1845)
Hughes, Edward. *Civil Service Reform 1853–5*, in *History* vol. XXVII (London, 1942)
Hunt, Roland, and Harrison, John. *The District Officer in India* (London, 1980)

Ingram, E. *The Beginning of the Great Game in Asia 1828–34* (Oxford, 1979)
'Investigator', *Mr. Hook's Life of David Baird*, in *Asiatic Journal* vols X and XI (London, 1833)
Islam, Shamsul. *Chronicles of the Raj* (London, 1979)
Ivory, James. *Autobiography of a Princess* (London, 1975)

Jackson, Robert, *Thirty Seconds at Quetta* (London, 1960)
Jacquemont, Victor. *Letters from India* (London, 1936)
Josty, J. P. *The Art of the Book in India* (London, 1982)

Kak, B. L. *The Fall of Gilgit* (London, 1977)
Kaul, G. L. *Kashmir Then and Now* (Srinagar, 1972)
Kaye, Sir John William. *History of the Sepoy War*, 9th ed. (London, 1880)
 Lives of Indian Officers 2 vols (London, 1867)
 History of the War in Afghanistan 2 vols (London, 1851)
Kaye, M. M. *The Golden Calm* (Exeter, 1980)
Keay, John. *The Gilgit Game* (London, 1979)
 Where Men and Mountains Meet (London, 1977)
Keene, Henry George. *Fifty-Seven* (London, 1888)
Kincaid, Dennis. *British Social Life in India* (London, 1938)

Bibliography

Kipling, Rudyard. *A Choice of Kipling's Prose*, intro W. Somerset Maugham (London, 1952)
  Kim (London, 1901)
  Plain Tales from the Hills (London, 1888)
  Rudyard Kipling's Verse 3 vols (London, 1919)
Knight, E. F. *Where Three Empires Meet* (London, 1905)
Kohfeldt, Mary Lou. *Lady Gregory* (London, 1985)
Kopf, David. *British Orientalism and the Bengal Renaissance* (Berkeley, 1969)
Korbel, Josef. *Danger in Kashmir* (Princeton, 1954)

Lago, Mary, and Furbank, P. M. *Selected Letters of E. M. Forster* 2 vols (London, 1983, 1985)
Lang, John. *Wanderings in India* (London, 1859)
Lane-Fox, Robin. *Alexander the Great* (London, 1973)
Le Fèvre, Georges. *An Eastern Odyssey* (London, 1933)
Lewis, Jared. *E. M. Forster's Passages to India* (Columbia, 1979)
Lord, John. *The Maharajahs* (London, 1972)
Lorimer, E. O. *Language Hunting in the Karakoram* (London, 1939)
Lothian, Sir Arthur Cunningham. *Kingdoms of Yesterday* (London, 1951)
Lunt, Maj. General James. *Bokhara Burnes* (London, 1969)
Lutyens, Mary. *The Lyttons in India* (London, 1979)

Macaulay, Major-General Colin. *Two Letters Addressed to the Rt. Hon. Lord Harris* (London, 1816)
Mackenzie, Colin. *Storms and Sunshine in a Soldier's Life* (London, 1884)
Mackenzie, Mrs Colin. *Life in the Mission, the Camp and the Zenana* (London, 1853)
Mackenzie, Compton. *All Over the Place* (London, 1948)
  My Life and Times: Octave Nine (London, 1970)
Maclagan, Michael. *'Clemency' Canning* (London, 1962)
Maclean, Fitzroy. *A Person from England* (London, 1958)
Maillart, Ella. *Oasis Interdites* (Paris, 1937)
Malleson, George Bruce. *History of the Indian Mutiny* 3 vols (London, 1878–80)
Mason, Philip (see also Woodruff, Philip). *A Matter of Honour: An Account of the Indian Army, its Officers and Men* (London, 1974)
Masson, Charles, *Narrative of Various Journeys in Baluchistan, Afghanistan and the Panjab* 3 vols (London, 1842)
Masters, John. *Bugles and a Tiger* (London, 1959)
  The Road Past Mandalay (London, 1961)
Maude, Francis Cornwallis. *Memories of the Mutiny with which is Incorporated the Personal Narrative of John William Sherer* 2nd ed. (London, 1894)
McCormick, A. D. *An Artist in the Himalayas* (London, 1895)
McRae, Malcolm. *Sir Charles Trevelyan's Indian Letters 1859–1865*, in *The English Historical Review* vol. LXXVII (London, 1962)
Metcalf, Thomas R. *The Aftermath of Revolt* (Princeton, 1965)
Michell, George. *The Hindu Temple* (London, 1977)
Mill, James. *The History of British India* 3rd ed. (London, 1830); revised H. H. Wilson, 9 vols, 4th ed. (London, 1840–8)
Miller, Keith. *Continents in Collision* (London, 1982)
Mirsky, Jeannette. *Sir Aurel Stein* (Chicago, 1977)
Mitchell, A. G. *Hindu Gods and Goddesses* (London, 1982)
Montgomery, Brian. *A Field-Marshal in the Family* (London, 1973)

Monty's Grandfather (Poole, 1984)
Moore, R. J. 'The Composition of "Wood's Education Despatch"', in *The English Historical Review* vol. LXXX (London, 1965)
  Sir Charles Wood's Indian Policy (Manchester, 1966)
Moorhouse, Geoffrey. *Calcutta* (London, 1971)
  India Britannica (London, 1983)
  To the Frontier (London, 1985)
Moravia, Alberto. *Un'idea dell' India* (Milan, 1962)
Morison, Margaret Cotter. *A Lonely Summer in Kashmir* (London, 1904)
Mudford, Peter. *Birds of a Different Plumage* (London, 1974)
Murphy, Ray. *Edward Lear's Indian Journal* (London, 1953)
Muthiah, S. *Madras Discovered* (Madras, 1981)

Naipaul, V. S. *Among the Believers* (London, 1981)
  An Area of Darkness (London, 1964)
Newby, Eric. *A Short Walk in the Hindu Kush* (London, 1958)
Norris, J. A. *The First Afghan War* (Cambridge, 1967)

O'Dwyer, Sir Michael Francis. *India as I Knew it* (London, 1925)
Orgill, Douglas, and Gribbin, John. *Brother Esau* (London, 1982)
Orwell, George. *Burmese Days* (London, 1935)
  Collected Essays (London, 1961)
Ouspensky, P. D. *A New Model of the Universe* (London, 1931)

Panigrahi, D. N. *Charles Metcalfe in India* (Delhi, 1968)
Panter-Downes, Mollie. *Ooty Preserved* (London, 1967)
Parks, Fanny. *Wanderings of a Pilgrim in Search of the Picturesque* 2 vols (London, 1850)
Pasolini, Pier Paolo. *L'odore dell'India* (Milan, 1962)
Pemble, John. *The Raj, the Indian Mutiny and the Kingdom of Oudh* (Hassocks, 1977)
  (ed.) *Miss Fane in India* (London, 1985)
Perkins, Roger. *The Kashmir Gate* (Chippenham, 1983)
  The Punjab Mail Minder (Newton Abbot, 1979)
Philips, C. H. *The Correspondence of Lord William Bentinck* (Oxford, 1977)
Phillimore, Colonel R. H. *Historical Records of the Survey of India* (Dehra Dun, 1945)
Pinney, Thomas, (ed.). *The Letters of Thomas Babington Macaulay* 6 vols (1974–1981)
Postans, Marianne. *Cutch, or Random Sketches* (London, 1839)
Prinsep, Val C. *Imperial India* (London, 1879)

Ramaswami, N. S. *The Madras Club 1832–1982* (Madras, 1982)
Roberts, C. E. Bechhofer. *The Mr. A. Case* (London, 1950)
Roberts, Field-Marshal Earl. *Forty-one Years in India* (London, 1897)
  Letters Written during the Indian Mutiny (London, 1924)
Roberts, Emma. *Scenes and Characteristics of Hindostan* 3 vols (London, 1835)
Rosselli, John. *Lord William Bentinck* (London, 1974)
Rushdie, Salman. *Midnight's Children* (London, 1981)
  Shame (London, 1983)
Russell, Wilfrid. *Indian Summer* (Bombay, 1951)
Russell, William Howard. *My Diary in India* 2 vols (London, 1860)

Sale, Florentia. *A Journal of the Disasters in Afghanistan* (London, 1843)
Savory, Isobel. *A Sportswoman in India* (London, 1909)

Bibliography

Schofield, Victoria. *Bhutto, Trial and Execution* (London, 1979)
    Every Rock, Every Hill (London, 1984)
Schomberg, Colonel R. C. F. *Between the Oxus and the Indus* (London, 1935)
Scott, Paul. *The Raj Quartet* 4 vols (London, 1966–71)
Shellim, Maurice. *The Daniells in India* (Calcutta, 1970)
    Patchwork to the Great Pagoda (Calcutta, 1973)
Shepherd, J. W. *A Personal Narrative of the Outbreak and Massacre at Cawnpore during the Sepoy Revolt* (Lucknow, 1886)
Sherer, J. W. *Daily Life during the Indian Mutiny* (London, 1898)
Sherson, Erroll. *Townshend of Chitral and Kut* (London, 1928)
Singer, André. *Lords of the Khyber* (London, 1984)
Singh, N. Iqbal. *The Andaman Story* (New Delhi, 1978)
Sleeman, John. *Rambles and Recollections* 2 vols (London, 1844)
Slessor, Marshal of the Royal Air Force Sir John. *The Central Blue* (London, 1956)
Smith, George. *Bishop Heber* (London, 1895)
Smith, H. Bosworth. *Life of Lord Lawrence* (London, 1883)
Spear, Percival. *Delhi* (Oxford, 1937)
    India, a Modern History (University of Michigan, 1961)
    Twilight of the Mughuls (Cambridge, 1951)
Staley, Elizabeth. *Monkey Tops* (Bangalore, 1981)
Stein, Sir Aurel. *On Alexander's Track to the Indus* (London, 1929)
Stephens, Ian. *Horned Moon* (London, 1966)
    Pakistan (London, 1967)
Stocqueler, J. H. *Handbook to India* (London, 1844)
Stokes, Eric. *The English Utilitarians in India* (Oxford, 1959)
Stone, S. J. *In and Beyond the Himalayas* (London, 1896)
Strachey, Sir John. *India: Its Administration and Progress* (London, 1903)
Strachey, Sir John, and Strachey, Sir Richard. *The Finances and Public Works of India* (London, 1882)
Sud, O. C. *Complete Guide to Simla* (Simla, 1976)
Surtees, Virginia. *Charlotte Canning* (London, 1972)
Sykes, Sir Percy. *A History of Afghanistan* vol. II (London, 1940)

Tayler, William. *Thirty-Eight Years in India* (London, 1881)
Taylor, Colonel Meadows. *Confessions of a Thug* (London, 1839)
Tayyeb, A. *Pakistan: A Political Geography* (Oxford, 1966)
Temple, Sir Richard. *Men and Events of My Time in India* (London, 1882)
    The Story of My Life 2 vols (London, 1896)
Theroux, Paul. *The Great Railway Bazaar* (London, 1975)
Thompson, Edward. *The Other Side of the Medal* (London, 1925)
Thomson, Captain Mowbray. *The Story of Cawnpore* (London, 1859)
Thomson, W. *Memoirs of the Late War in Asia*, 2 vols (London, 1838)
Thornhill, Mark. *Personal Adventures of a Magistrate* (London, 1884)
Thornton, Edward. *History of the British Empire in India*, 6 vols (London, 1841–5)
Tollygunge Club. *Calcutta 200 Years* (Calcutta, 1981)
Toye, Hugh. *The Springing Tiger* (London, 1959)
Train, George Francis. *Young America Abroad* (Boston, 1857)
Trevelyan, C. E. *The Application of the Roman Alphabet to all the Oriental Languages* (Serampore, 1834)
    Christianity and Hinduism Contrasted (London, 1882)
    On the Education of the People of India (London, 1838)

The Irish Crisis (London, 1848)

The Letters of Indophilus to the Times (London, 1858)

The Organization of the Permanent Civil Service (London, 1853), with Stafford Northcote

Report upon the Inland Customs and Town Duties of the Bengal Presidency (Calcutta, 1834)

Trevelyan, George Macaulay. *Sir George Otto Trevelyan* (London, 1932)

Trevelyan, George Otto. *Cawnpore* (London, 1865)

The Competition Wallah (London, 1864)

Interludes in Verse and Prose (London, 1905)

The Ladies in Parliament etc. (London, 1888)

The Life and Letters of Lord Macaulay (London, 1876)

Trevelyan, Humphrey. *The India We Left* (London, 1972)

Public and Private (London, 1980)

Trevelyan, L. R. *A Year in Peshawur and a Lady's Ride into the Khyber Pass* (London, 1880)

Trevelyan, Raleigh. 'Return to Gilgit', in *Country Life* (28 Dec. 1978)

Trevelyan, R. C. *Collected Works* (London, 1939)

The Three Encounters of Buddha (London, 1932)

Trevelyan, W. R. F., 'Polo in Gilgit', in *Blackwood's Magazine*, vol. CCXXIX (Edinburgh, 1931)

'Quetta, 31st May 1935: A Personal Account', in *Blackwood's Magazine* vol. CCXIX (Edinburgh, 1936)

Trotter, L. J. *The Earl of Auckland* (London, 1890)

Trousdale, William (ed.). *The Gordon Creeds in Afghanistan* (London, 1984)

Tuker, Lt. General Sir Francis. *While Memory Serves* (London, 1950)

Tully, Mark, and Jacob, Satish. *Amritsar* (London, 1985)

Vachell, Horace Annesley. *The Hill* (London, 1905)

Vibart, Colonel Edward. *The Sepoy Mutiny as Seen by a Subaltern from Delhi to Lucknow* (London, 1898)

Victoria and Albert Museum. *The Indian Heritage*, catalogue (London, 1982)

Vigne, G. T. *Travels in Kashmir* (London, 1842)

Weller, Jac. *Wellington in India* (London, 1972)

Welsh, Colonel James. *Military Reminiscences* 2 vols (London, 1830)

Wilkinson, Theon. *Two Monsoons* (London, 1976)

Williams, L. F. Rushbrook. *The Black Hills* (London, 1958)

Williams, Ronald. *Montrose: Cavalier in Mourning* (London, 1975)

Wolpert, Stanley. *A New History of India* (Oxford, 1982)

Woodham-Smith, Cecil. *The Great Hunger* (London, 1962)

Woodruff, Philip (see also Mason, Philip). *The Men Who Ruled India: The Founders and the Guardians* (London, 1953–4)

Wright, Maurice. *Treasury Control of the Civil Service* (Oxford, 1909)

Wynne, Martin (ed.). *On Honourable Terms* (London, 1985)

Yalland, Zoë. *A Guide to the Kacheri Cemetery and the Early History of Kanpur* (London, 1983)

Yapp, M. E. *Strategies of British India* (Oxford, 1980)

Young, Gavin. *Slow Boats to China* (London, 1981)

Younghusband, Captain Frank E. *The Heart of a Continent* (London, 1896)

Bibliography

Yule, Colonel H., and Burrell, A. C. (eds). *Hobson-Jobson: A Glossary of Anglo-Indian Colloquial Words and Phrases etc* (London, 1886)

Zobi, Antonio. *Notizie storiche sull'origine . . . pietre dure* (Florence, 1841)
Zwalf, W. (ed.). *Buddhism: Art and Faith*, British Museum and Library catalogue (London, 1985)
  The Shrines of Gandhara (London, 1979)

Index

Page references in *italic* type indicate illustrations in the text.